OXFORD ISLAMIC LEGAL STUDIES

Series Editors:
Anver M. Emon, Clark Lombardi, and Lynn Welchman

SHARI'A AND SOCIAL ENGINEERING

OXFORD ISLAMIC LEGAL STUDIES

Series Editors:
Anver M. Emon, Clark Lombardi, and Lynn Welchman

Satisfying the growing interest in Islam and Islamic law, the *Oxford Islamic Legal Studies* series speaks to both specialists and those interested in the study of a legal tradition that shapes lives and societies across the globe. Islamic law operates at several levels. It shapes private decision making, binds communities, and it is also imposed by states as domestic positive law. The series features innovative and interdisciplinary studies that explore Islamic law as it operates at each of these levels. The series also sheds new light on the history and jurisprudence of Islamic law and provides for a richer understanding of the state of Islamic law in the contemporary Muslim world, including parts of the world where Muslims are minorities.

ALSO AVAILABLE IN THE SERIES

Narratives of Islamic Legal Theory
Rumee Ahmed

Religious Pluralism and Islamic Law
Dhimmis and Others in the Empire of Law
Anver M. Emon

Domestic Violence and the Islamic Tradition
Ayesha S. Chaudhry

Shariʿa and Social Engineering

The Implementation of Islamic Law in Contemporary Aceh, Indonesia

R. MICHAEL FEENER

OXFORD
UNIVERSITY PRESS

OXFORD
UNIVERSITY PRESS

Great Clarendon Street, Oxford, OX2 6DP,
United Kingdom

Oxford University Press is a department of the University of Oxford.
It furthers the University's objective of excellence in research, scholarship,
and education by publishing worldwide. Oxford is a registered trade mark of
Oxford University Press in the UK and in certain other countries

First Edition published in 2013

Impression: 1

Published in the United States of America by Oxford University Press
198 Madison Avenue, New York, NY 10016, United States of America

British Library Cataloguing in Publication Data
Data available

Library of Congress Control Number: 2013945314

ISBN 978–0–19–967884–6

Printed and bound in Great Britain by
CPI Group (UK) Ltd, Croydon, CR0 4YY

For John & Irene

When a city becomes renowned for having received the Word of God, the world will reckon that the city ought to be, as a result, so much better governed, that such order will prevail as to accord right and justice to one and all. Therefore, if things turn out to be no better than anywhere else, or worse than this, as if the truth of God were not to be found there at all, what is one to say?

John Calvin
Sermons on Micah

About the Author

R. Michael Feener is Research Leader of the Religion and Globalization Research Cluster at the Asia Research Institute, and Associate Professor of History at the National University of Singapore. Previously he taught at Reed College, and the University of California, Riverside. He has also held visiting professor positions and research fellowships at Harvard University, Kyoto University, École des Hautes Études en Sciences Sociales (Paris), the University of Copenhagen, The Doris Duke Foundation for Islamic Art (Honolulu), and the International Institute for Asian Studies (IIAS) in Leiden. Born in Salem, Massachusetts, he was trained in Islamic Studies and foreign languages at Boston University as well as in Indonesia, Egypt, and the Yemen. His books include *Muslim Legal Thought in Modern Indonesia*, *Shiʿism in Southeast Asia: ʿAlid Piety and Sectarian Constructions* (with Chiara Formichi), *Proselytizing and the Limits of Pluralism in Contemporary Asia* (with Juliana Finucane), *From the Ground Up: Perspectives on Post-Tsunami and Post-Conflict Aceh* (with Patrick Daly and Anthony Reid), *Mapping the Acehnese Past* (with Patrick Daly and Anthony Reid), *Islamic Connections: Muslim Societies of South and Southeast Asia* (with Terenjit Sevea), *Islamic Law in Contemporary Indonesia: Ideas and Institutions* (with Mark Cammack), and *Islam in World Cultures: Comparative Perspectives.*

Preface

Aceh, on the northern tip of Sumatra, has long been viewed as a bastion of Islam in Southeast Asia. This image has been even further reinforced since the turn of the twenty-first century with the formalization of provisions for the implementation of Islamic law in this "Special Autonomous Region" of Indonesia. This book examines the state Shariʿa project in contemporary Aceh as an experiment in social engineering, and argues for the development of a new analytic perspective on contemporary calls for the implementation of Islamic law as future-oriented agendas for social transformation. A particular focus here is on the direction and management of social change through the work of legal, educational, and religious institutions to reinterpret and regulate of aspects of Islamic belief and practice, as well as of public morality. These critical investigations are pursued through detailed critical examinations of the institutional architecture, ideological underpinnings, and day-to-day operations of this contemporary Islamic legal system.

The implementation of Islamic law in twenty-first-century Aceh emerged out of fiercely contested politics, and this context has significantly shaped the establishment and reception of the formal institutions of the number legal system in Acehnese society. In light of this, there have been a number of recent studies exploring the politics of Shariʿa in Aceh, particularly in relation to attempts by the Indonesian state to assert control over the province in its campaigns to suppress and eradicate the challenge posed by the Free Aceh Movement (I. Gerakan Aceh Merdeka/GAM). For most analysts of these political and military dynamics, the critical point is the contest over control of the state and its resources.[1] However, as important as the contestation of political elites is for contextualizing these developments, they are not in themselves sufficient for understanding the complex, embedded discourses on public morality, personal piety, social order, doctrinal rectitude, and economic development that diversely configure to inform agendas for the implementation of Islamic law. The present work aims to complement the expanding body of scholarship on Islamic law to address important questions concerning what particular individuals and groups hope to accomplish after taking hold of the reins

[1] This body of work is engaged with at various points in the chapters that follow, where particular studies will be cited in full.

of government. For many supporters of state Shariʿa the point is not only to gain power, but to use the apparatus of the state to promote agendas of social change based upon Islamic ideals.

In order to develop a higher-resolution picture of the design, evolution, and everyday workings of Aceh's Islamic legal system, this book focuses on state Shariʿa institutions as sites for the instantiation of visions of Islamic law as an instrument of social engineering. This aspirational and prescriptive orientation toward law in contemporary Aceh is something that I have found to be consistently highlighted in their legal documents and official publications, as well as in many conversations that I have had with officers of various ranks employed in the State Shariʿa Agency (I. Dinas Syariat Islam/DSI), the "Shariʿa Police" (I. Wilyatul Hisbah/ WH), the Ulama Council (I. Majelis Permusyawaratan Ulama/MPU), and the Religious Courts (I. Mahkamah Syariah), as well as with teachers and students in many of Aceh's Islamic schools. The importance of the work of social engineering is, for many of them, something that was keenly felt in response to the political violence and natural disaster that Aceh has suffered during their lifetimes. The combined trauma of prolonged armed conflict and the great earthquake and tsunami of 2004 had devastating effects on Acehnese society, but some of the broader patterns of responses by individuals, organizations, and the state took shape in ways that are by no means unique either to Indonesia or to Islam. A recent work of American Christian theological response to the disasters of the 9/11 terrorist attacks and Hurricane Katrina, for example, also struggles with the problem of how in such times of crisis citizens may come to look to the state as "the only institution capable of defining the problem and dealing with it."[2]

Aceh's state Shariʿa institutions are important sites in which visions of Islamic law and its role in society are constructed through changing patterns of practice that serve to integrate elements from multiple strands of religious, intellectual, and ideological influence, while also responding to contingent social and political factors.[3] To get at the micro-mechanisms of these developments, the chapters that follow draw on a broad range of empirical material including archival documents, local publications, observations of everyday operations, and interviews with those directly

[2] Gabriel A. Santos, *Reforming the Broken Body: Church and State after Disaster* (Eugene, OR: Cascade Books, 2009), 282.

[3] Of course, they are not the only place where such cultural work is performed. For more on non-state dimensions of the engagements with Islam in contemporary Aceh, see R. Michael Feener, David Kloos, and Annemarie Samuels (eds.), *Islam and the Limits of the State: Reconfigurations of Ritual, Doctrine, and Authority in Contemporary Aceh* (Leiden: Brill, forthcoming).

involved with these institutions. These diverse sources are brought together in a series of chapters organized around particular institutions, each of which demonstrates a particular aspect of state Shariʿa as a project of social engineering. Under this rubric, the diachronic development of each institution successively traces over the same chronology (centered on developments from the mid-twentieth century) from a series of different perspectives. Before this, however, it is necessary to first establish some of the major narrative points, institutions, and individual actors that lie beneath this palimpsest.

HISTORICAL BACKGROUND

Aceh has a long and complex history—and one that is relatively well documented in contrast to those of many other Indonesian societies. A substantial discussion of the particular legacies of Aceh's past that are important for understanding contemporary developments of Islamic law will be presented in Chapter 2. Before that, however, a brief introduction to the major outlines of this history may be necessary here for readers unfamiliar with the broader contexts of Aceh and Indonesia.[4]

The story begins with Aceh as a major early center of Islam in the region that provided royal patronage for religious institutions, learning, and literary production, and attracted scholars (ulama) from across the Muslim world to its court. Historical memories of, and textual legacies attributed to, seventeenth-century Aceh have contributed to the popular image of a "Golden Age" of Islam in Aceh that has come to serve as a major point of reference in discourses of Aceh's Islamic identity ever since. However, by the eighteenth century, the strength of the Aceh sultanate had waned significantly, and political power was increasingly devolved to a class of local aristocracy known in Acehnese as the *ulèëbalang*. In the nineteenth century, new tensions emerged between the *ulèëbalang* and the ulama, particularly throughout the decades of war that followed the Dutch invasion of Aceh in 1873. In response to this attack, the Acehnese waged a long, and ultimately unsuccessful, war of anti-colonial resistance cast in terms of a *jihād* in the defense of Islam against invading infidels. As the local ulama emerged as symbolic leaders of this opposition to the expansion of the colonial state in Aceh, the Dutch cultivated collaborations with a number of *ulèëbalang* in attempts to neutralize the resistance and consolidate their control over "pacified" areas. The rivalries between the

[4] For ease of reference, there is also a timeline of major developments in the modern history of Aceh provided in Appendix II.

ulama and the *ulèëbalang* grew steadily through the early decades of the twentieth century and eventually exploded after the end of World War II.

Under the Japanese wartime occupation of Aceh, new models of mobilizing the ulama in support of state programs and projects were introduced that have come to be of lasting importance to the politics of Islam in the region ever since. At the war's end, the establishment of Indonesian independence in August 1945 was soon followed by a "Social Revolution" that radically transformed societies in Aceh and neighboring areas of Sumatra. The end result of that was the near total extinction of the *ulèëbalang*, and Aceh's ulama then found themselves in a situation in which there were no significant local contenders to their claim of social and political authority. The absence of external rivals, however, served to heighten internal tensions among various groups of Islamic religious leaders, particularly along fault lines defined by modern agendas of religious and social reform.

Over the middle decades of the twentieth century, relations between "Traditionalist" and "Modernist" ulama became increasingly fraught through steepening competition for the hearts and minds of Aceh's Muslim community.[5] The Traditionalists upheld established models of Shāfiʿī jurisprudence and Khālidī-Naqshbandī Sufism as central to religious education in the local Islamic boarding schools known as *dayah*. The leading figure of Acehnese Traditionalist ulama of that time was Tgk. Muda Waly (d. 1961) of the Dayah Darussalam at Labuan Haji (West Aceh). The Traditionalist ulama were, however, increasingly the target of sharp critiques by Islamic Modernists associated with an organization called PUSA (Persatuan Ulama-Ulama Seluruh Aceh). PUSA's charismatic leader was Daud Beureueh (d. 1987), who in 1953 became the head of an armed struggle against the central Indonesian government for the creation of an Islamic state known as the Darul Islam.[6] As the conflict dragged on the Indonesian state granted a series of concessions, including the re-designation of Aceh Province as a "Special Area" (I. *Daerah Istimewa*) in 1959, and a pardon for Daud Beureueh in 1962.

[5] Throughout this book, the terms Modernist, Traditionalist, Revivalist (as well as their related forms of Modernism, etc.) are capitalized to indicate their use as technical terms. Here these technical terms are used in accordance with a set of definitions developed in conversations between colleagues involved in a research project on "Islam and Social Dynamics in Indonesia" at the National University of Singapore, in which Professor M.C. Ricklefs was Principal Investigator and I was co-PI. The definitions of these terms are provided in Appendix III on "Key Analytical Terms," and they are also employed in: M.C. Ricklefs, *Islamisation and its Opponents in Java, c. 1930 to the Present* (Singapore: NUS Press, 2012), 514–16.

[6] This rebellion against the Republic of Indonesia came to be linked together with other armed campaigns under the same name for the establishment of an 'Islamic state' of Indonesia. Seen C. van Dijk, *Rebellion under the Banner of Islam: The Darul Islam in Indonesia* (Martinus Nijhoff, 1981), 309–36; Chiara Formichi, *Islam and the Making of the Nation: Kartosuwiryo and Political Islam in Twentieth-Century Indonesia* (KITLV Press, 2012), 109–243.

With this re-integration into the Indonesian Republic, Aceh was deeply affected by the dramatic political reconfiguration of the nation following the attempted coup and subsequent mass violence of 1965. With the establishment of Suharto's stridently anti-communist New Order that followed, Aceh's ulama were organized into a state-sanctioned Ulama Council with the aim of providing Islamic legitimation for various government policies. The first leader appointed for Aceh's Ulama Council was Tgk. Abdullah Ujong Rimba (d. 1983), a Traditionalist scholar who had briefly associated himself with Daud Beureueh and the Darul Islam but soon thereafter, proclaimed the movement to be an invalid challenge to the legitimate authority of the Indonesian state. Ujong Rimba thence came to play an important role in the building of a coalition of Acehnese ulama who supported the New Order and its projects of national development.

The most prominent figure involved with managing relationships between Aceh's Islamic religious leadership and the Indonesian central government was, however, Ali Hasjmy (d. 1998). Hasjmy came from a Modernist background, and in his youth he had been associated with PUSA. In 1953, he was arrested on suspicion of supporting the Darul Islam and brought to Jakarta, where he became a prominent collaborator in central government efforts to end the rebellion and establish control over Aceh. He later returned home as appointed governor of the newly re-established Indonesian province of Aceh in 1957, where he began work on a number of new initiatives for the state management of Islamic affairs in the service of national interests. This included the establishment of a number of new institutions of governance and education organized around a concept of Islamic propagation (Ar./I. *daʿwa*) that combined elements of modernizing religious reform, Indonesian nationalism, and economic developmentalism. These measures contributed significantly to the domestication of potential Islamic opposition to the centralizing state over the decades that followed, and laid the foundations for many of the major components of Aceh's Islamic legal system as it was developed in the early years of the twenty-first century. By that time, *daʿwa* projects for religious proselytization and social reform involved increasingly close interaction between Islamic student activists and New Order government officials. Through these developments, new visions of Islam as integral to the agenda of national development (I. *Pembangunan*) emerged by the turn of the twenty-first century and took a prominent place in Indonesian public discourse.

In the meantime, however, the discovery of natural gas in North Aceh in the 1970s served to once again heighten the problematic place of Aceh in Indonesian national politics—albeit with a new kind of challenge. By that time the cause of Acehnese discontent with the national leadership in

Jakarta was no longer primarily about Islamic governance. Rather it came from local demands that the people of Aceh should enjoy a greater share of the wealth being extracted from their land in the form of these extremely lucrative natural resources. This was the context in which the Free Aceh Movement (GAM) proclaimed its campaign for Acehnese independence from Indonesia in 1976. Well after its leader Hassan di Tiro fled to exile abroad in 1979, GAM continued its fight through decades of violent struggle against the Indonesian armed forces. While many involved with the movement in its early stages shared earlier links to the Darul Islam, GAM did not emphasize Islam in most of its public rhetoric, and instead, it framed its cause as one of ethnic nationalism and liberation from an exploitative relationship to the central Indonesian state.

The conflict lasted for decades, resulting in widespread public misery. The death toll on both sides rose even further with a renewed increase in violence during the 1990s. After the fall of Indonesia's New Order regime in 1998, the rapid succession of short-term Indonesian presidents that followed began more active explorations of new options that could help them put an end to the situation in Aceh. In addition to a marked escalation of military intervention at the time, the leadership in Jakarta also began contemplating other means of facilitating the re-integration of Aceh within the Indonesian Republic. With the declaration of "Special Autonomy" at the turn of the new millennium, the implementation of Islamic law came to prominence as a central plank in these new strategies. The primary architects and agents involved with developing Aceh's Islamic legal system during this period—including the founding head of the State Shariʿa Agency (DSI), Alyasa Abubakar, and the long-serving head of the Ulama Council (MPU), Muslim Ibrahim—shared a broad background of education and teaching in Indonesia's system of State Islamic Studies Institutes (I. Institut Agama Islam Negeri/IAIN), as well as involvement with various *daʿwa* programs. They were thus seasoned exponents of the position that Islam held great potential for contributing to the promotion of state-sanctioned agendas of social stability, national integration, and economic progress.

These Acehnese Muslim academics, politicians, and religious leaders vigorously promoted the idea that the state implementation of Shariʿa could serve as both a solution to the ongoing conflict with GAM, and as the basis for re-establishing social order. Working with officials of the central government in Jakarta, they came to oversee the development of a new Islamic legal system in Aceh. In the process, the jurisdiction of Aceh's Islamic courts was formally expanded, a number of new state Shariʿa institutions were established, and new legislation was passed dealing with issues of public morality, as well as with various aspects of Islamic religious belief and practice. All of this, however, made only a modest impact on Acehnese society during these early years when the region was still wracked with violent clashes between GAM and the Indonesian military.

The situation changed dramatically in the wake of the massive earthquake and tsunami that devastated coastal regions of Aceh on 26 December, 2004. The overwhelming destruction resulted in the reconfiguration of priorities on all sides, which had the effect of accelerating developments in the peace process. The signing of the Helsinki Peace Accords in 2005 was followed by the promulgation of a new Law on Governing Aceh (LOGA) in 2006, which re-established and further defined the legislative and institutional foundations of Aceh's Islamic legal system under the provisions of Aceh's "Special Autonomy" status. At the same time, new life was breathed into the letter of the law through a broad-based wave of religious revival. The combination of a heightened sense of Islamic religiosity and the euphoria of a new peace in a region long plagued by conflict contributed to new visions of Aceh's future that came to be elaborated in a burgeoning public discourse on post-disaster/post-conflict "reconstruction."

SHARIʿA AND SOCIAL ENGINEERING

Much of the public discourse on reconstruction was framed in terms introduced to Aceh by the personnel of numerous and diverse international disaster relief and development agencies that arrived and set up shop in the wake of the tsunami. Many of these institutions and individuals shared a basic working model in which immediate assistance with post-disaster recovery was only the first step in a broader project of social reconstruction. The model was one of "linking relief, rehabilitation and development" (LRRD) through projects that created infrastructure, fostered capacity building, and established new models of governance. The Agency for the Reconstruction and Rehabilitation of Aceh and Nias (BRR) that was established to coordinate these projects in Aceh publicly proclaimed its mandate with the popular slogan: "Build Back Better." During the reconstruction period, the metaphor of "building" to describe these processes of social transformation assumed a prominent place in the public imagination of post-tsunami/post-conflict Aceh. This was expressed not only rhetorically, but physically as well. Just as international aid donors and development agencies publicly signaled their contributions to a new Aceh through the visible signs of new structures (homes, schools, hospitals, and public buildings), so too did Aceh's religious leaders through the construction of imposing mosques, Islamic schools, Shariʿa courthouses, and offices for institutions of the state's Islamic legal system. The cumulative effect of all this new construction was a constant visual reinforcement of the idea of a "total reconstruction" of Acehnese society.

Discursively, this was often spoken of as a work of re-building "from the ground up." Practically speaking, however, much of this actually moved along vectors from the top down. This is what is referred to throughout this book as the use of Islamic law as a tool of "social engineering." As demonstrated in the chapters that follow, the model of social reconstruction promoted by the architects and agents of Aceh's state Shariʿa system has been one in which the elements of Islamic law formally implemented are not simply reflections of established patterns of religious belief and practice, or even a longing to recover a past "golden age." Instead, the project was self-consciously formulated to produce a "new" Aceh, one in which reformed Islamic values formulated by modern-educated Muslim academics could serve to facilitate social stability and development.

Well beyond the realms of official government policy, the top-down vector of reconstructing Islamic Aceh is also widely reflected across the physical landscape. The image on the cover of this book depicts one example of a very familiar sight in post-disaster/post-conflict Aceh: that of a large mosque under construction. A number of the illustrations to the following chapters also aim to convey the dramatic and pervasive effect made and sustained by this peculiar "edifice complex" of the reconstruction period. In a majority of cases, the first element completed in mosque construction projects was a large dome, often with a glittering exterior finish that contrasts sharply with the unfinished concrete and rebar structure below. Often, construction slowed down considerably, or even stopped completely, after the dome was finished. The grand mosque of Lhokseumawe depicted in the photograph on the cover of this book has remained in such a state for at least seven years. The overall effect has been symbolic of one characteristic feature of the broader enterprise—that of prominently signaling grandiose aspirations through highly visible and dramatic public statements, while often failing to fully develop the structures necessary to support them.

The reconstruction of Islam and society in Aceh thus remains very much an unfinished project, and its progress to date is often described as disappointing even by many of the people most active in the design and administration of the state Shariʿa system. Nevertheless, the story of Islamic law in Aceh is important for the insight it provides into the future-oriented and instrumentalist aspects of calls for the state implementation of Shariʿa in the contemporary Muslim world. Against the dramatic backdrop of social reconstruction following the twin traumas of violent conflict and natural disaster, the development of Aceh's Islamic legal system as an interventionist agenda of steering social transformation emerges in sharp relief. The chapters that follow provide close historical and ethnographic explorations of the particular forms that this experiment with state Shariʿa have taken there, with an eye to demonstrating the complexities involved with the formulation, interpretation, and implementation of Islamic law in the twenty-first century.

The primary aim of this book is thus to argue for the importance of taking seriously the future-oriented dimensions of contemporary projects for the state implementation of Islamic law, as well as the complexities of the intellectual influences, political contexts, and socio-economic factors that inform them. At the same time, however, I have also striven to produce an empirically grounded and critically nuanced account of the particular aspirations and efforts of those Muslims in Aceh who have been most directly involved in pursuing this ambitious, and highly contested, agenda of state Shariʿa. It is hoped that this work can thus also serve to complement existing and forthcoming scholarship on other aspects of life in post-disaster/post-conflict Aceh in developing a more comprehensive picture of a complex contemporary society in the midst of dramatic social disruption and reconstruction.

Acknowledgements

Despite the feelings of solitude that one can sometimes feel during late nights and early mornings at the desk, no work of scholarship is ever the sole production of the author. We write not only for our colleagues but often with them as well, as echoes of their voices join the conversation through comments scribbled on rough drafts, new materials sent by post and over the internet, critiques in the seminar room, and more casual conversations. This work in particular has benefited from a great many stimulating interactions over the past seven years, and fully detailing all of the debts incurred in the process could fill as many pages as the book itself. There are, however, several people and institutions that I would like to particularly thank here.

I first went to Aceh with Tony Reid, soon after taking up a new job at the Asia Research Institute (ARI) of the National University of Singapore (NUS). That trip to Aceh proved to be the first of many, during which I was given a practicum crash course introduction to the world of relief, reconstruction, and development agencies. My exposure to this came through working with Tony and Patrick Daly on the establishment of a new research center (the International Centre for Aceh and Indian Ocean Studies/ICAIOS), and assisting with programs run by the Aceh Research Training Institute (ARTI). I am grateful to Michael Leigh, Laura Yoder, Leena Avonius, Saiful Mahdi, Harold Crouch, Linda Poskitt, and all of the ARTI and ICAIOS staff for all that I have been able to learn through this experience. My work with ICAIOS and ARTI also brought me into contact with many teachers and students in Aceh, particularly those at the IAIN Ar-Raniry and Universitas Syiah Kuala in Banda Aceh, Universitas Malikussaleh and the Sekolah Tinggi Agama Islam Negeri in Lhokseumawe, and Universitas Al Muslim in Bireuen. These friends and colleagues have taught me much in the course of researching and writing this book, and I am very grateful for their generosity in sharing their time and their thoughts with me over the past six years. Special thanks here go to Yusny Saby, Hamid Sarong, Alyasa Abubakar, Muslim Ibrahim, Rusjdi Ali Muhammad, Amirul Hadi, Hasbi Amiruddin, Rani Usman, Darni Daud, Daud Yoesoef, Mujiburrahman, Hasnul Arifin Melayu, Muslim Zainuddin, Jufri Ghalib, Armiya Ibrahim, Tgk. Abdullah Nafi, T. Kamaruzzaman, Nurdin A.R., Ibu Ani, Yenny Rahmayati, and Ivan Arisandi. I owe an immense debt of gratitude to Mahdi Abdullah Syihab and his team at the Pasee Institute of Research

(PIR) in Lhokseumawe: Syarqawi, Damanhur, Saifuddin Dhuhri, Hamdani, Elidar Sari, Nanda Amalia, and her family. They not only provided me with generous hospitality and stimulating discussions during my regular visits to Lhokseumawe over the years, but also provided invaluable research assistance during the intervals between my trips through newspaper clippings, collecting ephemera, and making arrangements for my visits to various state Shariʿa institutions, as well as conducting and transcribing supplementary interviews. Pak Mahdi also accompanied me on many of my interviews, focus-group discussions, and visits to the archives—and his presence provided true blessings of friendship, in addition to a wealth of interesting conversation and a great deal of technical assistance with recording and transcribing.

I was also extremely fortunate in finding tremendous support for this research back at NUS, particularly under the mentorship of Merle Ricklefs in the Department of History. His guidance and encouragement helped me to begin thinking about the time that I was spending in Aceh in terms of a research project of my own, in addition to the organizational, administrative, and teaching work that I was doing there. Beyond providing a great wealth of valuable advice on research, writing, and academic life, Merle also helped to support this work financially as a part of his larger research project entitled *Islam and Social Dynamics in Contemporary Indonesia*, which was supported by the NUS Faculty of Arts and Social Sciences and the Singapore Ministry of Education.[1] This grant also helped to bring in other researchers on Indonesian Islam to the History Department at NUS to work on aspects of this larger project, including Chaider Bamualim and Amelia Fauzia. Our regular meetings to discuss work-in-progress have enriched my own thinking about the developments in Aceh discussed in this book.

Further stimulation, critique, and encouragement were provided by my colleagues at NUS and by a steady stream of visiting research fellows at ARI. For this I would like to thank: Ben Arps, Arunasalam Balasubramaniam, Julius Bautista, Gary Bell, Anne Blackburn, Chee Heng Leng, Ken Dean, Kees van Dijk, Mike Dowdle, Chiara Formichi, Juliana Finucane, Johan Fischer, Michael Gilsenan, Kikue Hamayotsu, Ian Harris, Noorhaidi Hasan, Tineke Hellwig, Janet Hoskins, Noboru Ishikawa, Arif Jamal, Robin Jeffrey, Leigh Jenco, Gavin Jones, Nico Kaptein, Pattana Kittiarsa, Lily Kong, Rodolphe de Koninck, Michael Laffan, Thomas Larsson, Charles Leary, Stephen Legomsky, Francis Lim, Al Makin, Pierre-Yves Manguin, Gabriele Marranci, Levi McLaughlin, Duncan McCargo, Kate McGregor, Michelle

[1] This three-year research grant was generously funded by the Singapore Ministry of Education's Academic Research Fund (MOE AcRF #R-110-000-029-750).

Miller, Judith Nagata, Ng Zhiru, Barbara Nowak, Victor Ramraj, Ronit Ricci, Rachel Rinaldo, Kathryn Robinson, Jeffrey Samuels, Timothy Simpson, Vineeta Sinha, George Souza, Nasir Tamara, Arun Thiruvengadam, Bryan Turner, Pieter van der Veer, Geoff Wade, Johannes Widodo, Thongchai Winichakul, Xiang Biao, Mayfair Yang, and Zhong Yijiang. I would also like to say a special word of thanks here to ARI's Director Prasenjit Duara, whose intellectual energy, leadership, and friendship have been inspiring. ARI and NUS also provided great support for research assistance to help with organizing and filing all the data collected for this project, and to help in preparing this text for publication. For this I am grateful to Mok Mei Feng, Renee Lee, Suhaili Osman, Maisarah Abdul Malek, Nur Hani Bte Zainal, Mohd Faisal, Andrew Yeo, and especially Hongyan Li.

Outside Singapore I was given precious time to write during visiting fellowships hosted by the Institut d'études de l'Islam et des sociétés dumonde Musulman (IISMM)/École des hautes études en sciences sociales (EHESS) in Paris and the Kyoto University Center for Southeast Asian Studies (CSEAS). During these periods of writing leave in France, Japan and other travels abroad I also benefited from the use of materials in the libraries of these host institutions, and others, including Cornell University, the Koninklijk Instituut voor Taal-, Land- en Volkenkunde (KITLV) in Leiden, the Carsten Niebuhr Library at the University of Copenhagen and the Kongelige Bibliotek in Denmark, Sophia University, Tenri University, and the University of Tokyo in Japan, and the Arsip Propinsi in Banda Aceh.

As I worked these materials into my discussions of Islamic law in contemporary Aceh I was also able to present aspects of the book in progress at a number of lectures, seminars, and conferences, and I would thus like to thank the colleagues who attended and responded to my work at CSEAS, the Sophia University Institute of Asian Cultures, the Tokyo University Institute for Advanced Studies on Asia, Leiden University, the Nordic Institute of Asian Studies at Copenhagen, the Sciences Po Centre d'études et de recherches internationales, IISMM, and the Centre Asie du Sud-est at EHESS in Paris, the Helsinki Collegium for Advanced Studies at the University of Helsinki, the Weatherhead East Asian Institute at Columbia University, the Asian Law Centre at the Melbourne Law School, and the University of Washington Law School, as well as the Association for Asian Studies (AAS) annual meeting in Honolulu, and the European Association for Southeast Asian Studies conference (Euro SEAS) in Naples.

Among the many colleagues abroad, I would like to thank Dina Afrianty, Omar Farouk Bajunid, John Bowen, Léon Buskens, Melissa Crouch, Kees van Dijk, Oman Fathurahman, Greg Fealy, Andrée Feillard, Joshua Gedacht, Byron Good, Mary-Jo Good, Kristina Großmann, Claude Guillot,

Wael Hallaq, Masashi Haneda, Carol Hau, Yoko Hayami, Robert Hefner, Bernard Heyberger, Engseng Ho, Virgina Hooker, Reza Idria, Ludvik Kalus, Midori Kawashima, Clive Kessler, Hiroko Kinoshita, David Kloos, Yasuko Kobayashi, Junko Koizumi, Yasushi Kosugi, Hiroko Kushimoto, Elizabeth Lambourn, Tim Lindsey, Nathalie Maugiron, Justin McDaniel, Ed McKinnon, Brinkley Messick, Ken Miichi, Julian Millie, Antje Missbach, Kosuke Mizuno, Kazuo Morimoto, Mariko Naito, Takahiro Nakajima, Kojiro Nakamura, Mitsuo Nakamura, Hisako Nakamura, Moch. Nur Ichwan, Euis Nurlaelawati, Benjamin Otto, Jan Michiel Otto, Paul Powers, Peter Riddell, Abdullah Saeed, Annemarie Samuels, Hiromu Shimizu, Yuki Shiozaki, Jim Siegel, Catherine Smith, Yumi Sugahara, Amanda Whiting, John Wolff, Paul Wormser, Yo Nonaka, and Nishi Yoshimi.

As the work was being drafted a number of friends and colleagues provided detailed feedback on various chapters, including: Ismail Alatas, Ed Aspinall, Dan Birchok, Robin Bush, Mark Cammack, Philip Fountain, Barry Hooker, Marion Katz, Jeremy Kingsley, Hal Nevis, David Powers, Tony Reid, Arskal Salim, Martin Saxer, Eka Srimulyani, Eric Tagliacozzo, Martin van Bruinessen, and Muhammad Qasim Zaman. Raj Brown, Patrick Daly, Faisal Devji, Victor Ramraj, Merle Ricklefs, Francis Robinson, Merlin Swartz, Wu Keping, and Liang Yongjia read through the entire text, as have the editors of this series Anver Emon and Clark Lombardi. All of these readers have made valuable criticisms on earlier drafts, and the book in your hands is much improved for it. I have attempted to respond to all of their points, but where I have failed to do so here the fault is all my own.

Last, but far from least, I would like to thank my family for all their steadfast support of me, no matter what kind of work I was pursuing. My parents have seen me through years of wanderings on unfamiliar paths, but they have never given up on me as lost and always provided a home to which I could return. My wife, Mayuko, and my two children have been wonderful companions with whom I have been happy to share my journeys in more recent years. They have not only brought much laughter, joy, and comfort to my life, but they have also been incredibly patient and understanding of the fact that I had to be away from them so often in Aceh and elsewhere as I worked on this book. I could not have done it without them, and now that it is done I am very happy to be able to spend even more time with them.

Contents

Illustrations

Permissions

I would like to thank the following publishers and archive sources for permission to reproduce some of the material included in this book.

An earlier draft of Chapter 9 has appeared in the form of an article: "Social Engineering through Sharīʿa: Islamic Law and State-Directed Daʿwa in Contemporary Aceh," *Islamic Law and Society* (2012) 19(2) 275–311. That material is reproduced here with permission from Brill.

The sketch figure on "The Role of the ʿUlamāʾin National Development toward Islamic Ideals," comes from the Aceh Provincial Archives (Arsip Propinsi Aceh No. 255/40 - 1971), and is used here with permission from the Badan Arsip.

The cartoon of the "Specter of a 'Deviant Sect' Leading Youth Astray," was previously published in *Modus Aceh* 50.VIII, 11–7 (April 2011): 2, and is reproduced with permission from the publisher.

The sketch of a thief punished by amputation in Aceh, c. 1670 has been previously published in: Thomas Bowrey, *A Geographical Account of Countries Round the Bay of Bengal, ed. Richard Temple* (Cambridge: Hakluyt Society, 1905). Image reproduced with permission from the Hakluyt Society.

1

Introduction

The ulama ordered the people of the land to repent,
All at once
All sinfulness was forbidden,
All were ordered to obey God's commandments
At that time, everyone was terrified,
and obeyed the orders of the ulama
The sultan decreed that anyone who disobeyed
was to be to be struck down
The community held firm to their faith,
and what was ordered did not encounter opposition

Do'Karim
Hikayat Prang Gômpeuni

In the late nineteenth century, after a terrifying dream vision of his realm being devastated by an unstoppable inundation, the sultan of Aceh called the kingdom's Islamic scholars (ulama) to court. One of these scholars, Tgk. Kuta Karang, interpreted the nightmare not only as a portent of the imminent attack of the Dutch, but also as a sign of divine retribution for the sins of the community.[1] Read today, the Sultan's dream—quoted from the prologue of late nineteenth-century Acehnese vernacular epic—seems to eerily foreshadow the combined calamities of war and natural disaster, as well as the attempts to deal with them through official policies of impositions of religious order, that have shaped Aceh's modern history ever since. However, well before both the 2004 tsunami and the 2005 Helsinki Peace Accords that put an end to decades of violent conflict between the Indonesian central government and the Free Aceh Movement (GAM), Edwin Wieringa analyzed this episode as forming part of a "sermon" situated within a well-established tradition of Islamic

[1] Edwin Wieringa, "The Dream of the King and the Holy War against the Dutch: The 'Kôteubah' of the Acehnese Epic, 'Hikayat Prang Gômpeuni,'" *Bulletin of the School of Oriental and African Studies* 61(2) (1998) 298–308. My translation here differs somewhat from that published in the article.

moral exhortation in Acehnese literature. It calls attention in a dramatic way to the relationships between religious and political leadership, as well as to the intertwined perceptions of public manifestations of religiosity and conceptions of cosmic order in this region of the Muslim world.[2] Reiterations of these elements of public discourse characterized the rapid transformation of Acehnese society over the first decade of the twenty-first century, as appeals to the Shariʿa as a means to protect the community from calamity became resonant in new and powerful ways there in the early years of the twenty-first century. As one prominent local Islamic activist has expressed it: "If the Muslim community in Aceh neglects the Shariʿa today, we worry that God will once again afflict us with disaster and tragedy."[3]

ISLAMIC LAW AND SOCIAL ENGINEERING

The contemporary project of the state implementation of Islamic law has been significantly re-shaped by recent social transformations in Aceh following the devastating earthquake and tsunami of December 2004 and the subsequent end of a protracted violent conflict between the central Indonesian government and the armed separatist Free Aceh Movement (GAM). In this context, the attempt to build a more stable moral and legal order based on Shariʿa norms was folded into broader projects for the "total reconstruction" of society. International organizations involved in this work brought with them a sense that this post-disaster/post-conflict moment presented an unprecedented opportunity to address long-standing social issues in Aceh—and each brought to the situation its own vision of how their work could not only help Aceh to recover from trauma, but to actually "Build Back Better."[4] This rhetoric of not simply physically re-building, but actively "re-making" Aceh during its recovery from disaster and conflict helped to re-energize the work of state Shariʿa institutions which had only a minimal impact on society during the first years of the twenty-first century.

[2] For example, James Siegel has remarked on this in relation to the Dutch invasions of Aceh in the late nineteenth century. See James T. Siegel, *Shadow and Sound: The Historical Thought of a Sumatran People* (Chicago: University of Chicago Press, 1979), 231–2.

[3] Hasanuddin Yusuf Adan, *Syariʿat Islam di Aceh: Antara Implementasidan Diskriminasi* (Banda Aceh: Adnin Foundation, 2008), 44.

[4] This was the slogan of the Indonesian government's Rehabilitation and Reconstruction Agency for Aceh and Nias (BRR), and it was also used widely by many NGOs and foreign development agencies involved with projects in post-disaster Aceh. The relationship between their rhetoric of reconstruction and discourses on Shariʿa implementation in Aceh are discussed in detail in the book, particularly in Chapter 2 and Chapter 9.

At the turn of the millennium, the project for the state implementation of Islamic law had been introduced as part of a new strategy by the Indonesian central government to undermine local Acehnese support for GAM. Behind that immediate political context, however, was a complex history of earlier attempts on the part of the state to use law, and Islamic law in particular, as tools for stimulating and channeling social change in desired directions. As will be discussed further in the chapters that follow, over the second half of the twentieth century Indonesian legal discourse developed a strong instrumentalist tone. Under Suharto's "New Order" (I. *Orde Baru*) government, an increasing number of legal scholars, judges, and government official embraced what was called "Development Law Theory" (I. *Teori Hukum Pembangunan*), pioneered by Mochtar Kusuma-Atmadja.[5] From the mid 1970s, this legal theory became a pillar of state policy mandating that law was to be employed as a "tool" (I. *alat*) for national development.[6] Over the decades that followed, all segments of Indonesia's legal system, including the state-administered areas of Islamic law, were put into service in the pursuit of development goals formulated by an ascendant class of technocrats.

This vision of law as an instrument of social engineering grew out of the engagement of Indonesian thinkers with works in the field of "sociological jurisprudence" produced in Europe and the United States by thinkers including Eugen Ehrlich and Roscoe Pound.[7] It was, in fact, through the Indonesian-language translation of Pound's introductory handbook on the Philosophy of Law that the very term "social engineering" was introduced to students in law schools throughout the country.[8] Indonesian (mis)appropriations of the term, however, eventually went far beyond the gradual, "organic" models of law and social change advocated by Pound himself and instead came to be used for more activist, state-directed programs of economic and social development. Underlying all this remained a broader "sociological" conception of the function of law in

[5] For an introduction to this strand of Indonesian legal discourse, see Shidarta, ed. *Mochtar Kusuma-Atmadja dan Teori Hukum Pembangunan: Eksistensidan Implikasi* (Jakarta: Epistema Institute, 2012).

[6] This point was clearly stressed in two of the major defining documents of official state policy in this period, the "1973 Main Outlines of National Direction" (*Garis-garis Besar Haluan Negara Republik Indonesia Tahun*/GBHN, 1973), and the "Five Year Development Plan for 1974–1979" (*Replita II – Tahun 1974/75 s.d. 1978/79*).

[7] Pound himself wrote a preface to the first English translation of Ehrlich's *Fundamental Principles of the Sociology of Law* (Cambridge, MA: Harvard University Press, 1936).

[8] Roscoe Pound, *Pengantar Filsafat Hukum*, translated by Moh. Radjab (Jakarta: Bhratara, 1963). This first edition of the Indonesian translation was published in cooperation with the Franklin Press (Jajasan Penerbitan Franklin, Djakarta-New York). Based upon the second, expanded edition of Pound's text (1954), it was re-printed several times over second half of the twentieth century, and found a stable place within the basic curriculum.

society that looked beyond the spheres of legislation and formal legal institutions to encompass fields of education and "socialization."[9] It was these areas in particular that came to attract the attention and the energies of campus-based Islamic activists who, over the latter decades of the twentieth century, brought together mutually-reinforcing currents of Islamic reform, Indonesian nationalism, and economic developmentalism together in what I refer to subsequently as the "*daʿwa* paradigm"—based upon the popular term in contemporary Indonesian Islam referring to religious revival and propagation.

Many of these *daʿwa*-oriented Muslims went on to careers in the New Order government or in higher education, and from these positions they came to transform the public profile of Islam, and dominant visions of Islamic law in Indonesia. Within this broader national context, Aceh had a particular distinction as a laboratory for developing mechanisms for the state management of Islam. It was there that the New Order government experimented with a series of new institutions, beginning in the 1960s with the establishment of the nation's first Faculty of *Daʿwa* at a state institution of higher education and an official Council of Ulama. These measures were pursued with the explicit intention of using Islam both as a means of maintaining social and political order, and as an instrument to steer social change in directions that facilitate the goals of national economic development.

These developments over the second half of the twentieth century laid the basic institutional foundations for the creation of Aceh's Islamic legal system at the turn of the twenty-first. However, as will be discussed later, while legal provisions for the state implementation of Islamic law in Aceh were put in place by the Indonesian government in 1999, it was not until after the tsunami and the end of the conflict in 2005 that the new laws and institutions that they created became more visible and active in the province. By that time, the broader contexts of the project of state Shariʿa had shifted dramatically. The trauma of the natural disaster accelerated the peace process toward ending the conflict between GAM and the Indonesian government. The new stability also facilitated the entry and work of an entire panoply of new organizations and institutions from abroad that carried with them ambitious visions for a "total reconstruction" of Aceh.

The rapidly changing political, social and environmental conditions of Aceh over recent decades have thus shaped both the form and function of Aceh's state Shariʿa institutions as they were deployed in a project of social engineering. As will be shown in what follows, many of those

[9] The specific course of these developments will be presented and analyzed in greater detail in Chapter 9.

Acehnese Muslims involved with this viewed the opportunity to promote the formal implementation of Islamic law as a chance to advance their own visions of religious reform and social improvement.[10] The ambitions of some of the state-affiliated and *daʿwa*-oriented architects and agents of Aceh's twenty-first-century state Shariʿa system were rather lofty—and they were further inflated as Islamic leaders came to adopt for their own aspects of the rhetoric of "total-reconstruction" brought to Aceh in the post-disaster/post-conflict period by international development organizations and NGOs. The actual responses of various segments of Aceh's internally diverse Muslim community to this Islamizing agenda, however, present a rather different situation than that of the idealized receptivity to the voices of Islamic religious authority recited in the nineteenth-century Acehnese poem quoted in the epigram to this chapter. For rather than having the population fall into line in obeying the new religious dictates of the state, the twenty-first-century implementation of Islamic law has been highly contested, with its proponents having to continuously struggle against segments of the population that are either ambivalent, or in some cases even actively opposed, to their work.

The focus of this book is on the institutions and actors involved with this twenty-first-century project for the state implementation of Islamic law in pursuit of social transformation. The individual chapters are structured as studies of the major components of this system and their changing configurations. The discussions of these dynamic institutional elements treat key aspects of their respective organizational structures, diachronic development, everyday operations, and the personnel associated with these institutions. Taken together, the book explores the overall design and operation of the major components of Aceh's contemporary Islamic legal system. In doing so, it critically examines how these institutions have taken shape by building on aspects of late-twentieth-century Muslim discourse on *daʿwa* agendas for social change and incorporating aspects of global models of disaster relief, reconstruction, and development. Both of these streams of influence have contributed significantly to shaping the ways in which the architects and agents of the state Shariʿa system have attempted to use Islamic legislation and legal institutions as tools to steer society in directions reflecting their visions of religious reform.

The instrumentalist approach to Islamic law that characterizes the project of state Shariʿa in contemporary Aceh reflects both a significant reconfiguration of the Islamic legal tradition, and the specific local contexts of social reconstruction in the post-disaster/post-conflict period. Indeed, the dramatic transformations of this particular setting serve to

[10] These developments will be discussed further in Chapters 2 and 9.

strikingly amplify broader trends of Muslim legal thought in the modern period. The most important development to note for our purposes here is that there has been a marked shift in the relative emphasis on the idea of law as serving the maintenance of stability and preservation of order through its systematization of already established practice, vis-à-vis one in which law is seen as a tool to be employed in future-oriented projects of social engineering.[11] While these developments have yet to receive much attention in discussions of Islamic law in the modern period, they should be considered as a further example of what Nathan Brown has characterized as important, fundamental shifts in the meaning of the Shariʿa as it became embodied in modern institutional frameworks of law, education, and governance.[12]

Of course, to some degree, Islamic law has long been involved with attempts to actively shape aspects of social life in Muslim communities.[13] However, in the modern period the social-control technologies of the nation-state have facilitated new kinds of experiments in legal instrumentalism deployed in support of state-directed agendas for social change. In the process, control of these developments has tended to slip from the hands of the ulama as a relatively autonomous guild of scholar jurists to government bureaucrats—Foucault's "technicians of behavior, engineers of conduct, [and] orthopædists of individuality."[14] Such modernizing transformations have indeed, as Wael Hallaq expressed it, irreversibly "altered the nature of the law."[15] However, while it is clear that these institutional and ideological transformations have disfigured the classical traditions of jurisprudence, it has not put an end to further reinterpretations of, and calls for, the practical implementations of Shariʿa in society. Indeed, if anything, there has been a marked rise in both since the mid-twentieth century. How then, are we to understand Muslim calls for and state projects of implementing Islamic law within the context of modern nation states?

[11] These transformations of Indonesian legal thought occurred through a complex of local reinterpretations of the "sociological jurisprudence" of Eugen Ehrlich and Roscoe Pound, and critical interventions into discourses on "living law" associated with Dutch scholars of customary law (D. *adatrecht*). These developments will be discussed in more detail in Chapter 9.

[12] Nathan J. Brown, "Shariʿa and State in the Modern Middle East," *International Journal of Middle East Studies* 29(3) (August 1997) 359.

[13] J.N.D. Anderson, "Law as a Social Force in Islamic Culture and History," *Bulletin of the School of Oriental and African Studies* 20(1/3) (1957) 13–40.

[14] Michel Foucault, *Discipline and Punish: The Birth of the Prison*, transl. Alan Sheridan (New York: Vintage Books, 1977), 294.

[15] Wael B. Hallaq, "Can the Shariʿah be Restored?" in Yvonne Y. Haddad and Barbara F. Stowasser (eds.), *Islamic Law and the Challenges of Modernity* (Walnut Creek: Altamira Press, 2004), 21–53.

MODERN INSTITUTIONS OF ISLAMIC LAW

This work takes an empirical approach to the study of Islamic law in society by looking to structures and interpretations that specific groups of Muslims themselves identify with the Shariʿa, rather than imposing a normative litmus test of current practices against particular aspects of the classical tradition.[16] In doing so, it critically examines the roles of state-affiliated ulama, "Shariʿa bureaucrats," and the codification of statutory legislation as significant instantiations of contemporary Muslim visions of what constitutes Islamic law. Such work calls for an historical and ethnographic, rather than a doctrinal approach to the description and interpretation of developments in Aceh. This study thus examines the working of the state Shariʿa system as it was designed and implemented in Aceh at the turn of the twenty-first century. The research for it has included close readings of a wide range of local publications on issues of Islamic law and society and of archival materials, as well as of the voluminous official documents of Aceh's state Shariʿa apparatus, other government offices, Islamic organizations, and NGOs in Aceh. This textual material is, furthermore, contextualized in relation to extensive direct observation of the day-to-day workings of the various institutions involved with the implementation of Islamic law there over the course of frequent shuttling back and forth between Aceh and Singapore from 2006–2012. During this period, I attended court sessions at the Mahkamah Syariah, visited offices of the State Shariʿa Agency (DSI), the Ulama Council (MPU), and the Wilayatul Hisbah (WH), and I accompanied law enforcement officials on patrol. I also learned about diverse forms of contemporary Islamic education at both Traditionalist and Modernist schools, and attended sermons, lectures, and professional "training sessions" run by various government offices and NGOs. These occasions have provided ample opportunities for both formal interviews and myriad informal conversations with judges, lawyers, court administrators, civil servants, police and Wilayatul Hisbah officers, preachers, teachers, and students of both traditional Acehnese *dayahs* and modern Islamic schools.[17]

[16] Rudolph Peters, "From Jurists' Law to Statute Law or What Happens When the Shariʿa is Codified," in B.A. Roberson (ed.), *Shaping the Current Islamic Reformation* (London: Frank Cass, 2003), 93; Ron Shaham, "Western Scholars on the Role of the ulama in Adapting the Shariʿa to Modernity: A Critical Review," in Meir Hatina (ed.), *Guardians of Faith in Modern Times: Ulama in the Middle East* (Leiden: E.J. Brill, 2009), 171–92.

[17] Where formal interviews are quoted or referenced in the chapters that follow, I have given the actual names of individuals only for prominent public figures who have served as heads of particular institutions, and for well-known local academics. For lower-ranking officers and administrators involved with Aceh's state Shariʿa institutions, I have preserved their anonymity but indicated their job description, branch office, and gender to provide some context for their statements.

The focus of this work is thus squarely on those who have designed, created, and implemented the province's Islamic legal system. Of course, not all Muslims in Aceh agree with either their vision, or with the practical application of their work—as has been made clear in the pages of Aceh's vibrant free press in the condemnations of international human rights groups, and the evaluations of many previous academic observers.[18] The perceptions and experiences of Islam, and state Shariʿa in particular, by other segments of contemporary Acehnese society—including those of NGO organizers, women's rights activists, bloggers, diaspora dissidents, punk rockers, and "ordinary Muslims" who are either ambivalent about or directly opposed to the formal implementation of Islamic law—have already received extensive academic treatment elsewhere, and I have discussed them further in another publication.[19] However sympathetic one may personally be to such critical perspectives, it would nevertheless be a serious oversight to ignore or cynically discount the voices of those who advocate and defend the project of state Shariʿa in Aceh. They, too, comprise a significant element within a highly-contested public sphere on the shape and direction of Acehnese society. The present work is thus intended to complement the expanding body of recent and forthcoming work on culture and politics in contemporary Aceh by adding a new dimension of engagement with the aspirations for and attempts at the practical implementation of the Islamic legal system by its officials and supporters.[20] In order to maintain this focus on an under-examined dimension of Shariʿa implementation in contemporary Aceh—and to keep the work to a reasonable length—this book does not retread over discussions that have been previously published elsewhere. Instead, footnotes at various points will serve to refer readers to examples of the

[18] For more on this, see R. Michael Feener, "Hand, Heart and Handphone: State Shariʿa in the Age of the SMS," *Contemporary Islam* 7 (2013) 15–32.

[19] R. Michael Feener, David Kloos, and Annemarie Samuels (eds.), *Islam and the Limits of the State: Reconfigurations of Ritual, Doctrine, and Authority in Contemporary Aceh* (Leiden: Brill, forthcoming).

[20] For in-depth treatments of other aspects of Muslim experience in contemporary Aceh, see Dan Birchok, "Sojourning on Mecca's Verandah: Place, Temporality, and Islam in an Indonesian Province," Ph.D. dissertation (Ann Arbor: University of Michigan, 2013); David Kloos, "Becoming Better Muslims: Religious Authority and Ethical Improvement in Aceh, Indonesia," Ph.D. dissertation (Amsterdam: Vrije Universiteit, 2013); Annemarie Samuels, "After the Tsunami: The Remaking of Everyday Life in Banda Aceh, Indonesia," Ph.D. dissertation (Leiden University, 2012); Kristina Großmann, "Handlungsräumemuslimischer Aktivistinnen: Nach der Einführung der Syariat Islam und dem Tsunami in Aceh, Indonesien," Ph.D. dissertation (Frankfurt am Main: Johann Wolfgang Goethe-Ūniversität, 2012); Catherine Smith, "War, Medicine and Morality in Aceh: An Ethnography of 'Trauma' as an Idiom of Distress," Ph.D. dissertation (Canberra: Australian National University, 2012); Dina Afrianty, "Local Women's NGOs and the Reform of Islamic Law in Aceh: Case Study of MISPI," Ph.D. dissertation (Melbourne: University of Melbourne, 2010); and Sehat Ihsan (Milano-Bicocca University, dissertation in progress).

extensive existing work on those segments of Acehnese society that have been in opposition or indifferent to the agenda of state Shariʿa, rather than engaging in any extensive rehearsal of that material.

The political dimensions of debates over Islamic law in Aceh are of course important, and as such they have received considerable commentary in recent academic work on the subject.[21] In the last years of the twentieth century, the basic provisions allowing for the formal establishment of Aceh's contemporary Islamic legal system were clearly set out by the Indonesian central government in an attempt to gain the upper hand in the ongoing and increasingly violent campaign against GAM at the turn of the twenty-first century. However, as evidenced in archival materials discussed in the chapters that follow, much of the shape of the legislation and institutions put in place actually drew on models that had been experimented with and developed by state-affiliated Islamic leaders in Aceh over the preceding half century. In this sense, the politics of the conflict in the post-Suharto period (i.e., after 1998) provided a new opportunity for some of Aceh's local Islamic leadership to push forward agendas for religious and social reform of their own that drew on decades of discourse on *daʿwa* and development.

There is thus more to the story of Shariʿa in Aceh than just politics. The conflict-era provisions for the formal implementation of an Islamic legal system may very well have been a top-down process initiated and directed by political elites. However, the religious and ethical dimensions of the project have a history of their own, and potentially also a longer future ahead of them than do the alternating successes and failures of any particular political parties. Although there are clearly some parties in Aceh who have attempted to manipulate the public symbolism of the Shariʿa for short-term political gain, not all do. Rather, many of the proponents of the agenda to employ Islamic law as a tool of social engineering in Aceh clearly view the process as a gradual one of change on the scale of generations,

[21] See, for example, Moch. Nur Ichwan, "The Politics of Shariʿatization: Central Governmental and Regional Discourses of Shariʿa implementation in Aceh," in R. Michael Feener and Mark E. Cammack (eds.), *Islamic Law in Contemporary Indonesia: Ideas and Institutions* (Cambridge, Mass.: Harvard University Press, 2007), 193–215; Arskal Salim, *Challenging the Secular State: The Islamization of Law in Modern Indonesia* (Honolulu: University of Hawaii Press, 2008), 149; Edward Aspinall, *Islam and Nation: Separatist Rebellion in Aceh, Indonesia* (Stanford, CA: Stanford University Press, 2009); Michelle Ann Miller and R. Michael Feener, "Emergency and Islamic Law in Aceh," in Victor Ramraj and Arun Thiruvengadam (eds.), *Law and Emergency Powers in Asia: Exploring the Limits of Legality* (Cambridge: Cambridge University Press, 2010), 213–36; Arfiansyah, "The Politicization of Shariʿah: Behind the Implementation of Shariʿah in Aceh, Indonesia," Ph.D. dissertation (Montreal: McGill University, 2010).

and not electoral cycles.[22] As will be discussed in the chapters that follow, their heavy emphasis on education reflects their ambition to have a lasting impact on "moods and motivations" and not just on short-term strategic issues or particular government policies of current interest.[23] For a more nuanced understanding of the role of Islamic law in contemporary Acehnese society, it is then necessary to adopt a broader perspective with expanded temporal horizons toward aspirational visions of Aceh's future, as well as to its troubled past.

SHARIʿA AND SOCIETY IN ACEH

The story of Islamic law in contemporary Aceh is one with a complex historical prologue that needs to be considered in any serious attempt to understand the particular forms and functions of the institutions comprising the current state Shariʿa system. The next chapter presents a critical overview of the ways in which ideas of Islam as a definitive element of Acehnese identity have taken shape in the region's history. This material serves to contextualize the ways in which both the Indonesian central government and local Islamic leaders appeal to Islam in policy discussions and public debates over the implementation of Islamic law in contemporary Aceh. There, attention is paid to the emergence of particular discourses that define Acehnese society in relation to "Islam." These include appeals to the implementation of Islamic law as testimony to the legitimacy of rulers, evolving understandings of acceptable Sufi doctrine and practice, the growth of modern visions of Islamic reform, and patterns of state involvement in the management of Islamic religious affairs.

In the latter half of the twentieth century, aspects of all these developments have come together in relation to a new "*daʿwa* paradigm" at the intersection of Indonesian nationalism, economic development, and Islamic reform that has been influential in the formation of Aceh's Islamic legal system. This is particularly evident in the ways that the architects and agents of state Shariʿa have attempted to use law as a tool of social engineering. The project has included a set of legislative priorities, conceptions of doctrinal purity, public morality, and an instrumentalist vision of law as a tool of modernizing agendas of development, rather than as a reflection of existing social norms and practices. Drawing on

[22] One of the most egregious examples of the blatant political manipulation of Islamic law in post-disaster/post-conflict Aceh has been the passing of the 2009 Shariʿa Criminal Code (*Qanun Jinayat*), discussed in Chapter 5.

[23] The phrase is, of course, taken from Clifford Geertz's classic essay, "Religion as a Cultural System," in *The Interpretation of Cultures* (New York: Basic Books, 1973), 87–125.

language that had established itself in Indonesian civil law discourse over the second half of the twentieth century, Acehnese supporters of the state implementation of Islamic law referred to the project using the English-language phrase "social engineering." The idea of law in relation to "social engineering" was introduced to Indonesia largely through the writings of the American legal philosopher Roscoe Pound. Pound's work gained a significant place on the curricula of many of the country's secular law schools starting in the 1960s.[24] Indonesian jurists, however, soon developed their own, more activist, understandings of the term than Pound had proposed to develop a model of law that fit with the priorities of political stability and economic development under the direction of a strong centralized state.[25] By the end of the twentieth century, these ideas had permeated Indonesian discourse well beyond the faculties of law schools and came to be embraced by many of the Muslim intellectuals involved with the design and promotion of Aceh's Islamic legal system.

While the basic legal framework that made the formal implementation of Shariʿa possible in Aceh was established with the Special Autonomy Laws of 1999 and 2001, the project gained a new lease of life after the 26 December 2004 tsunami and the end of the conflict with GAM. It was in that context that the idea of Shariʿa implementation as an exercise in social engineering was amplified through its resonance with an increasingly pervasive rhetoric of "total reconstruction." This book presents a detailed description and critical analysis of the aims, structure, and function of the major institutions of state Shariʿa in contemporary Aceh.

Each of the chapters that follow treats one aspect of this system, covering: educational institutions, ulama organizations, substantive legislation, Shariʿa courts, government bodies for monitoring and enforcement (WH), and the State Shariʿa Agency (DSI). Each chapter then provides an overview of diachronic developments relevant to the particular institution being discussed. In some cases this includes some longer historical treatments of developments over the course of the twentieth century, such as in the chapters on Islamic education, ulama councils, legislation, and Shariʿa courts. For those new institutions created only at the turn of the twenty-first century, the historical treatment is considerably less extensive, although there, too, specific mention will be made to the transformation of the Islamic legal system in the wake of

[24] Pound's *Introduction to the Philosophy of Law*, which first appeared in Indonesian translation as: *Pengantar Filsafat Hukum* (Jakarta: Bhratara, 1963).

[25] Shidarta, "Posisi Pemikiran Teori Hukum Pembangunan dalam Konfigurasi Aliran Pemikiran Hukum (sebuah diagnosis awal)," in Shidarta, ed. *Mochtar Kusuma-Atmadja dan Teori Hukum Pembangunan: Eksistensi dan Implikasi* (Jakarta: Epistema Institute, 2012), 9–80.

the great earthquake and tsunami of 26 December 2004. This structure means that in a number of cases, the same time periods of Aceh's history are covered in multiple passes, each time with a particular thematic and institutional focus but in a way that builds upon the earlier tellings to provide increasing levels of nuance to the story. The chronology of these developments is important, but it is not the dominating framework for the discussions in this book. Rather, the chapter structure of the book is designed to provide windows onto the design and operational mechanics of specific institutions within this contemporary Islamic legal system.

Chapter 3 looks at the ways in which understandings of Islam central to the development of Aceh's contemporary Shariʿa system were developed and transmitted through Islamic educational institutions in Aceh. After tracing the outlines of major developments in both Traditionalist and Modernist-style schools in twentieth-century Aceh, this chapter focuses on the pivotal role of the Banda Aceh campus of the State Institute for Islamic Studies (IAIN) in the contemporary Islamic legal system. This local branch of the Indonesian national system of Islamic higher education has played a primary role in the design, development, leadership, and day-to-day operations of the state institutions responsible for the implementation of Islamic law under the current state Shariʿa system.

In Aceh, the state implementation of Islamic law has been not just (or even primarily) about the establishment of institutions operating in the formal legal sphere, but more broadly concerned with fostering new subjectivities embodying a particular constellation of "Islamic values" that are viewed as conducive to directing social change in desired directions. The focus of this chapter is thus on how educational institutions in Aceh have contributed to the development and dissemination of specific models for thinking about Islam, law, and society in Aceh in ways that highlight conjunctures of institutional and ideological innovations that inform both the substantive content and the institutional architecture of the contemporary Islamic legal system.

Another major institution involved in the promotion of official understandings of Islamic law appropriate to its instrumentalist deployment by the state has been the Ulama Council. Chapter 4 discusses the processes by which Aceh's ulama have been organized by the Indonesian state both as a means of social control in a politically troubled region, and as an instrument for the promotion of particular governmental policies of "development." It also addresses the extent to which the ulama have attempted to use this institutional foundation and its resources to advance their own agendas for social change. These discussions begin by tracing the evolving dynamics of Islamic leadership in Aceh during the mid-twentieth-century "Darul Islam" (DI) insurrection against the Indonesian central government. From there the chapter traces subsequent attempts by the central government in Jakarta to engage with local Islamic scholars at various times to support the integration of the region into the Indonesian state. It then examines the current work of Aceh's official Ulama Council with a focus on the role it has played in public debates over the perceived threat posed by "deviant teachings" (I. *ajaran sesat*). The work of the MPU along these lines is an example of state intervention into the definition of "acceptable" forms of Islamic belief and practice, advanced in the idiom of a paternalistic rhetoric of "protecting" the community from the onslaught of perceived external threats. The Ulama Council's work on the production and dissemination of modern Islamic discourses of social transformation reflects trends both at the Indonesian national level and more broadly across the region, where concern with the perceived spread of heterodoxy has been on the rise over the past decade. Within the more specific context of Aceh, however, these developments also build upon distinct local traditions of Islamic reform as well as governmental strategies for national development and the further integration of Aceh into the Indonesian state.

Chapter 5 discusses the development of Islamic legislation in Aceh over the past half-century, as well as the form and content of the laws currently in force. This discussion highlights the continuities between Aceh's current Islamic legislation (referred to locally as "*qanun*"), and a succession of earlier attempts at legislating select issues of public morality to reflect Shariʿa norms. Following initial attempts at promulgating Shariʿa-based legislation in the early 1960s, proposed regulations concerning alcohol, gambling, and relations between the sexes consistently dominated the agenda of draft Shariʿa by-laws in Aceh during the first years of the New Order period (1966–1998). It was, however, only in the contexts of post-New Order de-centralization and new attempts at resolving the conflict between GAM and the Indonesian central government at the turn of the twenty-first century that new legal frameworks were constructed under the rubric of "Special Autonomy" that enabled the establishment of such laws in a more definitive way as part of the new Islamic legal system in Aceh. Tracing the successive development of these earlier attempts at legislating aspects of Islamic law in Aceh demonstrates the extent to which the particular concerns and goals of the current Shariʿa system are not unprecedented impositions by the Indonesian central government, but actually reflect earlier attempts of certain segments of Aceh's Islamic leadership to advance an agenda of prescriptive social reform through the modern legislative apparatus of the state.

The changing political contexts of the post-Suharto period opened a window of opportunity in which actors associated with both the local

Acehnese and Indonesian central governments saw mutual interests in advancing the project of state Shariʿa. Much common ground for this was set by the broader acceptance of the *daʿwa* paradigm across academic, activist, and bureaucratic circles over the last decades of the twentieth century. As the political configurations further shifted in the post-disaster/post-conflict period, however, new dynamics took hold and the processes of legislation changed considerably. It was at this time that a radically new set of items was placed on the legislative agenda of Aceh's Provincial Assembly (DPRA), most dramatically with the much-debated 2009 Islamic criminal code (*Qanun Jinayat*), and the ambiguity of its current legal status. The chapter thus concludes with a discussion of this controversial document, and the role that this document has played in attempts to reshape the broader discursive spheres of culture and politics in Aceh well beyond the limits of the formal legal sphere.

Chapter 6 shifts attention to the institutions tasked with implementing these laws, starting with Aceh's Islamic religious courts. It traces their development from the period of the Japanese wartime occupation (1942–1945) to the present, highlighting significant changes in the definition of the jurisdiction of Islamic courts over the past seventy years. In addition to a discussion of the jurisprudence of the courts in their actual handling of both family law and penal cases, particular attention is paid to the ways in which Aceh's Islamic courts are integrated within Indonesia's national legal system. As a concrete example of both of these aspects of the structure and functioning of Aceh's religious courts, the chapter includes an extended discussion of a Shariʿa criminal case that was first heard in a local court in Lhokseumawe (North Aceh), and then passed to an appellate Shariʿa court at the provincial level in Banda Aceh before being sent on for cassation by the Indonesian Supreme Court in Jakarta (Mahkamah Agung). The Supreme Court's handling of this case in particular presents a striking confirmation of the place of Aceh's Islamic legal system within the broader Indonesian national framework. At the same time, however, the particular selection of cases that the Shariʿa courts do handle continues to reflect considerations of public pedagogy that stress the importance of setting proper examples to reinforce the standards of public morality prescribed by the *qanun*.

Chapter 7 discusses the establishment of a new governmental body created at the turn of the twenty-first century and tasked with the job of coordinating the work of the other state institutions involved with the implementation of Islamic law in Aceh. After an overview of the structure and operations of the State Shariʿa Agency (Dinas Syariat Islam/DSI), the chapter presents a critical examination of the underlying vision of Islamic law that animates the enterprise. The ideals informing the work of the

DSI connect back to the *daʿwa* paradigm developed in Indonesia since the 1960s, as well as to the particular ways in which *daʿwa* was institutionalized in Aceh over the same period. A number of the major tropes of official discourses on state Shariʿa in Aceh reflect both genealogical links with developments in Islamic Modernist and Revivalist movements elsewhere in Indonesia during the last decades of the twentieth century, and aspirations for re-making an Acehnese society in accordance with these particular visions of Islam as a comprehensive system for establishing and maintaining social order. In line with this vision, the implementation of Islamic law is expressed in terms of a program that brings the benefits of accountability, transparency, openness, and the rule of law through the enforcement of higher aspirations for personal morality. The discussion of the ways in which these ideals are promoted by the DSI highlights the further shift toward instrumentalist visions of Islamic law and its deployment for state-directed projects of social engineering as a coordinated effort at public education supported by the various institutions of the contemporary Islamic legal system.

Chapter 8 treats the mechanisms for the monitoring and enforcement of Shariʿa norms in contemporary Aceh with a focus on the institution known locally as the Wilayatul Hisbah (WH), which is often described as Aceh's "Shariʿa police." This examination of the work and the experience of WH officers calls particular attention to the fundamental importance of conceptions of public pedagogy at work in this new institution for the enforcement of Islamic law, and its intended contribution to the project of social engineering. As the most high-profile and polemicized institution of state Shariʿa in contemporary Aceh, the WH also presents us with dramatic examples of the interface between the formal legal apparatus and society in the contestation over the ways in which Shariʿa values are to be engaged in state programs of social control. After introducing the legal foundation and operational structure of the WH, the focus of the chapter shifts to the personnel of this institution. Based upon interviews and extensive interaction (both on and off-duty) with male and female WH officers from across the province, this chapter engages narratives of their own motivations in the job and experiences of their work in the field, as well as their relations to other government bodies and vigilante groups. These rarely heard perspectives serve to set the stage for the concluding section of the chapter, which presents a window onto the heated public debates over the WH and its work in contemporary Aceh.

The final chapter (9) builds on the empirical data presented in the chapters that precede it to develop a more sustained discussion of the idea of Shariʿa as a tool of social engineering in contemporary Aceh. In doing so it traces the various lines of influence that have shaped this forward-oriented, instrumentalist vision of Islamic law in society—including strains of twentieth-century American sociological jurisprudence, *da'wa*-inspired Islamic activism, and the international reconstruction and development rhetoric of "building back better." These and other diverse elements have come together in unexpected and powerful ways to shape the discourse and practice of Islamic law in contemporary Aceh in the post-disaster/post-conflict period. While the basic legal framework that made the expanded implementation of Shari'a possible in contemporary Aceh was established with the special autonomy laws of 1999 and 2001, the idea of Shari'a implementation as an exercise in social engineering was amplified through resonance with an increasingly pervasive rhetoric of "total reconstruction" after 2004.

Today, an increasing number of Muslim societies across the world have become de-stabilized by political turmoil and natural catastrophe, leading many to look for models of building a new society out of the ruins of tragic pasts of conflict, repression, and/or physical devastation. In the muddled sea of global media pundit commentary that was blown to billows by the breezes of the "Arab Spring" in 2011, the very notion that ideals and visions of the future informed by "Islam" might play a role in remaking societies in the course of post-authoritarian transitions was greeted with various admixtures of fear and disdain. Such readings of the situation, however, were generally based upon a frame of analysis that focused simply on identifying manageable ideological labels for those who were emerging as potential players in new spheres of political contestation. By comparison, critical and contextualized examinations of just what such broad constructions as "Islam" (or "Democracy" for that matter) might actually contain and convey for particular actors in various countries received little attention.

This book attempts to frame new lines of discussion about appeals to Islam as a source of values, and about how Islamic law in particular is viewed as a potential tool for transforming society. The point here is that there is more to Muslim politics than simply "seizing the state," and that much can be learned by paying attention to what various actors imagine might actually be gained through the control of certain elements of the state apparatus. For in some cases, those promoting the formal implementation of Islamic law have viewed the project in avowedly instrumentalist terms—in which the goal is not simply one of taking control, but further toward the use of state power and resources as tools to promote agendas of social change. In order to get at this, of course, studies of Islamic law in contemporary societies need to move beyond the abstractions of political ideology and elite power plays. As important as these aspects of recent developments are, they are not in themselves sufficient for understanding the idealistic motivations, and the strategic choices made in their pursuit, by advocates of state Shariʿa in contemporary Muslim societies. These ideals, furthermore, are themselves multiple and variously configured "on the ground" in ways that are not sufficiently captured by reading appeals by Islamist politicians to Shariʿa as a kind of shorthand for the rule of law.[26] To get at this we also need to consider the complex, embedded discourses on public morality, personal piety, social order, doctrinal rectitude, and economic development that diversely configure to inform agendas for the implementation of Islamic law.

The chapters that follow are designed to deliver windows onto precisely these aspects of the project of state Shariʿa in contemporary Aceh by presenting detailed, "thick" descriptions of various segments of the Islamic legal system there.[27] While the empirical details of these discussions are unique, the story that they tell can provide more than just an interesting case study. Indeed, Aceh presents a remarkable site for investigating the impact of instrumentalist, future-oriented visions of Islamic law on modern Muslim calls for the state implementation of Shariʿa. This is because the dramatic social and political contexts of "total reconstruction" in the post-disaster/post-conflict period there serve to significantly amplify discourses of instrumentalism and aspiration for ethically-informed social transformation that resonate with ideals held by Islamists in many other parts of the world.

The immense physical destruction of the natural disaster, washing over the already tattered social fabric of a land plagued by decades of violent conflict, produced a compelling vision of "creative destruction"—one reflecting a not-uncommon conception of opportunity found among modern humanitarian movements. As Michael Barnett has recently described it:

> Devastation invites reformers to imagine new arrangements that can peel away the causes of suffering and create the spiritual and material foundations for a better world. Few humanitarians enter a world of ruin with the goal of putting the pieces back together the way they were; instead, they treat the ruin as an opportunity to seek justice and human improvement.[28]

[26] Cf. Noah Feldman, "Why Sharia?" *New York Times* (16 March 2008): <http://www.nytimes.com/2008/03/16/magazine/16Shariah-t.html?pagewanted=all>, accessed 23 August 2012; *The Fall and Rise of the Islamic State* (Princeton: Princeton University Press, 2008).

[27] Here I must make another nod to Geertz, who in turn gestures to Gilbert Ryle. Clifford Geertz, "Thick Description: Toward an Interpretive Theory of Culture" in *The Interpretation of Cultures*, 3–30.

[28] Michael Barnett, *Empire of Humanity: A History of Humanitarianism* (Ithaca: Cornell University Press, 2011), 227.

Such opportunities for both spiritual renewal and social improvement in the wake of the great wave were glimpsed by local Muslim academics and activists, as well as by the myriad agents of international aid and development organizations that flocked to Aceh to undertake the immense work of reconstruction. For the former, the post-disaster/post-conflict context provided a critical juncture for invigorating the province's fledgling Islamic legal system, as well as for heightened expectations of wide-ranging social transformation in accordance with *daʿwa*-inspired ideals that had been taking shape in Aceh for decades. Through an explication of these historical developments and critical analysis of the current work of the institutions that have been established to implement the Shariʿa in contemporary Aceh, this book seeks to open up new lines of critical discussion on one of the most complex experiments with the implementation of Islamic law in the contemporary world.

2

Islam in Visions of Aceh's Past (and Future)

> Sultan al-Mālik al-Ẓāhir ranks among the most noble and generous of kings. He belongs to the Shāfiʿī school of law. He is a patron of Muslim legal scholars who come to his court to read the Qur'ān and to discourse [on religion]. He frequently campaigns against the unbelievers. He is humble and walks on foot to the congregational prayer on Fridays. The people of his country also belong to the Shāfiʿī school of law. They too are keen in fighting unbelievers and enthusiastically accompany the sultan on his campaigns. They overwhelm the infidels living near them, who must then pay a tax in settlement.
>
> Ibn Baṭṭūṭa,
> *Riḥla*

The history of Aceh is one of the most extensively documented of any region in island Southeast Asia.[1] The earliest written and archaeological sources we have for settlements on the northern end of Sumatra date back to the late first millennium, and they already point to its pivotal position as a site of cultural and commercial contact with a wide range of other societies stretching from China to India and the Middle East.[2] From the late thirteenth century, these diverse cultures met there under the broad umbrella of an expanding trans-regional Islamicate civilization of the post-Abbasid period to make the northern tip of Sumatra not only one of the first, but also one of the most influential centers of Islam in the region.[3]

[1] For a rich sample of accounts of visits to Aceh dating back to the thirteenth century, see: Anthony Reid, *Witnesses to Sumatra: A Travellers' Anthology* (Kuala Lumpur: Oxford University Press, 1995).

[2] E. Edwards McKinnon, "Beyond Serandib: A Note on Lambri at the Northern Tip of Aceh," *Indonesia* 46 (1988) 74. For more on the archaeological heritage of Aceh, see Francine Brinkgreve and Retno Sulistianingsih (eds.), *Sumatra: Crossroads of Cultures* (Leiden: KITLV Press, 2009).

[3] On Aceh's place within the broader context of the development of regional Muslim cultures in Southeast Asia, see R. Michael Feener, "Southeast Asian Localisations of Islam and Participation within a Global Umma, c. 1500–1800," in Anthony Reid and David Morgan (eds.), *The New Cambridge History of Islam*, vol. 3 (Cambridge: Cambridge University Press, 2010), 470–503.

Much has been written on Acehnese history, and a considerable amount of new work is currently being developed in this field. This is not the place for a comprehensive review of that literature.[4] It is important here, however, to present an introduction to those aspects of the history of Islam in the region that have significantly informed the modern developments that are the main focus of this book. These include discussions of appeals to the implementation of Islamic law as testimony to the legitimacy of rulers, evolving understandings of acceptable Sufi doctrine and practice, and the growth of modern visions of Islamic reform, as well as patterns of state involvement in the management of Islamic religious affairs. Building on this background, subsequent chapters will go on to tell the story of a series of inter-related trajectories of developments of Islam, law, and society in Aceh, picking up generally from the mid-twentieth century and continuing on through the first decade of the twenty-first.

SUMATRAN SULTANATES

The earliest Islamic polity for which we have significant evidence in Southeast Asia was established at Pasai (on Aceh's north coast, near present-day Lhokseumawe) at the end of the thirteenth century. Pasai developed a court culture in which the Arabic language held pride of place, and which maintained contacts with Muslim sultanates in Cairo, Delhi, and elsewhere.[5] The fourteenth-century Maghribi traveller Ibn Baṭṭūṭa attests to the remarkable degree to which this Sumatran city was connected with other parts of the global *umma*.[6] In the quote from him at the opening of this chapter describing Pasai's sultan and his realm, it is clear that the formation of the sultanate's Islamic identity involved diverse elements, ranging from adherence to an established "school" (Ar. *madhhab*) of Islamic law and participation in global traditions of Islamic learning and literature, to armed struggle against non-Muslim outsiders.

Pasai's pre-eminence as a center of Islamic culture in northern Sumatra waned over the course of the fifteenth century, and was eclipsed in the sixteenth with the rise of the Sultanate of Aceh at the northern tip of

[4] On the current state of the field, see R. Michael Feener, "The Acehnese Past and its Present State of Study," in R. Michael Feener, Patrick Daly, and Anthony Reid (eds.), *Mapping the Acehnese Past* (Leiden: KITLV Press, 2011), 1–24.

[5] For Pasai and its development as an early site of Islamicate civilization in Southeast Asia through processes of Malay-Muslim "*alchimie culturelle*," see Claude Guillot and Ludvik Kalus, *Les monuments funéraires et l'histoire du sultanat de Pasai à Sumatra, XIIIe-XVIe siècles* (Paris: Association Archipel, 2008).

[6] Ibn Baṭṭūṭa, *Riḥla - Tuḥfat al-nuẓẓar fī gharā'ib al-amṣār wa ajā'ib al-asfār* (Beirut: Dār al-sharq al-ʿarabī, n.d.), 478–81.

the island.[7] Like Pasai before it, the sultanate of Aceh defined itself as an Islamic port polity through the patronage of religious scholars from abroad, as well as by military campaigns against infidels. Expressions of the sultanate's role as a patron and defender of Islam entailed not only expansionary campaigns into the Sumatran hinterland, but also—and more importantly—crusades to combat Portuguese maritime expansion in the region.[8] Aceh's vigorous attempts to assert control over trade through the Straits of Malacca also came to mutually reinforce the designs of other Muslim states to confront the Portuguese and their intervention into Indian Ocean trade at that time. Cooperation on this common front facilitated a degree of official interaction between the sultanate of Aceh and the Ottoman Empire during the sixteenth century.[9] These contacts have come to serve as a significant point of reference in assertions of Aceh's connections to a broader Muslim world at a number of critical points in its later history.[10]

By the turn of the seventeenth century, Portuguese power was on the wane and Aceh emerged as the dominant commercial and cultural center of the region, supplanting Malacca which held the position previously, and defining new models of Malay-Muslim culture that have had a lasting impact on the subsequent development of Islam in Southeast Asia.[11] Its most famous ruler, Iskandar Muda (r. 1607–1636), launched campaigns for the Islamization of neighboring regions in Sumatra, and staged elaborate observances of Friday prayers and other Islamic religious

[7] During this period of transition, other smaller states also attempted to assert themselves as new, but ultimately short-lived, centers of trade along the Acehnese side of the Straits of Malacca—including Peudada (near present-day Bireuen). Ludvik Kalus and Claude Guillot, "Note sur le sultanat de Peudada, fin XVe-début XVIe [Épigraphie islamique d'Aceh. 5]," *Archipel* 83 (2012) 7–15.

[8] Anthony Reid has discussed the formative influence of opposition to the Portuguese during the establishment of the Acehnese sultanate, and a significant degree of valorization of militant struggle came to be a defining mark of the Acehnese character: "Islam in South-East Asia and the Indian Ocean littoral, 1500–1800: Expansion, Polarisation, Synthesis," *The New Cambridge History of Islam*, vol. 3, (Cambridge: Cambridge University Press, 2010), 427–69.

[9] Giancarlo Casale, *The Ottoman Age of Exploration* (Oxford: Oxford University Press, 2010), 56–9; İsmail Hakkı Göksoy, "Ottoman-Aceh Relations as Documented in Turkish Sources," in R. Michael Feener, Patrick Daly, and Anthony Reid (eds.), *Mapping the Acehnese Past* (Leiden: KITLV Press, 2011), 65–96.

[10] This was the case both in the nineteenth century, when Aceh appealed to the Ottomans for assistance support against Dutch incursions, and again in the wake of the 2004 tsunami, which attracted a number of Turkish aid workers and organizations to Aceh. For the nineteenth century connections, see Ismail Hakkı Kadı, Andrew Peacock, and Annabel Teh Gallop, "Writing History: The Acehnese Embassy to Istanbul, 1849–1852," in R. Michael Feener, Patrick Daly, and Anthony Reid (eds.), *Mapping the Acehnese Past* (Leiden: KITLV Press, 2010), 163–82.

[11] Leonard Andaya, *Leaves of the Same Tree: Trade and Ethnicity in the Straits of Melaka* (Honolulu: University of Hawai'i Press, 2008), 108–45.

holidays.[12] Iskandar Muda adopted many aspects of court culture from the contemporary Mughal Empire to bolster his authority as a Muslim sovereign,[13] and established an institution for the state management of Islam analogous in some ways to that of the office of the Ottoman *Sehülislam*.[14]

The Acehnese court was an important regional patron of Islamic scholarship during the seventeenth century. Prominent ulama working there included both foreign scholars attracted by its increasing wealth, like Nūr al-Dīn al-Rānīrī (d. 1658), as well as Sumatran-born scholars who had studied at major centers of Islamic learning in South Asia and the Middle East like ʿAbd al-Raʾūf al-Sinkgkel's (d. 1693). The latter's surviving works include the *Mirʾāt al- ṭullāb fī tashīl maʿrifa t al-aḥkām al-Sharʿiyya lil-mālik al-wahhāb*, in which he advanced a Shariʿa-based argument for the legitimacy of a woman to serve as the head of a Muslim state (*khalīfa*).[15] This was no mere theoretical issue for Aceh's Muslims at that time, as Aceh was ruled by a succession of four queens (*sulṭānas*) from 1641–1699.

The seventeenth-century sultanate is often hailed as a "Golden Age" of Islam in Aceh, and held up by some as an historical precedent for the contemporary Shariʿa system in the province. Popular expressions of this vision often repeat the claim that, at that time, "the Shariʿa was applied comprehensively, for both civil and criminal affairs."[16] Such views, however, have not gone unchallenged in contemporary Aceh. One young Acehnese academic and activist has, for example, compiled accounts of corporal punishments carried out in Aceh during that time for drinking, adultery, apostasy, theft, banditry, and murder. These punishments often took forms unknown to the established traditions of Islamic courts and applied in ways that neglected or even contradicted formal rules of *fiqh*, leading him to argue that the "sadistic" (I. *sadis*) punishments inflicted for these crimes were generally dealt with by local custom law (I. *adat*)

[12] See Denys Lombard, *Le sultanat d'Atjéh au temps d'Iskandar Muda, 1607–1636* (Paris: École Française d'Extrême-Orient, 1967).

[13] James T. Siegel, *Shadow and Sound: The Historical Thought of a Sumatran People* (Chicago: University of Chicago Press, 1979), 24–5, Vladimir Braginsky, "Structure, Date and Sources of *Hikayat Aceh* Revisited: The Problem of Mughal-Malay Literary Ties," *Bijdragen tot de Taal-, Land- en Volkenkunde* 162 (4) (2006) 441–67.

[14] Ito Takeshi, *"The World of the Adat Aceh: A Historical Study of the Sultanate of Aceh"* Ph.D. dissertation (Canberra: Australian National University, 1984), 259–62.

[15] Amirul Hadi, *Islam and State in Sumatra: A Study of Seventeenth-Century Aceh* (Leiden: Brill, 2004), 60.

[16] This particular wording of the common claim is taken from: Mukhtar Aziz, "Tinjauan Historis Pelaksanaan Syariat Islam di NAD," in T.H. Thalhas (ed.), *Pendidikan dan Syariat Islam di Nanggroe Aceh Darussalam dan 8 Undang-Undang Terkait* (Jakarta: Galura Pase, 2007), 73.

or political expediency rather than by the formal procedures of Islamic jurisprudence.[17]

NEW DYNAMICS OF LOCALIZATION

Contemporary appeals to the precedent of the "Golden Age" of the seventeenth-century sultanate obscure the legacy of major formative developments in the political and social systems of Aceh over the intervening centuries. Aceh's pre-eminent position as a regional center of Islam and its active engagement with the broader Muslim world declined in the late seventeenth century, as interventions by the Dutch East India Company (VOC) catalyzed realignments of trade relationships that hastened Aceh's decline as both a port and a polity. With the abdication of the last *sulṭāna*, Keumalat Shah (r. 1688–1699), power passed from the established dynasty of the Aceh sultanate into the hands of prominent Arab migrants, and thence to ethnic Buginese claimants to the throne.[18] Over the course of the eighteenth century, the area of Aceh's effective political control over territories beyond the capital receded considerably. In this context, various local lords (Ac. *ulèëbalang*) emerged as the de facto rulers of their respective territories.[19]

The resulting decentralization facilitated the emergence of complex new social and cultural dynamics. It was, for example, during the eighteenth and nineteenth centuries that traditions of literature and Islamic texts written in the Acehnese language developed substantially. This corpus added a level of more localized vernacular expressions of Islam complementing the works of religious scholarship produced and studied in Malay and Arabic that had been dominant there through the seventeenth century.[20] Another major vector for the development of new models of Islam in Aceh followed a course northward from the Minangkabau region. There, new forms of

[17] Ayang Utriza Nway, "Adakah Penerapan Syariat di Acheh: Tinjauan Sejarah Hukum di Kesultanan Acheh," *Jurnal Gelombang Baru* IV (2009) 17–62.

[18] T.J. Veltman, "Nota over de Geschiedenis van het Landschap Pidië," *Tijdschrift van het Bataviaasch Genootschap van Kunsten en Wetenschappen* 58 (1919) 71–88.

[19] K.F.H. van Langen, "De Inrichting van het Atjehsche Staatsbestuur onder het Sultanaat," *Bijdragen tot de Taal- Land- en Volkenkunde van Nederlandsch-Indië* 37(1) (1888) 382–471.

[20] It must be noted, however, that the rise of textual production in Acehnese did not mean the end of Malay as a medium of Islamic scholarship, and a number of scholars from Aceh continued to produce Malay-language works in the Islamic religious sciences through the eighteenth and nineteenth centuries. Into the twentieth century some of these works continued to be published and studied in local *dayah*, particularly through the compilations by Ismāʿīl b. ʿAbd al-Muṭṭalib al-Āshī, the *Jamʿjawāmiʿ al-muṣannafāt* (Cairo: Muṣṭafā al-Bābī al-Halabī, 1925), and the *Tāj al-muluk* (Cairo: Muṣṭafā al-Bābī al-Halabī, 1938).

Figure 2.1. An Acehnese mosque at Peudada: This structure reflects aspects of architectural styles known from the seventeenth century, as well as the addition of an ornamental false dome, reflecting more "modern" styles that became popular in Aceh from the end of the nineteenth century and ubiquitous during the twenty-first century reconstruction boom. (Photo by R. Michael Feener)

Sufism were carried by Muslim migrants drawn to the new economic and commercial possibilities of the pepper plantations that were proliferating on the west coast of Sumatra in the late eighteenth and early nineteenth centuries.[21]

Forms of Sufi cosmology had been known and much debated in Aceh long before this, with debates over texts associated with the Shaṭṭariyya Sufi order dominating the discourse for much of the seventeenth century.[22]

[21] During this period, the sultanate's increasing inability to control further stretches of the west coast opened the possibility for other parties to establish their own trading ports there, and some *uléëbalang* established their own trade in pepper, particularly with American merchant vessels from Salem, Massachusetts. For more on this, see: James W. Gould, "America's Pepperpot, 1784–1873," *Essex Institute Historical Collections* XCII (1956) 83–152; XCII (1956) 203–51; XCII (1956) 295–348; and George Granville Putnam, *Salem Vessels and Their Voyages—Series I: A History of the Pepper Trade with the Island of Sumatra* (Salem, Massachusetts: The Essex Institute, 1924). A vernacular Acehnese depiction of life in the new pepper plantations that supplied this trade can be found in Leubè Isa's *Hikajat Ranto*, see G.W.J. Drewes, *Two Acehnese Poems: Hikajat Ranto and Hikajat Teungku di Meuke* (The Hague: Martinus Nijhoff, 1980), 6–41.

[22] There is an extensive (and often repetitive) literature of international scholarship on Acehnese Islamic polemics of this period, focused particularly on the works of four authors: Ḥamza Fanṣūrī, Shams al-Dīn al-Sumaṭrānī, Nūr al-Dīn al-Rānīrī, and ʿAbd al-Raʾūf Singkel. For an overview of work on this topic published in Dutch, English, and Indonesian,

Subsequently vibrant traditions of Sufi belief and practice identified with the Shaṭṭariyya spread across Aceh and West Sumatra.[23] Werner Kraus has argued that by the nineteenth century, understandings of the Shaṭṭariyya had blended with aspects of local religious belief and practice to produce a strongly localized form of Sufism in Aceh.[24] These localized Sufi traditions are today often indiscriminately referred to as *wujūdiyya* and associated with the concepts of the "unity of Being" (Ar. *waḥdat al-wujūd*) and the "perfect man" (Ar. *al-insān al-kāmil*). These concepts had been central to Shaṭṭarī teachings in earlier centuries, but have since come under attack by reformers for their alleged "pantheism."[25]

At the same time, aspects of other Sufi traditions and orders came to be integrated into the mix on Sumatra's west coast.[26] One of the most influential of these was introduced by the West Sumatran scholar Da'ūd Sunur (d. 1858) who settled in the Acehnese port town of Trumon after returning from an extended period of study in Mecca.[27] Upon arrival there he became a pioneer of trends in Sufi reform that were to transform the face of Islam in Aceh over the nineteenth and early twentieth centuries.[28] Michael Laffan has suggested that Da'ūd Sunur may have been affiliated with the Naqshbandiyya order, which represented a new force in reshaping understandings of Islam across the archipelago at that time.[29] In

see Peter Riddell, *Islam and the Malay-Indonesian World: Transmission and Responses* (Honolulu: University of Hawai'i Press, 2001).

[23] See Oman Fathurahman, *Tarekat Syattariyah di Minangkabau; Teksdan Konteks* (Jakarta: KITLV, 2008); Fakhriati, *Menelusuri Tarekat Syattariyah di Aceh Lewat Naskah* (Jakarta: Departmen Agama RI Badan Litbangdan Diklat Puslitbang Lektur Keagamaan, 2008).

[24] Werner Kraus, "The Shattariyya Sufi Brotherhood in Aceh," in Arndt Graf, Susanne Schröter, and Edwin Wieringa (eds.), *Aceh: History, Politics and Culture* (Singapore: ISEAS Publishing, 2010), 212–24.

[25] For the earlier background of internal Sufi reform that prefigured Modernist critiques of Ibn'Arabi, see Alexander Knysh, *Ibn'Arabi in the Later Islamic Tradition: The Making of a Polemical Image in Medieval Islam* (Albany: State University of New York Press, 1999).

[26] Werner Kraus, *Zwischen Reform und Rebellion: Über die Entwicklung des Islams in Minangkabau (Westsumatra) zwischen den beiden Reformbewegungen der Padri (1837) und der Modernisten (1908): Ein Beitragzur Geschichte der Islamisierung Indonesiens* (Wiesbaden: Franz Steiner Verlag, 1984), 77–9.

[27] Suryadi, "Shaikh Daud of Sunur: Conflict between Reformists and the Shattariyyah Sufi Order in Rantau Pariaman in the First Half of the Nineteenth Century," *Studia Islamika* 8(3) (2001) 57–124.

[28] Edwin Wieringa, "A Tale of Two Cities and Two Modes of Reading: A Transformation of the Intended Function of the Syair Mekah dan Madinah," *Die Welt des Islams* 42(2) (2002) 190–1.

[29] Michael Laffan, *The Makings of Indonesian Islam: Muslims, Orientalists and Entwined Visions of a Sufi Tradition* (Princeton University Press, 2011), 43. See also L.W.C. van den Berg, "Over de devotie der Naqsjibendijah in den Indischen Archipel," *Tijdschrift voor Indische Taal-, Land-, en Volkenkunde* 28(2) (1883) 158–75; K.F. Holle, "Mededeelingen over de devotie der Naqsjibendijah in den Ned. Indischen Archipel," *Tijdschrift voor Indische Taal-, Land-, en Volkenkunde* 31 (1886) 67–81; Martin van Bruinessen, *Tarekat Naqsyabandiyah di Indonesia: Survei Historis, Geografis dan Sosiologis* (Bandung: Mizan, 1992).

Aceh, as elsewhere, Naqshbandiyya introduced new practices to existing repertoires of Sufi devotionalism, and it became known especially for the importance it placed upon directed spiritual exercises (Ar./Ac. *suluk*) and ritualized "retreat" for purposes of prayer and meditation (Ar. *khalwa*/Ac. *kaluët*).[30] These ritual practices could at times become highly politicized, and during the Dutch war, a Naqshbandī shaykh in Samalanga prescribed seven days of *kaluët* as penance for any Acehnese who had entered into territory controlled by the Dutch "unbelievers."[31]

"HOLY WAR" AND WORLDLY POWER STRUGGLES

Nineteenth-century changes to established forms of religious belief and practice in Aceh took shape within contexts of new political realities that carried considerable consequences for the modern reconfiguration of Acehnese Islamic identity. The most dramatic of these developments was clearly the Dutch invasion of Aceh in 1873, and the decades of armed resistance that followed.[32] For the Acehnese, the legacies of conflict, both during and since the wars against the Dutch, have fostered popular perceptions that incorporate the idea of violent resistance against outside aggression into a conception of a strong Acehnese Islamic identity.[33]

The Dutch wars in Aceh opened new opportunities for local ulama to reassert their authority. The *uléëbalang* had often collaborated with the Dutch to maintain local control over their territories, and in the process, lost prestige in the eyes of the people. While some Acehnese ulama were also willing to collaborate, others opted for an oppositional stance and deployed the symbols of Islam in their campaigns of resistance against the invading infidels.[34] One of the most powerful means of doing this

[30] For more on this aspect of the devotional practice of the Khālidiyya, see Butrus Abu-Manneh, "Khalwa and Rabita in the Khalidi Order," in M. Gaborieau, A. Popovic, and T. Zarcone (eds.), *Naqshbandis: cheminements et situation actuelle d'un order mystique musulman* (Istanbul: Éd. Isis, 1990), 283–302.

[31] C. Snouck Hurgronje, *The Achehnese*, vol. II, trans. A.W.S. O'Sullivan (Leiden: E. J. Brill, 1906), 116.

[32] For more on the broader colonial contexts of this, see Anthony Reid, *The Contest for North Sumatra: Atjeh, the Netherlands, and Britain, 1858–1898* (Kuala Lumpur: University of Malaya Press, 1969).

[33] Tropes of violent resistance continue to be expressed in Aceh today, even in official government publications on Acehnese culture. See, for example: *Aceh Tanah Rencong* (Banda Aceh: Pemerintah Provinsi Nanggroe Aceh Darussalam, 2008).

[34] The Dutch orientalist C. Snouck Hurgronje is often credited (or castigated) as central in making this division crucial to shaping the contours of the Dutch wars in Aceh. For Snouck's own statements on the dynamics of religious and social leadership in Aceh during the Dutch wars, see: Snouck, *Achehnese* I, 187, and E. Gobée and C. Adriaanse (eds.), *Ambtelijke Adviezen van C. Snouck Hurgronje: 1889–1936* ('s-Gravenhage: Martinus Nijhoff, 1957), 47–396.

was to draw on the traditions of more activist Sufism that had taken root in the region over the course of the eighteenth and early nineteenth centuries—including the Sumatran scholar 'Abd al-Ṣamad al-Palimbānī (al-Jāwī)'s treatise on *jihād*.[35] Over the late nineteenth century, there developed a body of "holy war" texts in Acehnese verse, generally referred to as *Hikayat Prang Sabi*.[36] Through these evocative narratives of heroism, calls to join the fight against infidel intruders, and promises of heavenly rewards for martyrdom, the idea of Islam not only as a central, but also as a confrontational and oppositional aspect of Acehnese identity was further consolidated.

In the twentieth century, vigorous wartime assertions of the centrality of Islam for defining the Acehnese and their way of life gave powerful cultural expression to the idea of the ulama as militant defenders of Aceh against external threats. In this, the status of the ulama as authoritative local leaders was increasingly contrasted with that of the traditional aristocracy (Ac. *ulèëbalang*), who came to fill positions of worldly power within the Dutch colonial administration as it consolidated control over parts of Aceh in the early decades of the twentieth century. As their prestige vis-à-vis the *ulèëbalang* increased, the ulama also turned their attention toward the development of new institutions. While the apparatus of the colonial state provided new sources of support to maintain the position of some *ulèëbalang*, the ulama came to solidify their own autonomous position through the establishment of Islamic educational institutions known in Acehnese as *dayah*. These Islamic religious boarding schools came to serve as the primary organizational structures of Acehnese Islam in the early twentieth century.[37] They provided the ulama with avenues of considerable social influence in particular local communities, while simultaneously facilitating the integration of the broader population

[35] One early exemplar of the Acehnese genre of "Holy War" texts—Nya' Ahmat's 1894 exhortation to *jihād* against the incursion of the Dutch entitled *Nasihat ureuëng muprang*—draws on the work of Palimbānī's *Naṣīḥat al-muslimīn wa tadhkirat al-mu'minīn fī faḍā'il al-jihād fī sabīl Allāh* (Snouck, *Achehnese* II, 119).

[36] There is a considerable body of modern writing on Acehnese *Prang Sabi* texts—and in fact, this particular genre of texts has received attention disproportionate to its place within the broader tradition of Acehnese literature. See, for example: H.T. Damsté, "Hikajat Prang Sabi," *Bijdragen tot de Taal-, Land- en Volkenkunde* 84 (1928) 545–609; A. Hasjmy, *Hikajat Prang Sabi mendjiwai Perang Atjeh Lawan Belanda* (Banda Aceh: Pustaka Faraby, 1971); Teuku Ibrahim Alfian, "Aceh and the Holy War (Prang Sabil)," in Anthony Reid (ed.), *Verandah of Violence: The Background to the Aceh Problem* (Singapore: Singapore University Press, 2006), 109–20; and Amirul Hadi, "Exploring Acehnese Understandings of Jihad: A Study of the *Hikayat Prang Sabi*," in Feener, Daly, and Reid, *Mapping the Acehnese Past*, 183–98.

[37] Acehnese *dayah*, like analogous institutions of *pondok pesantren* across the Indonesian archipelago, went through formative phases of expansion and consolidation during this period. The specific development of Acehnese *dayah* will be treated more extensively in Chapter 3.

under a generally shared range of understandings of Islam that drew upon the established traditions of Shāfiʿī *fiqh* and Naqshbandī Sufism.

CONTESTING VISIONS OF ISLAM

Over the first decades of the twentieth century, transformations of the internal dynamics of Acehnese society were driven by new tensions arising from debates over differing visions of what constitutes proper Islamic belief and practice. During this period, Acehnese Muslims returning from periods of study abroad began bringing home some of the modernizing visions of Islam that were then gaining ground in West Sumatra, Java, Egypt, and elsewhere.[38] These reform-minded activists were sharply critical of Aceh's *dayah* and the traditions of Sufism and jurisprudence that those schools maintained and transmitted.

In some instances, tensions erupted in violence, as was the case in a 1927 row between conservative ulama and *madrasa* activists in Sigli that left four persons wounded.[39] Less physical challenges to Traditionalist forms of Islam filled a number of new spaces in the expanding public sphere at that time. Authors writing in modern, romanized forms of the Indonesian language were publishing pamphlets aggressively denouncing Traditionalist positions and attacking popular forms of Sufi belief and practice in the 1930s and 1940s.[40] High-profile public debates were also staged in many Acehnese cities at that time, some of the most dramatic of which featured the *madrasa*-educated reformist Tgk. Sufi squaring off against the doyen of Aceh's Traditionalists, Tgk. Muda Waly.[41]

As these developments were taking place, agendas of modernizing Islamic reform were eagerly taken up by some *uléëbalang*. A number of those *uléëbalang* also found common ground with other Islamic Modernists against the Traditionalist ulama, with whom relations

[38] For an overview of these developments in broader contexts of Muslim history during this period, see R. Michael Feener, "New Networks and New Knowledge: Migrations, Communications and the Refiguration of the Muslim Community in the Nineteenth and Early Twentieth Centuries," in Robert Hefner (ed.), *The New Cambridge History of Islam*, vol. 6 (Cambridge: Cambridge University Press, 2010), 39–68.

[39] M. Isa Sulaiman, "Les Ulèebalang, les Ulémas, et les enseignants de madrasah: La lutte pour le pouvoir local en Aceh de 1942 à 1951," Ph.D. dissertation (Paris: Écoles Des Hautes Études en Sciences Sociales, 1985), 84.

[40] For example, Hasbi Ash Shiddieqy's *Penutup Mulut* and Abdullah Ujong Rimba's *Pedoman Penolak Salek Buta*. Sulaiman, "Les Ulèebalang, les Ulémas, et les enseignants," 85. For more on the development of religious discourse in Aceh at that time, see: James T. Siegel, *The Rope of God* (Berkeley: University of California Press, 1969), 98–133.

[41] John Bowen has discussed similar debates occurring in the Gayo highlands at this time. See *Muslims through Discourse: Religion and Ritual in Gayo Society* (Princeton: Princeton University Press, 1993), 21–32.

often continued to be strained in the decades since the Dutch wars. For example, the first Acehnese branch of the Islamic Modernist organization Muhammadiyah was founded by the *uléëbalang* T. Muhammad Hasan and T. Cut Hasan.[42] Notwithstanding the role of these *uléëbalang*, the leading roles in Acehnese movements for Islamic reform soon came to be dominated not by *uléëbalang* but rather by a different kind of ulama. These new ulama were trained in the new style of *madrasa* schools spreading across the archipelago and engaged with broader discourses of reform that were at that time circulating between this region, South Asia, and the Middle East. In the wake of the Dutch wars, these Modernist ulama articulated a new vision of Islam, and of Islam's potential role in ordering society. They convinced many that a modern form of Shari'a could serve as the foundation for a reconstitution of society.[43]

In the early years of the twentieth century, Islamic Modernist organizations were established in various parts of the Indonesian archipelago, including the Muhammadiyah and al-Irsyad (Java) and the Sumatra Thawalib (West Sumatra). In the 1920s, these organizations established branch offices and schools in various parts of Aceh. However, none of these movements was successful in developing a mass local following there.[44] Islamic Modernism only flourished in Aceh after the establishment of a distinctly Acehnese movement for Islamic reform, the Persatuan Ulama-ulama Seluruh Aceh (PUSA). PUSA worked to establish its own modern educational institutions, such as the Normaal Islam Instituut at Sigli that trained cadres to fill positions in a modern system of administration.[45] PUSA graduates exhibited, literally, a new "style" of Islam in Aceh, one in which trousers and neckties were preferred over sarung and turbans. PUSA's vision of Islam was not a "conservative" one, but rather a forward-looking, "progressive" agenda that emphasized public morality, as well as regimes of personal discipline that could facilitate the development of greater social order. This had the effect of attracting a certain degree of relative indulgence, if not necessarily respect, from Dutch colonial officials—so much so that some opponents criticized the Muslim Modernists for being a tool of colonial domination.[46] From the

[42] In fact, when the largely reformist organization, Persatuan Ulama Seluruh Aceh (PUSA), was first founded in 1939, it also received significant support from the *uléëbalang*. Alfian, "The Ulama in Acehnese Society," in Ahmad Ibrahim, Sharon Siddique, and Yasmin Hussain (eds.), *Readings on Islam in Southeast Asia* (Singapore: Institute of Southeast Asian Studies, 1985), 84.

[43] Jim T. Siegel, "Syariat Islam di Acheh," *Jurnal Gelombang Baru* IV (2009) 105–6.

[44] More on PUSA and its role in the development of Islam in modern Aceh will be discussed in Chapters 3 and 4.

[45] Alfian, "Ulama in Acehnese Society," 85.

[46] Anthony Reid, *Blood of the People: Revolution and the End of Traditional Rule in Northern Sumatra* (Kuala Lumpur: Oxford University Press, 1979), 26.

1940s, however, most *madrasa* graduates became increasingly open in expressing anti-Dutch sentiment and aspirations for independence.[47]

While thoroughly grounded with leadership from local Acehnese communities, PUSA was often antagonistic toward aspects of Acehnese tradition, and its members aggressively critiqued a range of customary practices that had come to be associated with Islam as blameworthy "innovations" that had to be suppressed.[48] They were also stridently opposed to the forms of Sufism that had become so widely established in Aceh at that time. The Khālidiyya line of the Naqshbandiyya Sufi order in particular had come to inform widely shared patterns of Islamic belief and practice across communities of Traditionalist Muslims in Aceh.[49] As networks of Traditionalist Islamic schools known locally as *dayah* expanded and multiplied over the course of the twentieth century, adherence to the authoritative teachings of the Khālidiyya-Naqshbandiyya and its prescribed ritual techniques became integrated into the basic fabric of those institutions.[50]

The paramount figure in the establishment of Khālidī Sufism as central to Traditionalist Islam in Aceh was Tgk. MudaWaly (d. 1961).[51] Muda Waly grew up in South Aceh, where he attended Dutch colonial schools, while at the same time studying the Qurʾān and the Islamic religious sciences from his father and later at the Traditionalist Islamic schools (I. *pesantren*) Jamiʿah Al-Khairiyah in Labuan Haji and Bustan al-Huda in Blang Pidie.[52] After a brief spell looking for appropriate teachers to continue his studies within Aceh, he left for West Sumatra to attend the new "modern style"

[47] Sulaiman, "Les Ulèebalang, les Ulémas, et les enseignants," 86–7.

[48] Edward Aspinall, *Islam and Nation: Separatist Rebellion in Aceh, Indonesia* (Stanford, CA: Stanford University Press, 2009), 29.

[49] This sub-tradition of the Naqshbandiyya traces its origins to Iraq and the teachings of Shaykh Khālid al-Kurdī (d. 1827). For more on its introduction to and development in Indonesia, see Werner Kraus, "Some Notes on the Introduction of the Naqshbandiyya-Khalidiyya into Indonesia," in M. Gaborieau, A. Popovic, and Th. Zarcone (eds.), *Naqshbandis: Historical Developments and Present Situation of a Muslim Mystical Order* (Istanbul and Paris: Éd.Isis, 1990), 691–706; Martin van Bruinessen, "After the Days of Abû Qubays: Indonesian Transformations of the Naqshbandiyya-Khâlidiyya," *Journal of the History of Sufism* 5 (2007) 225–51.

[50] The development of *dayah* within the broader history of Islamic education in Aceh will be further discussed in Chapter 3.

[51] Tgk. Muda Waly's own roots, however, were farther down the coast in the Minangkabau region of West Sumatra. He was the son of a local religious functionary (Ac. *leubè*), Tgk. Muhd. Salim bin Malin Palito, who had his own Islamic education in West Sumatra, where he also married into the family of two prominent ulama—Shaykh Khatib Ali and Shaykh Jamil Jaho. Sulaiman, "Les Ulèebalang, les Ulémas, et les enseignants," 66–7.

[52] The life and work of this figure has yet to attract the scholarly attention it deserves. At present, the most cited published source for his biography is the account produced by his son: Muhibbuddin Waly, *Ayah Kami: Maulana Syeikh Haji Muhammad Waly al-Khalidy, Teungku Syeikh Haji Muda Waly* (Singapore: JBW Printers & Binders Pte. Ltd., 1993). The basic material presented here is drawn largely from this source as well.

Normal Islam School that had been founded at Padang by Mahmud Yunus.[53] However, he dropped out after three months, disappointed by the school's relative inattention to religious (as opposed to more "general") subjects and its "modern" styles of dress and deportment. He nevertheless stayed on in West Sumatra after this, where he quickly rose to prominence in public debates through his defense of Traditionalist Sufism and jurisprudence against the critiques of these established modes of belief and practice that were launched with increasing force by Islamic Modernists at that time.

From Padang, Tgk. Muda Waly departed for the *ḥajj* in 1939, spending a total of three months in Arabia before heading back to Sumatra. It was only upon his return that Tgk. Muda Waly was initiated into the Nasqshbandiyya Sufi order under Shaykh ʿAbd al-Ghānī al-Kamfarī. Back in South Aceh, Tgk. Muda Waly founded a *dayah* named Darussalam at Labuan Haji. There he institutionalized Naqshbandī-Khālidī practices of *suluk* and *khalwa* in ways that were to become standard in Traditionalist Islamic schools (Ac. *dayah salafi*) all across Aceh over subsequent decades. By that time, however, other new Islamic schools were also being founded on Aceh's west coast, including modern-style *madrasas* connected with PUSA.[54] Ideological differences between PUSA and non-PUSA ulama also came to index political sentiment over the years that followed. During the Japanese occupation of Aceh in World War II, Tgk. Muda Waly became increasingly critical of PUSA ulama who cooperated with the Japanese.[55]

The relationship of PUSA with the Japanese occupational forces was a complex one, dating from even before the actual invasion of Sumatra. In the run up to that operation, a "fifth column" of Acehnese activists (including a number of leading figures from PUSA) known as the *Fujiwara Kikan* or "Komite F" worked to prepare for the coming of the Japanese.

[53] Eka Srimulyani, *Mahmud Yunus' Islamic Educational Thought: Tracing and Contextualizing Islamic Educational Reform in Indonesia* (Banda Aceh: Ar-Raniry Press, 2008).

[54] Over time, these new Modernist schools drew increasing numbers of students away from Traditionalist *dayah*. The dramatic shift in both resources and status of these two kinds of schools is reflected in their current physical conditions, as evidenced by the illustration following in contrast with the photo of new construction at a Modernist Islamic school in Samalanga presented in Chapter 3.

[55] Traditionalist opposition to the Japanese and their PUSA collaborators took an even more dramatic form in the uprising at Bayu (North Aceh). That revolt, led by Tgk. ʿAbdoel Djalil, was violently crushed by Japanese forces in late 1942. Tgk. ʿAbdoel Djalil's most famous quote was "throwing out the dogs to let the pigs in" (Ac. *geulét asèë, geutrimòng-boeï*)—in reference to the replacement of the Dutch by the Japanese as the new foreign power attempting to dominate Aceh. For an overview of the uprising at Bayu, and notes on some variations of this famous quotation as it circulated in Aceh at the time, see A.J. Piekaar, *Atjeh en de Oorlog met Japan* ('s-Gravenhage-Bandung: N. V. Uitgeverij W. van Hoeve, 1949), 304–8.

Figure 2.2. Student housing at Dayah Darussalam, Labuan Haji (West Aceh): Current conditions at what was formerly the most important center of Traditionalist Islam in Aceh make for a striking contrast to the current building boom at other *dayah* that have embraced aspects of Modernist reform. (Photo by R. Michael Feener)

As the Japanese took control in Aceh, PUSA's anti-Dutch stance, and its penchant for modern organization and mobilization styles further facilitated its active cooperation with the Japanese occupational administration, at least at first.[56] However, PUSA was not the only beneficiary of new policies under the Japanese military administration. Like the Dutch before them, the Japanese attempted to develop strategies to play off the divisions between the ulama and the *uléëbalang* in establishing their own authority over Aceh—thus capitalizing on, and ensuring the continuation of, local fissures among the Acehnese.

Under the Japanese occupation, PUSA was able to claim important positions within the new structures of state authority.[57] In 1943, the

[56] Anas M. Yunus, *Gerakan Kebangkitan Aceh Kumpulan Karya Sejarah M. Junus Djamil* (Bandung: Bina Biladi Press, 2009), 381–4. This is a reprint of a work by one of the members of the *Fujiwara Kikan*, which Saya Shiraishi has identified as having been being initially commissioned by the Japanese administration. Saya Shiraishi, "Aceh under the Japanese Occupation: Rival Leaders in Aceh Besar and Pidie," M.A. thesis (Tokyo: International Christian University, 1975), 33–5.

[57] These developments were, however, by no means certain at the outset. In fact, after initially favoring PUSA, the Japanese came (for a time) to look more toward the *uléëbalang* as their preferred collaborators, and thus the PUSA-affiliated members of the *Fujiwara Kikan* were temporarily marginalized from positions of power. A number of *uléëbalang* were also appointed to formal administrative posts as *gunchōs* and the local assembly (Jp. *shū-san gikai*) was comprised almost exclusively of *uléëbalang* as well. As time wore on,

Japanese established a number of new institutional forms for the official management of Islam.[58] In March of that year, they created a council of ulama to support its policies, and PUSA's charismatic leader, Daud Beureueh, was a prominent and persuasive speaker on the Council's official propaganda tours across Aceh.[59] In addition to the establishment of the Ulama Council, other changes under the Japanese administration have also been important in laying the foundations for institutions that have come to play key roles in the implementation of a new state system of Islamic law in the twenty-first century.[60] Perhaps the most important of these was granting PUSA ulama control over a new system of Islamic religious courts (Jp. *shūkyō hōin*) established in 1944.[61] This added a dimension of state management of Islamic religious affairs that had not existed under Dutch colonial policy in Aceh.[62] It also served to contribute to a significant increase of the power of the ulama as it facilitated the initial entrance and ascent of *madrasa* graduates into the state bureaucracy.[63] In this sense, PUSA's reformist ulama emerged from the Japanese period in a strengthened position, and further consolidated their position over the early years of Indonesian independence.[64]

ACEH, ISLAM, AND THE INDONESIAN REPUBLIC

Soon after the end of the war Aceh's leading ulama—both Modernist and Traditionalist—joined together in signing a declaration urging Muslims to rally behind Soekarno and his opposition to the Dutch, and declaring the struggle for independence to be a "Holy War" (Ac. *prang sabi*).[65]

however, the Japanese renewed their engagement with PUSA ulama—leaving them with a relatively better position than the *uléëbalang* at the war's end. Shiraishi, *Aceh under the Japanese*, 17–30.

[58] Piekaar, *Atjeh en de Oorlog met Japan*, 275.

[59] Reid, *Blood of the People*, 114. Daud Beureueh has been the subject of a number of previous studies, and has gained increased attention by Indonesian writers in recent years. See, for example: M. Nur El Ibrahimy, *Tgk. M. Daud Beureueh: Perannya dalam Pergolakan di Aceh* (Jakarta: Gunung Agung, 1982); Kholid Santosa, *Jejak-jejak sang pejuangpemberontak: Pemikiran, gerakan dan ekspresipolitik S.M. Kartosuwirjo dan Daud Beureueh* (Bandung: Sega Arsy, 2006); Irfan Awwas, *Trilogikepemimpinan Negara Islam Indonesia* (Yogyakarta: Uswah, 2008).

[60] Sulaiman, "Les Ulèebalang, les Ulémas, et les enseignants," 90–5, 107–15.

[61] Piekaar, Atjeh en de Oorlog met Japan, 278.

[62] The history of Islamic courts in Aceh will be further discussed in Chapter 6.

[63] Shiraishi, "Aceh under the Japanese Occupation," 35–55.

[64] Sulaiman, "Les Ulèebalang, les Ulémas, et les enseignants," 191–224; Reid, *Blood of the People*, 200–11; Eric E. Morris, "Islam and Politics in Aceh: A Study of Center-Periphery Relations in Indonesia," Ph.D. dissertation (Ithaca: Cornell University, 1983), 147.

[65] Morris, "Islam and Politics," 122. Part of this involved the reiteration of calls to *jihād* that had developed into a significant genre of Acehnese language verse in the late

This coming together of different Muslim factions demonstrates the extent to which religious ideals have been at work in the motivations of Aceh's Islamic leaders in their engagement with projects of defending the Indonesian nation since its earliest formation. As Edward Aspinall has amply demonstrated, a commitment to Islamic religious ideas and support of the project of establishing an Indonesian state were by no means fundamentally opposed.[66] At the same time, the subsequent history of more tense dynamics of internal Muslim polemics on the role of Islam in the structure of the nation-state also presages in significant ways analogous developments among Acehnese Muslims in their debates over the institutional form and substantive content for the state implementation of Shariʿa at the turn of the twenty-first century.

Soon after the joint declaration, the two major blocs of Islamic leadership in Aceh went their separate ways in pursuing their aspirations for an independent Indonesia. Muda Waly and other Traditionalist ulama formed the *Barisan Hizbullah* militia to assist in the struggle against the return of the Dutch. They also mobilized politically within an Indonesian Traditionalist Muslim political party called PERTI (Pergerakan Tarbiyah Islamijah).[67] It was the Modernist PUSA, however, that was most successful in establishing itself as the dominant Islamic organization in Aceh during the early years of Indonesian independence. In doing so, it played an important role of reframing public discourse on the state implementation of Shariʿa in Aceh in relation to projects of modernizing reform.

At war's end, PUSA moved swiftly against its rivals, the *uléëbalang*, who were now branded as the last remaining allies of the fallen Dutch colonial order. From December 1945 to January 1946, violent clashes erupted across Aceh in what came to be known as the "Social Revolution" (I. *Revolusi Sosial*). By the end of it, most of the *uléëbalang* were killed, and those who survived fled from Aceh.[68] This left the field open for a reconstitution of a professional administrative class in Aceh, the ranks of which soon swelled with young Muslim professionals with allegiance to PUSA. At the forefront of this new ascendency of Aceh's Modernist Muslims was PUSA

nineteenth century. See M. Isa Sulaiman, "Islam et propaganda anti-néerlandaise: Abdullah Arief et le Seumangat Atjeh, 1945–1946," *Archipel* 30 (1985) 207–17.

66 Aspinall, *Islam and Nation*.

67 An introduction to Perti and an overview of the development of its politics can be found in Alaiddin Koto, *Pemikiran Politik Perti (Persatuan Tarbiyah Islamiyah), 1945–1970* (Jakarta: Nimas Multima, 1997). For more on the Perti political activism of Muda Waly in particular, see Martin van Bruinessen, *Tarekat Naqsyabandiyah di Indonesia* (Bandung: Mizan, 1992), 143–6.

68 For more on these developments, see Reid, *Blood of the People*. A selection of declarations, proclamations, military announcements, legislative motions, letters and other documents related to the early contests for Acehnese autonomy are collected in Alibasjah Talsya, *Sedjarah dan Dokumen-dokumen Pemberontakan di Atjeh* (Jakarta: Penerbit Kesuma, 1955).

charismatic leader, Daud Beureueh, who emerged from the war not only as Aceh's foremost Islamic reformist leader, but also as its military governor and chief administrator. With Daud Beureueh at its head, PUSA capitalized on their newly privileged position in society to energetically promote its reformist vision of Islam in the making of a new, modern Aceh.[69]

With the achievement of independence from colonial control and wartime occupation, followed as it was by the elimination of their only significant rivals to power, the leadership of PUSA had every reason to expect that it would be in a position to pursue its agenda of social and religious reform in Aceh while maintaining their de facto control over most of the administrative apparatus of the state.[70] Daud Beureueh even claimed that President Soekarno himself had verbally promised that Aceh would be left alone to implement Shari'a as the law of the land.[71] The tale of this promise supposedly made at a private meeting during the president's visit to Aceh in 1947 was to become one of the foundational texts arguing for the state application of Islamic law over the decades that followed. The purported breaking of that promise was also later invoked as justification for the armed rebellion that Daud Beureueh and his followers in PUSA launched against the central Indonesian government in 1953.[72] This is referred to as the "Darul Islam" movement, and it came to be linked together with other armed campaigns under that name for the establishment of an Islamic state in other regions of Indonesia at that time.[73] The immediate cause of the Darul Islam revolt in Aceh, however, was the local reaction to administrative changes that dissolved the province of Aceh and annexed the territory to the province of North Sumatra, with its capital in Medan. This resulted in PUSA losing its control over local administration, provoking sharp reactions by its members and

[69] This included a stepping up of its earlier campaigns against customary practices. See for example, the 1948 PUSA proclamation on Traditionalist funerary practices, recently reprinted in Analiansyah and Jamhuri, *Syariat Islam di Nanggroe Aceh Darussalam: Inventarisasi Dokumen* (Banda Aceh: Dinas Syariat Islam Provinsi Nanggroe Aceh Darussalam, 2008), 4–5.

[70] Aspinall, *Islam and Nation*.

[71] The dialogue between Soekarno and Daud Beureueh is presented in its dramatic and now canonical form in M. Nur El Ibrahimy, *Tgk. M. DaudBeureueh*, 64–5.

[72] C. van Dijk, *Rebellion under the Banner of Islam: The Darul Islam in Indonesia* (The Hague: Martinus Nijhoff, 1981), 299, 309–10, 335–6. In 1959, many of these Darul Islam-affiliated civil servants were re-integrated into the Regional Administration of Aceh under the Indonesian Republic.

[73] The other Darul Islam movements were located in West Java, South Sulawesi, and South Kalimantan: van Dijk, *Rebellion under the Banner of Islam*. For an in-depth treatment of the visions of an Islamic state animating developments in the West Java Darul Islam movement, see: Chiara Formichi, *Islam and the Making of the Nation: Kartosuwiryo and Political Islam in Twentieth-Century Indonesia* (Leiden: KITLV Press, 2012), 109–243.

its leadership—leading eventually to the declaration of armed opposition to the central Indonesian state.[74]

While PUSA's Modernist leadership proclaimed Aceh as part of the Darul Islam, leading Traditionalists in Aceh, including Tgk. Muda Waly, Tgk. Hasan Kreung Kalé, and the Habib Muda Seunagan continued to cooperate with the Indonesian republican government.[75] Under the rubric of the organization Safīnat al-Salāma wa'l-Najāḥ, these Traditionalist ulama released a fatwa ruling that Daud Beureueh's rebellion was *ḥarām*. Over the years that followed, the conflicts between PUSA-affiliated Modernists and Traditionalist Muslims in Aceh grew increasingly violent. In this escalation of intra-Muslim hostility, Muda Waly founded a *dayah*-based Traditionalist militia to oppose the Darul Islam rebels on Aceh's west coast.[76] Today, his surviving followers still reminisce about the ways in which Darul Islam attempts to assassinate him were foiled by divine intervention.[77]

The Darul Islam movement waged a long struggle to establish a modern Islamic state in Aceh, but it was ultimately unsuccessful. Agreements to end hostilities were reached with most of the rebel leaders in 1959, when Aceh was granted the status of a "special" province with concessions of autonomy in the fields of religion, *adat*, and education. However, Daud Beureueh and an inner circle of his followers continued their resistance until 1962, when he was granted a pardon.[78] Even then, however, he both refused to formally surrender and maintained his demands for the state implementation of Islamic law in Aceh, arguing that:

> It is already high time that aspects of the divine law must be applied. The evils and crimes such as gambling, adultery, drugs and alcohol—as well as wasting time with traditional diversions, games and pastimes—appear to be thriving in our society, staining our law and our way of life. They must be completely eradicated.[79]

[74] Herbert Feith, *The Decline of Constitutional Democracy in Indonesia* (Ithaca: Cornell University Press, 1962), 345–6.

[75] Dan Birchok, "Locating the Descendants of ʿAlī in Southwest Aceh: The Places of ʿAlid Piety in Late 20th-century Seunagan," in Chiara Formichi and R. Michael Feener (eds.), *Shiʿism in Southeast Asia: ʿAlid Piety and Sectarian Constructions* (London: Hurst, forthcoming).

[76] Sulaiman, "Les Ulèebalang, les Ulémas, et les enseignants," 289–90.

[77] Interview with Tgk. Bakongan, July 2008 at Trumon (Aceh Selatan). Similar stories are also common, for example in the town of Nigan (Nagan Raya), where another student of Muda Waly, Tgk. Yahya, was based. Personal communication with Dan Birchok, 15 March 2012.

[78] For more on these developments, see van Dijk, *Rebellion under the Banner of Islam*, 269–339.

[79] Daud Beureueh, "Muqaddimah Pelaksanaan Unsur-unsur Sjariʿat Islam (1962)," reprinted Analiansyah and Jamhuri (eds.), *Syariat Islam Di Nanggroe Aceh Darussalam: Inventarisasi Dokumen* (Banda Aceh: Dinas Syariat Islam Provinsi Nanggroe Aceh Darussalam, 2008), 98.

At the turn of the twenty-first century when the agenda for state implementation of Islamic law in Aceh came to receive new support, it was precisely these same areas of personal morality and the modernizing rationalization of everyday practice that were emphasized once again as being central to the project of Shariʿa in reforming society. In fact, efforts in this direction were common in many parts of Indonesia at that time, but the particular political contexts of special autonomy in Aceh allowed such work to take more official forms in Aceh than they did elsewhere.

ACEH AND ISLAM UNDER INDONESIA'S NEW ORDER

The pardon of Daud Beureueh and the formal end of the Darul Islam movement was soon followed by the collapse of Soekarno's founding regime of the Indonesian Republic and the establishment of Suharto's New Order in 1965. The dynamics of interaction between Aceh and the Indonesian central government underwent a new evolution during this period, as visions of the role of Islam in defining Acehnese identity became increasingly prominent in official discourse. The most prolific and high-profile figure in producing the New Order narrative of Acehnese Islam was Ali Hasjmy.[80]

Ali Hasjmy was born on 28 March 1914 at Montasiek (Aceh Besar), where he was primarily educated in the Dutch colonial schools. After that, he continued his studies in West Sumatra, where he was exposed to the new models of modern Islamic education being developed by reformers there.[81] Inspired by these new visions of Islam, upon his return Hasjmy affiliated with Islamic reformist organizations in Aceh, including PUSA, as a youth activist.[82] He also became active in the spheres of politics and the media, and during the war he was trained as a journalist under the Japanese to work on their fortnightly propaganda organ, *Atjeh Sinbun*, of which he was promoted to Editor in 1944. At the war's end, Hasjmy strengthened his ties to the emerging leadership of the independent Indonesian Republic, and recast his paper in their cause under the title *Semangat Merdeka* ("Spirit of Freedom") in October 1945.[83] He also found work in the bureaucracy of the new Indonesian government, rising to the

[80] For Ali Hasjmy's role in the development of official visions of Aceh's history, see Dan Birchok, "Soujourning on Mecca's Verndah."

[81] Hasbi Amiruddin, "Prof. H. A. Hasjmy (Rektor IAIN Ar-RaniryPeriode 1977–1982)," in *Biografi Rektor IAIN Ar-Raniry: Kepemimpinan IAIN Ar-Raniry dari Masa ke Masa* (Banda Aceh: Ar-Raniry Press, 2008), 59–62.

[82] van Dijk, *Rebellion under the Banner of Islam*, 275.

[83] Reid, *Blood of the People*, 108–9, 189.

rank of deputy head of the North Sumatra Social Welfare Office in Medan. In 1953, however, he was arrested there on suspicion of collaborating with the Darul Islam. The following year, he was released and transferred to Jakarta where he began close collaboration with Indonesian government officials in their attempts at dealing with their "Aceh problem."[84] Hasjmy was seen as a possible asset in this because of his past ties with PUSA, and in Jakarta he was groomed to serve as the new governor of Aceh when the province was administratively re-established in January 1957.[85]

Upon his return to Aceh, Hasjmy faced considerable resistance both from those involved with the Darul Islam, and from those who petitioned Jakarta to recall this governor because they perceived him as being too close to the former rebels. However, he succeeded over time in consolidating his position as the leader of the Indonesian province of Aceh through deft negotiation with diverse parties. His warming relations with some former colleagues in PUSA in particular were to prove valuable for him, since at that time much of the administrative bureaucracy was still in the hands of former Darul Islam affiliates. However, he also reached out to non-PUSA affiliated ulama in attempts to build broader (or even rival) constituencies to support him in the task set for him by Jakarta.[86] In doing this, Hasjmy also benefited from strategic collaboration with the leading military commander (I. *Panglima*) in Aceh, Sjammaun Gaharu.[87]

Over the course of his career in Aceh, Ali Hasjmy helped form a number of modern Islamic institutions, all designed to garner broader Muslim support for the assertion of Indonesian national control over the province. In 1959, he headed a committee charged with the task of preparing for the establishment of an institution of higher education dedicated to the study of Islamic law—a project that was eventually realized with the establishment of the State Institute for Islamic Studies (IAIN) Ar-Raniry'sFaculty of Shariʿa in 1960.[88] Over the years that followed, Ali Hasjmy also continued working with Islamic religious leaders, developing new structures through which they could contribute their authority in support of various government policies and programs and in which they also saw opportunities to utilize the resources of the state to further their own agendas for the definition and management of Islamic ideals in Aceh.

[84] A. Hasjmy, *Semangat Merdeka: 70 Tahun Menempuh Jalan Pergolakan & Perjuangan Kemerdekaan* (Jakarta: Bulan Bintang, 1985), 435–69.

[85] As already noted, one of the great sources of grievance for Aceh's Darul Islam movement had been the merger of Aceh under the administration of the province of North Sumatra, with its capital in Medan in 1951.

[86] Hasjmy, *Semangat Merdeka*, 482

[87] van Dijk, *Rebellion under the Banner of Islam*, 332–3.

[88] Amiruddin, "Prof. H. A. Hasjmy," 64. The development of IAIN and its role in the state implementation of Islamic law is discussed in detail in Chapter 3.

The path through this rocky period of Indonesian history was not, however, straight and smooth for Hasjmy as he experimented with various measures to build support for the Indonesian state among Aceh's Islamic leadership in the late 1950s and early 1960s. As new patterns of engagement between Aceh's Islamic leaders and the Indonesian central government were consolidated, the ulama became active allies to the military in its campaigns against the Indonesian Communist Party (PKI) in the province.[89] In fact, when the strongly anti-communist Indonesian government supported the establishment of a provincial Ulama Council, the first fatwa that it issued was a condemnation of communism as being forbidden by Islamic law (*ḥarām*).[90]

Hasjmy worked closely with the Ulama Council over the years that followed, serving as its Deputy Head from 1969, and taking over as Head of the Council in 1982. His role in this organization was a major factor in its deployment in the service of supporting government programs ranging from tourism policy to birth control. Hasjmy's formalization of working ties between Islamic religious authority and the state was appreciatively noted by one Acehnese observer, writing "at that time government programs did not run into any obstacles in their implementation because the way had been cleared for them by Ulama Council *fatwas*."[91] Hasjmy actively promoted the New Order's emerging developmentalist ideals and argued that they were in line with proper understandings of Islam.[92]

Even after the end of his term as governor in 1964, Hasjmy remained a major player in the development of Indonesian state-affiliated Islamic institutions in Aceh. Some of these, like the Ulama Council, originated locally in Aceh.[93] Others were attempts at introducing local offices of bodies that had their origins elsewhere in Indonesia. One of the most ambitious examples of the latter was the Union for the Improvement of Islamic Education (Gabungan Usaha Perbaikan Pendidikan Islam/ GUPPI). The origin myths of GUPPI point to a local *pesantren* movement organized in West Java in 1950.[94] However, this grassroots organization seems to have met with little success in expanding its activities until it was

[89] Harold Crouch, *Political Reform in Indonesia after Soeharto* (Singapore: ISEAS Press, 2010), 282.

[90] The Majelis Ulama will be discussed in detail in Chapter 4.

[91] Amiruddin, "Prof. H. A. Hasjmy," 64.

[92] Hasjmy, *Semangat Merdeka*, 490–1.

[93] Aceh's Ulama Council is the oldest state-affiliated body of its kind in Indonesia, and in fact in its original formulation in 1965 served as the model for the national Majelis Ulama Indonesia (MUI) when that was later founded by Suharto in 1975.

[94] For more on the role of the GUPPI in New Order politics, see Heru Cahyono, *Peranan Ulama dalam Golkar, 1971–1980: Dari Pemilu sampai Malari* (Jakarta: Pustaka Sinar Harapan, 1992); and Arief Subhan, "Jamʿiyat Istijmāʿ al-juhūd li iṣlāḥ al-tarbiyya al-Islāmiyya (GUPPI): Tajdīd fī al-tarbiyya al-Islāmiyya ʿan ṭarīq al-siyāsa," *StudiaIslamika* 5(3) (1998) 129–54.

taken over by Ali Moertopo and other political agents of Suharto's political machine (Golkar) to mobilize it in support of the New Order government for the 1971 Indonesian general elections.[95] At GUPPI's national convention in Jakarta that year, the organizing committee issued a formal statement contrasting the "secularism" of earlier regimes with "true" understandings of the Indonesian national ideology, *Pancasila*, claiming that the centrality of belief in God (I. *Ketuhanan Yang Maha Esa*) made clear that religion and the state could never be separate.[96]

These invocations of religion in redefining the "true" nature of the Indonesian nation were furthermore explicitly linked to the doctrine of the "dual function" (I. *dwifungsi*) of the Indonesian military. According to this doctrine, the army should not only defend the country. It should also play a role in setting and implementing national policies. Its role in defense was thus set together with a broader mandate of domestic social control to facilitate national programs of development in all fields of life, "... in ideology, politics, economy, spiritual development and culture."[97] In an address to the 1971 GUPPI national convention, Lieutenant General Amir Machmud asked the ulama to participate in the New Order government development policies, emphasizing in particular their importance in helping to create and maintain social stability.[98] In this way, the ulama were placed in a pivotal position between the government and the military in directing an Islamically-inflected vision of national development, as graphically illustrated in Figure 2.3 by the figure at the center of this didactic diagram from a GUPPI internal document sent to Aceh in the run-up to the 1971 Indonesian elections:

The Indonesian government was particularly sensitive to the role of Islam in managing potential social conflict in Aceh. In the run-up to the 1971 elections, the central administration of GUPPI in Jakarta formally appointed a "leadership board" for a branch in Aceh that included the head of the Iskandar Muda army division based there, the governor as its official patron, and the influential ulama Tgk. Abdullah Ujong Rimba as "advisor" to a board made up of high-ranking police officers and lawyers.[99] This

[95] See, for example Sapardjo, *Tugas dan Tudjuan GUPPI dalam Rangka Koordinasi sesama Golongan Fungsional, and Pendjelasan Perdjuangan GUPPI dalam rangka Pemilu* (Un published MS, Arsip Propinsi Aceh – 254/40).

[96] On the permutations of official interpretations of *Pancasila* in Indonesian political history: Luthfi Assyaukanie, *Islam and the Secular State in Indonesia* (Singapore: ISEAS Press, 2009), 98.

[97] Majelis Ulama Indonesia di Aceh, Berkas Musyawarah Gabungan Usaha Perbaikan Pendidikan Islam (GUPPI) yang berlangsung dar tanggal 25 s/d 28 January 1971 di Jakarta – Arsip Propinsi Aceh No. 254/40.

[98] Arsip Propinsi Aceh No. 254/40.

[99] Surat keputusan Mo. KKP-019/GUPPI/1971 dari Pimpinan Konsulat Atjeh Gabungan Usaha Perbaikan Pendidikan Islam – GUPPI – Anngota: Sekber Golkar (Arsip Propinsi Aceh No. 254/40).

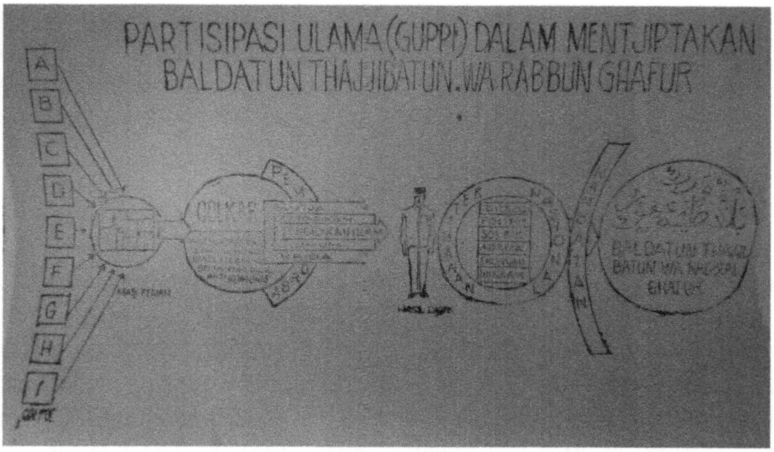

Figure 2.3. The role of the ulama in national development, 1971: This diagram from an official GUPPI document situates the ulama (the human figure depicted here) as a key part of the mechanisms by which the Indonesian government and military work to develop society toward the Qur'ānic ideal of "a good land under a forgiving Lord" (Ar. *baldat ṭayyiba wa rabb ghafūr*). Arsip Propinsi Aceh No. 255/40—used with permission from the Province of Aceh Archives

was soon followed up by a branch meeting in Banda Aceh in which all local members of GUPPI declared their commitment to ensuring the electoral success of Golkar (the political organization of the New Order government) in their aspiration toward achieving the Qur'ānic goal of living in "a good land under a forgiving Lord" (I. *Baldatun Thajjibatun Wa Rabbun Ghafur/Ar. balda ṭayyiba wa rabb ghafūr*).[100] As will be discussed subsequently, this Qur'ānic quotation is also often deployed by proponents of Aceh's contemporary Shari'a system as well.[101] Although not all of Aceh's Islamic leadership was supportive of GUPPI at the time and such projects for mobilizing Muslim support for the New Order state

[100] Document from the Aceh Provincial Archives (Arsip Propinsi Aceh – 255/40). This Qur'ānic phrase (*Sabā'*/34:15) has long been a central trope within modern Indonesian Islamic reformist discourse. It was broadly popularized by usage in Muhammadiyah circles in the early mid-twentieth century. It thence became a common plank in the rhetorical scaffolding of campus-based *da'wa* groups in the decades after that, and it continues to resonate in contemporary Acehnese debates over the direction of social change, where it appears frequently in popular print media and online fora. See, for example, Safrina, "Luka Aceh Syariat Atau Aceh Lukai Syariat," 5 November 2010, <http://lidahtinta.wordpress.com/2010/11/05/luka-aceh-syariat-atau-aceh-lukai-syariat>, accessed 27 August 2012; and "Islam dan Perdamaian: Dari Hudaibiyah ke Helsinki," Aceh Forum Community, 29 June 2006, <http://www.acehforum.or.id/archive/index.php/t-2447.html>, accessed 17 July 2012.

[101] See, for example, Alyasa Abubakar, *Penerapan Syariat Islam di Aceh: Upaya Penyusunan Fiqih dalam Negara Bangsa* (Banda Aceh: Dinas Syariat Islam, 2008), 58.

were not uniformly successful in delivering desired electoral results, these initiatives played an important role in establishing the foundation for a "*da'wa* paradigm" bringing rhetorics of Islamic reform, Indonesian nationalism, and economic development together in powerful new ways.

DA'WA AND DEVELOPMENT

In order to ensure that the vision of the ideal society promoted by the ulama was truly in line with that of the New Order government, a raft of state initiatives was launched for the continuing education of Islamic religious leaders. This included various short training programs and seminars in which the ulama were given instruction on their desired roles in supporting "mental and spiritual development." The Islamic leaders were also reminded in no uncertain terms of the responsibility that the government placed on their shoulders for the success or failure of local implementations of the central government's development policies.[102]

Although GUPPI as an organization faded in importance over the course of the 1970s, the New Order state continued to mobilize the support of Islamic religious leaders along similar lines. Aceh was an important laboratory for developing mechanisms for the state management of Islam. This was particularly clear with the institution of an official Ulama Council (*Majelis Ulama*), which was established in Aceh a decade before an analogous institution was created at the national level in 1975. Over that interval, the Council developed new programs for "Upgrading Ulama" (using this English-language term) that pressed upon local Muslim leaders the importance of their work in drawing upon religious resources to ensure political stability and economic development.[103] This theme was repeatedly drilled into the cadres of local preachers and Ulama Councils over the years that followed.[104] Always ready to give a speech, Ali Hasjmy was the most prominent spokesman for the cause at "Upgrading Ulama" events across the province during the 1960s and 1970s.[105]

[102] This point was, for example, driven home sharply in the conclusion to a lecture given to a group of ulama from the economically disenfranchised region of West Aceh in 1972. Arsip Propinsi Aceh No. 256/40.

[103] Samples of the materials presented at such "upgrading workshops" can be found in the Provincial Archives at Banda Aceh: *Berkas Mengenai Up-Grading Majelis Ulama Kabupaten Aceh Barat yang Berlangsung Tanggal 13 s/d 17 Maret 1971 di Meulaboh* (Arsip Propinsi Aceh No. 156/40).

[104] In Aceh, this included a high profile event opened by the Minister of Religious Affairs in 1976 (Arsip Propinsi Aceh No. 277/41 – *Berkas Sehubungan Dengan Penataran Muballigh se-DAISTA yang Diadakan padat gl. 5 s/d 9 Feburari 1976 di Banda Aceh*).

[105] He repeated this message in dozens of similar addresses across the province, a typical exemplar of which is Ali Hasjmy, "Para Ulama Haruslah Aktif Membantu Pembangunan Negara," a public lecture delivered at the closing ceremony of yet another upgrading

Indeed, well after the end of his second term as governor in 1964, Hasjmy had remained a major public figure in Aceh.[106] One of his first major "post-retirement projects" was the establishment of a Faculty of Dakwah at the Banda Aceh campus of the State Institute for Islamic Studies (IAIN).[107] This was a significant innovation at the time, as Aceh was the first campus anywhere in Indonesia's national system of Islamic higher education to establish a separate faculty specifically for Islamic propagation (Ar. *daʿwa*).[108] Upon the opening of the Dakwah Faculty in 1968, Hasjmy was appointed as its first dean. To support this endeavor, he not only marshaled his political clout, but also his skills in publicity by publishing extensively on the subject of Islamic propagation.[109]

Over the course of his political career, Hasjmy was active in writing and publishing a wide range of texts on Islam, as well as essays on Acehnese history and culture, collections of his own poetry, self-celebrating memoirs, & etc.[110] In these publications, Hasjmy strove to construct both images of Aceh's glorious past, and its bright Indonesian and Islamic futures. As one appreciative commentator characterized it, Ali Hasjmy believed that a solid relationship between Aceh and Jakarta would

workshop for ulama and mosque preachers (Ar./I. *khatib*) in West Aceh on 27 February 1973 (Arsip Propinsi Aceh – 264/40).

[106] He also maintained a prolific publication record that spanned not only diverse genres, but also presented various different "faces" for diverse audiences as he addressed topics ranging from traditional Acehnese literature to the future of Islam.

[107] For the early history of the Dakwah Faculty, see Institut Agama Islam Negeri (IAIN), *Sewindu Fakultas Dakwah* (Banda Aceh: IAIN Jamiʿah Ar-Raniry, 1975).

[108] *Risalah: Fakultas Dakwah dan Publisistik I.A.I.N. Djami'ah Ar-Raniry Darussalam* (Aceh: Bahagian Publikasi Fakultas Dakwah, Publisistik Darussalam Banda Atjeh, 1969). In other IAIN, studies of *daʿwa* came under the Fakultas Ushuluddin (Ar. *uṣūl al-dīn*). Outside of the IAIN system, there were also broader Indonesian attempts at institutionalizing *daʿwa* around that time, often framed explicitly as an important means to counter fears of the continuing influence of communism among the population. See, for example: *Pusat Daʿwah Islam Indonesia* (Jakarta: Sekreteriat Pusat Daʿwah Islam Indonesia, Masjid Istiqlal, 1970), 8–12.

[109] See, for example, A. Hasjmy, *Dustur Da'wah—Menurut Al-Quran* (Jakarta: Bulan Bintang, 1974); "Tugas Fakultas Dakwah: Membina Manusia Pembangun," in *Majalah Pengetahuna/Kebudayaan Sinar Darussalam* (Banda Aceh: Yayasan Pembina Darussalam/Studiklub Islam Darussalam, 1975); *Ulama Aceh Mujahid Pejuang Kemerdakaan dan Pembangun Tamadun Bangsa* (Jakarta: Bulan Bintang, 1997); and essays collected in: Ali Hasjmy, *Kapita Selekta Islam (Kumpulan Pidato-Ceramah-Khuthbah)* (Banda Aceh: Privately Printed, Yayasan Ali Hasjmy, no date).

[110] A full bibliography of his prodigious output in all of these fields has not yet been compiled—something that would be a necessary first step toward developing a more comprehensive picture of his views on all these subjects. Work on such subjects will also have to take into consideration that he also published texts under various pseudonyms, including Al-Hariry, Asmara Hakiki, Aria Hadiningrum, and presumably others built upon the initials AH (and perhaps even more that do not follow this pattern). A significant amount of primary material for such research, including some of Hasjmy's correspondence, is housed at the A. Hasjmy Library and Museum, located at Jln. Jend. Sudirman No. 28/29, Lamtemen, Banda Aceh.

depend upon a coming together of Islam and nationalism—one that would spring from a combination of the national ideology of *Pancasila*, select aspects of Aceh's own rich heritage, and a broad conception of what he referred to as "*Islamisme*."[111] This coincided well with emerging views in Jakarta in the 1970s, where *dakwah* (Ar. *da'wa*) was increasingly seen by the New Order as a potential means to facilitate its own agendas of developmentalism.[112] Ali Hasjmy worked to promote this vision not only through the Faculty of Dakwah, but also through the State Institute for Islamic Studies (IAIN) as a whole. From 1977 to 1982, he held the position of Rector for the institution, and it was during this time that many of the figures who were later to emerge as prominent leaders in Aceh's twenty-first-century Islamic legal system, including Muslim Ibrahim (Head of Aceh's Ulama Council) and Alyasa Abubakar (Head of the State Shari'a Agency), were students there.[113]

The IAIN Banda Aceh campus was, however, by no means the only state-affiliated institution where *da'wa* was coming to shape visions of the future development of society over the latter decades of the twentieth century. Indeed, reformed visions of Islam were then increasingly being promoted as being in line with national development goals, as well as evolving conceptions of Indonesian national identity.[114] The connections between *da'wa* and developmentalism were, however, particularly pronounced in Aceh. In many ways, Aceh can be seen as a kind of social laboratory for New Order experiments with the state management of Islam, as will be discussed further in the chapters that follow, particularly in relation to the Ulama Council and the Faculty of Dakwah at the IAIN.

The New Order government in Jakarta established a new generation of technocrats as its local representatives in Aceh. These technocrats were entrusted not only with the implementation of economic development projects, but also with counteracting rival ideologies that could serve to inspire opposition. These technocrats came to feel that they had a significant stake in the consolidation and perpetuation of Aceh's

[111] Roeslan Abdulgani, "Prof. Ali Hasjmy sebagai Pembangun Jembatan Kepercayaan antara Pusat dan Daerah Berdasarkan Islamisme-Nasionalismesesuai Pancasila," in Badruzzaman Ismail (ed.), *A. Hasjmy, Aset Sejarah Masa Kini Dan Masa Depan: Delapan Puluh Tahun Melalui Jalan Raya Dunia* (Jakarta: Bulan Bintang, 1994), 21.

[112] Pierre Labrousse and Farida Soemargono, "De l'Islam comme morale du développmement: L'action des bureaux de propagation de la foi (Lembaga Dakwah) vue de Surabaya," *Archipel* 30 (1985) 219–28.

[113] Interview with Yusny Saby, 27 January 2011 at Banda Aceh.

[114] For more on these broader Indonesian developments, see Robert W. Hefner, "Islam, State, and Civil Society: ICMI and the Struggle for the Indonesian Middle Class," *Indonesia* 56 (October 1993) 1–36; and Bernhard Platzdasch, *Islamism in Indonesia: Politics in the Emerging Democracy* (Singapore: ISEAS Press, 2009).

position within the broader Indonesian nation. A 2001 International Crisis Group report aptly characterized Aceh's late twentieth-century technocrats as:

> ... educated in state universities and rose through the civil service and military, in some cases reaching high rank. Though strongly aware of their distinctive Acehnese identity, these people were nonetheless able to thrive within the centralised bureaucracy and political system of Soeharto's New Order. Members of this group now [2001] form an influential constituency in favour of broad autonomy for Aceh within Indonesia, as opposed to independence, though they share the general discontent in the province at its treatment by Jakarta.[115]

Many of these technocrats were, furthermore, also descendants of ulama. This included even Aceh's governor from 1986 to 1993, Ibrahim Hasan, who was regarded locally as being sympathetic to *da'wa* agendas for the further Islamization of society.[116] At the same time, his position also reflected broader national trends of increasing political accommodation between the Indonesian state and Islamic religious leaders.[117]

Although the New Order technocrats tended to be viewed by outside observers as proponents of developmentalist modernity within a paradigm of secularization, for at least some of the technocrats, their visions of development were informed by particular understandings of religion, and in particular by contemporary *da'wa* discourse. In a peculiarly prescient work from the late 1970s, Stuart Schlegel profiled one pious Muslim technocrat in Aceh and argued that he represented what Schlegel termed "Golkar Islam."[118] Since that time there have been an increasing number of bureaucrats and government officials emphasizing the centrality of Islam to the reform and control of Acehnese society. These views not only came to be shared by those directly employed by the state, but also began to seep out and have broader resonance among a growing

[115] International Crisis Group, "Aceh: Can Autonomy Stem the Conflict?" ICG Asia Report No. 18 (27 June 2001): 2. <http://www.crisisgroup.org/~/media/Files/asia/south-east-asia/indonesia/Aceh%20Can%20Autonomy%20Stem%20the%20Conflict.pdf>, accessed 28 August 2012.

[116] Tim Kell, *The Roots of the Acehnese Rebellion, 1989–1992* (Ithaca: Cornell Modern Indonesia Project, 1995), 30.

[117] Mizan Sya'roni, "Muslim-Government Relation in the Indonesian New Order: Making Sense of the Nahdlatul Ulama's Withdrawal from Practical Politics," in *Islam and Development: A Politico-Religious Response* (Yogyakarta: Permika Montreal, 1997), 255–92.

[118] The reference is to the government's political organization to which all Indonesian civil servants had to join in lieu of political party membership under Suharto's New Order (1965–1998). Stuart A. Schlegel, "Technocrats in a Muslim Society: Symbolic Community in Aceh," in Gloria Davis (ed.), *What is Modern Indonesian Culture?* (Athens: Ohio University Center for International Studies, 1979), 232–48.

middle class who found their material prospects improving to various degrees under the economic policies of the New Order.[119]

This expanding middle class was to become an important constituency for those advancing agendas for the formal establishment of the Shariʿa over the final years of the twentieth century. These individuals were simultaneously Acehnese Muslims with a strong sense of local identity and participants in broader trends of Islamic revival that were gaining ground across Indonesia for decades.[120] In recognizing this, it becomes clear that simplistic models of co-optation by Jakarta are insufficient to deal with the complexity of these developments. The motivations of these actors reflect not only the extent to which they may have been beholden to structures of established political power, but also the aspirational appeal of Shariʿa as a model of divinely ordained justice and a means of addressing worldly needs for security and stability. These aspirations are spontaneously cited in Acehnese discourses on Islamic law, both in individual conversation, as well as in the broader public sphere and in popular media.[121]

The general sense that Shariʿa carries with it ideals and values both consistent with God's will and compatible with modern visions of development has considerably facilitated the reception of the current Shariʿa system in some sectors of Acehnese society.[122] It has also created a situation in which the idea of the Shariʿa is upheld as an absolute good even by those who take up positions critical of the work of the state institutions tasked with its implementation. Even local critics of particular aspects of the current Islamic legal system in Aceh often refer to abstracted ideals

[119] For a critical perspective on Aceh's Indonesianized middle class, see Otto Syamsuddin Ishak, *Dari Maaf ke Panik Aceh: Sebuah Sketsa Sosiologi-Politik* (Jakarta: Tifa, Lembaga Studi Pers dan Pembangunan, 2008).

[120] For contemporary views of this emerging Muslim middle class in Indonesia, see the chapters by Abdurrahman Wahid and Aswab Mahasin in Richard Tanterand Kenneth Young (eds.), *The Politics of Middle Class Indonesia* (Clayton: Monash University Centre of Southeast Asian Studies, 1990), 22–4, 138–44.

[121] This is particularly among circles affiliated with private Islamic schools (both the "Traditionalist" *dayah* and "Modernist" *madrasa*) and with various Muslim organizations, as well as a significant number of university students. I have highlighted some representative expressions of public positions both in favor of and opposed to state Shariʿain "Hand, Heart and Handphone: State Shariʿa in the Age of the SMS," *Contemporary Islam* 7 (2013) 15–32.

[122] Studies of the public sphere in Indonesia have tended to focus almost exclusively on more liberal NGOs and the role that they played in promoting civil society over recent decades. These have undoubtedly been important players, but there is a need to further develop our understandings of the public sphere by devoting attention to the religious NGOs of various types that have also proliferated in recent Indonesian history. This is common even in many of the papers published by the Aceh Institute, one of the most dynamic independent institutions of local academics in Aceh. See, for example: Harist Muzani, "Syariat tanpa Simbol," (12 December 2010), <http://www.acehinstitute.org/index.php?option=com_content&view=article&id=385:syariat-tanpa-simbol&catid=74:paradigma-islam>, accessed 18 July 2011.

of Shariʿa in making their arguments.[123] This tension between forms of Islamic idealism, pragmatic critique and political positioning has been a central dynamic in many Muslim societies since the mid-twentieth century. In Aceh, this played out in particularly striking ways in the struggles between the Indonesian central government and the "Free Aceh Movement" (GAM) in the latter years of the twentieth century.

ACEHNESE VISIONS OF ISLAM AND INDEPENDENCE

The discovery of natural gas in the area of Lhokseumawe (North Aceh) brought brighter visions of future prosperity for Aceh.[124] However, the structures put into place to exploit these resources quickly came to follow patterns that had long served to channel the economic benefits of Aceh elsewhere.[125] As the situation developed in the 1970s, local resentment mounted over the national government's appropriation of Aceh's wealth.[126] It was in this context that, in 1976, Hassan Muhammad di Tiro proclaimed Aceh's independence from Indonesia and formed GAM to initiate an armed campaign for secession.[127]

GAM's military successes were at first far from impressive. By 1979, Hassan di Tiro and a number of other leaders of the movement fled into exile abroad in the face of an intense Indonesian counter-insurgency

[123] For example in December 2006, a local "civil society" organization, the Yayasan Insan Cita Madani (YICM), conducted a survey to gauge public opinion on the state implementation of Islamic law in Aceh. Its results revealed both widespread dissatisfaction with the current laws and institutions in place, and an overwhelming (87 percent) agreement with the statement that "*Pemberlakuan Syariʿat Islam solusi bagi kehidupan masyarakat Aceh.*" See Andi Mahdi (ed.), *Polemik Penerapan Syariat Islam di Aceh* (Banda Aceh: Yayasan Insan Cita Madani, 2007). In a focus group discussion convened on the topic at the YICM office on 26 June 2008 the most frequent topics that arose were the need for more wide-reaching public education about Islamic law at the village level and more regularized mechanisms of enforcement, not for "less Shariʿa."

[124] "Although Indonesia has a number of hydrocarbon fields, the field located in the region of Aceh was its most valuable at the time and was a major contributor to state income." Damien Kingsbury, *The Politics of Indonesia* (New York: Oxford University Press, 2005), 151.

[125] Nishi Yoshimi, "Among Bangsa, Keturunan and Daerah: Peace-building and Group Identity in the Law on Governing Aceh, 2006," in Yamamoto Hiroyuki, Anthony Milner, Kawashima Midori, and Arai Kazuhiro (eds.), *Bangsa and Umma: Developments of People-grouping Concepts in Islamized Southeast Asia* (Kyoto: Kyoto University Press, 2011), 169.

[126] For more on the economy of Aceh and its relation to New Order development projects, see Nazamuddin, Agussabti and Syamsudin Mahmud, "Economic Modernization and its Influence on the Social System in Aceh," in Arndt Graf, Susanne Schröter, and Edwin Wieringa (eds.), *Aceh: History, Politics and Culture* (Singapore: ISEAS Publishing, 2010), 82; Manfred Rist, "Economic Development of Aceh since 1945," in Graf, Schröter, and Wieringa, *Aceh: History, Politics and Culture*, 107–11.

[127] Kell, *The Roots of the Acehnese Rebellion*, 14–18.

campaign.[128] Thereafter, GAM's leaders repeatedly reframed the movement. For example, from 1986 to 1990, about 500 GAM members went to Libya for military training.[129] During this period, Libya was promoting a particular vision of "Third World" liberationism in which Islam could form an important part of various local identity movements—but in which particular jurisprudential and theological interpretations were deliberately downplayed.[130] Not surprisingly, the emphasis of GAM's agenda over the period that followed was squarely on a struggle for national liberation, rather than a religious revival.[131] While Islam would remain a critical aspect of GAM's vision of Acehnese identity, the aim of its struggle was not the creation of any particular vision of an "Islamic" state or society. Like Libya's profile as a vanguard of third-world liberationism on the global stage, GAM's particular agenda for Aceh was also increasingly facing a considerable ideological challenge in the form of Revivalist visions of Islam that sought to restore the centrality of religious visions for the remaking of a society in crisis as the twentieth century drew toward a close.

The rise of GAM and the Indonesian military's moves to suppress it initiated another period of armed conflict between Aceh and the central government in Jakarta. There were some significant elements of continuity in this, as most of those involved in the early formation of GAM held Islam to be an important aspect of Acehnese identity, and many also had previous personal or familial ties to supporters of the Darul Islam. However, as GAM evolved over the decades that followed, Islam came to be increasingly marginal as the movement came to be framed as an ethno-nationalist separatist cause.[132] Unlike the Darul Islam movement of the previous generation, GAM did not develop any explicit agenda for the consolidation of the formal role of Islam in the independent Aceh for which they were struggling.[133]

[128] For more on the involvement of the Acehnese diaspora in conflict, see Antje Missbach, *Separatist Conflict in Indonesia: The Long-Distance Politics of the Acehnese Diaspora* (Abingdon: Routledge, 2011).

[129] Damien Kingsbury, "Political Reconstruction in Aceh," in Matthew Clarke, Ismet Fanany, and Sue Kenny (eds.), *Post-Disaster Reconstruction: Lessons from Aceh* (London: Earthscan, 2010), 63.

[130] Dirk Vandewalle, *Libya since Independence* (Ithaca: Cornell University Press, 1998), 132–3.

[131] There were clearly significant elective affinities between GAM and ideological trends in Libya during that time, but there is no clear evidence of any distinct causal vector between the two in either direction.

[132] Aspinall, *Islam and Nation*, 13.

[133] There were occasionally broad rhetorical appeals to Islam as a basis for the constitution of an independent Aceh made by some GAM leaders in the earlier stages of the movement. However these statements never developed into a systematic vision for an Islamic state, and indeed the appeals to Islam were increasingly downplayed over the later history of the movement. Ed Aspinall, personal communication, 25 July 2012.

GAM's vision of Aceh's future diverged increasingly from those of many of Aceh's Islamists, who at that time were coming more and more to identify Islam with Indonesian nationalism, rather than with any form of Acehnese exceptionalism that would cut its ties with the broader Indonesian *umma*. During that time, significant developments in conceptions of Islam and Indonesian identity were taking place at the national level.[134] This was particularly the case with regard to the role of Islamic religious revival in evolving understandings of Indonesian nationalism that coalesced under the developmentalist *daʿwa* paradigm of the New Order state. This in turn marked an important aspect of transitions in the relationship between the Acehnese and the Indonesian state in the late twentieth century.

The conflict over control of Aceh and its wealth led to energetic debates about Acehnese identity, and about the role that Islam should play in society.[135] Through the nexus of *daʿwa* and developmentalism, by the last decades of the twentieth century many of Aceh's Islamic intellectuals had come to believe that the structures of the New Order state would serve their interests better than would an independent nation under GAM. At the same time the New Order regime came increasingly to appeal to Islam in its campaigns for hearts and minds, as well as for votes. This continued even during the pronounced upsurge in violence during the 1990s and into the early years of the twenty-first century.[136] Despite the great trauma suffered by the Acehnese population during that period, there was also a strengthening of the position of those who viewed Islam as the bond that cemented the relationship between Aceh and the broader Indonesian nation. As Edward Aspinall has characterized the situation:

> Especially after the fall of Soeharto, government supporters appealed to Islamic unity to undercut separatism. In turn, the urge of identity differentiation pushed Acehnese nationalists to emphasize other factors and even to

[134] For the development of New Order forms of Indonesian Islamist nationalism at this time, see R. Michael Feener, *Muslim Legal Thought in Modern Indonesia* (Cambridge: Cambridge University Press, 2007), 106–17.

[135] Writing of the situation in the 1980s, Eric Morris, argued that "... the conflict has been about how one group of leaders rather than another has come to be in a position to formulate the symbols of group identity, to provide the definition of what it means to be Acehnese" (*Islam and Politics*, 13). Likewise, Edward Aspinall has noted: "During the conflict years, the two sides strove to 'fill the heads' of the Acehnese with different visions of their place in the world and in history" (*Islam and Nation*, 3, 194).

[136] Aceh was not unique in this case, and in fact, Golkar was involved with local movements for the implementation of Islamic law in other parts of Indonesia during the initial stages of post-Suharto de-centralization. One striking example of this was in another former Darul Islam area, South Sulawesi. Muhamad Hisyam, "The Preparatory Committee for Implementation of Sharia (KPPSI): An Islamic Resurgence in South Sulawesi," in Ikuya Tokor (ed.), *Islam in Southeast Asia: Transnational Networks and Local Contexts* (Tokyo: Tokyo University of Foreign Studies, 2009), 14.

> attack government attempts to Islamize public affairs. The transition from Islam to nationalism was complete.[137]

Islam had thus fully emerged as a major means for the Indonesian state to challenge GAM's claims of representing the ideals of the Acehnese people.[138] Of course, those presented with these broad formulations from on high were often left to struggle on their own over the implications that such a constructed dichotomy held for them in navigating their daily lives.

Some in Jakarta viewed the state support of Islam in terms of finally fulfilling the aims of the earlier Darul Islam, drawing on a vision of the Acehnese as being inherently defined by their adherence to Islam. While in part calling on stereotypical visions of Aceh's past, appeals to Islam were increasingly being used in Aceh itself in conversations that were more directly concerned with the future.[139] The growing identification of Islam as the potential solution to, and not simply the cause of, Acehnese grievances found resonance within the Indonesian armed forces at that time as well. Over the 1990s, reconfigurations of authority within ABRI had resulted in the emergence of an increasingly visible segment of military leadership that was sympathetic to Islamist visions of Indonesian nationalism.[140] The Indonesian military were to eventually become more involved with groups in Aceh dedicated to the application of Islamic norms in the governing of everyday life. In the meantime, however, the Indonesian military was more often a source of disorder and destruction than an embodiment of any religious vision of social order.[141]

[137] Aspinall, *Islam and Nation*, 13.

[138] Kell, *The Roots of the Acehnese Rebellion*, 57.

[139] This, for example, was the dominant rhetoric of Syamsul Hadi, an influential proponent of the current Islamic legal system in Aceh and former Indonesian Supreme Court justice who opened a series of discussions of the topic with high ranking officials from the Ulama Council and members of the provincial assembly (DRPA) with dramatic appeals to the "longing" for the Shari'a that he felt was burning in the hearts of many Acehnese (closed door sessions in the DPRA Head's office and the MPU Central office, Banda Aceh, 27 May 2008).

[140] Jun Honna, "Military Ideology in Response to Democratic Pressure during the Late Suharto Era: Political and Institutional Contexts," *Indonesia* 67 (April 1999) 95.

[141] The violence and misrule in Aceh were closely monitored by the International Crisis Group (ICG). See "Aceh: Can Autonomy Stem the Conflict," "Aceh: How Not to Win Hearts and Minds," *Indonesia Briefing* (23 July 2003), <http://www.crisisgroup.org/~/media/Files/asia/south-east-asia/indonesia/B027%20Aceh%20How%20Not%20to%20Win%20Hearts%20and%20Minds.pdf>, accessed 28 August 2012; and, "Aceh: Why the Military Solution Still Won't Work," *Indonesia Briefing* (9 May 2003), <http://www.crisisgroup.org/~/media/Files/asia/south-east-asia/indonesia/B026%20Aceh%20Why%20The%20Military%20Option%20Still%20Wont%20Work.pdf>, accessed 28 August 2012.

ISLAM AND SOCIAL CONTROL

As the conflict with GAM re-ignited and the violence escalated in the 1990s, lawlessness was rampant in Aceh. After the fall of Suharto in 1998, Indonesian military operations continued and even increased in intensity.[142] Indeed, the violence suffered by the general population in many parts of Aceh was even greater during the *Reformasi* period than it had been under the New Order, and it left many severely traumatized.[143] The brutality of the Indonesian armed forces during this period served to drive more of the population to side with GAM.[144]

With a non-functioning court system and in the absence of any outside mechanisms for ensuring the protection of basic human rights, an undisciplined military often acted with impunity. As Elizabeth Drexler has characterized the situation, "every failed attempt to hold perpetrators accountable was followed by renewed instability, underlining the state's inability to subordinate violence to the law."[145] Michelle Miller has further documented that in this context of rampant public disorder, there was a further disturbing rise in the trend for the local population to resort to extra-legal means for settling disputes and grievances.[146]

The situation was clearly unsustainable, and on 8 November 1999, a massive rally was held at Banda Aceh's iconic Baiturrahman mosque demanding a referendum on Acehnese independence. Speakers included a number of prominent Islamic preachers, some of whom were prominent figures associated with local Islamic organizations based in Traditionalist *dayah*.[147] In an attempt to prevent secession, Indonesian military operations in Aceh were also supplemented with other strategies by the rapid succession of presidents in power during the post-Suharto "*Reformasi*" period. These measures came to include granting Aceh

[142] On the later stages of the conflict: Michelle Ann Miller, *Rebellion and Reform in Indonesia: Jakarta's Security and Autonomy Policies in Aceh* (Abingdon: Routledge, 2009).

[143] A.E. Priyono, "Post-DOM Aceh: The Escalation of State Terror and Resistance of Civil Society Movements," in Stanley Adi Prasetyo, A.E. Priyono, and Olle Törnquist (eds.), *Indonesia's Post-Soeharto Democracy Movement* (Jakarta: DEMOS, 2003), 513–41; Byron Good and Mary-Jo Del Vecchio-Good (PIs), *Psychosocial Needs Assessment of Communities Affected by the Conflict in the Districts of Pidie, Bireuen and Aceh Utara* (Jakarta: International Organization for Migration, 2006).

[144] Edward Aspinall, "Modernity, History and Ethnicity: Indonesian and Acehnese Nationalism in Conflict," in Damien Kingsbury and Harry Aveling (eds.), *Autonomy and Disintegration in Indonesia* (London: RoutledgeCurzon, 2003), 128–47.

[145] Elizabeth F. Drexler, *Aceh, Indonesia: Securing the Insecure State* (Philadelphia: University of Pennsylvania Press, 2008), 125.

[146] Miller, *Rebellion and Reform*, 108.

[147] Particularly prominent were the Rabithah Thaliban Aceh (RTA) and the Himpunan Ulama Dayah Aceh (HUDA). See Miller, *Rebellion and Reform*, 32; and Aspinall, *Islam and Nation*, 131–3.

the right to special autonomy over a number of key aspects of local administration, including provisions for the application of Islamic law in the province.[148] One main objective of this was to undermine support for both GAM and the student-led movement for a referendum (SIRA) among the ulama and the broader Muslim population.[149] The grant of autonomy opened up opportunities for other parties within Aceh to advance their own goals of formalizing Islam within the structures of the state.

Working within this framework, a group of academics from the Banda Aceh State Institute for Islamic Studies (IAIN) began working together with Acehnese politicians and officials from Jakarta to develop more specific structures and substance for the development of an Islamic legal system in the province.[150] The idea of the Shariʿa as a source of social order held considerable appeal for a number of Islamic academics and activists who saw it as the best solution for a society in such desperate need of some form of stability. Hasanuddin Yusuf Adan, an IAIN lecturer educated at the International Islamic University Malaysia, was one prominent voice of the views expressed in such circles at that time:

> We need religious values to provide social control ... and our faith should be grown out of the pure sources of Islam (I. *sumber agama murni*) ... The sure way to save our community and our homeland is through strengthening *social control* [English term used in original], which is expressed in religious terms by instructing (I. *menasihati*) each other and following the advice we receive (I. *salingmena'atisetiapnasihat*).[151]

The forms that such religiously grounded norms of social control could take, however, tended toward more coercive means than simple "advice." This included the promulgation of new legislation based on Shariʿa norms, and the establishment of new state institutions for applying them.

THE GREAT WAVE AND ITS WAKE

Over the first years of the twenty-first century, the foundations of a new Islamic legal system were laid in Aceh. Legislation was enacted to regulate Islamic belief and ritual worship, as well as issues of public morality

[148] The legal frameworks for this special autonomy and the legislation establishing elements of the new Islamic legal system will be treated extensively in Chapter 5.

[149] Edward Aspinall, "Whither Aceh?" *Inside Indonesia* 62 (April–June 2000):<http://www.insideindonesia.org/edition-62-apr-jun-2000/whither-aceh-3007555>, accessed 30 July 2012.

[150] Interview with Yusny Saby, 17 November 2008 at Banda Aceh.

[151] Hasanuddin Yusuf Adan, *Politik dan Tamaddun Aceh* (Banda Aceh: Adnin Foundation Aceh, 2006), 95–6.

including gambling, alcohol consumption, and relations between the sexes; the Ulama Council (MPU) was given additional powers; the religious courts were given expanded jurisdiction; the Wilayatul Hisbah (WH), a body for policing Shariʿa offenses, was created; and a State Shariʿa Agency (DSI) was established to coordinate various aspects of implementation. All of this, however, was in many ways still an untested experiment at that time. With the conflict between GAM and the Indonesian military still ongoing, attention, energies, and resources were largely directed elsewhere. The new laws went unenforced by the formal apparatus of the state, and the fledgling institutions founded to support them had limited reach in society.[152]

The situation changed dramatically, however, following the devastating Boxing Day earthquake and tsunami of 2004.[153] The shock of this unforeseen tragedy redefined priorities, transformed conversations about the future of Acehnese society, and accelerated ongoing negotiations to bring an end to the conflict. This was formally concluded in July 2005 with the signing of the Helsinki Agreement.[154] These developments contributed to the establishment of a level of stability which allowed for attention to be refocused on issues of social order under a civilian administration, and set the stage for a reworking of the earlier special autonomy measures that provided for the state implementation of Islamic law. It also greatly facilitated the work of international NGOs to carry out massive projects of reconstruction in Aceh. This in turn brought together conditions to actualize discourses of linking immediate disaster relief with more ambitious projects of fostering social change and economic development that had become common in post-disaster relief and international aid circles during the 1990s.[155] Consequently, enormous amounts of money

[152] There were, however, instances of local vigilante action against perceived offenses of the Shariʿa in various parts of Aceh during this period—and the attention that they received in the local and international media came to play a significant role in the public discourses on Islamic law that developed over the years that followed. These developments will be discussed further in Chapter 8.

[153] Kerry Sieh, "The Sunda Megathrust: Past, Present and Future," in Patrick Daly, R. Michael Feener, and Anthony Reid (eds.), *From the Ground Up: Perspectives on Post-Tsunami and Post-Conflict Aceh* (Singapore: ISEAS Press, 2012), 1–22.

[154] See Edward Aspinall, *The Helsinki Agreement: A More Promising Basis for Peace in Aceh?* (Washington: East-West Center, 2005). Overviews of diverse aspects of the peace process can be found in Aguswandi and Judith Large (eds.), *Reconfiguring Politics: The Indonesia–Aceh Peace*, special issue of *Accord: An International Review of Peace Initiatives* 20 (2008), <http://www.c-r.org/our-work/accord/aceh/index.php>, accessed 30 July 2012. A more extended treatment of the process from the perspective of someone closely involved with the GAM delegation at Helsinki can be found in Damien Kingsbury, *Peace in Aceh: A Personal Account of the Helsinki Peace Process* (Jakarta: PT Equinox Publishing, 2006).

[155] For critical interventions into the discourse of linking relief, reconstruction, and development (LRRD) in response to natural disasters and "complex political emergencies," see Margaret Buchanan-Smith and Simon Maxwell, "Linking Relief and Development: An Introduction and Overview," *Institute of Development Studies Bulletin* 25(4)

flowed in, allowing a range of international NGOs to field-test their latest theories of linking disaster relief and recovery to more forward-directed development projects.[156] Under the popular motto of "building back better," the post-disaster reconstruction looked beyond purely physical rebuilding to also include a broad range of programs aimed at addressing economic and social conditions that were seen as contributing to the vulnerability of the community. As will be discussed shortly, these new visions of disaster as creating opportunities for wide-ranging reform came to inspire new ways of thinking about the implementation of Islamic law as a project of social engineering among *daʿwa*-oriented academics and activists in Aceh in the post-disaster/post-conflict period.

At the same time, the earthquake and tsunami also triggered a wide-ranging religious revival across Aceh, in which diverse supernatural readings of the meaning of the catastrophe were developed.[157] As will be discussed further in Chapter 9, these broad-based religious reactions were selectively drawn upon by the state and other major players behind the transformations of Aceh as justifications for particular visions of post-disaster social reconstruction in which Shariʿa was invoked as the surest means to prevent further disasters from striking Aceh.[158]As expressed in one Friday sermon at the iconic Baiturrahman mosque in Banda Aceh:

> We have to always be on guard against those disasters that are caused by our own iniquities. At the same time we must be aware of our responsibilities to exert control over those actions that can lead to disaster, because the loss that will result does not just affect the offender, but disaster also strikes those who have not sinned.[159]

(1994) 2–16; Richard Longhurst, "Conceptual Frameworks for Linking Relief and Development," *Institute of Development Studies Bulletin* 25(4) (1994) 17–23; Paul Spiegel, "The Relief-Reconstruction-Development Dynamic: A New approach to the Concept of Linking Relief, Reconstruction, and Development," *Refuge* 17(4) (October 1998) 33–7; Ian Smillie, "Relief and Development: The Struggle for Synergy," *Thomas J. Watson Jr. Institute for International Studies Occasional Papers #33* (Providence: Brown University, 1998); Philip White and Lionel Cliffe, "Matching Response to Context in Complex Political Emergencies: 'Relief,' 'Development,' 'Peace-building' or Something In-Between?" *Disasters* 24(4) (2000) 314–42.

[156] For critical reflections on aspects of these projects for reconstruction and development, see the essays by John Telford, Ian Christoplos, and Treena Wu; Patrick Daly and Yenny Rahmayati; Wolfgang Fengler, Ahyalhsan, and Kai Kaiser; Daniel Fitzpatrick and Saiful Mahdi in Daly, Feener, and Reid, *From the Ground Up*, 25–155.

[157] For studies of broader dimensions of religious responses to the disaster, see Reza Idria, "Muslim Theological Perspectives on Natural Disasters: The Case of Indonesian Earthquakes and Tsunami of 2004," M.A. thesis (Leiden: Leiden University, 2010); as well as the essays by Arndt Graf and Edwin Wieringa in Graf, Schröter, and Wieringa(eds.) *Aceh*, 287–99; 316–33.

[158] Michelle Ann Miller, "The Role of Islamic Law (Sharia) in Post-Tsunami Reconstruction," in Matthew Clarke, Ismet Fanany, and Sue Kenny (eds.), *Post-Disaster Reconstruction: Lessons from Aceh* (London: Earthscan, 2010), 35.

[159] Ali Mochtar Ngabalin, "Refleksi Musibah Orang Aceh," *Gema Baiturrahman* (3 January 2011): 2.

Figure 2.4. New mosque construction in North Aceh: The post-tsunami reconstruction boom included the building of hundreds of new mosques across the province—nearly all of which were large structures with elaborate domes. The elaborate decoration of these domes was generally completed first and in quite a number of cases construction slowed considerable thereafter, leaving congregants to pray beneath them in unfinished spaces of bare concrete and rebar. (Photo by R. Michael Feener)

Official government publications also cited the neglect of religious duties and widespread moral degradation as the cause of the natural disasters, citing Qur'ānic verses on the fate of earlier communities who had turned away from God.[160]

At the same time, a number of Aceh's Islamic leaders were swept up in the broader trends of seeing the post-disaster reconstruction as an opportunity to create a "New Aceh" (I. *Aceh Baru*).[161] Their vision of what this new society might look like, however, diverged at various points from those of some of the newly-arrived NGOs that were advocating ideals of human rights, gender justice, and other liberal causes as prominent aspects of their work. Seeing such ideas as potential threats to religious

[160] For example: M. Hasbi Amiruddin (ed.), *Aceh: Serambi Mekka* (Banda Aceh: Pemerintah Provinsi Nanggroe Aceh Darussalam, 2008), 378–88.

[161] As highlighted, for example, in Bustami Abubakar (ed.), *Ulama dan Politik: Menyongsong Aceh Baru* (Lhokseumawe: Lembaga Studi Islam dan Masyarakat Aceh/ STAIN Malikussaleh, 2011), xiv.

values, they rallied to Islam as a way of countering the deleterious effects of this second devastating wave of *globalisasi*.[162] In their shared opposition to the perceived promotion of a "liberal" social ethos, a further convergence of interests was established between segments of Aceh's Islamic leadership and the Indonesian state through the reinvigoration of Shariʿa implementation with a focus on public morality as a means of social control.[163]

Beyond the strengthening of existing institutions for the administration of Islamic law in Aceh, assertions of the need for the vigorous enforcement of Shariʿa norms to confront the challenges of the new open society of the post-disaster/post-conflict period took a wide range of direct forms, ranging from spontaneous outbursts of vigilante justice in local communities to the more coordinated efforts of organizations such as the "Anti-Sin League" (Badan Anti Maksiat/BAM). BAM was established by an Acehnese with close ties to the police and military and was based on a paramilitary structure, including its own intelligence division and uniforms for its field operatives. The organization rose to public prominence in the first years after the tsunami by carrying out raids on locations where gambling, alcohol consumption, and improper mixing of the sexes were believed to have taken place. At the same time, however, it claimed a mandate of not only "forbidding wrong" but also "commanding right" through programs of promoting the recitation of the Qurʾān and other forms of devotionalism.[164] The purpose of this, its founder explained, was to engender forms of religious awareness that could facilitate the building of a better society: "If people are pious and consistent in performing religious devotions, all else runs smoothly. It's like if someone is used to driving his own car—when he is at the wheel he knows how to steer it."[165] In the deployment of this aspirational project for promoting a particular form of religious awareness, BAM was not only an intimidating adjunct to the coercive apparatus of the Indonesian

[162] Muslim Thahiry, Khairizzaman, and Abidin Nurdin (eds.), *Wacana Pemikiran Santri Dayah Aceh* (Banda Aceh: BRR, PKPM Aceh & Wacana Press, 2006), 99, 118, et passim.

[163] These particular developments took place against the broader backdrop of a rapprochement between *daʿwa*-oriented Islamic activists and the New Order state that had been gaining ground since the late 1980s. Aspinall, *Islam and Nation*, 211; M.C. Ricklefs, *Islamisation and Its Opponents in Java: A Political, Social, Cultural and Religious History, c. 1930 to the Present* (Singapore: NUS Press, 2012), 254.

[164] For a magisterial study of the historical development of ideas of "commanding right and forbidding wrong" (Ar. *al-amr bi'l-maʿrūf wa'l-nahy ʿan al-munkar*) in Muslim societies, see Michael Cook, *Commanding Right and Forbidding Wrong in Islamic Thought* (Cambridge: Cambridge University Press, 2000).

[165] Interview with Fachruddin bin Asmiy (leader of BAM), 3 September 2008 at the Lambaro Skep mosque, Banda Aceh.

state.[166] For, in addition to the role that BAM clearly played along that line, its engagement with the promotion of a more encompassing religious subjectivity was simultaneously engaged with other, less forceful, agendas for re-establishing Islam as the primary source of Acehnese identity and as the model for the governance of society. BAM's methods were by no means models of civility, but they were nonetheless engaged with the emergence of a new and Islamicizing public sphere in post-disaster/post-conflict Aceh.[167]

As the religious revival crested, however, public enthusiasm for more aggressive promotion of Shariʿa waned and other visions of Aceh's future came increasingly to the fore. This was perhaps most dramatically signaled by the election of former GAM figures as governor and as the dominant party in the provincial legislature in 2006 and 2009, respectively.[168] Most former GAM politicians ran on platforms that did not include the strengthening of state Shariʿa as a prominent item, something that was palpable in its absence when viewed alongside most Indonesian national parties running in the election, for which the Shariʿa was more of a central issue. Michelle Miller has even quoted a "senior GAM representative" as going so far as to state that, "[i]f we win [the election] we will put an end to sharia. But we have to be careful about how we approach this matter because most Acehnese people accept it."[169]

To date, however, there has not been an "end" to Shariʿa in Aceh. All the substantive legislation that was passed before the ascendance of GAM politicians remains on the books, and none of the institutional structures for applying those laws have been dismantled.[170] Indeed, even in the face of government policies that have attempted to curb the allocation

[166] For more on the role of *preman* (criminal thugs with ties to military, police, and government agencies) in the politics of Suhato's New Order and the subsequent Reformasi period, see Tim Lindsey, "The Criminal State: Premanisme and the New Indonesia," in Grayson J. Lloyd and Shannon L. Smith (eds.), *Indonesia Today: Challenges of History* (Lanham, Md.: Rowman & Littlefield, 2001), 283–97; Loren Ryter, "Youth, Gangs and the State in Indonesia," Ph.D. dissertation (Seattle: University of Washington, 2002); and "Reformasi Gangsters," *Inside Indonesia* (April 2005), <http://www.insideindonesia.org/weekly-articles-82-apr-jun-2005/reformasi-gangsters-2407177>, accessed 30 July 2012.

[167] At the same time, BAM's close relationship to the "uncivil state" reflects broader national patterns in Indonesia, as demonstrated by Robert Hefner in *Civil Islam: Muslims and Democratization in Indonesia* (Princeton: Princeton University Press, 2000), 167–213.

[168] Damien Kingsbury, "Political Reconstruction in Aceh," in Matthew Clarke, Ismet Fanany, and Sue Kenny (eds.), *Post-Disaster Reconstruction: Lessons from Aceh* (London: Earthscan, 2010), 69–75.

[169] Miller, "The Role of Islamic Law," 34.

[170] Even the most controversial piece of Islamic legislation in contemporary Aceh, the 2009 Islamic Criminal Code (*Qanun Jinayat*), remains, in principle, on the books. The refusal of Governor Irwandi Yusuf to sign the bill into law himself, however, reflects the ongoing resistance of former GAM leadership to promote the further Islamization of Aceh's legal system. For more on this, see Chapter 5.

of state resources to the Islamic legal system and widespread popular disappointment with aspects of the way in which it has been practically implemented, the Shariʿa maintains a significant resonance among the wider public. As will be discussed in the chapters that follow, this has itself been facilitated by the wide-ranging efforts to raise "awareness" (I. *kesadaran*) of Islam which have been characteristic of all the institutional structures of Aceh's twenty-first-century Islamic legal system.

The continuing appeal of Islamic law as an ideal for the ordering of society clearly transcends the tribulations of short-term electoral cycles, and is felt across a number of party lines. Indeed, the very abstraction of the concept of Shariʿa serves to facilitate diverse and dynamic conversations on social issues in contexts of contested political control. To more fully appreciate its role in contemporary society, there is a need then to supplement the extensive work that has already been done on the politics of Islamic law in Aceh to engage with its broader social and cultural dimensions.[171] The politics have clearly been an important aspect of recent developments, and it is by no means my intention to deny this reality. There is, however, more to the situation than the much-discussed dimensions of intra-party competition and co-optation by the state. Another major field of activity relevant to these developments is that of education, which will be examined in the next chapter in relation to both the formation of aspirational visions of Islam among Muslims in Aceh, and the institutional structures responsible for training the officials, bureaucrats, and staff of Aceh's contemporary Islamic legal system.

[171] This territory is as rich, complex, and challenging, and no single scholar could hope to cover all its aspects. This book focuses largely on macro-level institutions and the religious and ideological visions that motivate the people who work within them. More fine-grained treatment of the micro-dynamics that are also involved are being developed in the recently completed dissertations by Dan Birchok, David Kloos, Annemarie Samuels, and Catherine Smith, as well as the studies collected in R. Michael Feener, David Kloos, and Annemarie Samuels (eds.), *Islam and the Limits of the State: Reconfigurations of Ritual, Doctrine, Community and Authority in Contemporary Aceh* (Leiden: Brill, forthcoming).

3

Reconfigurations of Religious Education and Authority

All this can be very well compared to the labour of an architect who, while erecting a building, proceeds gradually with his plan. He begins with gathering an adequate number of masons and other labourers and procuring the required material; he then levels the ground, lays the foundation and raises the walls brick by brick. The roof is laid when the walls are ready and thus after continuous and extensive hard labour, he completes the construction of the building.

Abu'l-Aʿla Maududi
The Islamic Law and Constitution

Maududi (d. 1979) was one of the pioneers of modern Islamic revival and his vision for remaking society in the image of a reformed understanding of religion has been widely influential across the Muslim world.[1] At the

[1] Southeast Asia has not been an exception, and in fact, important points of contact between the Islamist visions of Maududi and that of Indonesia's M. Natsir can be traced across the pages of the English-language journal *Progressive Islam* during the 1950s. See Terenjit Sevea, "Making Medinas in the East: Islamic Connections and *Progressive Islam*," in R. Michael Feener and Terenjit Sevea (eds.), *Islamic Connections: Muslim Societies in South and Southeast Asia* (Singapore: ISEAS, 2009), 149–74. In particular, the imprint of Maududi's totalizing conception of remaking state and society in the image of Islam found significant resonance with Natsir and other Indonesian Islamists associated with the party he led, known as Masjumi. While the some of Maududi's views did influence Indonesian Muslim activists and intellectuals, their impact was, however, also framed by engagements with much more diverse sources of inspiration from other modern Muslim thinkers, as well by the political contexts of their reception. Rémy Madinier, *L'Indonésie, entre démocratie musulmane et Islam intégral: Histoire du parti Masjumi, 1945–1960* (Paris: Karthala, 2012), 420; M. Kamal Hassan, "The Influence of Mawdūdī's Thought on Muslims in Southeast Asia: A Brief Survey," *The Muslim World* 93 (July/October 2003) 429–64. Starting from the 1970s, Indonesian translations of Maududi's works were being published by the Dewan Daʿwah Islamiyah Indonesia (DDII). Audrey R. Kahin, *Islam, Nationalism and Democracy* (Singapore: NUS Press, 2012), 179. Maududi's was also the subject of an entire chapter in an Indonesian volume on "Islam and Development" published at the end of the New Order period. Achmad Zaini, "Mawdudi's Conception of the Islamic State," in *Islam and Development: A Politico-Religious Response* (Yogyakarta: Permika Montreal, 1997), 163–99. For more on the legacy of Natsir and his associates in the DDII in evolving visions of Islamic law and society in Indonesia: Feener, *Muslim Legal Thought*, 81–117.

center of his vision was a program of what he referred to as "cultural engineering" in which the primary mode for transforming society was not only a political project, but more fundamentally a matter of Islamic education.[2] Maududi's broad vision works on the scale of generations to gradually spread the vision of a reconstituted Islamic society and deepen the conviction of individual believers so that they can collectively come together in Islamizing all aspects of life. For this reason, Maududi dedicated a substantial section of his treatise on the Islamization of law in Pakistan to education, foregrounding the importance of teaching and public pedagogy in facilitating substantial legal change.[3] The quotation at the beginning of the chapter (drawn from that work) presents this idea in a visual metaphor of first sweeping the ground to a flat level and then physically rebuilding the structures of society—an image that is particularly striking when read in the context of post-tsunami Aceh.

This chapter critically examines the ways in which modern developments of Aceh's Islamic educational institutions have played a role in shaping conceptualizations of Islam as both the putative essence of Acehnese tradition and as a blueprint for Aceh's future. This includes investigations of the transformation of traditional Islamic schools and the innovations brought by the modern *madrasa* model and the development of new institutions of higher education in Indonesia. Over nearly a century of modernizing reforms advanced by the initiatives of Islamic organizations and the interventions of state management there has been a significant transformation of basic conceptions of religious education, from established models of transmitting and maintaining tradition to programs for consciously molding the shape and direction of social change.

This re-envisioning of the aims and methods of Islamic education has had an impact not only on self-described "Modernist" institutions, but also upon schools which are often labeled "Traditionalist," including Acehnese *dayahs* and *pesantrens* all across Indonesia. In these developments, a major role was played by Indonesia's State Institutes of Islamic Studies (IAIN). As will be discussed later, the branch campus of this system in Banda Aceh has played a crucial role in the development of Aceh's contemporary Islamic legal system. In tracing the trajectories of reconfigurations of Islamic education in Aceh over the past century, this chapter will highlight

[2] Seyyed Vali Reza Nasr, *Vanguard of the Islamic Revolution: The Jama'at-i Islami of Pakistan* (London: I.B. Tauris, 1994), 78; Muhammad Qasim Zaman, *The Ulama in Contemporary Islam: Custodians of Change* (Princeton: Princeton University Press, 2002), 103.

[3] Abu'l-A'la Maududi, *The Islamic Law and Constitution* (Lahore: Islamic Publications, n.d.), 94–100.

conjunctures of institutional and ideological innovations that have come together to inform both the substantive content and the dynamics of the socialization of new visions of Islamic law in contemporary Aceh.

TRADITIONS OF ISLAMIC EDUCATION IN ACEH

Given the region's rich history as a center of Muslim learning and literature, as well as its strong sense of Islamic identity, there has been a tendency among many modern scholars and social commentators to assume certain long-term continuities in the pattern of state involvement with religious institutions in Aceh. Such modern understandings of Aceh's history, however, often retroject relatively recent Islamic institutional forms upon earlier periods of Aceh's history. Aceh holds a reputation for being a pre-eminent center of Islam in Southeast Asia, and we know that a number of Muslim scholars from the Middle East and South Asia were attracted to Aceh by its reputation and promise of royal patronage since at least the sixteenth century.[4] Nevertheless, we have very little information about the institutional frameworks in which such scholars worked in Aceh. Furthermore, our understanding of developments in Aceh over the long period between the oft-discussed "golden age" of Iskandar Muda and the late nineteenth century is strikingly underdeveloped.[5] As a result, we simply do not know very much at all about the more proximate origins of the institutions of religious education that are most common in Aceh today: the *meunasah* and the *dayah*.

Today, the *meunasah* is a ubiquitous feature of Acehnese villages. The contemporary *meunasah* is a site for Islamic education, but of a very rudimentary type where children are taught to memorize and recite passages from the Qur'ān and given basic instruction in Islamic belief and practice. In Aceh, the *meunasah* has come to be a central village institution, and traditionally it had many other roles to play in local communities well beyond that of Qur'ānic education. The *meunasah* of late-nineteenth-century Aceh was described as, "a sleeping-place for the men, a rest-house for strangers and a house of prayer or chapel, the *meunasah* also serves as a place of assemblage on various special

[4] Hoesein Djajadiningrat, "Critisch Overzicht van de in Maleische Werken Vervatte Gegevens over de Geschiedenis van het Soeltanaat van Atjeh," *Bijdragen tot de Taal-, Land- en Volkenkunde* 65 (1911) 157, 160–1.

[5] I have argued for the need for new work in this intervening "long eighteenth century" in "The Acehnese Past and its Present State of Study," in R. Michael Feener, Patrick Daly, and Anthony Reid (eds.), *Mapping the Acehnese Past* (Leiden: KITLV Press, 2011), 11–14.

Figure 3.1. A rural *meunasah* in North Aceh. In many Acehnese villages the *meunasah* is the largest building. As such it provides space for community meetings and ceremonies, while also providing a physical point of reference for orienting the community around a center for religious observance and education, as well as for local governance. (Photo by R. Michael Feener)

occasions."[6] The integration of the *meunasah* into local social life had political dimensions as well, and Isa Sulaiman noted the traditional dependence of the religious leader (Ac. *imeum*) of the village *meunasah* upon the local aristocracy (Ac. *ulèëbalang*) in the twentieth century. The village-level *meunasah* of the more recent past then was in some sense more associated with traditions of local political organization than with the religious authority of the ulama (see Figure 3.1).

In earlier periods, however, the *meunasah* seems to have been associated with more substantial study of the Islamic religious sciences. One of the earliest recorded uses of the term is found in the Acehnese poem *Hikayat Pocut Muhamat*. This text provides an evocative depiction of studies at a

[6] The village *meunasah* maintained these non-educational functions in communal life well into the twentieth century, and in 1969, Jim Siegel described the *meunasah* as "a building that men use as a meeting place to discuss village problems and to pray together during the fasting month. At night unmarried adolescent boys sleep there." James T. Siegel, *The Rope of God* (Berkeley: University of California Press, 1969), 52. Such practice appears to have its origins in pre-Islamic institutions of "nocturnal separation" of the sexes that are also known from other parts of Sumatra. However, in some parts of Aceh along the southwest coast, the *meunasah* is a space gendered as female for many purposes, particularly in villages that have more recently constructed new style mosques (Ar./I. *masjid*) for use by the men. Dan Birchok, personal communication, 17 July 2012.

meunasah (referred to in the text by the variant form *beunasah*)[7] as a site of Islamic religious education in West Aceh during the mid-eighteenth century:

> The teacher (Ac. *teungku*) had six hundred pupils; and all was a buzz of activity
> Some were reciting the Qur'ān, and others reading the *Masā'il*
> Some were studying the *Ajurrūmiyya*, others were translating the *Fātiḥa*,
> Some were reading Malay (Ac. *jawoë*) texts, others were engaged in discussion
> In the western pavilion (Ac. *rangkang*) they were studying [Arabic] grammar; and in the eastern pavilion spelling
> In the upstream pavilion they studied Sufism (Ac. *teusawoh*) from the subtle wisdom found in the *Ḥikam* and the *Iḥyā'*
> Everyone studied according to his capacity; some from Arabic works, others from texts in Malay
> The *teungku* was the master, and there was a tutor (*wakī*) in each pavilion who would look over the shoulders of students to examine their work[8]

This snapshot presents a picture of active engagement with texts in both Arabic and Malay starting from primary-level instruction in Qur'ānic recitation and the rudiments Arabic language, as well as basic catechism. At a higher level, the only works directly named here would be grouped under the rubric Sufi texts,[9] and it is curious to note that among the specific titles and more general fields of study mentioned by the poet, we do not find a single reference to a work of Islamic law or jurisprudence (*fiqh*).[10] By the late nineteenth century, however, standard works of Shāfiʿī

[7] Although many Muslims in Aceh today claim that the term *meunasah* is derived from the Arabic *madrasa*, this does not seem to be the case. In this text, one of the earliest descriptions of an Islamic school in Aceh, we get hints of a rather different etymology where the form *beunasah* appears to be related to terms used for religious institutions in other parts of the Malay Muslim world, including the term *balasoh* in Patani. Christopher M. Joll, *Muslim Merit Making in Thailand's Far-South* (Dordrecht: Springer, 2012), 215. I would like to thank Martin van Bruinessen and John Wolff for calling this to my attention and sharing their thoughts on the matter with me.

[8] G.W.J. Drewes (ed.), *Hikajat Potjut Muhamat* (The Hague: Martinus Nijhoff, 1979), 134–5. My translation here differs some what from that of Drewes. I have also rendered the titles of Arabic texts in standard transliteration, rather than in their Acehnese forms for easier identification. Drewes provides more detailed references to these texts in notes: see page 269.

[9] i.e. the classical Arabic works of al-Ghazālī (d. 1111), *Iḥyā' ulūm al-dīn*; and Ibn ʿAṭā'Allāh (d. 1309), *Kitāb al-ḥikām*.

[10] Of course, the source available to us here is a poem, not a complete catalog of studies at this institution, and thus cannot be taken to mean that no *fiqh* was studied there. The omission is, however, striking to a modern reader accustomed to the primacy given to Shāfiʿī jurisprudence by Acehnese in their current descriptions of *dayah* education. *Fiqh* has, of course, been central to Islamic education since the development of the first *madrasas* in eleventh-century Iraq, and its local primacy among other Islamic religious sciences is reflected in Acehnese sayings dating back to at least the nineteenth century such as "The study of jurisprudence produces saints" (*èleumèë pikah – le èëlia*). C. Snouck Hurgronje, *The Achehnese*, vol. II, trans. A.W.S. O'Sullivan (Leiden: E.J. Brill, 1906), 8.

fiqh were noted as central to Acehnese Islamic education. The curriculum of that time included Arabic grammar (Ac. *euleumèe alat*), jurisprudence (Ac. *euleumèe fikah*/Ar. *fiqh*), sufism (Ac. *tassawoih*/Ar. *taṣawwuf*), as well as studies of primary texts (Ac. *hadéh*/Ar. *ḥadīth* and *tafeusé*/*tafsīr*).

Both in terms of the material taught and the modes of instruction employed, Aceh's Islamic educational institutions generally paralleled Traditionalist schools elsewhere in Southeast Asia. Studies typically followed patterns also known in other parts of the Indonesian Archipelago and centered around the importance of transmitting particular texts in face-to-face encounters between students and their teacher, with commentary from the latter being added at various points.[11] In the late nineteenth century, the *teungku rangkang* were reported to tutor students in Malay-language *fiqh* texts, including the *Ṣirāt al-Mustaqīm* of al-Rānīrī, a Gujarati-Arab scholar who had worked at the court of Aceh in the seventeenth century.[12] More advanced students read Arabic works from the Shāfiʿī school, including Nawāwī's (d. 1277) *Minhāj al-Ṭālibīn* and commentaries on that work such as Anṣārī's (d. 1520) *Fatḥ al-Wahhāb*, Ibn Ḥajar's (d. 1567) *Tuḥfat al-Muḥtāj*, and the Maḥallī's (d. 1459) *Kanz al-Rāghibīn*.[13] Most of these standard Shāfiʿī texts are the same found in Traditionalist Islamic educational institutions in Java and other parts of the Indonesian Archipelago.[14] However, options beyond the established works of the Shāfiʿī school have also long played some part in Islamic legal practice in Aceh. For example, in the late nineteenth century Snouck Hurgronje reported that an appendix to Acehnese author Muḥammad Zayn b. Jalāl al-Dīn's work on marriage law sets forth rulings adopting the Ḥanafī position allowing for the marriage of underage girls without a living father or grandfather.[15]

At the turn of the twentieth century, Islamic learning beyond the elementary-level education provided by the village *meunasah* was increasingly pursued in other institutions that had come to be referred

[11] This method of teaching is referred to in Java as *bandungan*, with the teacher reading and commenting on an Arabic text, entertaining a certain degree of questioning and discussion as he goes. Snouck, *Achehnese*, vol. II, 29–30.

[12] Al-Rānīrī's work and its legacy in Aceh are discussed further in Chapter 5.

[13] Snouck, *Achehnese*, vol. II, 8–10.

[14] For surveys of curricula at the end of the nineteenth and the twentieth centuries, respectively, see L.W.C. van den Berg, "Het Mohammedaansche Godsdienstonderwijs op Java en Madoera en de daarbij gebruikte Arabische Boeken," *Tijdschrift voor Indische Taal-, Land- en Volkenkunde* 31 (1886) 518–55; and Martin van Bruinessen, "Kitab Kuning: Books in Arabic Script Used in the Pesantren Milieu," *Bijdragen tot de Taal-, Land- en Volkenkunde* 146 (1990) 226–69.

[15] Snouck read this as an instance of *madhhab* eclecticism (Ac. *balé' meudeuhab*), and notes that in the late nineteenth century, the study of *fiqh* was still thriving in Aceh, despite the disruption of more than three decades of war against the Dutch. Snouck, *Achehnese*, vol. II, 22–3.

to as *dayahs*. Popular etymology in Aceh derives this term from an Arabic word commonly used to refer to Sufi lodges (Ar. *zawiya*). Through the end of the nineteenth century, it was used to refer to sites for the recital of litanies and the performance of other supererogatory ritual.[16] The *dayah* as a school for the teaching of Islam had institutional foundations and contexts rather different from the village *meunasah*, and was organized primarily around charismatic teachers, rather than being directly rooted in the micro-dynamics of local village life.[17] For example, in the last years of the nineteenth century, an expanding network of schools was centered on Tgk. di. Lam Nyòng (a.k.a. Nya' Him).[18] In the twentieth century, a similar position came to be held by Tgk. Muda Waly of Labuan Haji. By that time, these schools were increasingly coming to be referred to by the term "*dayahs*" and a number of them were being established as institutions in more routinized forms that outlived their charismatic founders, often run by descendants and students of their founding teachers. It is from this period that we can trace a significant expansion of *dayahs* across Aceh, in which these lineage institutions were complemented by various new startups.[19]

With this expansion came a degree of differentiation, with some *dayahs* distinguishing themselves in certain areas of specialization. Even today, there is a sense among many in *dayah* circles that some of these institutions have their own "special" features that attract students of particular interests. Nearly all *dayahs*, however, incorporate some aspects of Sufi devotionalism and thus the name continues to reflect some aspects of its purported etymology. Generally speaking, most Acehnese *dayahs* today participate in traditions broadly associated with the Naqshbandiyya, and many with the Khālidī sub-branch of that order in particular. As local centers of both Islamic education and religious authority, *dayahs* have been important institutions in the formation of established understandings of Islam and its role in the structuring of Acehnese society. These networks of Traditionalist Muslim authority have, however, faced increasingly powerful challenges both by the introduction of secular models of schooling introduced under Dutch colonialism and by the advent of Islamic Modernist programs for reforming religious

16 Snouck described the "*déah*" of the late nineteenth century as a kind of more substantial, stone-floored building serving as village chapels or erected near venerated gravesites (*Achehnese*, vol. I, 63–4).

17 M. Isa Sulaiman, "Les Ulèebalang, les Ulémas, et les enseignants de madrasah: La lutte pour le pouvoir local en Aceh de 1942 à 1951," Ph.D. dissertation (Paris: École des Hautes Études en Sciences Sociales, 1985), 22.

18 "Almost all the teachers of the North and East Coasts owe their schooling wholly or in part to him." Snouck, *Achehnese*, vol. II, 27.

19 Sulaiman, "Les Ulèebalang, les Ulémas, et les enseignants de madrasah," 64.

education in the region over the course of the twentieth century. The latter in particular have served to shape perceptions of Islam for subsequent generations, and contributed significantly to the foundations of Aceh's contemporary Islamic legal system.

MODERNIZING MUSLIM SCHOOLS

During the early decades of the twentieth century, the consolidation of colonial control over Aceh allowed the Dutch to turn their attention to the establishment of new civilian institutions.[20] This included considerable efforts directed toward the construction of "native schools" which introduced the accoutrements of modern-style education—blackboards, chairs, writing tables, etc.—to segments of the local population.[21] At first, the "un-Islamic" origins of these schools, not to mention their form and contents, attracted the antipathy of many Acehnese Muslims. Their association with Dutch colonialism was particularly marked in the reactions of Aceh's Traditionalist ulama, who pronounced that attending such schools would lead one to unbelief (Ac. "*sekolah kaphé*").[22] Despite these negative cultural reactions, the colonial school system quickly expanded to the point that Aceh had a relatively high degree of village school attendance.[23] By 1935, over 33,000 children were enrolled in Aceh's colonial *volkschools*, comprising a "slightly higher" proportion than in the central region of Dutch colonialism in Java.[24]

Over the first decades of the twentieth century, other forms of modern education were also taking shape in Aceh, particularly a new type of Islamic school, designated by the term *madrasa* (see Figure 3.2).[25] These *madrasas*

[20] Non-military aspects of colonial Aceh are highlighted in Jean Gelman Taylor, "Aceh Histories in the KITLV Images Archive," in R. Michael Feener, Patrick Daly, and Anthony Reid (eds.), *Mapping the Acehnese Past* (Leiden: KITLV Press, 2011), 199–239.

[21] Sulaiman, "Les Ulèebalang, les Ulémas, et les enseignants de madrasah," 58–62. For a broader overview of Dutch colonial education in the Indies, see Lee Kam Hing, *Education and Politics in Indonesia, 1945–1965* (Kuala Lumpur: University of Malaya Press, 1995), 3–26.

[22] Reform-minded Acehnese Islamic scholars from the early twentieth century have frequently called attention to this "Traditionalist" opposition to modern learning, and Hasbi Ash Shiddieqy recalled being forbidden by his father even to study the Roman alphabet because of its associations with "unbelief." Nourouzzaman Shiddiqi, *Jeram-Jeram Peradaban Muslim* (Yogyakarta: Pustaka Pelajar, 1996), 217.

[23] Eric Morris gives figures of 12.3 percent, as opposed to an overall average of only 4.3 percent across the Netherlands East Indies. Eric E. Morris, "Islam and Politics in Aceh: A Study of Center-Periphery Relations in Indonesia," Ph.D. dissertation (Ithaca: Cornell University, 1983), 80.

[24] Anthony Reid, *Blood of the People: Revolution and the End of Traditional Rule in Northern Sumatra* (Kuala Lumpur: Oxford University Press, 1979), 21–2.

[25] For an introduction to the modern *madrasa* as it developed in the region, see Arief Subhan, "The Indonesian Madrasah: Islamic Reform and Modernization of Indonesian Islam in the Twentieth Century," in Azyumardi Azra, Kees van Dijk, and Nico J.G. Kaptein

Figure 3.2. A modern *madrasa* classroom in rural Aceh Besar: Outfitted with desks and chairs that mark a "modern" schoolroom, this scene is typical across Aceh today. A century ago, however, such an arrangement was a prominent marker of the radical reforms introduced by proponents of Modernist Islamic education. (Photo by R. Michael Feener)

followed models of combined religious and secular curricula within a modern institutional setting of graded classes in schoolrooms furnished with chairs, writing tables, blackboards, and all the accouterments of "modern" education. In Aceh, the first modern-style *madrasa* was established by Tuanku Raja Keumala, an Islamic scholar with close connections to the court of Aceh's last sultan, ʿAlāʾ al-dīn Muḥammad Da'ud Shah. In 1915, he applied to the Dutch military governor for permission to establish a new school named Madrasah Khairiyah at Kutaraja (present-day Banda Aceh). Upon approval, the school was built in the neighborhood of the Baiturrahman mosque and an Acehnese scholar who had studied at Mecca, Tgk. Muhammad Saman Siron, was appointed as its first director.[26]

At first the development of these new visions of Islamic education were largely linked with the spread of modern Islamic reform movements from outside Aceh. In the first decades of the twentieth century, new streams of Islamic thought began trickling into Aceh from a number of different

(eds.), *Varieties of Religious Authority: Changes and Challenges in 20th Century Indonesian Islam* (Singapore: Institute of Southeast Asian Studies, 2010), 127–38.

[26] Ismuha, "Ulama Aceh dalam Perspektif Sejarah," in Taufik Abdullah (ed.), *Agama dan-Perubahan Sosial* (Jakarta: CV. Rajawali, 1983), 23–4.

directions including the Middle East, South Asia, and other parts of the Indonesian archipelago. The *madrasa* model adopted in Aceh drew much of its organizational structure, curriculum, and teaching methods from models that were then being developed in neighboring West Sumatra.[27] This included the development of curricula that included "general subjects"—such as mathematics and geography—taught with Arabic-language textbooks. Some of these materials were imported from Egypt, particularly in the first few years, but soon these texts began to be supplemented by other Arabic works produced by Sumatran authors, including the Minangkabau reformist Mahmud Yunus.[28] Yunus was a pioneer of modernizing Islamic education in Indonesia, and he had a direct and powerful influence upon the first generation of Acehnese reformists who founded Persatuan Ulama Seluruh Aceh ("All Aceh Ulama Union"/ PUSA). The contemporary Acehnese scholar Eka Srimulyani has referred to Yunus' "focus on behavioral and spiritual aspects in practical life," in connection with his model of reforming Islamic education as essential for effecting social change.[29] In this nexus of education reform and agendas for wider ranging social transformation of the community, Modernist Islamic activists succeeded to a remarkable degree in setting the ground for discussions of Islam in Aceh for nearly a century. The dissemination of this orientation toward Islam and its role in society was greatly facilitated by the spread of madrasas there over the course of the twentieth century.

In the 1920s, two *madrasas* were also established in Tapak Tuan and Labuan Haji by West Sumatran Modernists affiliated with the Sumatera Thawalib—an institution that pioneered such innovations as the use of school desks, scheduled classes, and systematized curriculum in Muslim Southeast Asia.[30] These two experiments with Modernist Islamic education in Aceh were, however, unsuccessful and folded in the early 1930s in the face of strong opposition from local Traditionalists.[31] Within a decade, however, momentum for modernizing reform was building locally among

[27] Mahmud Yunus, *Sejarah Pendidikan Islam* (Jakarta: Hidakarya Agung, 1985), 179. For an overview of these developments in English, see Taufik Abdullah, *Schools and Politics: The Kaum Muda Movement in West Sumatra, 1927–1933* (Ithaca: Cornell University SEAP, 1971). For more on the role of Mahmud Yunus in movements for the modernization of Islamic education in Indonesia, see Karel Steenbrink, *Pesantren, Madrasah, Sekolah: Pendidikan Islam dalam Kurun Modern* (Jakarta: LP3ES, 1986).

[28] Yunus' textbooks on subjects like geography also inspired Acehnese authors to compose similar Arabic texts for use in local *madrasas*, such as Muhammad Nur El Ibrahimy's introduction to logic, *'Ilm al-manṭiq*. Ismuha, "Ulama Aceh dalam Perspektif Sejarah," 28–9.

[29] Eka Srimulyani, *Mahmud Yunus' Islamic Educational Thought: Tracing and Contextualizing the Islamic Educational Reform in Indonesia* (Banda Aceh: Ar-Raniry Press, 2008), 39, 57.

[30] Luthfi Assyaukanie, *Islam and the Secular State in Indonesia* (Singapore: ISEAS Press, 2009), 37.

[31] Morris, "Islam and Politics," 81.

a new generation of Acehnese Muslim leaders. In 1930, Tgk. Abd. Rahman Meunasah Meucap founded the Madrasah Al-Muslim Peusangan at Matang Glumpang Dua,[32] and Daud Beureueh led a number of prominent ulama to found the Madrasah Saadah Abadiyah in Sigli. Thereafter the floodgates were opened and new *madrasas* proliferated across the region.[33] By 1936, there were over 100 *madrasas* in Aceh, mostly along the North Coast road between Banda Aceh and Medan. For the generation of Islamic Modernists who drove these developments, the reform of Islamic education was an essential part of a broader agenda to redefine Acehnese conceptions of Islam and its role in society.[34] It was to facilitate this grand project of religious reform and social transformation that PUSA was formed.

PUSA's brand of Islam marked a sharp break with the traditional models of authority.[35] Led by Daud Beureueh, Tgk. Abd. Rahman, M. Nur Ellbrahimy, Tgk. Ismail Yakub, and Tgk. H. Mustafa Ali, PUSA's concern with education was clearly emphasized from the start, and its ties to Islamic Modernist schools in particular were signaled by the invitation of Mahmud Yunus to its founding conference on 5 May 1939.[36] Soon after its formation in 1939, PUSA further expanded its educational activities to Bireuen with the founding of the Normaal Islam Instituut, and the Ma'had Iskandar Muda at Lam Paku.[37] PUSA quickly emerged as the most active proponent of the *madrasa* model in Aceh.[38] With the support of PUSA, modern-style Islamic schools proliferated to the point that there were over 200 madrasas in Aceh by 1946.[39] The graduates of these *madrasas* came to form networks of reform-minded Muslims, many of whom entered into the local civil service in the early years of Indonesian independence.

[32] Ismuha, "Ulama Aceh dalam Perspektif Sejarah," 57–8. On Al Muslim and the PUSA curriculum, see Amiruddin Idris and Wildan, "Pelaksanaan Pendidikan di Kabupaten Bireuen: Tinjauan Historis terhadap Al Muslim Peusangan," in T.H. Thalhas and Choirul Fuad Yusuf (eds.), *Pendidikandan Syariat Islam di Nanggroe Aceh Darussalam dan 8 Undang-Undang Terkait* (Jakarta: Galura Pase, 2007). Al Muslim became established as a university in 2003.

[33] Mahmud Yunus, *Sejarah Pendidikan Islam*, 177; Ismuha, "Ulama Aceh dalam Perspektif Sejarah," 27.

[34] Morris, "Islam and Politics," 76.

[35] For an overview of PUSA's importance in the eyes of subsequent generations of Acehnese Modernist Muslims, see Ismuha, Baihaqi A.K. and Dalminis Noor, "Pengaruh PUSA terhadap Reformasi di Aceh," in Usman Said (ed.), *Agama, Perkembangan dan Pembangunan* (Jakarta: Proyek Pembinaan Perguruan Tinggi Agama/IAIN di Pusat – Direktort Pembinaan Perguruan Tinggi Agama Islam, 1980), 39–67; and Hamdiah Latief, "Persatuan Ulama Seluruh Aceh (PUSA): Its Contributions to Education Reforms in Aceh," M.A. thesis (Montreal: McGill University, 1992). PUSA will be discussed further in Chapter 5.

[36] Mahmud Yunus, *Sejarah Pendidikan Islam*, 178.

[37] Ismuha, "Ulama Aceh dalam Perspektif Sejarah," 31.

[38] Sarity Pawiloy, *Madrasah Islam Modern* (Banda Aceh: Pusat Latihan Penelitian Ilmu-Ilmu Sosial, 1974), 6.

[39] Morris, "Islam and Politics," 164.

STATE APPROPRIATIONS OF ISLAMIC EDUCATION

The proliferation of *madrasas* across Aceh over this period not only contributed to the reformulation of conceptions of authoritative Islamic knowledge, but also created a new institutional reality governed by modern models of management. After the revolution, the PUSA-dominated government of Aceh tied these modern Muslim schools firmly to the state apparatus as *madrasas* began to receive subsidies and the teachers of these schools became salaried state employees.[40] In 1947, Daud Beureueh, then serving as Indonesia's military governor of Aceh, extended state control over Acehnese *madrasas*—which were then re-designated as Sekolah Rakyat Islam (SRI) and entitled to receive state support from a newlycreated provincial Board of Religious Education (Lembaga Pendidikan Agama). In the 1960s, the Sekolah Rakyat Islam were reformed into Madrasah Ibtidaiyah Negeri (MIN), with a new balance of "general" and religious subjects (68 and 32 percent, respectively). By the mid-1970s, more than 200 such schools were operating, serving approximately 100,000 students across the province. During the same period, however, state primary schools (Sekolah Dasar/SD) with a more restricted religious component in their curricula (eight percent) expanded to over 800 units serving 170,000 pupils—leading to increasing frictions between advocates of the two models of education in the province.[41]

These developments in Aceh attracted the attention of Muslim activists and administrators in other parts of the new nation. Soon, the national Ministry of Religious Affairs began their own programs for the reform and state management of *madrasa* education. In Aceh, the Sekolah Guru Islam (formerly the Normal Islam School at Bireuen) was brought under control of Indonesian Ministry of Religious Affairs as a state school for religious teachers and court officials (Sekolah Guru Hakim Agama/SGHA Negeri) in 1951. That same year a four-year government Islamic teacher's college (Perguruan Guru Agama/PGA) was established for over 300 students, as well as a two-year advanced teacher's training institution (PGA Atas) for 50 students at Banda Aceh.[42]

Over the decades that followed, state involvement with *madrasas* progressed to the point that by 2002, about one fifth of Indonesia's 37,000 *madrasas* were under the direct supervision of the Indonesian Ministry of Religious Affairs.[43] A great many more, however, have also adopted the

[40] Baihaqi A.K. "Ulama dan Madrasah Aceh," in Taufik Abdullah (ed.), *Agama dan Perubahan Sosial* (Jakarta: CV. Rajawali, 1983), 154.

[41] Morris, "Islam and Politics," 278–9.

[42] Mahmud Yunus, *Sejarah Pendidikan Islam*, 181, 392.

[43] Arief Subhan, "The Indonesian Madrasah," 126–38.

official government guidelines that allocated 30 percent of the syllabus to studies of religious subjects and the remaining 70 percent to "general" education—a ratio that came to be widely accepted by Indonesian *madrasas*. This has also allowed for these schools to receive various forms of state subsidy, and for them to grant recognized diplomas. In 1975, movements in this direction were boosted by the issuing of a memorandum from three government ministries (*SKB Tiga Menteri*) proclaiming that all students in Islamic schools should be provided with six years of education in "general subjects" in addition to their religious studies. The general education requirement was later extended to nine years following the 1989 law on national education that transferred supervision over a greater number of Islamic schools to the Ministry of Education and Culture.[44] Since then, Indonesian state involvement with the management of *madrasas* has deepened even further. In the mid-1990s, the government opened its own public *madrasas*.[45] Subsidies for programs in private *madrasas* have also increased, although there are constant calls from segments of the Muslim community for more to be done in this regard.[46]

Parallel to these steps toward the centralizing reform of Modernist *madrasa* education were the stirrings of movements for the reform and revitalization of Indonesia's Traditionalist Islamic schools. In most parts of the country outside Aceh, Traditionalist Islamic schools are referred to not as *dayahs*, but rather by the Javanese term *pesantrens*. In the early years of Indonesian independence, attention was directed toward Islamic schools and the roles that they might play in nation building.[47] Over the decades that followed, these institutions became sites for experiments by both official and non-state actors with new means of supporting projects for economic and social development at the local level.[48] The 1970s and 1980s saw the rapid growth of cooperation between NGOs and the Traditionalist

[44] Donald J. Porter, *Managing Politics and Islam in Indonesia* (London: Routledge, 2002), 52; Robert W. Hefner, "Islamic Schools, Social Movements, and Democracy in Indonesia," in *Making Modern Muslims: The Politics of Islamic Education in Southeast Asia* (Honolulu: University of Hawai'i Press, 2009), 55–105.

[45] Azyumardi Azra, Dina Afrianty, and Robert W. Hefner, "Pesantren and Madrasa: Muslim Schools and National Ideas in Indonesia," in Robert W. Hefner and Muhammad Qasim Zaman (eds.), *Schooling Islam: The Culture and Politics of Modern Muslim Education* (Princeton: Princeton University Press, 2006), 180.

[46] Rosimanidar, "Wacana Madrasah Modern Dalam Persaingan Global," in Ridwan Hasan (ed.), *Islam and Globalization: Challenges & Opportunities to the Future Renaissance* (Aceh: Unimal Press, 2010), 499–506.

[47] Karel A. Steenbrink, *Pesantren, Madrasah, Sekolah: Pendidikan Islam dalam Kurun Moderen* (Jakarta: LP3ES, 1986), 97.

[48] For studies of developments along these lines in Javanese pesantren, see Manfred Oepen and Wolfgang Karcher with Robert Kingham (eds.), *The Impact of Pesantren in Education and Community Development in Indonesia* (Berlin: Fredrich-Naumann Stiftung, 1988).

Muslim organization Nadhlatul Ulama (NU) in this direction.[49] At the same time, Islamic reformist organizations including the Muhammadiyah were also taking a new look at *pesantren* education and its potential for pursuing their own goals for educating a modern Muslim public. A major move in this direction came in 1982, when the central Muhammadiyah leadership established the first such school to be directly managed by the organization, the Pondok Hajjah Nuriyah Shabran at Sukoharjo.[50] Since the 1980s, both Modernist *madrasas* and schools identifying themselves with the more Traditionalist model of *pesantrens* have proliferated to produce a remarkable resurgence of Islamic education all across Indonesia.

As the Indonesian state expanded its horizons of ambition to assert greater control over Traditionalist Islamic schools, it used its mechanisms of financial support to encourage *pesantrens* to adopt general education requirements into their curriculum, following the model of the modern *madrasa* system. This further fueled ongoing debates about the proper balance between "religious" and "general" subjects in the *madrasa* curriculum. A 1962 policy had stipulated that the ideal balance would be 68 percent general and 32 percent religious subjects, respectively. Under Suharto's New Order, the government further renewed its attention to *pesantrens* in attempts to harness their potential to support programs for national development.[51] In 1975 new governmental guidelines further adjusted the balance to 70/30, which moved things further toward the model of a *madrasa* and reformed *pesantren* as Indonesian "public school[s] with an Islamic identity."[52]

Over the decades that followed, it became increasingly common for larger *pesantrens* to actually have schools following the *madrasa* model located on campus to provide students with the accreditation of having followed the national curriculum.[53] At the same time, however, these modernizing moves have proceeded alongside the development of other state measures that aim to support the study of the Arabic texts at the heart of Traditionalist curricula, including contests of *kitāb* reading to promote the study of *fiqh* and other Islamic religious sciences.[54] The

[49] Martin van Bruinessen, "Traditionalist and Islamist Pesantrens in Contemporary Indonesia," in Farish A. Noor, Yoginder Sikand, and Martin van Bruinessen (eds.), *The Madrasa in Asia: Political Activism and Transnational Linkages* (Amsterdam: Amsterdam University Press, 2008), 226–9.

[50] M.T. Arifin, *Gagasan Pembaharuan Muhammadiyah dalam Pendidikan* (Jakarta: Pustaka Jaya, 1987), 223–32.

[51] For more on these developments, see: Manfred Ziemek, *Pesantren dalam Perubahan Sosial* (Jakarta: P3M, 1986), 175–254.

[52] Arief Subhan, "The Indonesian Madrasah," 131.

[53] Azra, Afrianty, and Hefner, "Pesantren and Madrasa," 178.

[54] Mina Hattori, "The Tradition of Kitab Learning at *Pondok Pesantren* in Indonesia" (Tokyo: Sophia University Institute of Asian Cultures Working Paper Series, 2012), 68–9.

combined effects of these developments served to shape the education of a growing portion of Aceh's population who acquired both a strong sense of Islamic religious identity and a familiarity with modern structures of pedagogy and state policy. This potent combination reflects key aspects of what I have referred to earlier as the "*daʿwa* paradigm" that was to become central in the development of the province's Islamic legal system at the end of the twentieth century.

FURTHER REDEFINITIONS OF ACEHNESE *DAYAHS*

These broader Indonesian developments of national-level Islamic education policy were, moreover, further contextualized within the specific contexts of Aceh. In 1959, Special Autonomy provisions granted Aceh a greater degree of control over the administration of religion, custom, and education (I. *keagamaan, peradatan, dan pendidikan*).[55] This allowed for experimentation in new forms of managing Islamic education, including projects for the reform of the province's Traditionalist *dayahs.* Over the second half of the twentieth century the overall number of *dayahs* in Aceh remained relatively constant, but schools referred to by that name increasingly came to experience and embody significant innovations in both form and function.[56]

One of the most high-profile experiments along these lines was the creation of a new, state-affiliated "modern *dayah*" named after Tgk. H. Muhammad Panté Kulu (d. 1891), author of one of the major texts of the *Prang Sabi* tradition. This school was opened in the new "student city" (Kota Pelajar Mahasiswa/Kopelma) of Darussalam on the outskirts of Banda Aceh in 1968. The student city was established on the eastern edge of the provincial capital as a project spearheaded by then Governor Ali Hasjmy in cooperation with the leadership of the Indonesian armed forces in Aceh.[57] It was conceived of as part of their efforts to enhance stability and facilitate government development projects.[58] Toward this end, they

[55] *Surat Keputusan Perdana Menteri Republic Indonesia No. 1/missi/59 tgl. 26 Mei, 1958.*

[56] In 1966, there were 455 *dayahs* in Aceh, with a total of 20,715 students; in 2005, the total number had grown only slightly to 520 *dayahs* across the province, with the heaviest concentrations along the north coast and the road between Pidie and Langsa. *10 Tahun Darussalam dan Hari Pendidikan* (Banda Aceh: Yayasan Pembina Darussalam, 1969), 415; Muslim Thahiry, Khairizzaman, and Abidin Nurdin (eds.), *Wacana Pemikiran Santri Dayah Aceh* (Banda Aceh: BRR, PKPM Aceh & Wacana Press, 2006), 146.

[57] Plans first laid under A. Hasjmy's term as governor in 1962, with Letnan Kolonel Njaʿ Adam Kamil, Kepala Staf KodamI/Iskandar Muda as the Head of the Organizing Committee. *10 Tahun Darussalam*, 293–307.

[58] A. Hasjmy, "Konsepsi Ideal Darussalam," in *10 Tahun Darussalam dan Hari Pendidikan* (Banda Aceh: Yayasan Pembina Darussalam, 1969), 25–78.

created a consolidated (and thus more easily administered and policed) district as home to three new schools: a general university, a campus of the State Institute for Islamic Studies (IAIN) system, and the creation of this "modern *dayah*."

The Dayah Moderen Tgk. Cik Panté Kulu was officially opened with a ceremony that included a formal address by then President Suharto, and charged with the mission of becoming an institute of Islamic higher education that would produce a new vanguard of ulama with "broad knowledge and capabilities, as well as deeply held piety."[59] Its initial teaching staff included prominent ulama such as Abdullah Ujong Rimba. The programs of study included two degree programs, a three-year "BA" and a five-year MA (Drs.).[60] These degree programs were structured according to a model of standardized classes and graded examinations, both of which were radical innovations in the structure of Acehnese *dayahs* at that time.

The new syllabi designed for the school also represented a major shift away from the standard *dayah* curriculum in Aceh. Few of the standard Shāfiʿī texts familiar to Traditionalists appear, and instead, the mandatory reading list is dominated by authors generally favored by Modernist and Revivalist reformers, including: classical Ḥanbalī texts that had gained a new popularity among reform-minded Muslims of the twentieth century such as the works of Ibn Qudāma (d. 1223) and Ibn Kathīr (d. 1373), Ibn Rushd's (d. 1198) work of cross-*madhhab* jurisprudence, the *ḥadīth* studies of the early modern Yemeni reformer al-Shawkānī (d. 1839), and twentieth-century Egyptian proponents of a moderated Islamic Modernism including ʿAbd al-Wahhāb al-Khallāf (d. 1956) and Muṣṭafā al-Marāghī (d. 1945). The largest imprint of an Indonesian author on the syllabus was by Hasbi Ash Shiddieqy (d. 1975)—a modern scholar from Lhokseumawe who was also central in producing material for the curriculum of the State Institute of Islamic Studies IAIN.[61]

For all of its innovative curriculum and prominent state support, however, the Dayah Tgk. Cik Panté Kulu failed in both attracting top students and producing the kinds of new ulama that it had hoped for. The school thus eventually dropped out of the public spotlight, and was

[59] Ismuha, "Ulama Aceh dalam Perspektif Sejarah," 95.

[60] *Kurikulum/Syllabus Fakultas Syariʿah Perguruan Tinggi Islam Dayah Tgk. Chik Panté Kulu, 31 December 1973* (Arsip Propinsi Aceh – 269/41).

[61] *Kurikulum/Syllabus Fakultas Syariʿah Dayah Tgk. Chik Panté Kulu Darussalam Banda Aceh, Tahun 1974* (ArsipPropinsi Aceh: MajelisUlama Indonesia DI Aceh, No. 269/41). For more on Hasbi Ash Shiddieqy and his role in the development of the IAIN curriculum, see R. Michael Feener, "Indonesian Movements for the Creation of a "National *Madhhab*,'" *Islamic Law and Society* 9(1) (2001) 83–115.

left to wither on the vine.[62] The basic idea, however, of a reformation of *dayah* education continued to inspire some Acehnese administrators and academics. As recently as 2008, Hasbi Amiruddin of the Banda Aceh campus of the Indonesian State Institute for Islamic Studies (IAIN) called for the creation of a new institution for Islamic higher education which he called Perguruan Tinggi Dayah Manyang,[63] and which reprised many of the ideas originally at the heart of the Dayah Tgk. Cik Panté Kulu experiment.

In the meantime, other attempts at *dayah* reform have managed to have a more significant and sustained impact on Islamic education in Aceh. In these developments, institutions situated in the areas around Banda Aceh and along the North Coast have risen to prominence, further emphasizing a major shift in the geography of Islamic authority in modern Aceh. As noted in Chapter 2, over the nineteenth and the early twentieth centuries, major developments in Sufi reform that resulted in the widespread acceptance of the Naqshbandī, and later the Khālidī Sufi order across Aceh's Traditionalist *dayah* community spread up from the Minangkabau region to new centers established along Aceh's West Coast.[64] The paramount position of these networks that came to be centered around Tgk. Muda Wali's *dayah* at Labuan Haji and politically affiliated with PERTI was forcefully challenged over the middle decades of the twentieth century by the ascendancy of PUSA, whose network of Modernist *madrasas* were concentrated along Aceh's north coast.[65] In that area, Samalanga has emerged to a position of particular prominence.[66]

There were at least 19 *dayahs* established in Samalanga in the early twentieth century. Less than 50 years later, only six of them remained open, but among those that did outlive their founders were schools that emerged as pioneers in the modernizing reform of *dayah* education, such as the Dayah Nurus-Syariah and the Ma'had al Ulum Diniyah Islamiyah Mesjid Raya (a.k.a. "Mudi Mesra"). Mudi Mesra was by far the largest *dayah* in Samalanga and it drew students from all across Aceh who were attracted by the school's reputation for dynamism, as well as by the prestige it gained through the increasing amount of resources that it could draw upon in supporting its work. Mudi Mesra was an early recipient of

[62] In 1985, the institution was reworked to form the Perguruan Tinggi Tgk. Chik Panté Kulu, but in a form that no longer emphasized aspects of the traditional *dayah* model. Hasbi Amiruddin, *Menatap Masa Depan Dayah di Aceh* (Banda Aceh: Yayasan Pena, 2008), 144.

[63] Hasbi Amiruddin, *Menatap Masa Depan Dayah di Aceh*, 14–143.

[64] And, in fact, most of the major shaykhs associated with these Sufi reforms, from Da'ūd Sunūr to Tgk. Muda Waly and Muhammad Yatim al Khalidiy were themselves ethnically Minang—or, as such migrants are referred to in Acehnese, *jame'* ("guests").

[65] Mannan Nur, *Studi Tentang Dayah di Samalanga* (Banda Aceh: Pusat Penelitian Ilmu-Ilmu Sosial, 1975), 37.

[66] Muslim Thahiry, Khairizzaman, and Abidin Nurdin, *Wacana Pemikiran Santri Dayah Aceh*, 142.

Figure 3.3. A traditional-style teaching pavilion in a *dayah* at Samalanga: As these simple, open-air structures are generally unfurnished, students sit on the floor. (Photo by R. Michael Feener)

Indonesian government aid for Islamic education.[67] Such incentives have encouraged structural and curricular reform including the development of more standardized forms of classes for both male and female students, as well as a spate of new modern construction that now dwarfs the nearby traditional-style *rangkang* pavilions (as seen clearly in the photos).

The introduction of English language classes and other general subjects alongside religious instruction at Mudi Mesra coincided with government-sponsored reforms in the 1970s in which all *pesantren* students were obligated to complete general education requirements.[68] At the same time, requests for data on Traditionalist Islamic education for official Department of Religion reports led to the formalization of procedures for recording grades, student evaluations, and other administrative matters. Government-backed projects to modernize the administration of *pesantrens* continued to strengthen over the decades that followed.[69] These trends were

[67] Mannan Nur, *Studi Tentang Dayah di Samalanga*, 17–32.

[68] Azra, Afrianty, and Hefner, "Pesantren and Madrasa," 176.

[69] In 1981, a new handbook for *pesantren* management was published under the auspices of the Department of Religious Affairs. It drew on the findings of a major conference on the subject held in 1971, and the experience of trying to implement its recommendations over the years that followed. Mustofa Syarif, *Administrasi Pesantren* (Jakarta: PT Paryu Barkah, 1981). Further documents related to this project can be found in Suparlan Suryopratondo,

Figure 3.4. New construction for Islamic education at Samalanga: Just across the road from the simple pavilions shown in the previous photo, a four-story concrete building is being erected with modern-style classrooms, computer clusters, and administrative offices. (Photo by R. Michael Feener)

further accelerated in the post-disaster/post-conflict period in relation to state programs for Shariʿa implementation, as Aceh's burgeoning popular press ran an almost daily feed of calls from both *dayah* leaders and government officials for closer cooperation in upgrading Islamic education.[70]

There again, the contexts of special autonomy allowed for developments in Aceh to take their particular shape. Much of the concrete work in this direction has been facilitated by a special body known as the Badan Dayah, which was established in 2008 within the governor's office for the support of *dayah* education.[71] Together with other sources of state funding for education, an increasing number of *dayahs* across Aceh have

Abd. Rachman Saleh, Marwan Saridjo, and Mustofa Syarif (eds.), *Kapita Selekta Pondok Pesantren* (Jakarta: PT Paryu Barkah, 1976).

[70] e.g., "Manajemen Dayah Harus Diubah," *Serambi* (7 August 2008), 10; "Bangkitkan Pendidikan Dayah," *Waspada* (27 April 2009), 24; "Dayah Harus Direvilitasi," *Rakyat Aceh* (20 July 2009), 4.

[71] The political motivations behind this have been complex—combining advocacy for agendas of education reform and economic development to appeals for the defenses of Aceh's cultural identity. This has included, for example, the establishment of *dayahs* along the border with North Sumatra province to protect Aceh from deviant understandings and Christian missionary encroachment: "Bangun Dayah Sambil Bentengi Perbatasan," *Rakyat Aceh* (27 October 2009), 3.

come to receive assistance in various forms, including hard infrastructure, teaching materials, and salary subsidies for teachers.[72] In the specific case of Samalanga, Mudi Mesra illustrates a particularly striking series of developments that have served in significant ways as templates for reform and development programs at many other Acehnese *dayahs*.[73] This has included the establishment of a new "college" for Islamic higher education,[74] and a primary school that follows a model of "integrated" (I. *terpadu*) Islamic and general subjects curricula that has become increasingly popular across Indonesia over the past three decades.[75]

The spread of "integrated schools" (I. *pesantren terpadu*) represents a further manifestation of the influence of the *madrasa* model of Islamic education in Indonesia.[76] *Pesantren terpadu* adopt the Indonesian state curriculum, while also promoting a vision of education in the service of social change associated with modern conceptions of *tarbiya* (education) and *daʿwa* (religious propagation). On the national level, the expansion of *pesantren terpadu* has been connected to reformist networks of Hidayatullah and the PKS.[77] In Aceh, too, these groups have made some inroads over the past decade. However, here these new players came into a field with its own model of integrated Islamic education. One of the major local institutions of this type in Aceh is the Dayah Terpadu Inshafuddin, which was founded at Lambaro Skep (Banda Aceh) in 1974 under the direction of Tgk. Amin Hasyim. Its foundations were rooted in organizational reconfigurations of religious authority in Aceh during the early years of the New Order, when a number of Traditionalist ulama who had belonged to PERTI developed relationships with academics

[72] "Tgk. Dayah Akan Dapat Gaji," *Rakyat Aceh* (22 December 2010), 3; "Dayah Terima Kitab Seumeubeut," *Rakyat Aceh* (27 January 2008), 7.

[73] Alumni of Al Aziziyyah have been active in establishing new *dayahs* across Aceh in a sort of franchise modeled on the experience of their studies in Samalanga. For example: "Dayah Mabdaul Ulum Al Aziziyyah," *Aceh Independen* (6 March 2009), 14.

[74] The STAI al-Aziziyyah at Samalanga opened in 2003, with majors in Syariah and Dakwah, and its vision of modern education for more socially engaged ulama. While most of its students and teachers are Mudi Mesra graduates, the formal curriculum is modeled on that of the IAIN. The influence of the IAIN on the reform of *pesantren/dayah* education will be discussed further subsequently. *Panduan Program Strata Satu (S-1) Sekolah Tinggi Agama Islam (STAI) Al-Aziziyah Samalanga Tahun Akademik 2005–2006* (Samalanga: Sekolah Tinggi Agama Islam Al-Aziziyah, 2005), 5; "Dayah Samalanga Menuju Era Baru," *Tabloid Tabangun Aceh* (7 August 2007), 5.

[75] Siti Zalikha Ibrahim, "Santri Menemukan Jati Diri," in Ahmadun Yosi Herfanda (ed.), *Menuju Syariat Islam Kaffah: Pikiran dan Pengalaman Santri Aceh dalam menuntut Ilmu dan Hubungannya dengan Perbuatan Nyata* (Banda Aceh: Lepena, 2008), 27–80, 30–1.

[76] Hasbi Amiruddin, "Dayah: Lembaga Pendidikan Tertua Masyarakat Aceh," in T.H. Thalhas and Choirul Fuad Yusuf (eds.), *Pendidikan dan Syariat Islam di Nanggroe Aceh Darussalam* (Jakarta: Galura Pasê, 2007), 26–7.

[77] Noorhaidi Hasan, "Islamizing Formal Education: Integrated Islamic Schools and a New Trend in Formal Education in Indonesia," *S. Rajaratnam School of International Studies, Working Paper No. 172* (Singapore: RSIS, 2009); Hefner, "Islamic Schools," 65, 101.

from the IAIN to form a new organization for the reinvigoration of *dayah* education.[78] Inshafuddin was officially commissioned on 4 February 1968 at a conference held at Seulimeum, and its first campus was opened in 1974. Five years later, it expanded considerably upon receiving a significant land grant from the governor's office. Close collaboration between the provincial government and the Dayah Inshafuddin leadership eventually led to the official integration of general and religious subject curricula in 1998.[79]

Further development of the Dayah Terpadu Inshafuddin took place after the 2004 disaster and subsequent dynamics of reconstruction. The physical structure of the *dayah* was devastated by the tsunami, but soon thereafter, new waves washed over the school in the form of disaster recovery and rehabilitation aid. In the wake of the tsunami, the *dayah* was not only physically rebuilt but facilities were also substantially improved with the help of Swiss donors.[80] The Dayah Terpadu Inshafuddin also continues to maintain strong ties to the IAIN, and it is managed by a notarized foundation (I. *yayasan*) in a modern model of administration that formalizes oversight of the school by a committee. This is in contrast to the situation in most traditional *dayahs* where the head teacher (Ac. *teungku/abuya*) exercises ultimate control. Over recent decades, such "rationalized" forms of administration have become increasingly widespread in both Acehnese *dayahs*, and in Traditionalist Islamic schools across many other parts of Indonesia as well.[81]

In the post-disaster/post-conflict period, a number of other schools promoting modernizing models of reformed Islamic education have also been upgraded and some others newly established in Aceh. One significant new player in this field is Gontor 10, a new branch campus of the famous "*pondok modern*" in Central Java.[82] This Islamic school was founded in

[78] Muslim Thahiry, Khairizzaman, and Abidin Nurdin, *Wacana Pemikiran Santri Dayah Aceh*, 143–4; Baihaqi A.K., "Ulama dan Madrasah Aceh," 148.

[79] "Dayah Warisan Ulama Aceh," *Aceh Independen* (24 April 2009), 14.

[80] In Aceh, *dayah terpadu* are known not only for innovations in their curricula, but for distinctive aspects of on-campus facilities. For example, these schools generally have a centralized kitchen that prepares meals for all students, rather than following the traditional model in which students cook for themselves. These additional facilities make the costs of sending a student several times higher than that for a student at a traditional *dayah*—and this contributes to some broad trends in the class affiliations of students and graduates from these two kinds of institutions (Interview with Yusny Saby, 17 November 2008 at Banda Aceh).

[81] Hasbi Amiruddin, *Menatap Masa Depan Dayah di Aceh*, 56–7.

[82] Lance Castles, "Notes on the Islamic School at Gontor," *Indonesia* 1 (June 1966), 30–45; Ali Saifullah HA, "Darussalaam: Pondok Modern Gontor," in *Pesantren dan Pembaharuan* (Jakarta: LP3ES, 1985), 134–54. More on the driving force behind the institutional and curricular innovations of this *pesantren*, Imam Zarkasyi, and selections from his own writings on Islamic education can be found in Ahmad Fuad Effendi, Amir Hamzah Wiryosukarto, et al., *K.H. Imam Zarkasyi dari Gontor: Merintis Pesantren Modern* (Ponorogo: Gontor Press,

1926, and since then it has attracted students with its innovative "modern" curriculum, its openness to global currents of Islamic reform, and its close ties to international Islamic organizations including the Muslim World League (*Rābiṭa al-ʿālam al-islāmī*).[83] Over nearly a century, Gontor has expanded and opened a number of branch campuses in other parts of Indonesia. The ranks of former students at Gontor schools include a number of prominent Indonesian Muslim figures, ranging from liberal Muslim intellectuals like Nurcholish Madjid, to radical Islamists, including Abu Bakar Baasyir.[84]

A number of Gontor alumni from Java came to Aceh as disaster relief volunteers in 2005, where they saw potential for developing Islamic education through the founding of a branch campus of Gontor there. At first, they met with various obstacles ranging from GAM commanders demanding protection money (Ac. *Pajak nanggröe*) to resistance from some of Aceh's traditional Islamic leadership who derided Gontor as "Muhammadiyah"—referring to the Islamic Modernist organization established in Java nearly a century ago. Some even accused the school's Modernism of lying outside the fold of acceptable understandings of Islam (Ar. *ahl al-sunna wa'l-jamāʿa*). Eventually, however, they succeeded in establishing a campus near Seulimeum, on a site not far from the location of the conference that had launched the Inshafuddin project in 1968.[85] As this was the tenth campus of the Gontor system, the new school is called "Gontor 10." It enrolled its first class of 15 *santri* at the end or 2005, and since then it has expanded to over 250 students, including a number of tsunami orphans who received scholarships. The 44 teachers currently working at the school are all alumni of Gontor's central campus in Java, thus reflecting another dimension of the increasing integration of Aceh into the broader Indonesian nation under the aegis of Islam.[86]

The establishment of a branch of this Modernist school system based in Java finds its place within a wider range of Indonesian Islamic institutions that have recently been established in Aceh. This trend, however, may actually be seen as something of a reversal of relationships between

1996). For more on Nurcholish Madjid and Abu Bakar Baasyir—representing two dramatically different strains of Indonesian Islam, respectively, see R. Michael Feener, *Muslim Legal Thought in Modern Indonesia* (Cambridge: Cambridge University Press, 2007), 133–7; and M.C. Ricklefs, *Islamisation and its Opponents in Java: A Political, Social, Cultural and Religious History, c. 1930 to the Present* (Singapore: NUS Press, 2012), 180–4.

83 van Bruinessen, "Traditionalist and Islamist Pesantrens," 223.

84 Martin van Bruinessen, "Divergent Paths from Gontor: Muslim Educational Reform and the Travails of Pluralism in Indonesia," in Freek L. Bakker and Jan Sihar Aritonang (eds.), *On the Edge of Many Worlds* (Zoetermeer: Uitgeverij Meinema, 2006), 152–62.

85 Interview with Ahmad Saifullah, 19 November 2008 at Gontor 10, Seulimeum.

86 "Darul Amin Gontor 10 Meunasah Baro, Seulimeum, Aceh," *Wardun: Warta Dunia Pondok Modern Darussalam Gontor* 61 (2008), 66–8.

Aceh and more central regions of administrative and political power in Indonesia. For most of the twentieth century, Islamic organizations founded outside of Aceh had met with considerable difficulties in establishing local branches there. For example, the Muhammadiyah, which was founded in Central Java and well-developed in West Sumatra, advanced ideas of Islamic reform that, as already noted, inspired movements for modernizing reform in Aceh. However, the Muhammadiyah itself encountered considerable difficulties in establishing and maintaining branches in Aceh. Instead, advocates of Islamic Modernist reform in Aceh came to found their own local organization in the form of PUSA. Through the end of the twentieth century, PUSA and other local Muslim organizations played roles in Aceh analogous to the national structures of the Muhammadiyah and NU in other parts of Indonesia. Furthermore, prior to the major transformations of the post-disaster/post-conflict period, there were more vectors of institutional influence in the opposite direction, with several new Islamic institutions first developed in Aceh being adopted at the national level across Indonesia. Major examples of this include the Council of Ulama (which will be discussed further in the next chapter), and the creation of Indonesia's first Faculty of Daʿwa within the national system of Islamic higher education (IAIN).

HIGHER ISLAMIC EDUCATION IN ACEH

The establishment of the IAIN grew out of a series of attempts to set up Islamic colleges during the Japanese wartime occupation and the early years of Indonesian independence.[87] In 1950, this took the shape of the Perguruan Tinggi Agama Islam Negeri (PTAIN), which was established at Yogyakarta with the mission of:

> ... providing higher education and becoming a center for the development and deepening of Islamic religious knowledge. In working toward this goal, it is also charged with laying down a foundation for the formation of moral

[87] For general background on the IAIN system and its development, see Johan Hendrik Meuleman and Henri Chambert-Loir, "Les Instituts islamiques publics indonésiens," in Nicole Grandin and Marc Gaborieau (eds.), *Madrasa: La Transmission du Savoir dans le Monde Musulman* (Paris: Éditions Arguments, 1997), 199–216; Margaret Gillett, "The IAIN in Indonesian Higher Education," *Muslim Education Quarterly* 8(1) (1990) 21–32; Dadi Darmadi, "IAIN dalam Wacana Intelektual Islam Indonesia," in Komaruddin Hidayat and Hendro Prasetyo (eds.), *Problem dan Prospek IAIN: Antologi Pendidikan Tinggi Islam* (Jakarta: Departemen Agama RI, 2000), 333–68; Johan Meuleman, "The Institut Agama Islam Negeri at the Crossroads: Some Notes on the Indonesian State Institutes for Islamic Studies," in Johan Meuleman (ed.), *Islam in the Era of Globalization: Muslim Attitudes towards Modernity and Identity* (Jakarta: INIS, 2001).

> and educated people who have an awareness of their responsibilities for the prosperity of Indonesian society and the world in general, all upon the basis of *Pancasila*, culture, Indonesian nationality, and reality.[88]

Over the years that followed, the public profile of the PTAIN grew, and it was eventually renamed as the Institut Agama Islam Negeri (IAIN) and given redefined mandates for its work in Islamic education and national development in 1960.[89] The IAIN system rapidly expanded to the point that by 1973, there were dozens of IAIN campuses spread across the country. Two years later, however, major restructuring of the IAIN began and the number of campuses was consolidated to just thirteen.[90]

During much of the New Order period, the IAIN—and especially its main campuses in Jakarta and Java—came to be an influential force in the promotion of an academic study of Islam informed by social science and text-critical methodologies.[91] As such, the IAIN developed an image of being a major bastion of modern and "moderate" Islam in Indonesia. Its intellectualized and depoliticized visions of Islam, moreover, fit well with New Order priorities of stability and economic development. The IAIN has also served as an important part of national programs for the reform of *pesantren* education.[92] As a national resource for the "transformation and modernization" of *pesantren*, the IAIN has functioned as the primary avenue for further studies available to students of Islamic schools and many of its alumni have in turn gone back to work as *pesantren* teachers after graduation.[93]

During the latter decades of the twentieth century, IAIN academics were also key players in facilitating the engagement of *pesantrens* with state and NGO rural development projects, as discussed earlier.[94] These developments were aided by the fact that, at that time, the IAIN had already established itself as the primary track by which Muslims from a Traditionalist background could enter into the national circles of academics and professionals. Within Aceh in particular, it has also shaped avenues of interaction between government officials and *dayah* leaders.[95]

88 *Buku Tahunan IAIN "Al-Djami'ah Al-Islamijah Al-Hukumijah" 1960–1962* (Jogjakarta: IAIN "Al-Djami'ah Al-Islamijah Al-Hukumijah," 1962), 12.

89 *Peraturan Peresiden Republik Indonesia* no. 11 tahun, 1960; *Penetapan Menteri Agama* no. 43 tahun 1960; *Peraturan Menteri Agama* no. 15 tahun 1961; *Penetapan Menteri Agama* no. 35, tahun 1960.

90 Azra, Afrianty, and Hefner, "Pesantren and Madrasa," 189.

91 Feener, *Muslim Legal Thought*, 118–50.

92 Porter, *Managing Politics and Islam in Indonesia*, 52.

93 Fuad Jabali and Jamhari (eds.), *IAIN dan Modernisasi Islam di Indonesia* (Jakarta: UIN Jakarta Press, 2003), 91–134.

94 For more on this see also Oepen and Karcher, with Kingham (eds.), *The Impact of Pesantren Education*; Feener, *Muslim Legal Thought*, 172–4.

95 This is not to say, of course, that all Traditionalist schools have accepted reforms along these lines, and in fact there are some high profile examples of schools that have not. Florian

Barry Hooker has called particular attention to the role of the IAIN, as an important institution operating at the national level, in expanding the ability of the Indonesian state to promote official understandings of the Shariʿa.[96] This holds true at both the national level, and with more specific reference to Aceh. There is, however, also a significant degree of diversity in the ways that specific IAIN campuses function locally, particularly those located outside of Java.[97] The "Ar-Raniry" campus of the IAIN was established at Banda Aceh in 1963, following guidelines set out by a founding committee led by then-governor Ali Hasjmy and Sjammaun Gaharu, the highest-ranking Indonesian military officer in the province.[98] With the aim of facilitating the further integration of Aceh more firmly within the Indonesian agenda of national development, the founding of an IAIN campus in Banda Aceh should also be seen as a reflection of broader efforts to put an end to the Darul Islam revolt there.[99] In a speech on the 17th anniversary of its founding, Hasjmy linked the occasion to celebrations earlier that week for *Pancasila* Day and the commemoration of the founding of the Indonesian Army, proclaiming that IAIN, too, has an important role to play in the continuing project of nation building.[100]

The Ar-Raniry campus at Banda Aceh was the third IAIN established by the Indonesian government (following those of Jakarta and Yogyakarta).[101] It was initially comprised of three faculties: Theology (I. *Usuluddin*), Islamic law (I. *Syariah*), and Education (I. *Tarbiyah*), but even at its inception, plans were already being laid for the establishment of a fourth faculty on campus—one which had no precedent in the other IAIN at that time. This was a Faculty of Dakwah (Ar. *daʿwa*),[102] and this innovation at IAIN's Aceh campus later spread across the national system. Each of these faculties came to play some role in the implementation of Islamic law in Aceh. The Shariʿa Faculty, for example, has been led by a number of deans who have also been important

Pohl, "Religious Education and Secularization: Indonesia's Pesantren Tradition and Civil Society," Ph.D. dissertation (Philadelphia: Temple University, 2007), 163–4.

96 M.B. Hooker, *Indonesian Syariah: Defining a National School of Islamic Law* (Singapore: ISEAS, 2008), 288.

97 Fuad Jabali and Jamhari, *IAIN dan Modernisasi Islam di Indonesia*, 116–17.

98 *10 Tahun Darussalam*, 228–9.

99 Ali Hasjmy, *Semangat Merdeka: 70 Tahun Menempuh Jalan Pergolakan dan Perjuangan Kemerdekaan* (Jakarta: Bulan Bintang, 1985), 490–1; IAIN Ar-Raniry, *Die Natalis Ke-I Djamiʿah Ar-Raniry* (Banda Aceh: Panitia Perajaan Dies Natalis Ke-I I.A.I.N., Djamiʿah Ar-Raniry Darussalam, 1963), 31–2.

100 A. Hasjmy, "Laporan Tahunan Rektor," *Buku Tahunan Hari Jadike-XVII IAIN Jamiʿah Ar-Raniry* (Banda Aceh: IAIN, 1980), 3–4.

101 M. Hasbi Amiruddin (ed.), *Aceh: Serambi Mekka* (Banda Aceh: Pemerintah Provinsi Nanggroe Aceh Darussalam, 2008), 342.

102 Institut Agama Islam Negeri (IAIN), *Kenang2-an Die Natalis Ke-IDjamiʿah Ar-Raniry* (Banda Aceh: Panitia Perajaan Dies Natalis Djamiʿah Ar-Raniry Darusaalam, 1963), 16–17.

figures in the development of Islamic legal thought at the national level, including Hasbi Ash Shiddieqy (d. 1975) and Ismail Muhammad Syah (a.k.a. "Ismuha", d. 1995).[103] Its graduates have also come to provide the bulk of the staffing for Aceh's religious courts (I. Pengadilan Agama/later Mahkamah Syariah).[104] Beyond the Shariʿa courts, most of Aceh's newer Islamic legal institutions—such as the State Shariʿa Agency (DSI) and the Wilayatul Hisbah (WH)—draw most of their personnel from alumni of IAIN's Tarbiyah and Dakwah faculties.[105]

The Arabic-derived term *tarbiya* is used to designate faculties of education within the IAIN system. It is also used to refer to broader trends within modern Indonesian Islam associated in particular with campus-based Revivalist movements. Although this broad rubric encompasses a considerable range of ideological positions, Bernhard Platzdasch has succinctly identified the most basic goal shared by Indonesian *tarbiya* groups, i.e. that "each Muslim had to endeavor to improve the moral life of the community, and bring about public life in accordance with Islam."[106] In his inaugural lecture as professor in IAIN Banda Aceh's Tarbiyah Faculty on 9 October 1999, then rector Safwan Idris proclaimed that "the development of Shariʿa is the vision for Aceh's future," and emphasized that one of the most important aspects of special autonomy for Aceh was the development of a system of education that could support and empower the pursuit of these goals.[107] The staff of the IAIN Tarbiyah Faculty have been particularly supportive of this project, and in the post-disaster/post-conflict period, its lecturers have called for the government to invest ever more resources toward the "grand engineering of this social development" (I. *rekayasa besar pembangunan masyarakat ini*).[108]

[103] For more on these two figures and their role in developing material for the IAIN national curriculum, see Feener, *Muslim Legal Thought*, 59–61; Mark E. Cammack and R. Michael Feener, "Joint Marital Property in Indonesian Customary, Islamic, and National Law," in Peri Bearman, Wolfhart Heinrichs, and Bernard G. Weiss (eds.), *The Law Applied: Contextualizing the Islamic Shariʿa* (London: I.B. Tauris, 2008), 92–115.

[104] Graduates of the Syariah Faculties of branch junior colleges of the IAIN system in Aceh, however, tend to find employment with the DSI, the WH, and in local religious affairs offices for marriage registration (Kantor Urusan Agama/KUA). Interview with STAIN administrator, 23 May 2008 at Lhokseumawe.

[105] The State Shariʿa Agency and the Wilayatul Hisbah will be discussed in more detail in Chapters 7 and 8, respectively.

[106] Bernhard Platzdasch, *Islamism in Indonesia: Politics in the Emerging Democracy* (Singapore: ISEAS Press, 2009), 54.

[107] Safwan Idris, *Mengemban Amanah Allah: Reaktualisasi Syariat Islam dan Masa Depan Pendidikan di Aceh* (Pidato Pengukuhan Jabatan Guru Besar Tetap dalam Ilmu Pendidikan pada Fakultas Tarbiyah IAIN Ar-Raniry, Banda Aceh, 1999), 3–4.

[108] Muhibuddin Hanafiah, "Ketika Ulama Merespon Zaman," *Aceh Independen* (20 February 2009): 10.

An important dimension of the work of the Tarbiyah Faculty, and across Banda Aceh's IAIN more broadly, involves developing models of "education as moral persuasion" as part of the broader work of implementing Islamic law.[109] Here, there has been considerable emphasis on aspects of Islamic education well beyond curricular reform, including the mobilization of *dayah* and *madrasa* to support economic and social development in line with national priorities and as means of countering the deleterious effects of "globalization" on the moral character of Aceh.[110] As one *dayah* activist has put it:

> The shaping of a proper sense of morality and the implantation of strong Islamic values among members of the community—from early childhood through their adult years—is an important function of the *dayah* in protecting their communities from the dangerous influences of other religions and foreign cultures.[111]

This emphasis on Islamic education as a means to establish and reinforce acceptable parameters of social control highlights yet another key aspect of Aceh's contemporary Islamic legal system.

The IAIN Faculty of Dakwah has arguably been even more central to the development of Islamic law in contemporary Aceh than has the Faculty of Tarbiyah. As already mentioned, plans for the creation of this novel unit within the State Institute for Islamic Studies were in place even at the very founding of the Banda Aceh campus at Kopelma Darussalam.[112] At the conclusion of his second term as governor in 1964, Ali Hasjmy served for two years as Minister of the Interior before formally retiring from government service. He nevertheless remained a major public figure in Aceh for years thereafter, and one of his first major "post-retirement" positions was as the founding dean of the Dakwah Faculty in 1968. Its establishment was a significant innovation at the time, as Aceh was the first campus anywhere in Indonesia's national system of Islamic higher education to establish a faculty of this kind.[113]

[109] Eka Srimulyani, "Syariat Islam melalui Tiga Educational Networks (Keluarga, Sekolah dan Masyarakat)," in Eka Srimulyani (ed.), *Filosofi Pendidikan Berbasis Syariat dalam Educational Networks* (Banda Aceh: Dinas Syariat Islam Provinsi Nanggroe Aceh Darussalam, 2008), 13.

[110] See, for example, the papers by Nurhayati, Ramlan, Susi Yusrianti, Ismail, Husaini, Rosamanidar, and Syarifah Rahmah in Ridwan Hasan (ed.), *Islam and Globalization: Challenges & Opportunities to the Future Renaissance* (Lhokseumawe: Unimal Press, 2010).

[111] Siti Zalikha H. Ibrahim, *Menuju Syariat Islam Kaffah* (Banda Aceh: Lapena Institute for Culture and Society, 2008), 27–77.

[112] In the years between the opening of the campus and the establishment of its fourth faculty, *daʿwa* was administered as a major (I. *jurusan*) within the Usuluddin Faculty.

[113] For more on the history of the Dakwah Faculty of IAIN Banda Aceh, see: *15 Tahun Institut Agama Islam Negeri Jamiʿah Ar-Raniry Darussalam Banda Aceh, 5 Okt 1963 – 5 Okt 1978* (Banda Aceh: Panita Harijadi Ke-XV IAIN Jamiʿah Ar-Raniry, 1978), 66–71.

To support this endeavor, Hasjmy not only marshaled his political clout, but also his skills in publicity, giving frequent speeches and publishing extensively on the subject.[114] *Daʿwa*, he argued, was at its heart infused with a sense of mission to propagate a comprehensive understanding of Islam that could serve to order all aspects of human life (I. *cita Islam yang menyeluruh*).[115] Along these lines he stressed that *daʿwa* was an "applied science" (I. *ilmu untuk diamalkan*) that could serve as a much needed "medicine" (I. *obat*) for a sick society, so that the Muslim community could become united and strong in order to combat the threatening evils of communism, socialism, and materialist moral decadence.[116]

Over the decades that followed, Hasjmy produced an immense amount of material in support of the idea of *daʿwa* as a central component of both Indonesia's national development vision, and of Aceh's future as an exemplary Muslim society. In a lecture for a training session of mosque officials for the provincial Ulama Council in 1981, Hasjmy dramatically presented a vision of crisis facing the Muslim community at the then recent turn of the fifteenth century of the Islamic calendar.[117] He began with a screed against the "Modern Age of Ignorance" (I. *Jahiliyah Modern*) in which Muslims are threatened on all sides by both the secularization of the capitalist world and the atheism of the communist bloc. In this lecture he quoted liberally from both Sayyid Quṭb and Muḥammad b. ʿAbd al-Wahhab (among others) to argue that material progress was not only in itself meaningless, but positively dangerous when unaccompanied by the spiritual development necessary to serve as the foundation for a morality that could successfully address the challenges of modernity.[118] To address

[114] Much of Ali Hasjmy's writing on this subject was repetitive. The basic outlines of his vision of *daʿwa* can be found in: *Dustur Daʿwah—Menurut Al-Qur'an* (Jakarta: Bulan Bintang 1974); *Dakwah Islamiyah dan Kaitannya dengan Pembangun Manusia* (Pidato Pengukuhan sebagai guru besar luar biasa dalam Ilmu Dakwah); and *Pokok-pokok pikiran sekitar Dakwah Islamiyah: Sebuah Tinjauan tentang Sifat, Sasaran, dan Cara-cara Pelaksanaan Dakwah* (Banda Aceh: Majelis Ulama Propinsi Daerah Istimewa Aceh, 1981).

[115] A. Hasjmy, *Di Mana Letaknya Negara Islam?* (Surabaya: Bina Ilmu, 1984), 33–43, 299.

[116] Institut Agama Islam Negeri (IAIN), *Risalah Fakultas Dakwahdan Publisistik I.A.I.N. Djamiʿah Ar-Raniry Darussalam* (Aceh: Bahagian Publikasi Fakultas Dakwah/Publisistik Darussalam Banda Atjeh, 1969), 22.

[117] The idea of the need for Islam to be "renewed" at each century is a well-established tradition in the history of Islamic reform movements, based on a prophetic tradition that, "[a]t the head of every century, God shall raise for this community one who will revive its religion" (*Sunan* Abī Da'ūd 37: 4278). The turn of the fifteenth century of the *Hijra* in particular (1400H/1979 CE) marked a key moment in the global Islamic revival of the late twentieth century.

[118] A. Hasjmy, "Kemungkinan-kemungkinan Islam di Abad XV," in *Bahan-bahan Penataran Imam dan Khatib* (Banda Aceh: Majelis Ulama se Daerah Istimewa Aceh, 1981). This speech drew on the talk of his inaugural lecture as professor of Dakwah at IAIN, entitled "Dakwah Islamiyah dan Kaitannya dengan Pembangunan Manusia."

these challenges, he called for a return of Islam to its position of centrality in public life in ways that not only had specific relevance to Aceh, but also broader resonances across discourses of Islamic reformers elsewhere in Indonesia at that time.[119]

Hasjmy served as rector of Banda Aceh's IAIN from 1987 to 1982, during which time the nexus of *daʿwa* ideals and national development fueled significant changes on campus. Over the years that followed, student enrollment underwent a significant increase, and various programs expanded, including the upgrading of Arabic language studies with the appointment of a teacher from al-Azhar.[120] It was also during that same time, for example, that the first batch of IAIN students to be sent abroad for graduate studies on scholarships provided by Mobil Oil returned to campus. This included Safwan Idris, who would later become rector, overseeing the IAIN during some of the most violent years of the conflict between GAM and the Indonesian government until his shocking assassination in 2000.[121] A number of other students at IAIN during Hasjmy's tenure as rectoralso went on to play defining roles in the creation of Aceh's Islamic legal system.[122] Among them were Muslim Ibrahim (who served as the head of the reconstituted Ulama Council during the post-disaster/post-conflict period), and Alyasa Abubakar (founding Director of the State Shariʿa Agency/DSI).[123] During their time on campus during these years, IAIN students were immersed in an atmosphere in which *daʿwa* was actively promoted as the organizing rubric for both Islamic idealism and pragmatic engagement with issues of social development.[124]

[119] For example in the Indonesian Prosperous Justice Party (PKS), which draws heavily on *daʿwa* and *tarbiya* circles for its support, and which emphasizes both of these aspects of Islam heavily in the training materials distributed to new cadres. See, for example, Departemen Kaderisasi DPP Partain Keadilan Sejahtera, *Manajemen Tarbiyah: Anggota Pemula* (Jakarta: PT Syaamil Cipta Media, 2003).

[120] A. Hasjmy, "Laporan Tahunan Rektor," 5–8, 12.

[121] This tragic event is dramatically narrated in Hasbi Amiruddin, "Prof. H. A. Hasjmy (Rektor IAIN Ar-Raniry Periode 1977–1982)," in *Biografi Rektor IAIN Ar-Raniry: Kepemimpinan IAIN Ar-Raniry dari Masa ke Masa* (Banda Aceh: Ar-Raniry Press, 2008), 150–3.

[122] Interview with Yusny Saby, 27 January 2011 at Banda Aceh.

[123] Both of these figures will be treated more extensively later in the chapters dealing with the Ulama Council (MPU) (Chapter 5) and the State Shariʿa Agency (DSI) (Chapter 7).

[124] Roeslan Abdulgani, "Prof. Ali Hasjmy sebagai Pembangun Jembatan Kepercayaan antara Pusat dan Daerah Berdasarkan Islamisme-Nasionalisme sesuai Pancasila," in Badruzzaman Ismail (ed.), *A. Hasjmy - Aset Sejarah Masa Kini Dan Masa Depan: Delapan Puluh Tahun Melalui Jalan Raya Dunia* (Jakarta: Bulan Bintang, 1994), 21.

IAIN ALUMNI AND THE ISLAMIC LEGAL SYSTEM

Visions of *daʿwa* along the lines of those promoted by Hasjmy were also an increasingly important part of broader Indonesian public discourse during the New Order period. Indeed, in many ways, *daʿwa* emerged as an important common rubric within which the state could present the Islamic bona fides of its various modernizing social programs and Islamist groups could express their agendas for the further Islamization of society while remaining safely outside the dangerous sphere of party politics.[125] With the spread of Dakwah Faculties across the IAIN system over the New Order period, the IAIN came to play an important role in the development of these national discourses of *daʿwa* and development.[126] After the fall of Suharto in 1998 and the subsequent decentralization, some IAIN campuses came to express their visions for the Islamization of society through support of local measures to enforce Shariʿa norms through regional regulations (I. *Peraturan Daerah/PerDa*).[127] With the granting of "Special Autonomy" to Aceh soon after that, many of the faculty and alumni of the Banda Aceh IAIN saw an exceptional opportunity to pursue their Islamizing visions of social reform—a chance to harvest the fruit of their work over the preceding decades that attempted to "implant" (I. *menanamkan*) what they viewed as desirable, "modern" understandings of Islam and its law among a generation of Acehnese Muslims.[128]

In the early years of the twenty-first century, IAIN graduates and faculty members figured prominently in public discourses on Shariʿa in contemporary Aceh, contributing a steady stream of lectures, speeches, academic publications, and writings for the popular press that propound visions of Islam in line with the ideals of *daʿwa*, social stability, and economic development. In this work, they were clearly building upon the

[125] For more on these developments, see Feener, *Muslim Legal Thought*, 102–9.

[126] The "strategic" (I. *strategis*) role to be played by religious and moral education in supporting other sectors of national development was emphasized, for example, by Minister of Religious Affairs Muhammad M. Basyuni, in his foreword to T.H. Thalhas and Choirul Fuad Yusuf (eds.), *Pendidikan dan Syariat Islam di Nanggroe Aceh Darussalam dan 8 Undang-Undang Terkait*, xvi.

[127] Such was the case to some extent also, for example, in Makasar (South Sulawesi). Muhamad Hisyam, "The Preparatory Committee for Implementation of Sharia (KPPSI): An Islamic Resurgence in South Sulawesi," in Ikuya Tokoro (ed.), *Islam in Southeast Asia: Transnational Networks and Local Contexts* (Tokyo: Tokyo University of Foreign Studies, 2009), 13. However there, as in Aceh itself, not all IAIN faculty supported the agenda of state Shariʿa, and some actually emerged as prominent voices opposed to the formal implementation of Islamic law. Mujiburrahman, "The Politics of Shariah: The Struggle of the KPPSI in South Sulawesi," in Martin van Bruinessen (ed.), *Contemporary Developments in Indonesian Islam: Explaining the "Conservative Turn"* (Singapore: ISEAS, 2013).

[128] Syahrizal Abbas, *Syariʿat Islam di Aceh: Ancangan Metodologis dan Penerapannya* (Aceh: Dinas Syariʿat Islam Provinsi Aceh, 2009), 49–50.

foundation that had been laid by the work of the IAIN over the preceding decades. Ali Hasjmy's role in institutionalizing the *da'wa* paradigm at the Banda Aceh IAIN campus has left a lasting impact on the character of this school. With the prolonged chaos of armed conflict between GAM and the central government during the 1990s, IAIN faculty members including Safwan Idris, Daniel Djuned, and Alyasa Abubakar reopened discussions of Islam in ways that highlighted its potential role in fostering social stability and development. As will be discussed in what follows, as they did so they also picked up again on a well-established list of specific concerns that had been emphasized in Aceh through earlier Ulama Council *fatwas* and draft regional regulations since the 1960s.[129] This included concerns about alcohol, gambling, and inappropriate mixing of the sexes, as well as the definition of proper Islamic religious belief and practice.

They were encouraged in this work by government officials and prominent politicians in Jakarta, particularly after the fall of Suharto in 1998. In early 1999, a proposal for the implementation of aspects of Islamic law in Aceh was submitted to Yusril Ihza Mahendra, then head of the Islamist "Crescent and Star Party" (Partai Bulan Bintang/PBB) in Jakarta. He responded to the IAIN group from Aceh with a request that they go back and re-draft their proposal to aim for a more complete implementation of Islamic law, stating that under the watch of Habibie as Indonesia's interim president the situation was favorable for a more ambitious plan for formally instituting the Shari'a in Aceh.[130] The genesis of the current system of state Shari'a in Aceh was, in this sense, by no means simply an "unwanted gift from Jakarta"—although its critics both in Aceh and abroad have often criticized it as such.[131] Rather, the project was born out of complex—and diversely motivated—interactions between a group of local Muslim academics building on developments that had been taking shape in Aceh for decades, and various political players at the national level opportunistically exploiting the situation. In this case, local desires for a source of social stability and legal certainty, as well as agendas for Islamizing reform, found common cause with attempts by the central government to undermine local support for the separatist campaign of GAM.

[129] However, it needs also to be noted that there were some IAIN faculty who were critical of various aspects of the formalization of Shari'a in Aceh at that time. See Moch Nur Ichwan, "Official Ulema and the Politics of Re-Islamization: The Majelis Permusyawaratan Ulama, Shari'atization and Contested Authority in Post-New Order Aceh," *Journal of Islamic Studies* 22.2 (2011) fn. 26.

[130] Interview with Muslim Ibrahim, 12 April 2011 at Banda Aceh.

[131] John Bowen, *Islam, Law and Equality in Indonesia: An Anthropology of Public Reasoning* (Cambridge: Cambridge University Press, 2003), 232.

These particular developments, moreover, should be seen against the background in which Islam was often regarded as an important source of bonds between Aceh and the broader Indonesian nation for much of the twentieth century.[132] Such sentiments are particularly prevalent among both the ranks of pious New Order technocrat administrators and IAIN graduates—two groups that expanded in both numbers and influence in Aceh and all across Indonesia over the last decades of the twentieth century. In a focus group discussion on religious leadership with members of the IAIN Banda Aceh Faculty of Shariʿa, for example, there was a clear emphasis on the necessary role of what one participant called "ulama *struktural*"—Islamic authorities with institutional support who could facilitate more "positive" communication with other offices of government.[133] Comments such as these from IAIN academics in Aceh call attention to the diversity across the various branches of Indonesia's system of state Islamic colleges and universities. For while the flagship IAIN campuses in Jakarta and Yogyakarta are often associated with visions of a "substantive" Islam that looks beyond more "formalistic" understandings of the tradition, the general tone at some other branches is not necessarily so ambivalent toward more institutionalized forms of Islam.[134]

STATE POLICY AND *DAʿWA* IDEALS IN MODERN MUSLIM HIGHER EDUCATION

Over the past 50 years, the IAIN has played a significant role in reshaping visions of Islam and its role in Indonesian society, contributing significantly to broader trends in which nation-making and state educational projects have come to be seen as also reflecting Islamic religious aspirations.[135] In Aceh, in particular, the IAIN has played a pivotal role in the redefinition of the relationship between local religious leadership and the Indonesian state. These developments ultimately contributed to the project of implementing Islamic law as part of broader strategies to end the conflict between the central government and GAM. In part, this was accomplished by the re-channeling of aspirations for modernizing Islamic reform that

[132] As argued persuasively in Edward Aspinall's *Islam and Nation: Separatist Rebellion in Aceh, Indonesia* (Stanford, CA: Stanford University Press, 2009).

[133] Focus group discussion, 29 May 2008 at Banda Aceh.

[134] The Indonesian phrase *Islam Substantif* was the title of a popular book by the long-serving Rector of the Jakarta IAIN campus: Azyumardi Azra, *Islam Substantif: Agar Umat Tidak Jadi Buih* (Bandung: Mizan, 2000).

[135] Azra, Afrianty, and Hefner, "Pesantren and Madrasa," 173.

had earlier been championed by PUSA and the Darul Islam through institutions of the Indonesian state.

Since the 1960s, the Banda Aceh campus of the IAIN has produced a large and ever increasing number of preachers, teachers, and state officers that combine strong personal commitments to Islamic religious ideals with political sympathies to the Indonesian nation. The influence of the IAIN was, furthermore, spread to other segments of Acehnese society through the involvement of its faculty and graduates with programs for the reform of *dayah* education, as well as through their engagement with and/or employment in various institutions tasked with the formal implementation of Islamic law, including the Shariʿa Courts (MS), the Ulama Council (MPU), the State Shariʿa Agency (DSI), and the enforcement officers of the Wilayatul Hisbah (WH).

The unifying rubric of *daʿwa* provides both inspiration and legitimation for the work of all of these institutions in the specific context of contemporary Aceh. At the same time, it also reflects significant global trends that should be noted to further contextualize the national-level developments described in this chapter. Abu'l-Aʿla Maududi (quoted at the beginning of this chapter) has had an enormous influence on the development of Islamist thought over the course of the twentieth century. One aspect of his legacy that has heretofore been under-recognized is his role in modern re-conceptualizations of Islamic higher education. In a recent essay on this subject, Muhammad Qasim Zaman has called attention to Maududi's contribution to discussions in Saudi Arabia that led to the establishment of the Islamic University of Medina in 1961. The overarching vision of this institution, and one that has since been echoed by many modern Islamist educators, has been to design and establish schools to serve as instruments of *daʿwa*:

> The significance of this vision lies not only in its desire to produce "good" Muslims and to promote Islam in the world through them and with the backing of the state; it is also important for conceiving of a new kind of ulama—products not of traditional madrasas but of modern, albeit Islamic, universities—who alone would be able to challenge and reverse processes of Westernization.[136]

This "*daʿwa* paradigm" of modern Islamic education could also be characterized by a tendency to de-privilege specialized studies of jurisprudence and its ancillary Islamic sciences as they have traditionally

[136] Muhammad Qasim Zaman, "Epilogue: Competing Conceptions of Religious Education," in Robert W. Hefner and Muhammad Qasim Zaman (eds.), *Schooling Islam: The Culture and Politics of Modern Muslim Education* (Princeton: Princeton University Press, 2006), 256.

been defined—a phenomenon that I have discussed elsewhere in terms of "Islamism and the eclipse of Islamic jurisprudence."[137] This in turn has facilitated some radical re-considerations of who may be counted among the ranks of legitimate religious authorities. Yūsuf al-Qaraḍāwī, for example, has claimed that "graduates of Shari'a Faculties and departments of Islamic studies, as well as everyone who has a [serious] interest in the Shariʿa sciences and Islamic culture and is active and productive as a scholar" can be considered among the ranks of contemporary ulama.[138]

Commenting on the actual impact that re-conceptualizations of religious authority have had in Egypt, Wael Hallaq has characterized the blurring of boundaries between ulama and modern Islamists as resulting in "hybridized interpretive mechanisms that are no longer loyal to the Azharite juristic hermeneutic."[139] In the discourses on Islam, law, and society that have emerged in such contexts, one can see the contours of a significant re-definition of the primary concerns of modern Muslim communities. The defining dynamics are thus no longer primarily centered on traditions of law as interpreted by scholar-jurists, but also on projects invoking *daʿwa* as a means of activist social transformation.

In contemporary Aceh, such reconfigurations of religious authority and the visions of Islam which they produce and promulgate have been even further removed from established models of Islamic legal reasoning—to the point that the very conception of Shariʿa itself has been re-centered around a modern *daʿwa* paradigm. Within this new discourse, traditionally trained ulama and modern Muslim intellectuals have been engaged in ongoing conversations about and contestations over Islamic law and its role in governing both individuals and society. The next chapter will examine the ways in which these developments have taken shape in relation to the establishment of institutionalized forms of modern Muslim religious authority in Aceh.

137 Feener, *Muslim Legal Thought*, 81–117.

138 Quoted in Zaman, "Competing Conceptions of Religious Education," 263.

139 Wael Hallaq, *Sharīʿa: Theory, Practice, Transformations* (New York: Cambridge University Press, 2009), 476.

4

Institutionalizing the Ulama

And when we think we lead, we are most led.

Byron,
The Two Foscari[1]

The changing conceptions of what constitutes Islamic religious authority described in the last chapter have had a significant effect on the formal institutions involved with the implementation of Islamic law in Aceh. This chapter discusses the processes by which the ulama have been organized into modern institutions for both religious reform and social control over the past century. It begins by tracing the formation of modern voluntary associations for Islamic reform in the first half of the twentieth century, and thence follows the subsequent attempts by the government to mobilize local Islamic leaders to support the integration of the region into the Indonesian state. The patterns of engagement between the ulama and the formal institutions of the state have been complex, involving diverse motivations and shifting strategic calculations of mutual interests. The power dynamics have also fluctuated in ways that have determined the relative ability and limitations of government officials and religious leaders to set the agenda for the state institutions of Islam in Aceh—thus contributing to significant ambiguity at times as to who is actually leading whom. Tracing these developments allows us to better grasp the ambiguities of the relationship between the ulama and the modern state that complicate any attempt to create an easy narrative of either independent authority or co-optation.

As discussed in the previous chapter, in the earliest decades of the twentieth century, Aceh's established religious leadership encountered new challenges to their authority that did not come from foreign infidel occupiers, but rather from fellow Muslims who took up modernizing agendas of reform in the name of Islam. At that time, several new associations and organizations promoting Islamic education and social

[1] G.G. Byron, *The Two Foscari: An Historical Tragedy* (Paris: A. & W. Galignani, 1822), 63.

issues were founded in Sumatra, including PERTI, which as previously discussed in Chapter 2, eventually came to be associated primarily with Traditionalist ulama in Aceh.[2] The leading organization of modernizing Islamic reformers in the Netherlands East Indies at that time was the Muhammadiyah. After its founding in Java in 1912, the Muhammadiyah expanded across the Archipelago, and in particular to West Sumatra, which became a major center for its further dissemination into surrounding regions.[3] In Aceh, the reformist ideas of the Muhammadiyah were first taken up by a number of *ulèëbalang*, who had been exposed to what Anthony Reid has described as "a modern and somewhat nationalist religious education" in West Sumatra.[4] Although the Muhammadiya has a formal organization attracted few members from the broader Acehnese population, the basic ideas of modernizing reform that it promoted resonated in various sectors beyond the small circles of *ulèëbalang*. In particular, the new *madrasa* model of modern Islamic education was eagerly embraced by a new generation of Acehnese ulama in the early decades of the twentieth century. A number of them came together to give more concrete form to their aspirations to reform Islam and Islamic education with the founding of PUSA (Persatuan Ulama Seluruh Aceh/All Aceh Ulama Union) in 1939.

During the Japanese occupation, PUSA's influence expanded and the organization emerged from the end of the war in a position of relative strength and became even more dominant following the massacre and exodus of many *ulèëbalang* in the "Social Revolution" of 1946. With this, PUSA and its supporters consolidated their control of local administration during the first years of Indonesian independence. However, when the province of Aceh was dissolved into neighboring North Sumatra by the central government in 1951, PUSA's disappointment over their loss of control fueled the rise of the Darul Islam rebellion in Aceh. As the rebellion dragged on over the years that followed, Soekarno searched for potential allies, at times turning toward the Traditionalist ulama of Aceh's *dayahs* who resisted much of the PUSA agenda of modernizing religious reform.[5]

[2] PERTI was founded in 1928, and reformed into a political party in 1945. Donald Hindley, *The Communist Party of Indonesia, 1951–1963* (Berkeley: University of California Press, 1964), xv.

[3] In addition to Aceh, Minangkabau Muhammadiyah activists also played important roles in the spread of Modernist reform further south along Sumatra's west coast. For more on this, see G.F. Pijper, "Nieuwe godsdienstige denkbeelden in Benkoelen," *Fragmenta Islamica: Studiën over het Islamisme in Nederlandsch-Indië* (Leiden: E. J. Brill, 1934), 159–82.

[4] Anthony Reid, *Blood of the People: Revolution and the End of Traditional Rule in Northern Sumatra* (Kuala Lumpur: Oxford University Press, 1979), 25.

[5] The relations between Aceh's Traditionalist Islamic leaders, the Indonesian State, and the Darul Islam have been discussed in Chapter 2.

Attempting to forge links with Traditionalist ulama, however, required some significant adjustment to Soekarno's general tone in public statements on Islam that tended to be sharply critical of what he disparagingly referred to as a "mentality of imitation" (I. *taklid*/Ar. *taqlīd*) and to Traditionalist *fiqh* more generally.[6] At times, however, Soekarno was able to shift his tone to speak in a language that could be interpreted as more accommodating of Muslim religious concerns, at least in contexts where other interests might overlap. When Soekarno did appeal to Islam it was, however, generally to a non-Traditionalist view, often also drawing on non-Muslim sources such as Lothrop Stoddard's *New World of Islam*[7] to redefine Islam in terms of modern notions of "progress," while sharply critiquing *fiqh* and railing against traditional practices and the segregation of women.[8]

Bernhard Dahm has described Soekarno as having turned, temporarily at least, somewhat toward Islam as a source of personal refuge during his exile in Endeh (Flores) from 1934–1941.[9] It was, for example, from that seat of exile that Soekarno carried out a correspondence on various Islamic issues with A. Hassan, the prolific public spokesman of the reformist group PERSIS (Persatuan Islam).[10] Over the years that followed it is clear that Soekarno came to recognize the strategic potential for

[6] B.J. Boland, *The Struggle of Islam in Modern Indonesia* (The Hague: Martinus Nijhoff, 1971), 123–34.

[7] Originally published in 1921, Soekarno commissioned an Indonesian translation of this work that was published with a new chapter added at the end entitled: "The Rise of the New World of Islam in Indonesia." This additional chapter was written by Abubakar Atjeh. See Abubakar Atjeh, "Kebangkitan dunia baru Islam di Indonesia," in Lothrop Stoddard, *Dunia baru Islam* [Indonesian translation of *The New World of Islam*] (Jakarta: Panitia Penerbit, 1966), 295–332.

[8] Examples of Soekarno's often harsh critiques of traditional Islamic understandings can be found throughout his published writings. For a sample in English, see Sukarno, *Under the Banner of Revolution* (Jakarta: Publication Committee, 1966), 309–28; 333–9; 353–86; 387–428; 461–76. His penchant for modernizing reform is also highlighted in the speech delivered at the conferral of his honorary degree in *daʿwa* from the Jakarta campus of the IAIN in 1964. Ibrahim (ed.), *Pengantar Hukum Islam di Indonesia* (Jakarta: Departemen Agama, 1965), 33–45.

[9] Bernhard Dahm, *Soekarno and the Struggle for Indonesian Independence*, revised and updated edition of *Sukarnos Kampf um Indonesiens Unabhängigkeit* (Ithaca: Cornell University Press, 1969), 174–96.

[10] Sukarno, *Under the Banner*, 309–28. For more on A. Hassan and PERSIS, see Howard M. Federspiel, *Islam and Ideology in the Emerging Indonesian State: The Persatuan Islam (PERSIS), 1923–1957* (Leiden: Brill, 2001). However, in his later autobiographical reflections on his time in Endeh, Soekarno made no mention at all of Islam—and in fact, the only spiritual consolation he claimed to have taken there was in visions of Brahma, Vishnu, and Shiva while gazing across his yard at a breadfruit tree. Sukarno and Cindy Adams, *Soekarno: An Autobiography*, as told to Cindy Adams (Indianapolis: The Bobbs-Merrill Company, Inc., 1965), 135–6.

cultivating the support of ulama in Aceh.[11] This included engaging with Traditionalist leaders in the circle around Tgk. Muda Waly as a check against the PUSA-affiliated block that had joined the Darul Islam.[12] However, Soekarno generally found it easier to work with Muslims of a more Modernist orientation, and in dealing with issues in Aceh, Soekarno found a sympathetic counterpart in the person of Ali Hasjmy.[13]

Hasjmy's work of engaging Aceh's Islamic religious leadership in attempts to consolidate support for Indonesian government rule in Aceh engaged both Modernists who had formerly been his colleagues in PUSA, and Traditionalist ulama. Hasjmy was greatly aided in this work through his collaboration with Tgk. H. Abdullah Ujong Rimba. Ujong Rimba was sympathetic to some points of the reformist program, particularly in the modernizing of Islamic education, while at the same time maintaining his commitment to *fiqh* of the Shāfiʿī *madhhab* and to "recognized" forms of Sufism. From this position he built and maintained strategic alliances with both PUSA and non-PUSA ulama across Aceh through an intricate, decades-long balancing act. Working together with Ujong Rimba, Hasjmy made significant progress in forging relationships with an increasing number of Modernist and Traditionalist ulama. Through the 1950s and over the decades that followed, much of Aceh's Islamic religious leadership—both Modernist and Traditionalist—had come to be either reconciled with or directly engaged with the state.[14]

One key point on which cooperation between Traditionalist and Modernist ulama could be firmly grounded was on opposition to communism. In the wake of the attempted coup in 1965, one of the first mass killings of suspected communists in Indonesia took place in Aceh. Early that October, several thousand were killed in outbreaks of violence that soon came to be tragically repeated across the country.[15] In Aceh, as

[11] With particular reference to Aceh, PERTI and Tgk. Muda Waly were considered important local allies of the Indonesian central government in their campaigns against Daud Beureueh's Darul Islam movement. Dan Birchok, personal communication.

[12] Interview with Tgk. Bakongan, July 2008 at Trumon (Aceh Selatan).

[13] Hasjmy wrote a panegyric to Soekarno entitled "I am your Soldier - for Soekarno" (*Aku Serdadumu–Untuk Bung Karno*) in 1945. Today, the text of this poem is prominently displayed on a wooden plaque in the reception area of the Ali Hasjmy Library in Banda Aceh. However, elsewhere in his writings, Hasjmy hints at some of the more ambiguous aspects of his relationship with Soekarno. See, for example Hasjmy's narrative of dancing with "flirtatious girls" from Maluku at one of Soekarno's garden parties in Jakarta, an experience that left him with memories that Hasjmy described as "beautiful and very confusing." *A. Hasjmy, Semangat Merdeka: 70 Tahun Menempuh Jalan Pergolakan & Perjuangan Kemerdekaan* (Jakarta: Bulan Bintang, 1985), 511–12.

[14] Edward Aspinall, *Islam and Nation: Separatist Rebellion in Aceh, Indonesia* (Stanford, CA: Stanford University Press, 2009), 195.

[15] Robert Cribb, *Historical Atlas of Indonesia* (Honolulu: University of Hawaii Press, 2000), 169–71.

in many other parts of Indonesia at the time, the ulama emerged as an important source of support for the establishment of the New Order and continued to see an important convergence of interests with the strong anti-communist stance of Suharto's government over the decades that followed.

THE FORMATION OF ACEH'S ULAMA COUNCIL

In 1965, the government of the "Special Region" (I. *Daerah Istimewa*) of Aceh inaugurated a council of religious leaders as a new institutional mechanism for the management of Aceh's Islamic religious leadership. This took the form of a state-affiliated Ulama Council that was initially called the Majelis Ulama Daerah Aceh (MUDA).[16] One of the top priorities for this council was to institutionalize Muslim resistance to any resurgence of communism following the failed coup attempt and subsequent mass violence that led to the collapse of Soekarno's government and the establishment of Suharto's "New Order." From the beginning, it was closely linked to the Indonesian military—as were all of the major state-affiliated institutions for the management of Islam in Aceh.[17] Indeed, when the council convened its first conference (I. *musyawarah*) that December its inaugural public proclamation was a sharp condemnation of communism as "unbelief—and legally forbidden (Ar. *ḥarām*) to Muslims."[18] In its mission to fortify Aceh against communism by using the Shariʿa, the Ulama Council actively sought to build a broad coalition of support among Aceh's Islamic leadership. Much of its work was spearheaded by figures with connections to PUSA and the recently founded Banda Aceh campus of the IAIN. The Ulama Council also appointed three "Honorary Directors"

[16] For more on the founding conference of Aceh's Ulama Council, see Ismuha, "Ulama Aceh dalam Perspektif Sejarah," in Taufik Abdullah (ed.), *Agama dan Perubahan Sosial* (Jakarta: CV. Rajawali, 1983), 97. The meeting was attended by Ujong Rimba, T.H. Hasan, Ismuha, Ibrahim Husein, M. Yasin, Tgk. Zamzami Yahya, Tgk. Abd. Jalil Takengon, and 57 other participants. Ismuha, *Sejarah Singkat Majelis Ulama Propinsi Daerah Istimewa Aceh* (Banda Aceh: Majelis Ulama Propinsi Daerah Istimewa Aceh, 1983), 6–13. A collection of primary documents from the first three decades of the Majelis Ulama is also published in Badruzzaman Ismail (ed.), *Amal Bakti Empat Windu Majelis Ulama Aceh Tahun 1965–1997* (Aceh: Majelis Permusyawaratan Ulama Provinsi Nanggroe Aceh Darussalam, 2002).

[17] Moch. Nur Ichwan, "Official Ulema and the Politics of Re-Islamization: The Majelis Permusyawaratan Ulama, Shariʿatization and Contested Authority in Post-New Order Aceh," *Journal of Islamic Studies* 22.2 (2011) fn. 36.

[18] This first statement of the Ulama Council is regularly reproduced in published collections of MPU fatwas. See, for example, *Kumpulan Fatwa-fatwa Majelis Ulama Propinsi Daerah Istimewa Aceh tahun 1965 s/d 31 Maret 1979* (Banda Aceh: Sekretariat Majelis Permusyawaratan Ulama, 2006), 1–6.

(I. *Ketua Kehormatan*) that included Daud Beureueh, Tgk. H. Hasan Kreung Kalé, and of course Ali Hasjmy.[19]

Aceh's Ulama Council is one of the oldest state-affiliated bodies of its kind in Indonesia, and in fact it later came to serve as a model for the national Majelis Ulama Indonesia (MUI) when that was later founded by Suharto in 1975.[20] Over the intervening decade, the work of Aceh's Ulama Council pioneered programs that were later also implemented at the national level. Under Sjammaun Gaharu's tenure as commander of the Indonesian armed forces in Aceh, an urgent emphasis was placed upon economic development as part of the broader program to secure the integration of Aceh. This included a five-year plan to improve production facilities and infrastructure as well as the mandate to create the new center of higher education at the student city of Kopelma Darussalam, on the outskirts of Banda Aceh.[21] Aceh's Ulama Council came to play a significant role in promoting particular policies in some of these areas, but more important was its role in advancing a broader vision of Islam that could facilitate both social stability and economic development.[22]

The position of this Ulama Council as an institution for the administration of Islam was strengthened under provincial legislation in 1966, which provided a new legal foundation for the Council, now re-defined as the Majelis Permusyawaratan Ulama (MPU) of the Special Region of Aceh. As noted by Arskal Salim, this law did, in fact, commission the Ulama Council with the task of "maintaining local security and political stability."[23] At the same time, however, it also stipulated a more activist role for the Council to "foster the unity of the ulama ... in efforts to channel the "fire" (I. *api*) of Islam, [and] to make it a positive and '*militan*' [term used in Indonesian original] force contributing to the Indonesian

[19] Hasjmy, *Semangat Merdeka*, 711–12.

[20] For more on the founding of Indonesia's national Ulama Council, see Mohammad Atho Mudzhar, *The Fatwas of the Council of Indonesian Ulama: A Study of Islamic Legal Thought in Indonesia, 1975–1988* (Jakarta: INIS, 1993), 46–7.

[21] *Dua Windhu Kodam-I/Iskandar Muda* (Jakarta: Sejarah Militer Kodam-I/Iskandar Muda, 1972), 244–7.

[22] This was in fact a function of Aceh's Ulama Council from soon after its founding. In 1966, new guidelines for the organization explicitly set forth its responsibility for fostering political stability, security, and public order. *Peraturan Daerah Propinsi Daerah Istimewa Aceh No. 1/ 1966 tentang Pedoman Dasar Majlis Permusjawaratan Propinsi Daerah Istimewa Aceh*, II.5.3–4. These aims were further clarified in a proclamation from the governor of Aceh in 1970 (SK No. 347/1970 – 22 Oktober). Ismuha, *Sejarah Singkat*, 36. For some broader contextualizing discussions of the ways in which Islamic thought came to reflect and inform discussions of economic development and government policy in New Order Indonesia, see Feener, *Muslim Legal Thought*, 118–81.

[23] Arskal Salim, *Challenging the Secular State: The Islamization of Law in Modern Indonesia* (Honolulu: University of Hawaii Press, 2008), 146.

revolution based on *Pancasila*, in accordance with the function of religion as a foundational element of Nation and Character building."[24]

A significant part of the Ulama Council's work in its first year of existence involved the review and restatement of earlier state Shariʿa policies that had been previously promulgated in Aceh. For example, in October 1966, it issued a review of an earlier (1958) provincial regulation on the prohibition of alcohol that sought to both strengthen existing sanctions and to revoke licenses for the trade in and consumption of alcohol that had been made available for special venues and non-Muslims under the earlier law.[25] The following year, the Ulama Council built upon these foundations by issuing a call for the further state implementation of "elements" of Islamic law (I. *Unsur-unsur Syariat Islam*) by enacting provincial by-laws (I. *peraturan daerah*) as well as gubernatorial decisions and instructions covering the fields of doctrine, ritual practice, ethics, education, *daʿwa*, religious property, commercial transactions, public symbolism of Islam, and other social issues.[26] Over the years that followed, the Ulama Council also engaged with prominent leaders of Aceh's Traditionalist Muslim community—including two of Tgk. Muda Waly's sons (Djamaluddin Waly and Muhibbudin Waly)—for support in both promoting campaigns for the promotion of public morality, and for their assistance in policing the boundaries of what could be considered acceptable forms of Sufi thought and practice.[27]

By 1975, Tgk. Ujong Rimba could write with pride about the role that Aceh's Ulama Council had come to play in promoting both the observance of Islamic law in Aceh and its support of various development programs. He was also gratified to see that the work of Aceh's Ulama Council was inspiring new developments across Indonesia more broadly, noting the fact that ten years after the establishment of an Ulama Council in Aceh, President Suharto was now urging Indonesia's provincial governors to take the lead in forming similar institutions in their provinces, while

[24] *Peraturan Daerah Propinsi Daerah Istimewa Aceh No. 1/1966 tentang Pedoman Dasar Majelis Permusyawaratan Ulama Propinsi Daerah Istimewa Aceh*, I.4.

[25] These recommendations were, in their main outlines, manifested in positive law soon thereafter. A week later, the provincial government issued a new law on the subject: *Peraturan Daerah Aceh No. 6/1966*. The earlier regional regulation was: *Peraturan Daerah Aceh No. 17/1958 tentang Larangan Membuat, Memasukkan, Memperdagangkan, Menyimpan dan Meminum Minuman Keras di Daerah Propinsi Daerah Istimewa Aceh*. The history of Islamic legislation in modern Aceh is discussed in more detail in Chapter 4.

[26] "Keputusan Musyawarah Alim Ulama se-Daerah Provinsi Daerah Istimewa Aceh tahun 1967," in *Kumpulan Fatwa-fatwa Majelis Ulama*, 25–7.

[27] *Surat Keputusan Pimpinan DPR Propinsi Dista tentang Pembentukan Panitia Khusus II, Dengan Tugas Menyusun Konsepsi Pembinaan Akhlak* (Arsip Propinsi Aceh No. 246/39); *Bundel Mengenai Perkembangan Ilmu Tharikat/Kebatinan dalam Daerah TK. II* Aceh Barat (Arsip Propinsi Aceh No. 311/51). I would like to thank Dan Birchok for calling these documents to my attention.

also allowing for the establishment of a national council of ulama.[28] The function of this new Indonesian Ulama Council (Majelis Ulama Indonesia/ MUI) was to serve as "translator" (I. *penerjemah*) between the government and the Muslim community to ensure the success of regional and national development programs.[29]

In Aceh, the Ulama Council (re-designated as a branch of the Indonesian MUI after 1975) worked to translate these new national ideals of economic development in terms that would resonate with local religious sensibilities.[30] In a circular letter on national education, the leadership of Aceh's Ulama Council stressed that faith (Ar. *iman*) and piety (Ar. *taqwa*) are pre-requisites for the creation of a new breed of "*homo developmenticus*" (I. *manusia pembangunan*).[31] The work of the Ulama Council thus included establishing religious legitimation for controversial programs such as the central government's ambitious family planning program.[32] It was also extended to the task of ensuring the political stability necessary for economic development, as an internally circulated bulletin of the MUI emphasized to all of its local branches in the run-up to the 1977 general elections.[33] Beyond this, Aceh's Ulama Council has experimented with a broad range of *daʿwa*-related social programs.[34]

[28] Ujong Rimba, *Risalah Majlis Ulama Daerah Istimewa Aceh: Sumbangan Pikiran untuk Musyawarah Majlis Ulama se Indonesia yang berlangsung di Jakarta sejak tanggal 21 s/d 27 Juli, 1975* (n.p. - typescript KITLV Library, Leiden #Mq1176NI).

[29] This mandate was elaborated at length in the speeches of high-ranking officials at the MUI's inaugural conference in July 1975. See Husein Segaf, Suminto, Chatibul Umam, and Ali Ibrahim (eds.), *Ulama dan Pembangunan* (Jakarta: Panitia Musyawarah Nasional I Majelis Ulama Seluruh Indonesia, 1976), 65–280.

[30] In 1974, this view was stressed by high-ranking Indonesian officials on visits to Aceh, such as the Menteri Kesejahteraan Rakyat, who referred to the developmentalist vision of the 1973 GBHN in urging Aceh's ulama to develop interpretations of Islam that could facilitate economic growth. "Pentingnya Seminar Mengali Ajaran2 Agama untuk Mendorong Pembangunan," *Harian Duta I.23* (5 November 1974), 1, 4.

[31] Majlis Ulama Daerah Istimewa Aceh, *Surat perihal Pembaharuan Sistim Pendidikan Nasional* (No. 420/MU/101), 9 February 1979.

[32] Discussions of this last issue were, for a long time, on the agenda of the Ulama Council, which realized just how controversial an issue it was. From its first appearance in their published statements of 1972, through to its first cautious statements on the subject in 1974, the MU came to play an important role in legitimizing the program in the eyes of Acehnese Muslims. The steps on this path can be traced in detail through the materials collected in: *Kumpulan Fatwa-fatwa Majelis Ulama*.

[33] "Pernyataan Majelis Ulama Indonesia tentang Pemilu tahun 1977," *Bulletin Majelis Ulama Indonesia—Untuk Informasi dan Komunikasi Intern 12* (Banda Aceh: Sekretariat MUI, March 1977), 7–8. A copy of this sent to the Aceh branch is held in the provincial archives: Arsip Propinsi Aceh - 338/53.

[34] This included, for example, the formation of a "Special Team" consisting of security officers (ABRI), health officials, and Islamic preachers to address what was perceived to be an increase in prostitution during that period. Abdullah Ujong Rimba, *Rencana dan Program Dakwah dalam rangka Penanggulangan Wanita Tuna Susila (WTS) di Banda Aceh - May 1980*), Arsip Propinsi Aceh - 339/53.

The emphasis on the importance of fostering "spiritual development" as a central responsibility of the Ulama Council was another point on which Indonesia's national-level Ulama Council reflected concerns similar to those of its provincial predecessor in Aceh.[35]

Over the course of the 1970s and 1980s, Aceh's Ulama Council worked with the Dakwah Faculty of the Banda Aceh IAIN on outreach programs designed to promote this state vision of economic developmentalism combined with rationalizing religious reform.[36] The agenda for one such program sent to the sub-district of Bandar Baru in Pidie in 1974, for example, included public sermons on village industrialization, family planning, and the modernization of animal husbandry, as well as fostering Islamic morality and "the purification of faith from superstition."[37] The Ulama Council also literally "cleared the way" for major economic development projects by pronouncing religious justification for the exhumation of Muslim graves at sites slated for natural gas extraction.[38] Another important component of the MUI's work in supporting government programs was in helping to secure and maintain the stability that was seen as a pre-requisite for economic growth. In this capacity, the Ulama Council continued to be closely involved with the Indonesian military in Aceh over the decades that followed.[39]

INDONESIAN ISLAM AND ACEHNESE SEPARATISM

In the 1970s, the greatest threat to the stability needed for the New Order's economic development programs came from the Free Aceh Movement (GAM). To address this problem, Aceh's Ulama Council worked in various

[35] As is clearly seen, for example, in the documents prepared locally for presentation to the second national conference of the MUI held at Jakarta in 1980: *Berkas Sehubungan dengan MUNAS Ke II MUI* (Arsip Propinsi Aceh – 304/50).

[36] For a concise statement of the developmentalist agenda of the Indonesian National Ulama Council (MUI) that was reflected in such local programs in Aceh, see H. Soedirman, "Dasar Pikiran Majelis Ulama Indonesia tentang Proyek-proyek Pembangunannya," *Majelis Ulama: Untuk Informasidan Komunikasi Intern 8* (August 1982) 7–16.

[37] *Majelis Ulama Propinsi Daerah Istimewa Aceh dalam rangka Terima Jabatan Gubernur Kepala Daerah Istimewa Aceh 1968 s/d 1977* (Banda Aceh: Sekretariat Majelis Ulama Daerah Istimewa Aceh, 1977), 14.

[38] "Majlis Alam Ulama Tinjau Proyek L.N.G.," *Harian Duta* II.78 (23 May 1975), 1, 4. This sort of thing clearly appears to have happened on more than one occasion in the 1980s. Ali Hasjmy, chairman of the Aceh branch since 1982, described how the ulama literally served the government in preparing the ground for development projects. "... on several occasions the Public Works Office has asked us [the Ulama Council] to come to areas through which roads will be built." Quoted in Tim Kell, *The Roots of the Acehnese Rebellion, 1989–1992* (Ithaca: Cornell Modern Indonesia Project, 1995), 51.

[39] Ismuha, *Sejarah Singkat*, 51–2, 106–7.

ways to counter local Muslim support for that separatist cause. A general appeal published by the Ulama Council in 1978 warned of the dangers posed by separatism, while calling for those who supported GAM to return to the fold and work together to develop Aceh within the Indonesian nation.[40] Over the years that followed, the MUI ran a slate of programs for preparing preachers to work in their local communities by ensuring that their messages emphasized the importance of national unity and political stability.[41] Aceh's Ulama Council was even called upon at times to provide legitimation for the Indonesian military's anti-insurgency campaigns.[42]

In 1982, Ali Hasjmy replaced Tgk. Ujong Rimba as chairman of Aceh's Ulama Council. During Hasjmy's tenure in this position, he made a priority of mobilizing Aceh's Ulama Council to spearhead Indonesian government efforts to suppress GAM.[43] The public statements that they issued asserted the importance of Islam to the Indonesian nation and depicted separatism as a threat to Islamic ideals of unity. In 1985, for example, Aceh's Ulama Council published a fatwa on "national consciousness" (I. *kesadaran bernegara*) that reaffirmed its readiness to carry out *da'wa* programs to promote the idea that the entire Indonesian Muslim community "... unite in support of the government's struggle to develop the nation based on *Pancasila*, the 1945 constitution, and the guidance of God."[44] The alignment of Aceh's ulama with the Indonesian government's attempts to quell the GAM separatist threat was, however, by no means total—and there remained some local Islamic leaders who actually supported GAM in various ways. Many others, however, were more ambivalent on the issue of ultimate allegiances. Instead, they appeared to have followed pragmatic patterns of collaboration with whichever side was more firmly in control of their area, while focusing largely on their educational and pastoral roles in local communities.[45]

Significant sectors of Aceh's Islamic leadership remained a major source of local support for Aceh's continuing place within Indonesia over the

[40] Majlis Ulama Daerah Istimewa Aceh, *Seruan Kepada Seluruh Masyarakat Aceh* (No. 856/MU/1978).

[41] *Berkas Penataran Imam dan Khatib Se Propinsi Daerah Istimewa Aceh Tanggal 25 s/d 28 Januari 1981 di Banda Aceh* (Arsip Propinsi Aceh No. 309/50).

[42] Kell, *Roots*, 77. Kell's observations have also been noted in this connection by Aspinall, *Islam and Nation*, 206.

[43] Kell, *Roots*, 77–8.

[44] "Keputusan Rapat Kerja Komisi "B" (Fatwa/Hukum) Majelis Ulama Indonesia Propinsi Daerah Istimewa Aceh Tanggal 21 s/d 24 Jumadila wal 1405H/ 11 s/d 14 Februari 1985 M di Banda Aceh – Pernyataantentang Kesadaran Bernegaradan Bela Negara," reprinted in *Kumpulan Fatwa-fatwa Majelis Ulama Daerah Istimewa Aceh* (Banda Aceh: MPU, 2005), 221–3.

[45] For more on the diverse position of Aceh's ulama over the course of the conflict, see Shane Joshua Barter, "Ulama, the State, and War: Community Islamic Leaders in the Aceh Conflict," *Contemporary Islam* 5 (2011) 19–36.

decades that followed.[46] In their attempts to gain legitimacy and attract more support from the broader Muslim population, the Indonesian authorities welcomed and even encouraged rulings from the MUI that reflected issues of considerable symbolic importance to many Acehnese Muslims. These included fatwas on issues of Islamic morality, and in particular rulings aimed at addressing the social ills of gambling, alcohol, and sexual misbehavior. These very issues, not coincidentally, were prominent elements in the programs of Shariʿa implementation that had been advanced earlier in the 1960s—and that were to be revived again later under Aceh's new *qanun* legislation in the early twenty-first century.[47]

A number of scholars have observed that Shariʿatization in Aceh was a top-down project used by the central government in Jakarta as part of attempts to win the hearts of the Acehnese Muslims and to delegitimize the Free Aceh Movement. Moch. Nur Ichwan, for example, characterizes state Shariʿa as primarily a "political strategy," emphasizing that the introduction of state Shariʿa was "part of a project of the central government to win the support of the Acehnese people against the GAM."[48] This was clearly the case for some government officials in Jakarta. At the same time, however, this is only part of the story. This view suggests that national politics was a primary factor that motivated the local Islamic leaders who were most directly involved in the design and development of Aceh's contemporary Shariʿa system. Yet, it does not entirely account for the fact that there were other motivations at work in this as well. This perspective on state Shariʿa in Aceh tends to discount the possibility of other motivations driving the action of those local Islamic leaders who are committed to the project. As discussed at the close of the last chapter, during the New Order period, there were sections of Aceh's Islamic leadership that were willing to accommodate the sovereignty of the Indonesian state and saw in this a potential means for pursuing their own religious goals of establishing a place for Islamic law in the lives of Muslims in contemporary Aceh.

The motivations were complex, and at times, conflicting interests were at play among different elements of Aceh's Islamic leadership. Arskal Salim

[46] In September 1995, for example, a 68-strong delegation from Aceh attended a state reception at the presidential palace to pray for Suharto's well-being. Donald J. Porter, *Managing Politics and Islam in Indonesia* (London: Routledge, 2002), 94–5.

[47] For example, in 1991, Aceh's provincial MUI issued a fatwa on the drink known as "Green Sands," which called for Acehnese to stop selling or consuming this low-alcohol brew. "Keputusan Rapat Kerja Komisi'B' (Fatwa/Hukum) Majelis Ulama Indonesia Propinsi Daerah Istimewa Aceh Nomor 451/344/1991 M/1411 H tentang Minuman yang Mengandung Alkoholseperti Green Sands," *Kumpulan Fatwa-fatwa Majelis Ulama Daerah Istimewa Aceh* (Banda Aceh: MPU, 2005), 237–9.

[48] Moch. Nur Ichwan, "Official Ulema," 2–3.

has contrasted the position of the Modernist urban ulama associated with the MUI to that of the Himpunan Ulama Dayah Aceh (HUDA).[49] While the former put a high priority on the proposal for Shariʿa to be implemented under a provision for special autonomy within the Indonesian nation, the latter (mostly Traditionalist) ulama called for both the implementation of Shariʿa and for a referendum on Acehnese independence in 1999.[50] There were thus some clear divides in terms of the political agendas of different segments of Aceh's Islamic leadership. It should, however, also be noted here that at the same time representatives of Aceh's most prominent Traditionalist Muslim organizations including HUDA, the Rabithah Taliban Aceh (RTA), and even Majelis Ulama Nanggroe Aceh (MUNA—which is affiliated with former GAM leaders) expressed support for the project of Shariʿa implementation.[51] Reform-minded Islamic Modernists and Revivalists, as well as many Traditionalist Muslim leaders were thus widely in agreement on both the general proposition that Shariʿa should play a significant role in the future definition of Acehnese society, and the movement for the state to play a role in its formal implementation. The differences between them were thus not about whether or not the state should be involved with the formal implementation of Islamic law. Rather, the issue that divided the various camps of Aceh's Islamic religious leadership was the issue of whether or not Aceh should build its governmental institutions together with, or separate from, the Indonesian nation.[52]

THE MAJLIS PERMUSYAWARATAN ULAMA (MPU)

The referendum demanded by HUDA and SIRA was never held.[53] As it became clear that there was no possibility for a referendum on independence, the Indonesian military in Aceh stepped up its pressure on religious leaders to support their campaign against GAM. Subsequently, an increasing number of ulama came to focus their energies on the possibility of implementing the Shariʿa in Aceh as a special autonomous region within

[49] Salim, *Challenging the Secular State*, 151.

[50] These latter ulama were affiliated with the movement known as Sentral Informasi Referendum Aceh (SIRA).

[51] Eka Srimulyani, personal communication, 6 August 2012.

[52] Indeed, significant segments of the Acehnese public had by that time grown rather cynical of the MUI, seeing it to be merely an extension of the Indonesian state that they sought to exit from. Sri Suyanta, *Pola Hubungan Ulama dan Umara: Kajian Tentang Pasang Surut Peran Ulama Aceh* (Jakarta: Universitas Islam Negeri Syarif Hidayatullah, 2005), 113–16.

[53] Stanley Adi Prasetyo and Teresa Birks, "Background and Political Situation in Aceh," in Olle Törnquist, Stanley Adi Prasetyo, and Teresa Birks (eds.), *Aceh: The Role of Democracy for Peace and Reconstruction*, 2nd edition (Jogjakarta: PCD Press, 2010), 62–3.

Indonesia. On the national level, this proposal was aggressively pursued by a number of Muslim legislators as well as a circle of reform-minded politicians associated with then-president B.J. Habibie.[54] However, as noted in the previous chapter in connection with the IAIN, this "Jakarta strategy" was also seen as an opportunity for local Muslim academics and activists in Aceh to realize their own goals for the Islamization of society that had been pursued in various ways by PUSA and its heirs for decades. Plans for this involved a new vision and structure for the Ulama Council, on that built upon the foundations laid since 1965, but now reconfigured in relation to the political realities of Aceh's "Special Autonomy."

In 1999, with the end of the New Order and the beginning of the "Era of Reform" (I. *Reformasi*), the Indonesian government offered a new law on special autonomy for Aceh that granted the province rights directly to control matters of religion, custom (I. *adat*), and education, as well as other aspects of local policy and administration.[55] This allowed for the reformulation of existing Islamic institutions, including the Ulama Council. A regional regulation passed the following year strengthened the existing provincial branch of the MUI and changed its name back to the Majelis Permusyawaratan Ulama (MPU). The MPU was then re-defined as an organization "working parallel to and in equal partnership with" (I. *mitra sejajar*) the provincial government and the legislative assembly.[56] The scope of the MPU's potential powers wasconsolidated by subsequent legislation which gave the MPU even greater influence in the formation and review of state policy, and by a flood of funds from the office of governor Abdullah Puteh in 2002.[57]

The new role of the MPU in provincial affairs was further specified in *Qanun No.9/2003*, which clarifies that the Ulama Council has the authority to give its opinion and issue fatwas on official matters "whether requested to by the provincial government or not."[58] Its duties include providing concrete policy advice to the government on legal, social, economic, and

[54] Aspinall, *Islam and Nation*, 207–11. Before succeeding to the presidency in 1999, Habibie had gained a reputation as a supporter of mobilizing Muslim support for the New Order, particularly through the networks of reform-minded Muslim technocrats discussed earlier in relation to the Indonesian "*daʿwa* paradigm." For more on Habibie and his role in late New Order Muslim politics: Robert W. Hefner, "Islam, State, and Civil Society: ICMI and the Struggle for the Indonesian Middle Class," *Indonesia* 56 (October 1993), 1–36.

[55] *Undang-undang Republik Indonesia No. 44/1999 tentang Penyelenggaraan Keistimewaan Propinsi Daerah Istimewa Aceh.*

[56] *PerDa 3/2000*, III.3.1–2.

[57] For more on the money politics of Abdullah Puteh, and the corruption that characterized his tenure, see M. Isa Sulaiman and Gerry van Klinken, "The Rise and Fall of Governor Puteh," in Henk Schulte Nordholt and Gerry van Klinken (eds.), *Renegotiating Boundaries: Local Politics in Post-Suharto Indonesia* (Leiden: KITLV Press, 2007), 225.

[58] *Qanun Provinsi Nanggroe Aceh Darussalam No. 9/2003 tentang Hubungan Tata Kerja Majelis Permusyawaratan Ulama dengan Eksekutif, Legislatif dan Instansi lainnya*, V.9–11.

development issues. The Legislative branch of the government is required by the same law to ask for input from the MPU on any legislation that may touch upon issues of Shariʿa.[59] At the same time, however, the Provincial Legislative Assembly (DPRA) is by no means bound to comply with the recommendations of the MPU on any piece of proposed legislation.[60] The 2003 law also gives extensive elaboration on the relations between the MPU, the police, and military officials, where the MPU is tasked with providing "judgments and suggestions" (I. *pertimbangan dan saran-saran*) to law enforcement agencies and being involved with the education and training of the police force. The police are, for their part, obligated to work with the MPU for education and training police staff in the areas of Islamic law and public order, and similar points are made for the MPU's relations with local military command (*KODAM Iskandar Muda*).[61]

The definition and powers of the MPU as outlined in this *Reformasi*-era regional legislation were for the most part confirmed by the Law on Governing Aceh (LOGA) that was promulgated after the Helsinki Agreement that put an end to the conflict between GAM and the Indonesian government. However, one major change in the 2006 LOGA was an addition to the official formulation of the composition of the MPU. It stipulates that the Council is to be constituted of both ulama and "Muslim intellectuals who understand Islamic religious knowledge" (I. *cendekiawan Muslim yang memahami ilmu agama Islam*). The same law also mandates that special consideration be made for the representation of women on Aceh's Ulama Council.[62]

The work of the MPU is structured according to a number of "Commissions" (I. *Komisi*) charged with responsibility for: (1) Fatwa and Shariʿa laws, (2) Research and development, (3) Education, (4) Economic policy, (5) Women's and family empowerment, (6) Youth programs, and (7) Communal harmony and political issues.[63] The overall organization is led by an executive director, working together with a Plenary Council

[59] *Qanun No. 9/2003*, II.2–3; III.4.3; IV.6–7.

[60] Abidin Nurdin, "Ulama dan Proses Legislasi: Mengkaji Legitimasi Lembaga Ulama Aceh," in Arskal Salim and Adlin Sila (eds.), *Serambi Mekkah yang Berubah: Views from Within* (Jakarta: Pustaka Alvabet, 2010), 108–9.

[61] *Qanun No. 9/2003*, V.3.14–15.

[62] Law on Governing Aceh/*LoGA: Undang-Undang Republik Indonesia No. 11/2006 tentang Pemerintahan Aceh,* (138.1); (138.2–3); (140.1.a); (140.1.b). For more on female Islamic religious leadership in contemporary Aceh, including participation in other ulama organizations, including HUDA and Inshafuddin, see Eka Srimulyani, "Teungku Inong Dayah: Female Religious Leaders' Authority and Agency in Contemporary Aceh," in R. Michael Feener, David Kloos, and Annemarie Samuels (eds.), *Islam and the Limits of the State: Reconfigurations of Ritual, Doctrine, and Authority in Contemporary Aceh* (Leiden: Brill, forthcoming).

[63] The most recent legislation on the structure and function of the MPU is *Qanun Nomor 2/ Tahun 2009 tentang Majelis Permusyawaratan Ulama.*

(I. *Dewan Paripurna*). Members serve a term of five years, with the possibility of one renewal for a maximum of ten years in office. They are drawn from across the province through a series of vertically stacked selections. It begins at the local level with each village nominating potential members, then among those selected, five are chosen from each sub-district (I. *kecamatan*), and thence combined to a pool from which five are selected from each district (I. *kabupaten*). This results in a total pool of 260, from which 26 are chosen as members of the Plenary Council at the provincial level.

In addition to the religious specialists, the MPU also includes a Secretariat that handles matters of general administration and budget management. The administrative staff members often do not have educational backgrounds in the Islamic religious sciences, and are generally graduates of national, non-confessional schools.[64] Most of them, however, generally share a pronounced interest in Islamic education and are supportive of government agendas, not only for Islamic propagation but also for the state enforcement of Shariʿa religious norms.[65] Beyond these broad points of consensus, however, are a number of issues on which the members of the Ulama Council are divided, and the management of these diverse opinions is a key issue of concern both for the leadership of the Council, and for the provincial government.

In line with the broad definition of membership stated in the legislation that governs the MPU, the council is constituted by men (and some women) from a diverse range of backgrounds, among whom there are considerable differences in their exposure to the study of technical religious sciences. There is no formal testing of Islamic knowledge or ability to deal with Arabic sources, but each member must sign a statement swearing that they are able (I. *mampu*) to carry out the work of an Islamic scholar.[66] Beyond one's qualifications in religious learning, however, considerable emphasis is placed upon the character and maturity of those who would serve on the MPU. While the statute stresses the possession of religious knowledge and education credentials, within the organization more importance is placed upon moral and religious qualities in confirming an individual as a member of the Ulama Council. The personal religious practices and

[64] A considerable number of the office staff interviewed mentioned that most of what they knew of Islam was "self-taught" (I. *otodidak*). Many, however, had also spent at least some time in a Traditionalist *dayah*. Others expressed more eclectic religious backgrounds when pressed to articulate their own orientations toward Islam. For example, one young woman working in the finance department of the local MPU branch office in North Aceh identified herself as sympathetic to both "neo-Modernist" (I. *Pembaharuan*) and Sufi approaches to Islam (interview on 24 November 2008 at Lhokseumawe).

[65] Interview with an office clerk in the Banda Aceh office of the MPU, December 2008.

[66] Interview with Muslim Ibrahim, 12 April 2011 at Banda Aceh.

ethical character of candidates as role models for the community are more formally specified at the local (I. *kabupaten*) level offices of the MPU.[67]

In the years prior to the re-designation of the MPU under the special autonomy provisions, the Aceh branch of the national MUI was dominated by reform-minded (Modernist and Revivalist) Muslims drawn from the ranks of former PUSA affiliates, and later from the IAIN while others came from Modernist pedigrees of *Gontor* schools and Muhammadiyah activism.[68] However, Traditionalist Muslims have come to play more significant roles within the organization since then.[69] The foundation for this more balanced composition was actually established at the very founding of the Ulama Council in 1965, as symbolized by the choice of Tgk. Abdullah Ujong Rimba as its leader. In this position, Ujong Rimba was able to provide both sympathy for and credibility in Traditionalist circles while also being supportive of key aspects of PUSA's educational reform agenda. Today, a number of leadership positions in various local branches of the MPU are held by figures coming out of *dayah* backgrounds who emphasize a Traditionalist (Shāfiʿī) perspective on jurisprudence.[70] Thus although reform agendas do hold a prominent position on its agenda, the present-day MPU comprises the only major institution of state Shariʿa in Aceh that is not overwhelmingly dominated by reform-minded Muslims.

ISLAMIC LAW AS EDUCATION

The complex task of managing this diverse body within the MPU has been taken up by Muslim Ibrahim as the first head of the reconstituted Ulama Council in Aceh.[71] Over the first decade of the twenty-first century,

[67] For example, a former head of the North Aceh branch of the MPU, Tgk. H. Amirullah M. Diah has listed the following qualifications that must be possessed for one to be counted among the ulama: (1) One must be a Muslim possessed of religious knowledge, faith, piety, good works, noble character, sincerity, and devotion to God, (2) Instruct the community and maintain a proper balance between worldly and religious concerns, (3) Enjoin the good and forbid wrong, and (4) Serve as an "informal leader" [English in original] with a steady mindfulness of God. "Makalah Peran Majelis Permusyawaratan Ulama dalam Penerapan Syariʿat Islam," unpublished PowerPoint slides presented at the MPU Kab. Aceh Utara, 2009; *Profil Permusyawaratan Ulama Kabupaten Aceh Utara* (official brochure of the district MPU, printed at Lhokseumawe, n.d.).

[68] Interview with faculty from the Gontor 10 campus, 7 December 2008 at Seulimeum.

[69] Interview with MPU staff member, 13 February 2008 at Banda Aceh.

[70] Interview with district-level MPU member, 5 December 2008 at Lhokseumawe.

[71] Muslim Ibrahim was born in North Aceh in 1950 and attended government Islamic schools in Lhokseumawe before continuing on to IAIN for his first degree in *Tarbiya*. From there he continued his studies spent in Egypt, where he spent over a decade (1973–1984) taking a second degree at al-Azhar, followed by a Masters in *Tarbiya* and a doctorate in the field of comparative Islamic jurisprudence (Ar. *fiqh al-muqarran*) at ʿAyn Shams University.

he has done this through a balancing act that echoes in many ways that of Ujong Rimba in the earlier history of Aceh's Ulama Council. Although Muslim Ibrahim's own Islamic education was largely Modernist, he has carefully cultivated relationships with the Traditionalist ulama of the *dayah* community. This is reflected in his public statements on issues of Islamic legal interpretation in which he regularly attempts to balance Traditionalist and Modernist opinions.[72]

While occasionally giving preference to certain rulings favored by Traditionalists on some particular issues, the general approach to Islam held by Muslim Ibrahim and much of the central leadership of the MPU is nevertheless generally oriented toward modernizing reform. In this there are clear echoes of broader Muslim discourses of *daʿwa* and public education as the means for both religious and social reform that stretch back several decades to developments in Egypt when Muslim Ibrahim was a student there. At that time, the agenda of the Muslim Brotherhood was reconfigured to emphasize *daʿwa* and education.[73] Under the leadership of Ḥasan al-Huḍaybī (d. 1973) and thereafter, increasing stress was laid upon fostering a greater "awareness" of Islam as a crucial means of laying the groundwork for Islamizing agendas of social change. The goal was thus not one of revolutionary change, but rather of an ordered, gradual progress toward the goal of redefining society in a particular image of Islam.[74] Muslim Ibrahim has likewise repeatedly advocated precisely this kind of a "gradualist" (I. *penahapan*) approach to the implementation of Islamic law in Aceh.[75]

Upon his return after more than a decade of studying in Cairo, Muslim Ibrahim taught at the IAIN in Banda Aceh, and became active on the Ulama Council—then a provincial branch of the MUI. One of his responsibilities was the translation of Arabic works for the Council, and in addition to a slew of contemporary writings on particular issues of *fiqh*, he also produced an Indonesian translation of an Arabic edition of Dale Carnegie's *How to Win Friends and Influence People*. While the "Islamic" application of such a work might not be intuitive to many, this American managerial self-help guru has subsequently come to be cited in broader Indonesian

[72] Examples of this can be found particularly in his regular contributions to Aceh's leading daily newspaper, *Serambi*, under the rubric of "Konsultasi Agama Islam."

[73] For a general overview of the *daʿwa* milieu in Egypt at that time, see Carrie Rosefsky Wickham, *Mobilizing Islam: Religion, Activism, and Political Change in Egypt* (New York: Columbia University Press, 2002), 119–49.

[74] On al-Huḍaybī and the re-orientation of the Muslim Brotherhood's ideology during his tenure, see Barbara H.E. Zollner, *The Muslim Brotherhood: Hasan al-Hudaybi and Ideology* (Abingdon: Routledge, 2009).

[75] His most extended treatment of the topic can be found in: Muslim Ibrahim, *Penahapan dalam Legislasi dan Penerapan Syariʿat Islam* (Jakarta: Cahaya Ilahi, 2006).

discourses on "socialization" (I. *sosialisasi*).[76] The Indonesian rhetoric of *sosialisasi* has, as will be discussed further in the chapters that follow, emerged as a key organizing principle in the state implementation of Islamic law in contemporary Aceh and is closely connected to evolving conceptions of religious propagation and public pedagogy.

This approach to the "socialization" of Shariʿa and its role in society frames the pronounced emphasis on education (Ar./I. *tarbiya*) and *daʿwa*, even over the technical aspects of jurisprudence and positive law, in the work of the MPU and other institutions of state Shariʿa in Aceh. This vision of Shariʿa implementation primarily as a mode of mass education, rather than one that stresses coercive sanctions, is something that has also been emphasized by prominent visitors to Aceh hosted by the Ulama Council. One striking example of this came from the Grand Mufti of Syria, Dr. Ahmad Badr al-Din Hassan, at an event chaired by Muslim Ibrahim at the IAIN Banda Aceh in October 2009. The confirmation of the MPU's agenda by this external authority was widely published in the local press, quoting the Mufti's call to emphasize the teaching and inculcation of Islamic moral values, rather than coercive punishment in the application of Islamic law.[77]

The subsuming of law under a more dominant rubric of education can be traced across much of the discourse of the MPU and its staff.[78] Muslim Ibrahim has even referred to law (I. *hukum*) as a kind of "strong education" (I. *pendidikan keras*), because, as he puts it, "for some people, education in school is not sufficient to cultivate proper understandings and behavior."[79] In this understanding of law as a means for inculcating positive values, coercive enforcement is not employed primarily as a punishment for particular crimes that were committed, but rather as a means of generating a deterrent effect. As one clerk working in the administrative section of the MPU central office put it, "in certain cases, force must be used, for example, on the issue of headscarves and modest dress—there, coercion is necessary in order to raise awareness of the seriousness of the issue."[80]

The educational function of Aceh's Shariʿa legal system is stressed in a broad range of ways by people involved in its various institutions,

[76] See, for example, "10 Tips Meningkatkan Kemampuan Sosialisasi Anda ala Dale Carnegie," <http://www.scribd.com/doc/5593201/Dale-Carnegie-Tips>, accessed 29 March 2012.

[77] "Grand Mufti Suriah: Syariat Islam tidak Mengedepankan Hukuman," *Serambi* (15 October 2009), 1.

[78] It is also apparent in the work of the other state Shariʿa institutions in contemporary Aceh, as will be discussed in the chapters that follow.

[79] Interview with Muslim Ibrahim, 12 April 2011 at Banda Aceh.

[80] Interview with MPU office staff member, 18 November 2008 at Banda Aceh.

including the MPU. The MPU works together with various governmental institutions in Aceh, including the State Shariʿa Agency (DSI), to coordinate programs for the *sosialisasi* of official versions of Islamic law, including approval of the syllabus and the development of *daʿwa* materials as well as providing advice on the management of funds to be spent on honoraria for preachers and physical improvements to Islamic schools.[81] They also develop guidelines for Islamic education and proselytizing in schools, ranging from *dayahs* to universities, as well as for preaching in government workplaces and more informal settings in towns and villages.[82] Branches of the MPU also coordinate with their local Religious Affairs Offices (Kantor Urusan Agama/KUA) to define a basic syllabus of religious knowledge that every Muslim must be tested in before they are able to have their marriages officially registered.[83]

FATWAS AND OTHER ADVICE

Like its predecessor under the New Order, one of the MPU's main functions is to "give direction on religious issues on which there are differences of opinion."[84] This was, not coincidentally, also a major part of the founding mission statement of PUSA. The means of "clarifying" and communicating the message of Islam is pursued through the promotion of public discourse across a broad range of genres—from the mass media to official fatwas. During the 1990s, the Indonesian National Council of Ulama (MUI) began to take steps toward initiating more ambitious programs for *daʿwa* and development.[85] At the provincial level, Aceh's Ulama Council was moving even further along those lines at the time. In 1995, Aceh's Ulama Council

[81] Amirullah M. Diyah, Mustafa Ahmad, & Azhari Ali, *Pokok Pikiran MPU Aceh Utara* (white paper issued by the North Aceh MPU, 3 February 2006).

[82] Tgk. H. Jamaluddin A (team leader/Ketua), *Konsep Pendidikan Agama Islam di Semua Jenjang Pendidikan dan Kerjasama Lembaga Pendidikan Formal dengan Lembaga Pendidikan Informal* (Bireuen: Official document issued by the Majelis Permusyawaratan Ulama Kabupaten Bireuen, 2008).

[83] Majelis Permusyawaratan Ulama (MPU), *Materi Pembakalan Pembinaan Calon Linto dan Dara Baro (CALINDA)*, (Lhoksuemawe: Majelis Permusyawaratan Ulama Kota Lhokseumawe, 2007). This booklet includes an end sheet containing a printed form for a test of Islamic religious knowledge to be filled out and signed by the imam of the local mosque that administers the test, as well as an official from the KUA.

[84] LOGA 140.1.b. See also Abidin Nurdin, "Ulama dan Proses Legislasi: Mengkaji Legitimasi Lembaga Ulama Aceh," in Arskal Salim and Adlin Sila (eds.), *Serambi Mekkah yang Berubah: Views from Within* (Jakarta: Pustaka Alvabet, 2010), 110.

[85] Mohamad Atho Mudzhar, "The Ulama, the Government, and Society in Modern Indonesia: The Indonesian Council of Ulama Revisited," in Johan Meuleman (ed.), *Islam in the Era of Globalization: Muslim Attitudes towards Modernity and Identity* (Jakarta: INIS, 2001), 315–26.

issued a fatwa on the general topic of "enjoining right and forbidding wrong" (Ar. *al-amr bi'l-ma'rūf wa'l-nahy 'an-munkar*). It stressed the need for the ulama to work together with government authorities to address a list of social ills, namely sexual impropriety, alcohol, and gambling.[86]

The production of fatwas for Acehnese Muslims has long been linked to broader doctrinal controversies and informed by political contexts both within and beyond the region.[87] The official Ulama Council founded under the independent Indonesian state in 1965 has clearly been no exception. However, the ways in which its work has related to the political agenda of the state that sponsored it have by no means been completely predictable or uniform over time. Although the Ulama Council was founded by a governmental initiative, that did not guarantee that it always took the official line of the New Order state. There is indeed considerably more to the story than simple co-optation. As Robert Hefner has highlighted in a recent work on Shari'a politics:

> ... there is no reason to assume that all social movements are state centric in orientation. As with movements in other religious traditions, Islamic social movements tend to be as much concerned with changing citizens and society as they are with challenging the state.[88]

Keeping this important point in mind, we can see more clearly that participation within the state-affiliated Ulama Council involved complex configurations of diverse motivations including active attempts by Islamic leaders to create an Islamic society and an expression of Muslim identity, while also asserting their membership and participation within the independent Indonesian state.

M.B. Hooker has highlighted the major role that the national-level MUI has played in "the bureaucratization of Islam" while also noting that the influence of this bureaucratization on specific policy statements has, by

[86] "Keputusan Rapat Kerja Komisi 'B' (Fatwa/Hukum) Majelis Ulama Indonesia Propinsi Daerah Istimewa Aceh Nomor 01/I/1990," *Kumpulan Fatwa-fatwa Majelis Ulama Daerah Istimewa Aceh* (Banda Aceh: MPU, 2005), 320–2. This presents a further reiteration of a familiar repertoire of concerns that would come to be codified in the legislation of Aceh's twenty-first century Islamic legal system. These laws will be discussed further in Chapter 5.

[87] For example, 'Abd al-Salām b. Idrīs al-Āshī was the translator of the bilingual (Arabic and Malay) compilation of fatwas produced in Mecca in 1892. This text includes a number of fatwas dealing with cases arising in Aceh, ranging from the permissibility of various pre-Islamic cultural practices to the politics of living under a non-Muslim occupational government. Nico J.G. Kaptein (ed.), *The Muhimmāt al-Nafā'is: A Bilingual Meccan Fatwa Collection for Indonesian Muslims from the End of the Nineteenth Century* (Jakarta: INIS, 1997), 10–12.

[88] Robert W. Hefner, "Islamic Schools, Social Movements, and Democracy in Indonesia," in Robert W. Hefner (ed.), *Making Modern Muslims: The Politics of Islamic Education in Southeast Asia* (Honolulu: University of Hawai'i Press, 2009), 70.

no means, been invariably in support of Indonesian government policy, and in fact, at times they were in clear opposition.[89] On the latter point, he cites the research of Mohammad Atho Mudzhar, who has characterized the fatwas issued by the MUI during the New Order period as ranging widely between those clearly supportive of government policies (e.g., family planning), to others that have actually contradicted government policies (e.g., Christmas celebrations).[90] In general, however, the MUI has continued to express a strong sense of nationalism, as well as an emphatic commitment to defending the Indonesian *umma* from any perceived threat.[91] They have also been increasingly pro-active in determining which issues should be addressed rather than waiting for the government to request a fatwa—and in their specific pronouncements, they have exhibited an increasing tendency to prioritize their religious positions, rather than policy concerns. The situation then is one of an official body of "state ulama" who have come to use that position to promote their own interpretations of Islam.

Given the role played by the military in its formation and the close connection with other branches of the Indonesian state throughout the New Order and during the conflict with GAM, it needs to be asked whether Aceh's Ulama Council has followed a different path in negotiating its relationship with the state. Examining the fatwas and other public statements that they have produced presents its own complex picture of shared interests in broad social and political matters (e.g., anti-communism and Indonesian nationalism) alongside decisions on specific religious issues reflecting the doctrinal positions of local ulama. The MPU disseminates its interpretations of Islam and rulings on such diverse issues not only through fatwas but also various other means, including official statements of "advice" (I. *tausiyah*), reports on various topics issued by MPU committees, handbooks, sermon materials for preachers, academic publications, and more popular forms of public media.[92] These materials are moreover not only produced

[89] M.B. Hooker, *Indonesian Islam: Social Change through Contemporary Fatawa* (Crows Nest, NSW: Allen & Unwin, 2003), 60.

[90] Mohamad Atho Mudzhar, *Islam and Islamic Law in Indonesia: A Socio-Historical Approach* (Jakarta: Office of Religious Research, Development and Training—Ministry of Religious Affairs, 2003), 146–7. For his more detailed study of the fatwas produced by the MUI under the New Order, see *The Fatwas of the Council of Indonesian Ulama*.

[91] John Olle, "The Majelis Ulama Indonesia versus 'Heresy': The Resurgence of Authoritarian Islam," in Gerry van Klinken and Joshua Barker (eds.), *State of Authority: The State in Society in Indonesia* (Ithaca: Cornell University Southeast Asia Program, 2009); Stuart Fenwick, "Yusman Roy and the Language of Devotion: 'Innovation' in Indonesian Islam on Trial," *Studia Islamika* 18.3 (2011) 497–529.

[92] The latter cover the broadest range of topics, from the reform of established religious practice, to the rampant problem of corruption in governmental administration and electoral politics/*Kajian Komisi "A" Majlis Permusyawaratan Ulama (MPU) Kota Lhokseumawe No. 247/2006 tentang Korupsi, Kolusi dan Nepotisme (KKN) serta Money Politik* (Commission report—MPU Kota Lhokseumawe, 2006).

by the central MPU office in Banda Aceh, but by various district-level (I. *kabupaten*) branches as well.[93]

In his study of the national-level MUI, Nur Ichwan has identified a "reformist strategy" in which fatwas and *tausiyahs* were employed to bring Indonesian Muslims closer to its understanding of "orthodoxy."[94] We have already described the ways in which Aceh's Ulama Council was called upon to support the broad agenda of the New Order developmentalist state. In the next section, we will trace their opinions on more specific issues of Islamic interpretation to demonstrate the ways that Aceh's Islamic religious leadership used the facilities made available to them through the Ulama Council to propagate their own understandings of Islam through governing individual practice and public behavior.

RULINGS ON RELIGION AND SOCIETY

Much of the public discourse of Aceh's Ulama Council is centered on issues of social order and morality. Their positions on such issues circulate through diverse media, ranging from reports of its sub-committees on the acceptability (or not) of men and women shaking hands,[95] to circular letters asking local religious leaders for their help in informing their communities that Islam prohibits stealing electricity through undocumented splices off of the power grid.[96] The MPU also frequently makes pronouncements on what it considers to be the acceptable types of public events, with repeated instructions that distinguish "sinful" (I. *maksiat*) from "permissible" (I. *mubah*), and "proper Islamic" (I. *Islami*) forms of entertainment.[97] These categories are also used in

[93] For example, the North Aceh office of the MPU produces a quarterly glossy illustrated magazine entitled *Nida' Al-Islam* containing articles produced by local scholars on issues ranging from the interpretation of classical texts to thematic essays on contemporary social issues.

[94] Moch. Nur Ichwan, "Ulama and Politics: Majelis Ulama Indonesia in the Early Reformation Era," in Moch. Nur Ichwan, and Noorhaidi Hasan (eds.), *Moving with the Times: The Dynamics of Contemporary Islam in a Changing Indonesia* (Yogyakarta: UIN Sunan Kalijaga, 2007), 92–7.

[95] Majelis Permusyawaratan Ulama (MPU), *Berjabat Tangan (Mushafahah) antara Laki-laki dan Perempuan Ajnabiyah menurut Hukum Islam* (Lhokseumawe: Majelis Permusyawaratan Ulama Kota Lhokseumawe, 2005).

[96] This particular missive (sent to *imeum masjid, imeum meunasah*, and leaders of *dayah* and *pesantren*) was sent out by the Majelis Permusyawaratan Ulama (MPU) Kota Lhokseumawe on 31 August 2006.

[97] For example: *Kesimpulan Musyawarah Ulama Kabupaten Aceh Utara dan Kota Lhokseumawe tentang Keramaian Malam* (Circular letter issued on 20 July 2006). For a report on the public action taken in response to this fatwa, see "5,000 Terompet Disita," *Rakyat Aceh* (2 January 2008), 2.

provincial-level *tausiyah* on the permissible forms of public observance for events ranging from solar new year celebrationsto the commemoration of the 2004 earthquake and tsunami.[98]

The MPU also issues public statements on weightier issues of social justice that appeal as much to universal human values as to specifically Islamic conceptions of morality.[99] Specific examples of this range from the condemnation of the robbery and violent assault of a local Chinese businessman and his family, to calls for the Saudi Arabian government to mete out harsh penalties to its own citizens charged with the abuse of Indonesian domestic workers.[100] The MPU has also engaged with broader discussions of social issues, issuing statements condemning terrorism and the chronic problem of corruption.[101]

Much of the activity for Aceh's Ulama Council is focused on providing guidance on matters of Islamic religious belief and practice. Fundamental to this is the Council's assertion of the exclusive right of authorized religious specialists to decide on issues of Islamic law and its interpretation.[102] This was re-emphasized in a fatwa issued in 2008 that not only recognized the legitimacy of rulings based on the opinions of scholars adhering to an established "school" (Ar. *madhhab*), but also made the acceptance of such opinions from officially-recognized ulama obligatory (Ar. *wājib*) for those who were not qualified to exercise independent judicial reasoning (Ar. *ijtihād*) themselves.[103] Such a ruling

[98] *Taushiyah Majelis Permusyawaratan Ulama (MPU) No. 6/ 2008 tentang Peringatan Tsunami dan Menyambut Tahun Baru* (Tahun Baru Hijriyah dan Miladiyah).

[99] The Council also issues specific instructions for acceptable modes of democratic participation, generally issued as *tausiyah* in anticipation of local elections. In such circulars, it is stated that choosing local leadership is obligatory (Ar. *wājib*) according to Islam, and Muslims are urged to exercise their right to vote. There are also guidelines for choosing the candidate for which one should vote. In such texts, it is stated that acceptable candidates should generally meet the criteria of being free of the taint of corruption, committed to the prosperity of the community and economic development, able to uphold the standards of Islamic morality and the duty to "enjoin good and forbid evil," as well as being fit to perform the duties of prayer leader (Ar./I. *imam*) or preacher (Ar./I. *khatib*), and able to read and understand the Qur'ān. Statements along these lines have been repeated in numerous *tausiyah* over recent years. These particular examples are taken from *Taushiyah Majelis Permusyawaratan Ulama (MPU) Kota Lhokseumawe No. 247/2006 tentang Pemilihan Kepala Daerah dan Walikota/Wakil Walikota Lhokseumawe.*

[100] See, for example, "Ulama Kutuk Insiden Perampokan Ranto Peureulak," *Serambi* (21 November 2010), 13; and "Ulama Hukum Berat Penyiksa Sumiati," *Waspada* (19 November 2010), 3.

[101] "MPU Aceh: Teror Termasuk Dosa Besar," Waspada Online (1 July 2010), <http://www.waspada.co.id/index.php?option=com_content&view=article&id=127022:mpu-aceh-teror-termasuk-dosa-besar&catid=13&Itemid=26>, accessed 12 October 2011; "Ulama Aceh Bahas Fiqih Anti Korupsi," *Waspada* (28 November 2008), 7.

[102] *Keputusan Rapat Kerja Komisi 'A' Majelis Ulama Provinsi Daerah Istimewa Aceh tentang Talfiq* (16 July 1978).

[103] *Fatwa Majelis Permusyawaratan Ulama Provinsi Nanggroe Aceh Darussalam No. 451/1167/2008 tentang Beberapa Masalah Aqidah, Syari'ah (Fiqh) dan Akhlak.*

could be seen as potentially strengthening the authority of Traditionalist ulama. In Aceh, however, Modernist scholars in the line of PUSA have for nearly a century been considered by many local Muslims to be ulama as well—and thus they would not be bound themselves to adhere to only to rulings based upon the established interpretations of the traditional "schools" (Ar. *madhhab*/pl. *madhāhib*) of Islamic jurisprudence. Rather, their own pronouncements as ulama could (in light of this ruling) also be regarded as valid opinions to be followed by ordinary Muslims. This, again, points to the complex balancing act of Traditionalist and Modernist interests in the composition and work of Aceh's Ulama Council.

At the same time, the MPU has also attempted to recognize aspects of diversity within the Muslim community in handling issues on which it acknowledges legitimate differences of judicial opinion. For example, in 1975, the small local Muhammadiyah branch in the district of Singkil (on the border between Aceh and the province of West Sumatra) requested a fatwa on the permissibility of the reading of a second *khutba* during the prayers marking the end of the fasting month—hoping for a ruling in favor of their Modernist position on the issue. After listing proof texts in support of both positions, the resulting fatwa ruled that in order to preserve Muslim solidarity and national unity, either position could be held as valid, with the proviso that it is forbidden to impose the interpretation of any one group on another.[104]

Sentiments of this type have been echoed repeatedly for decades in the fatwa decisions and published statements of Aceh's Ulama Council.[105] In some cases, tolerance is demonstrated for aspects of ritual worship that are the subject of debate among jurists. On the other hand, the MPU tends to take a somewhat harder stance against other practices that are well established as local tradition, but without authoritative textual grounding in Islamic scholarship. Such is the case with *kenduri kematian*, referring to ritual funerary feasts held at the home of a deceased person's family at specified intervals on nights following his or her death. The MPU has officially criticized such practices, stating that they placed unnecessary burdens upon families already suffering hardship. The Council's prohibition of this practice was, however, tempered with words cautioning against taking harsh measures to put an end to something that is so deeply grounded in Acehnese social life. Thus, for example, one local circular on

[104] *Fatwa Majelis Ulama Provinsi Daerah Istimewa Aceh tentang Khutba Hari Raya* (8 December 1975).

[105] As, for example, in the following Lhokseumawe City Ulama Council's circular on the practice of *qunut*: Tgk. Hamdani Daudand Tgk. Azhari, *Pembahasan Masaalah Qunut dalam Shalat* (Lhokseumawe: Majelis Permusyawaratan Ulama Aceh Utara, 2006).

the subject clearly states that the practice of *kenduri kematian* is forbidden by Islam, and that those who respect this prohibition will earn heavenly rewards. At the same time, however, it advises agents of religious reform that they have to proceed wisely in confronting a practice with such deep roots in their local communities.[106] This approach is striking when compared to the much more uncompromising tone of PUSA proclamations on the subject issued over 50 years ago urging that *kenduri kematian* be abandoned "as quickly as possible."[107] Indeed, when comparing the positions of the twenty-first-century MPU with those of its predecessors under both PUSA and the Darul Islam, there is a sense of moderation on some issues that had previously served to sharply delineate "Modernist" from "Traditionalist" Muslims in Aceh.

SUFISM AND ITS MALCONTENTS

As an institution bringing together advocates for modernizing Islamic reform and Traditionalists from Aceh's *dayah*, the MPU has had to walk a particularly challenging path in dealing with debates over the legitimacy of forms of belief and practices associated with Sufism. As discussed in previous chapters, Sufi traditions have long histories in Aceh, and the practices of the Naqshbandī order in particular are deeply rooted in many *dayah*. However, there are also trends of Islamic Modernist reform in Aceh that are highly critical of beliefs and practices associated with Sufism. In an attempt to balance the concerns of its various constituencies, the dominant tone of the MPU's discourse in dealing with the issue has tended to be one of moderate Sufi reform, rather than a comprehensive condemnation. Here again, the efforts of an official institution of Aceh's state Shariʿa system have been directed toward managing processes of social change.

Debates over various aspects of Sufi practice have occupied the attention of Aceh's Ulama Council since the first years of its existence. In 1972, Aceh's Ulama Council formed a "Special Committee" tasked with studying the historical development and contemporary practices of Sufi orders in Aceh, and issued a fatwa forbidding the building of any structures over gravesites.[108] Two years later, a new fatwa was issued

[106] Dewan Paripurna Ulama, *Kenduri Kematian* (Lhokseumawe: Majelis Permusyawaratan Ulama (MPU) Kota Lhokseumawe, 2004), 9.

[107] *Maklumat Bersama* (Kutaradja/Banda Aceh: PUSA, 1948).

[108] *Keputusan Komisi A Majelis Ulama Provinsi Daerah Istimewa Aceh mengenai Maslah Thariqat* (22 March 1972); *Keputusan Komisi A Majelis Ulama Provinsi Daerah Istimewa Aceh mengenai Bangunan diatas Kuburan* (23 March 1972). This, of course, did not put an end to the practice, and the decision prohibiting such construction had to be officially repeated on

against any Sufi practices that "would interfere with the progress of national or provincial-level development projects."[109] This ruling was justified with an enumeration of various "excesses" of Sufism that place it beyond the bounds of the "pure creed" (I. *aqida murni*) of Islam, and was structured as an explicitly modern reformist critique that cast Sufism as both a vestige of heresies accumulated over time, and as a potential future threat to political and economic stability. In particular, it argues that participation in Sufi ritual practice "fosters a condition of mental stagnation and apathy that is clearly apparent to any observer. Such a condition is dangerous for national development and national security."[110]

The fears of ecstatic mystics causing social disruption and distracting Muslims from the pursuit of national development goals were occasionally confirmed for some by media reports of abuses, secrecy, and violent emotional outbursts among circles of Sufi practitioners. To take one relatively recent example, in 2008, the local press was abuzz with the story of a "blood bath" in which a crazed devotee struck out wildly at fellow participants in a *suluk* ritual in North Aceh.[111] At that time, the activities of a local branch of the Naqshbandiyya order raised concerns among some reform-minded activists and officials in Kebun Ubi, Aceh Tamiang. In response, other groups of ulama argued that "Sufism" was not the problem here. The Persatuan Dayah Inshafuddin, for example, appealed to a 1961 Ministry of Religion statement recognizing the legitimacy of the *Naqshbandī* order and used the opportunity to argue further that the same degree of state recognition should be extended to all other "acceptable" (Ar. *muʿtabara*) orders as well.[112] In response, the MPU issued a fatwa that did not condemn, but rather upheld in principle the

several occasions since, including in a letter to the Resident (I. *Bupati*) of Pidie (MU PDIA Surat No. 769/MU/1976).

[109] This *fatwa* directly references the 1973 National Plan (GBHN). *Keputusan Komisi A Majelis Ulama Provinsi Daerah Istimewa Aceh* (7 November 1974).

[110] This report is included as an appendix published in: *Kumpulan Fatwa-fatwa Majelis Ulama Propinsi Daerah Istimewa Aceh tahun 1965 s/d 31 Maret 1979* (Banda Aceh: Sekretariat Majelis Permusyawaratan Ulama, 2006), 135–60. In 1975, the East Aceh branch of the Majelis Ulama held its own workshop on the issue of Sufi orders (I. *thariqat*), which concluded that "[i]n general, Sufism carries with it tendencies for creating a cult of the individual around its teachers, and thus deviates from the principal teachings of Islam." *Hasil Keputusan Raker Majelis Ulama Keb.Aceh Timor yang Berlangsung dari tanggal 31 January s/d 2 Pebruari 1975 di Langsa, Arsip Propinsi Aceh – 272/41.*

[111] "Peserta Suluk Mengamuk, Tiga Santri Tewas Ditikam; Dayah Sa'adatun Banjir Darah," *Metro Aceh* (13 September 2008), 1. The practice of *suluk* has been at the center of modern polemics about the legitimacy of Sufi practice in Southeast Asia for more than a century. In fact, Michael Laffan has identified this issue at the very beginning of influential critiques printed at Singapore in al-Imam in 1908. Michael Laffan, "Understanding al-Imam's Critique of Tariqa Sufism," in Azyumardi Azra, Kees van Dijk, and Nico J.G. Kaptein (eds.), *Varieties of Religious Authority: Changes and Challenges in 20th Century Indonesian Islam* (Singapore: ISEAS Press, 2010), 27–35.

[112] For more on the ways in which recognition of acceptable Sufi orders has been configured in Indonesian Islamic legal discourse more broadly, see Michael F. Laffan,

right for members of that local branch to continue their Sufi practices since they belonged to a recognized and acceptable order.[113] In August 2010, the provincial office of the MPU issued a fatwa outlining the criteria that Sufi orders must meet in order to be officially "recognized," and listed the name of ten specific orders that were deemed to have met these requirements.[114] Aceh's Ulama Council dealt with issues related to Sufism with more nuanced approaches to traditions with long-established roots in the region.

More aggressive "anti-Sufi" agendas by Islamic Modernists and Revivalists in Aceh have thus been restrained in the face of resistance from Traditionalist Muslims who have maintained certain established local traditions of Sufi belief and practice. For example, in a recent statement on a well-known eighteenth-century Malay work, the *Durr al-Nafīs* of Muḥammad Nafīs al-Banjārī was singled out as a text that has been frequently misinterpreted, resulting in the spread of misinterpretations of Islamic doctrine.[115] Consequently, the MPU recommended that this text not be taught to those with inadequate religious knowledge.[116] It was not, then, Sufism as such, but rather perceived "Sufi excesses" and the potential for complex models of Sufi cosmology to be misunderstood by uneducated Muslims that were the major concerns of the Council.

In this context, teachings associated with local imaginations of the "monistic" Sufi cosmology of the *wujūdiyya* have been a frequent object of criticism by those seeking to purify Islamic belief and practice in Aceh.[117]

"Lightning Angels and Prayers for the Nation: Reading the Fatwas of the Jamiʿah Ahlith Thoriqoh al-Muʿtabaroh," in R. Michael Feener and Mark E. Cammack (eds.), *Islamic Law in Contemporary Indonesia: Ideas and Institutions* (Cambridge, Mass.: Harvard University Press, 2007), 66–80.

[113] *Fatwa Majelis Permusyawaratan Ulama Nanggroe Aceh Darussalam No. 07/2008 tentang Thariqat Naqsyabandiyah di Kebun Ubi, Aceh Tamiang.*

[114] "MPU Keluarkan Fatwa Thariqat Muktabarah," *Serambi* (9 August 2010), 3. This list was comprised of the following orders: Naqshbandiyya, Qādiriyya, Khālidiyya, Khalwatiyya, Muḥammadiyya, Shādhiliyya, Shaṭṭariyya, Dasūqiyya, Akhbāriyya, and al-Mufarradiyya. Merle Ricklefs notes that this list differs somewhat from that of the orders recognized by the Nahdlatul Ulama (NU) on Java, with the notable absence of the Sammāniyya, Tijāniyya, and especially the "Qādiriyya wa Naqshbandiyya" order (personal communication, 10 August 2012).

[115] *Muḥammad Nafsb. Idrīs b. al-Ḥusayn al-Banjārī, al-Durr al-nafīs fī bayān waḥdat al-afʿāl wa'l-asmā' wa'l-ṣifāt wa'l-dhāt al-taqdīs* (multiple printings in Cairo, Mecca, and various places in Southeast Asia over the past century and a half). Into the twentieth century, however, this work was sometimes printed in the margins of editions of another Malay Sufi text that is generally not considered as problematic by self-appointed contemporary enforcers of "orthodoxy"—ʿAbd al-Ṣamad al-Palimbānī (al-Jāwī)'s work drawing on Abū Ḥāmid al-Ghazālī's Bidāyat al-hidāyat. *Hidāyat al-Sālikīn fī Sulūk Maslak al-Muttaqīn* (Cairo: Muṣṭafāal-Bābī al-Ḥalabī, 1923).

[116] *Majelis Permusyawaratan Aceh, Kesimpulan Mubahasah Ulama Aceh Terhadap Pemahaman yang Menimbulkan Bidʿahdan Syubhat* (3 August 2009).

[117] For example, in 2010, a major meeting of prominent Acehnese ulama was convened at Dayah Malikussaleh in Pantonlabu (North Aceh). Under the leadership of the doyen of

As discussed in Chapter 2, traditional forms of belief about the "unity of Being" (Ar. *waḥdat al-wujūd*) have a long history in Aceh, dating back to at least the seventeenth century. However, in the modern period, the term *wujūdiyya* has come to serve as a general term of disparagement for any form of esoteric belief or practice that arouses suspicion, regardless of any historical connection it may have to local form of traditions associated with Ibn ʿArabī.[118] This often results in rather piecemeal (and frequently recycled) elements being combined in various forms in the cases brought against various groups. For example, in calling for the North Aceh MPU to issue a fatwa against a group known as the "*Salek Buta*," one local *dayah* leader, Tgk. Mustafa of Dayah Paloh Gadeng (Kreung Geukuh), claimed that the group's main text of reference was the "*Kitāb Insān Kāmil*"—in an obvious rhetorical attempt to associate this contemporary movement with a now discredited tradition widely regarded as "heterodox" by contemporary Indonesian Muslims.[119] Thus in such cases where local Sufi practice cannot establish clear links with an order recognized as "acceptable" to broader contexts of Islamic orthodoxy, its treatment often loses the nuance of internal debates on Sufi reform and instead slides into the field of public polemics of "deviant teachings" (I. *aliran/ajaran sesat*).

DEFENDING ISLAM AGAINST THREATS OF DEVIANCE

Fatwas on various groups identified as "deviant" (I. *sesat*) by Aceh's Ulama Council stretch back to the 1970s, often in the form of decisions that emphasized the potential threat that such groups posed to social stability (see Figure 4.1).[120] Local newspapers in Aceh regularly print stories about

Aceh's *dayah* ulama, Abuya Muhibuddin Wali, the Mubahasah Tinggi announced its decision to uphold the established creed of "*Ahlussunnah Waljamaah*" (Ar. *ahl al-sunna wa'l-jamāʿa*—which, in contemporary Indonesia, generally encompasses in principle both *Āshʿarī* and Māturīdī *kalām*), while condemning the more speculative cosmology associated with the Sufi conception of *waḥhdat al-wujūd*. "Gubernur Minta Ulamatidak Lepas Tangan," *Serambi* (18 May 2010), 1.

[118] For the earlier historical background of polemics on the *wujūdiyya* in Aceh, see Syed Muhammad Naguib al-Attas, *Rānīrī and the Wujūdiyah of 17th Century Aceh* (Kuala Lumpur: Monographs of the Malaysian Branch Royal Asiatic Society, 1966).

[119] "Penganut Sekta Salek Buta Sesatdan Murtad," *Rakyat Aceh* (6 January 2010), 1–2. The generic title supplied here refers to the concept of a "perfect man" who has complete progression along the Sufi path, which is associated with the doctrines of Ibn ʿArabī (d. 1240) and al-Jīlī (d. c.1428).

[120] In many such cases, these concerns are directly indexed to the central government's master plan for economic development (*Garis-Garis Besar Haluan Negara*/GBHN). See, for example, *Keputusan Raker Komisi 'A' Majelis Ulama Provinsi Daerah Istimewa Aceh tentang Ajaran Makrifatullah dan Ajaran Ahmad Arifin* (16 July 1978).

Figure 4.1. The specter of a "deviant sect" (I. *aliran sesat*) leading youth astray: The concerned Muslim elder exclaims, "Oh! How is it possible that there are such deviant sects in the Land of Sharia!" Cartoon by Olexs/Firmansyah, *Modus Aceh* 50.VIII, 11–17 April 2011: 2– Reproduced with permission.

petitions made to local MPU branches to ban various groups, publications, and activities that are perceived as a threat to dominant contemporary conceptions of Islamic orthodoxy.[121] The preoccupation with policing the borders of Islam to protect the community from the dangers of deviant teachings is not unique to Aceh.[122] During the New Order period, Indonesian national discourses on deviant sects were also often couched in terms of the need to preserve public order and maintain the unity of the Muslim community.[123] The persecution of heresy has assumed even more prominence in the profile of the MUI at the national level during the post-Suharto period.[124] Well beyond the MUI, moreover, there has also been a significant increase in attempts to "impose conformity of Islamic

[121] "MPU Larang Ajaran Hendri Dikembangkan di Abdya," *Serambi* (20 July 2007), 1; "Aktifkan Pengajian Antisipasi Ajaran Sesat," *Aceh Independen* (25 March 2009), 4; "Ekses Ceramah Menyesatkan: MPU Akan Panggil Tgk. Kasim," *Harian Aceh* (6 June 2009), 5.

[122] It is also, for example, a major issue across the Straits in contemporary Malaysia. See Hiroko Kushimoto, "*Ajaran Sesat* (deviant teachings): The Official Views on Sufism in Malaysia," Proceedings of the KIAS/SIAS Joint International Workshop "Struggling Muslims in the Modern and Present-day Eras: Political, Social, and Religious Aspects of their Endeavours" (Tokyo: Sophia University, 22 February 2012).

[123] M.B. Hooker, *Indonesian Syariah: Defining a National School of Islamic Law* (Singapore: ISEAS, 2008), 31.

[124] Olle, "The Majelis Ulama Indonesia versus 'Heresy'," 107.

belief" at various local levels in Indonesia since the turn of the twenty-first century, as Merle Ricklefs has extensively documented.[125]

Attention to such matters has increased over recent years in Aceh as well with stories about various perceived threats to Islamic "orthodoxy" regularly taking hold of local media attention.[126] These reports have produced a strong sense of vulnerability in some sectors, leading to calls for the revitalization of the mission pioneered by the Prophet in developing a strong community through the "implantation" of proper belief into the souls of its members.[127] In an appeal for more urgent attention to the defense of proper doctrine from deviant interpretations, one Acehnese *dayah* leader has written:

> Often Muslims are confused amid the myriad understandings of and challenges to Islamic belief. In such a situation, one needs the ability and discrimination to evaluate each and every stream of thought that confronts him.[128]

Prominent Muslim academics and leading officers of Aceh's Islamic legal institutions have also perceived the need for such work, with the MPU making the issue of ensuring doctrinal integrity a central aspect of the state Shariʿa project.[129] The DSI has gone even further to stress that the state has a primary obligation (I. *kewajiban*) to promote orthodox understandings of belief and to police public discourse against threats of doctrinal deviance.[130] For its part, the MPU has enthusiastically performed its self-appointed role of protecting the community from the dangers of deviant teachings.[131] One prominent figure in the organization has expressed the urgency of its work in this area by characterizing what is perceived as a colossal wave of assaults on the integrity of Islamic belief and practice as a tragedy more devastating than the actual tsunami of 2004.[132] Another has likened deviant teachings to "poison" that must be sucked out

[125] M.C. Ricklefs, *Islamisation and Its Opponents in Java: A Political, Social, Cultural and Religious History, c. 1930 to the Present* (Singapore: NUS Press, 2012), 318–40.

[126] This included, for example, the circulation of CDs and other digital media containing suspect teachings. "Soal CD Pendangkalan Akidah: MPU Bireuen Didesak Keluarkan Fatwa," *Serambi* (20 November 2010), 9.

[127] Iskandar Ibrahim, "Syariat Islam Yang Solutif," in Syamsul Rijal (ed.), *Syariat Islam dan Paradigma Kemanusiaan* (Banda Aceh: Dinas Syariat Islam, 2008), 101.

[128] Daud Zamzani, Nuruzzahri Yahya, Hasanoel Bashry HG, Muchtar A. Wahab, and Ismail Ya'kub, *Pemikiran Ulama Dayah Aceh* (Banda Aceh: BRR, 2007), 3.

[129] Fauzi Saleh, "Eksistensi Akidah dalam Penegakan Syariah: Kesiapan Mental Menerima Penerapan Syariat Islam," in Syamsul Rijal (ed.), *Syariat Islam dan Paradigma Kemanusiaan* (Banda Aceh: Dinas Syariat Islam, 2008), 348; Muslim Ibrahim, "Sejarah Syariʿat Islam di Bumi Aceh," in Rusjdi Ali Muhammad (ed.), *Kontekstualisasi Syari ʿat Islam di Nanggroe Aceh Darussalam* (Banda Aceh: Ar-Raniry Press, 2003), 36–7.

[130] Alyasa Abubakar and Marah Halim, *Hukum Pidana Islam di Provinsi Nanggroe Aceh Darussalam* (Banda Aceh: DSI, 2007), 52–4.

[131] "Ulama Jadi Benteng Masuknya Aliran Sesat," *Rakyat Aceh* (10 November 2007), 3.

[132] "Moral Pemimpin Patut Dipertanyakan," *Rakyat Aceh* (19 December 2010), 4.

of a wound, or a computer virus that must be "deleted" before it corrupts the entire system—something very small, but extremely dangerous.[133]

In one of the earliest pieces of substantive Shariʿa legislation passed in Aceh's contemporary Islamic legal system, the Ulama Council was assigned responsibility for identifying and preventing the spread of deviant teachings.[134] The highest-level statement on the subject to date has been an MPU fatwa issued in 2007, in which the Ulama Council defined its role more explicitly as that of not only being "responsive" to threats of deviant teachings as they arise, but also "proactive and anticipative" in dealing with perceived dangers to the faith. The 2007 fatwa also outlines specific procedures for investigating religious groups suspected of adhering to deviant teachings, complete with a list of substantive criteria for determining their status. It also establishes guidelines for appropriate modes of corrective action against any groups judged to be deviant by these measures.[135]

Under the broad rubric of doctrinal deviancy, the MPU has published rulings on a wide variety of alternative models of Islamic belief in practice, ranging from the Tablighi Jamāʿat (which it sanctioned as a movement for *daʿwa*, whose members should be considered as proper Muslim co-religionists), to the circulation of apocalyptic "chain letters" attributed to the caretaker of the prophet Muḥammad's grave in Medina (which the MPU rejected as dangerous superstition in opposition to Islamic orthodoxy).[136] Some suspect groups that have attracted the attention of the MPU (such as the Ahmadiyya) were relatively established with a long-term presence in Indonesia.[137] More typically, however, the targets of local campaigns against "deviant teachings" have generally been smaller communities without clearly identifiable trans-regional branches. The groups suspected of professing deviant teaching have been small and for the most part locally based. In a number of such cases, the authorities have brought in the leaders of such groups to explain their beliefs and to demonstrate their distinctive ritual practices. Their testimony is then often portrayed in a mocking tone in the local newspapers and tabloids.[138]

[133] Interview with State Islamic College teaching staff, 25 June 2008 at STAI Al-Aziziyah, Samalanga.

[134] *Qanun Provinsi Nanggroe Aceh Darussalam No. 11/2002 tentang Pelaksanaan Syariʿat Islam dalam Bidang Aqidah, Ibadahdan Syiʿar Islam*, III.6.

[135] *Fatwa Majelis Permusyawaratan Ulama Nanggroe Aceh Darussalam No. 04/2007 tentang Pedoman Identifikasi Aliran Sesat*. This fatwa has also been subsequently reprinted as a small, shirt pocket-sized booklet and widely circulated by the provincial MPU in 2011.

[136] *Tausiyah Majlis Permusyawaratanulama Kota Lhokseumawe No. 94/2004 tentang Surat Selebaran*.

[137] For example: Ahmadiyah 'Haram' di Aceh," *Rakyat Aceh* (26 November 2008), 1–2.

[138] "4 Pengikut Tgk. Aiyub Disidangkan MPU Bireuen," *Serambi* (4 April 2011), 13; "Tgk Ahmad Silet Bantah Bawa Aliran Sesat,"*Serambi* (10 May 2009), 19; "Dilarang Lakukan Pengajian: Tengku Syahrul Mengaduke Dewan," *Serambi* (9 March 2007), 19.

In some other cases, however, the MPU has actually intervened to stop the vigilante persecution of some groups suspected of adhering to deviant teachings by members of local communities. For example, in August 2010, a large mob attacked a house in Aceh Tamiang, and dragged over a dozen people found on the site to the local police station. The attack was incited by rumors that the building was actually the base for a group spreading "deviant teachings." However after an inspection was carried out by the local MPU at the request of the Wilayatul Hisbah (WH or the Shariʿa police), it was determined that the practices of the group were not, in fact, heretical and the group agreed to work to clarify and correct any aspects of their practice that may have appeared to be in error.[139] However it must be noted that there is also nothing on record to suggest that any official action was taken against the participants in the mob action that had initiated the incident.

In 2011, recognizing the strength of public sentiment against the perceived threats of deviant religious groups, Aceh's government—at that point led by prominent former members of GAM—attempted to capitalize on this opportunity to establish some much-needed Islamic credentials. This started with a series of high-profile public statements about a group known as *Millata Abraham*, which was accused of not only disparaging Muḥammad's role as the final and perfect prophet, but also of paying large sums to those who agreed to join their group.[140] On 4 April, the deputy governor, Muhammad Nazar, publicly called for the MPU to deliver a fatwa on the issue.[141] However, on 6 April, before the MPU could respond to their request, the provincial government issued both a gubernatorial regulation and a joint decision with the provincial military command, police commissioner, public prosecutor, and head of the Department of Religious Affairs officially condemning the *Millata Abraham* as "deviant."[142] As the

[139] "Diduga Ajaran Aliran Sesat: Ratusan Orang Gerebek Rumah Warga," *Serambi* (2 August 2010), 19.

[140] They appear to have first become the object of state censure in 2010, when their group was condemned as heretical by the North Aceh MPU, the State Sharīʿa Agency (DSI), and the North Aceh Majelis Adat's offices in Lhokseumawe. "MPU Acutdan Dinas SI Sepakat: Kutuk Aliran Sesat," *Rakyat Aceh* (19 October 2010), 4; "Aliran Millata Abraham Hancurkan Islam," *Rakyat Aceh* (21 October 2010), 13. An extensive interview with the leader of Millata Abraham, Zainuddin, was published in an edition of the news weekly *Modus Aceh* that was almost completely dedicated to covering the issue of "deviant teachings" (50.VIII, 11–17 April 2011), 9–10.

[141] "Wagub Aceh: Pengikut Aliran Sesat Digaji Rp 15 Juta," *Serambi* (4 April 2011), 1.

[142] *Peraturan Gubernor Aceh No. 9/2011 tentang Larangan Kegiatan Aliran Millata Abraham di Aceh*, and *Keputusan Bersama Gubernor Aceh, Panglima Komando Daerah Militer Iskandar Muda, Kepala Polisi Daerah Aceh, Kepala Kejaksaan Tinggi Aceh, dan Kepala Kantor Wilayah Kementerian Agama Aceh Nomor 450.1/165/2011, KEP/216/IV/2011, KEP/65/IV/2011, KEP-073/N.1/Dsp.5/04/2011, KW.01.1/4/HM.00.1/766/2011 tentang Larangan Kegiatan Aliran Millata Abraham di Aceh.*

police began the work of apprehending followers of that group on the following day, the governor's office issued another major statement on the subject of "deviant sects" (I. *aliran sesat*), this time publishing a list of 14 groups deemed to be deviant, and a pledge to allocate more state resources for the implementation of Shariʿa and more funding for religious education to deepen the faith of local Muslims to protect them from falling prey to deviant teachings.[143]

Among the groups listed there as "deviant" were, however, some groups that were in fact recognized as legitimate by significant segments of Aceh's Muslim community.[144] The MPU thus soon received complaints from representatives of some groups who objected to government censure of their beliefs and practices, and to being listed alongside other groups that they agreed were "clearly deviant."[145] Given the tensions that the affair aroused between the provincial government and ulama from local *dayah*, it was inevitable that the head of the MPU would have to enter the fray. His engagement in the affair reveals some of the internal complexities and potential contradictions involved with official attempts to define, promote, and administer particular forms of Islam through contemporary Aceh's state Shariʿa system.

As head of the MPU, Muslim Ibrahim had voiced support for the governor's prohibition of the *Millata Abraham* and advocated strengthening measures against the group through the promulgation of a *qanun* on the subject defining some sanctions to be imposed.[146] At the same time, he also expressed far less enthusiasm for the governor's expanded list of 14 "deviant sects." In responding to the pushback from some Muslim groups who found themselves included on the list, Muslim Ibrahim explained that the MPU had no involvement with determining which particular groups appeared on the governor's list—thus attempting to absolve the MPU from responsibility for the final decision. However when the governor, Irwandi Yusuf, was pressed for justifications of the selection of particular groups included on the list, he replied that his office had simply followed the general guidelines for determining deviancy in

[143] "Polisi Masih Amankan Anggota Millah Abraham," *Serambi* (7 April 2011), 1; "Puluhan Ribu Massa Demo Aliran Sesat," *Serambi* (8 April 2011), 1.

[144] The list of 14 read: 1. Ajaran Milata Abraham, 2. Darul Arqam, 3. Ajaran Kebatinan Abidin, 4. Aliran Syiah, 5. Ajaran Muhammad Ilyas bin M Yusuf, 6. Tarikat Haji Ibrahim Bonjol, 7. Kelompok Jamaah Qur'an Hadits, 8. Ajaran Ahmadyah Qadiyan, 9. Pengajian Abdul Majid Abdullah, 10. Ajaran Ilman Lubis, 11. Tarikat Mufarridiyah, 12. Ajaran Ahmad Arifin, 13. Ajaran Makrifatullah, 14. Pengajian Al-Quran dan Hadits.

[145] This included a delegation from the Pengajian Al-Quran dan Hadits, members of Banda Aceh's Shiʿite philosophy discussion group, who protested that they did not fit the criteria for being labeled deviant. "MPU tidak Infokan Nama Aliran Sesat," *Serambi* (13 April 2011), 1–2.

[146] "Puluhan Ribu Massa Demo Aliran Sesat," *Serambi* (8 April 2011), 11.

the MPU's 2007 general fatwa on the subject.[147] The uncomfortable exchange of public statements on this hot-button issue reflected the increasing tension between the scholars of the Ulama Council and the former GAM-dominated executive leadership of the provincial government over the question of who held legitimate authority in the determination and defense of Islamic orthodoxy in contemporary Aceh.

THE ULAMA, ISLAMIC EDUCATION, AND SOCIAL ENGINEERING

The tussle between the governor's office, the leadership of the MPU, and various independent Islamic groups over who has the ultimate authority to determine the limits of acceptable Islamic belief and practice represents a critical juncture to reflect on the relative role of religious vis-à-vis political leaders in determining the agenda of state Shari'a in contemporary Aceh. The question thus becomes one of who is leading the agenda of state Shari'a in contemporary Aceh?

The spread of "deviant teachings" has been a marked concern of Islamic religious leaders who were invested by the community with the authority to determine the limits of acceptable belief and practice. The rising popular anxiety over perceived threats to Islam has served to make the issue an attractive one for Indonesian state officials and political candidates seeking to rally new sources of support for their positions. In some cases, mutually reinforcing momentum was successfully built as state officials marshaled their resources to repress a group—like *Millata Abraham*—that could be judged as deviant by the vast majority of Aceh's leading religious scholars. However, when the state took it upon itself to produce its own list of heresies without consulting the ulama, they met with a significant public backlash. This show of relative independence of the official Ulama Council from the broader offices of the state in this instance reflects not only the special position of the Aceh's ulama as established in the provincial legislation on the MPU, but also a pronounced trend at the national level since the end of the New Order in 1998.

At the same time, however, it also serves to reassert one of the central roles assigned to Aceh's Ulama Council at its founding. In a volume commemorating more than three decades of work by Aceh's Ulama Council, there is a clear emphasis on the MPU's role in implementing Islamic law as a tool to be employed for the transformation of Acehnese society. The language used for this is striking, with the ulama characterized

[147] Interview with Muslim Ibrahim, 12 April 2011 at Banda Aceh.

as "agent of reform" and "agent of development" (English in original), who take up the crucial task of "engineering" (I. *merekayasa*) change to foster development and the prosperity of the *umma*.[148] Here the explicit language of social engineering is used to define the work of Aceh's Ulama Council. The charged political contexts of that institution's founding and its close relationship with the governor's office and the Indonesian military under the New Order may suggest that the goals of such social engineering projects would be determined by the concerns of the ruling elite, rather than by the ulama who were purportedly co-opted into this official body. However, a case such as that of the reaction of both the MPU and the broader Muslim community to the governor's list of 14 deviant groups makes it clear that, in the post-Suharto period at least, the situation is not so straightforward.

As noted earlier, Indonesia's national-level Ulama Council centered in Jakarta could, at times, directly contradict state priorities when they felt strongly enough that religious or broader social concerns mandated otherwise. As the authoritarian control of the central government collapsed at the end of the twentieth century, it became increasingly apparent that the state needed the legitimacy that the ulama could lend them somewhat more than the religious leaders needed the institutional and financial support of the government. In this context, then, the ulama had greater liberty to express their independence in determining answers to religious questions. With the emergence of the idea that the state implementation of Islamic law could serve to undermine GAM and attract support for the Indonesian government in Aceh, Aceh's Ulama Council has also come to be more assertive in their statements on the interpretation of Islam and its role in shaping the development of Acehnese society.

Religious leaders have diverse motives for participation in state institutions, and varied concerns can inform their actions within them. There have clearly been significant examples of self-serving political opportunism among some of the figures involved in Aceh's Ulama Council since its founding at the dawn of Suharto's New Order. However, that should not preclude us from also recognizing that others within the organization saw their involvement as providing opportunities to draw on the resources of the state to further their own goals of promoting Islamic ideals in society. The founding of Aceh's Ulama Council was a calculated measure to create an official body that could produce and disseminate interpretations of Islam to facilitate social change in desired directions. Under the authoritarian control of the New Order and the local command

[148] Badruzzaman Ismail (ed.), *Amal Bakti Empat Windu Majelis Ulama Aceh Tahun 1965–1997* (Aceh: Majelis Permusyawaratan Ulama Provinsi Nanggroe Aceh Darussalam, 2002), 119.

of the Indonesian military in its campaigns against GAM, much of the work of Aceh's Ulama Council was directed from the outside by other segments of the Indonesian state. Nevertheless, some of Aceh's Islamic leadership were able to use the resources made available to them through the institution to pursue their own agendas of religious reform.

With the weakening of the central state in the post-Suharto period and the concomitant strengthening of self-consciously Islamic elements across various branches of the Indonesian military and civil administration, the Ulama Council has been increasingly assertive of its position as the source of official statements on Islamic religious affairs in Aceh. In some ways, the situation here—and in Indonesia more generally—could be compared to developments in Egypt at the same time. Nathan Brown had noted that there, state efforts to organize, regulate, and steer Islamic discourse have led to a situation in which, "the attempt to subsume the Sharia has resembled a boa constrictor working to digest an elephant: the shape of the serpent dramatically changes as a result of the audacious effort."[149] The public statements of the MPU have played an important role in defining Islamic law in Aceh. However, this dynamic discourse is also situated within the broader legal context framed in the provincial level legislation that both defines the powers of state Shari'a institutions and elaborates the substantive content of the law they are tasked with administering. The next chapter will explore the historical development, contemporary dynamics, and substantive content of legislation in Aceh's Islamic legal system.

[149] Nathan Brown, "Egypt: Cacophony and Consensus in the Twenty-first Century," in Robert Hefner (ed.), *Sharia Politics: Islamic Law and Society in the Modern World* (Bloomington: Indiana University Press, 2011), 117.

5

The Legislation of Islam

> Society requires not only that the passions of individuals should be subjected, but that even in the mass and body as well as in the individuals, the inclinations of men should frequently be thwarted, their will controlled, and their passions be brought into subjection... In this sense the restraints on men, as well as their liberties, are to be reckoned among their rights.
>
> Edmund Burke
>
> *Reflections on the Revolution in France*[1]

Codification has frequently been viewed as one of the most transformative modern innovations in Islamic law, representing not only a means of standardization but also allowing for an entirely new pattern of state involvement in the interpretation and application of Shariʿa.[2] Joseph Schacht considered codification, "the most important manifestation of Islamic modernism"[3]—reflecting a particular trajectory of reform framed by a re-conceptualization of the state and its role in administering religion and public order. Bernard Botiveau has gone even further in stressing what he sees as the "secularizing" transformation that processes of codification have had upon traditional Islamic law and its place in modernizing Muslim societies.[4]

Programs for legal reform in the Ottoman Empire during the nineteenth century are often cited as the earliest landmarks in these developments.[5] Over the course of the twentieth century, the idea that there was a need to compile a fixed body of statutes out of the diverse rulings of *fiqh* appears to have found expression in an increasing number of Muslim societies.

[1] Edmund Burke, *Reflections on the Revolution in France – and on the proceedings in certain societies in London relative to that event*, (London: Penguin Books, 1986), 151.

[2] Murteza Bedir, "Fikih to Law: Secularization through Curriculum," *Islamic Law and Society* 11.3 (2004) 378–401; Wael B. Hallaq, *Sharīʿa: Theory, Practice, Transformations* (New York: Cambridge University Press, 2009), 367–70.

[3] Joseph Schacht, "Problems of Modern Islamic Legislation," *Studia Islamica* 12 (1960) 99.

[4] Bernard Botiveau, *Loi Islamique et droit dans le sociétés arabes* (Paris: Karthala, 1993), 144.

[5] For an overview of early developments along these lines, see Roderic H. Davison, *Reform in the Ottoman Empire, 1856–1876* (Princeton: Princeton University Press, 1963).

Rudolph Peters has argued that, in the process, the production of statements of substantive law has generally shifted away from being the preserve of the ulama as scholar/jurists to a function of politicians and state officials.[6] As discussed in Chapter 3, however, contemporary Aceh presents a case in which academics associated with a modern "Islamic college" (IAIN) have also played a considerable role in both the general shaping of the Shariʿa system, and in the drafting of particular pieces of legislation.[7]

ISLAM AND LAW IN MODERN INDONESIA

In Indonesia, calls for the formal implementation of Islamic law have been present among some sectors of the Muslim community since the emergence of the independent republic in the mid-twentieth century. Advocates of this had attempted to establish this through the insertion of a clause in the preamble of the 1945 constitution that came to be known as the "Jakarta Charter" (*Piagam Jakarta*). This controversial formulation stipulated that Muslims within the new nation would be obliged to observe Islamic law.[8] In a last-minute revision before the constitution was proclaimed, however, this wording was struck from the preamble, purportedly as a concession to the Christian populations of the eastern archipelago. This was viewed by some Muslim Indonesians as a betrayal of their aspirations for independence and an ungracious recompense for their participation in the struggles that led to it.[9]

[6] Rudolph Peters, "From Jurists' Law to Statute Law or What Happens When the Shariʿa is Codified," in B.A. Roberson (ed.), *Shaping the Current Islamic Reformation* (London: Frank Cass, 2003), 95.

[7] Aceh, furthermore, does not seem to be the only example of a place in which a faculty associated with a state-backed institution of Islamic higher education has played a significant role in shaping a contemporary Islamic legal system. One needs to look no further afield than across the Straits of Malacca to see one of the most striking cases of this anywhere in the world—where the International Islamic University of Malaysia has come to exercise a practical monopoly on the training and certification of judges for that country's Islamic courts. For more on this, see the articles by Farid S. Shuaib, Najibah M. Zin, and Amanda Whiting in Mark E. Cammack, R. Michael Feener, and Clark B. Lombardi (eds.), *Islamic Law and Islamic Legal Professionals in Southeast Asia*, a special issue of *Pacific Rim Law & Policy Journal* 21.1 (2012) 85–161.

[8] "*ke-Tuhanan, dengan kewadjiban mendjalankan Sjariʿat Islam bagi pemeluk-pemeluknja…*" Muhammad Yamin, *Naskah Persiapan Undang-undang Dasar 1945*, vol. 1 (Jakarta: Yayasan Prapanca, 1959–1960), 145. See also B.J. Boland, *The Struggle of Islam in Modern Indonesia* (The Hague: Martinus Nijhoff, 1971), 26, and Appendix I. This phrase came to be referred to as the "Seven Words" in later constitutional debates.

[9] Aspects of the debates over the constitutional status of this document, as well as appendices containing relevant primary materials, can be found in H. Endang Saifuddin Anshari, *Piagam Jakarta, 22 Juni 1945: Sebuah Konsensus Nasional tentang Dasar Negara Republik Indonesia, 1945–1949* (Jakarta: Gema Insani Press, 1997). A shorter version of this work in English can be found in the same author's M.A. thesis, "The Jakarta Charter of

Their disappointment fueled a series of attempts to further Islamize the Indonesian state and society over the decades that followed, including the campaigns of the Masjumi party and the *daʿwa* movement that absorbed the former's energies and channeled them into campaigns of Islamic propagation in the latter decades of the twentieth century.[10] One of the leading spokesmen for both was M. Natsir, who explicitly framed the issue in terms of the right of Muslims to be subjected to Islamic law. In particular, he demanded that as Muslims comprised the overwhelming majority of citizens in the newly independent Indonesia, the Shariʿa was the only possible means through which to ensure social justice and social stability.[11]

In Aceh, the demands that the Shariʿa be applied as part of the formal legal apparatus of the Indonesian state in the 1950s escalated beyond the realm of party politics and eventually took militant form in the Darul Islam (DI) rebellion led by Daud Beureueh. Despite years of armed struggle, the Darul Islam was ultimately unable to achieve its goals of creating a state governed by Shariʿa in Aceh. As the threat of the DI was neutralized, however, the Indonesian central government soon came to develop its own plans for how the formal administration of Islamic law could serve to steer Acehnese society in desired directions. The sources and influences on these developments were complex, involving the Indonesian military leadership, local Acehnese politicians, IAIN academics, and Islamic activists who had formally been associated with the DI and PUSA.

This chapter presents a critical analysis of the legislation of Islamic law in Aceh since Indonesian independence in 1945. In doing so, it notes the points of continuity, as well as the distinct breaks between the formal structures of regulating Islamic belief and practice promoted by the DI and those established subsequently under the Indonesian central government. The ways in which Jakarta had understood the Islamic ideals of the Acehnese DI were important factors in the history of subsequent state management of religious affairs in the province as they unfolded over the following decades. At the same time, however, much of the substance of Islamic legislation in Aceh today is rooted in local formulations stretching back to PUSA through the development of *daʿwa* discourses at the IAIN. Against this background, this chapter will examine legislation that provides both the form and substance of contemporary Aceh's Islamic legal system.

June 1945: A History of the Gentleman's Agreement between the Islamic and the Secular Nationalists in Modern Indonesia" (Montreal: McGill University Institute of Islamic Studies, 1976).

[10] See Boland, *The Struggle of Islam*, 105–12.

[11] M. Natsir, *Demokrasi di bawah Hukum* (Jakarta: Penerbit Media Daʿwah, 2002—based upon lectures given in 1966), 5–15.

EARLY ISLAMIC LEGISLATION IN ACEH

With the more confident assertion of Indonesian state control over Aceh, cautious first steps were taken to introduce new legislation reflecting Islamic ideals of public morality. The first substantive pieces of legislation in this direction took the form of district-level (I. *kabupaten*) statutes on the production, sale, and consumption of alcohol. By the end of 1961, several local laws were passed to strengthen state control through provisions for licensing and taxation. These provisions, however, were far from a blanket prohibition and in some districts "strong drink" (I. "*miras*'—*minuman keras*) was defined as including all forms of local spirits (I. *tuak*), but excluded wine and beer.[12]

It was not until the following year that measures for the formalization of Islamic law were taken up at the provincial level. The way was cleared for this by an executive order issued under the authority of the Indonesian military command in Aceh. The provisions of this were explicit about two points: (1) that this was a measure to promote stability in the region under the broader umbrella of Indonesian national law, and (2) the details of precisely which "elements" were to be applied were to be determined by the regional government.[13] This last point was taken up by the local legislature and under the direction of A. Hasjmy, who began working out the agenda of Islamic legislation.[14] The framework for this was defined by the ranking Indonesian military officer in the province, Lt. Col. Sutjipto, who announced that Shari'a policy in Aceh must be administered in a way that is in line with the aims of the Main Outlines of National Direction (GBHN) and not in conflict with any higher-level national legislation.[15]

The first major piece of legislation introduced along these lines was a 1963 law on the topic of "*Syiar Islam*." This term and its broad-ranging formulations will be discussed in more detail in what follows. In the case of this particular law, the term *syiar* was used with reference to stipulations about the observance of Islamic holidays, the closing of shops and offices for Friday prayers, and measures making it obligatory for all persons [Muslim and non-Muslims alike] to "respect the

[12] For example *Peraturan Daerah Tingkat Ke II Atjeh Timur No. 4/ Tahun 1961 tentang Mengatur Pedjualan Minuman Keras; and Peraturan Daerah Tingkat Ke II Atjeh Tengah No. 36/ Tahun 1961 tentang Mengatur Pendjualan Makanandan Minuman Keras.*

[13] *Keputusan Penguasa Perang No. KPTS/PEPERDA -061/3/62 tentang Kebidjaksanan Pelaksanaan Unsur-unsur Sjari'at Islam bagi Pemeluk-pemeluknja di Daerah Istimewa Atjeh.*

[14] *Pernyataan No.B-71/1/DPRD-RG/1962.*

[15] See Analiansyah and Jamhuri, *Syariat Islam Di Nanggroe Aceh Darussalam: Inventarisasi Dokumen* (Banda Aceh: Dinas Syariat Islam Provinsi Nanggroe Aceh Darussalam, 2008), 208.

atmosphere of the fasting month" (I. *menghormati suasana bulan puasa*) by refraining from eating, drinking, smoking, or opening food stalls and restaurants during daylight hours. Such measures, the law states, were intended "to strengthen religious feeling and spirit and to implant in the hearts of citizens a sense of faith that can serve to ensure proper mental development."[16]

ISLAMIC LEGISLATION UNDER INDONESIA'S "NEW ORDER"

As noted in previous chapters, the explosion of anti-communist reactions that accompanied the establishment of Suharto's New Order contributed new momentum for the state institutionalization of Islam in Aceh. The first piece of provincial legislation passed in 1966 formalized the establishment of Aceh's Ulama Council.[17] Soon thereafter, substantive legislation of Islamic issues, including the perennially popular topic of alcohol, proceeded apace, with a new provincial-level law passed to supersede the various district-level regulations of the preceding years. This law took a much stronger stance on the issue, re-defining "strong drink" (*miras*) as "any intoxicating liquid" and stipulating more substantial sanctions than those that had been on the books in Aceh to date.[18]

One significant milestone in this process was the drafting of the 1968 bill on the implementation of "Elements of Islamic Shariʿa" (I. *Unsur-unsur Sjariʿat Islam*). The draft bill mandated that the provincial government had to support and encourage Islamic worship (Ar. *ʿibādāt*) to preserve Islamic morality (Ar. *akhlāq*), and to foster the promotion of "*syiar* Islam," as well as mandates for the government to be more active in the fields of education, *daʿwa*, and upholding the duty to "enjoin the right and forbid wrong" (Ar. *al-amr biʾl-maʿrūf waʾl-nahy ʿan al-munkar*).[19] The aspects of this legislation relating to Islamic education were strongly emphasized

[16] *Peraturan Daerah Istimewa Atjeh No. 1/Tahun 1963 tentang Pelaksanaan Sjiar Agama Islam*, (5.2).

[17] *Peraturan Daerah Propinsi Daerah Istimewa Atjeh No. 1/Tahun 1966 tentang Pedoman Dasar Majlis Mermusjawaratan Propinsi Daerah Istimewa Atjeh.*

[18] *Peraturan Daerah Propinsi Daerah Istimewa Atjeh No. 6/Tahun 1966 tentang Larangan Membuat, Memasukkan, Memperdagangkan, Menjimpan dan Menimbun Minuman Keras*, (I.1.d). These included a sentence of six months and a fine of Rp. 10,000 (in the currency of that time).

[19] *Peraturan Daerah Propinsi Daerah Istimewa Aceh No. 6/Tahun 1968 tentang Ketentuan-ketentuan Pokok Pelaksanaan Unsur-unsur Sjariʿat Islam* (I.2.a-i). The law also established a state Islamic institution to administer matters of religious property (I. *Baitul Mal*).

in the substantive provisions of the text itself, with a focus on facilitating religious belief and practice, education, and combating the threat of "deviant teachings." The bill also called for the regional government to work together with the Ulama Council to "implant (I. *menanam*) into the hearts of its citizens, from an early age, a sense of faith and love toward the religion of Islam."[20] Although Traditionalist and Modernist reformers debated particular points of some rules in the provincial legislative assembly (DPRA), they were in broad agreement that there was a need to codify measures designed to facilitate public expressions of Islamic belief and practice in the form of positive law.[21] In the end, however, this draft Shariʿa legislation was not approved by the Interior Minister, who saw this as inconsistent with Indonesian national law of the time.[22] While not formally enacted in 1968, many of the provisions of this bill came to define key planks in the platform of state Shariʿa as it took shape in Aceh at the turn of the twenty-first century.

Over the intervening decades, the Indonesian central government came gradually to endorse other provincial-level initiatives for the further Islamization of Acehnese society. While framed locally in terms of Aceh's special identification with Islam, these developments in the formal regulation of Islam were largely in step with trends at the national level over the final decades of the twentieth century. They reflected in particular a fundamental change in Indonesian legal culture in the second half of the twentieth century, with a pronounced shift toward a more instrumentalist view of law to promote particular agendas of social change under the rubric of what came to be known in Indonesia as "Development Law Theory" (I. *Teori Hukum Pembangunan*).[23] The New Order prominently announced this new pillar of state policy in two major pronouncements of the mid-1970s: the 1973 Main Outlines of National Direction (GBHN) and the Five Year Development Plan (I. *Replita*) for 1974–1979, which stated that law was to be used as a "tool" (I. *alat*) and "instrument" (I. *sarana*) in the

[20] *Per Da 6/1968*, (III.5.1-3).

[21] The discussions of this bill leading to its approval by the provincial legislature are recorded in *Sidang Ke-IV Dewan Perwakilan Rakyat Daerah Gotong Rojong Propinsi Daerah Istimewa Atjeh* (Banda Aceh: Secretariat D. P. R. D. - GR Prop. Daerah Istimewa Aceh, 1968), a copy of which is preserved in the Arsip Propinsi Banda Aceh.

[22] A. Basiq Djalil, Peradilan *Agama di Indonesia: Gemuruhnya Politik Hukum (Hk. Islam, Hk. Barat, dan Hk. Adat) dalam Rentang Sejarah Bersama Pasang Surut Lembaga Peradilan Agama Hingga Lahirnya Peradilan Syariat Islam Aceh* (Jakarta: Kencana Prenada Media Group, 2006), 165.

[23] For an overview of the development of Development Law Theory and its place in the broader history of Indonesian legal thought, see Sidharta, "Posisi Pemikiran Teori Hukum Pembangunan dalam Konfigurasi Aliran Pemikiran Hukum (sebuah diagnosis awal)," in Shidarta, ed. *Mochtar Kusuma-Atmadja dan Teori Hukum Pembangunan: Eksistensi dan Implikasi* (Jakarta: Epistema Institute, 2012), 9–80.

service of national development.[24] This fundamental shift toward utilitarian prescription as the dominant legal ideology in Indonesia allowed the state to legitimize its various agendas of restructuring and reform in a wide range of areas, including the articulation of official understandings of Islamic law as a tool of social engineering.

This is an important, though little-acknowledged aspect of the background to the 1974 Marriage Act.[25] In the spirit of the 1973 GBHN, the first draft of this law sought to unify family law through rationalization and standardization in the form of a proposal to transfer authority over issues of marriage law for all Indonesian citizens to the civil court system, a move which would have stripped the country's Islamic courts of most of their effective jurisdiction. This prompted a significant backlash from some Muslim leaders, in response to which the government proposed a new bill—one that took the opposite approach of formalizing the administration of family law through the reform of the state's Islamic legal apparatus. Like the earlier bill which had met with so much resistance from segments of the Muslim community, the new 1974 Marriage Act was designed to both facilitate greater unification in the national legal system and to change the behavior of citizens through modernizing agendas of social reform. The aim was to foster stable families through the formal regulation of divorce and polygamy, the control of population growth, and the formal establishment of legal rights for women.[26] In doing this through the idiom of Islamic law, however, this reform measure gained broad acceptance among the country's Muslim population. Through this experience, lessons were learned that came to inform the place of Islam in New Order social development policies over the decades that followed.

The 1974 Marriage Act enhanced role of Indonesia's Islamic Religious Courts (I. *Peradilan Agama*) in the administration of family law. This in turn led to further changes in the structure and management of these institutions that included the recruitment of new staff. In the process, judges with a background in traditional Islamic educational institutions (I. *pesantren*) were replaced by graduates of modern academic institutions, and especially by those of the IAIN.[27] The modernization

[24] *Garis-Garis Besar Haluan Negara Republik Indonesia Tahun 1973; Rencana Pembangunan Lima Tahun Kedua – Tahun 1974/75 s.d. 1978/79.*

[25] *Undang-undang Republik Indonesia No.1/Tahun 1974 tentang Perkawinan.*

[26] Mark E. Cammack, Lawrence A. Young, and Tim Heaton, "Legislating Social Change in an Islamic Society: Indonesia's Marriage Law," in Tim Lindsey (ed.), *Indonesia: Law and Society, second edition* (Annandale: The Federation Press, 2008); Azyumardi Azra, "The Indonesian Marriage Law of 1974: An Institutionalization of the Shariʿa for Social Change," in Arskal Salim and Azyumardi Azra (eds.), *Shariʿa and Politics in Modern Indonesia* (Singapore: ISEAS Press, 2003), 88.

[27] For more on the rise of IAIN Syariah faculty graduates as judges in the 1970s and 1980s, see Euis Nurlaelawati, Modernization, *Tradition and Identity: The Kompilasi Hukum Islam*

and professionalization of Indonesia's Islamic judiciary was subsequently advanced even further through the 1989 Religious Judicature Act.[28] Over the decade that followed these measures, the first judges coming from backgrounds in the IAIN and the religious courts were recruited to the Indonesian Supreme Court.[29]

The transformations of Indonesia's Islamic courts under the New Order also involved the codification of a set of rules to be applied by them in the form of the 1991 *Compilation of Islamic Law* (I. *Kompilasi Hukum Islam*/KHI). Like other modern projects for the codification of Islamic law, a major goal was to produce a uniform body of rules that could be easily applied by the courts.[30] While the process was led by Supreme Court judges and officials at the Ministry of Religious Affairs, the drafting process included the participation at various levels of scholars of Islamic law selected from IAIN campuses across the country.[31] Aceh's Islamic leadership was thus not only aware of, but some were also participants in various stages of the process that led to the 1991 *Kompilasi*. Several of them would later emerge as prominent figures in Aceh's twenty-first-century Islamic legal system.[32] Through the process, they gained new experience with state attempts to direct changes in behavior through an instrumentalist approach to Islamic legislation.

As noted in Chapter 3, these IAIN-based academics were part of a generation that came of age in a world in which ideas of *daʿwa*-driven social transformation were ascendant in Indonesia as well as elsewhere in the Muslim world. For example, Alyasa Abubakar—who was later to become the founding Director of Aceh's State Shariʿa Agency (DSI)—was an active participant in a regular seminar to discuss "custom (I. *adat*) that contradicts the Shariʿa" held at the Banda Aceh IAIN in the mid-1970s.[33] The idea that

and Legal Practice in the Indonesian Religious Courts (Amsterdam: Amsterdam University Press, 2010), 58–9.

[28] *Undang-undang Nomor 7/Tahun 1989 tentang Peradilan Agama*. For more on these developments, see Mark Cammack, "Indonesia's 1989 Religious Judicature Act: Islamization of Indonesia or Indonesianization of Islam?" in Arskal Salim and Azyumardi Azra (eds.), *Shariʿa and Politics in Modern Indonesia* (Singapore: ISEAS Press, 2003), 96–124; Mark E. Cammack, "The Indonesian Islamic Judiciary," in R. Michael Feener and Mark E. Cammack (eds.), *Islamic Law in Contemporary Indonesia: Ideas and Institutions* (Cambridge, MA: Harvard University Press, 2007), 146–69.

[29] This happened even though there was initial resistance from older members of the court, all of whom came from backgrounds of a "secular" legal education. See Sebastiaan Pompe, *The Indonesian Supreme Court: A Study of Institutional Collapse* (Ithaca: Cornell Southeast Asia Program, 2005), 387–8.

[30] Yahya Harahap, "Informasi Materi Kompilasi Hukum Islam: Mempositifkan Abstraksi Hukum Islam," in Cik Hassan Bisri (ed.), *Kompilasi Hukum Islam dan Peradilan Agama dalam Sistem Hukum Nasional* (Jakarta: Logos Wacana Ilmu, 1999), 27–35.

[31] Bustanul Arifin, "Kompilasi: Fiqih dalam Bahasa Undang-undang," *Pesantren* 2(2) (1985) 25–30.

[32] Interview with Hamid Sorong, 21 June 2010 at Banda Aceh.

[33] These seminars brought together young students like Alyasa with leading reformist figures including Ismuha and A. Hasjmy. Some of the proceedings of their discussions

inculcating Islamic piety can serve as a means for transforming individuals and society for the better was reflected in diverse ways at the time in Aceh, including in the form of a 1990 law establishing formal requirements of Qur'ānic literacy for all primary school graduates in the province.[34] As the Islamization of society in Aceh—and in Indonesia more broadly—progressed over the 1990s, further developments in the official state ideology of law as a "tool of development" laid the groundwork for the social engineering project of Aceh's Islamic legal system in the twenty-first century. In 1993, the announcement of a new statement on "Main Outlines of National Direction" (GBHN) placed a renewed emphasis on legal instrumentalism and on its "socialization" (I. *sosialisasi*) as a developmental priority. At the same time, it also allowed for a broader consideration of legal pluralism under the aegis of the Indonesian state—something which some observers have seen as opening the door for further development of substantive Islamic law in various parts of the country.[35] By the end of the century, however, the Suharto regime was rapidly unraveling and the framework of the conversation was shifting from one of legal pluralism to state de-centralization.[36]

ISLAMIC LAW AND SPECIAL AUTONOMY

After the fall of Suharto in 1998, the loosening of centralized control over local governance emerged as a major theme in the new national movement for political and social reform (I. *Reformasi*).[37] The 1999 Act on Local Governance set the basic terms for the devolution of some

on issues included the use of numerological divination to determine the compatibility of young couples to be married, as well as on the holding of ritual meals on set days after the death of a family member are recorded in: Institut Agama Islam Negeri (IAIN), *Seminar Adat yang Bertentangandengan Syariʿat* (Banda Aceh: Lembaga Research dan Survey IAIN Jamiʿah Ar-Raniry Darussalam, Banda Aceh, 1975).

34 Arskal Salim, *Challenging the Secular State: The Islamization of Law in Modern Indonesia* (Honolulu: University of Hawaii Press, 2008), 149.

35 Translation in Nur Ahmad Fadhil Lubis, "The State's Legal Policy and the Development of Islamic Law in Indonesia's New Order," in Arskal Salim and Azyumardi Azra (eds.), *Shariʿa and Politics in Modern Indonesia* (Singapore: ISEAS, 2003), 55. For the reaction of Muslim leaders in Aceh to the 1993 GBHN, see Majelis Permusyawaratan Rakyat, *Ketetapan-ketetapan Majelis Permusyawaratan Rakyat Indonesia Tahun 1993* (Jakarta: B7 Pusat, 1993), 19–20.

36 For more on the broader political, social and economic aspects of this process, see Coen J.G. Holtzappel, "The Regional Governance Reform in Indonesia, 1999–2004," in Coen J.G. Holtzappel and Martin Ramstedt (eds.), *Decentralization and Regional Autonomy in Indonesia: Implementation and Challenges* (Singapore: ISEAS, 2009), 1–48.

37 On the legal and political dimensions of Reformasi, see Petra Stockmann, *Indonesian Reformasi as Reflected in Law: Change and Continuity in Post-Suharto Era Legislation on the Political System and Human Rights* (Münster: LIT Verlag, 2004), and Harold Crouch, *Political Reform in Indonesia after Soeharto* (Singapore: ISEAS Press, 2010).

governmental powers to the district and municipality levels.[38] Although authority over religious affairs was not among the areas devolved to district-level governments, some local leaders nevertheless interpreted de-centralization as empowering them to implement regional regulations (I. *peraturan daerah/perda*) relating to morality, dress, and other aspects of life traditionally covered by Islamic law. They were now, however, justified on paper at least as measures to address socially pressing issues and to preserve public order.[39] In her survey of these regional regulations, Robin Bush identified 78 pieces of legislation in 52 jurisdictions dealing with issues that are popularly perceived as "Islamic" concerns, including prostitution, gambling, alcohol, modest dress, the administration of religious almsgiving (Ar. *zakāt*), and official requirements of Qur'ānic literacy.[40] These topics overlap almost seamlessly with the measures for implementing aspects of Islamic law in Aceh over the second half of the twentieth century, and this same constellation of concerns also largely defined the scope of Aceh's Islamic system in the post-Suharto era.

The legal and political contexts for Islamic legislation in Aceh were, however, considerably different from those of other parts of Indonesia during the *Reformasi* period. There it was not a general policy of de-centralization, but rather the specific dynamics of Indonesian attempts to suppress the separatist agenda of GAM that framed developments. The turn of the millennium witnessed a new turn in Jakarta's strategy at ending the conflict, one that included not only aggressive military operations, but also political strategies aimed at undermining popular support for GAM.[41] The 1999 law on special autonomy for Aceh was passed soon after the referendum in East Timor that resulted in its secession from the Indonesian republic, and represented an attempt by the Indonesian government to stave off the possibility of a similar situation in Aceh.[42] As a special autonomous region within Indonesia, Aceh was then given

[38] *Undang Undang Republik Indonesia Nomor 22/Tahun 1999 tentang Pemerintahan Daerah*. For an overview of the political restructuring mandated by this law, see *Marco Bünte, Regionale Autonomie in Indonesien: Wege Zur Erfolgreichen Dezentralisierung* (Hamburg: IFA, 2003), 127–41.

[39] Arskal Salim, "Muslim Politics in Indonesia's Democratisation: The Religious Majority and the Rights of Minorities in the Post-New Order Era," in Ross McLeod and Andrew MacIntyre (eds.), *Indonesia: Democracy and the Promise of Good Governance* (Singapore: ISEAS Press, 2007), 115–27.

[40] Robin Bush, "Regional Shari'a Regulations in Indonesia: Anomaly or Symptom" in Greg Fealy and Sally White (eds.), *Expressing Islam: Religious Life and Politics in Indonesia* (Singapore: ISEAS Press, 2008), 174–91.

[41] Michelle Miller and R. Michael Feener, "Emergency and Islamic Law in Aceh," in Victor Ramraj and Arun Thiruvengadam (eds.), *Law and Emergency Powers in Asia: Exploring the Limits of Legality* (New York: Cambridge University Press, 2010), 213–36.

[42] H.M. Kaoy Syah and L. Hakiem, Keistimewaan Aceh Dalam Lintasan Sejarah, *Proses Pembentukan UU No. 44/1999* (Jakarta: Pengurus Besar Al Jami'yatul Washliyah, 2000), 165.

authority over key areas that had not been devolved elsewhere in the country, and in particular, the fields of religion and education.[43]

This special autonomy legislation opened the door for the development of substantive Shariʿa legislation and the institutional mechanisms for its implementation. Discussions of the form and content of a new Islamic legal system for Aceh were held in Jakarta starting in 2000, and over the years that followed dozens of local Muslim leaders were brought to Jakarta and hosted by the Ministry of Religious Affairs, the National Assembly (DPR), and the Supreme Court.[44] There, Jakarta-based backers of Shariʿa as a solution to the Aceh conflict including Yusril Ihza Mahendra worked with academics from the Banda Aceh IAIN and the law faculty of Syiah Kuala University to develop these plans.[45] The basic framework for establishing a new Islamic legal system for Aceh was further consolidated by a second law on Aceh's special autonomy issued in 2001, which conferred (at least in principle if not in practice) broader powers of self-governance to the province.[46] Over the next two years, the Provincial Legislative Assembly (DPRA) passed several new pieces of legislation (now referred to as "*qanun*") that provided the substance of an Islamic positive law and defined the new institutions by which these new laws would be implemented.

These new laws were developed through the collaboration of academics from the IAIN, local officials and Muslim technocrats, and politicians and public officials in Jakarta. However, in all this there was a notable lack of involvement by the leadership of Aceh's traditional *dayahs*.[47] Some of the Modernist academics involved in the process in fact expressed considerable antipathy toward the idea that *madhhab*-based traditional jurisprudence could play any significant role in the development of Islamic positive law for a

[43] *Undang-Undang Nomor 44 Tahun 1999 tentang Penyelenggaraan Keistimewaan Daerah Istimewa Aceh.*

[44] One prominent figure from the Indonesian Supreme Court in Jakarta involved in these developments was Syamsul Hadi, who remained a strong supporter of the further Islamization of Aceh's Islamic legal system over the years that followed. On a visit to the head of Aceh's provincial assembly on 27 May 2008, he urged proponents of the further Islamization of the legal system there to "take advantage" of the current situation in Aceh to press for further Islamic legislation, and endorsed the idea of establishing *ḥudūd* penalties that were then being discussed in relation to a new draft Shariʿa criminal code (*Qanun Jinayat*).

[45] Interview with Hamid Sorong, 29 May 2008 at Banda Aceh.

[46] *Undang Undang Republik Indonesia Nomor 18/Tahun 2001 tentang Otonomi Khusus bagi Provinsi Daerah Istimewa Aceh sebagai Provinsi Nanggroe Aceh Darussalam* formally changed Aceh's name to Nanggroe Aceh Darussalam (NAD/"State of Aceh, Abode of Peace"), and for this reason it is often referred to by international scholars as the "NAD Law." This term was, however, resented by some Acehnese nationalists sympathetic to GAM. See, for example Taufik Al Mubarak, *Aceh Pungo* (Banda Aceh: Bandar Publishing, 2009), 193–4.

[47] Interview with Rusjdi Ali Muhammad, 26 January 2011 at Banda Aceh.

modern state.[48] Others, however, have developed more nuanced views on the possibilities for the future development of *fiqh* in the context of Aceh's state Shariʿa system. This is most prominently exemplified in the work of Alyasa Abubakar, who was appointed the first head of the State Shariʿa Agency (DSI) in 2001. While frankly acknowledging that the structures and power dynamics of a modern nation call for models of jurisprudence radically different from those employed under pre-modern states, he sees this in terms of a progressive "paradigm shift" in conceptualizations of Islamic law and its role in governing society. Through appeals to principles of general public interest (Ar. *maṣlaḥa*) to justify new laws on problems not mentioned in scriptural sources, and a robust reinvigoration of Islamic conceptions of governance (Ar. *siyāsa*), Alyasa envisions a new conception of jurisprudence. The aim here is to infuse state legislation with the values of Islamic law, so that in the future Shariʿa would become part of national regulations that were to be observed by the *umma* "as citizens, and not only because they were Muslim by religion."[49] This is, of course, a radical reframing of established models of *fiqh*, and one that has yet to be realized even within Alyasa's own circle of academics involved in Aceh's state Shariʿa institutions. Indeed, the initial formulations of Islamic legislation under the *Reformasi*-era special autonomy provisions were far more modest.

The first regional regulation on Islam passed in Aceh during the post-Suharto period was Regional Regulation (I. *Peraturan Daerah*/Per Da) Number 5, issued in 2000. It begins with considerations stressing the need for Islamic values to be firmly established in Acehnese society. Those values were seen to be imperative as the religious life of its people was deemed essential to ensure justice and prosperity, as well as a means of preparing them to face the challenges of globalization.[50] Pursuant to this, the law itself obliges all Muslims to observe Islamic law in its totality (I. *secara kaffah*) and outlines the broad areas to be covered by Shariʿa, including doctrine and religious practice, transactions, ethics, education, marriage law, inheritance, the regulation of religious property, criminal law, *daʿwa*, *syiar*, and "enjoining good/forbidding wrong."[51] This list repeats verbatim what was found in the draft legislation of 1968. Many other sections not only repeat similar concerns (e.g., regulating relations between the sexes and policing popular entertainments), but also use

[48] Syahrizal Abbas, "Pelaksanaan Syariʿat Islam di Aceh Dalam Kerangka Sistem Hukum Nasional," in Syahrizal (ed.), *Dimensi Pemikiran Hukum dalam Implementasi Syariat Islam di Aceh* (Banda Aceh: Dinas Syariat Islam Provinsi Nanggroe Aceh Darussalam, 2007), 11.

[49] Alyasa Abubakar, *Penerapan Syariat Islam di Aceh: Upaya Penyusunan Fiqih dalam Negara Bangsa* (Banda Aceh: Dinas Syariat Islam, 2008), 10–11, 63–9.

[50] *Peraturan Daerah Nomor 5 Tahun 2000 tentang Pelaksanaan Syariat Islam di Provinsi Daerah Istimewa Aceh*, (*Menimbang* a, c).

[51] *PerDa 5/2000*, (IV.5.2).

nearly identical language such as in the stipulation that "[e]very person is free to perform *daʿwa* with the aim of promoting the development of the Islamic religion, and the unity of the Muslim community."[52] The remarkable consistency of both substantive concerns and rhetorical expression of Islamic law in Aceh over the past half century is striking, and it calls attention to significant aspects of continuity linking Aceh's current Islamic legal system to earlier measures that aimed to implement the Shariʿa and reform society through the formal apparatus of the Indonesian state.

The emphasis in the 2000 law is, moreover, clearly on aspects of religious propagation (*daʿwa*) and education (*tarbiya*), emphasizing the obligation of government to work on "instilling the values of faith and piety in its citizens from an early age."[53] This broad mandate is further elaborated in terms of both formal educational programs and more informal means of Islamic propagation. It states that the provincial government is responsible for establishing and developing schools that emphasize religious and moral instruction, and other formal institutions of *daʿwa*, while at the same time empowering individual Muslims to pursue similar programs of propagation to strengthen the community. In this initial statement of the aims of Aceh's new Islamic legal system, the emphasis is clearly on the instrumental use of law to support the socialization of religious values. The actual substance of what Islamic values were to be taught and propagated was, however, left to be defined by future legislation and administrative policy decisions. From 2002, a cascade of *qanun* and provincial-level executive instructions were issued to (re-)define the roles and responsibilities of—as well as the formal restrictions placed upon—the institutions tasked with administering Islamic law in Aceh: the Ulama Council (MPU),[54] the Shariʿa Courts (*Mahkamah Syariah*),[55] the State Shariʿa Agency (DSI),[56] and the enforcement units referred to locally as the

[52] *PerDa 5/2000,(I.2.a-i)*/(III.10). [53] *PerDa 5/2000,*(IV.6.2).

[54] *Qanun Aceh Nomor 2 Tahun 2009 tentang Majelis Permusyawaratan Ulama.*

[55] *Qanun Provinsi Nanggroe Aceh Darussalam Nomor 10 Tahun 2002 tentang Peradilan Syariat Islam; Keputusan Presiden Republik Indonesia Nomor 11 Tahun 2003 tentang Mahkamah Syarʿiyah Provinsi di Provinsi Nanggroe Aceh Darussalam; Keputusan Bersama Gubernur, Kepala Kepolisian Daerah, Kepala Kejaksaan Tinggi, Ketua Mahkamah Syarʿiyah Provinsi, Ketua Pengadilan Tinggidan Kepala Kantor Wilayah Departemen Kehakiman dan HAM Provinsi Nanggroe Aceh Darussalam Nomor: 26/PKS/2004, Nomor: SKEP/62/ VIII/2004, Nomor: B-1229/N.1/08/2004, Nomor: MSY. P/K/HK.009/614/2004, Nomor: W1. D1.UM.01.10-1116, Nomor: W1.UM.01.08-1604 tentang Operasionalisasi Kewenangan Mahkamah Syarʿiyah; Keputusan Ketua Mahkamah Agung Republik Indonesia tentang Pelimpahan Sebagian Kewenangan dari Peradilan Umum kepada Mahkamah Syarʿiyah Provinsi di Provinsi Nanggroe Aceh Darussalam Nomor: KMA/070/SK/X2004.*

[56] *Peraturan Gubernur Provinsi Nanggroe Aceh Darussalam Nomor 41 Tahun 2009 tentang Susunan Organisasi dan Tata Kerja Unit Pelaksana Teknis Dinas Pada Dinas Syariat Islam Provinsi Nanggroe Aceh Darussalam.*

Wilayatul Hisbah (WH).[57] Further institutional legislation passed during this period dealt with the administration of *zakāt* and Islamic religious properties.[58]

In 2002, *Qanun 11* took things considerably further in an aim to broadly redefine the public profile of Islamic religious observance in Acehnese society. One of its most striking features was made clear in its very title, in which the word "*syiar*" (Ar. *shiʿār*) is placed right alongside *ʿaqīda* (belief) and *ʿibādāt* (practice), as if *syiar* itself was also a central aspect of Islamic religious experience and expression, with a similarly well-established place within the tradition. However, while *ʿaqīda* and *ʿibādāt* have long been central categories of Islamic religious expression, *syiar* has not traditionally enjoyed such a status. In fact, its usage here reflects a significant new configuration of popular understandings of Islam in twentieth-century Southeast Asia.

Qanun 11 does not provide any detailed statements on the specifics of what is considered proper Islamic belief and practice. Rather, it mandates in general terms that "[t]he provincial, district, and municipal governments, and social institutions are obligated to support and foster the belief of the Muslim community and to guard it against the influence of deviant understandings and sects."[59] Similar needs for institutional safeguards to establish and preserve orthodoxy figure prominently in the *qanun's* treatment of *ʿibādāt*: "Every person in the Province of Aceh must respect the sincere observance of [Islamic] ritual practice."[60] The tropes of "respect" and "protection" pervade the discourse of many advocates of Shariʿa implementation in contemporary Aceh, and they play an important role in the formulation of understandings of *syiar* Islam.

In the General Stipulations of *Qanun 11*, *syiar* is defined as "all activities that contain values of religious devotion for the glorification and elevation of the carrying out of Islamic teachings" (I.1.5). In the articles that comprise this section of the *qanun*, *syiar* covers areas related to the official state regulation of emblematic or symbolic aspects of Islam.

[57] *Qanun Provinsi Nanggroe Aceh Darussalam Nomor 11/Tahun 2002 tentang Pelaksanaan Syariʿat Islam Bidang Aqidah, Ibadah dan Syiar Islam.*

[58] *Instruksi Gubernur Daerah Istimewa Aceh Nomor 05/INSTR/2000 Tahun 2000 tentang Pembudayaan Kemakmuran Masjid dan Meunasah dalam Provinsi Daerah Istimewa Aceh; Qanun Aceh Nomor 10 Tahun 2007 tentang Baitul Mal.*

[59] *Qanun 11/2002*, (III.4.1).

[60] *Qanun11/2002*, (IV.11). In the "General Stipulations" (Ketentuan Umum) "worship" (I. *ibadah*/ Ar. *ʿibādāt*) is defined as prayer and fasting during the month of Ramadan" (Bab 1, Pasal 1.8 – 192). However, the boundaries of what is considered *ibadah* elsewhere in this piece of legislation are more porous that this might suggest, with (for example) statements like: "During the month of Ramadhan the community is urged to perform special evening prayers (I. *shalat tarawih*) and carry out other supererogatory acts of worship" (Bab IV, Pasal 10.3).

Under this rubric, for example, one finds broadly framed provisions on the observance of Islamic holidays, the use of *Jawi* (modified Arabic script) and dates according to the Islamic (*hijrī*) calendar in both personal and official documents, as well as the "obligation to wear Islamic dress" (I. *wajib berbusana Islami*).[61] The organizing logic that places these diverse matters under the rubric of *syiar* here frames an orientation toward Islam as definitive of social norms and communal identity.

Qanun 11 also introduces a new institution for the enforcement of Islamic law in Aceh: the Wilayatul Hisbah (WH). The WH is defined here as a state body tasked with addressing infractions of Aceh's Shariʿa legislation through the mechanisms of "reprimand" (I. *tegur*) and "advice" (I. *nasehat*).[62] This legislation does not, however, give them authority to prepare and pursue indictments, and thus they must work together with the civilian police and the public prosecutor's office in order to bring a case to the Shariʿa Court. There are stipulations for *taʿzīr* (discretionary) penalties for various offenses against legislated standards of Islamic religious belief and practice (*ʿaqīda* and *ʿibādāt*), as well as for violations of provisions identified with "*syiar* Islam"—which covers such matters as the holding of deviant opinions, "insulting Islam," neglecting Friday prayers, eating, drinking, or smoking in public during the daylight hours of Ramadan, providing facilities for Muslims to do so, and for immodest dress.[63] *Syiar* is thus clearly a central term in the rhetoric of state Shariʿa in Aceh, and its role in the overall project of state Shariʿa in Aceh is discussed at length in Chapter 7.

In terms of defining offenses against the Shariʿa that could be more easily enforced and prosecuted under the legal system of a modern state, the most significant pieces of legislation in contemporary Aceh are three *qanun* passed in 2003: No. 12 on the consumption of alcohol, No. 13 on gambling, and No. 14 on *khalwat* ("improper covert association" between unmarried members of the opposite sex).[64] The foundation for these three laws was laid in a series of gubernatorial instructions on these same three areas of public morality issued by then (and later disgraced) governor Abdullah Puteh.[65] The form that the laws took in the legislature

[61] *Qanun 11/2002*, (V.12–13). [62] *Qanun 11/2002*, (VI.14.1–5).

[63] The penalties for these offenses range from two to twelve strokes of the cane (*cambuk*), four months to two years in prison, and up to Rp. 3,000,000 (US$313) in fines. *Qanun 11/2002*, (VIII.20–23).

[64] This English-language glossing of the term is borrowed from William Roff's work on analogous developments of regulating Islamic morality in the Malay Peninsula. See "Patterns of Islamization in Malaysia, 1890s–1990s: Exemplars, Institutions and Vectors," *Studies of Islam and Society in Southeast Asia* (Singapore: NUS Press, 2009), 98.

[65] *Instruksi Gubernur Propinsi Nanggroe Aceh Darussalam Nomor 04/INSTR/2002 Tahun 2002 tentang Larangan Judi (Maisir), Buntut, Taruhandan Sejenisnya yang*

was, however, heavily influenced by the input of Islamic leaders with ties to IAIN's Dakwah Faculty, including Azhar Basyari.[66] These three laws were the first (and to date only) enforceable provisions on Islamic criminal law in Aceh's state Shariʿa system, and they contain stipulations for sanctions that reflect classical Islamic jurisprudential categories of both mandatory punishments stipulated as "limits [set by God]" (Ar. *ḥadd*/ pl. *ḥudūd*) and "discretionary punishments" (Ar. *taʿzīr*) to be determined by worldly authorities. In the texts of Aceh's Shariʿa legislation, however, it is the latter category of "discretionary punishments" that dominates, and in many places the intent behind the exercise of this discretionary power by the state reflects a pronounced concern for "blocking the means [to sin]" (Ar. *sadd al-dharāʾiʿ*), or, as Hashim Kamali has expressed it, "preventing an evil before it actually materializes."[67]

The first piece of Islamic "criminal" legislation to be passed as part of Aceh's state Shariʿa system was *Qanun 12* on alcohol, which prohibits the consumption of intoxicating drink as an offense against the Shariʿa, as well as being something that ruins one's physical and mental health, and is detrimental to social life for giving rise to other kinds of sin. This law supersedes earlier measures aimed at the control of alcohol consumption, and it extends the prohibition to include the production, provision, sale, import, distribution, transport, storage, stock, trade, gift distribution, and promotion of all intoxicating beverages.[68] It also attempts to close earlier loopholes by forbidding any other government institutions to license hotels or any other business to trade in alcohol.[69] *Qanun 12* also calls for communal support in the campaign to eradicate alcohol in Aceh, while also stipulating formal, state-enforced sanctions for those convicted of offenses against this law. With regard to the latter, it stipulates a set range of fines and prison terms—setting a *ḥudūd* penalty for drinkers at 40 strokes, and *taʿzīr* penalties between three months to one year in prison and/or fines between Rp. 25,000,000–75,000,000 (US$2,611–7,833) for those who have otherwise facilitated the provision and consumption of

Mengandung Unsur-Unsur Perjudian dalam Propinsi Nanggroe Aceh Darussalam; Instruksi Gubernur Provinsi Nanggroe Aceh Darussalam Nomor 05/INSTR/2002 Tahun 2002 tentang Tata Pergaulan/Khalwat antara Pria dan Wanita dalam Provinsi Nanggroe Aceh Darussalam; and *Surat Edaran Gubernur Provinsi Nanggroe Aceh Darussalam 536/20976 Tahun 2002 tentang Larangan Minuman Beralkohol (Khamar).*

66 Interview with Hamid Sorong, 21 June 2010 at Banda Aceh.

67 Mohammad Hashim Kamali, *Principles of Islamic Jurisprudence* (Cambridge: Islamic Texts Society, 1991), 311.

68 *Peraturan Daerah Propinsi Daerah Istimewa Aceh Nomor 4 Tahun 1999 tentang Larangan Minuman Beralkohol di Propinsi Daerah Istimewa Aceh; Nomor 4 Tahun 2000 tentang Perubahan Pertama atas Peraturan Daerah Nomor 4 Tahun 1999.*

69 *Qanun Provinsi Nanggroe Aceh Darussalam Nomor 12 Tahun 2003 tentang Minuman Khamar dan Sejenisnya.*

alcohol. In support of this, the law also contains a section on the technical aspects of caning (I. *cambuk*).[70]

Qanun 13 prohibits gambling as both an offense against Islamic law and as a means to shield the community from the negative social effects associated with it. Like *Qanun 12* on alcohol, the law also prohibits any governmental body from granting any license for gambling, and enjoins citizens to join their campaign against this scourge. However, as gambling—unlike wine drinking—is not considered a *ḥadd* crime, this law characterizes its sanctions as *taʿzīr*, with penalties ranging from between 6–12 strokes for gamblers, and between three months to one year in prison and/or fines between Rp. 15,000,000–35,000,000 (US$1,566–3,655) for those who providing venues for or otherwise facilitated gambling in Aceh.[71]

Taʿzīr sanctions are also specified for violations of *Qanun 14*, on *khalwat/mesum*, which is defined as "the close contact in a secluded place of two legally responsible adults (Ar. *mukallaf*) of the opposite sex who are marriageable, but unmarried." The law further states an additional gloss on the basic definition that reads: "any actions, activities, and situations that could lead to fornication (Ar. *zinā*)" are to be considered *khalwat*.[72] Here the role of law in "blocking the means" to greater sins and the social ills they occasion is even more directly emphasized than it is in *Qanuns 12* and *13*. The penalties stipulated for *khalwat* consist of between 3–9 strokes and/or a fine of Rp. 2,500,000–10,000,000 (US$261–1,044) for those convicted of *khalwat*, and for those who otherwise facilitated *taʿzīr* penalties between 2–6 months in prison and/or fines between Rp. 5,000,000–15,000,000 (US$522–1,566).

These three *qanun* have, to date, defined the only areas of Islamic penal law to supply cases to Aceh's Shariʿa Courts (Mahkamah Syariah/MS). Even so, few arrests were made and no formal sentences were executed for violations of Islamic law for almost two full years after these laws were enacted. Indeed, it was only after the massive destruction of the 2004 earthquake and tsunami that the institutions of state Shariʿa came to assert a more active role in attempt to manage the dramatic social and political transformations that swept over Aceh in the post-disaster/post-conflict period.[73] By that time, however, the social contexts of Aceh's

[70] This issue will be addressed in Chapter 7 in connection with the role of the Wilayatul Hisbah (WH) in the formal administration of corporal punishment in Aceh's Islamic legal system.

[71] *Qanun Provinsi Nanggroe Aceh Darussalam Nomor 13 Tahun 2003 tentang Maisir (Perjudian).*

[72] *Qanun Provinsi Nanggroe Aceh Darussalam Nomor 14 Tahun 2003 tentang Khalwat (Mesum)*, II.2.

[73] Michelle Ann Miller, "The Role of Islamic Law (Sharia) in Post-Tsunami Reconstruction," in Matthew Clarke, Ismet Fanany, and Sue Kenny (eds.), *Post-Disaster Reconstruction: Lessons from Aceh* (London: Earthscan, 2010), 33.

Islamic legal system had changed dramatically. In the wake of the tsunami and the subsequent reinvigoration of peace negotiations, the conflict between GAM and the Indonesian central government came to an end. The relatively stable peace that ensued, combined with a local Islamic religious revival and a massive influx of foreign aid and development workers bringing with them echoes of global discourses on "reconstruction" and "development" came together in a perfect storm and served to powerfully amplify strains of earlier Indonesian *daʿwa* discourse on Shariʿa as a tool of social engineering.

POST-CONFLICT SHARIʿA LEGISLATION

If the Special Autonomy Law of 1999 and the subsequent development of *qanun* as regional Islamic legislation were linked to Indonesian strategies for victory against GAM's separatist campaigns, the dynamics of the situation in Aceh were reconfigured with the signing of the Helsinki Memorandum of Understanding and the formal end of the conflict in 2005. With the peace came a new law redefining the administration of Aceh as a special autonomous region: the Law on Governing Aceh (LOGA).[74] The LOGA is a massive document containing provisions for the administration of the province in areas ranging from *adat* to economics. For our purposes here, however, discussion will be limited to those sections of the law dealing specifically with the implementation of Shariʿa. Of fundamental importance for these developments is the reassertion of Aceh's special status as an autonomous region within Indonesia. As such, its local authority was confirmed over key areas for the contemporary Islamic legal system including not only "religious life," but also "*adat* based upon Islam," and education "in accordance with Shariʿa," and the role of the ulama in developing state policy.[75]

The LOGA defines the Shariʿa in a formulation that reflects a strong consistency with earlier state definitions of Shariʿa stretching back to the 1968 draft law on "Elements of Islamic Shariʿa."[76] There are also links to previous Islamic legislation in the LOGA's reaffirmation and further definition of the roles and responsibilities of the MPU.[77] These particular areas are, moreover, framed within a broader system in which "*Ke-Islam-an*" ("Islamicity") is cited as the first foundation (I. *asas*) of government.[78] At the same time, however, the LOGA also outlines the

[74] *Undang Undang Republik Indonesia Nomor 11 Tahun 2006 tentang Pemerintahan Aceh* (Law on Governing Aceh/LOGA).

[75] LOGA,V.17.2. [76] LOGA,XVII.125.2. [77] LOGA,XIX.138–40.

[78] LOGA,IV.20.a.

electoral system for a new, democratic Aceh that includes the possibility for independent candidates and local political parties to stand for election.[79] These provisions provided opportunities for former GAM figures who have since succeeded in winning both the governor's office and a plurality of seats in the provincial legislature since the passing of the LOGA in 2006.[80] This has in turn fueled new dynamics in the further development of Shariʿa legislation, as dramatically manifested in the debates over a unified code of Islamic criminal law (*Qanun Jinayat*, discussed shortly), and the promulgation of new Shariʿa by-laws at the district level in various parts of Aceh.[81]

In the 2008 legislative session, over 80 draft *qanun* were in development by the provincial assembly (DPRA), of which 28 were actively discussed. Among them, most bills containing provisions on substantive Shariʿa issues were placed well behind those considered more important priorities by the legislature in the run-up to the 2009 elections, including laws on education, administration, and the regulation of local political parties.[82] Even then, however, the politics of Shariʿa legislation continued to play a role—as evidenced in *Qanun No. 3/2008* on local political parties, which stipulated that tests of Qurʾānic literacy be administered to candidates standing for public office.[83]

The place of Islamic legislation in the work of the DPRA was, however, to change dramatically following the success of *Partai Aceh* (PA) in the April 2009 elections.[84] The PA, which was formed and represented largely by former GAM members, took 33 of 69 seats and was thus set to dominate the incoming government. The outgoing majority was, by contrast, dominated by representatives of the nationalist Golkar party, and their long, virulent animosity toward GAM made the loss all the more painful. In their last, lame-duck days in session, Aceh's provincial lawmakers brought the issue of a unified Islamic criminal code (*Qanun Jinayat*) up for discussion. In the process, revisions were made to earlier drafts to reflect the input of

[79] LOGA,X.67.1.

[80] See Gunnar Stange and Roman Patock, "From Rebels to Rulers and Legislators: The Political Transformation of the Free Aceh Movement (GAM) in Indonesia," *Journal of Current Southeast Asian Affairs* 29(1) (2010) 95–120.

[81] The most prominent of these being the measure passed in West Aceh in August 2010 that sought to further specify the requirements for modest Muslim dress in that district. *Peraturan Bupati Aceh Barat No. 5/2010 tentang Penegakan Syariat Islam dalam Pemakaian Busana Islami di Kabupaten Aceh Barat.*

[82] Discussion at the DPRA Banda Aceh, 27 May 2008.

[83] Melissa Crouch, "Stretching the Scope of Special Autonomy in Aceh: The Controversial Qurʾan Requirement for Election Candidates," *The Australian Journal of Asian Law* 11(1) (2009) 135–41.

[84] See Blair Palmer, "Services Rendered: Peace, Patronage and Post-Conflict Elections in Aceh," in Edward Aspinall and Marcus Mietzner (eds.), *Problems of Democratisation in Indonesia: Elections, Institutions and Society* (Singapore: ISEAS, 2010), 286–306.

previously marginal Islamist voices—the most striking of which involved the application of dramatic corporal punishments (both *ḥudūd* and *taʿzīr*), including death by stoning for those convicted of committing adultery (*zinā*). This new version, with its high-profile and controversial sanctions for sexual offenses, was passed just days before the end of that year's legislative session and the inauguration of a new legislature dominated by former GAM leaders.[85]

A NEW ISLAMIC CRIMINAL CODE

Discussions of the need for revision and reform of the *qanun* on alcohol, gambling, and *khalwat* had been taking shape in Aceh since soon after they were passed in 2003. These discussions engaged both NGO activists and Islamic leaders associated with state Shariʿa institutions. Things accelerated, however, after the popular GAM figure Irwandi Yusuf was elected governor in the first elections after the passing of the LOGA in 2006. By May of the following year, Governor Irwandi asked the State Shariʿa Agency (DSI) to begin work on developing a law that could revise and replace the existing *qanun* with a unified code of Islamic criminal offenses (*jinayat*). This initiated a long process that, from its earliest stages, involved a diverse range of participants, including a number of IAIN academics and "ulama, as well as NGO activists from human rights and gender justice organizations.[86] Out of these conversations, two lengthy bills came to be drafted: one on the substantive content of Islamic criminal law (*Qanun Jinayat*) and another on Islamic criminal procedure (*Qanun Acara Jinayat*).

In the course of these developments the Director of the State Shariʿa Agency, Alyasa Abubakar, emerged as a leading figure in the initial drafting of both bills. Beyond his leading role in the work of the drafting committees, Alyasa also published a number of books through the DSI office in Banda Aceh that elaborated on the need for more comprehensive legislation on penal law and criminal procedure.[87] The long and contentious process of

[85] *Qanun No.--- / 2009 tentang Hukum Jinayat and Qanun No.--- / 2009 tentang Hukum Acara Jinayat.* No formal numbering has yet been given to these bills due to their current status.

[86] Kristina Großmann, "Women's Rights Activists and the Drafting Process of the Islamic Criminal Law," in R. Michael Feener, David Kloos, and Annemarie Samuels (eds.), *Islam and the Limits of the State: Reconfigurations of Ritual, Doctrine, and Authority in Contemporary Aceh* (Leiden: Brill, forthcoming).

[87] Alyasa Abubakar and Marah Halim, *Hukum Pidana Islam di Provinsi Nanggroe Aceh Darussalam* (Banda Aceh: Dinas Syariat Islam Provinsi Nanggroe Aceh Darussalam, 2006); Alyasa Abubakar, *Penerapan Syariat Islam di Aceh*; Alyasa Abubakar, *Wilayatul Hisbah: Polisi*

drafting eventually resulted not just in a revision of existing legislation on alcohol, gambling, and *khalwat*, but also a considerable expansion to cover new areas of legislating morality, including provisions on adultery (Ar. *zinā*), false accusation of adultery (Ar./I. *qadhf*), and rape (I. *pemerkosaan*).[88] Over the course of the drafting process, later versions came to reflect increasingly assertive Islamist influences, not only in the much-discussed stipulation of *ḥudūd* penalties, but also in the application of the gold standard for the payment of fines.[89] The aspects of this law that most sharply mark this hard-line turn were added only in the very last stages in the process, reflecting a remarkable instance of both the marginalization of civil society groups, and the manipulation of legislative processes so serve particular political agendas.[90] In the end, Alyasa claimed that the draft that eventually came to be passed by the provincial legislature was not in line with his original vision for the project.[91]

The version of the *Qanun Jinayat* that was passed by the outgoing legislature on 14 September 2009 upset many more in Aceh as well, and sparked heated debate well beyond the walls of the provincial assembly. It was strongly criticized in many circles, as local activists castigated the move as one of a "spiteful" lame-duck cohort of political losers that played upon highly charged religious symbolism, rather than upon the substance and values of the Shariʿa. If the DPRA were serious about promoting Islamic law, one of them argued, they would do better to take on important matters that could not be handled by local communities at the village level, including measures against systemic corruption and the development of state education programs.[92] International organizations also decried the law as giving legal sanctions to violations of human rights.[93]

Pamong Prajadengan Kewenangan Khusus di Aceh (Banda Aceh: Dinas Syari'at Islam Provinsi Aceh, 2009).

88 Numerous drafts were circulated by diverse parties in 2008 and 2009. A comprehensive chart comparing the rulings of *Qanun* 12, 13, and 14 of 2003, along with a draft of one version prepared by the State Shariʿa Agency (DSI) can be found inAlyasa, *Penerapan Syariat Islam di Aceh*, 105–68.

89 This emphasis on a "gold standard" reflects the influence of groups such as the *Hizbut Tahrir Indonesia* (HTI), whose message has been spread in Aceh through the distribution of their weekly pamphlet, *Buletin Daʿwah Al Islam*, at Friday congregational prayers at an increasing number of mosques in Aceh over recent years.

90 Großmann, "Women's Rights Activists and the Drafting Process."

91 Interview with Alyasa Abubakar, 23 September 2010 at Banda Aceh.

92 Thayeb Loh Angen, "Membangun Peradaban Aceh Baru," *Harian Aceh* (13 November 2009), 10.

93 See, for example, Human Rights Watch, *Policing Morality: Abuses in the Application of Shariʿa in Aceh, Indonesia* (New York: HRW, 2010). Available online at: <http://www.hrw.org/sites/default/files/reports/indonesia1210WebVersionToPost.pdf>, accessed 22 May 2012; Amnesty International, "Indonesia: Repeal Cruel New Stoning and Caning Law," *Amnesty International Public Statement*, 17 September 2009. <http://www.amnesty.

Commenting on these developments, Arskal Salim concluded that this decision by the outgoing DRPA was politically driven, "determined by the fact that the outgoing DPRA was less interested in whether the *qanun* would be implemented . . . and more in being able to claim that they were the legislators who introduced tougher Islamic penal laws."[94] As one local activist expressed the dilemma that was to follow, the disgruntled outgoing legislature left some "homework" (I. *pekerjaan rumah*/"PR") for the new government to deal with.[95] Indeed, the passing of the *Qanun Jinayat* did create considerable political headaches for the new government composed of former GAM leaders who had other priorities and different views on the role that Islam and Islamic law should play in the rebuilding of Acehnese society in the post-conflict period. The Lieutenant Governor, Muhammad Nazar, stated to the press that "[t]he provincial government prefers a more educational penalty for adulterers, rather than stoning."[96] Governor Irwandi, for his part, made repeated public statements that he would not sign the bill into law, despite mobilizations of protest from some segments of the Muslim community against this stance.[97]

Debates over the *Qanun Jinayat* thus went on well after the legislators who passed it had been replaced. These included challenges to the specific contents of the law from a broad range of perspectives, and heated public arguments over its legal standing and enforcement in Aceh. Indonesian national law stipulates that if after 30 days the governor has not signed a measure passed by the legislature, it automatically goes into effect.[98] This can only be precluded ifthe governor sends the bill back to the legislature for further review. He did not do so, however, and so the *Qanun Jinayat* thus remains "on the books" despite Irwandi's statements that he was not inclined to do anything that would support enforcement of its provisions.[99]

The *Qanun Jinayat* represents a new element in the development of Aceh's contemporary Islamic legal system. While arising out of broad-based discussions of the need to reform earlier Shariʿa legislation, its final form was radically recast in an aggressive stance toward highly symbolic criminal sanctions. In this, the *Qanun Jinayat* is comparable to

org/en/news-and-updates/news/indonesia-must-repeal-cruel-new-stoning-caning-law-20090917>, accessed 5 July 2012.

[94] Arskal Salim, *Politics, Criminal Justice and Islamisation in Aceh* (Melbourne: Melbourne Law School Asian Law Centre, 2009) <http://www.lindseyfederation.law.unimelb.edu.au>, accessed 2 February 2011.

[95] Interview with Irwan Adabi, 26 January 2011 at Banda Aceh.

[96] Erwinda Maulia and Hotli Simanjuntak, "Government to Review Aceh's Stoning By-law," *The Jakarta Post* (17 September 2009), 1.

[97] "Gubernur Belum Terapkan Qanun Jinayat: Ribuan Massa Demo Akbar," *Rakyat Aceh* (9 November 2009), 1–2.

[98] *Undang-Undang No.10/2004 tentang Tatacara Undang-undang,* Pasal 43.

[99] "Revisi Raqan Jinayat tak Masuk Prioritas," *Serambi*(4 May 2010), 1.

modern developments in other Muslim societies where, as Rudolph Peters has argued, "the introduction of *ḥudūd* had a highly symbolic character and did not result in a drastic change of the penal system."[100] The impetus here then is not strictly legal, but more broadly political and cultural—in a way such that formal legislation comes to serve as an important means of signifying the Islamic credentials of a state or society.[101] This situation makes it clear that we need to look beyond the formal dimensions of state legal institutions in order to better understand the significance of Islamic law in contemporary Acehnese society. The limits of black-letter law and formal operational procedures in the interpretation and application of Shariʿa are also apparent in the workings of Aceh's system of Shariʿa Courts, which will be discussed in the next chapter.

[100] Rudolph Peters, *Crime and Punishment in Islamic Law: Theory and Practice from the Sixteenth to the Twenty-first Century* (New York: Cambridge University Press, 2005), 160.
[101] Nathan J. Brown, "Sharia and State in the Modern Middle East," *International Journal of Middle East Studies* 29.3 (August 1997) 371.

6

The Jurisdiction and Jurisprudence of Shariʿa Courts

> With us, law is nothing unless close behind it stands a warm, living public opinion. Let that die or grow indifferent, and statutes are waste paper, lack all executive force.
>
> Wendell Phillips
> *"Harper's Ferry"*[1]

In Aceh, as in many Muslim societies, the Shariʿa has long played an important role in defining social norms and setting criteria for the ethical evaluation of public behavior. As is clear in the case of the *Qanun Jinayat* discussed in the previous chapter, however, rapid political reconfigurations can give rise to serious tensions between proponents of newly-imposed rules appealing to Islamic ideals and established models for the regulation of morality in Muslim communities. That particular case resulted in new legislation that was technically "on the books," but did not find resonance with either those holding the reins of state, or with significant sectors of the population. Without sufficient political or popular will, the provisions of the *Qanun Jinayat* remain effectively a dead letter. It is unclear as to whether the controversial physical punishments stipulated in the bill will be applied in Aceh at some point in the future. At present, however, this particular attempt at using formal legislation to further Islamize society can be seen as a spectacular failure. In fact, it could be argued that the passing of a version of the *Qanun Jinayat* that included the stoning penalty has actually had a negative effect on the broader project of Shariʿa social engineering, as a backlash over the politics of its passing has contributed significantly to popular cynicism about the state implementation of Islamic law. Within this highly charged political context, the work of applying the *qanun* passed by the local legislature is assigned to the Aceh's Shariʿa Courts (I. *Mahkamah Syariah*).

[1] Wendell Phillips, *Speeches, Lectures and Letters* (Boston: Lee & Shepard Publishers, 1884), 264.

This chapter focuses on these Shariʿa Courts as pivotal state institutions of Aceh's Islamic legal system. It begins by outlining some of the most important points in the historical development of Shariʿa courts in Aceh, highlighting significant changes in the political foundations of the courts, their formal jurisdiction, and the enforcement of their decisions. Drawing on official documents and court observation, as well as conversations with judges, lawyers, clerks, and private individuals involved with cases, the sections that follow proceed to examine the organization, administration, caseload, and jurisprudence of the Shariʿa Courts in contemporary Aceh. The chapter then concludes with a detailed examination of one particular example of a *khalwat* case that went through the processes of appeal and cassation from a local Shariʿa Court in North Aceh to the Indonesian Supreme Court in Jakarta. This discussion aims to both provide a concrete example of how an Islamic law criminal case is handled by a contemporary Acehnese Shariʿa Court, and to demonstrate the ways in which the local application of the *qanun* is managed within the broader Indonesian national framework.

THE STATE ADMINISTRATION OF ISLAMIC LAW IN ACEH

The increased integration of Aceh's Shariʿa Courts into the Indonesian legal system that has occurred (and in fact accelerated) under the current "Special Autonomy" provisions opens a new chapter in the long and complex history of the administration of Islamic law in Aceh. The institutional mechanisms for implementing Islamic law in the region have varied considerably over time. Based on the titles of individuals recorded on tombstones in North Aceh, Claude Guillot and Ludvik Kalus have sketched an outline of offices for the administration of Islamic law in fifteenth-century Pasai (North Aceh) that were drawn from models developed in medieval Muslim societies of South Asia and the Middle East.[2] As the political center of gravity in the region shifted from Pasai to the area around Banda Aceh in the sixteenth century, Muslim scholars from around the Indian Ocean littoral were attracted there by the patronage of Aceh's sultans.[3] Over the centuries that followed, these connections facilitated

[2] Claude Guillot and Ludvik Kalus, *Les monuments funéraires et l'histoire du sultanat de Pasai à Sumatra, XIIIe–XVIe siècles* (Paris: Association Archipel, 2008), 102–16.

[3] Hoesein Djajadiningrat, "Critisch Overzicht van de in Maleische Werken Vervatte Gegevens over de Geschiedenis van het Soeltanaat van Atjeh," *Bijdragen tot de Taal-, Land- en Volkenkunde* 65 (1911) 157, 160–1.

the introduction of aspects of new models for the state management of Islam that were then being developed in the Mughal and Ottoman empires.

Early European visitors to Aceh frequently commented on the important role that ulama played at court, often imagining their power as analogous to that of more familiar Christian clerical officials. In a number of these sources, the high-ranking Islamic scholar responsible for mediating with foreign merchants and diplomatic envoys was referred to as "the Bishop."[4] Takeshi Ito sees this as a position analogous in some ways to that of the high Islamic religious office of the Ottoman *Sehülislam*, reflecting the tendency of Aceh's sultans to adopt Islamic symbols and institutions developed elsewhere to bolster their authority as rulers of Muslims.[5] Between 1636–1644, the highest ranking religious scholar at Aceh's court was a new arrival from Gujerat, Nūr al-Dīn al-Rānīrī.[6] Al-Rānīrī produced a Malay-language manual of *fiqh* that presented a basic introduction to established rulings in Arabophone Muslim scholarship to Southeast Asian Muslims. The work translated norms of Shāfiʿī Islamic jurisprudence that were well established across many areas of the Muslim world, butreflected little in terms of how its rulings were applicable to local conditions in Aceh. Thus, for example, it provided guidance on the permissibility of eating camel (*ḥalāl*) and giraffe (*ḥarām*), but said nothing about any of the large Sumatran fauna that abounded in the forests of Aceh at that time.[7] Nevertheless, this work served as the foundational text for the study of Islamic jurisprudence in the Malay language for centuries—introducing Southeast Asian Muslim scholars to normative understandings of *fiqh* common across many areas of the expanding Muslim world at that time.[8]

Of course, a *fiqh* manual of this type cannot be taken as definitive of the actual Islamic legal system in Aceh during al-Rānīrī's day.[9] To get a sense

[4] For example, Jacob Compostel, a Dutch envoy to Iskandar Muda in 1636, reported that "the great Bishop" held a court of law once a week, and Balthasar Bort reported in 1659 that the officer known as the Leube Kita Kadi was both "Archbishop" and judge. Takeshi Ito, "The World of the Adat Aceh: A Historical Study of the Sultanate of Aceh," Ph.D. dissertation (Canberra: Australian National University, 1984), 159–63.

[5] Ito, "The World of the Adat Aceh," 259–62.

[6] The most extensive biographical study of al-Rānīrī produced to date can be found in Paul Wormser, *Le Bustan al-Salatin de Nuruddin ar-Raniri: Réflexions sur le role culturel d'un étranger dans le monde Malais au XVII*^e^ *siècle* (Paris: Cahiers d'Archipel, 2012), 41–56.

[7] Nūr al-Dīn Muḥammad Jīlānī b. ʿAlī b. Ḥasanjī b. Muḥammad b. Ḥumayd al-Rānīrī, *Ṣirāṭ al-mustaqīm fī fiqh madhhab al-shāfiʿī* (Cairo: al-Bābī al-Ḥalabī, 1937), 336.

[8] The text exists today in many manuscript holdings across Indonesia and beyond, as well as in numerous printed editions, both on its own (as in the edition cited in footnote 7) and in the margins of a popular eighteenth-century work that was specifically commissioned by the sultan of Banjarmasin to clarify various points in al-Rānīrī's work: Muḥammad Arshad b. ʿAbd. Allāh al-Banjārī, *Sabīl al-muhtadīn lil-tafaqquh fī amr al-dīn* (Singapore: al-Ḥaramayn, n.d./frequent reprints), 2 vols.

[9] As Norman Calder has critically demonstrated, "A work of *fiqh* does not describe an executive legal system." *Islamic Jurisprudence in the Classical Era* (Cambridge: Cambridge University Press, 2010), 162.

of the institutional frameworks for the implementation of Islamic law in Aceh in the pre-modern period, we must then turn to other contemporary sources.[10] The seventeenth-century sultanate maintained a system of four courts with specified jurisdictions: a "civil" court, a "criminal" court, a "religious" court with a *qāḍī* as presiding judge, and the court at what a French visitor to Aceh at that time referred to as the "*alfandèque*" (Ar. *funduq*/I. *pondok*) that handled commercial disputes between merchants.[11] Under this system, infractions of the Shariʿa come largely under the jurisdiction of the *qāḍī* court, including matters of personal status, as well as certain violations of standards of public morality—with a particular emphasis on alcohol and gambling.[12] It is clear, however, that the jurisdiction of the Shariʿa court was not unbounded, but rather functioned within a broader system of religious and more worldly courts, each with their own specialized and limited spheres of judicial competence.

At the same time, the public symbolism of Islam was clearly a matter of great importance to the Acehnese court, as evidenced by the grandiose forms of ritual observance noted in both local documents and in travelers' accounts.[13] Visitors repeatedly remarked upon the strict enforcement of law by Aceh's sultans and sultanas during the seventeenth century. In his discussion of the law as applied in Aceh in 1602, François Martin noted that the penalty for theft was the amputation of hand(s), and feet for repeat offenders. At the same time, however, he also described a number of other forms of physical mutilations for those found guilty of adultery that do not correspond to established Islamic criminal penalties (Ar. *ḥudūd*) for that crime.[14] The use of severe forms of physical punishment in seventeenth-century Aceh is visually epitomized by the image of the quadruple amputee sketched by Thomas Bowrey during his time there in the 1670s (see Figure 6.1).[15] This, however, is by no means an indication that the law imposed was in any way "Islamic." Indeed, there seems to have been a marked emphasis in particular on dramatic physical punishments for those who would challenge social order and

[10] Ito, "The World of the Adat Aceh," 154–8.

[11] Augustin de Beaulieu, *Mémoires d'un voyage aux Indes Orientales, 1619–1622*, ed. Denys Lombard (Paris: Maisonneuve et Larose, 1996), 200–4.

[12] Denys Lombard, *Le Sultanat d'Atjéh au temps d'Iskandar Muda* (Paris: École Française d'Extrême-Orient, 1967), 80–1.

[13] Public spectacles of Islamic ritual observance were noted, for example, by Peter Mundy who was on hand to witness the lavish celebration of the end of Ramadan in 1637. Anthony Reid, *Witnesses to Sumatra: A Travellers' Anthology* (Kuala Lumpur: Oxford University Press, 1995), 82–90.

[14] This included castration for men and the mutilation of the face for women. Reid, *Witnesses to Sumatra*, 60.

[15] Thomas Bowrey, *A Geographical Account of Countries Round the Bay of Bengal*, ed. Richard Temple (Cambridge: Hakluyt Society, 1905).

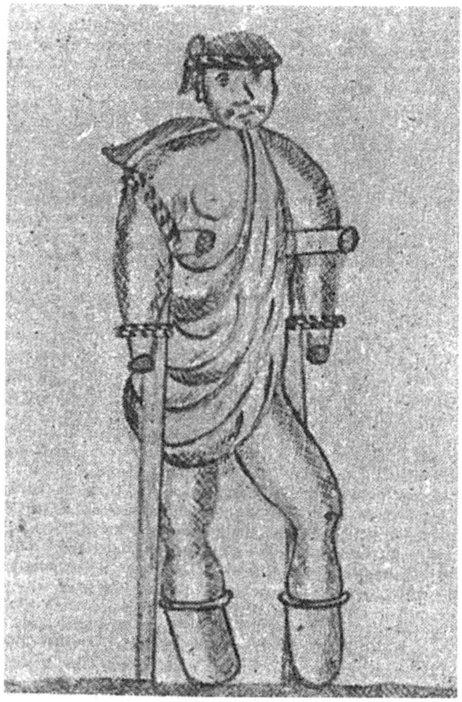

Figure 6.1. A thief punished by amputation in Aceh, c. 1670. Thomas Bowrey, *A Geographical Account of Countries Round the Bay of Bengal*, ed. Richard Temple. (Cambridge: Hakluyt Society, 1905)

royal privilege. William Dampier, for example, described law in Aceh as "very strict" during his stay in Aceh (1688–1689), noting in particular the practice of amputation, but also several other brutal forms of execution that are unknown to Islamic law.[16] Such images of Acehnese severity were apparently not merely the products of non-Muslim European perceptions, as a Mughal account of Aceh written at the turn of the seventeenth century also remarked on the peculiarly high degree of state surveillance over sexual impropriety and the dramatic forms of violent punishment meted out to incorrigible offenders.[17]

Sources that were intended to aid judges in applying Islamic law in this period include the *Mir'at al-ṭullāb*, composed by al-Rānīrī's successor at the Acehnese court, ʿAbd al-Ra'uf Singkel (d. 1693).[18]

[16] Reid, *Witnesses to Sumatra*, 112–13.

[17] Muzaffar Alam and Sanjay Subrahmanyam, *Writing the Mughal World: Studies on Culture and Politics* (New York: Columbia University Press, 2012), 108–9.

[18] The work was commissioned by Sulṭāna Safiyat al-Din Shah (r. 1641–1675) herself. Peter G. Riddell, *Islam and the Malay-Indonesian World: Transmission and Responses*

This text was in turn taken as the basis for the mid-eighteenth-century work of Jalāl al-dīn b. Muḥammad Kamāl al-dīn Turasānī, titled *Safīnat al-ḥukkām fī takhlīsh al-khashshām*, which covers matters of family, contract, and criminal law, as well as aspects of the procedure and administrative structures that should ideally be used to apply the Shariʿa under the sultan. This text has attracted the attention of some modern Acehnese, who refer to it as a precedent for the application of Islamic law by modern state structures.[19] Ali Hasjmy was among the first to call attention to the *Safinat al-Ḥukkām* in the context of modern Shariʿa politics.[20] Soon thereafter, Syiah Kuala University produced a Romanized edition of the text.[21] Copies of this edition are, however, hard to come by in Aceh today, and so in 2004, Aceh's State Shariʿa Agency (DSI) published a massive new Romanized version, which they hailed as "concrete proof" (I. *bukti nyata*) that the Islamic courts in Aceh had their own traditions of Islamic procedural law.[22] The precedent, however, is a rather tenuous one for present-day policies. The specifics of administering Islamic law presented in this text bear almost no resemblance to the current system in place—and it is devoid of anything that resembles the modern legislation of Islam in the special autonomous province of contemporary Aceh. It is clear that the formal application of Islamic law has long and historically visible roots in Aceh. However, the particular mechanisms of administering Islamic law in earlier periods differed considerably from those of Aceh's contemporary Islamic legal system, thus strengthening the sense that what is going on now is much more about visions of the future than of the past.

(London: Hurst & Company, 2001), 129. A facsimile edition was published locally as Teungku Sjeich Abdurrauf alias Teungku Tjhik Sjiah Kuala, *Mir'at at-Tullab Fi Tashil Maʿrifat Ahkam Ash-Syarʿiyyah li'l Malik Al-Wahhab: Tjermin bagi mereka jang menuntut Ilmu Fiqih pada memudahkan mengenai segala Hukum Sjaraʿ Allah* (Banda Aceh: Universitas Syiah Kuala, 1971).

[19] Hasbi Amiruddin, *Perjuangan Ulama Aceh di Tengah Konflik* (Yogyakarta: Ceninnets Press, 2004), 31–2.

[20] A. Hasjmy, "Islam Menjiwai Alam Pikiran Melayu Lama: Sebuah Studitentang Naskah Tua *Safinatul Hukkam*," in *Apa Tugas Sastrawan sebagai Khalifah Allah* (Surabaya: Bina Ilmu, 1984), 105–9.

[21] This text was the first to appear in an apparently short-lived series of such editions. The second of these was of a text compiled in 1890 that claims to present the Kanun Meukuta Alam Sultan Iskandar Muda.

[22] Jalaluddin At-Tarusani, *Safinat Al-Hukkam fi Takhlish Al-Khashsham* (Banda Aceh: Dinas Syariʿat Islam Provinsi Nanggroe Aceh Darussalam, Fakultas Syariʿah IAIN Ar-Raniry, 2004).

COLONIAL RE-CONFIGURATIONS OF ISLAMIC COURTS

In general, Indonesia's Islamic courts trace their modern origins to an 1882 Dutch regulation that authorized a system of religious tribunals (D. *priesterraaden*).[23] These courts were authorized to decide cases of family law, but were only established on the islands of Java and Madura.[24] The Dutch generally did not seek to regulate the administration of Islamic law beyond these territories.[25] In Aceh, the Dutch did establish a "*Raad Oelama*" in 1919. This institution was not, however, an independent Islamic religious court but rather an advisory board (D. *adviescollege*) of religious scholars that could be consulted by the colonial government on matters of family and inheritance law.[26]

Major modern innovations in the development of Islamic courts in Aceh came during the Japanese occupation of Sumatra during World War II. At that time, the Japanese made a number of significant concessions in acknowledgement of the assistance of an Acehnese Muslim "fifth column" (known as the Fujiwara Kikan) in establishing a beachhead for them in Aceh.[27] This included the establishment of a system of Islamic courts, a move that transferred crucial aspects of local governance from the *ulèëbalang* over to the ulama—particularly in the matter of dividing and distributing shares of estates in cases of death and divorce.[28] In developing these new institutions for the modern administration of Islamic affairs, the Japanese provided institutional resources to influential PUSA ulama who were energized by currents of modernist Islamic reform in the early twentiethcentury.[29] PUSA presented their own detailed plan for a new Islamic legal system in Aceh to the Japanese administration in

[23] *Staatsblad No. 152/1882 - Ordonnantie van den Gouverneur Generaal bevattende bepalingen omtrent de samenstelling enz. der priesterraden op Java en Madura.* Reprinted in Thoralf Hanstein, *Islamisches Recht und Nationales Recht: Eine Unstersuchung zum Einfluß des Islamischen Rechts auf die Entwicklung des modernen Familienrechts am Beispiel Indonesiens* (Frankfurt: Peter Lang, 2002), 140–1.

[24] Earlier colonial developments leading up to the 1882 decree in Java are summarized in Kobayashi Yasuko, *Indonesia tenkaisuru isuramu* (Nagoya: Nagoya Daigaku Shuppannkai, 2008), 121–49.

[25] The one major exception to this was the case of South Kalimantan, where the Dutch established the Kerapatan Kadi in 1937. Daniel S. Lev, *Islamic Courts in Indonesia: A Study in the Political Bases of Legal Institutions* (Berkeley: University of California Press, 1972), 79.

[26] J.J. van de Velde, *De Godsdienstige rechtspraak in Nederlandsch-Indië, Staatsrechtlijk beschouwd* (Leiden: Drukkerij A Vros, 1928), 26–8.

[27] Harry J. Benda, *The Crescent and the Rising Sun: Indonesian Islam under the Japanese Occupation, 1942–1945* (The Hague: W. van Hoeve Ltd., 1958), 106.

[28] Eric E. Morris, "Islam and Politics in Aceh: A Study of Center-Periphery Relations in Indonesia," Ph.D. dissertation (Ithaca: Cornell University, 1983), 102.

[29] A.J. Piekaar, *Atjèh en de Oorlog met Japan* ('s-Gravenhage: W. van Hoeve, 1949), 224.

December 1943. This was intended not only to establish Islamic institutions within the formal structure of the state, but also to further advance their own position vis-à-vis the *ulèëbalang*.[30] On 13 February 1944, the Japanese authorities in Aceh responded with the establishment of their own model of an Islamic "Religious Court" (Jp. *shūkyō hōin*) with jurisdiction over appeals from the district and sub-district level *Qāḍī*Courts that had also been established under the occupation. The creation of this new system of religious courts was proclaimed by the Japanese administration as a significant demonstration of their "respect and esteem for Islam."[31] It also turned out to be a successful means by which to consolidate local Muslim support for programs of social control and resource management directed by the local administrative apparatus of a state whose center was located outside of Aceh itself.

INDEPENDENT INDONESIA'S RELIGIOUS COURTS

With Indonesian independence in 1945, some new attempts were made to unify the different Islamic religious court structures that had previously been established across the archipelago under a unified national system.[32] In Aceh, however, PUSA ulama strove to assert local control over the *shūkyō hōin*.[33] The following year, Aceh's local Representative Assembly formalized the jurisdiction of these courts over divorce, inheritance, religious endowments, donations, and cases related to Islamic religious property administered by the institution of the *Baitul Mal*.[34] At the same time, these courts in Aceh were also renamed as "Mahkamah Syariah." The Arabic-derived designation for these courts was, and has been ever since, viewed by many both within and beyond Aceh as signaling an increased

[30] Anthony Reid, *Blood of the People: Revolution and the End of Traditional Rule in Northern Sumatra* (Kuala Lumpur: Oxford University Press, 1979), 128.

[31] *Aceh Syu Rei (UU) no. 12, Syowa 19, 2 Gatsu, 13 Nichi*, Pasal 1: 2.2 in Analiansyah and Jamhuri, *Syariat Islam Di Nanggroe Aceh Darussalam: Inventarisasi Dokumen* (Banda Aceh: Dinas Syariat Islam Provinsi Nanggroe Aceh Darussalam, 2008), 325–6.

[32] Under independent Indonesia's new legal system, Islamic religious courts with limited jurisdiction over limited aspects of family law existed alongside a much more extensive system of civil courts which handled criminal and commercial cases for all Indonesian citizens in addition to personal status law for non-Muslims. For an overview of the place of Islamic law within the broader Indonesian national legal system, see Jan Michiel Otto, ed. *Sharia Incorporated: A Comparative Overview of the Legal Systems of Twelve Muslim Countries in Past and Present* (Leiden University Press, 2010), 533–490.

[33] M. Isa Sulaiman, "Les Ulèebalang, les Ulémas, et les enseignants de madrasah: La lutte pour le pouvoir local en Aceh de 1942 à 1951," Ph.D. dissertation (Paris: Écoles Des Hautes Études en Sciences Sociales, 1985), 216.

[34] *Keputusan No. 35 Sidang Pekerdja Dewan Perwakilan Aceh Pada Hari Rabu Tanggal 3 December, 1947*, in Analiansyah and Jamhuri, *Syariat Islam*, 329–31.

"Islamization" of the legal system. A similar reading is also common for the re-designation of provincial legislation as "*qanun*."[35]

Over the first decade of Indonesian independence, Aceh's Mahkamah Syariah developed in dynamic tension with national-level attempts to manage the Islamic religious courts that had been administered by the Dutch and Japanese in other parts of the country. In 1957, Aceh's provincial government issued a new regulation on Aceh's Shariʿa Courts that affirmed the courts' jurisdiction over cases of marriage, divorce, reconciliation, inheritance, religious endowments, charitable gifts, and religious property. At the same time, it placed these courts under the supervision—and funded from the budget—of the Indonesian Department of Religious Affairs (I. *Departemen Agama*/DepAg).[36] Aceh's local Muslim leaders pressured DepAg to approve their draft regulations for the Mahkamah Syariah, and as a result Aceh was the first area of independent Indonesia to have an officially recognized Islamic court. Soon thereafter, however, a new Indonesian government regulation was issued to provide for the establishment of Islamic religious courts in many more areas that did not have previously recognized Islamic Courts (I. *Pengadilan Agama*)—that is, everywhere in the country outside of Java, Madura, and South Kalimantan.[37] This regulation was based on the one passed for Aceh earlier in that year.[38] The jurisdiction of these newly recognized Islamic courts was, however, more limited than what many of Aceh's Islamic leaders had hoped for.

Over the decade that followed, there were repeated attempts to further extend the jurisdiction of the Islamic religious courts in Aceh. In 1958, the local legislative assembly issued a resolution calling for the Mahkamah Syariah to also handle cases related to theft, adultery, false accusations of adultery, gambling, and other Shariʿa criminal matters.[39] Although

[35] The terms used to refer to both these Islamic courts and the legislation they apply draw on precedents established in the nineteenth-century Ottoman Empire under the *Tanzimat* reforms. These developments were, however, originally reflections of quite the opposite process there. In the context of the modernizing Ottoman Empire, these terms marked not the expansion but rather the contraction of the place of Islamic law in the broader legal system and reflected new trends toward a restructuring and secularizing of social institutions. Elyse Semerdjian, *Off the Straight Path: Illicit Sex, Law, and Community in Ottoman Aleppo* (Syracuse University Press, 2008), 69–70.

[36] *Peraturan Pemerintah Nomor 29/ Tahun 1957 tentang Pembentukan Pengadilan Agama/Mahkamah Sjariʿjah di Propinsi Aceh, Pasal 2.*

[37] *Peraturan Pemerintah No. 45, Tahun 1957 tentang Pembentukan Pengadilan Agama/ Mahkamah Sjariʿjah di luar Djawadan Madura.* This law revoked the separate provisions for Aceh outlined in Law No. 29 passed earlier that year (*Peraturan Pemerintah Nomor 29/ Tahun 1957*) and thus placed Aceh under the same system now applicable for other Islamic courts in Indonesia.

[38] Dan Lev also noted that the Aceh law was, in turn, modeled after an earlier draft from East Sumatra. *Islamic Courts*, 89.

[39] *DPRD/Res/58/No. 1 in: Analiansyah and Jamhuri, Syariat Islam*, 412–14.

such motions for broadening the jurisdiction of Aceh's Islamic religious courts were blocked by the central government in Jakarta, this did not discourage other attempts over the years that followed. For example, in 1967, Aceh's Ulama Council issued a statement urging the government to expand the jurisdiction of the Shariʿa courts to include broader substantial authority over cases of inheritance and joint marital property (Ac. *Hareuta sihareukat*), and to remove any authority over related matters from the jurisdiction of the civil courts.[40] Daniel Lev has called attention to the expansionist agenda of Aceh's Shariʿa Courts at the time, remarking that since the early years of Indonesian independence, "the courts have consistently gone beyond their statutory mandate." Judges in other parts of the country, he adds, were generally critical of such "over-reaching."[41] By the 1970s, however developments in the Indonesian capital were moving in directions that led to both expanded jurisdiction and greater national oversight for all of the country's Islamic religious Courts.

As discussed in the previous chapter, provisions in 1974 Marriage Law contributed to a dramatic increase in the caseload of the Religious Courts. In response to this, the Department of Religious Affairs began a series of efforts to restructure the country's Religious Courts. These measures included increasingly ambitious programs for standardizing nearly all aspects of the court, ranging from the design and furnishings of its physical facilities, to the format of official paperwork and workflow procedures, as well as standardized reference works to be stocked in the courts' library, and technical equipment for observing the new moon to determine the beginning and end of Ramadan.[42] The Department of Religious Affairs explicitly formulated these reforms as mechanisms for greater control over the administration of Islamic law by local courts.

The Department of Religious Affairs also addressed the definition and hierarchy of jurisdiction with a 1981 reclassification of Islamic courts. In Aceh, this reclassification produced a new formalization and distribution of local Islamic courts (now no longer known as "Mahkamah Syariah," but rather designated by the national standardized term for "religious courts" "Pengadilan Agama"). Under this new structuring, Aceh's courts were organized according to the same hierarchies of jurisdiction applied by the Indonesian government at the national level, with six Level IIB Courts

[40] *Keputusan Musyawarah Alim Ulama Se-Daerah Provinsi Daerah Istimewa Aceh* (26 November 1967), reprinted in: *Kumpulan Fatwa-Fatwa Majelis Ulama Propinsi Daerah Istimewa Aceh Tahun 1965 s/d 31 Maret 1979* (Banda Aceh: MPU, 2006), 22.

[41] Lev, *Islamic Courts*, 204.

[42] For a sense of the aim and scope of standardization at that time, see *Standardisasi Pengadilan Agama* (Jakarta: Direktorat Pembinaan Badan Peradilan Agama Islam, 1980).

(at Lhoksukon, Idi, Kuala Simpang, Nagan Raya, Blangkejeren, and Calang), eight Level IIA Courts (at Sigli, Sabang, Takengon, Langsa, Lhokseumawe, Kutacane, Meulaboh, and Tapak Tuan), as well as one first-level court and an appeals court at Banda Aceh.[43]

At the same time, larger reconfigurations of Indonesia's legal system beyond the framework of the Department of Religious Affairs were also having a significant impact on the structure and hierarchy of Islamic religious courts. The Indonesian Supreme Court (Mahkamah Agung/MA) had, in theory, held the authority to review Islamic court decisions since 1970.[44] However, no real attempts were made to exercise this authority until 1977, when the Supreme Court issued a new regulation on its handling cassation from the Religious Courts.[45] Although this initially met with considerable opposition from the Department of Religious Affairs, the position of the Indonesian Supreme Court at the apex of the nation's Islamic legal system was soon consolidated, and in 1979, the Court appointed a special panel of six justices to handle cassation from the Islamic courts.[46] As Barry Hooker has demonstrated, with the transfer of the courts from the auspices of the Department of Religious Affairs to the Supreme Court, Indonesia's Islamic Courts are integrated into the national secular system, and are thus bound by it.[47] Sebastiaan Pompe has interpreted these measures as further attempts to extend centralized control over the lower courts of all jurisdictions across Indonesia.[48]

Other reforms proceeded apace over the years that followed, including a 1985 regulation recognizing the appointment of female judges to Indonesia's Islamic courts.[49] The most comprehensive formal restructuring

[43] *Keputusan Menteri Agama Republik Indonesia Nomor 13/Tahun 1981 tentang Klasifikasi Pengadilan Tinggi Agama dan Pengadilan Agama se Indonesia*, republished in *Himpunan Peraturan Perundang-Undangan Produk Departemen Agama RI, Tahun 1981* (Jakarta: Proyek Perencanaan Peraturan Perundangan Keagamaan Tahun Anggaran 1981/1982, 1982), 49–58.

[44] Mark E. Cammack, "Islamic Law in Indonesia's New Order," *International and Comparative Law Quarterly* 38(1) (1989) 66.

[45] *Keputusan Mahkamah Agung Nomor 1/Tahun 1977 tentang Jalan Pengadilandalam Pemeriksaan Kasasi dalam Perkara Perdata dan Perkara Pidana oleh Pengadilan Agama dan Pengadilan Militer; Surat Edaran Mahkamah Agung No. 04/1977 perihal Pelaksanaan Jalan Pengadilan Pemeriksaan Kasasi dalam Perkara Perdata dan Pidana oleh Peradilan Agama dan Peradilan Militer*, reprinted in: *A. Basiq Djalil, Peradilan Agama di Indonesia: Gemuruhnya Politik Hukum (Hk. Islam, Hk. Barat, dan Hk. Adat) dalam Rentang Sejarah Bersama Pasang Surut Lembaga Peradilan Agama Hingga Lahirnya Peradilan Syariat Islam Aceh* (Jakarta: Kencana Prenada Media Group, 2006).

[46] Cammack, "Islamic Law in Indonesia's New Order," 67.

[47] M.B. Hooker, *Indonesian Syariah: Defining a National School of Islamic Law* (Singapore: ISEAS, 2008), 290.

[48] Sebastiaan Pompe, *The Indonesian Supreme Court: A Study of Institutional Collapse* (Ithaca: Cornell Southeast Asia Program, 2005), 215–37.

[49] Euis Nurlaelawati, *Modernization, Tradition and Identity: The Kompilasi Hukum Islam and Legal Practice in the Indonesian Religious Courts* (Amsterdam: Amsterdam University Press, 2010), 34.

of Indonesia's Islamic courts, however, came in 1989 with the passage of the Religious Judicature Act. This legislation vested the courts with new powers and mandated changes in the organization and staffing of the courts modeled after the parallel system of civil courts. The jurisdiction of the courts was also expanded to include inheritance cases.[50] In many ways, however, these developments marked the culmination and formalization of processes by which Islamic religious courts across the country had been gradually standardized into structures analogous to those of the country's civil courts.[51]

In terms of the substantive law to be applied by these reformed Islamic courts, the major innovation of this period came in 1991 when Suharto issued a presidential instruction on the *Compilation of Islamic Laws (Kompilasi Hukum Islam*/KHI). This text, however, has been the subject of some controversy in Indonesia. While some Islamist activists hailed the measure as a significant mark of progress toward the state implementation of Islamic law, others have been quite critical of the substantive content of the Islamic laws contained in the KHI.[52] Since the fall of Suharto in 1998, critiques of the KHI as a regressive holdover from a defunct authoritarian regime have also becomeincreasingly pronounced.[53] In her study of the decisions of Religious Courts (Pengadilan Agama) in Jakarta and West Java, Euis Nurlaelawati speaks of an "ambivalence" toward the KHI among Religious Court judges—and more broadly across society at large—arguing that "the application of the KHI has not met its goal of directing society to solve its familial problems in the courts, that is to obtain a legal guarantee of certainty."[54] Beyond this, she further argues that in the court decisions of her case studies *fiqh* texts are cited by many judges as more authoritative references than the KHI. As will be discussed further in what follows, the situation has developed in rather different directions in contemporary Aceh.

[50] Mark E. Cammack, "Indonesia's 1989 Religious Judicature Act: Islamization of Indonesia or Indonesianization of Islam," *Indonesia* 63 (April 1997) 143–68.

[51] Mark E. Cammack, "The Indonesian Islamic Judiciary," in R. Michael Feener and Mark E. Cammack (eds.), *Islamic Law in Contemporary Indonesia: Ideas and Institutions* (Cambridge, MA: Harvard University Press, 2007), 154–7.

[52] Habiburrahman, *Rekonstruksi Hukum Kewarisan Islam di Indonesia* (Jakarta: Kencana Prenada Media Group, 2011). I would like to thank Mark Cammack for calling this work to my attention.

[53] See, for example: Marzuki Wahid and Rumadi, *Fiqih Madzhab Negara: Kritik Atas Politik Hukum Islam di Indonesia* (Yogyakarta: LKiS, 2001); and Siti Musdah Mulia, with Mark E. Cammack, "Toward a Just Marriage Law: Empowering Indonesian Women through a Counter Legal Draft to the Indonesian Compilation of Islamic Law," in Feener and Cammack (eds.), *Islamic Law in Contemporary Indonesia*, 128–45.

[54] Nurlaelawati, *Modernization, Tradition and Identity*, 224.

With the collapse of Suharto's "New Order," a spate of further reforms to Indonesia's legal system was introduced.[55] The most sweeping change came when a major restructuring of Indonesia's judiciary was announced with the passing of *Law No. 35/1999*.[56] This law initiated a process whereby the nation's Islamic Courts were removed from the administrative authority of the Department of Religious Affairs and brought under the direct supervision of the Supreme Court (MA).[57] In 2003, a Presidential Decision under President Megawati Sukarnoputri (*No.11/2003*) and a Decision from the head of the Indonesian Supreme Court (*KMA/070/SK/X/2004*) transferred control over Aceh's Islamic Courts from the Ministry of Religious Affairs to come under the jurisdiction of the Indonesian Supreme Court as part of the "one roof" (I. *satu atap*) policy.[58] The structures of this administrative supervision were further consolidated in 2004, thus firmly establishing the situation of all Indonesia's Islamic courts under the "one roof" of the Supreme Court.[59] These developments inform the broader legal and administrative backdrop for changes in Aceh's Shariʿa Courts under its twenty-first-century special autonomy laws.[60]

In terms of jurisdiction, the re-structuring of Aceh's Islamic Courts during the *Reformasi* period picked up with *Qánun No. 10/2002*, which restored some wider jurisdiction to Aceh's Islamic religious courts over areas including select aspects of criminal law (*jinayat*).[61] This same law also re-designated these courts as "Mahkamah Syariah," a usage that distinguished them from the Islamic religious courts in other parts of

[55] For a brief contextualized overview of these developments, see: Tim Lindsey and Mas Achmad Santosa, "The Trajectory of Law Reform in Indonesia," in Tim Lindsey (ed.), *Indonesia: Law and Society*, 2nd edition (Annandale: The Federation Press, 2008), 2–22.

[56] Arskal Salim, "Epilogue: Shariʿa in Indonesia's Current Transition: An Update," in Arskal Salim and Azyumardi Azra (eds.), *Shariʿa and Politics in Modern Indonesia* (Singapore: ISEAS, 2003), 215.

[57] This move initially met with considerable resistance from the Department of Religious Affairs, although such opposition was eventually overwhelmed, and the Religious Courts across the country were formally transferred to the supervision of the Supreme Court in June 2004. Cammack, "The Indonesian Islamic Judiciary," 156–7.

[58] Tim Lindsey and M.B. Hooker, with Ross Clarke and Jeremy Kingsley, "Shariʿa Revival in Aceh," in Feener and Cammack (eds.), *Islamic Law in Contemporary Indonesia*, 251.

[59] *Keputusan Presiden Republik Indonesia Nomor 21/Tahun 2004 tentang Pengalihan Organisasi, Administrasi dan Finansial di Lingkungan Peradilan Umum dan Peradilan Usaha Negara dan Peradilan Agama ke Mahkamah Agung*. A summary of the plans informing these changes was published in English—presumably for the benefit of the international donors that supported the reform program: *Blueprint for the Reform of the Supreme Court of Indonesia* (Jakarta: The Supreme Court of Indonesia, 2003), 53–7.

[60] Laws of 1999, 2001, and 2006, as discussed in Chapter 5.

[61] *Qanun Provinsi Nanggroe Aceh Darussalam Nomor 10/Tahun 2002 tentang Peradilan Syariat Islam*, (III.49). In the official "Clarification" (I. *Penjelasan*) of this *qanun*, the law's authority over Shariʿa criminal offenses was laid out in greater detail, specifying the application of *ḥudūd* penalties for cases involving theft, brigandage, adultery, false accusations of adultery, alcohol, and apostasy, as well as *qiṣāṣ* (retaliation) for murder and battery, and *taʿzīr* punishments for those found guilty of gambling, *khalwat*, or neglecting one's duties of

Indonesia and reclaimed the name used for the courts by PUSA during the early years of Indonesian independence. Most of these changes were later affirmed by the 2006 Law on Governing Aceh (LOGA), including the expanded jurisdiction of Aceh's Shariʿa Courts and their administrative supervision by the Indonesian Supreme Court. Accordingly, funding and technical support for Aceh's Shariʿa Courts remain situated within the general hierarchy of the Indonesian national system wherein the Supreme Court provides funding, technical support, and administrative authority. The Supreme Court also maintains the authority for selecting and confirming judges in Aceh's Shariʿa Courts, as well as its role in the cassation and review of cases coming up from those courts.[62] With the redefinition of Aceh's special autonomy status in the LOGA, the position of the Mahkamah Syariah as "special courts" (I. *pengadilan khusus*) within the broader Indonesian legal system was also confirmed in the 2006 national law amending Indonesia's 1989 Religious Judicature Act. This measure helped to further establish the position of the MS within the reformed framework of the Indonesian national legal system.[63] Thus while their official mandate is to apply the *qanun* passed by the provincial legislature under Aceh's Special Autonomy provisions, the Mahkamah Syariah are fully financed and directly administered from Jakarta under the supervision of the Indonesian Supreme Court (Mahkamah Agung).

POINTS OF REFERENCE

While thus deeply integrated into Indonesian's national system of Islamic courts, Aceh's Shariʿa Courts also retain a number of distinctive features, aside from their more expansive jurisdiction. Aceh's own complex modern history has informed the development of patterns that set some aspects of its courts apart from those that have been studied elsewhere in Indonesia. This is seen, for example, in the composition of its personnel. Indonesia's Islamic court system employs an extensive schedule of rotation whereby judges move frequently to diverse parts of the country. This has facilitated

obligatory prayer and fasting. Such "Clarifications" are, however not legally binding and in practice the only forms of physical sanction that have been applied by the courts have been *taʿzīr* canings for violations of the *qanun* on alcohol, gambling, and *khalwat*.

[62] *Undang-Undang Republik Indonesia Nomor 11/Tahun 2006 tentang Pemerintahan Aceh*, (LOGA) 1, 131, 135–6.

[63] Aceh's Shariʿa Courts are explicitly defined as such in the official 'Clarification' (I. *Penjelasan*) to *Undang-undang Republik Indonesia Nomor 3/20006 tentang Perubahan atas Undang-Undang Nomor 7/1989 tentang Peradilan Agama*, 2.3A. For more on this: Mardani, *Hukum Acara Perdata Peradilan Agama dan Mahkamah Syariʿah* (Jakarta: Sinar Grafika, 2009).

a considerable degree of standardization and centralization across the Indonesian judiciary since the New Order period.[64] In principle, then, the appointment and career trajectories of Islamic Court judges was to be centrally managed for the entire nation from Jakarta. In Aceh, however, these aspects of the Shariʿa Court judiciary were often framed in de facto provincial terms as the violence of the conflict and the tense local political situation have placed considerable practical limits upon the extent to which judges from outside the province could be rotated in.

During the decades of armed conflict between GAM and the Indonesian government, Aceh's courts tended to fall outside regular national circuits of rotation. As judges from other parts of the country refused being posted to Aceh for fear of the violence, local judges have tended to stay in Aceh for longer periods and it thus became a regular pattern for local judges to, at most, move between different courts within the province. These conditions have unintentionally facilitated a relatively more direct sense of connection between Shariʿa court judges and the local communities that they serve. This is evidenced, for example, in the participation of judges in various non- or semi-official religious and social activities outside the court.[65] For instance, it is not uncommon for Mahkamah Syariah judges to also volunteer as preachers, teachers of Qur'ān recitation, and even corpse washers.[66] Nevertheless, even in this situation, standards of professional distance are still applied to preserve a necessary measure of dignity and impartiality. As one senior judge expressed it: "We have to act according to the regulations of our position. We can't be like other people, going to coffee shops, for example—we can't do that."[67] It took several years after the formal end of the conflict for standard rotation procedures to kick in, and it was only then that more of Aceh's Shariʿa Court judges

[64] John R. Bowen, "Fairness and Law in an Indonesian Court," in Feener and Cammack (eds.), *Islamic Law in Contemporary Indonesia*, 170–92.

[65] This is also reflected in some aspects of court practice, such as the use of language. The Acehnese language became a potent symbol of identity during the conflict, and today, it continues to be used in a relatively wider range of contexts than are vernacular languages in many other parts of Indonesia. On occasion, the parties appearing before the Shariʿa court will use Acehnese or "code-switch" between Acehnese and Indonesian in expressing themselves—particularly when discussing emotionally charged issues of divorce. When this happens, there is generally little problem in understanding the testimony, as most judges and court clerks also know Acehnese. Once the party has finished speaking, however, one of the judges "translates" what was said by restating the point in formal Bahasa Indonesia to be entered into the official court record. For a more language-focused study of the processes of transformation that happens as such reports are written in another Sumatran context, see Curtis E. Renoe, "Legal Texts and Truths: The Interactive Production of Fact in Indonesian Criminal Trials," Ph.D. dissertation (New Haven: Yale University, 2002).

[66] Those judges involved with the last of these activities tend to be women, who have said that it is an important duty to ensure that female corpses are properly prepared for a Muslim burial. Interview with Shariʿa Court judge, 26 January 2009 at Banda Aceh.

[67] Interview with Shariʿa Court judge, 20 January 2009 at Bireuen.

were transferred to other provinces of Sumatra and some even as far as Maluku.

The legacy of Aceh's modern history of Islamic reform on the religious background of Shariʿa Court judges has been even more influential on the character of these institutions. As discussed earlier, the Shariʿa Courts were first established under the Japanese as a concession to the Islamic Modernists associated with PUSA, prominent members of which had actively collaborated during early stages of Japan's wartime occupation of northern Sumatra. Since then, Modernist Muslims have comprised the overwhelming majority of Aceh's Shariʿa Court judges. Today, nearly all of Aceh's Shariʿa Court judges have degrees from IAIN—many from the Banda Aceh campus, but also from the branches in Medan, Padang, Palembang, Pekanbaru, and elsewhere.[68] Very few of them, however, have spent much time studying in traditional *dayahs*, and some are even candid in expressing their criticism of what they perceive to be the inflexibility of Traditionalist *fiqh*. This situation contrasts sharply with what has been described, for example, in West Java, where there is a higher number of older judges who come out of *pesantren* backgrounds.[69] In her study of those Shariʿa courts, Euis Nurlaelawati sees the impact of this connection to *pesantren* reflected in the citation of Arabic *fiqh* texts in court decisions to add legitimacy to the rules stated in the 1991 *Compilation of Islamic Law* (KHI).[70] In some cases, she even found that the only references cited were to *fiqh* texts, sometimes even without any reference at all to the KHI or any piece of Indonesian state legislation.[71]

In Aceh, however, specific *fiqh* texts are rarely, if ever, cited in Mahkamah Syariah decisions. In general, the closest thing one encounters with reference to *fiqh* are formulaic gestures appealing to "general axioms of Islamic jurisprudence" (I. *sesuai dengan kaedah fiqhiyyah*), and a similarly vague gesture in the standard formula that marks the beginning of the

[68] Many of the Shariʿa Courts" clerical staff have IAIN backgrounds as well. Interview with Shariʿa Court administrative officer, 9 January 2009 at Banda Aceh.

[69] Nurlaelawati, *Modernization, Tradition and Identity*, 163–6. Though not directly recruited from the *pesantrens* but from the IAIN and other educational institutions, judges in Indonesia'sreligious courts generally have a certain linkage with *pesantren* and come from traditional religious backgrounds. See page 180.

[70] Most of the citations were of titles on the list of 13 official recommended references that were compiled in 1958 by the Ministry of Religious Affairs and continued to serve as authoritative references before the 1991 KHI. These are: (1) al-Bājūrī, *Ḥāshīyat kifāyat al-akhyār*, (2) al-Malībārī, *Fatḥ al-mu'in*, (3) ʿAlī b. Ḥijazī b. Ibrahīm al-Sharqāwī, *Ḥāshiyaʿalā al-taḥrīr*, (4) al-Qalyubī, *Sharḥ kanz al-rāghibīn*, (5), al-Anṣārī, *Fatḥ al-Wahhāb*, (6) al-Haytāmī, *Tuḥfat al-muḥtāj*, and (7) *Targhīb al-mushtaqq*, (8) Sayyid Uthmān b. Yaḥya, *al-Qawānīn al-sharʿiyya*, (9) Daḥlān, *al-Qawānīn al-sharʿiyya*, (10) al-Shamsurī, *al-Farāʾid*, (11) al-Bāʿalawī's *Bughyat al-Mustarshidīn*, (12) al-Jazīrī's *al-Fiqh ʿalā al-madhāhib al-arbaʿa*, and (13) al-Sharbinī's *Mughnī al-Muḥtāj*.

[71] Nurlaelawati, *Modernization, Tradition and Identity*, 16–17, 139, 172.

official texts of Mahkamah Syariah decisions: "Considering the 'Shariʿa proof texts' (I. *nash-nash Syarʿiyah*) and the state law relevant to this case, the Court decides . . ." For example, in the compiled decisions of the Lhokseumawe Shariʿa Court for 2006–2007, there are only a handful of specific citations to be found, and all of them refer to exactly the same sentence in a single work of *fiqh*. This passage is from al-Sharqāwī's *Ḥāshiya ʿalā al-Taḥrīr*,[72] and it is generally presented in Indonesian-language translation, without the original Arabic being reproduced in the text of the court's decisions:

> Considering the text on page 105 of Sharqāwī's *Ḥāshiya ʿalā al-taḥrīr* that reads: "Whenever a conditional divorce has been stipulated, the divorce is effected whenever the stipulated condition has been fulfilled."

This citation is invariably used to provide additional justification for the application of "conditional divorce" (I. *talak-taklik*).[73] Given the fact that it is used consistently for this purpose, and in such a uniform way, one cannot help but have the impression that this single sentence is the only part of Sharqāwī's text with which most Islamic Court judges in Aceh are familiar.

Aceh's religious court decisions differ from those of some other parts of Indonesia, not only in the near absence of references to Arabic-language *fiqh* texts, but also in the ubiquity of references to Indonesian law. The most common citations to Indonesian national law are to sections 49 and 89 of the 1989 Religious Judicature Act on court procedure and definition of jurisdiction. There are also, however, frequent references to the text of the 1991 *Compilation of Islamic Law* (KHI).[74] Indeed, among long-serving Shariʿa Court judges in Aceh, there seems to be relatively little of the animosity toward the KHI that Nurlaelawati reported for her case studies closer to the Indonesian capital.[75] It would thus appear that despite their unique disposition under the terms of Aceh's "Special Autonomy" provisions, the province's Shariʿa Courts operate in ways that mark them as particularly close to the standard national models prescribed by the central Indonesian state.

[72] This text is included in the list of 13 authoritative *fiqh* texts officially recommended for consultation by Indonesia's religious courts.

[73] For more on the position of conditional divorce in Indonesia's Islamic religious courts, see Hisako Nakamura, Conditional Divorce in Indonesia, *Harvard Law School Islamic Legal Studies Program Occasional Publications* No. 7 (July 2006).

[74] The most common of such references in the cases I have examined from Aceh are to *Peraturan Pemerintah Nomor 9/tahun 1975*, Section 19(f) and Section 116(g) of the *Kompilasi Hukum Islam* on "irreconcilable differences" ("*antara suami dan isteri terus-menerus terjadi perselisihan dan pertengkaran dan tidak ada harapan akan hidup rukun lagi dalam rumah tangga*").

[75] Interviews with Shariʿa Court judges, 25 June 2008 at Lhokseumawe, and 26 January 2009 at Banda Aceh, respectively.

PHYSICAL FACILITIES

In the 1990s, John Bowen described the Islamic Court in Takengon (Central Aceh) as "a one-storey wooden structure on a quiet residential street in the center of town," with the case archives collecting dust in small back room.[76] In the early twenty-first century, the situation has changed dramatically there. The Takengon Shariʿa Court is now housed in a new, imposing, multi-storied concrete building topped with an ornamental dome. Unlike the previous building, which was near shops, schools, and the mosque, the new courthouse is built at a considerable distance outside of the town center, in a new administrative district surrounded by the new buildings of other government offices, many of which were still under construction when I last visited in 2009. It contains not only large courtrooms, but also spacious accommodation for a library of printed reference works, a case archive, administrative offices and computer facilities, as well as special rooms to serve as space for out-of-court mediation of family disputes. The facilities at the new Shariʿa Court building in the provincial capital (Banda Aceh) are even more impressive—with carpeted, air-conditioned offices for the senior staff.

The new buildings in Takengon and Banda Aceh are striking examples of the dramatic physical improvements of some Mahkamah Syariah buildings in Aceh over the past decade (see Figures 6.2 and 6.3). The Indonesian Supreme Court in Jakarta has funded these upgrades since the religious courts came under its supervision under the "one roof" policy. This direct funding from the national level has provided a high level of support for the Shariʿa Courts in Aceh. In this regard they have been protected from the budgetary cutbacks that the provincial government has imposed on other sections of Aceh's Islamic legal system over recent years. While there are plans and ongoing construction for a system-wide upgrade of all of Aceh's Mahkamah Syariah buildings, at present, many Islamic Courts are still housed in single-storey buildings with modest and, in many cases, rather dilapidated furnishings. Nevertheless many judges and clerks serving in those courts that have yet to be improved do express hopes that they too will soon enjoy the benefits flowing from Jakarta as a concrete marker of the growing integration of the Indonesian national system for the administration of Islamic law.

[76] Bowen, "Fairness and Law," 172.

Figure 6.2. The Mahkamah Syariah building at Lhokseumawe: Constructed according to the standard layout of Islamic Courts during the New Order period. (Photo by R. Michael Feener) These modest facilities contrast sharply with those of the new generation of Sharia Court buildings in Aceh, as seen in the next photo.

Figure 6.3. The new Mahkamah Syariah building at Banda Aceh, a considerably grander structure dating from the period of post-disaster/post-conflict reconstruction. (Photo by R. Michael Feener)

THE WORK OF THE COURTS

In terms of their actual day-to-day operation, Aceh's Shariʿa Courts appear to be little different from Islamic Courts in other Indonesian provinces. The vast majority of the cases before the court continue to be related to divorce, followed far behind by cases dealing with inheritance, determinations of joint marital property, and a smattering of cases on *waqf* administration.[77] In her observation of the Religious Court in South Jakarta (regarded as one of the busiest in the country), Nurlaelawati reported that judges there hear seven divorce cases a day on average.[78] Banda Aceh's Mahkamah Syariah does not lag far behind with an average caseload of six per day.[79] In fact, the Mahkamah Syariah there can sometimes hear (or at least call for administrative matters) up to nine cases on particularly busy days.

There have, however, been some peculiarities that distinguish Aceh's caseload from those of other Indonesian Religious Courts over the past decade. For example, the first years after the tsunami saw a significant rise in numbers of inheritance cases—some of which were rather complicated from a technical perspective because of the relatives who had died or were missing, thus raising issues of verification that there were no other living claimants with legitimate claims on the estate. Analogous issues also arise in cases of inheritance where joint marital property (Ac. *hareuta sihareukat*/I. *harta bersama*) is involved. At the same time, some of Aceh's Mahkamah Syariah heard a considerable number of cases petitioning for the dissolution of marriages that were contracted soon after the disaster—often between recent widows and widowers who came together as a result of the shared trauma of having lost families and only began to recognize serious issues of incompatibility after the immediate trauma of the disaster had faded.[80] There was also a bump in the number of petitions

[77] Of these various types of cases, the category of "joint marital property" (I. *harta bersama*; Ac. *Laba sihareukat/hareuta sihareukat*; Jv. *gono-gini*) is the least familiar to scholars of Islamic law working outside of Indonesia. For an overview of its place in the work of Indonesia's Shariʿa Courts, see Mark E. Cammack and R. Michael Feener, "Joint Marital Property in Indonesian Customary, Islamic, and National Law," in Peri Bearman, Wolfhart Heinrichs, and Bernard G. Weiss (eds.), *The Law Applied: Contextualizing the Islamic Shariʿa* (London: I.B. Tauris, 2008), 92–115.

[78] Nurlaelawati, *Modernization, Tradition, and Identity*, 188–9.

[79] Interview with Shariʿa Court administrative officer, 9 January 2009 at Banda Aceh.

[80] The particular contexts of post-tsunami Aceh are even more dramatically reflected in recent rulings on matters of inheritance. In some cases, the provincial appeals court has taken steps to address situations of pre-deceased heirs that demonstrate a remarkable degree of "contextualization" applied to justify addressing immediate concerns of social justice, even when doing so would seem to contradict provisions well-established in traditional Islamic jurisprudence. For a translation and discussion of one case of this type, see "Estate of H. Zainal Bachri: Case No. 13/2008, Provincial Islamic Court for Aceh, decided 26

for the validation of marriages for which official documentation had been lost in the disaster. Generally, such certification of marriage is a necessary pre-condition to be established before a couple can file for divorce. In cases where official documentation was no longer available, it became the general procedure that the marriage could be recognized based on the testimony of two witnesses, and the taking of oaths by both husband and wife.[81]

Although there has been some talk of developing a new Acehnese *qanun* on family law and procedure, the Mahkamah Syariah mainly uses the same substantive legislation and procedures as those used by Religious Courts elsewhere in Indonesia.[82] In general, several appearances before the court are necessary before a divorce will finally be granted.[83] The first session is often rather informal in tone, with the judges offering "advice" to the couple in hopes that some reconciliation may be achieved even before the start of official proceedings. Thus before the parties are sworn in, judges will often say a few words about how much God abhors divorce, the joys that marriage can bring to a couple, as well as the challenges of marriage, especially for young couples who are just starting off. In some cases, they even urge the couple to recall their original feelings of love for one another; and on several occasions, I have seen both husband and wife choking back tears at this. One judge in Banda Aceh estimated that in about 20 percent of the divorce cases that she has heard, this actually had the effect of couples deciding to reconcile without further proceedings.[84] If the couple does not reconcile at this first session, the court schedules a second hearing at least one week later to give couples a chance to "cool their heads." Multiple hearings are also a standard feature of cases for divorce on grounds of desertion, but in this case it is almost expected that the deserting party will not appear in court. Generally, a divorce is granted after repeated failures of the absent party to respond to the summons. In cases where the husband and wife both return to court, the proceedings

March 2008 (*Putusan Mahkamah Provinsi Nomor 13/2008*) in Haider Ala Hamoudi and Mark E. Cammack, *Islamic Law in Modern Courts* (Alphen aan den Rijn: Wolters Kluwer, 2013).

[81] As, for example, in the case of a 20-year-old marriage between an Acehnese man and a Chinese convert from Roman Catholicism: A. Muslim/Mary bte. Tjong Tjun, heard at the *Mahkamah Syariah* Banda Aceh, 28 May 2008.

[82] Mardani, *Hukum Acara Perdata*, 36.

[83] In 2003 and again in 2008, the Indonesian Supreme Court issued regulations mandating that all couples filing for divorce had to first participate in mediation (I. *mediasi*). *Peraturan Mahkamah Agung Republik Indonesia Nomor 2/Tahun 2003 tentang Prosedur Mediasi di Pengadilan; Peraturan Mahkamah Agung Republik Indonesia Nomor 1/Tahun 2008 tentang Prosedur Mediasi di Pengadilan*. I would like to thank Mark Cammack for calling these regulations to my attention.

[84] Interview with Shari'a Court judge, 28 May 2008 at Banda Aceh.

range from a simple official pronouncement of divorce where both parties wish to separate, to more sharply contested cases.

In deciding the cases before them, many of Aceh's Shariʿa Court judges place considerable importance on the discretion that they exercise. In doing this, the particular sections of legislation cited in a decision often reference the general aims of the law, rather than anytechnical points of jurisprudence. A typical formulation of such runs:

> Considering that according to Islamic law marriage is a physical and spiritual bond between a man and a woman as husband and wife, with the intention of building a happy, stable family and a peaceful household in accordance with God's command in the Qur'ān (*al-Rūm*/30: 21), Section 1 of the *1974 Marriage Act*, and Section 3 of the *1999 Compilation of Islamic Laws* (KHI).[85]

As one Shariʿa Court judge in Lhokseumawe characterized his work of resolving specific cases in terms of these broader aims, "We don't only focus on legal texts, but we must also look to more broadly to the specific conditions of each case—at the individuals involved, other contextual factors."[86] This is a vision of justice that is far from blind, and one that considers aspects of "sociological jurisprudence" to be crucial to the work of the courts.[87]

CRIMINAL CASES

With the passing of *Qanuns 12, 13* and *14* in 2003, Shariʿa criminal offenses related to alcohol, gambling, and *khalwat* have also come under the jurisdiction of the Mahkamah Syariah. Such cases have, however, comprised only a very small portion of the courts' caseload to date; and that proportion has further shrunk over recent years. Across Aceh, there has been a sharp decrease in cases involving *Qanuns 12, 13,* and *14* since their numbers peaked in 2005–2006. There was virtually no official enforcement of these three *qanun* before the great earthquake and tsunami of 26 December 2004. In 2005, the number of such cases heard by Aceh's Shariʿa Courts surged to a total of 107, but then dropped precipitously to half that number in 2008. Most of the province's 21 Shariʿa Courts did not

[85] Similar formulations are found throughout divorce cases handled by the courts in Aceh. This particular wording is quoted from *Putusan Nomor 151/Pdt.G/ 2006/MSy-Lsm* (Lhokseumawe, 25 January 2007).

[86] Interview with senior Shariʿa Court judge, 20 January 2009 at Lhokseumawe.

[87] The influence of modern visions of sociological jurisprudence originating outside of the Islamic legal tradition for Aceh's contemporary state Shariʿa system will be discussed further in Chapter 9.

Table 6.1.

Types of cases filed				
Year	Alcohol	Gambling	*Khalwat*	Total
2005	20	79	8	107
2006	21	31	8	75
2007	13	18	27	58
2008	10	35	5	50

Statistics compiled by Muhammad Yusuf, Panitera/Sekretaris Mahkamah Syariʿiyah Aceh, 5 June 2009

hear a single new case of these types in 2008 and the first half of 2009.[88] Since then, the numbers have stayed low across the province, although there is considerable variation across the individual Shariʿa Courts at the district level.[89]

This is not to say, however, that there were actually fewer incidents related to alcohol, gambling, and *khalwat*. In fact, news about "criminal" (Ar. *jināya*) offenses against Aceh's Islamic legislation—and of *khalwat* in particular—appears on average about two out of any three days in the public media.[90] However, by far most of the incidents of this type are settled outside of the formal structures of Aceh's Shariʿa Courts. For example, in 2010, the WH Banda Aceh officially responded to a total of 104 incidents. Of these, slightly more than half (57) were dealt with by bringing the offenders to the WH offices for "moral instruction" (I. *nasehat*), and 45 were turned over to community leaders to be "settled by local custom" (I. *adat*). The remaining two were developed into dossiers submitted to the public prosecutor's office to prepare a formal case, but only one of them actually ended up being heard in court. Similar patterns have been noted in other parts of Aceh since 2008 as well. For example, a judge in Lhokseumawe noted in that year that there were over 100 reported *jināya* cases in that city that never made it to court.[91] Other officials have noted in particular that *khalwat* occurs every day, but that by far the majority

[88] Statistics compiled by Muhammad Yusuf, *Panitera/Sekretaris Mahkamah Syariʿiyah Aceh*, 5 June 2009.

[89] Interviews with Armia M.H., 26 January 2011 at Banda Aceh and with Rusjdi Ali Muhammad, 26 January 2011 at Banda Aceh.

[90] Sulaiman Tripa, *Perang Melawan Khalwat di Aceh: Pelaksanaan Qanun Khalwat dan Profil Kasus Khalwat dalam Harian Serambi Indonesia*, 15 January 2007–15 January 2008 (Banda Aceh: Pustaka Novum, 2008), 19.

[91] Interview with senior Shariʿa Court judge, 25 June 2008 at *Mahkamah Syariah* Lhokseumawe.

of them are "settled by *adat*."[92] As will be discussed further in Chapter 9, "settling by *adat*" is a loose euphemism that, depending on the case and the location in which it occurs, can refer to anything from a stern lecture from village elders to forcing the couple to marry, as well as various forms of physical and emotional abuse.

The relatively small incidence of *jināya* cases formally presented at court may not, in fact, be all that unusual when seen in the context of deeper historical patterns in the implementation of Islamic law. Calling attention to the historically low rate of cases going to court, Wael Hallaq has remarked, "many more were informally resolved at the local level, with the intervention of the elders, the imam, the household matriarch or others of equal prestige and authority."[93] There may then be some degree of similarity here to pre-modern patterns. But the social effects of such trends for handling *jināya* offenses can play out rather differently in the context of a contemporary society under a modern nation state. Indeed, while there is a tendency among many academic commentators to view the use of "custom" (I. *adat*) as more flexible and harmonious than are the more formal mechanisms of Islamic law, this well-worn trope in academic discussions of law in Indonesian Muslim communities stands in need of some empirical qualification. In the case of Aceh, the *adat* sanctions for offenses like *khalwat* can often be considerably more severe than the fixed penalties set forth in the official legislation of the *qanun*. For example while the text of *Qanun No.14* on *khalwat* stipulates penalties of 3–9 strokes of the cane (I. *cambuk*) and/or a monetary fine, cases of "village justice" popularly glossed as being handled "in accordance with *adat*" (I. *diselasaikan secara adat*) can involve things including being forcibly dunked into filthy sewer water, beaten with wooden clubs, and subjected to various forms of traumatic public humiliation.[94]

At the same time, the low number of cases going to court also reflects the execution of strategic decisions by officers of the state. These decisions are moreover shaped by the broader vision of Islamic law as a tool of social

[92] H. Armia Ibrahim, *Proses Hukum Terhadap Pelanggaran Qanun-Qanun Syariʿat Islam* (Banda Aceh: Bahan Pembekalan Qanun-Qanun Syariʿat Islam Bagi Ulama/Tokoh Perempuan se Kota Banda Aceh, 2010).

[93] Wael B. Hallaq, *Sharīʿa: Theory, Practice, Transformations* (New York: Cambridge University Press, 2009), 163.

[94] For example: "Nikah Siri Bawa Petaka—Dituduh Mesum, Janda-Duda Mandi Air Parit," *Metro Aceh* (30 October 2008), 1–2; "Mulut Pezina Dibroti Warga," *Metro Aceh* (7 May 2009), 1–2. Officials at the State Adat Council (MAA) protest that such measure should not be considered as "proper *adat*." As one official expressed it: "Such things are not proper *adat* sanctions, but rather expressions of the community's reaction toward those who have committed such acts" (Interview, 13 April 2011 at Banda Aceh). Such distinctions, however, are by no means operative in many local communities that assert their own autonomy in dealing with cases of *khalwat* and other infractions against the Shariʿa.

engineering. For example, in 2008, the Mahkamah Syariah in Banda Aceh heard only one criminal case. At that time the court took up this particular case of gambling only after a long consultation with the Lieutenant Governor, Nazar (who generally handled issues relating to Islamic law for Governor Irwandi at the time). In these discussions, it was agreed that the court should take the case as a public sign that would serve to foster awareness and appreciation of Shariʿa.[95] Considerations of calibrating the number of Islamic law criminal cases handled by the courts in order to achieve optimum social effect are a serious topic of discussion among the officers of Aceh's state Shariʿa institutions. In 2011, I was present in the office of one district-level Shariʿa office where local officers were frankly discussing what they thought might be the optimum time interval between public canings. Their conversations centered around the question of how to strike an effective balance between canings—spacing these performances of punishment as public pedagogy apart just enough so as not to bore or turn people off to the idea of such sanctions for infractions of Islamic morality, and yet not so infrequent that the idea would drop out of public discourse and popular consciousness. Attempting to steer a middle course between appearing overly aggressive (and alienating segments of the community) and apathetic (thus fueling the popular critique that the government is not "serious" enough about Shariʿa implementation), a loose consensus emerged among some that six to seven weeks might be an effective interval between public canings.[96] This was, however, only an informal deliberation among staff at one district WH office and as far as I have been able to ascertain, there is no official policy in place that would manage the timing of public canings in such a way.

Though the application of canings for violations of Aceh's *qanun* against alcohol, gambling, and *khalwat* are rare, they are by no means insignificant. In fact, in consideration of conversations like the one just referred to, their calculated rarity can even serve to lend them a social impact greatly disproportionate to their relative share of the caseload in the Islamic Courts. This, in fact, is precisely the intention of the some of the architects and agents of Aceh's Islamic legal system and a reflection of their broader vision of how the state enforcement of religious law can serve as a powerful instrument of public education directed toward official projects of social reform. The selective application of canings, however, is

95 Interview with Shariʿa Court judge, 24 September 2008 at Banda Aceh. However, according to some Shariʿa Court judges, such concerns also had to be placed in proper perspective relative to more important matters for the court to deal with at that time, including lingering issues of marital status and inheritance from the massive backlog of post-disaster/post-conflict cases.

96 Informal group discussion among local WH officers, 14 April 2011.

not without its own risks. Public reaction to the perceived discriminatory tendency toward highly symbolic punishment has compromised the overall effectiveness of state efforts to "socialize" Shariʿa norms in society.

One of the most common critiques of Aceh's Islamic legal system is in fact precisely related to the perception that laws are not uniformly applied and enforced. As evocatively expressed by a middle-aged woman whose home was destroyed by the tsunami: "The current implementation of Shariʿa is not fair (Ac. *hana adé*), why is it only the little people that get punished, but when the elites (Ac. *awak rayeuk*) get caught, they never receive a caning?"[97] Many have been particularly aggrieved by the fact that public officials and prominent politicians who have been caught in violation of Aceh's Islamic laws in well-known cases have not been caned.[98] The argument that caning penalties are not fairly applied is a common one in many public fora in Aceh, and it is often accompanied by calls to carry out sentences for Shariʿa violations committed by provincial elites. As one contributor to the "Text Messages (sms) to the Editor" page of a local low-brow tabloid asked:

> When, sir, will you actually carry out the punishments on public officials who violate the Shariʿa—like the Representative of the Assembly from Lhokseumawe who has clearly been convicted by the court? And when will you amputate the hands of those who steal the people's money through their corruption?[99]

The specific case of the local politician convicted of *khalwat* referred to in this quote was one of the first times that a public figure was sentenced to caning, and also (not coincidentally) one of the first Shariʿa criminal cases from Aceh to pass through provincial appeal and cassation to the Indonesian Supreme Court in Jakarta.[100] As both an example of a contemporary Shariʿa Court decision on a case of Islamic criminal law, and an illustration of the progress of a case through the appeals process, this particular incident merits some further discussion. The detailed presentation and critical analysis of the case presented here is based upon

[97] "Pelaksana Syariah Tak Adil Rakyat Kecil Dihukum, Orang Berada Lolos," *Harian Aceh* (6 November 2007), 2.

[98] Such as the 2006 case involving a member of the local legislative assembly (DPRD) in Aceh Tamiang. "Razia Jilbab Diprotes Warga Aceh Tamiang," *Waspada* (24 October 2007), 3.

[99] "Hukuman Cambuk Tak Adil," *Metro Aceh* (15 November 2010), 6.

[100] This case represents one of a very small number of Shariʿa criminal cases to have gone up from Aceh to Indonesia's Supreme Court. The first four cases to do so (two involving gambling, and one involving alcohol in addition to the case discussed here) were published as: *Yurisprudensi Mahkamah Syariʿah Provinsi Nanggroe Aceh Darussalam Perkara Jinayat* (Banda Aceh: Mahkamah Syariʿah Provinsi NAD, 2007). In none of these cases were the applicants successful in having the decision of the lower courts reversed at the provincial or national levels.

official documentation from the first order, appeals, and Supreme Court decisions.

AN OFFICE AFFAIR

This *khalwat* case was brought against Zainal Abidin b. T.M. Ali (Defendant 1), a male member of the local legislative assembly representing the Islamist Crescent and Star Party (Partai Bulan Bintang/ PBB), who was found alone in the party offices on a Sunday afternoon with the local party treasurer, Cut Meurah Raziah (Defendant 2). On 11 September 2005, the Lhokseumawe "Shariʿa Police" (I. Wilayatul Hisbah/ WH) received reports of suspicious activity. As the case file reports the incident, at around 16:30 (WIB) a local WH officer received information by telephone from a witness alleging that a member of the local assembly (DPRD) was in *khalwat* (Ac. *meusum*) with a woman at the PBB office. Thereupon Said Zulkarnaini, Commandant of the WH Unit, led a team of ten WH officers to the PBB party office. Upon arriving there, another witness brought some of the WH officers around the right-hand side of the building. The WH officers then attempted to peer in, but all the windows of the office were tightly shut and the dark green curtains had been drawn across them, so the witness was unable to see inside. Subsequently, the witness headed to the left-hand side of the building, where he could not see inside as the curtains were also closed. However, the witness noticed that the air-conditioning compressor on that side of the building was running, which led him to believe that there must have been someone inside the office. The WH officer and the witness who had called in the initial report of the incident then headed for the front door and knocked at least six times while announcing "*salam*," but no one came to the door. The witness then tried opening the door by turning the handle downwards at least twice while pushing the door as hard as he could. However the door would not open as it was locked. When he pushed down on the handle a third time, however, the door "suddenly opened" from the inside.

The door had been opened by a woman, Cut Meurah. The witness then introduced himself and asked for permission to enter and inspect the premises. Upon entering, another witness, Irwan, noticed that the woman looked embarrassed and rather nervous while absent-mindedly flipping through a newspaper that she was holding upside-down. The witness also noticed that the woman's lipstick was smudged, and that a motorcycle was parked in the reception area of the office. It was further noted that the woman's white handbag was placed on Zainal's desk. After the premises had been inspected it was clear that no one else other than the two defendants were on site. One of the witnesses asked to see some identification, whereupon Zainal forbade Cut Meurah from showing her identity card.[101] When confronted by the WH officers, Zainal was indignant and threatened to use his contacts and influence to have the officers fired. They nevertheless continued with their investigations and filed their report with the Public Prosecutor (I. *Jaksa*), who issued formal charges for the case to the Mahkamah Syariah at Lhokseumawe on 28 January 2006.

The hearing was held on 8 May 2006 and both defendants appeared together in court, bringing with them a total of five lawyers. Testimony was heard from a large number of witnesses, including four WH officers who had been present at the scene, three other high-ranking members of the Crescent Star Party, the owner of the kiosk in front of the party office building, and four "mitigating witnesses" called by the counsel for the defense. A member of the local Ulama Council (MPU) was also called as an "expert witness" to provide an authoritative definition of "*khalwat*," which he explained as:

> the withdrawal of two non-*muḥrim* [i.e. potentially marriageable] people of the opposite sex to a place or a building that facilitates their meeting at any time without restriction;
>
> That the legal basis for forbidding *khalwat* in Islam is God's rule: "*wa lā taqrabū al-zina*," [Qur'ān 17 (*Banī Isrā'īl*): 32] which means do not do anything which draws one close to fornication;
>
> That the definition of *khalwat* is the withdrawal to a private place without a third party or any other restriction—for example, an office on the side of a road in which in one room is a non-*muḥrim* couple and in which they could engage in activities without another person watching them as the door and windows are closed. Such a situation would qualify as *khalwat*.[102]

The first defendant (Zainal) then testified himself, stating that he was in the office for a meeting that he had convened for that Sunday afternoon to discuss financial matters in preparation for the support of the party's planned social service programs for that coming Ramadan. He also claimed that he had tried to contact other party members and staff via phone and text messages beforehand about the meeting. When he arrived at the office, however, he found only Cut Meurah's motorbike parked inside the reception area. At first he did not see her there and so he went on inside to perform his ablutions for mid-afternoon prayers. It was then that he heard the ruckus between Cut Meurah and the WH officers who were trying to gain entrance.

The Public Prosecutor (I. *Jaksa*) called for both of the defendants to be sentenced to five strokes of the cane (I. *cambuk*), and for them to be held

[101] *Keputusan 04/JN/2006/MSy.Lsm.*

[102] *Keputusan 04/JN/2006/MSy.Lsm.*

responsible for the court fees related to the case. The defense, on the other hand, requested that the charges to be dropped and the reputations of the defendants restored. The court found the facts of the case to be that the two defendants were indeed a non-*muḥrim* couple alone in a secluded place, and that this fulfilled the definition of *khalwat* as provided by the expert witness from the MPU. The court also made a point of highlighting as an exacerbating factor that as an elected member of the legislative assembly and a teacher, respectively, both of the accused should be "setting examples for the community." Citing sections I.4, I.5 and I.22 of *Qanun No. 14/2003*, as well as the expert witness from the MPU clarifying the technical definition of *khalwat*—but without any reference to *fiqh* texts—the court found them both guilty and sentenced them in accordance with the recommendations from the Public Prosecutor.

The decision was appealed by the defendants and heard by the provincial-level Shari'a Court in Banda Aceh, which upheld the decision on 25 August 2006 with the revision that the number of strokes for the woman be reduced from five to three.[103] The parties then applied for cassation to the Indonesian Supreme Court in Jakarta, which rejected their argument and upheld the decision of the provincial Shari'a Court in a decision issued on 25 April 2007.[104] Following the Supreme Court ruling, a date for the execution of the caning sentence was set. On the appointed day (13 December 2007), the stage on which this was to take place was set up on an open field in the city of Lhokseumawe. A crowd gathered that morning in anticipation of the event, and there were even (unconfirmed) rumors that the convicted Zainal Abidin was himself milling on the outskirts of the park while preparations were being made. Nonetheless, neither he nor Cut Meurah came forward to receive the punishment, and there was no legal way that they could have been compelled to stand for their sentence. This is because there were at that time no provisions for the arrest and detention of offenders against the *qanun* in Aceh. Some have cited this as a shortcoming of Aceh's Islamic legislation that compromises the ability to effectively enforce the law.[105] However, the absence of any such provision can also be seen as consonant with the general emphasis on moral exhortation and public pedagogy over punitive measures in the

[103] The rationale for this was that the punishments for the two parties should be different to reflect the fact that since Defendant 1 was the head of the office in which the incident took place he should bear the ultimate responsibility for any violations of the law that take place there (*Putusan No. 03/JN/2006/1\4Sy-Prov*).

[104] *Putusan No. 02K/AG/JN/2007.*

[105] This was, in fact, one of the major procedural issues that some involved with the application of Islamic law in Aceh had hoped would be addressed by a new law of Shari'a criminal procedure (*Qanun Acara Jinaya*).

basic structure of Aceh's contemporary Islamic legal system—a topic that will be discussed further in Chapter 8.[106]

The actual legal questions addressed by the court of first instance in this case were limited to the determination of two points in the Acehnese *qanun* on *khalwat* (*No. 14/2003*): the status of a "legal subject" under the jurisdiction of Islamic law in the province, and the definition of *khalwat*. With regard to both, the Court presented fairly straightforward clarifications to demonstrate that the law is clearly applicable to the actions of both the accused parties at the time of the incident. With regard to the first point, the court simply noted that both of the accused were adult Muslims acting under their own free will. For the second, the court accepted the expert witness testimony from a member of Aceh's Ulama Council (MPU). In its decision, the court noted that the offense is both prohibited by the law of the state (I. *peratutran perundang-undangan yang berlaku*) and forbidden (Ar. *ḥarām*) with regard to Shariʿa.

The chief judge of the panel that originally decided the case in Lhokseumawe later clarified that the general reference to "relevant Shariʿa texts and indicators" (I. *nash-nash dalil-dalil syarʿi yang berhubungan*) in the decision was to emphasize and strengthen the statutory legal prohibition—adding that it was an example of the way in which the ideals of Shariʿa and the positive law of the Acehnese *qanun* could be seen as mutually complementary (I. *saling melangkapi*).[107] That being said, the court's decision of this case—and indeed, its jurisprudence in nearly all of the criminal and family law cases that it handles—is marked by a near-total absence of any citations to works of *fiqh* or the appeal to any technical form of Islamic jurisprudential reasoning. Once the court of first instance had decided the case, the higher courts involved with its appeal and cassation confirmed the original ruling with only minimal amendment.

The Supreme Court's handling of this case in particular presents a striking confirmation of the place of Aceh's Islamic legal system within the broader Indonesian national framework. With historical roots stretching back to the earliest days of Indonesian independence and a considerable degree of integration within the national court structure, Aceh's Shariʿa Courts are the most established institutions of its contemporary Islamic legal system. As such, they have also been the least actively involved with the particular projects of social engineering specific to Aceh's Shariʿa agenda under the current special autonomy. In fact, their handling of

[106] The idea of establishing procedures for arrest and detention was to become one of the major aims of the draft *qanun* on Shariʿa criminal procedure (*Qanun Acara Jinayat*) discussed in Chapter 5. The procedures, politics, and problematics of applying caning penalties in Aceh will be further discussed in Chapter 8.

[107] Interview with Dr. H. Zulkifli Yus, 17 September 2008 at Takengon.

family law cases demonstrates the remarkable degree to which the courts rely on national norms as defined in the 1974 Marriage Act and the 1991 KHI. Even in the areas of criminal law that distinguish the works of Aceh's Shariʿa Courts from other Islamic courts in Indonesia, it is clear that for the most part, the courts have not been particularly aggressive in taking on new cases—although in some particular venues the local leadership of first-instance courts have been more open than others to dealing with infractions against Aceh's *qanuns* on gambling, alcohol, and *khalwat*. Moreover, the cautious decisions that Aceh's Shariʿa Courts issued on such cases have tended to be accepted within the broader parameters of the Indonesian legal system in the few instances where they have progressed through cassation to the Supreme Court in Jakarta.

Aspects of the select Shariʿa criminal cases that Aceh's Shariʿa Courts do handle, however, continue to reflect considerations of the importance of setting proper examples to promote and reinforce the standards of public morality prescribed by the legislation discussed in the previous chapter, and which are characteristic of the social engineering project of state Shariʿa more generally. This point is clearly enunciated in the court's emphasis on the point that, as an elected official of a self-identified "Islamic" political party and a teacher, both Zainal and Cut Meurah should be held responsible for setting a public example. Thus again we have a significant indication that the emphasis of the administration of state Shariʿa in Aceh is less on the systematic formal prosecution of every infraction, but rather on ensuring a vivid public awareness of the ethical imperatives that the law is designed to promote in society at large. In the next two chapters, the focus will shift from the Shariʿa Courts to discuss two rather different institutions that are of much more recent origin, and which were designed with a much more explicit mandate to employ the formal legal apparatus of the state as a tool to promote an Islamizing transformation of society.

7

State-directed *Daʿwa* and the Shariʿa Bureaucracy

> Islam regards law as a tool, not as an end in itself. Law is a tool and an instrument for the establishment of justice in society, a means for man's intellectual and moral reform and his purification. Law exists to be implemented for the sake of establishing a just society that will morally and spiritually nourish refined human beings.
>
> Ayatollah Khomeini
> *Islamic Government*[1]

The conception of law expressed in the quote represents an important, but still little-analyzed aspect of modern Islam. From Iran to Indonesia, and in many other parts of the world, instrumentalist visions of the Shariʿa have informed agendas of social reform and political struggle. Over the past half-century, these developments have reconfigured Islamic jurisprudence as thinkers negotiated complex engagements with modern strains of legal thought of non-Muslim origin.[2] In the particular case of Indonesia, the development of Muslim legal thought in an instrumentalist mode also progressed parallel to broader transformations in the dominant philosophy of law at the national level.

In his study of legal culture during the first decades of independent Indonesia, Daniel Lev remarked on what he perceived to be a transition from the colonial conservatism of "customary law" (D. *adatrecht*) to "revolutionary law." By the second half of the twentieth century, there were stirrings of new visions of the way in which law could be used to actively promote social change.[3] The dynamics that drove these processes

[1] Ayatollah Khomeini, *Islam and Revolution: Writings and Declarations of Imam Khomeini*, trans. by Hamid Algar (Berkeley: Mizan Press, 1981), 80.

[2] For more on these developments with Indonesian Islam, see R. Michael Feener, *Muslim Legal Thought in Modern Indonesia* (Cambridge: Cambridge University Press, 2007).

[3] Daniel S. Lev, "Judicial Institutions and Legal Culture in Indonesia," in Claire Holt, with Benedict R. O'G. Anderson and James Siegel (eds.), *Culture and Politics in Indonesia* (Ithaca: Cornell University Press, 1972), 255–97.

will be discussed further in Chapter 9. The most important point of these developments to consider here is that by the end of the twentieth century, law had come to be seen in Indonesia as an important means not only for the preservation of order but also as an instrument to facilitate particular developmental goals.[4]

ISLAMIC LAW AND INSTRUMENTALISM

Under the New Order there was a growing convergence between the rhetoric of social transformation used by technocrats advocating economic development programs and that of Islamic activists associated with the *daʿwa* movement. Over the latter decades of the twentieth century, both of these concerns combined with strains of Indonesian nationalism into a configuration that I have already referred to as Indonesia's "*daʿwa* paradigm." As noted in Chapter 2, *daʿwa* activists and state-affiliated Islamic organizations at that time proclaimed that the aim or their movement was to create "a good country under the blessings of God" (Ar. *balda ṭayyiba wa rabb ghafūr*).[5] To reach this goal, they argued (again, in ways parallel to those of more secular nationalist technocrats) that the key was education. Their project was thus one of changing the mentality of the nation's Muslim community (I. *merubah mental umat bangsa*).[6]

In Aceh, Ali Hasjmy was central to the promotion of these emerging currents of Indonesian Islam during the New Order period. In the flood of published writings and public speeches that he gave on the subject, Hasjmy aggressively advanced the idea that Islam was an all-encompassing "way of life" that included distinct configurations of personal piety, social mores, and political commitments. He also stressed that the realization of these ideals needed to be pursued through modern organizational structures. Hasjmy explicitly modeled his approach on modern Christian prototypes, and later claimed that he wrote much of the text of his most sustained discussion of *daʿwa* while his wife was being treated in a missionary hospital in Jakarta.[7]

The idea of *daʿwa* as a program for social change was to become central to re-conceptions of Islamic law and its political role in

[4] Nur Ahmad Fadhil Lubis, "The State's Legal Policy and the Development of Islamic Law in Indonesia's New Order," in Arskal Salim and Azyumardi Azra (eds.), *Shariʿa and Politics in Modern Indonesia* (Singapore: ISEAS, 2003), 55.

[5] A. Surjadi, *Daʿwah Islam dengan Pembangunan Masjarakat Desa* (Bandung: Rivanty, 1971), 94–9.

[6] H. Zainal Abidin Ahmad, *Memperkembang dan Mempertahankan Pendidikan Islam di Indonesia* (Jakarta: Bulan Bintang, 1976), 108–13.

[7] A. Hasjmy, *Dustur Daʿwah Menurut Al-Qurʾan* (Jakarta: Bulan Bintang, 1974).

twenty-first-century Aceh.[8] This instrumentalism is expressed by some in even stronger terms, with the rhetoric of using Islam as a "weapon" in the crusade for social reform.[9] In pursuit of their ideals of Shariʿa social reform, Acehnese academics, Muslim religious leaders, and government officials have called for more active involvement from both families and local communities in carrying out programs of transformative *daʿwa*.[10] Such multi-layered strategies for the Islamization of society make for a blurring of clear boundaries between vectors "imposed from above" or "from below." Indeed, in the case of Aceh we find a situation in which the dynamics of *daʿwa*-driven social reform have oscillated between the two in complex ways over time: From the activism of PUSA reformists to the provincial government initiatives of Ali Hasjmy, as well as later from the social visions of local academics and activists to the state Shariʿa structures established in Aceh after the fall of the New Order.

As expressed in one of the official publications of Aceh's State Shariʿa Agency (DSI), the project of implementing Islamic law requires "comprehensive support at all levels so that the real socialization of the Shariʿa can be realized in both public and private life."[11] In this view, *daʿwa* is seen as an obligation upon all Muslims, to be carried out to promote the Shariʿa through "raising awareness" (I. *peningkatan kesadaran*).[12] This approach to *daʿwa* is in fact seen as the central goal of Aceh's Islamic legal system by many of its advocates. As one such voice expressed in Aceh's leading daily newspaper, "Creating a collective awareness among society at large is the main objective of the Shariʿa... Punishments are not the end, but only a means. The ultimate aim is the fostering of morality and the upholding of justice."[13]

While the efforts of individual Muslims are necessary, however, proponents of Aceh's contemporary Islamic legal system do not regard them as sufficient to guarantee success. For this, the formal legal institutions of the state are necessary:

> The *daʿwa* movement cannot proceed effectively without the support of power. The support needed is none other than the authority of the state. The *daʿwa* movement will lose its meaning without the support of such power.

[8] Mahbub Fauzie, "Dakwah dan Sosial Umat Islam," *Serambi* (17 April 2009), 30. The author is an alumnus of the Dakwah Faculty at the Banda Aceh IAIN.

[9] "Dakwah Jadi 'Senjata' Pemantapan Syariat," *Serambi* (16 August 2008), 28.

[10] "Penerapan SI Harus Dimulai dari Keluarga Sendiri," *Rakyat Aceh* (11 January 2009), 3.

[11] Fakhri, "Syarʿiat Islam Yang Kaffah: Suatu Pendekatan Komunikasi," in Zaki Fuad Chalil (ed.), *Melihat Syariat Islam Dari Berbagai Dimensi* (Banda Aceh: Dinas Syariat Islam, 2007).

[12] Muhammad, "Partisipasi Masyarakat dalam Penegakan Hukum Pada Qanun-Qanun Aceh," in Syamsul Rijal (ed.), *Syariat Islam di Aceh: Problematika Implementasi Syariah* (Banda Aceh: Dinas Syariat Islam, 2009), 169.

[13] "Ada Apa Dengan Syariat Islam di Aceh," *Serambi* (3 August 2007), 4.

> The Shariʿa will be upheld by the *daʿwa* movement supported by the legal authority of the state.[14]

The belief in the necessity of state power to effectively direct social change pervades rhetoric of government officials in contemporary Aceh, both within and beyond the special institutions tasked with implementing Islamic law.[15] As Tun Azhari, a senior member of the Lhokseumawe city council expressed it in 2009, "As I see it, if the government is seriously committed, all can be accomplished. This is no society that cannot be ordered by such means."[16]

THE MAKING OF A SHARIʿA BUREAUCRACY

As discussed in previous chapters, Aceh had been a site of a series of Indonesian experiments in the state administration of Islam since the 1960s—including the establishment of an official Ulama Council and the creation of a separate "Faculty of Daʿwa" in the State Institute for Islamic Studies (IAIN). Most of Aceh's local Islamic leadership, moreover, have tended to see more opportunities for success than they did dangers of co-optation in these developments. They were consequently inclined to press for more, rather than less, state involvement with religious affairs, as evidenced by their continuing efforts to promulgate new Islamic legislation and to expand the formal jurisdiction of the Shariʿa courts. Such initiatives coming up from local Islamic leaders, rather than down from the governor's office or the regional military command were, however, as often dampened as they were encouraged by the Indonesian central government in the middle decades of the twentieth century. By the 1990s, however, new configurations of power in Jakarta had emerged through the development of what Platzdasch has described as an increasingly "powerful rapport" between New Order nationalists and IndonesianIslamists.[17] These developments have informed the contexts in

[14] Syukrinur A. Gani, "Syariat Islam dan Dakwah," in Zaki Fuad Chalil (ed.), *Melihat Syariat Islam Dari Berbagai Dimensi*, (Banda Aceh: Dinas Syariat Islam, 2007), 20.

[15] In the non-Islamic legal sphere, this has its roots in the rise of "Development Law Theory" during the New Order period. The main figure of this school of Indonesian legal thought, Mochtar Kusuma-Atmadja, consistently emphasized the importance of state power in discussions of law and social control. For more on Development Law Theory, see Shidarta, "Posisi Pemikiran Teori Hukum Pembangunan dalam Konfigurasi Aliran Pemikiran Hukum (sebuah diagnosis awal)," in Shidarta (ed.), *Mochtar Kusuma-Atmadja dan Teori Hukum Pembangunan: Eksistensi dan Implikasi* (Jakarta: Epistema Institute, 2012), 9–80.

[16] Quoted in "Razia Pelanggaran Syariat Harus Ditingkatkan," *Serambi* (27 March 2009), 9.

[17] Bernhard Platzdasch, *Islamism in Indonesia: Politics in the Emerging Democracy* ((Singapore: ISEAS Press, 2009), 56, 128–35.

which the state implementation of Shariʿa came to be seen as part of plans to put an end to the escalating conflict between the central Indonesian government and the Free Aceh Movement (GAM).

There have been, however, considerable dissenting voices as well. In fact, strident criticisms of the work of Aceh's state Shariʿa institutions are regularly published in the editorial sections of local newspapers and magazines as well as in the digital fora of myriad blogs and Facebook pages.[18] In the editorial pages of the daily newspaper *Harian Aceh*, for example, the Acehnese novelist Thayeb Loh Angen writes: "Islam is a great religion and it is not appropriate for it to be institutionalized by any government or, more frankly, to be subjected to any worldly power. One feels today as if the state Shariʿa bureaucracy is forcing adherence to Islam."[19] Many other critics have referred to Aceh's contemporary Islamic legal system as an "unwanted gift from Jakarta" and call for attention and resources to be redirected to other priorities, including the improvement of infrastructure and the provision of welfare services.[20]

As vocal as such critiques have been, the establishment of a formal Islamic legal system for the province was welcomed by other significant segments of society, particularly among *daʿwa* activists and IAIN academics who had been developing their own ideas of how the Shariʿa could serve as the solution to the rampant lawlessness that plagued Aceh during the prolonged conflict period. For a community traumatized by decades of violence, the Shariʿa came to be seen as a potential source of peace and stability. It was in this context that collaborations emerged between IAIN academics in Aceh and politicians in Jakarta to lobby to promote their vision of Islamic law as a means to end the conflict and restore stability.[21] Proponents of stronger state intervention in the administration of Islam were able to significantly advance their cause in the last years of the twentieth century, and developments along these lines accelerated considerably after the collapse of the Suharto regime in 1998.

[18] Such material is easily located on the web. See, for example, *Syariat Islam Akan Membawa Aceh Makin Tertinggal*, <http://www.topix.com/forum/world/malaysia/T0VS2NMLQI3J75M0S>, accessed 22 August 2012. In such interactive digital fora that accommodate comments, one can easily see the wide range of opinion expressed in Aceh and beyond on the pros and cons of the contemporary Islamic legal system.

[19] Thayeb Loh Angen, "Membangun Peradaban Aceh Baru," *Harian Aceh* (13 November 2009), 10.

[20] Early critiques of along these lines have been noted by John Bowen in *Islam, Law and Equality in Indonesia: An Anthropology of Public Reasoning* (Cambridge: Cambridge University Press, 2003), 232.

[21] These included Muhammad Yus, Kaosyah, Razali Amna, Mujib Budiman, Yusuf Hanfiyya, Ramli, and Usman Hasan, among others. Interviews with Yusny Saby, 27 January 2011 at Banda Aceh; and with Hamid Sorong, 21 June 2010 at Banda Aceh.

The local elections in June 1999 brought a new ruling coalition to Aceh's provincial legislative assembly, in which the local branch of Suharto's well-established Golkar political machine struggled to maintain power in the new environment of post-New Order "Reform" (I. *Reformasi*). One of its primary strategies for this was coalition building with political parties sympathetic to *daʿwa* interests.[22] Under the rapid succession of presidents over the years that followed, military operations were supplemented by other strategies aimed at resolving the conflict, including granting Aceh the right to special autonomy that provided the broader legal structure for the application of Islamic law in the province.[23] As the violence of the conflict with GAM had escalated, the Indonesian government began considering more comprehensive approaches to enhance the success of its military operations. Part of this included looking to Islam as part of a solution to the "Aceh problem," and this led some in Jakarta to engage sectors of Aceh's Islamic leadership as a means to undermine the appeal of GAM and legitimate Indonesian control over the province.

When Suharto's successor, B.J. Habibie, made a visit to Banda Aceh in 1999, he spoke at the great mosque about his commitment to putting an end to the conflict. While he was there, IAIN academics including Alyasa Abubakar impressed upon him the significant role that the Shariʿa could play in this, if only Aceh were granted the permission to formally implement Islamic law.[24] Habibie, who had made a reputation for himself as being sympathetic to *daʿwa* and the state support of Islamic institutions, proved receptive to the idea.[25] Soon thereafter, Alyasa and other IAIN faculty began an active campaign of publicizing the idea of Shariʿa as a solution to the conflict in the local media. Prominent Muslim academics in Aceh, including Alyasa Abubakar, Muslim Ibrahim, Rusjdi Ali Muhammad (all from the IAIN), and Tgk. Daud Zamzamy representing the *dayah* ulama engaged with Jakarta in discussions that eventually lead to the special autonomy measures that facilitated the development of Aceh's contemporary Islamic legal system.

[22] Edward Aspinall, *Islam and Nation: Separatist Rebellion in Aceh, Indonesia* (Stanford, CA: Stanford University Press, 2009), 144.

[23] For further detailed discussions of these complex political developments, see the essays by M. Isa Sulaiman, Edward Aspinall, William Neesen, Damien Kingsbury and Lesley McCulloch, Kirsten E. Schulze, Aleksius Jemadu, Michelle Ann Miller, and Rodd McGibbon in Anthony Reid (ed.), *Verandah of Violence: The Background to the Aceh Problem* (Singapore: Singapore University Press, 2006), 121–359.

[24] Interview with Alyasa Abubakar, 23 September 2010 at Banda Aceh.

[25] For Habibie's involvement with *daʿwa*-oriented Islamic activists and his role in developing new patterns of Indonesian state engagement with Islam, see Robert W. Hefner, "Islam, Sate, and Civil Society: ICMI and the Struggle for the Indonesian Middle Class," *Indonesia* 56 (October 1993), 1–35.

Working within this new legal framework, the first slate of Shariʿa legislation discussed in Chapter 5 was drafted and passed by Aceh's provincial assembly. At the same time, the governor's office in Banda Aceh also began to redefine existing institutional structures and to create new ones to support the state implementation of Islamic law. In 2001, governor Ramli Riduan proclaimed the need to establish a provincial-level government body to coordinate the implementation of Shariʿa in Aceh. This quickly grew from a small section within the government's office to a full-scale state agency (I. *dinas*).[26]

When Abdullah Puteh took office as Aceh's governor in November 2002 he consolidated his base of local support with further appeals to the formalization of the role of Islam in the provincial government.[27] A month after he assumed office, new financial autonomy measures led to a flood of new funds to support the implementation of Islamic law and by 2002, the new State Shariʿa Agency (I. *Dinas Syariat Islam*/DSI) had received 42 billion rupiah (US$4,387,646) from the governor's "special education fund." As Isa Sulaiman and Gerry van Klinken have characterized Puteh's term as governor, "religion and custom were manipulated to support the government's conflict resolution strategies, while the elite was smothered with money and facilities to keep them on side."[28] The corruption during Puteh's time in office was scandalous, even by Indonesian standards, and eventually led to criminal convictions. For some, this has served as further evidence of the use of the Shariʿa as an instrument of political manipulation.[29]

Despite Puteh's fall, however, the issue of Shariʿa came to increasing prominence in the government's public pronouncements on the conflict with GAM over the years that followed. Aceh's reconfigured Ulama Council issued a fatwa against "sedition" in August 2003, and in February 2004,

[26] The first head of the DSI argued that it not be dealt with adequately by any lower-level government office (I. *badan* or *kantor*). Alyasa Abubakar, *Syariʿat Islam di Provinsi Nanggroe Aceh Darussalam: Paradigma, Kebijakan dan Kegiatan* (Banda Aceh: Dinas Syariat Islam, 2003–5th edition, 2008), 153. This is the most oft-republished work issued by the DSI, having appeared in five editions since its first printing in 2003, with each edition expanding upon previous versions.

[27] For Abdullah Puteh's statements on the "necessity" of implementing Shariʿa in Aceh, see Sri Suyanta, *Pola Hubungan Ulamadan Umara: Kajian Tentang Pasang Surut Peran Ulama Aceh* (Jakarta: Universitas Islam Negeri (UIN) Syarif Hidayatullah, 2005), 234.

[28] Between 2001 and 2003, Aceh's routine expenditure increased from 3,475 to 9,520 billion rupiah (US$363,493,723–995,815,900). M. Isa Sulaiman and Gerry van Klinken, "The Rise and Fall of Governor Puteh," in Henk Schulte Nordholt and Gerry van Klinken (eds.), *Renegotiating Boundaries: Local Politics in Post-Suharto Indonesia* (Leiden: KITLV Press, 2007), 235–48.

[29] Critiques of the forms that Shariʿa has taken in Aceh have proliferated since the time of Abdullah Puteh. For a distillation of many of the most popular lines of argument, see Reza Idria, "Mesin Syariat," *Jurnal Gelombang Baru* IV (2009) 12.

the top Indonesian military commander in the province proclaimed that "whoever supports Islamic Shariʿa also supports the extermination of GAM ... because GAM's actions deviate greatly from the Islamic faith." GAM leaders, for their part, retorted, saying that the state implementation of Shariʿa was "a plot by the central government to depict the Acehnese as fanatics in the eyes of the outside world."[30] In these escalating polemics over the place of Islam in the governance of Aceh, the state worked to give ever more concrete form to institutions for the management of religious affairs, including the DSI.[31]

THE STATE SHARIʿA AGENCY (DSI)

There are a number of government bodies that deal with the administration of aspects of Islamic law and religious affairs in Indonesia.[32] The DSI, however, is a completely new kind of institution. It is unique to Aceh and has a mandate that covers distinctive aspects of the Islamic legal system for this special autonomous region. The legal foundations of the State Shariʿa Agency were established with legislation passed in 2001, and in the year that followed, district-level DSI offices began to be established across the province.[33] Its main purpose is to plan and coordinate the implementation of Islamic law in the province.[34]

The DSI is structured into four main sections, in addition to a secretariat and the technical logistics unit. Of them, only one is primarily involved with activity in the formal legal sphere. This is the Legal Division, which has sub-sections tasked with draft legislation and coordinating the work other state institutions involved with Shariʿa implementation and enforcement. The Legal Division has, however, actually tended to be the least active of any in the agency. A considerably more vibrant division of the DSI is that which is dedicated to propagation and religious practice (I. *dakwah dan peribadatan*). It is tasked with administering *daʿwa* programs, providing facilities for ritual observance, supporting and maintaining houses of worship, facilitating the work of other religious

[30] Aspinall, *Islam and Nation*, 207–14. The first quotation in this paragraph is quoted by Aspinall from *Serambi*, 23 February 2004.

[31] Harold Crouch, *Political Reform in Indonesia After Soeharto* (Singapore: Institute of Southeast Asian Studies, 2010), 285.

[32] In addition to the Religious Courts (Pengadilan Agama), this includes the Department of Religious Affairs (DepAg) and the Office for the Registration of Muslim Marriages (Kantor Urusan Agama).

[33] *Peraturan Daerah Nomor 33/ 2001 tentang Pembentukan Susunan Organisasidan Tata Kerja Dinas Syariat Islam Propinsi Daerah Istimewa Aceh.*

[34] Alyasa Abubakar, *Syariʿat Islam*, 155.

institutions, and promoting "*syiar* Islam" (which will be discussed further later in the chapter). The remaining sections of the DSI deal with the administration of institutional, personnel, and material resources for the development of religion in society, and the handling of records and information management. The DSI also initially supervised the work of Aceh's new "Shariʿa police" (Wilayatul Hisbah/WH), until that unit was transferred to the supervision of the civilian police force (I. *polisi pamong praja*) in 2008.[35]

At its founding, the DSI recruited civil servants who were already working in the provincial-level offices of other government agencies. Many of them were drawn from the Department of Information, particularly from its Communications section. Their background in information management and communications has been important to the work of the DSI in promoting its vision of Shariʿa to the public.[36] Upon assuming their duties, these civil servants were required to attend training sessions to develop their understandings of Islam in line with the DSI's vision of the role that Islamic law could play in the reform of Acehnese society.[37] As it expanded, however, the Agency also locally recruited new staff from the IAIN, largely graduates from the Daʿwa and Tarbiya Faculties with backgrounds that had prepared them for the work of Islamic proselytization, but not necessarily for the civil service. Today, these graduates comprise the majority of the Agency's staff across the province.

The work of the DSI spans a broad range of activities for promoting Islamic moral values and ritual observance in Acehnese communities. This includes, for example, sponsoring public preaching programs, supporting mosque activities and basic Islamic education, providing educational and financial assistance for new Muslim converts, and sending officials out to give inspirational and instructional talks to the regular morning assemblies (I. *apel pagi*) held at various government offices, as well as providing training and the payment of honoraria to village-level Qurʾān teachers and religious functionaries.[38] The DSI also conducts special activities at various points in year, including "*safaris*"—a kind of official

[35] The WH will be discussed separately as the main topic of Chapter 8.

[36] Interview with Alyasa Abubakar, 23 September 2010 at Banda Aceh.

[37] "Dinas Syariat Islam Gelar Safari Pekan," *Serambi* (17 September 2008), 21; "Dakwah Ramadhan Digelar di 40 Gampong," *Rakyat Aceh* (12 August 2010), 3.

[38] "Imum Meunasah Dibekali," *Rakyat Aceh* (7 August 2007), 2; "Pembekalan Wawasan Imeum Selesai," *Serambi* (31 August 2007), 4; "68 Tengku Imeum Gampong Terima Honor," *Rakyat Aceh* (30 May 2008), 3; "Ratusan Tengku Seumebeut Terima Honor," *Rakyat Aceh* (2 July 2008), 4; "180 Pengurus Masjid Diberi Pelatihan," *Rakyat Aceh* (21 November 2009), 3; "Dinas SI Sosialisasi Qanun," *Serambi* (4 August 2009), 17; "Tahun 2010, Dinas Syariat Islam Pijay Kerja Ekstra," *Serambi*(16 July 2009), 25; "Dinas Syariat Islam Bantu Muallaf," *Serambi* (2 July 2009), 33.

roadshow to disseminate information about the state implementation of Islamic law at the district and sub-district levels.

Local DSI offices at the district level also organize their own public teaching sessions on Islamic topics (I. *pengajian*) and administer the selection of "model villages" (I. *desa percontohan*)—a program designed to encourage local communities to "compete in goodness" (Ar. *fāstabiqū al-khayrāt*) in exemplifying desired Islamic values.[39] Some district DSI offices also offer training programs for village-level functionaries responsible for enforcing Shariʿa morality at the local level (I. *muhtasib desa*). Like all the activities of district-level DSI offices—and following the administrative logic of post-Suharto decentralization—these programs are contingent upon the support of the district head (I. *bupati*), and as a result, there has not been any uniform implementation of such programs across the province as a whole. In some cases, lack of support by the *Bupati* has resulted in a significant decrease in the activities of local DSI offices. In others, surges of activity have been noted under the leadership of local officials who—out of various motivations—have chosen to prioritize the promotion of state Shariʿa in their districts.

TIGHT TROUSERS, FREE SKIRTS, AND DISTRICT-LEVEL PUBLIC MORALITY MEASURES

In 2009, the *Bupati* of West Aceh, Ramli Mansur, launched a high-profile (and sharply criticized) campaign to promote the image of rigorous Shariʿa observance in his district.[40] Local officials were quoted in the media saying that WH officers would apprehend any woman entering the district wearing tight trousers or jeans and that any woman caught wearing such would have them confiscated and shredded. In place of the confiscated apparel, the individual would be given a "properly fitting" skirt, provided free of charge by the local government.[41] The West Aceh WH office set up checkpoints on the road into downtown Meulaboh, stopping women who were considered to be in violation of this dress code.[42] These women

[39] Interview with Hasballa, Head of Dinas Syariat Islam West Aceh, 21 September 2010 at Meureubo.

[40] "Bupati Aceh Barat Minta Pendatang Pakai Rok," *Waspada Online* (29 May 2010), <http://www.waspada.co.id/index.php?option=com_content&view=article&id=118393>, accessed 22 December 2011.

[41] "Peringatan Bagi Kaum Perempuan—Pakai Celana Jeans Ketat Digunting," *Rakyat Aceh* (29 October 2009), 1–2. Local "skirt drives" were held to collect donations from the community for this purpose: "Asoh Buka Posko Pengumpulan Rok," *Harian Aceh* (28 June 2010), 14.

[42] "Tim WH Intensifkan Razia di Kota—Wanita Bercelana Jeans Dibagi Rok," *Serambi* (24 June 2010), 17.

were then given short lectures on the demands of Islamic modesty, and a skirt that they were required to change into (in a space provided and overseen by female WH officers) before being allowed to continue on their way.[43] Some local entrepreneurs established skirt rental stalls with crude changing booths along the roads just before the checkpoints for the convenience (and in the hope of cashing in on the worries) of female travelers who wished to avoid this humiliation.[44]

The aggressive stance taken toward this particular issue of female dress drew criticism from many sectors, both within and beyond West Aceh at that time. Some accused the *Bupati* of politicizing a hot-button issue for his own interests, and others raised questions about where he was getting all those free skirts from, and what was to become of the investments of local merchants who held inventories of women's trousers that would become illegal to wear or sell in the district.[45] Human rights and gender justice-oriented NGOs criticized the coercive enforcement targeted at women.[46] Some supporters of the new stricter measures on public modesty argued in response that the campaign against tight trousers was an important front in the crusade against the social ills of liberal globalization and materialistic hedonism central to the vision of Shari'a as an agent of positive social change.[47] Others claimed that in fact, the measure was actually designed to "protect" women from being targeted by moralistic vigilantes.

Undeterred by the barrage of criticism, the West Aceh local legislative assembly went ahead and passed a special, district-level (I. *kabupaten*) regulation on "Islamic clothing" in August 2010, which was accompanied by a further increase in the measures taken for its implementation by the local office of the WH.[48] In connection with these developments, the West Aceh office of the DSI also held a special training program for village-level volunteers to police Shari'a norms in local communities, referred to in Aceh as "*muhtasib desa*." Each village in the district was asked to send

[43] DediIskandar, "Razia Busana Ketat, WH Bagi Rok Gratis," *Prohaba* (21 August 2010), 1.

[44] "Gempar Buka Rental Rok di Perbatasan Aceh Barat," *Harian Aceh* (17 June 2010), 14.

[45] "Perempuan Aceh Barat Dilarang Pakai Celana," *Radio Nederland Online* (16 November 2009), archived at <http://id.shvoong.com/law-and-politics/law/1946717-perempuan-aceh-barat-dilarang-pakai>, accessed 22 May 2012.

[46] See, for example, Human Rights Watch, *Policing Morality: Abuses in the Application of Shari'a in Aceh, Indonesia* (New York: HRW, 2010). Available online at: <http://www.hrw.org/sites/default/files/reports/indonesia1210WebVersionToPost.pdf>, accessed 22 May 2012.

[47] Editorials on the issue had been circulating for several years before this particular program in West Aceh caught the headlines. A typical statement of the public arguments for such measures can be found in "Ideologi di Balik Pakaian Ketat," *Harian Aceh* (16 November 2009), 2.

[48] *Peraturan Bupata Aceh Barat No. 5/ 2010 tentang Penegakan Syariat Islam dalam Pemakaian Busana Islami di Kabupaten Aceh Barat.*

two representatives who would be willing to serve as the faces of Shariʿa enforcement in their communities. These individuals would be called upon to ensure that the new regulation would be observed. Those who responded to this call comprised both people who actively volunteered, as well as others who were "delegated" by their village heads (Ac. *geucik*). They received a small honorarium and were also given training and lectures on the importance of upholding proper Islamic standards of morality, as well as their special responsibilities to do so in their communities.[49]

They were also provided with a very thin packet of photocopied materials intended to provide them with information relevant to their duties. Among these references was the full text of the 2005 regulation on the execution of caning sentences, which lays out the technical details for applying such sanctions and the supervision of the process by the office of the Public Prosecutor (I. *Jaksa*).[50] The application of caning punishments does not, however, fall within the legal mandate of *muhtasib desa* in Aceh. Despite this, these village-level Shariʿa enforcement volunteers were provided with copies of this document on the practical aspects of administering corporal punishment. The prominent inclusion of this particular text among the very few pieces of legislation that were provided in their training packet by the local DSI office is indicative of broader structural problems in the mechanisms for the local implementation of Islamic law that will be discussed further in the next chapter. These problems are exacerbated by the ambiguities, gaps, and overlaps in the current legislation that regulates the roles and interactions of state Shariʿa offices, *adat* institutions, and village-level leadership in contemporary Aceh.

After the first regional regulation defining the outline of Aceh's state Shariʿa system was passed in 2000, further legislation followed that redefined and strengthened village-level structures for the application of customary law.[51] This new law mandated that *adat* institutions should serve as "tools of social control" (I. *alat social kontrol*) in the administration of local communities.[52] These overlapping goals have, in turn, facilitated

[49] Field notes taken at the West Aceh DSI office during a *muhtasib desa* training session, 21 September 2010 at Meureubo, West Aceh.

[50] *Peraturan Gubernor Provinsi Nanggroe Aceh Darussalam Nomor 10/Tahun 2005 tentang Petunjuk Teknis Pelaksanaan Uqubat Cambuk*. For more on the role of Public Prosecutor's office in relation to the implementation of Shariʿa in Aceh, see Marah Halim, "Sistem Penegakan Hukum dalam Pelaksanaan Syarʿiat Islam di NAD," in Syahrizal (ed.), *Dimensi Pemikiran Hukum dalam Implementasi Syariat Islam di Aceh* (Banda Aceh: Dinas Syariat Islam Provinsi Nanggroe Aceh Darussalam, 2007), 56–60, esp. 36-74.

[51] *Peraturan Daerah Nomor 5/Tahun 2000 tentang Pelaksanaan Syariat Islam di Provinsi Daerah Istimewa Aceh.*

[52] *Peraturan Daerah Propinsi Daerah Istimewa Aceh Nomor 7/Tahun 2000 tentang Penyelenggaraan Kehidupan Adat*, Pasal 4 (sic.).

a range of experiments from the DSI on utilizing village leadership and other local-level mechanisms for the enforcement of Islamic law.[53] The situation clearly gives the lie to conventional wisdom on "*adat* vs. Islam" as an oppositional dyad in discourses on law and society in Indonesia. At the same time, it also reflects the degree to which the shift to an instrumentalist paradigm of law has pervaded conversations on government administration and social change in the country, even down to the local level.

PUBLICATION AND PROPAGATION

The DSI's aspiration to utilize and regulate village-level leaders to assist with the implementation of Shari'a is clearly reflected in a handbook produced especially for local religious functionaries referred to in Acehnese as *imeum meunasah*.[54] The *imeum meunasah* are responsible not only for leading prayers, but also for ensuring the necessary "facilities" for ritual worship in the village, including providing water and prayer mats, maintaining the sound system, and managing the activities that support the implementation of Shari'a through the promotion of "*syiar Islam*" (Ar. *shiʿār*), particularly during Ramadan. They are also tasked with preparing local pilgrims for the *ḥajj*, facilitating disputes over issues of inheritance, and the administration of *zakāt*. The handbook provides both brief explanations of the general system and sample cases of distribution.[55] The *imeum meunasah* also officiates at local marriages (and helps in mitigating spousal disputes) through the village *adat* council, and assists with the registration of local marriages and divorces. Duties extend to interventions within families to address the needs of women and children, acting as a safeguard against domestic violence, and even chastising children who do not properly care for their aged parents.[56]

The DSI's official handbook for *imeum meunasah* opens by stating its explicit aim to standardize the different opinions on Islamic legal issues relevant to contemporary life.[57] It contains over 200 pages of instructions

[53] Alyasa Abubakar, *Syariʿat Islam*, 177.

[54] Saleh Suhaidy, *Buku Pegangan Teungku Imeum Meunasah* (Aceh: Dinas Syariat Islam Provinsi Nanggroe Aceh Darussalam, 2007, reprinted 2009).

[55] *Qanun No. 7/ 2004* authorizes him to perform these functions, and letters from the Bupati/Walikota serve to make him also function as the Head Officer of the local office of the *Baitul Mal*.

[56] Saleh Suhaidy, *Buku Pegangan Teungku Imeum Meunasah*, 170.

[57] In its attempt to do this, it draws on an extremely eclectic range of sources, ranging from twentieth-century reformist writers from Indonesia and abroad (Hamka, Hasbi Ash Shiddieqy, Sayyid Sabiq) to older Malay (Jawi) texts well-established in Traditionalist circles, such as the *Perukunan Melayu*, and even including references to an Indonesian translation of Daniel Lev's work on Indonesia's Islamic court system (op. cit.).

on various aspects of religious administration, including guidelines for ablutions, ritual prayer, fasting, almsgiving, pilgrimage, personal devotions, treatment of corpses, marriage, protecting women and children, inheritance, the administration of religious property and "*syiar* activities." The handbook presents the *imeum meunasah* with a streamlined system of belief in God, angels, books, prophets, the coming judgment, and the doctrines of personal will and pre-destination, as well as instructions on ritual performance (accompanied by visual aids) and sample Arabic texts for the preface to Friday sermons. It also contains templates for the blank forms necessary to administer *zakāt* and manage local mosque youth groups (I. *remaja masjid*), as well as flow charts outlining the necessary steps in preparing a corpse for burial. In 2008, the DSI gave 700 *imeum meunasah* from across the province a copy of this book, as the basic reference material for use in a four-day training program.[58]

The *Imeum Meunasah Handbook* was produced by the DSI's in-house publications department, which plays a critical role in the Agency's programs for *daʿwa* and "socialization" (I. *sosialisasi*).[59] Over the past decade, the Agency has published dozens of books of over a hundred pages in length, including other handbooks targeted at different audiences, such as government bureaucrats and the youth.[60] These publications are prefaced with a statement by the head of the DSI that clarifies the purpose of such work: "that the public discourse of implementing Shariʿa values will become more widespread and more easily understood so that it may be accepted by all and implemented in ways appropriate to their respective roles and responsibilities in society."[61]

The publications section of the DSI has also produced myriad booklets and pamphlets that are used to disseminate information on proper observance of the Shariʿa. Here, Indonesia's relatively high literacy rate opens possibilities for the use of such media in the service of state agendas for defining proper Islamic belief and practice to a degree that would not be possible in some

[58] Interview with Ziauddin Ahmad, 2 September 2008 at Banda Aceh.

[59] The concept of *sosialisasi* in the Indonesian and Acehnese contexts will be discussed further subsequently. In addition to the official DSI publications, the Agency also works closely with their "friends in the media" (I. *kawan-kawan dari pres*) to further assist them in spreading word of their programs for the socialization of Shariʿa values. Interview with local DSI official, 13 November 2007 at Tamiang.

[60] Misri A. Muchsin, Hasnuddin Yusuf Adan, Muhammad AR. Khairuddin, and Bukhari, *Buku Panduan Pelaksanaan Syariʿat Islam Bagi Birokrat* (Banda Aceh: Dinas Syarʿiat Islam, 2008); Sri Suyanta, Nurjannah Ismail, Muhammad Maulana, Emk Elidar, and Muhammad Yasir (eds.), *Buku Panduan—Pelaksanaan Syarʿiat Islam Untuk Remaja, Pelajardan Mahasiswa* (Banda Aceh: Dinas Syarʿiat Islam, 2008).

[61] This particular wording is taken from the preface to: Azman Ismail, *Syariat Islam di Nanggroe Aceh Darussalam* (Banda Aceh: Dinas Syariat Islam, 2007), vii.

other contemporary Muslim societies.[62] In addition to disseminating images illustrating acceptable styles of modest Muslim dress (see Figure 7.1), DSI publications also provide arguments explaining official views on the importance of such sartorial details for the success of the broader project of Shariʿa implementation. For example, a small DSI pamphlet on women's head coverings that was distributed in 2008 explains that:

> Clothing that conforms to the requirements made clear by God and His prophet must be accepted as a clear sign of Islamic identity for those that have faith. The work of the government in regulating dress is aimed at educating and fostering of religious awareness—not at punishing or making things difficult for people. These measures are intended to foster the spirit of Islam in everyday life, to the point that someday matters of modest dress will no longer need to be regulated by worldly institutions.[63]

The implementation of Islamic law is thus expressed as a program that, through the enforcement of laws regulating select aspects of individual behavior, works toward higher aspirations for public morality and social life. When this happens, so the official argument runs, the positive and constructive Shariʿa values of Aceh's Muslims will also come to be reflected in the public sphere as "good governance."[64]

Reflections of Shariʿa values in the public sphere proliferated across Aceh over the first decade of the twenty-first century in a variety of forms that together aim to foster "awareness" (I. *kesadaran*) of the centrality of Islam to social life. Even before the tsunami, the promotion of Islamic symbols factored into a number of construction and public works projects with, for example, the increasing use of calligraphic inscriptions of the "99 names of God" (Ar. *al-asmāʾ al-ḥusnā*) to adorn walls, lampposts, and other locations. Formal legislation served to promote the proliferation of Arabic script in various contexts as a visible marker of Islamic social order through provisions encouraging the use of the "Arab Melayu" (*Jawi*) script on the public signage of buildings, etc.[65] In the post-disaster

[62] At 99 percent of its youth population (aged between 15–24 years) literate, Indonesia ranks well ahead of many other large Muslim-majority countries. By comparison: Bangladesh 75 percent, Pakistan 71 percent, Nigeria 61 percent. World Bank, "Literacy rate, youth total (% of people ages 15–24)," <http://data.worldbank.org/indicator/SE.ADT.1524.LT.ZS/countries>, accessed 1 August 2012.

[63] Muhammad Suhaili Sufyan, *Busana Islami di Nanggroe Syariat* (Banda Aceh: Dinas Syariat Islam, 2008), 18.

[64] These particular aspects of "good governance" (English term in original) are expressed in Indonesian as *akuntabilitas, transparansi, keterbukaan*, and *aturan hukum* respectively. Jailani, "Implementasi Syariʿat Islam Di Aceh: Peluangdan Tantangan Membangun Sistem Pemerintahan yang Bersih dan Berwibawa," in Azman Ismail (ed.), *Syariat Islam di Nanggroe Aceh Darussalam* (Banda Aceh: Dinas Syariat Islam, 2007), 104–23.

[65] *Qanun Provinsi Nanggroe Aceh Darussalam No.11/2002 tentang Pelakasanaan Syariʿat Islam Bidang Aqidah, Ibadah, dan Syiʿar Islam*, V.12.2.

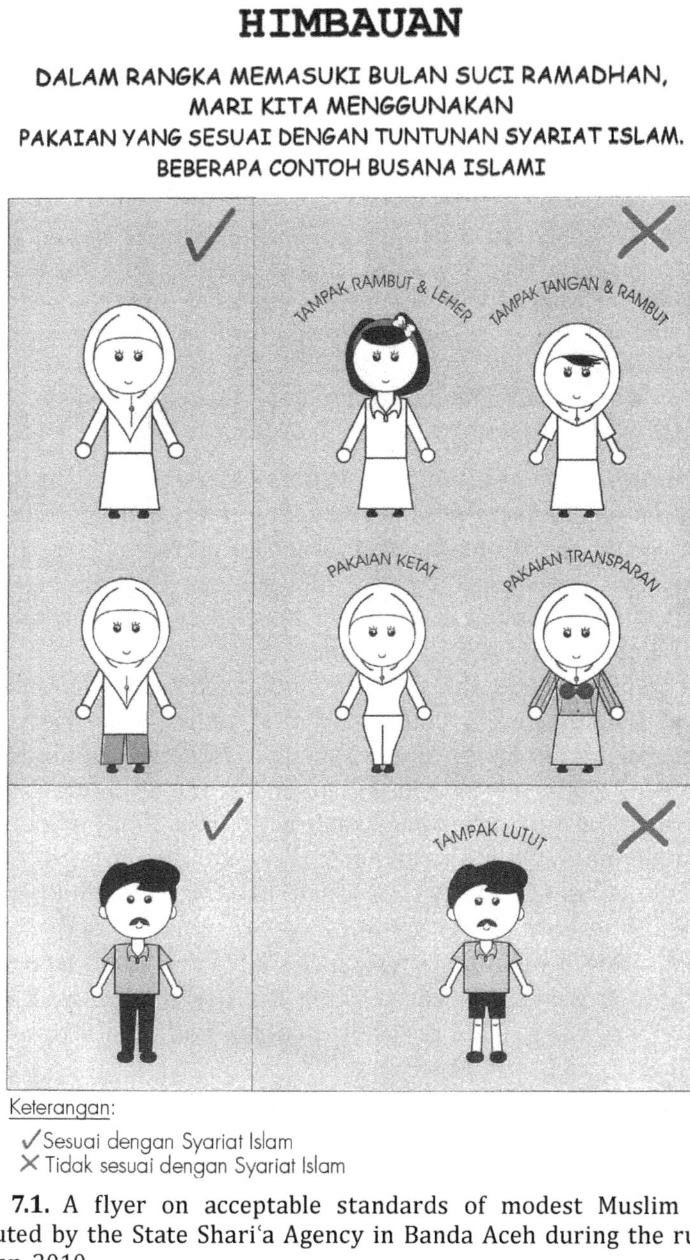

Figure 7.1. A flyer on acceptable standards of modest Muslim dress—distributed by the State Shari'a Agency in Banda Aceh during the run-up to Ramadan, 2010.

reconstruction phase, the prominence of Islamic symbolism in the built environment of Acehnese cities and towns was further bolstered by a building boom in large mosques with eye-grabbing ornamental domes.

Figure 7.2. A State Shariʿa Agency (DSI) sign announcing the prohibition of and penalties for *khalwat* at Bireuen. (Photo by R. Michael Feener)

One particularly striking way in which the DSI contributes to this new visual culture of Shariʿa is through billboards that serve as highly visible reminders of the Islamic legal order of society. Most people arriving in Aceh from outside do so either via the main road north from Medan or through the Sultan Iskandar Muda Airport at Banda Aceh. By either route, one is greeted by large billboards prominently announcing that you have arrived in a place where Shariʿa law is in effect. Within Aceh, the DSI has erected hundreds of other billboards as public reminders of the rules of social behavior regulated by the *qanun*. Some of the earliest of these were stylistically rather straightforward presentations of texts in Arabic and Indonesian, such as in the illustration in Figure 7.2 where quotations from the Qurʾān and *ḥadīth* serve to call attention to and reinforce the basic points and stipulated penalties of the *qanun* on *khalwat*.

Billboards of this kind have, moreover, come to be supplemented by others that take the form of colorful and dramatic paintings. Often produced by district-level offices of the State Shariʿa Agency, billboards of this type can be found even in relatively remote areas of the province. A striking example of this can be seen in Figure 7.3, which presents the prohibition on *khalwat* as stipulated in the *qanun* against the backdrop of vivid scenes of a young couple being apprehended by state officials in this world, and facing their religious punishment in the next.

Figure 7.3. A State Shariʿa Agency (DSI) billboard warning young couples of the dangers of *khalwat* near a wooded waterfall outside Tapaktuan, South Aceh. (Photo by R. Michael Feener)

THE "SOCIALIZATION" OF THE SHARIʿA

The production and proliferation of publications and billboards aimed at promoting the observance of Shariʿa across all segments of society comprises an important aspect of the DSI's work. Projects for the publicizing of Shariʿa through such means are referred to locally as *sosialisasi*, and the term has become the most common rubric for the activity of Aceh's Islamic legal institutions since 2007. The Indonesian-language term *sosialisasi* carries with it a range of meanings that may cause some confusion to those who read it exclusively in terms of its English cognate.

The standard dictionary of contemporary Bahasa Indonesia lists three separate definitions for *sosialisasi*, ranging from the state seizure of private assets to the processes of disseminating and publicizing information.[66] This latter definition is, in fact, perhaps the one that is most commonly seen in many Indonesian discourses. The contemporary usage of the term by officers of Aceh's Shariʿa institutions, however, goes beyond reference to the simple acquisition of existing norms and values to the deliberate promotion and "implanting" (I. *tertanamnya*) of aspirational standards

[66] *Kamus Besar Bahasa Indonesia* (Jakarta: Pusat Bahasa/PT Gramedia Pustaka Utama, 2008), 1371.

of religious and moral rectitude aimed at facilitating the development of society as a whole in the desired direction of "Islamization." This usage reflects yet another meaning of *sosialisasi*: one that refers to efforts at promoting new ideas in support for particular development projects.[67] In this sense of habituating of individuals to behave according to socially desirable norms in order to facilitate particular agendas of reform and improvement, the use of *sosialisasi* here echoes on a social level many of the established tropes in the literature of psychological developmental studies; particularly understandings of "processes whereby naïve individuals are taught the skills, behavior patterns, values, and motivations needed for competent functioning."[68]

In its common usage in contemporary Aceh, there is considerable and constant slippage between these last two conceptions of *sosialisasi*. Indeed, its very vagueness seems to be one of the primary attractions of the term, allowing for it to be used to describe DSI activities ranging from public preaching, publications, and poster campaigns to "model Shariʿa village" programs and the WH's spot inspections of women on the street whose clothes and head coverings do not fit their definitions of proper Islamic dress. In all of this, the DSI is most active outside of the formal legal sphere, particularly through programs fostering the habituation of individuals to a specific set of desirable social conventions. Its work in this direction thus combines modern modes of governmentality with classical conceptions of Islamic law. The result is a re-configuration of what Norman Calder has referred to as the "religious structure" of Shariʿa—incorporating "educational, recreational and aesthetic ends, as well as the merely practical."[69]

Understanding developments along such lines in contemporary Muslim societies demands a consideration not only of political, but also of pedagogic dimensions of modern Muslim religious discourse. Studies attempting to do this, however, have displayed a tendency to read *daʿwa* education as a project of "restoring cultural authenticity" and/or the promotion of Islamic identity politics.[70] These are undoubtedly important insights, but they can also distract us from noticing other important dimensions of contemporary Islamic agendas of education and socialization. In many contemporary Muslim societies, *daʿwa* programs

[67] *Kamus Besar Bahasa Indonesia*, 1331–2.

[68] Eleanor E. Maccoby, "Historical Overview of Socialization Research and Theory," in Joan E. Grusec and Paul D. Hastings (eds.), *Handbook of Socialization Theory and Research* (New York: The Guilford Press, 2007), 13–41.

[69] Norman Calder, *Islamic Jurisprudence in the Classical Era* (Cambridge: Cambridge University Press, 2010), 198.

[70] See, for example, Meir Hatina, "Restoring a Lost Identity: Models of Education in Modern Islamic Thought," *British Journal of Middle Eastern Studies* 33.2 (2006) 196.

are oriented not only—or even primarily—toward nostalgic dreams of recapturing an essentialized Islamic past, but rather toward visions of future-oriented social transformation. In such cases, modern projects of Islamic propagation are clearly more than just a search for "authentic" roots. They are also about actively striving toward the creation of new ideals of moral community.

The DSI's vision of transforming the future underlies its dominant emphasis on education. Their official publications call for schools and other educational institutions to work with them toward the idea of "implanting," "socializing," and "internalizing" (I. *tertanamnya, tersosialisasi dan terinternalisasi*) Islamic values in children from their earliest years, and to follow up in accordance with the development of students at higher levels.[71] To further work in this direction, the Agency also runs a range of educational programs, including "intensive courses" to teach students about the values of the Shariʿa and its role in protecting them from the dangers of drug use and sexual promiscuity.[72] Such work in formal educational institutions is furtherexpanded and reinforced through broader agendas of *sosialisasi*. The success of this agenda hinges on raising awareness of and internalizing "Shariʿa values" (I. *nilai-nilai syariat Islam*) in individual Muslims. This agenda of public pedagogy has been aggressively promoted not only by the DSI, but also by other official Islamic institutions in Aceh. For example, lieutenant governor Muhammad Nazar has called for his fellow IAIN alumni to devote themselves to more outreach work to promote Islamic education for greater awareness and understanding of the Shariʿa among the broader public.[73] He has also added elsewhere that for the implementation of Islamic law in Aceh to be considered successful, it must engage with the community to encourage the transformation of individual Muslims to collectively "build moral character and foster integrity in all activities."[74] The state's official legal apparatus has an important role to play in this work, but the point is not simply one of the formal enforcement of law. As the former head of the North Aceh district office of the DSI put it:

> What we do here is to persuade and motivate. We don't go on patrol to arrest and prosecute cases, but rather so that we are visible in the community and thus discourage people from doing wrong. People commit crimes because, first, there is an intent and, second, because there is an opportunity. It is extremely difficult to alter the contents of another person's heart except

[71] Alyasa Abubakar, *Syariʿat Islam*, 183–8.

[72] "Siswa Dibimbing Syariat Islam," *Serambi* (6 November 2007) 7.

[73] "Karang Taruna Diharapkan Ikut Tegakkan Syariat Islam," *Harian Aceh* (18 February 2009), 3.

[74] "Abaikan Agama, Aceh Semakin Hancur," *Rakyat Aceh* (2 February 2009), 1–2.

> through education and moral instruction, and that takes a long time. So we start with what is more in our power, and that is to remove the opportunities to sin.[75]

The idea of using the apparatus of the state to instill such motivation has been an animating principle underlying the various and diverse projects of Aceh's State Shariʿa Agency. This vision of "socializing the Shariʿa" has been perhaps most thoroughly elaborated in the prolific writings of DSI's founding director, Alyasa Abubakar.[76]

DAʿWA DISCOURSE AND THE DSI

Alyasa Abubakar has been one of the most prominent figures in the development of contemporary Aceh's state Shariʿa system. He is a graduate of both al-Azhar in Cairo and the Yogyakarta campus of the IAIN. The thesis that he submitted to the latter in 1989 was a critique of both traditional *madhhab*-based *fiqh* and modern *Salafi* attempts to "turn back the clock" to the time of the Prophet as being equally unable to meet the challenges facing Muslims in a rapidly changing Muslim world.[77] In developing these lines of argument further since then, he came to increasingly emphasize the need for developing future-oriented projects for the revival and re-interpretation of Islamic law to promote social transformation.[78]

After completing his graduate studies, Alyasa returned to teach at the Banda Aceh campus of the IAIN. There he became involved in conversations with other local academics about the potential of the Shariʿa as a solution to the problems of social instability that plagued the region during the escalating conflict of the 1990s. In March 2002, he was appointed as the first director of the new DSI to which he recruited a number of his colleagues and former students. Many of those involved in the design and application of Aceh's contemporary Islamic legal system share broad aspects of his vision of Shariʿa and its role in directing social transformation. Their views on such matters, moreover, were also shared by an increasing number of Indonesian Muslim leaders and organizations at the national level in the late twentieth century, particularly among *daʿwa* activists of Alyasa's generation who had graduated from universities in Java.

This *daʿwa* movement in late twentieth-century Indonesia was decentralized and internally diverse. Nevertheless its participants were

[75] Interview with Husnan Ibrahim, 19 November 2007 at Lhokseumawe.

[76] Interview with Alyasa Abubakar, 23 September 2010 at Banda Aceh.

[77] This work was later published as: *Ahli Waris Sepertalian Darah: Kajian Perbandingan terhadap. Penalaran Hazairin dan Penalaran Fiqh Madzhab* (Jakarta: INIS, 1998).

[78] Interview with Alyasa Abubakar, 23 September 2010 at Banda Aceh.

loosely united under a broad vision of Islam as a force for future-directed social transformation. Various groups working toward this aim by advancing agendas of pietization intended to transform individuals and communities. This was to be pursued through the careful regulation of ritual practice and the promotion of public symbols of Islam in order to foster a new awareness of the power of Islam to give order and meaning to life. The *daʿwa* programs of religious and social reform thus worked toward the cultivation of particular habits such as the adoption of forms of "Islamic dress" and the headscarf (I. *jilbab*) as means of both transforming individual behavior and creating a new sense of Islam's presence in public life.

One of the most important centers for these developments during the New Order period was Salman Mosque on the campus of the Bandung Institute of Technology (ITB).[79] Even in its architectural design, this mosque was intended to symbolize an uncompromisingly modern approach to Islam—one that strikingly brought a "clean" and angular aesthetic to frame the most prominent site of religious activity for a student body of aspiring technocrats (see Figure 7.4). The activists who based their work there strove to promote a vision of Islam that could serve as a central component in totalizing visions of economic development and social transformation. During the last decades of the twentieth century, the Salman mosque movement pioneered the popularization of many terms that have since become central to *daʿwa* discourses in the Indonesian public sphere.[80] Among Salman's signature contributions was the articulation of a constellation of concepts that served to reframe discussions of religion and its desired role in society, the most prominent of which were "*syiar*" and "Islam yang *kaffah*" (discussed shortly).[81]

In ways that to a considerable extent complemented the project of *daʿwa* associated with the Salman Mosque Movement, other important innovations in Indonesian Islamic activism were being developed in

[79] For a compilation of influential sermons delivered at ITB's Salman Mosque, see Muhammad Imaduddin Abdul Rahim, *Kuliah Tauhid* (Bandung: Pustaka-Perpustakaan Salman ITB, 1980).

[80] Yo Nonaka, "Isuraamuni motoduku jikohenkakuni yoru shakaikaikakuno kokoromi—Indonesia no daigakudaawaundouno rekishito shisou," Ph.D. dissertation (Tokyo: Keio University, 2011), 69–87.

[81] For introductions to the Salman Mosque movement and its place in the history of contemporary Indonesian Islam, see "Gerakan Kaum Muda Islam Mesjid Salman," in Abdul Aziz, Imam Tholkhah, and Soetarman S. (eds.), *Gerakan Islam Kontemporer di Indonesia* (Jakarta: Pustaka Firdaus, 1989); Rifki Rosyad, "A Quest for True Islam: A Study of the Islamic Resurgence Movement among the Youth in Bandung, Indonesia," M.A. thesis (Canberra: Australian National University, 1995); and Yo Nonaka, "Indonesiano daigakudaawaundou saikou: Saruman mosukuniokeru isuraamuundou no shisou to gendaitekiigi," *SOIAS Research Paper Series* 7 (Tokyo: Sophia University Institute of Asian Cultures, 2012).

Figure 7.4. The modern brutalist architecture of the Salman Mosque, on the campus of the Bandung Institute of Technology. (Photo by R. Michael Feener)

the latter decades of the twentieth century to promote the Islamization of individuals and society through new models of Islamic education (Ar. *tarbiya*). The Indonesian *tarbiya* movement built upon foundations developed in the Middle East by the Muslim Brotherhood, and developed in ways that brought together not only reform-minded Modernists, but also a significant segment of Traditionalists coming out of *pesantren* backgrounds.[82] The various Indonesian Islamic movements of that period organized around modern concepts of *daʿwa* and *tarbiya* shared broad common goals of spreading and deepening attachment to "Islamic values" among new generations of Indonesians, including *pesantren* teachers and students, as well as young Muslim professionals and technocrats. The intertwining lineages of Indonesian *daʿwa* and *tarbiya* activism have mutually reinforced the use of distinctive rhetorical terms and tropes that have come to dominate the discourse of state Shariʿa in contemporary Aceh. Some of the most prominent examples of this can be found in the ubiquitous use of the terms "*syiar*" and "Islam yang *kaffah*" in contemporary Indonesian Islamic discourse. These slogans actively promoted by the Salman Mosque movement and the associated broader

[82] Yon Machmudi, *Islamising Indonesia: The Rise of the Jemaah Tarbiyah and the Prosperous Justice Party (PKS)* (Canberra: Australian National University E Press, 2008), 62–7. <http://epress.anu.edu.au/wp-content/uploads/2011/03/whole_book10.pdf>.

circles of *daʿwa* and *tarbiya* activism that it inspired went on to become central to the project of Shariʿa as a tool of social engineering in Aceh.

SYIAR ISLAM AND A SHARIʿA SOCIETY

As noted in Chapter 5, the term "*syiar*" figures prominently in the title of the first piece of substantive Shariʿa legislation passed as part of Aceh's contemporary Islamic legal system in 2002. There it refers to "all activities that carry with them the values of religious worship to adorn and elevate the observance of Islam."[83] The State Shariʿa Agency lists the support of *syiar* prominently among its defined areas of activity, where it serves as a broad rubric covering such things as the design and construction of houses of worship, the organization of space and decoration, the presence of mosques and *meunasah*, the broader use of Arabic script and *hijrī* calendar dates, the use of formal openings and salutations in letters and official documents—all to promote a robust cultural identity reflecting the community's strength and commitment to Islam.[84] As Alyasa himself has explained it: "The regulation of *syiar* is intended to nudge members of the community closer toward realizing Islamic values."[85]

The State Shariʿa Agency places considerable importance on the role that the public symbolism of *syiar* can play in creating an atmosphere and environment supportive of Islamic religious belief and practice.[86] Configured variously across diverse DSI programs, *syiar* serves as a critical element in broad-ranging social transformation:

> *Syiar* can also play a role in politics by fostering a more humane, respectful, honest, and just political climate—and one that rejects the corruption of money politics [English term in the original]. In the field of law, *syiar* helps to foster a greater sense of respect for the law, even in small matters such as wearing a helmet when riding on a motorbike, obeying traffic signals, and courtesy toward pedestrians.[87]

[83] *Qanun Provinsi Nanggroe Aceh Darussalam Nomor 11/Tahun 2002 tentang Pelaksanaan Syariat Islam bidang Aqidah, Ibadah dan Syiʿar Islam*, I.5.

[84] Alyasa Abubakar, *Syariʿat Islam*, 167–77.

[85] Alyasa Abubakar, *Syariʿat Islam*, 236–7.

[86] Fauzi Saleh, "Eksistensi Akidah dalam Penegakan Syariah: Kesiapan Mental Menerima Penerapakan Syariat Islam," in Syamsul Rijal (ed.), *Dinamika Sosial Keagamaan dalam Pelaksanaan Syariat Islam* (Banda Aceh: Dinas Syariat Islam Provinsi Nanggroe Aceh Darussalam, 2007), 42.

[87] Alyasa Abubakar and Marah Halim, *Hukum Pidana Islam di Provinsi Nanggroe Aceh Darussalam* (Banda Aceh: Dinas Syariat Islam, 2006), 63. The English-language term italicized earlier is used in the original.

In Aceh, as in Indonesia more generally, the concept of *syiar* has come to be strategically deployed in efforts to create and reinforce "moods and motivations" in individuals commensurate with the vision of Islam promoted by the *daʿwa* and *tarbiya* movements.[88]

Today, most Indonesian Muslims no longer perceive "*syiar*" as a neologism. The popularity of the term *syiar* all across Indonesian public discourse on Islam today testifies to the extent that terms coming out of small circles of late twentieth-century campus-based activists have come to influence developments at the national level. As ubiquitous as the term is in contemporary Indonesian Islamic discourse, it should also be realized that *syiar* is a relatively recent addition to the popular lexicon. Its current usage in public preaching, print discourse, social media, and in the text of Aceh's contemporary Shariʿa legislation reflects the culmination of a rather erratic path through the history of Islam.

The Arabic root of the word (*sh*-ʿ-*r*) has associations with feelings, cognizance, perception, and (poetic) inspiration, as well as with hair. Forms based on this root can be found in several verses of the Qurʾān, in several of which *shaʿāʾir* is used to refer to religious "symbols" including the Meccan hills of *Ṣafā* and *Marwa*, the sacred month, animals dedicated for ritual sacrifice, and pilgrims to the *kaʿba*.[89] Subsequent elaborations of *shiʿār* in Islamicate technical vocabularies provide some illuminating perspective on the distinctive way in which the Indonesianized term "*syiar*" is deployed in contemporary Aceh. In its earliest recorded Arabic usages outside of the Qurʾān, *shiʿār* literally referred to rallying around the tribal banner—a display of communal solidarity through the ritual display of public symbols of identity. Taufik Fahd has identified the term "*shiʿār*" in the pre-Islamic period as referring to a signal for the gathering of war parties and other Bedouin expeditions.[90] After the coming of Islam it was used for caravans leaving for the *ḥajj*, as well as with reference to various stations of the pilgrimage ritual (Ar. *shaʿira/mashāʿir*). The latter in particular reflect aspects of the Qurʾānic usages just noted, as *shiʿār* came to be used for the "marking" of animals dedicated for ritual sacrifice, and later served more generally to imbue objects and situations with "a feeling of the sacred." Other than this definition of *shiʿār*, one of the most interesting notions of marking implied

[88] Again, here I am borrowing the term from Clifford Geertz' classic essay, "Religion as a Cultural System," in *The Interpretation of Cultures*, 87–125.

[89] *al-Baqara* (2), 158, *al-Māʾida* (5), 2, *al-Ḥajj* (22), 32.

[90] Such usage was later carried into other Islamicate languages. In Ottoman Turkish, *shiʿār* was used not only for particular, concrete badges and flags but also more generally as "a token by which friends know one another in battle." As in Persian, it was also the term for a "war cry." James W. Redhouse, *A Turkish and English Lexicon* (Constantinople: Printed for the American Mission by A.H. Boyajian, 1890/reprinted İstanbul: *Çağrı Yayınları*, 1992), 1126; S. Haim, *The Shorter Persian-English Dictionary* (Tehran: Farhang Moaser, 1985), 394.

by the term is its usage in reference to the marking of non-Muslims living in mixed societies such as that of Abbasid Baghdad where *shiʿār* was used for the distinguishing marks on the clothing of Jewish and Christian subject populations (Ar. *dhimmī*).[91] In other cases, however, the social dynamics of this "marking" were reversed—with *shiʿār* used more with reference to marks distinguishing the Muslim majority.[92] In Modern Standard Arabic, *shiʿār* and its plural forms are now used to refer to emblems, token features, distinguishing characteristics, mottos, or slogans—and the compound *shiʿār tijārī* denotes a trademark.

"Syiar Islam" in its Indonesian usage has a comparatively short history, traceable back only to the twentieth century. A prominent early use of the term comes from *Kartosuwiryo*, the leader of the Darul Islam movement centered in West Java to which the Acehnese rebellion of the same name was became affiliated in the 1950s. Before that, in July 1936, *Kartosuwiryo* published a pamphlet entitled *Sikap Hijrah*, in which he described the establishment of Muhammad as leader of the community at Medina as an act that for the first time made manifest the "*Sjiʿar-oel-Islam*."[93] Thereafter, scattered usage of the term with reference to the public symbolism of Islam and the distinctive identity of the Muslim community begins to appear in various Indonesian Islamic periodicals through the 1940s–1960s. For example, an editorial published in 1946 called for the establishment of new Islamic schools and prayer houses, "so that *syiar* Islam can manifest itself more clearly in the era of national development."[94] During these first years of Indonesian independence, the need for promoting and expanding *syiar* was stressed in public statements and the popular press by other prominent figures in the modern history of Indonesian Islam, including *Tjokroaminoto*.[95] In the 1970s, it rose further in prominence, and even appeared as the title of a monthly magazine briefly published at Jakarta (*Syiar Islam*).[96] The real popularization of *syiar* was, however, further

[91] T. Fahd, "Shiʿār," *Encyclopaedia of Islam*, 2nd Edition (Brill Online, 2012), <http://referenceworks.brillonline.com/entries/encyclopaedia-of-islam-2/shiar-SIM_6921>, accessed 26 June 2012.

[92] The Shāfiʿī jurist al-Māwardī (d. 1058), for example, used the term to refer to congregational prayers and to the *adhān*—and further argued that the *muḥtasib* has the duty to compel their observance. As we shall see in Chapter 7, mandatory (male) attendance at Friday prayers is a matter sometimes enforced by the Wilayatul Hisbah (WH) in contemporary Aceh. Abī al-Ḥasan ʿAlī b. Muḥammad b. Ḥabīb al-Baṣrī al-Baghdādī al-Māwardī, *Kitāb al-aḥkām al-sulṭāniyya wa al-wilāyāt al-dīniyya* (Beirut: al-Maktabat al-ʿAṣriyya), 264. I would like to thank Marion Katz for calling this passage in Māwardī's work to my attention.

[93] I would like to thank Chiara Formichi for pointing out this early usage of the term to me. For more on Kartosuwiryo and his role in the development of Islamist discourses in modern Indonesia, see her *Islam and the Making of the Nation: Kartosuwiryo and Political Islam in Twentieth-Century Indonesia* (Leiden: KITLV Press, 2012).

[94] "Memperloeas Sjiar Islam," *Berita Indonesia* (10 October 1946), 2.

[95] "Dunia Islam," *Antara News* (22 November 1949).

[96] I would like to thank Dan Birchok for calling my attention to this publication.

advanced through the activities of the campus-based Islamist organizations of that time, and particularly by the Salman Mosque Movement. The first Indonesian-language academic treatment of the Salman Mosque Movement tried to gloss the (at the time still largely unfamiliar) term "*syiar*" as: "A broad concept that views Islam as a totality, and that aims to concretely manifest the totality of its teachings in social life."[97]

The idea of a totalizing vision of Islam was sometimes also expressed in terms of a "way of life" or a "system" by those associated with the *da'wa* movements of the late twentieth century. Such usages reflected broader trends in global Islamic discourses of the late twentieth century. In Indonesia, however, the distinctive use of the phrase "Islam yang *kaffah*" also came into increasing prominence through its deployment by activists associated with *tarbiya* circles in the 1990s. This Indonesian-language phrase draws on the Qur'ānic verse that calls for believers to "fully" or "completely" (*kaffah*) embrace Islam (Ar. *udkhulū fī'l-Islām kāffatan*).[98] Despite its Qur'ānic origins, the phrase "*Islam yang kaffah*" has (like "*syiar*") only come into popular Indonesian usage over the past few decades, largely through its use by campus *da'wa* and *tarbiya* activists. Today, this phrase is repeated across an expanding range of Muslim discourses in the country from those of urban professionals associated with the Jakarta-based "Prosperity and Justice Party" (*Partai Keadilan Sejahtera*/PKS) to local movements such as the Islam *Kaffah* group based in the onion-farming village of Blumbang on the slopes of Central Java's Mt. Lawu.[99] The term "*Islam yang kaffah*" also appears prominently in the official "Clarification" (I. *Penjelasan*) of Aceh's *Qanun 11*, and it has become a central referent in the public discourse of those furthering programs for the Islamization of law in contemporary Aceh as a prominent keyword in the publications of the DSI.

The transformative ambitions of embracing "*Islam yang kaffah*" are far-reaching. In Alyasa's oft-reprinted manifesto on the aims and methods of state Shari'a, he argues that a comprehensive commitment to Islam can have the effect of making people "more honest, frugal, studious, diligent, loyal, intelligent and emotionally mature."[100] The project is in this sense a forward-looking movement aiming toward social transformation in a kind of modernizing "disciplinary revolution."[101] Alyasa's writings on the

[97] Aziz, et al., "Gerakan Kaum Muda Islam Mesjid Salman," 223.

[98] *Al-baqara* (2), 208. The prominent Indonesian Islamic radical preacher Abu Bakar Baasyir has even proclaimed this verse to be "the most crucial command in the Qur'an." See M.C. Ricklefs, *Islamisation and its Opponents in Java: A Political, Social, Cultural and Religious History, c. 1930 to the Present* (Singapore: NUS Press, 2012), 182.

[99] Ricklefs, *Islamisation and Its Opponents*, 417–18.

[100] Alyasa Abubakar, *Syari'at Islam*, 85–6.

[101] This term has been coined by Philip S. Gorski with reference to "the introduction and diffusion of disciplinary techniques, both new and old, and their social and political effects,"

subject call for the development of a "new understanding" (I. *pemahaman baru*) of Islam in which the law functions to help people to "become more perfect Muslims" (I. *untuk menjadi Muslim yang lebih sempurna*).[102] The ultimate aim then is to transform individuals to better prepare their souls for success in both this world and the next. However individuals, according to Alyasa, are not able to achieve this on their own. Instead he argues that the lower appetites of human beings, and Satan's persistent machinations to ensnare them, need to be countered with an equally powerful force—that of the state. As he writes: "Government involvement in the promotion of religious teachings to make individuals more observant of the Shariʿa is something that, logically speaking, is clearly needed—in fact, absolutely necessary... Human beings need to be watched, reminded and helped (I. *dibantu*) in this." He is also consistently and sharply critical of those who hold the "naïve view" (I. *pemikiran yang naïf*) that individuals could observe the Shariʿa on their own, without the intervention of the state.[103]

According to Alyasa, the role of the state is crucial in enhancing the effectiveness of the Shariʿa project. He emphasizes this critical function of government through his use of the expression "*Islam yang kaffah*" as a central trope in the rhetoric of Aceh's contemporary Islamic legal system. His elaboration of this key term in Indonesian *daʿwa* discourse includes attempts to pre-empt those who would question the need for this—or any other qualifying modifier—to be used in relation to Islam. In response to the questions: "Why does the world "*kaffah*" need to be added? Isn't "the Shariʿa" sufficient in itself? What difference does the addition of the word "*kaffah*" make?" Alyasa states that in the specific context of contemporary Aceh, the phrase "*Islam yang kaffah*" "is necessary in that it carries with it important political considerations, and is not just a reflection of some theoretical point. The intention behind using this term is to clearly signal that the implementation of the Shariʿa in Aceh is carried out with the involvement of the state."[104]

CHALLENGES AND LIMITS TO STATE SHARIʿA

The state itself, however, has not always been completely supportive of the project of implementing Islamic law in Aceh, and the rise and fall of local governments has had a direct impact on the flow of funds designated

in early modern Europe. *Disciplinary Revolution: Calvinism and the Rise of the State in Early Modern Europe* (Chicago: University of Chicago Press, 2003), 34.

102 Alyasa Abubakar, *Syariʿat Islam*, 87.

103 Alyasa Abubakar, *Syariʿat Islam*, 75–6.

104 The relative novelty of the use of the same term in Aceh is also addressed in the Chapter 4 of the same work. Alyasa Abubakar, *Syariʿat Islam*, 21–30.

to facilitate the work of state Shariʿa institutions. As already discussed, when governor Abdullah Puteh saw it to be in his political interests, he lavished a flood of money on the State Shariʿa Agency. By 2007, however, the situation was very different. With the election of Irwandi Yusuf as governor in 2006, the DSI's budget was drastically cut.[105] Activities were scaled back considerably in many sections of the Agency, and this often left employees with little to do at the office aside from reading newspapers and, when connections were up and functioning, surfing the internet. The funding cutbacks were oftdiscussed in the public media and many coffee shop conversations as indications that the state was not "serious" about the application of Shariʿa in society. For some this was a fact to be bemoaned.[106] For others, it is not necessarily such a bad thing, and there are many in Aceh who have been sharply and publicly critical of the state Shariʿa system.

Some, though relatively few in number, questioned the very legitimacy of a state agency being intrusively involved in issues of personal piety and public morality. Many more critics accept the idea that the state does have an important role to play in supporting Islamic belief and practice, but they nevertheless critique what they see as the hypocrisy and lack of professionalism of those staffing the Shariʿa bureaucracies. As one citizen expressed this in an "sms to the editor" to a local Acehnese newspaper:

> You in the DSI "inspect" others because of Islam, but I am surprised, have you ever "inspected" your own heart, your own words, or even your own sincerity with regard to the Shariʿa?[107]

Questions of the proper priorities in the development of Aceh's Islamic legal system are also frequently raised by critics of Aceh's contemporary Islamic legal system, asking why, for example, there has not been any

[105] "Plafon Anggaran Syariat Islam Dinilai Minim," *Serambi* (19 October 2010), 20; "Anggaran Habis, Syariat Islam Kandas," *Rakyat Aceh* (15 February 2010), 1–2.

[106] "Mahasiswa Minta Syariat Islam Ditegakkan," *Serambi* (7 December 2010), 17; "Penerapan Syariat Islam Menurun," *Waspada* (3 December 2010); "Dinas Syariat Islam dan MPU Dinilai Gagal," *Harian Aceh* (10 November 2010), 14; "Dewan Minta Dinas Syariat Islam Pro Aktif," *Rakyat Aceh* (4 November 2010), 5; "KAMMI Unjuk Rasa di Dinas Syariat Islam," *Serambi* (7 August 2010), 17; "Pelaksanaan Syariat Islam Masih Kabur," *Serambi* (7 August 2010), 21; "Penerapan Syariat Islam Belum Maksimal," *Serambi* (19 April 2007), 3; "Pelaksanaan Syariat Islam Kurang Bergema," *Serambi* (23 April 2007), 13; "Diaktifkan, Tim Terpadu Syariat Islam," *Serambi* (19 April 2007), 13; "Penerapan Syariat Islam Belum Optimal," *Waspada* (16 April 2007); "DSI Kota Serius Tegakkan Syariat," *Serambi* (21 April 2007), 2; "Dinas SI Diminta Perketat Pengawasan," *Rakyat Aceh* (3 September 2007), 3; "Penerapan SI Butuh Peran Negara," *Waspada* (6 November 2007), 17; "Syariat Islam Mati Suri di Tamiang," *Serambi* (29 August 2007), 3; "Penerapan SI di Subulussalam Lemah," *Waspada* (13 July 2007), 24; "Pembayaran Diyat Perlu Payung Hukum," *Serambi* (2 July 2007), 10; "PII dan Forsima Sosialisasikan Syariat Islam," *Serambi* (9 March 2007), 13; "Penegakan Syariat Islam Belum Sempurna," *Rakyat Aceh* (7 February 2007), 5.

[107] "Aspirasi," *Metro Aceh* (13 October 2009), 6.

specific legislation on popular issues such as governmental corruption and illegal deforestation.

Aceh's state Shariʿa officials have also been criticized for their inconsistency in their application of Islamic law, as well as a perceived tendency to apply physical punishments only to offenders from the lower or "marginal" classes.[108] On the island of Sabang, for example, public demands for the caning (I. *cambuk*) of a high-ranking government official convicted of *khalwat* were expressed with calls for justice to be carried out efficiently and without prejudice, in order to avoid the spread of negative perceptions about Islam in Aceh.[109] Others have been accused as well for "shutting their eyes" to problems such as gambling and black market lotteries (I. *togel*) run out of local coffee shops that are perceived to have the "backing" (I. *beking*) of high-ranking officers of the Indonesian military, police, and provincial government.[110] The DSI has itself even been accused of leading believers astray (I. *menyesatkan*) through their promotion of certain interpretations of Islam rather than others.[111]

Many of the critics of the Islamic legal system, however, call not for its dismantling, but rather its reform to better accomplish the aspirational values of justice.[112] Along these lines, the DSI has sometimes even attracted the criticism of other state Shariʿa institutions in Aceh, for example, in the public harangue by the Lhokseumawe branch of the MPU who blamed the Agency for being unable to stop local women from appearing in public dressed in tight clothing (I. *pakaian ketat*).[113] Others come from diverse parties demanding more, not less Shariʿa:

> Although there have been many setbacks, the hope is that the Shariʿa will continue to work on influencing change in all aspects of life in Aceh. In doing so, however, it must be applied in ways that are just, not discriminatory (I. *tak diskriminatif*), and for the benefit of all.[114]

[108] "Warga Tuding Dinas Syariat Islam Pilih Kasih," *Harian Aceh* (21 April 2007), 1, 11.

[109] "Ketua PN Sabang Tidak Dihukum: Masyarakat Minta Dinas Syariat Islam Dibubarkan," *Harian Aceh* (24 April 2007), 1.

[110] "Togel Marak di Bireuen: Dinas Syariat Islam Dituding 'Tutup Mata'," *Harian Aceh* (12 April 2007), 5.

[111] For example, it has been criticized for its Indonesian language renderings of Qurʾānic verses on banners and billboards used to promote its interpretations of Islam, not just for the translations, but also for the accuracy of technical references. See "Dinas Syariat Islam Dituding Menambah Ayat Al Quran," *Harian Aceh* (12 February 2009), 15.

[112] Irwan Adaby, "Harapan terhadap Syariat," *Serambi* (13 August 2008), 30.

[113] "Kinerja Dinas Syariat Islam Lamban," *Rakyat Aceh* (11 April 2007), 4. The *Dinas SyariatIslam* publicly responded to this, saying that their mandate is primarily to provide religious and moral lessons (I. *melakukan pembinaan*) and not to officially prosecute cases. "Dinas Syariat Islam Bantah Lamban dalam Bekerja," *Rakyat Aceh* (16 April 2007), 3.

[114] "Syariat Islam yang Kaffah," *Kontras* (25 February 2007), 2.

Many more broadly demand that the DSI and the provincial government consistently implement the measures already in place, and to put more effort into programs for the socialization of Shariʿa values.[115]

In December 2006, for example, a local NGO published a survey of public opinion that reported widespread disappointment with the state implementation of Shariʿa—with 82 percent of their sample reportedly disagreeing with the statement that "the implementation of Islamic law in Aceh has [positively] contributed to broader aspects of governance in Aceh." These disappointments did not, however, seem to have detracted from the belief of a majority of Acehnese that "Shariʿa" could, in some form, serve to constructively address the problems facing contemporary society. Indeed, an even higher portion (87 percent) of respondents to the same survey expressed agreement with the statement that "the implementation of Shariʿa is the solution for Acehnese society."[116] Based upon this data, the leaders of the organization that conducted the survey argued that in order to realizethe aspirations of the project of implementing the Shariʿa, the government would have to take the task more seriously than it has done to date.[117] Their argument was thus not that the state should get out of the business of implementing Islamic law altogether, but rather that the government should be doing a better job of it.

Others in Aceh have made more dramatic demands for the state to direct more attention and resources to the implementation of Islamic law, including violent demonstrations staged at the DSI Central Office in Banda Aceh. In 2008, about 100 student protesters complaining of the lack of effectiveness in implementing Shariʿa turned violent, vandalizing the front gate of the DSI building before marching to the governor's office to demand an audience.[118] Local chapters of Jakarta-based Islamist organizations such as HMI and KAMMI, as well as local groups like FOKUS Aceh, have staged demonstrations at DSI offices in other parts of the province as well

[115] "Pelaksanaan Syariat Islam Jalan Di Tempat," *Waspada* (29 March 2008), 12; "Kepala Dinas Syariat Islam Diminta Berani Tindak Bawahan," *Waspada* (14 March 2008), 16; "Ulama Diminta Tingkatkan Pelaksanaan SI," *HarianAceh* (11 August 2009), 1; "Syariat Islam di Agara Belum Maksimal," *Harian Aceh* (11 August 2009), 11; "MPU Aceh Evaluasi Pelaksanaan Syariat," *Serambi* (5 May 2009), 7; "Ketua MPU Aceh Barat: Penerapan Syariat Islam di Aceh Masih Ragu-Ragu," *Serambi* (24 December 2008), 22; "Pelaksanaan Syariat Islam Belum Maksimal," *Rakyat Aceh* (3 July 2009), 4; "Penerapan Syariat Islam Masih 'Dangkal'," *HarianAceh* (22 December 2009), 5.

[116] Yayasan Insan Cita Madani, *Hasil Survey YICM tentang Penerapan Qanun-Qanun Syariat Islam* (Banda Aceh: YICM, 2007). For a collection of documents on the survey and responses to the publication of its results, see Ampuh Devayan and Murizal Hamzah (eds.), *Polemik Penerapan Syariat Islam di Aceh* (Banda Aceh: YICM, 2007).

[117] Interview with Irwan Adabi, 26 January 2011 at Banda Aceh.

[118] "Unjuk Rasa Syariat Islam Ricuh: Polisidan Mahasiswa Kejar-kejaran," *Aceh Independen* (31 December 2008), 1–2.

to voice their view that the project of implementing Shariʿa has failed.[119] For Aceh's small but assertive groups of political Islamists, a radical reconstruction of the state is needed in order to facilitate the application of the Shariʿa:

> The DSI is certainly not an Islamic form of government... It is simply one bureaucratic unit... the implementation of Islamic law in Aceh needs to be carried out by a truly Islamic system of state, encompassing the legislative, judicial, and executive branches of government, not just a simple "Agency" (*Dinas*). Without the formation of a truly Islamic government, all the promises of political parties related to the implementation of the Shariʿa are nothing more than boasts.[120]

The provincial administration under governor Irwandi Yusuf has, however, not been very responsive to such requests. Aside from the botched attempt to get ahead of the MPU on the issue of "deviant teachings" discussed in Chapter 4, the general trend of his administration was to downplay the centrality of Shariʿa in both state policy and public discourse. This can be seen, for example, with the appointment of Ziauddin Ahmad as the new director of the DSI in 2008. Ziauddin was a career bureaucrat who had previously served in the Ministry of Information, and the Departments of Finance and Religious Affairs. In sharp contrast to Alyasa's academic background in the study of Islam, Ziauddin describes his own Islamic learning as something he pursued alongside his secular training for a professional career in the civil service. During his tenure at the DSI, Ziauddin maintained some of the most general points of Alyasa's vision with regard to support of Islamic education and "character building" through the inculcation of "ethical and religious understanding."[121] Ziauddin did so, however, with considerably less zest and without anything like the public profile and publication output of his predecessor.

The dramatic swing between these two styles of leadership was moderated to some degree in September 2010, when the governor appointed Rusjdi Ali Muhammad as the next director of the DSI. Rusjdi is an IAIN academic who has been involved with the development of Aceh's Islamic legal system since its inception. His vision has been to broaden the range of issues that the Agency should address, including not only

[119] "Maksiat Merajalela, SI Tamiang Hanya Razia Jilbab," *Waspada* (27 October 2007), 3; "KAMMI: Kinerja Dinas SI Menurun," *Waspada* (31 October 2008), 16; "Pemerintah Diminta Serius Terapkan Syariat Islam," *Serambi* (31 December 2008), 1–2; "Syariat Islam Lemah: KAMMI Demo Rumah Walikota," *Rakyat Aceh* (27 January 2009), 1–2; "HMI Kecewa Syariat Islam di Aceh 'Jalan Ditempat'," *Waspada* (21 February 2009), 11; "Minta Syariat Islam, Rumah Walikota Langsa Didemo," *Harian Aceh* (27 January 2009), 14.

[120] Affan Ramli, *Merajam Dalil Syariat* (Banda Aceh: Bandar Publishing, 2010), 73–5.

[121] Interview with Ziauddin Ahmad, 2 September 2008 at Banda Aceh.

aspects of daily practice such as ritual purity, but also social concerns such as cheating in the markets and corruption in public office.[122] Rusjdi has, in fact, a well-established record of promoting the message of the compatibility of reformed religious values and the pursuit of national development goals with publications testifying to his conviction that "the success of national development will help with the progress of fostering religious awareness in society in a mutually reinforcing way."[123] With this we have returned once again to the nexus of *da'wa*, development, and Indonesian nationalism that characterized the thought of IAIN academics and activists who supported the current project of Shari'a implementation at its inception, and thence back to the *da'wa* discourses promoted on the Banda Aceh IAIN campus since the days of Ali Hasjmy.

When interviewed in 2011 about his view of the situation since he stepped down as director of the State Shari'a Agency, Alyasa Abubakar remarked that he remained optimistic (I. *tetap optimis*) about the future of Islamic law in Aceh, stating that all that was needed was a shift back to a more favorable political climate.[124] That, however, may take some time to develop. In fact, popular sentiment seems to reflect a diminishing interest in any further strengthening of the state Shari'a system. The sense of a lack of progress indicated in the responses in the 2006 survey cited earlier has deepened over the years since then, and popular cynicism has grown particularly strong in the wake of the *Qanun Jinaya* debates. This has been compounded by cutbacks in funding for, and the consequent scaling back of, the public activities of state Shari'a institutions, as well as by the proliferation of both official reports and more widespread rumors of their officers being involved in cases of abuse and scandal. Many local Muslims have become increasingly disillusioned with actual results of the state implementation of Islamic law over the past decade, and vocal critiques of the institutions and ideology of the system are now common in Aceh's dynamic and diverse public sphere.[125] This has been the case not only for the DSI, but even more so for the Wilayatul Hisbah (WH). The next chapter will turn to consider this most hotly contested of Aceh's state Shari'a institutions.

[122] Interview with Rusjdi Ali Muhammad, 26 January 2011 at Banda Aceh.

[123] Rusjdi Ali Muhammad, *Revitalisasi Syar'iat Islam di Aceh: Problem, Solusi dan Implementasi* (Jakarta: Logos Wacana Ilmu, 2003), 85.

[124] Interview with Alyasa Abubakar, 26 January 2011 at Banda Aceh.

[125] For an overview of the wide range of opinions of Aceh's state Shari'a system expressed in one vibrant open forum, see R. Michael Feener, "Hand, Heart, and Handphone: State Shari'a in the Age of the SMS," *Contemporary Islam* 7 (2013), 15–32.

8

Sanctions and Socialization

> Only the man who has enough good in him to feel the justice of the penalty can be punished: the others can only be hurt, or with a finer realism regard themselves as temporary losers in a game which they may try again. The degree of goodness that can alone give a penalty the quality of punishment is something that the state cannot compel.
>
> William Ernest Hocking
> *The Coming World Civilization*[1]

This chapter discusses the coercive enforcement of Shariʿa norms of public morality in Aceh's Islamic legal system, with a focus on the Wilayatul Hisbah (WH). As the most high-profile and polemicized institution of Islamic law in contemporary Aceh, the WH has been at the center of tensions between the formal legal apparatus and some sectors of civil society over the promotion of Shariʿa standards of public morality through state programs of social control. While the name Wilyatul Hisbah derives from Arabic terms used for the application of Islamic law in medieval Muslim societies, the work of the WH in contemporary Aceh has been envisioned in ways that reflect modern understandings of the sociology of law.[2] This attention to the cultural contexts and social dynamics of law points to the extensive influence that trends in modern legal thought originating well outside of the Islamic tradition have had on the design and administration of Aceh's contemporary Shariʿa system.

[1] William Ernest Hocking, *The Coming World Civilization* (New York: Harper, 1956), 7. In the 1920s, William Hocking (quoted in the epigram to this chapter) co-taught philosophy seminars at Harvard with Roscoe Pound. William Ernest Hocking, *Present Status of the Philosophy of Law and of Rights* (New Haven: Yale University Press, 1926), viii. As will be discussed in Chapter 9, Pound's work on "sociological jurisprudence" made a major imprint on twentieth-century Indonesian understandings of law and society.

[2] The operative term at its root, *ḥisba*, was popularized through the work of Abū Ḥamid al-Ghazālī (d. 1111), whom Michael Cook identifies as having used it as "a general term (Ar. *ʿibāra shāmila*) for commanding right and forbidding wrong." Michael Cook, *Commanding Right and Forbidding Wrong in Islamic Thought* (Cambridge: Cambridge University Press, 2000), 429, 446–50.

POLICING THE SHARIʿA

The history of the mechanisms for the enforcement of Islamic law is a field that still requires much research. Over the medieval period, a number of institutions developed within diverse Muslim societies to deal with issues of public order within the framework of Islamic norms, including the judge (Ar. *qāḍī*), the police (Ar. *shurṭa*), and the market inspector (Ar. *muḥtasib*), whose public roles and responsibilities could at times overlap.[3] While the particular forms that these institutions have taken varied over time and place in Islamic history, they all consistently shared some connection with state power. They also provided for the use of discretionary corporal punishment (Ar. *taʿzīr*) to address offenses against norms of public morality but for which either there was no *ḥudūd* provision, or the stringent evidentiary requirements of *ḥudūd* could not be met.[4] *Taʿzīr* thus came to serve as "a conveniently-executed" mode of enforcement in the work of the *muḥtasib*.[5] In some contexts, such as under the Saljuqs, *taʿzīr* was moreover not only a "residual category" of Shariʿa offenses for general administrative convenience, but could also be used as a tool to be employed in pursuit of specific political ends.[6]

The reconfigurations of state power characteristic of modern nation-states brought with them new arrangements for policing the Shariʿa—and in many Muslim countries, this resulted in the elimination of pre-modern offices for the enforcement of public order and their replacement by modern style police forces. More recent movements for the "re-introduction" of Islamic criminal law have, however, been extremely critical of these modern historical developments. Calls for using the state apparatus to impose a moral order on society have sometimes also included appeals to establish special bodies to implement Shariʿa rules for public morality. In doing this, some modern Islamists have appropriated and reformulated classical conceptions of governance (Ar. *siyāsa*), combined with expansionary mechanisms for *taʿzīr*.[7]

[3] For a general introduction to these institutions, see: Emile Tyan, *Histoire de l'organisation judicaire en pays d'Islam*, (Leiden: E.J. Brill, 1960), 567–615.

[4] Rudolph Peters, *Crime and Punishment in Islamic Law: Theory and Practice from the Sixteenth to the Twenty-first Century* (New York: Cambridge University Press, 2005), 16; Anver M. Emon, "Ḥuqūq Allāh and Ḥuqūq al-ʿIbād: A Legal Heuristic for a Natural Rights Regime," *Islamic Law and Society* 13.3 (2006) 387–8.

[5] M.Y. Izzi Dien, "Taʿzīr," *Encyclopædia of Islam, Second Edition*, Brill Online, 2012, <http://referenceworks.brillonline.com/entries/encyclopaedia-of-islam-2/tazir-SIM_7475>, accessed 27 June 2012.

[6] Christian Lange, *Justice, Punishment, and the Medieval Muslim Imagination* (Cambridge: Cambridge University Press, 2008), 14, 216.

[7] Peters, *Crime and Punishment*, 144.

Commenting on the relation between these two concepts in the pre-modern Muslim traditions, Rudolph Peters has identified the primary aims of *taʿzīr* as the reform of the offender and as a deterrent for others, while *siyāsa* was exercised for the more general benefit of security and public order.[8] In a more recent paper, Marion Katz has extended this conversation significantly by highlighting the complex relationships between competing goals for the application of physical sanctions by Islamic legal scholars and the coercive power of the state. Through careful analyses of cases of sexual immorality from the Saljuq, Mamluk, and Ottoman periods, Katz demonstrates that in deciding to apply physical punishments, the state placed primary importance on "the supposed deterrent value of the punishment, the resulting gain in social order, and the consequent enhancement of the reputation of the ruler."[9] In doing so, however, the rulers not infrequently contradicted the opinion of Islamic jurists who argued for stricter adherence to the *ḥudūd* (sg. *ḥadd*) requirements and procedures detailed in their interpretations of the Shariʿa.[10]

The paramountcy of political considerations in the high-profile application of corporal punishments for offenses against Shariʿa norms of public morality is also clearly evident in Aceh's contemporary Islamic legal system. In this context, appeals to particular conceptions of *siyāsa* and *taʿzīr* have provided important conceptual resources for a thoroughly modern program of using law as a tool of social engineering. This agenda was the subject of an extensive academic justification in a recent dissertation produced at the Banda Aceh campus of the IAIN.[11] Official publications of the State Shariʿa Agency have also presented *taʿzīr* as an "adaptive and expansive" mechanism for the exclusive use of the state for addressing social ills.[12] Provisions for *taʿzīr* punishments were built into Aceh's contemporary Islamic legal system since its inception, and specific sanctions for offenses related to alcohol, gambling, and *khalwat* were elaborated in the *qanun* dealing with these issues in 2002. Nevertheless, no *taʿzīr* penalties were actually applied by the state until 2005.[13] By

[8] Peters, *Crime and Punishment*, 68.

[9] Marion Holmes Katz, "The Ḥadd Penalty for Zinā: Symbol or Deterrent? Texts from the Early Sixteenth Century," in Paul M. Cobb (ed.), *The Lineaments of Islam: Studies in Honor of Fred McGraw Donner* (Leiden: Brill, 2012), 374.

[10] Katz, "The Ḥadd Penalty for Zinā," 351–75.

[11] Achyar Zein, "Kriteria Tindak Pidana Dalam Al-Qurʾan," Ph.D. dissertation (Banda Aceh: Institut Agama Islam Negeri Ar-Raniry Darussalam, 2010).

[12] Alyasa Abubakar and Marah Halim, *Hukum Pidana Islam di Provinsi Nanggroe Aceh Darussalam* (Banda Aceh: Dinas Syariat Islam Provinsi Nanggroe Aceh Darussalam, 2006), 35–8.

[13] Arskal Salim, *Challenging the Secular State: The Islamization of Law in Modern Indonesia* (Honolulu: University of Hawaii Press, 2008), 159.

that time, however, the political and social contexts in Aceh had changed dramatically from what they were when the initial provisions for special autonomy and their implementation of Shariʿa were introduced in 1999. In the wake of the massive tsunami that struck Aceh in December 2004 came a series of dramatic social and political changes that significantly re-shaped the work of all the institutions of Aceh's Islamic legal system. The most important of these changes were a perceptible rise in the intensity of public religious discourse sparked by the trauma, the settling of the conflict between GAM and the Indonesian central government formalized by the signing of the Helsinki Agreement in July 2005, and the wide diffusion of discourses on comprehensive reconstruction promoted by government offices and NGOs in their various projects for disaster response and peace-building. Taken together, these developments energized the application of laws that had already been on the books for several years and the institutions that were created to administer them, particularly the WH.

THE WILAYATUL HISBAH (WH)

The basic provision for the establishment of a state institution for the enforcement of Islamic law in contemporary Aceh was contained in the 2000 law that framed the basic outline of the Shariʿa system, and allowed for "civil service investigators" (I. *penyidik pegawai negeri sipil*/PPNS) to investigate incidents of alleged infractions against Islamic law.[14] In 2002, *Qanun No. 11* elaborated basic regulations on the duties and responsibilities of the Wilayatul Hisbah. Its mandate in that legislation authorized WH officers to "admonish and advise" (I. *menegur dan menasehati*) those that they apprehended who were in violation of Aceh's Shariʿa laws. If, however, after such a reprimand the party did not repent or change their behavior, the WH were to turn the case over either to the police, or to a "civil service investigator" (PPNS) who could either prepare a formal case for submission to the Mahkamah Syariah or dismiss the matter if they deemed such a procedure unwarranted by the particular incident.[15] With the issuance of further gubernatorial instructions two years later, the authority of the WH beyond its ability to admonish and instruct those publicly violating Shariʿa norms was thus effectively restricted to receiving reports of violations from the community, ordering offenders

[14] *Peraturan Daerah Propinsi Daerah Istimewa Aceh Nomor 5/Tahun 2000 tentang Pelakasanaan Syariat Islam*, Pasal 20.

[15] *Qanun Provinsi Nanggroe Aceh Darussalam Nomor 11/Tahun 2002 tentang Pelaksanaan Syariat Islam bidang Aqidah, Ibadah dan Syiʿar Islam*, Pasal 15.

to stop what they were doing, asking them to present identification, and reporting the incident to the police.[16] These measures served to formally establish the work of the WH within the broader Indonesian legal system while also placing considerable restrictions on their activities for public enforcement of Aceh's Shariʿa legislation.

These basic arrangements were given further concrete shape in the 2006 Law on Governing Aceh (LOGA), which included provisions that called for local government to administer law enforcement under the organizational rubric of a civilian police force (I. Satuan Polisi Pamong Praja).[17] Upon his inauguration as governor in February 2007, Irwandi Yusuf acted upon the provisions of the LOGA to bring the WH under the supervision of the civilian police.[18] At the same time, the integration of the WH into the civilian police force also made it possible, for the first time, for some WH officers to become recognized as civil service investigators (PPNS). This provision in particular was read by some in the WH as opening the door to greater autonomy for the WH to make arrests and prepare their own cases for the Public Prosecutor to submit to the Shariʿa Courts, and over the years that followed, this did indeed become the case at some local WH offices.[19] Some of the first WH officers to be upgraded to the status of PPNS were women.[20] However, progress was slow, and by 2008, only 60 out of roughly 1,000 WH personnel across the province had been appointed as PPNS.[21] Critics of this new arrangement saw the slow progress of professionalization of WH staff as further evidence supporting their argument that the integration of the WH into the civilian police force was a policy aimed at restricting the WH's autonomy.

Under the rubric of the newly re-constituted civilian force, police officers routinely accompanied WH patrols and in some offices, and in some local posts WH officers were given new uniforms that symbolized their new position of partnership with the civilian police force.[22] The activities of the WH were also further regulated through new requirements that they produce formal reports from every incident that they handled, following the same guidelines and procedures established for the civil police.[23] On

[16] *Keputusan Gubernur No. 01 Tahun 2004 tentang Organisasi dan Tata Kerja Wilayatul Hisbah.*

[17] *Undang-Undang Republik Indonesia No.11/2006 tentang Pemerintahan Aceh* (LOGA) XXXV.244.1-2.

[18] Interview with Pamong Praja police officer, 26 January 2011 at Banda Aceh.

[19] "Desak WH Jadi Penyidik Sipil," *Rakyat Aceh* (15 May 2008), 2.

[20] Interview with a PPNS WH officer, 20 June 2010 at Banda Aceh.

[21] Interview with the WH Commandant, 4 September 2008 at Banda Aceh.

[22] "Polisi Akan Dampingi WH," *Serambi* (30 August 2007), 13; "WH Banda Aceh Kenakan Seragam Satpol PP," *Serambi* (26 April 2009), 3. The latter, however, was not the case uniformly for WH across the province. "Tiga Tahun Baju Dinas Tak Berganti," *Rakyat Aceh* (10 October 2010), 5

[23] Interview with WH officer, 20 June 2010 at Banda Aceh.

one level, these measures address some of the concerns that supporters of Aceh's Islamic legal system, including Alyasa Abubakar, had voiced about the need for the professionalization of the WH.[24] However, some WH officers themselves bristled over what they saw as a sacrifice of their autonomy in field operations. Some public supporters of a more vigorous enforcement of Shari'a have thus called for the re-establishment of the WH as an autonomous law enforcement body separate from the civilian police force. To date, however, no concrete measures have been taken to address these demands at the provincial level.[25]

STAFFING

Staffing has been a significant issue in the development of the WH since its establishment. Since it was first established under the aegis of the State Shari'a Agency, the WH has been staffed overwhelmingly with alumni of the IAIN, mostly from the Faculties of Da'wa and Tarbiya.[26] Some of the local WH district offices, however, also accepted candidates from local *dayah* who were able to pass the necessary entrance tests.[27] Most of them were hired as "contract" workers for a set time period, and paid at rates which could vary considerably depending on the local WH office. More professional recruits appointed as salaried civil servants (I. *pegawai negeri sipil*) have been markedly fewer in number. The competence and professionalization of WH recruits has, as a consequence, been a constant topic of public discussion

[24] Alyasa Abubakar, *Kajian Undang-Undang Pemerintahan Aceh dan Essay Tentang Perempuan, Perkahwinan dan Perwalian Anak* (Banda Aceh: Dinas Syariat Islam, 2007), 29.

[25] "WH Dikembalikan ke Dinas Syariat Islam," *Serambi* (15 April 2009), 17; "Kembalikan WH ke Dinas Syariat Islam," *Serambi* (15 May 2009), 22; "Kembalikan WH ke Dinas Syariat Islam," *Rakyat Aceh* (30 May 2009), 4; "Kembalikan WH ke Dinas Syariat Islam," *Rakyat Aceh* (7 June 2009), 6; "HMI Desak WH Dikembalikan ke Dinas Syariat Islam," *Harian Aceh* (27 December 2009), 5; "WH Kembali Digabung ke Dinas Syariat," *Serambi* (25 March 2010), 13; "WH Bireuen ke DSI," *Waspada Online* (25 March 2010), <http://www.waspada.co.id/index.php?option=com_content&view=article&id=99946>, accessed 4 November 2011; "WH Harus Dikembalikan ke DSI," *Serambi* (2 May 2010), 14; "MPU Abdya Dukung Pengembalian WH ke DSI," *Serambi* (5 May 2010), 24; "WH Harus Dikembalikan ke Dinas Syariat Islam," *Serambi* (28 June 2010), 3; "WH Minta Dikembalikan ke Dinas SI," *Rakyat Aceh* (5 October 2010), 3.

[26] Interview with Hamid Sorong, 29 May 2008 at Banda Aceh. Some of those working at the district- (I. *kabupaten*) level WH offices are graduates of the local "junior college" extensions of the IAIN as well (STAIN), many of whom have also spent time in *dayah* of a more "reformed" orientation, such as the Aziziyyah of Samalanga.

[27] *Muzakarah Ulama Se Kabupaten Aceh Utara Dilaksanakan pada tanggal 15 s/d 16 Juli 2009 oleh Majelis Mermusyawaratan Ulama (MPU) Kabupaten Aceh Utara di Gedung Hasbi Ash Shiddiqi, Moun Gedung Kota Lhokseumawe, Thema: "Melalui Muzakarah Ulama-Umara kita Tingkatkan Pemahaman Hukum Syari'ah"* (unpublished official report of the event compiled by the North Aceh MPU, 2009).

and debate in Aceh.[28] Often, the issue is couched in terms of the (lack of) "professionalism" of WH personnel, both by officials supportive of state Shari'a aiming to improve its institutional foundations,[29] and by critics who portray the WH collectively as uneducated and "emotionally immature" thugs operating with state sanction.[30] This latter view predominates in some local communities.[31] Indeed, even the teaching staff of local state Islamic junior colleges (Sekolah Tinggi Agama Islam Negeri/STAIN), from which many local WH recruits graduate, acknowledge the low standards for acceptance and the relative lack of specialized on-the-job training for new officers.[32]

Little public discussion exists, however, on the actual motivations of those who choose to apply to and join the WH. When asked why they chose to work for the WH, officers and administrative staff respond in diverse ways, sometimes citing multiple and simultaneous motivations. Some frankly acknowledge that when they joined the WH, it was the only practical option for them, given their backgrounds and aptitude. As one officer in Lhokseumawe expressed it:

> Basically, I was just looking for work because at that time I was unemployed and had no other options, however, after that, it turned out that I grew more and more interested and committed to the work of the WH.[33]

[28] "WH Rekrut Anggota Baru," *Rakyat Aceh* (11 August 2007), 2; "Pendaftaran Anggota WH Diperpanjang," *Serambi* (22 August 2007), 10; "264 Peserta Ikut Tes WH," *Serambi* (30 December 2008), 17; "Satpol PP WH Lhokseumawe Kurang Personil," *Rakyat Aceh* (18 December 2008), 4; "Dinas Syariat Rekrut 26 WH," *Serambi* (12 December 2008), 21; "Dinas Syariat Islam Aceh Barat Rekrut Tenaga Kontrak WH," *Harian Aceh* (12 December 2008), 15; "Rekrutmen Satpol PP dan WH Diam-diam," *Waspada* (29 November 2008), 7; "Kinerja Polhut dan WH Dipertanyakan," *Harian Aceh* (10 November 2008), 13; "Puluhan Calon WH Ujian Seleksi," *Waspada* (13 March 2008), 19; "Calon WH Pidie Dites Baca Khutbah," *Serambi* (8 February 2008), 15; "26 Petugas WH Aceh Barat Lulus Seleksi," *Serambi* (20 April 2009), 29; "Personil WH di Aceh Timur Belum Maksimal," *Rakyat Aceh* (12 March 2009), 7; "Kinerja WH Bireuen Dipertanyakan," *Prohaba* (19 January 2009), 2; "WH Pidie Diminta Perbaiki Kinerja," *Serambi* (10 December 2010), 19; "WH Aceh Besar Kekurangan Personil," *Harian Aceh* (1 July 2010), 3.

[29] "Kualitas WH Harus Ditingkatkan," *Serambi* (22 January 2010), 2; "Rekrutmen Wilayatul Hisbah Akan Diperketat," *Harian Aceh* (19 January 2010), 3.

[30] Fajran Zain, "WH Juga Manusia," in Fajran Zain (ed.), *Rangkeum 2009: Olah-pikir Aceh Institute di Media* (Banda Aceh: Aceh Institute Press, 2010), 187–91.

[31] See Benjamin Otto and Jan Michiel Otto, "Aceh's Wilayatul Hisbah (Shari'a Police): Practices and Perceptions," in R. Michael Feener, David Kloos, and Annemarie Samuels (eds.), *Islam and the Limits of the State: Reconfigurations of Ritual, Doctrine, Community and Authority in Contemporary Aceh* (Leiden: Brill, forthcoming).

[32] Notes from roundtable on Shari'a implementation at STAIN Malikussaleh 22 May 2008 at Lhokseumawe. This point was also stressed in interviews with faculty at the same institution two years later (23 June 2010 at Lhokseumawe), indicating that little progress had been made in addressing this issue over the intervening two years.

[33] Interview with an officer of the Lhokseumawe WH, 3 December 2008 at Lhokseumawe.

Many more, however, mention religious motivations as important factors in their decision to join the WH. These officers generally express more enthusiastic support for the state's project of implementing Islamic law in Aceh as an agenda of social reform.[34] Some go even further in stressing that the job is a way to fulfill the Islamic duty of "forbidding wrong" (I. *mencegah mungkar*/Ar. *nahy ʿan al-munkar*). One senior officer in Jantho even describes his work as a form of worship (Ar. *ʿibāda*),[35] while another officer in Lhokseumawe has explained:

> My motivation in joining the WH was to help in their campaign against violations of the Shariʿa in my community, and in Aceh more generally. In my experience, I think I have done some work toward that, at least in improving my own awareness and observance of the Shariʿa.[36]

WH officers with educational backgrounds in *daʿwa* and *tarbiya* have said that their work allows them to remain active in their chosen fields of study—giving concrete application to what they studied at the IAIN. In a number of cases, these alumni had worked as Islamic teachers and informal tutors for children in their communities before joining the WH.[37] In discussing how he saw his background in such work as preparing him for the joining WH, one officer in Bireuen explained:

> What drove me to choose the WH was that I had read in the newspaper that the work of the WH was to advise (I. *menasehati*) people and to promote the Shariʿa. These functions are also stipulated in the *qanun*. I used to carry out *daʿwa* in village prayer houses (Ac. *meunasah*) and so I wanted to take this opportunity to promote proper understanding of the Shariʿa in society more broadly.[38]

Others have spoken of the *daʿwa* aspects of working with the WH as deepening their own personal commitment to Islam. As a female officer concretely described her experience of working in the WH office at Bireuen:

> At first, I carried out *daʿwa* for myself. Maybe at that time I was just like others in the community who generally don't observe things like modest Muslim dress carefully enough. I would sometimes wear pants, for example. But now here I have tried to improve myself so that I can serve as an example to others.[39]

[34] Interviews with an officer of the provincial-level WH, 26 January 2009 at Banda Aceh; and an officer of the Bireuen WH, 24 December 2008 at Bireuen.

[35] Interview with a WH Section Commander, 14 April 2011 at Jantho.

[36] Interview with an officer of the North Aceh WH office, 5 January 2009 at Lhokseumawe.

[37] Interview with an officer of the WH provincial office, 26 January 2009 at Banda Aceh.

[38] Interview with an officer of the Bireuen WH office, 23 December 2008 at Bireuen.

[39] Interview with a member of the administrative staff, 23 December 2008 at the Bireuen WH office.

Once accepted as new recruits, WH officers are given a two-week training course designed by the State Shariʿa Agency (DSI). The program provides a general orientation and covers in a rather cursory way a diverse range of specific topics, with units dedicated to: the protection of human rights in implementing the law, gender equality, professional ethics, criminal psychology, and the basics of criminal procedure, as well as guidelines for the preparation of incident reports, conducting interrogation, securing a crime scene and collecting evidence, recording witness testimony, confiscation, detention, preparing a case, file management, administering investigations, submission of a dossier to the public prosecutor, and Shariʿa criminal legislation.[40] Of course, none of these topics can be dealt with in much detail in the short time allotted during the standard WH training course. Many new officers thus start their work with only a very shallow knowledge of the areas covered and come to learn more about some of them only on the job as they gain more experience.

RESOURCES

The number of new recruits undergoing even this rudimentary training has furthermore been significantly limited by decreases in the funding of WH operations over recent years. This has been the case at the provincial level since 2007 following the election of the former GAM member Irwandi Yusuf's term as governor.[41] Since that time the WH has been beset by a string of budgetary, logistical, and administrative difficulties. Indeed, even after the legislative assembly formally approved the annual budgets for WH officers' salaries, many field officers and administrative staff went unpaid for several months in 2007, 2008, and 2009.[42] Aside from personnel problems, the WH has also had to face the challenges of working with very limited equipment. In fact, many district-level offices only have one patrol vehicle to cover areas that can be quite large—and sometimes the operating budget for the office is insufficient to even keep that vehicle fueled.[43] In response to this situation, some public supporters of state

[40] Alyasa Abubakar, *Wilayatul Hisbah: Polisi Pamong Praja dengan Kewenangan Khusus di Aceh* (Banda Aceh: Dinas Syariʿat Islam Provinsi Aceh, 2009), 118–62.

[41] Irwandi was widely seen as having attempted to restrict the enforcement activities of the WH. Damien Kingsbury, "Political Reconstruction in Aceh," in Matthew Clarke, Ismet Fanany, and Sue Kenny (eds.), *Post-Disaster Reconstruction: Lessons from Aceh* (London: Earthscan, 2010), 74.

[42] "Legislatif Setujui Gaji WH," *Rakyat Aceh* (26 January 2007), 2; "Pemko Bersedia Menggaji WH," *Rakyat Aceh* (27 January 2008), 2; "WH Empat Bulan tak Bergaji," *Serambi* (25 April 2009), 13; "WH Aceh Barat Empat Bulan tak Terima Gaji," *Serambi* (8 April 2008), 17; "WH Aceh Barat Lima Bulan belum Bergaji," *Serambi* (13 May 2008), 21; "Nasib WH Bireuen, 4 Bulan Belum Terima Gaji," *Waspada* (27 April 2009), 23.

[43] Group discussion at the WH provincial office, 2 September 2008 at Banda Aceh.

Shari'a in Aceh have called for increases in funding for the WH and its activities.[44] However, allocations for the WH were subsequently cut even further, and in 2009, the annual budget for WH activities was not released until after the end of that calendar year.[45] In some cases, the lack of funds has even led to the temporary closing of local WH offices.[46] This gradual "starving of the beast" has seriously compromised the ability of the WH to fulfill its legal mandate, particularly at the provincial level—leading many within the WH and their supporters to complain that the provincial government is not serious in its support of Shari'a implementation.[47]

THE WORK OF THE WH

Despite the budgetary constraints, most WH offices across the province maintain some level of regular activity. For most civil servants (I. *pegawai negeri sipil*) and contracted personnel, the official workday begins at 8:00am with a morning assembly (I. *apel pagi*), after which many take a break for breakfast or coffee. After 9:00am, most are back to their desks processing paperwork or chatting with colleagues. When vehicles and fuel are available, the rest of the morning may be spent out on patrol until a break for lunch and mid-day prayers that generally lasts from about noon until 2:30pm. After that, the rest of the workday (until about 5:30pm) is usually spent at the office handling administrative tasks of filing reports, or planning for any upcoming special activities. On some days, there might be a second round of afternoon patrols. Only on very rare occasions are special patrols conducted after dusk.

When the WH takes to the streets on patrol, it is together with at least one accompanying officer from the civil police force in a joint operation (I. *pengawasan terpadu satpol*). The patrols can take a number of forms. The most common involve driving through areas where, for example, they suspect that young unmarried couples might be getting together. Whenever they set out to look for such situations, the WH never seem to have any trouble finding them. Even so, there are almost never any formal arrests made by the police officer that accompanies them. Most officers even make a point of not chasing any suspects who attempt to flee the scene of an incident, and for the WH such aggressive forms of apprehension are legally beyond their remit.[48] In fact, situations in which suspects run, or

44 "Dana WH Perlu Ditingkatkan," *Rakyat Aceh* (3 September 2007), 2.

45 "Dana WH Tahun 2009 belum Disalurkan," *Serambi* (7 January 2010), 3.

46 "Minim Dana, Kantor WH Ditutup," *Waspada* (23 June 2010), 7.

47 "Wilayatul Hisbah Terkendala Dana," *Waspada* (24 August 2010), 7.

48 Interview with a senior officer at the provincial-level WH office, 4 September 2008 at Banda Aceh.

Figure 8.1. A temporary roadside WH inspection point to enforce compliance with the law on "modest Muslim dress" at Meulaboh. (Photo by R. Michael Feener)

even just walk away, are much more the exception than the rule. When a young couple is approached by the WH, the general procedure is to ask for identification, record the names of both parties, and then to lecture them on the dangers that *khalwat* poses to both body and soul before sending them back home on their separate ways.

Other field activities of the WH include visits to investigate sites where members of the community have called in to report suspected violations of the Shariʿa, or setting up roadside spot-checks to monitor adherence to proper standards of modest Muslim dress (I. *busana Islam*) (see Figure 8.1). Over recent years, the WH have also mobilized for truancy patrols, sweeping through coffee shops and internet cafes for students skipping class and public servants from other departments who are away from their office during working hours.[49] These combined WH/police patrols will generally include both male and female officers, depending on the staffing of the local office. There is, however, one special patrol each week that is, by definition, gender segregated. *Qanun No. 11/2002* requires all adult male Muslims to attend mid-day congregational prays on Friday.[50]

[49] "Bolos Sekolah, Lima Pelajar SMA Ketangkap WH," *Metro Aceh* (20 November 2008), 1–2; "Warning! PNS Nongkrong Jam Kerja—Satpol PP Aktifkan Razia," *Rakyat Aceh* (14 October 2009), 5; "Satpol PP/WH Akan Razia Pegawai Bolos," *Serambi* (28 January 2010), 20; "Program 100 Hari Kasatpol PP dan WH—Siswa Bolos Ditangkap," *Rakyat Aceh* (28 January 2010), 1–2; "Bolos Sekolah, Lima Pelajar Ditertibkan," *Rakyat Aceh* (26 February 2009), 4.

[50] *Qanun Provinsi Nanggroe Aceh Darussalam Nomor 11/Tahun 2002 tentang Pelaksanaan Syariat Islam bidang Aqidah, Ibadah dan Syiʿar Islam*, IV.8.1.

Figure 8.2. Female WH officers on patrol in Banda Aceh. (Photo by R. Michael Feener)

When the male officers are thus occupied, the female officers often go out on patrol themselves (see Figure 8.2). As this is an aspect of the work of the WH that has yet to receive attention in the various media accounts of patrols that have appeared in the international press, an example of such a patrol warrants description in some detail here.[51]

On one Friday afternoon in September 2008/Ramadan 1429 H., 14 female officers boarded their patrol vehicles—two pickup trucks with double-sided wooden benches bolted to the beds—and left the Aceh Besar WH district office at Meuraxa. They stopped first to pick up two female police officers from the civil police station to accompany them on patrol—one for each of the trucks which thereafter went on their separate ways. As they drove around town, they broadcast appeals from the loudspeakers mounted on both trucks, announcing the legal obligation for all adult male Muslims to attend Friday prayers. These appeals repeated relevant articles of Aceh's *Qanun No. 11* on the need to attend prayers, and for shops and roadside stalls to be closed for the duration of services, interspersed with more general admonitions.

[51] A number of foreign journalists have followed WH patrols around Aceh over recent years, producing reports that tend to ignore the role of female officers. For example: "On Patrol with Aceh's Shariʿa Law Police," *BBC News online* (2 February 2010), <http://news.bbc.co.uk/2/hi/8481289.stm>, accessed 20 June 2012.

Operations like this are routinely conducted on Fridays, and especially during Ramadan. The route of this particular patrol wound its way around town to the old bus terminal at Setui, where a number of men were snoozing on benches in the waiting area. As the patrol rolled through the terminal, the officer with the megaphone shouted that all men there had to wake up and get themselves to the nearest mosque. Some did comply, but others barely budged and so when the patrol circled back around a few minutes later and found them still sleeping, the truck stopped and a half dozen female WH officers approached to stir them awake and to take down their names and issue official letters of warning. Some of the men seemed embarrassed, but others were apparently unfazed by all this.

From the bus terminal, the patrol continued on, and once the time for prayers had officially begun they put aside the megaphone and began rolling more quietly through various backstreets. When one officer noticed the front doors of one shop still slightly open, the patrol vehicle stopped. This was clearly a location already known to the WH women on patrol—a shopfront whose small signboard advertised itself as a hair salon. The truck stopped and the women walked over to the door that was slightly ajar, where they paused only for an instant before announcing themselves with the Muslim greeting of "Peace be upon you" (Ar. *al-salām ʿalaykum*) and entering into the dimly lit premises. Inside, they found the middle-aged proprietress along with three young women (two Acehnese from the small towns of Tamiang and Tangse, and the other, a Chinese Indonesian woman from Medan—the capital of the neighboring province of North Sumatra).[52] They were entertaining customers: two young Acehnese men dressed in T-shirts and baggy board shorts. The men were questioned by the WH as to what they were doing dressed like that at prayer time, and in such a location. As they did so, the WH officers pointed out that this "salon" did not have any styling chairs, but rather, was furnished only with a sofa and low coffee table near the entrance and a few rattan daybeds with vinyl-covered mattresses in the adjoining rooms.

Even for its professed purposes of legitimate business, however, there appeared to be problems at the salon. When the WH officers asked the proprietress to see her operating license, it was found to have expired, whereupon she was ordered to gather up her papers and to board the truck to be taken back to the WH office along with the other suspects found on site. The two young men protested vigorously as the WH officers confiscated the keys to their motorbikes parked outside and rode them

[52] On the perception of Medan in the moral geography of Acehnese Muslims, see Dan Birchok, "Sojourning on Mecca's Verandah: Place, Temporality, and Islam in an Indonesian Province," Ph.D. dissertation (Ann Arbor: University of Michigan, 2013), Chapter 2.

back to the station. After a lengthy argument, the two men clambered aboard the back of the truck, sitting back to back with the women facing out on the opposite side of the bench. The young women found on the premises boarded without protest. All, however, tried to shield their faces with their hands as they were driven back through town to the WH office.

Upon arrival at the WH office, the men and women apprehended at the salon were sent to separate rooms for questioning and processing—the proprietress to one, the young men to another, and the three younger women were then further divided, with the non-Muslim Indonesian Chinese woman taken for individual investigation, and the other two brought together to another office where they were questioned. The interrogation of the two young Acehnese women was led by a female WH officer who began addressing them with a soft voice, in an informal tone code-switching between the Acehnese and Indonesian languages. She asked if they were fasting, if they regularly said their prayers, and if they joined in Ramadan evening ritual recitation sessions (Ar. *tarāwīh*). They were also asked if they had ever attended a *dayah* or had any other kind of religious education, and then they were urged to attend the preaching sessions (I. *pengajian*) that often followed sunset prayers. Another officer in the room then chimed in, and with a considerably harder and less accommodating approach—issuing stern reprimands in rather officious-sounding, formal Indonesian. As familiar as this "good cop/bad cop" approach may seem to viewers of TV crime dramas, the point of it here was not to elicit a confession or to gather evidence on other suspects in the case. Rather, for the WH officers involved, the entire process was one of admonition and instruction (I. *pembinaan*). They later explained that the "interrogation" of such offenders was, in their eyes, a kind of "engaged *daʿwa*" (Ar. *daʿwa biʾl-hāl*) aimed at the repentance of the offenders, and securing a commitment that they would subsequently work to deepen their understanding and observance of Islam.

As is the case with most interrogations of this kind in contemporary Aceh, this incident did not end up as a case formally submitted to the Shariʿa Court. As discussed in Chapter 6, the number of cases of *khalwat* appearing before the courts has never been large, and has actually been decreasing since the first post-tsunami peak caseload in 2005–2006. In fact, senior officials at the WH and the DSI have publicly stated that not all such incidents should to be resolved through formal court hearings and the application of state sanctions.[53] However in those relatively rare cases when offenders are brought to trial and formally found guilty of offenses

[53] "Kadis Syariat Islam Aceh Utara: Tak Semua Pelaku Khalwat Harus Dicambuk," *Serambi* (3 April 2007), 9.

against the *qanun* on *khalwat*, alcohol, or gambling, the WH is obliged to take up another of its official roles in Aceh's state Shariʿa system: that of applying the punishment of public caning (I. *cambuk*).

CANING

Flogging (Ar. *jald*) is a well-established form of punishment within the Islamic tradition for both *ḥudūd* and *taʿzīr* offenses.[54] The use of a rattan cane for flogging reflects a convergence of Islamic and broader traditions of corporal punishment in both Muslim and non-Muslim Southeast Asian societies.[55] At present, caning is a legal punishment in neighboring Malaysia and Singapore, but it is not so in any region of Indonesia except the special autonomous region of Aceh. The reasons for the presence of caning penalties across the Straits of Malacca generally have more to do with the legacy of British colonialism than with any earlier Islamic or indigenous penal traditions, as the UK was one of the last countries to maintain flogging as a form of legal punishment, even after other European states had been abandoned it in favor of modern regimes of imprisonment.[56]

In Aceh, caning (I. *cambuk*) is the only form of *taʿzīr* corporal punishment applied in the contemporary Islamic legal system. Specific ranges for the number of strokes to be applied for various violations of the Shariʿa, and an initial set of technical guidelines for administering caning punishments were stipulated in regional regulations issued in 2002–2003.[57] These basic rules were further elaborated in an official gubernatorial instruction that was issued just before the first caning was applied in Bireuen in June 2005. There it is stipulated that although the ultimate authority for the administration of *cambuk* is the office of the public prosecutor (I. *Jaksa*), the actual caning is to be performed by an officer of the WH. The work

[54] For a brief synopsis of "classical doctrine" on flogging in the Islamic tradition, see Peters, *Crime and Punishment*, 35–6.

[55] In Malay, a number of different terms are used to refer to such punishments. In one of the earliest surviving Malay legal digests that incorporate both Islamic and autochthonous elements, it is generally referred to as *dera*. Liaw Yock Fang, *Undang-Undang Melaka* (The Hague: Martinus Nijhoff, 1976), 84. In contemporary Malaysia, the most common term is *sebat*, while in Aceh, *cambuk* is used to refer to caning in both official legislation and popular usage.

[56] Michel Foucault, *Discipline and Punish: The Birth of the Prison*, trans. Alan Sheridan (New York: Vintage Books, 1977), 10.

[57] *Qanun Provinsi Nanggroe Aceh Darussalam Nomor 11 Tahun 2002 tentang Pelaksanaan Syariat Islam bidang Aqidah, Ibadah dan Syiar Islam*, VIII.20.1; *Qanun Provinsi Nanggroe Aceh Darussalam Nomor 12 Tahun 2003 tentang Minuman Khamar dan Sejenisnya*, VII.26.1, VIII.31–35; *Qanun Provinsi Nanggroe Aceh Darussalam Nomor 13 Tahun 2003 tentang Maisir (Perjudian)*, VII.23.1; *Qanun Provinsi Nanggroe Aceh Darussalam Nomor 14 Tahun 2003 tentang Khalwat (Mesum)*, VII.22.1.

of the officer administering the strokes (I. *algojo*) is governed by strict regulations that range from the precise metrics of the rattan to be used and the limit of how far back the arm of the *algojo* can extend before each stroke, to the type of clothing that would modestly cover those being caned, and definitions of medical exemptions that would postpone the execution of caning sentences upon pregnant women and the infirm.[58] Various other precautionary measures are taken as well, with stipulations that the cane may only strike the back between the shoulders and the waist and that the proceedings would be stopped if the caning wounds the person, or if (s)he were to run off at any point.

These official stipulations to avoid excessive physical violence in the application of caning penalties are frequently published and discussed by officials in various institutions of the state Shariʿa system.[59] In part, such apologetics for the place of caning in Aceh's Islamic legal system address the high-profile criticisms launched by international human rights groups.[60] In a special pamphlet published for distribution at the first caning in 2005, Alyasa Abubakar attempted to demonstrate to his critics just how "humane" caning procedures were in Aceh by comparing the "restrained" forms practiced there with the more severe procedures administered in Pakistan, Malaysia, and Singapore—something that was documented in the pamphlet with a series of color illustrations depicting the application of caning penalties in those countries.[61] Most critics are, however, largely unconvinced by such arguments. This is not without reason, for there have clearly been cases in which the execution of caning sentences was carried out in ways that deviated from the government's strict procedural guidelines.[62] Furthermore, critiques of the official enforcement mechanisms of Aceh's Islamic legal system are often framed by broader considerations of the sometimes-violent forms of informal

[58] *Peraturan Gubernor Provinsi Nanggroe Aceh Darussalam Nomor 10/Tahun 2005 tentang Petunjuk Teknis Pelaksanaan Uqubat Cambuk.*

[59] They are often, for example, included in PowerPoint slideshows presented to various groups in Aceh by the Dinas Syariat Islam and the Mahkamah Syariah. H. Armia Ibrahim, *Proses Hukum Terhadap Pelanggaran Qanun-Qanun Syari'at Islam* (unpublished materials presented to an information and training session on Islamic law for female ulama and community leaders in Banda Aceh, July 2010).

[60] See, for example, Amnesty International, "Indonesian Government Must Repeal Caning Bylaws in Aceh," 22 May 2001, <http://www.amnesty.org/en/news-and-updates/indonesian-government-must-repeal-caning-bylaws-aceh-2011-05-20>, accessed 20 June 2012.

[61] Alyasa Abubakar, *Sekilas Syariat Islam di Aceh* (Banda Aceh: Dinas Syariat Islam, 2005).

[62] The most common deviation is disregard for the rule stipulating that the *algojo* may not extend his caning hand behind his back or above his shoulder, which results in considerably more painful strokes. Such was the case with a caning at Jantho (Aceh Besar) in January 2010—one of many that were filmed by local residents and uploaded to YouTube over recent years: <http://www.youtube.com/watch?v=glG7T1IO6SE,> accessed 28 June 2012.

moral policing carried out by groups of religious students, urban activists, and village communities in the name of Islam. The problem of vigilantism in relation to the application of Islamic law in Aceh will be discussed further later in the chapter. Before that, however, we turn to a discussion of what role caning is envisioned as playing within the official state Shariʿa system.

PHYSICAL PUNISHMENT AND PUBLIC PEDAGOGY

The officers and advocates of Aceh's Islamic legal system contend that the troubling incidents highlighted in international media and NGO reports are not problems inherent within the system itself, but rather, they are technical issues of practical application that need to be addressed in specific cases. For them, moreover, there is another dimension to caning that is not generally considered in the formulation of external critiques of corporal punishment—one in which the spectacle of the penalized body is rhetorically framed by reflections on the soul, and in which the physical punishment of an individual is applied as part of a broader program of public pedagogy.

The official "Clarification" (I. *Penjelasan*) to *Qanun No. 11/2002* provides some insight into the role that physical punishment is designed to play in Aceh's contemporary Islamic legal system:

> The threat of a caning penalty for those who commit violations of the Shariʿa is intended to both make the perpetrator more aware of the severity of his deed, and at the same time, to serve as a warning to society at large so that they do not do the same. The intent is that caning penalties will be effective in accomplishing both because the person punished in this way will feel shamed, but will not create undue hardship for his or her family. Caning penalties are also less expensive than incarceration, thus saving the government funds.[63]

One of the most striking things about this explanation of the official intent behind the application of caning for offenses against the Shariʿa is a total absence of any suggestion that it is aimed at inflicting physical pain as punishment. Rather, even before mention of the "rationalized" economic benefits of caning over imprisonment for both the state and to the families of convicted offenders, the emphasis is placed upon its supposed

[63] "Penjelasan atas Qanun Provinsi Nanggroe Aceh Darussalam Nomor 11/Tahun 2002 tentang Pelaksanaan Syariat Islam bidang Aqidah, Ibadah, dan Syiar Islam," in *Himpunan Undang-Undang, Keputusan Presiden, Peraturan Daerah/Qanun, Instruksi Gubernor berkaitan Pelaksanaan Syariʿat Islam, edisi ketujuh* (Banda Aceh: Dinas Syariat Islam, 2009), 313.

effectiveness in "raising awareness" (I. *kesadaran*) and creating a sense of shame (I. *malu*).

These pedagogic functions of caning are often explicitly stated and emphasized during the public execution of caning sentences in Aceh. For example, at a public caning held in front of the grand mosque of Jantho on a Friday in June 2011, the platform was decorated with a banner that read "With the Execution of Caning We Raise Public Awareness of the Implementation of Shariʿa in the District of Aceh Besar." Then, after the official program was opened with the recitation of verses from the Qurʾān, a preacher, brought in to give some brief "spiritual guidance" (I. *bimbingan rohani*), further emphasized the message. In his remarks, he reminded the audience that the point of caning is not to injure the body. Rather it should be viewed as:

> a lesson for us all . . . so that we might more carefully watch ourselves, and guard over our beloved sons and daughters . . . so that none of us become infected with the diseases (I. *penyakit*) of alcohol, drugs, or free mixing of the sexes, all of which could lead to fornication (Ar. *zinā*), something that has clearly been condemned by God.[64]

In this sense, caning as a penalty for infractions against Islamic law in contemporary Aceh represents a thoroughly modern approach to penal sanction—one in which the "temporal direction" of enforcement has shifted from attempts to punish crimes that have already been committed to future reform of both individuals and society at large.[65] In public pronouncements on caning, state Shariʿa officials regularly emphasize that the point of their work is not the application of painful punishments, but rather the betterment of society. In line with this view on the purpose of physical punishment in the Islamic legal system, officials have responded to public criticism over cases where sentences were passed but never executed by stating that, "the task of the DSI is not to cane people, but to improve society."[66]

Similar views are echoed at various levels of the system, and amplified by the voices of high-profile outsiders brought into Aceh to comment on developments there. In October 2009, the MPU and the IAIN hosted the Grand Mufti of Syria, Ahmad Badrouddin Hassan, in Banda Aceh. The day after his public lecture on campus, the province's leading daily

[64] I have transcribed these particular quotations from an anonymous video of this event that circulated on social media in and beyond Aceh shortly after the caning took place. Similar sentiments can also be seen and heard in the recordings of other canings that have been administered in Aceh since 2005.

[65] Foucault, *Discipline and Punish*, 126.

[66] "Banyak Eksekusi Cambuk belum Dilaksanakan: Kadis Syariat Islam Dituding Suap," *Serambi* (7 August 2009), 9.

newspaper ran a front-page report of his talks in Banda Aceh, highlighting his comments that: "the implementation of Shari'a in Aceh should not primarily emphasize punishment. What is more important is to educate people."[67] Physical punishments for violations of the Shari'a in Aceh are thus often officially portrayed as a tool of last resort within the broader agenda of implementing Islamic law as a project for "enjoining good and forbidding wrong" (Ar. *al-amr bi'l-ma'rūf wa'l-nahy 'an al-munkar*).[68] The rhetorical emphasis here is on casting caning not as a technology of retribution, but as a tool of reform.[69]

Within the system, caning is thus viewed as an effective element in a repertoire of means deployed in the project of engineering social change through the state application of Islamic law. The Commandant of the WH provincial office in Banda Aceh has explained why he sees caning as a particularly effective means for accomplishing this:

> Caning in Aceh is actually a means of education, not only a sentence or punishment. According to the Shari'a, the purpose of caning is not to injure someone, but rather is a lesson for the offender. For example, if one is caned, all of his family and neighbors will know that this has happened, and he will be stigmatized (I. *menyendang lebel*) as a person who had been caned. This will weigh heavily upon him, and his example will further be instructive to the community at large. That is the goal.[70]

Ideas of stigma and public shaming loom large in the official discourse on caning in Aceh's state Shari'a system. As expressed by Rusjdi Ali Muhammad during his tenure as head of the State Shari'a Agency, "the important thing [about caning] is the effect of shaming, both for the individual perpetrator in the face of the community, and as a deterrent example for those who witness it."[71] The head of Aceh's Ulama Council, Muslim Ibrahim, has also explicitly elaborated what he sees as the connection between shame (I. *rasa malu*) and deterrent effect (I. *efek jera*).[72] Not all agree, however, that this is in fact the case and some of the very people who have experienced firsthand being caned for violations of Aceh's *qanun* have made public statements directly challenging official

[67] "Grand Mufti Suriah: Syariat Islam tidak Mengedepankan Hukuman," *Serambi* (15 October 2009), 1.

[68] Interview with WH official, 26 January 2011 at Banda Aceh.

[69] However, there are others in Aceh who do express more interest in having corporal punishments inflict more pain than is the case at present. For example, one faculty member at STAIN Lhokseumawe argued in a group discussion there that current caning punishments are too light, asking his interlocutors why not set the number at 40 strokes "as in the time of the Prophet."Group discussion at STAIN Lhokseumawe, 22 May 2008.

[70] Interview with the Commandant of the WH, 4 September 2008 at Banda Aceh.

[71] Interview with Rusjdi Ali Muhammad, 26 January 2011 at Banda Aceh.

[72] Interview with Muslim Ibrahim, 27 May 2008 at Banda Aceh.

statements on the purported deterrent effect of corporal punishment and public shaming.[73]

Even these voices, however, have been unable to shake the faith in the idea of caning's effectiveness held by many of the architects and engineers of Aceh's Islamic legal system. Rather than re-thinking their basic premise, officials of Aceh's state Shariʿa bureaucracies have generally occupied themselves by tinkering with the technical details of existing mechanisms in efforts to enhance their effectiveness as a tool of social control. Many state officers involved with the implementation of Islamic law carefully consider the public impact of the application of caning penalties in ways that could maximize its deterrent effect. This has included discussions of how to achieve the maximum impact of the events in communicating the intended moral message. A local report on the subject published by the DSI reflects these concerns, emphasizing that for some sectors of society, the effect of witnessing or just hearing of a caning is relatively short-lived, and that after some time has passed, people begin backsliding to their old ways of sin. As one source quoted in that report expressed it:

> About a month or so after the execution of a caning sentence in Bireuen, the city appeared as if one that had been purged of sin. After that, however, the sin once again began quietly stretching out across the community.[74]

Since then, semi-official conversations about calibrating the system for the optimal deterrent effect of caning have continued, as discussed previously in Chapter 6.

These are, however, risky calculations that might not only fail to improve the situation, but may in fact even be counterproductive insofar as such considerations inform the selective application of the *qanun* by the formal state apparatus. This is something cited as a major point of protest by those critical of the state implementation of Islamic law in contemporary Aceh, who argue that WH operations and caning penalties are arbitrarily applied. As also discussed earlier, cases related to the Shariʿa criminal offenses of gambling, alcohol consumption, and *khalwat* have never taken up more than a very small portion of the caseload of the Aceh's Islamic courts. In fact, officials involved with other state Shariʿa institutions such as the WH and the DSI have stated that there is no reason why every such incident should be

[73] Quotes from some of these critics who have experienced caning themselves have been brought together in Sulaiman Tripa, *Perang Melawan Khalwat di Aceh: Pelaksanaan Qanun Khalwat dan Profil Kasus Khalwat dalam Harian Serambi Indonesia, 15 January 2007–15 January 2008* (Banda Aceh: Pustaka Novum, 2008).

[74] Bustami Abubakar, "Respon Masyarakat Bireun terhadap Pelaksanaan," in Syahrizal (ed.), *Dimensi Pemikiran Hukum dalam Implementasi Syariat Islam di Aceh* (Banda Aceh: Dinas Syariat Islam Provinsi Nanggroe Aceh Darussalam, 2007), 120.

formally processed through the court.[75] Nevertheless the relatively small number of cases related to gambling, alcohol, and *khalwat* that have resulted in caning punishments have had a notable impact on public perceptions of and discourse about the role of Shariʿa in society that has outweighed their relative position in the caseload of Aceh's state Islamic legal system. That being said, the kind of enthusiasm and even curiosity that public canings had created amongst the broader population has changed considerably since the first caning sentence was executed in Bireuen in 2005.[76] At that time, the event attracted a large crowd and significant attention by both local and international media. Such interest soon peaked, however, and three years later when half a dozen gamblers were caned in Sigli, the event attracted little public attention, much to the dismay of local DSI officials.[77]

In coffee shops and other informal settings all across Aceh, public conversations about caning have increasingly taken tones of disinterest and sometimes of outright derision over recent years. It is commonly heard, for example, that most people have become "bored" (I. *sudah bosan*) by the events—a sentiment that is compounded by the oft-repeated complaint that it is almost always the "little people" (I. *rakyat kecil*) and not government officials or other "elites" who are caned for their offenses. Indeed, even those who agree with caning in principle object to the perceived unfair discrimination in its application. As one village head from Bireuen expressed it:

> I really agree with the idea of caning, as long as it not only applied to the "little people" in society... Right now, those are the ones who suffer this penalty, and not others, including public officials who are clearly guilty of corruption.[78]

In other circles, however, one hears complaints in the opposite direction. Among some small but vocal circles of Acehnese Islamists, the problem is not that canings have become too routine but rather that they are not carried out frequently enough. As, for example, the local head of an Islamist youth association (Himpunan Mahasiswa Islam/HMI) in Bireuen complained in 2009, "The decrease in executions of caning penalties has had a negative effect, and led to increasing public violations of the Shariʿa, and of *khalwat* in particular."[79] Dissatisfaction in some circles arising from the perception

[75] "Tak Semua Pelaku Khalwat Harus Dicambuk," *Serambi* (3 April 2007), 5; "Warga Bireuen Pro Aktif Mengawal Syariat Islam," *Harian Aceh* (18 August 2009), 3.

[76] The BBC report of the event, for example, described the event as "more of a festival than a punishment exercise," where "crowds of people, including children, watched the proceedings." "Aceh Gamblers Caned in Public," *BBC News online* (24 June 2005), <http://news.bbc.co.uk/2/hi/asia-pacific/4618595.stm>, accessed 25 June 2012.

[77] "Enam Pelaku Maisir Dicambuk," *Rakyat Aceh* (19 April 2008), 1, 11.

[78] Bustami Abubakar, "Respon Masyarakat Bireun terhadap Pelaksanaan," 111.

[79] "Hukum Cambuk Mulai Pudar," *Waspada* (27 April 2009), 23.

that caning penalties are not applied regularly enough has, moreover, not only been channeled as criticism to the official state apparatus of the Islamic legal system, but has also contributed to discourses encouraging acts of vigilante enforcement of Shariʿa morality in Aceh.[80]

VIGILANTISM

Outbreaks of communal violence are, unfortunately, not uncommon in modern Indonesian history, and such incidents are popularly associated with religious fervor.[81] In the post-Suharto period, there has also been a marked rise in vigilantism in both rural and urban areas across the country.[82] In Aceh, incidents of vigilantism carried out in the name of the Shariʿa became increasingly common after the proclamation of the new special autonomy measure that was hailed locally as allowing for the application of Islamic law.[83] These violent incidents came to be referred to as "People's Tribunals" (I. *pengadilan rakyat*), and took various forms across the province at the turn of the twentieth century. *Pengadilan rakyat* were reported over alleged incidents of sexual immorality, alcohol and marijuana consumption, violations of the Ramadan fast, and petty theft. The punishments meted out for these offenses took a wide range of forms, including violent apprehension and beating by mobs and various forms of public humiliation such as shaving heads, "bathing" in filthy gutter water, and being dragged through the village in "parades of shame." Sometimes, however, vigilante action also included canings—the application of which far transgressed the limits of what was eventually outlined in the procedural regulations of the state. For example, one couple accused of *khalwat* were caned 100 times each by a village mob near Blang Pidie (South Aceh).[84]

[80] Mahdi Syihab has pointed to the ways in which disappointment with the measures taken by state institutions to apply Islamic law have been a significant factor in the motivations of *dayah* teachers and students (I. *santri*) involved in vigilante enforcement of Shariʿa morality in North Aceh. Mahdi Syihab, "Penegakan Syariat: Etnografi Aksi Razia Santri Dayah di Aceh Utara," in Arskal Salim and Adnin Sila (eds.), *Serambi Mekkah yang Berubah* (Banda Aceh: Aceh Research Training Institute, 2010), 57–91.

[81] For an overview of such developments at the national level, see John T. Sidel, *Riots, Pogroms, Jihad: Religious Violence in Indonesia* (Singapore: NUS Press, 2007). The situation on the ground in Aceh, however, has not followed the same broader patterns of paramilitary mobilization that Sidel describes as increasingly prevalent in other parts of the country over the past decade.

[82] Joshua Barker, "Vigilantes and the State," *Social Analysis* 50.1 (2006) 203.

[83] Edward Aspinall, *Islam and Nation: Separatist Rebellion in Aceh, Indonesia* (Stanford, CA: Stanford University Press, 2009), 210.

[84] Rusjdi Ali Muhammad, *Revitalisasi Syariat Islam di Aceh: Problem, Solusi, dan implementasi menuju Pelaksanaan Hukum Islam din Nanggroe Aceh Darussalam* (Banda Aceh: Ar-Raniry Press, 2003), 96.

Most often, these "People's Tribunals" were spontaneous affairs triggered by a sense of moral outrage in particular local contexts. This in itself was not a new situation in modern Aceh. Indeed, the province has been the site of a series of moral panics since at least the early period of Indonesian independence. During the 1950s, PUSA ulama raised the alarm over what they perceived as a troubling trend of local Muslims drinking "Jakarta Lemonade" (beer) and the free mixing of the sexes.[85] Half a century later, the burgeoning local press in Aceh fueled a further rise in moralistic public fervor with vivid daily reports of offenses against Shariʿa norms and editorial laments of the ever-worsening situation.[86] By that time, such concerns were increasingly elaborated in a discourse of "moral crisis" (I. *krisis moral*)—and of a spreading plague (I. *penyakit*) of immorality. The severity of the situation was also reflected in official publications issued by the State Shariʿa Agency:

> All of this constitutes a moral crisis that points to a weakness of faith. It is a disease that demands a cure so that Acehnese society can awake from this darkness. The best solution for this is for society to return to the belief and moral teachings of Islam.[87]

Calls to address the perceived moral crisis included appeals for direct and comprehensive engagement of the problem by the state and various sectors of society to "raise awareness" (I. *bangun kesadaran*) and to "channel all resources and energies to prohibit actions forbidden by God."[88] For some it appeared that the formal institutions of state Shariʿa in Aceh were for various reasons unable to effectively fulfill their legal mandate. In response, new "moral entrepreneurs" took it upon themselves to carry forth the crusade to enforce adherence to Islamic law.[89]

One high-profile example of this was Fakhruddin bin Hashmi, the leader of a movement known as the "Anti-Sin League" (Badan Anti Maksiat/ BAM), which he described himself as "helping the state" in the effort to implement the Shariʿa in Aceh. BAM was founded in the run-up to Ramadan

[85] Letter from Tgk. Ismail Yakub to S.M. Amin, quoted in Eric E. Morris, "Islam and Politics in Aceh: A Study of Center-Periphery Relations in Indonesia," Ph.D. dissertation (Ithaca: Cornell University, 1983), 192–3.

[86] For example: "Pelanggaran Syariat Islam Cenderung Meningkat," *Rakyat Aceh* (10 February 2009), 3; "Maksiat Marak di Lokasi Waduk," *Waspada Online* (15 July 2010), <http://www.waspada.co.id/index.php?option=com_content&view=article&id=130054:maksiat-marak-di-lokasi-waduk&catid=13:aceh&Itemid=26>, accessed 21 August 2012.

[87] Chairuddin Shobari, "Pelaksanaan Syariat Islam di Aceh Sebagai Instrumen Menghadapi Milenium ke III," in Syamsul Rijal (ed.), *Syariat Islam dan Paradigma Kemanusiaan* (Banda Aceh: Dinas Syariat Islam, 2008), 13.

[88] Zarkasyi, "Penerapan Syariat Islam di Aceh," in Siti Zalikha H. Ibrahim (ed.), *Menuju Syariat Islam Kaffah* (Banda Aceh: Lapena Institute for Culture and Society, 2008), 121.

[89] I borrow the term "moral entrepreneur" from Erich Good and Nachman Ben-Yehuda, *Moral Panics: The Social Construction of Deviance* (Oxford: Blackwell Publishing, 1994), 20.

in August 2006 to address the concerns voiced by activists associated with mosque-based youth groups in Banda Aceh. In particular, the movement was animated by reactions to a perceived erosion of morality in post-tsunami Aceh—a result of what Fakhruddin regarded as Aceh becoming "too open" to outsiders during the reconstruction period. At its founding, BAM was given a one-time "gift" of startup funds from the local government—on the sole condition that BAM would not engage in any public protests. For its part, BAM's leadership never felt the need to do so, since they enjoyed such warm relationships and direct access to the state, including the MPU, the DSI, the WH, the police, and the military. Fakhruddin was himself largely raised on and around Indonesian military bases in Aceh. These longstanding connections to the state security apparatus made a significant imprint on the organization and operations of BAM, which came to be structured in the form of units that included "Intelligence" and "Operational Command."

By 2008, BAM boasted over 300 members. Its headquarters was a moving camp that shifted from one mosque to another every six months or so.[90] BAM's operations in and around Banda Aceh included raids on locations selling alcohol, coffee shops where people play cards or dominos (popularly associated with gambling), and salons suspected as places of prostitution. BAM also conducted neighborhood sweeps in search of women who were not dressed according to the organization's standard of appropriately modest Muslim dress. Those caught in such operations were subjected to on-the-spot admonitions about the requirements of the Shariʿa and the importance to sexual morality for social order. BAM also engaged in more general forms of Islamic public education, including "lightning courses" (I. *pesantren kilat*) on Islamic belief and practice for high school students. Its activities in all of these areas, like the work of the DSI and the WH, which it in so many ways mirrored, were also often lumped under the rubric of "*sosialisasi.*"[91]

BAM's activities were, moreover, not just parallel to, but at times, actually integrated with those of the WH.[92] In fact, in earlier years, the WH even allowed BAM to use official vehicles for "joint operations" (I. *gerakan terpadu*), including patrols and raids on which they were accompanied by representatives of the WH, the DSI, and the police.[93] Coordinated

[90] At the time of the interview with Fakhruddin bin Hashmi, during which much of this information on BAM was collected (3 September 2008), the BAM headquarters was at the Lambaro Skep mosque in Banda Aceh.

[91] Interview with Fakhruddin bin Hashmi, 3 September 2008 at Banda Aceh.

[92] In this, these developments fit squarely within what Joshua Barker has discussed in terms of a well-established trend in Indonesian history for the state to actively cultivate relationships with vigilante groups where they perceived overlapping interests. Barker, "Vigilantes," 204.

[93] Interview with provincial-level WH staff, 5 January 2009 at Banda Aceh.

activity between BAM and the WH was sanctioned at the highest levels, and at times, WH collaborations could also extend to other organizations that played a role in the implementation of Shariʿa, including both state organizations such as the Ulama Council (MPU), the Mahkamah Syariah, and the Indonesian military (TNI), as well as non-state groups of students and teachers from *dayah*, and Islamic activists based on university campuses.[94] The WH has also conducted joint operations with other groups of *dayah* students (I. *santri*) outside of Banda Aceh, particularly in North Aceh.[95]

The WH are not, however, involved in all matters of community policing for alleged violations of Shariʿa. In fact, the WH are often called in only after vigilantes have already taken matters into their own hands. When they arrive at the scene on such cases, the role of the WH has sometimes been to assert protective custody over the suspects to shield them from further violent vigilante reprisals.[96] Unrestrained vigilantism has come to be seen as a serious problem by many senior figures involved with the state implementation of Islamic law in Aceh. As head of the State Shariʿa Agency that formerly oversaw the operations of the WH, Alyasa Abubakar emphasized that physical punishments should only be applied by formal state institutions and publicly criticized what he saw as the "excesses" of the "People's Tribunals" that sprung up to enforce Shariʿa norms of public morality before the official establishment of the WH.[97] Higher officials in the provincial government have also repeated such sentiments, including Lieutenant Governor Muhammad Nazar, who unequivocally announced in the local media that "local communities are not authorized to undertake patrols or raids to enforce Shariʿa morality, because such matters are to be left to the police and the WH."[98] Despite such strong public statements by representatives of the provincial government, the interface between state and local community policing is more ambiguous at the village level, where reactions to perceived offenses to Shariʿa morality can take various and at times violent forms.

94 Interview with WH Commandant, 5 January 2009 at Banda Aceh.

95 "Lagi, Santri Gelar Razia," *Serambi* (22 October 2007), 10.

96 "Saling Raba Tubuh di Tempat Gelap—Pasangan Mesum Kena Gimbal," *Metro Aceh* (1 December 2009), 2; "Digerebek Lalu Diarak Massa—Janda dan Penarik Ojek Bertindih di Semak Belukar," *Metro Aceh* (13 February 2010), 1–2.

97 Alyasa, *Sekilas Syariat*, 21.

98 "Wagub Muhammad Nazar: Masyarakat tak Berwenang Lakukan Razia Syariat," *Serambi* (23 November 2007), 1.

LOCAL CUSTOM AND COMMUNITY POLICING

Many of the punishments meted out by communities upon those perceived to have violated aspects of Islamic law in Aceh are considered to reflect "local custom" (I. *adat*). As noted earlier, however, the harshness of such measures appears to fly in the face of the common view of *adat* as a more accommodating alternative to Islamic law. Nevertheless, images of *adat* as a more flexible and humane alternative to Islamic law continue to be expressed not only by international academics and local NGO activists, but by some high-ranking officials of Aceh's state Shariʿa system as well. As noted by one ranking officer of the Banda Aceh WH:

> Sometimes communities prefer to deal with incidents on their own according to local custom (*adat*). In fact the reason that so few incidents are processed as formal court cases is that they are dealt with directly by local communities—which may include sanctions like in-kind fines of a goat to be sacrificed for a communal meal, or other sanctions defined by the leadership of the village.[99]

There is in practice, however, a wide range of possible *adat* solutions to particular incidences of offenses such as *khalwat*, many of which are considerably more fraught than that of hosting a communal meal of reconciliation.[100]

In addition to the forms of communal violence and public shaming mentioned earlier in relation to the "People's Tribunals," some cases of *khalwat* are resolved by forcing the couple to marry (if the woman is currently single). In some cases, opting for such "*adat* solutions" reflects local concerns for handling their own internal affairs, as well as a certain level of skepticism about the ability of the state apparatus to deal successfully with such problems.[101] Residents of one community who chose this option to deal with a case of *khalwat* in October 2007 explained that they refused to turn the couple over to the WH because they were not confident that the formal legal process could sufficiently chasten the offenders.[102] Reasoned considerations of restoring social order and affirming local autonomy have not, however, always been the primary factor in determining responses to incidents of *khalwat* at the village-level.

[99] Interview with WH Commandant, 26 September 2008 at Banda Aceh.

[100] In some communities, village leaders have even stipulated fines in terms of particular monetary amounts or heads of livestock.

[101] Otto & Otto, "Aceh's Wilayatul Hisbah."

[102] "Warga Nikahkan Pasangan Khalwat," *Waspada* (31 October 2007), 7.

Noting the high degree of indeterminacy in such cases, officials at the Aceh's state Adat Council (Majlis Adat Aceh/MAA) have attempted to distance what they see as "proper *adat*" from village vigilantism:

> [V]iolent acts carried out by a some sectors of the community for those in violation of the *qanun*, like shaving heads, "bathing" offenders in filthy water, carrying them around the village in a procession of shame, none of this is *adat*. It's just an emotional expression of the young villagers who are offended by those breaking the law.[103]

Despite the ongoing problems with official attempts at managing the ways in which local communities resort to "*adat* solutions," Aceh's state Shariʿa institutions have increasingly relied on village-level mechanisms to help them implement and enforce Islamic law. In many cases, this is a reflection of the sheer inability of local WH offices to fulfill their mandate given the limited resources at their command.[104] This reality has led a number of state Shariʿa officials to develop various models to enlist and regulate the support of village leaders in their work.

There are provisions allowing for local community and *adat* institutions to play a role in the implementation of Shariʿa found in various pieces of legislation passed during the early years of Aceh's "special autonomy."[105] These measures were positively endorsed by Alyasa Abubakar as head of the DSI to serve as the legal foundations for engaging with village-level and community leaders as force multipliers for the work of the WH.[106] As he expressed it in a Friday sermon delivered in Banda Aceh's iconic Baiturrahman Mosque:

> What is needed is for communities—under the village leadership, local *adat* council, and security apparatus—to admonish, control, and if necessary, to close down sites of "entertainment" (I. *hiburan*), and shops selling or renting books that could morally corrupt the youth by exposing them to things forbidden by Islam.[107]

The importance of mobilizing village leadership in the project of Shariʿa implementation was also a central feature of the DSI's handbook for

[103] Interview with a Majlis Adat Aceh official, 13 April 2011 at Banda Aceh.

[104] For example, in 2007, there were 25 cases of *khalwat* reported in the Pereulak, all of which were handed over by the WH to be settled by *adat*. "Penegakan Syariat Islam Diperketat di Aceh Jaya," *Serambi* (27 August 2007), 4.

[105] *Peraturan Daerah Propinsi Daerah Istimewa Aceh Nomor 7/Tahun 2000 tentang Penyelenggaraan Kehidupan Adat*, Pasal 3; *Qanun Nomor 5/Tahun 2003 tentang Pemerintahan Gampong dalam Provinsi Nanggroe Aceh Darussalam*, Menimbang b.

[106] Alyasa Abubakar and Marah Halim, *Hukum Pidana Islam di Provinsi Nanggroe Aceh Darussalam* (Banda Aceh: Dinas Syariat Islam, 2006), 124–34; Alyasa Abubakar, *Wilayatul Hisbah: Polisi Pamong Praja dengan Kewenangan Khusus di Aceh* (Banda Aceh: Dinas Syariat Islam, 2009), 27–35.

[107] Alyasa Abubakar, "Pembinaan Generasi Muda dalam Islam," in Azman Ismail (ed.), *Suara Khatib Baiturrahman* (Banda Aceh: Pengurus Masjid Raya Baiturrahman, 2006), 238.

imeum meunasah that was discussed in the previous chapter. There, stress is laid on the importance of local authorities in balancing public responses with the severity of the offense. In addition to this,it emphasizes the belief that village communities can be particularly effective in implementing Shariʿa. This, the handbook explains, is because sanctions issued by *adat* elders carry cultural authority and have a great psychological impact and deterrent effect since they cause perpetrators to feel a sense of shame in their local communities.[108]

Even more than with the *imeum meunasah*, the DSI and the WH have extensively fostered the creation of a new village-level institution to further aid them in the implementation of Shariʿa in local communities: the *muhtasib desa*. These are village residents who either volunteer or are appointed by village heads (Ac. *geucik*) as authorities responsible for handling offenses against the *qanun*. They sometimes receive training and honoraria from the local DSI offices, although these arrangements are far from being standardized across the province. The programs for certifying and supporting *muhtasib desa* have likewise not been uniformly developed in all areas of Aceh. North Aceh, for example, has had *muhtasib desa* established in villages since 2006. In other locations they have been introduced considerably later, if at all. The establishment and maintenance of *muhtasib desa* programs moreover depends largely on the support of the district-level government, as discussed in the previous chapter in relation to the high-profile campaign for the promotion of state Shariʿa by the District Head (I. *Bupati)* of West Aceh in 2009–2010.

WHITHER THE WH?

Aggressive assertions of coercive enforcement of Islamic law (such as that of the West Aceh *Bupati's* crusade against tight trousers) have met with considerable controversy in Aceh, and the WH in particular has become a lightning rod for public polemic. In the post-Suharto period, a combination of new legal mechanisms of institutional accountability, a press recently freed from censorship controls, and the development of a vibrant civil society has created new dynamics for the criticism of state institutions in the public sphere.[109] These have in turn significantly energized debates on the implementation of Islamic law in relation to human rights. Reports of

[108] Saleh Suhaidy, *Buku Pegangan Teungku Imeum Meunasah* (Aceh: Dinas Syariat Islam Provinsi Nanggroe Aceh Darussalam, 2007), 201.

[109] Michael Buehler, "Decentralisation and Local Democracy in Indonesia: The Marginalisation of the Public Sphere," in Edward Aspinall and Marcus Mietzner (eds.), *Problems of Democratisation in Indonesia: Elections, Institutions and Society* (Singapore: Institute of Southeast Asian Studies, 2010), 283.

human rights violations have been a regular feature of international media and NGO reportage on Aceh for decades. During the New Order period, the accusations of abuses tended to be directed toward the Indonesian military for its treatment of civilians during its campaigns against GAM. Since the turn of the twenty-first century, however, the focus of attention has been increasingly on issues related to the implementation of Islamic law.[110]

Such reports from outside observers play important roles in local debates on state Shariʿa in Aceh. In addition to providing evidentiary support for local critics of the Islamic legal system, they also stimulate defensive responses from its supporters. International conceptions of human rights have thus also come to be part of the official discourses of Islamic law in Aceh. In many cases, their response has not been to deny the universal claims of normative human rights discourse, but rather to implicitly accept them while arguing that, as it is applied in Aceh, Islamic law does not in fact violate such standards.[111] Such arguments, however, often reflect misreadings of foundational conceptions of "ends" in relation to "means" in contemporary human rights discourse—as, for example, in their appeals to justifications of caning as being aimed at promoting public benefit rather than being focused on physical punishment. Other defenders of Aceh's caning penalties construct arguments to justify current practice in Aceh through comparisons to other nations in which much more severe physical punishments are enacted by the state:

> Caning penalties in Aceh are not intended to torture (I. *menyiksa*), but only to create a sense of shame and a deterrent effect. This should not be seen as a violation of human rights (I. *Hak-hak Asasi Manusia*/HAM), in fact Islamic law specifically guarantees human rights. The United States and China, however, impose the death penalty![112]

[110] See, for example: *Human Rights Watch, Policing Morality: Abuses in the Application of Shariʿa in Aceh, Indonesia* (New York: HRW, 2010). Available online at: <http://www.hrw.org/sites/default/files/reports/indonesia1210WebVersionToPost.pdf>, accessed 22 May 2012; Jane Perlez, "In Aceh, Islamic Law is Taking Hold," *International Herald Tribune* (2 August 2006), 1, 4; "A Stone to Throw," *The Jakarta Post* (16 September 2009), 6; Norimitsu Onishi, "Extremism Spreads across Indonesian Penal Code," *New York Times* (27 October 2009): <http://www.nytimes.com/2009/10/28/world/asia/28stoning.html>, accessed 25 June 2012; Lynn Lee, "Aceh's Human Rights Record under Scrutiny," *The Straits Times* (2 December 2010), A16; Amnesty International, *The Indonesian Government Must Repeal Caning By-laws in Aceh*, 22 May 2001, <http://www.amnesty.org/en/news-and-updates/indonesian-government-must-repeal-caning-bylaws-aceh-2011-05-20>, accessed 20 June 2012.

[111] "Hukum Cambuk tidak Melanggar HAM," *Rakyat Aceh* (7 September 2007), 4; "Amnesty Internasional Minta Indonesia: Stop Hukum Cambuk di Aceh," *Waspada* (23 May 2011), 1; "Ulama Aceh Tanggapi Amnesty Internasional," *Waspada* (23 May 2011), 1.

[112] "Amnesty International Diminta Pahami Aceh," *Serambi* (24 May 2011): 1.

Despite such proclamations from high officials, it is clear that in some cases, WH field operations have in fact transgressed both basic international norms of human rights and the specific legal mandates of Aceh's state Shariʿa system.[113] The most egregious case involved a woman who was gang-raped by three WH officers after being taken into custody in Langsa in January 2010. This horrific incident was a particularly powerful lightning rod in attracting condemnation from both critics who would like to see the WH disbanded, and those who demanded more rigorous internal reform of the institution.[114] Well before this case, and ever since, the WH has been the most frequently criticized and hotly debated institution of Aceh's Islamic legal system. For some, this particular case of sexual violence perpetrated by self-appointed guardians of public morality was the low point in long catalogue of hypocrisy evident in their work.

Such complaints are frequently aired in the popular "SMS from the People" columns that have replaced more traditional "Letters to the Editor" sections of many local newspapers.[115] As one of these published text messages puts it:

> Lots of local officials violate the Shariʿa. We often see them going to sleep at motels during working hours and flirting with other men's wives. The WH do the same—putting on airs of religious learning while they are actually even more of a problem than civil servants.[116]

Many other voices in the din of this popular print forum call attention to what they see as the "unprofessional" and "arrogant" demeanor of WH officers in the field. Negative reaction to the way that some WH officers have conducted themselves has even led to incidents in which officers have encountered direct resistance, including both verbal and physical abuse in the course of conducting operations in certain areas.[117] The WH are also often resented by owners of cafés and other small businesses who complain of unwanted interference in their operations.[118]

In the open and highly polemical public forum of these popular newspaper pages, however, one finds expressions not only of opprobrium, but also voices of support for the WH and its role in the

113 "Polisi Syariah Digugat: Bertindak Melebihi Polisi," *Rakyat Aceh* (30 August 2008), 2.

114 "Oknum WH Mesum Harus Dihukum," *Rakyat Aceh* (21 April 2007), 11.

115 For a more extended discussion of this particular genre of popular print discourse in contemporary Indonesia and its use in public debates on Shariʿa implementation, see Feener, "Hand, Heart and Handphone," 21–6.

116 "Aspirasi," *Metro Aceh* (14 October 2009), 6.

117 For example: "Patroli WH di Pantai Meureudu Diprotes," *Serambi* (12 May 2010), 19; "Pemilik Kafe Bentrok dengan Aparat," *Waspada Online* (30 November 2010), <http://www.waspada.co.id/index.php?option=com_content&view=article&id=159605:pemilik-kafe-bentrok-dengan-aparat&catid=13&Itemid=26>, accessed 21 August 2012;

118 "Pengelola Kafé Keluhkan Sikap WH," *Harian Aceh* (26 October 2010), 14.

public enforcement of Islamic law. One common complaint against the WH has been that they are simply not effective in fulfilling their purported mandate.[119] Most of those advancing arguments along this line are not, however, opposed to the institution of the WH or of state Shariʿa per se. In fact, such critiques often come with appeals for the WH to be more active in policing public morality, sometimes going so far as to suggest particular locales and events that call out for increased patrolling. Others make more general claims about what they see as the importance of the work of the WH in the implementation of Islamic law:

> I salute the officers of the WH in Bireuen who strive to implement the Shariʿa by apprehending hundreds of Acehnese women not dressed in an appropriately Islamic way. We hope that this in not just a fleeting exercise, but that it will continue. The violators of the Shariʿa by-laws are not just the women in tight clothing, but also lots of others including men who do not attend Friday prayers—not to mention the many brothels operating under the cover of "salons," and the continuing close association between unmarried couples! We want all of these problems acted upon in the hope of making Aceh truly Islamic.[120]

While certainly not universally popular, the WH is nonetheless seen by at least some segments of the population as a potentially positive force in broader attempts to elevate existing standards of public morality and personal piety. Such aspirations (as referred to in the quote just cited in terms of making Aceh "truly Islamic") call our attention back once again to the ways in which contemporary Aceh's system of state Shariʿa is imagined by its architects, agents, and public supporters as a project of social engineering.

[119] "Tegakkan Syariat Islam, WH Langsa Harus Tegas," *Rakyat Aceh* (29 March 2007), 7; "WH dan Satpol PP Jalan di Tempat," *Aceh Independen* (1 December 2008), 6; "WH Diminta Serius Awasi Pelanggaran Syariat Islam," *Rakyat Aceh* (23 November 2009), 3; "Peran WH Belum Maksimal," *Harian Aceh* (8 June 2009), 5; "Kualitas WH Harus Ditingkatkan," *Serambi* (22 January 2010), 2; "Pemerintah dan WH Jangan Impoten," *Harian Aceh* (12 April 2010), 3; "WH Seperti Macan Ompong," *Rakyat Aceh* (21 April 2010), 4; "WH Pidie Diminta Aktif," *Serambi* (9 December 2010), 16.

[120] "Aspirasi," *Metro Aceh* (12 October 2009), 6.

9

Shariʿa and Social Engineering

> The goals of the modern utopist are supposedly immanent and within reach, and to postpone attaining them would be irresponsible, despite the "melancholy of fulfillment."
>
> Matei Calinescu
> *Five Faces of Modernity*[1]

The previous chapters have provided detailed descriptions and critical analyses of the major institutions of Aceh's Islamic legal system. These discussions have explored the ways in which the architects and agents of state Shariʿa have attempted to use law as a tool of social engineering, as well as some of the obstacles and resistance that this project has faced at times from various segments of both the state and society. Setting this twenty-first-century story in historical context has further demonstrated the important continuities at work in this, stretching back to a convergence of interests between modernizing technocrats, Islamic religious leaders, and the Indonesian military under the New Order. After the fall of the Suharto regime in 1998, elements of ongoing discourses of *daʿwa* and development came together into more concrete plans for the state implementation of Islamic law as one potential means for resolving the increasingly violent conflict between the Free Aceh Movement (GAM) and the Indonesian central government. The situation, however, became considerably more complex over the first decade of the new millennium as a result of an inter-related constellation of dramatic social transformations that included devastating natural disaster, the end of war, and the beginning of processes of reintegration, as well as the rapid opening of Acehnese society to a flood of new ideas on law, politics, economics, and religion.

[1] Matei Calinescu, *Five Faces of Modernity: Modernism, Avant-garde, Decadence, Kitsch, Postmodernism* (Durham: Duke University Press, 1987), 67.

BUILDING A "NEW ACEH"

While the basic legal framework that made the state implementation of Shariʿa possible in Aceh was first established by a law on special autonomy passed in 1999, the project was significantly energized after the 2004 tsunami and the end of the conflict with GAM. In that context, the idea of using Islamic law as a tool for social engineering was amplified through an increasingly pervasive rhetoric of "total reconstruction." The massive destruction wrought by the 2004 tsunami leveled many existing structures, both physical and organizational. At the same time, it also opened up space for rebuilding Acehnese society from the ground up. This work was greatly facilitated by the fact that the natural disaster and international responses to it catalyzed and accelerated efforts toward the settlement of a peace accord that ended the decades-long violent conflict between GAM and the central Indonesian government.[2] The newly established peace also allowed governments and a host of diverse non-governmental organizations (NGOs) to pursue their own projects of relief, rehabilitation, and development largely undisturbed by the kinds of violence that had previously made such interventions nearly impossible in Aceh.[3]

In the wake of the tsunami came a massive influx of foreign aid workers who brought with them ideas and models of both immediate disaster relief, and of reconstruction projects for the long-term transformation of society.[4] The efforts and agendas of international aid programs varied in many ways, but they generally shared a broad discursive framework that emphasized the goal of linking relief, rehabilitation, and development

[2] Earlier attempts at resolving the conflict had been plagued with difficulties—see Edward Aspinall and Harold A. Crouch, "The Aceh Peace Process: Why it Failed," *East-West Center Policy Studies* (Washington, DC: East-West Center, 2003); Michelle Ann Miller, *Rebellion and Reform in Indonesia: Jakarta's Security and Autonomy Policies in Aceh* (London: Routledge, 2009). Diverse aspects of the peace process that culminated with the 2005 Helsinki agreement are presented in the papers published in Aguswandi and Judith Large (eds.), *Reconfiguring Politics: The Indonesia–Aceh Peace Process, special issue of Accord: An International Review of Peace Initiatives* 20 (2008), <http://www.c-r.org/accord-article/reconfiguring-politics-indonesia-aceh-peace-process>, accessed 30 July 2012.

[3] Badan Rehabilitasi dan Rekonstruksi (BRR) & International Partners, *Aceh and Nias One Year after the Tsunami: The Recovery Effort and Way Forward* (Banda Aceh: BRR NAD-Nias, 2005), 14–15, 116–17.

[4] For extensive documentation of these massive relief and reconstruction efforts, see J. Telford, J. Cosgrave, and R. Houghton, *Joint Evaluation of the International Response to the Indian Ocean Tsunami: Synthesis Report* (London: Tsunami Evaluation Coalition, 2006). For a critical overview of these developments drawing on the TEC reports, see John Telford, "Disaster Recovery: An International Humanitarian Challenge?" in Patrick Daly, R. Michael Feener, and Anthony Reid (eds.), *From the Ground Up: Perspectives on Post-Tsunami and Post-Conflict Aceh* (Singapore: ISEAS Press, 2012), 25–39.

(LRRD) in response to the disaster.[5] The immense amount of funding available for reconstruction in post-tsunami Aceh created an unprecedented opportunity for various aid organizations to implement and test theories about disaster mitigation and vulnerability that they had been developing since the 1990s. This rhetoric of transformation built upon global discourses of developmentalism promoted by various government agencies and organizations like the World Bank. A defining trope of this was an emphasis on the importance of going beyond immediate post-disaster recovery and using the opportunity provided by the trauma to develop not only physical infrastructure, but also new modes of good governance that emphasized capacity building and sustainability.[6]

To coordinate the vast and diverse reconstruction efforts of international aid projects, and to facilitate links between relief, rehabilitation, and development in response to the disaster, the Indonesian government established a special, ministry-level body known as the Rehabilitation and Reconstruction Agency for Aceh and Nias (Badan Rehabilitasi dan Rekonstruksi/BRR).[7] The BRR was given a fixed, four-year mandate of operations by the Indonesian government, and a symbolic charge by former United States President Bill Clinton (in his capacity as the UN Special Envoy for Tsunami Recovery), to "Build Back Better"—a phrase that was to become a popular motto for reconstruction projects in Aceh.[8] The idea then was not only to manage the reconstruction of homes and physical infrastructure in disaster-affected areas, but also to construct and implement new models of quality assurance, transparency, good governance, and gender equity in post-tsunami Aceh.[9] In fact, of the originally proposed multi-billion dollar reconstruction budget, only half was directly allocated for humanitarian relief and reconstruction of facilities destroyed by the earthquake and tsunami. The remainder was budgeted "to address long-standing problems and for building a better Aceh."[10]

[5] For more on the LRRD paradigm and its role in shaping responses to disaster in Aceh, see Ian Christoplos and Treena Wu, "Linking Relief, Rehabilitation and Development (LRRD) to Social Protection: Lessons from Early Tsunami Response in Aceh," in Daly, Feener, and Reid (eds.), *From the Ground Up*, 40–56.

[6] See, for example, Multi Donor Fund, *Implementing Projects, Achieving Results: 18 Months of the Multi Donor Fund for Aceh and Nias—Progress Report III* (Jakarta: 2006).

[7] The BRR was formally established on 16 April 2005 "as a coordinating agency to ensure transparency, accountability, and speed in the reconstruction of Aceh and Nias." *BRR Fact Sheet* (Ref. 1003/10/3/BRRFactSheet-E.doc).

[8] *Badan Rehabilitasi dan Rekonstruksi (BRR) & International Partners, Aceh and Nias: Two Years after the Tsunami: 2006 Progress Report* (Banda Aceh: BRR NAD-Nias, 2006), iii.

[9] *Aceh and Nias: 2006 Progress Report*, 84–8.

[10] John Clark, et al., *Rebuilding a Better Aceh and Nias: Preliminary Stocktaking of the Reconstruction Effort Six Months After the Earthquake and Tsunami* (Jakarta: World Bank, 2005), xiv. The initial projections and plans for allocation of reconstruction aid funds were, of course, revised over the years that followed as priorities shifted. For an in-house

Figure 9.1. "Building Back Better": A new mosque under construction behind a much smaller wooden prayer house at Calang, Aceh Jaya. (Photo by R. Michael Feener)

Since 2005, this rhetoric of radical reconstruction spread across Aceh, far beyond the coastal areas affected by the tsunami (see Figure 9.1). The BRR's own reports and literature went so far as to proclaim that "the tsunami proved to be a blessing in disguise for Nanggroe Aceh Darussalam. It transformed this westernmost province of Indonesia. Not just physically either."[11] Combined with the euphoric discourses surrounding the dawn of a new peace in a region long plagued by violent conflict, reconstruction projects fostered the emergence of possibilities for creating a "new Aceh" that would transform the lives of a people who had suffered so much war and devastation.

The concept of "Building Back Better" was, however, understood in different ways by various parties in Aceh, and just what this new and improved Aceh might look like was a subject of extensive debate in a highly energized public sphere.[12] With the ending of armed conflict in 2005, Aceh was able, for the first time, to experience the new freedoms

account of the handling of these funds up until the end of the BRR's mandate in 2009, see BRR, *Finance: The Seven Keys to Effective Aid Management* (Jakarta: Multi Donor Fund/ UNDP, 2009).

11 BRR, *Tsunami: From Disaster to the Emergence of Light* (Jakarta: Multi Donor Fund/ UNDP, 2009), 95.

12 For an attempt at dealing with the connotations of this slogan in relief and development circles working in Aceh, see: James Kennedy, Joseph Ashmore, Elizabeth Babister, and Ian Kelman, "The Meaning of 'Build Back Better': Evidence From Post-Tsunami Aceh and Sri Lanka," *Journal of Contingencies and Crisis Management* 16.1 (2008) 24–36.

of post-Suharto Indonesia. Local newspapers, magazines, and broadcast media flourished, facilitating the emergence of vigorous debates on a wide range of social, legal, and political issues.[13] The great influx of NGOs and foreign aid organizations into post-conflict, post-tsunami Aceh brought new perspectives and voices to these conversations—often emphasizing concerns central to their own views on how restoring infrastructure and livelihoods could contribute to the promotion of broader projects of social change, economic development, and democratization. Their ideas were actively promoted not only through publications, but also through thousands of outreach sessions, focus group discussions, seminars, and workshops that cluttered the calendar of events in Aceh for most of 2005–2009. Through such programs, many Acehnese came to embrace new ideas about peace, human rights, gender justice, and democracy.

POST-TSUNAMI RELIGIOUS REVIVAL

Concurrent with these burgeoning discussions in NGO circles was a broad surge of religious revival in post-tsunami Aceh. The evocation of religious responses to natural disaster is of course by no means unique to either Aceh or to Islam.[14] The particular forms that responses may take in any religious tradition can, moreover, be as diverse as the individuals that comprise a community of believers. In an initial mapping of Acehnese interpretations of the earthquake and tsunami it was noted that while there were some who regarded these events as purely natural disasters, many Acehnese understood the tragedy as originating from God in diverse ways—either as divine retribution for the sins of the people, a test of their faith, or something pre-ordained regardless of human actions in the world.[15] Published collections of tsunami survivor narratives contain numerous accounts framed in expressly religious terms, with frequent references to the ways in which mosques (often the only buildings to survive the shocks of quake and wave) provided shelter and salvation from those fleeing the disaster.[16]

[13] Feener, "Hand, Heart and Handphone," 15–32.

[14] Some scholars of religion, in fact, have recently come to re-emphasize the important role that religion plays in dealing with situations of crisis, both on a personal and communal level. As Martin Riesebrodt has eloquently expressed it: "... religion is a system of practices especially concerned with warding off and overcoming crisis situations. Religion not only makes it possible for the inexplicable to be explained; it also maintains people's ability to act in situations in which they run up against their own limits." *The Promise of Salvation: A Theory of Religion* (Chicago: University of Chicago Press, 2010), 173.

[15] Julianto Saleh, *Pemaknaan Kejadian Tsunami dan Perilaku Keberagamaan Masyarakat Pasca Tsunami* (Banda Aceh: Pusat Latihan Penelitian Ilmu-Ilmu Sosial, 2005).

[16] See, for example, Damanhur bin Abbas, et al., *Tsunami dan Kisah Mereka* (Banda Aceh: Badan Arsip Provinisi NAD, 2006); Sri Widodo and Ikhwan Nursyujoko (eds.), 99 *Tangan Tuhan di Aceh: Misteri dan Keajaiban di Balik Tsunami* (Jakarta: Yayasan Air Mata,

Official publications from the Acehnese provincial government also elaborated upon what was perceived to be God's meaning and purpose behind such disasters, including: (1) to raise the quality of religious faith, (2) as a chance for those struck by tragedy to gain religious merit, (3) as a means of having one's sins forgiven, (4) as an opportunity for God to grant mercy to those who are patient in accepting their fate, and, (5) as God's test to see who truly has faith—"like gold that is tested by fire to separate the pure from the false."[17] Here again, there are myriad religious interpretations of the event. What is most striking about these various responses, however, is the relative emphasis on considerations of "opportunity" and the future lives of believers—rather than a sense of the disaster serving as a kind of retribution for past sins. Other Muslim voices in Aceh speak of Islam and the implementation of Shariʿa in particular as helping to prepare for and mitigate future disasters.[18] Some Acehnese even expressed beliefs about the disaster carrying other meanings for religious life: the devastation was seen as accelerating the peace process, which increased social stability and allowed for the consequent lifting of curfews, which in turn made it possible for people to pursue religious activities more freely and easily than they had been able to do during the conflict.[19]

In the preface to the Third Edition of the official handbook of the State Shariʿa Agency published in 2005, Alyasa Abubakar noted that the implementation in Islamic law in Aceh had indeed entered a "new phase" after the tsunami.[20] From that time, the state and other major players involved in the reconstruction of post-disaster/post-conflict Aceh energetically engaged with religious dimensions of social change. For example, the Consultative Group on Indonesia—composed of leaders from the National Development Planning Agency (Badan Perencanaan Pembangunan Nasional/BAPPENAS), the World Bank, and the international donor committee—designated "Supporting Religion and

2005). There are also, it should be noted, more worldly explanations for this—as some argue that the open design and/or more solid materials used in mosque construction accounted for the survival of those particular buildings while surrounding neighborhoods were leveled by the wave.

[17] Teuku Abdullah Sanny, *Tsunami Aceh* (Banda Aceh: Pemerintah Provinsi Nanggroe Aceh Darussalam, 2008), 157–63.

[18] Fakhri S., "Urgensi Syariat Islam Dalam Mengantisipasi Bencana Alam di NAD," in Syamsul Rijal (ed.), *Dinamika dan Problematika Penerapan Syariat Islam* (Banda Aceh: Dinas Syariat Islam, 2007), 50–72.

[19] Heru Cahyono, "Portret Kelembagaan Gampong yang Lumpuh di Meuria, Kecamatan Matangkuli, Kabupaten Aceh Utara," in Irine Hiraswati Gayatri (ed.), *Runtuhnya Gampong di Aceh: Studi Masyarakat Desa yang Bergejolak* (Yogyakarta: Pustaka Pelajar, 2008), 266.

[20] Alyasa Abubakar, *Syariʿat Islam di Provinsi Nanggroe Aceh Darussalam: Paradigma, Kebijakan dan Kegiatan* (Banda Aceh: Dinas Syariat Islam, 2003—Fifth Edition, 2008), vii. The prefaces of earlier editions are included in the front matter to this publication.

Culture" as a major rubric for reconstruction efforts in the immediate wake of the tsunami.[21] The BRR for its part actively encouraged transformation in the religious and cultural life of post-tsunami Aceh, as explained in one of its official publications:

> The risks were too great for BRR to focus merely on rebuilding damaged houses and infrastructure. The agency also needed to facilitate social transformation, and therefore geared all its programs and activities toward achieving social reconstruction... To achieve the above, BRR, in particular the Deputy for Religious, Social and Cultural Affairs, coordinated, developed and promoted cross-sectoral activities to strengthen and renew the spiritual and social life of the people.[22]

These activities included sponsoring training programs for female Muslim preachers taught by IAIN faculty, and a series of publications on Islamic issues written by ulama and NGO activists.[23] In a preface to one of these works, the ministerial-level Director of the BRR, Kuntoro Mangkusubroto, also commented on the issue of "spiritual development" as part of the broader processes of post-disaster reconstruction and development:

> Development encompasses more than just physical improvements, but also needs to include more intangible aspects of educating and enlightening the community (I. *umat*). The BRR welcomes the input of the ulama in both advising on and providing the spiritual substance of the ongoing work of building a "new Aceh."[24]

The Indonesian Government's initial "Master Plan" identified specific policy strategies to address religious aspects of the reconstruction of post-tsunami Aceh, with particular attention to the areas of religious education, the recruitment and training of religious officials, the construction of mosques and offices for state religious bureaucracies, and fostering "spiritual tranquility recovery."[25] These projects for religious reconstruction had the effect of bringing Islamic institutions and leadership further into the orbit of the Indonesian state in complex ways.

[21] Consultative Group on Indonesia, *Notes on Reconstruction: The December 26, 2004 Natural Disaster* (Jakarta: BAPPENAS, 2005), 45–53.

[22] BRR, Religion, *Social Culture: Revitalizing the Dignity of Society* (Jakarta: Multi Donor Fund/UNDP, 2009), 20.

[23] "BRR Latih Da'i Perempuan," *Serambi* (13 August 2007), 2.

[24] Daud Zamzani, Nuruzzahri Yahya, Hasanoel Bashry HG, Muchtar A. Wahab, and Ismail Ya'kub (eds.), *Pemikiran Ulama Dayah Aceh* (Banda Aceh: BRR, 2007), ix.

[25] *Regulation of the President of Republic of Indonesia Number 30 Year 2005 on Master Plan for Rehabilitation and Reconstruction for the Regions and People of the Province of Nanggroe Aceh Darussalam and Nias Islands of the Province of North Sumatra* (Jakarta: Republic of Indonesia, 2005), vol. IV, 4.

Through these newly strengthened connections, the ulama were engaged and employed to promote a new social vision of Islam in Aceh. This is reflected, for example, in the recommendations of a workshop for female ulama hosted at Banda Aceh's most luxurious hotel in June 2007, which called for the ulama to be "resolute toward the government on the issue of Shari'a implementation and more pro-active in society in promoting the understanding of Islamic law as a complete and total system (I. *syari'at Islam secara kaffah*)."[26]

On one level, such appeals to Islamic law and the role of the state in implementing its social vision echo the appeal of Shari'a as an abstract, idealized vision of justice and social order that have become increasingly popular among expanding circles of *da'wa* activists in Indonesia over the past two decades.[27] Indeed, it could be said that the implementation of Islamic law in Aceh as part of its "Special Autonomy" status has, to a significant degree, brought Acehnese understandings and practices of Islam more firmly in line with Indonesian national standards than at any other point in its history. This has become evident not only in the increasing convergence of Islamic discourses between Aceh and Jakarta, but also in the recent proliferation of branches of Indonesian Islamic organizations across the province over recent years. For most of Aceh's history, the major national Muslim organizations of Indonesia—including the NU and Muhammadiyah—had little success in Aceh. Since the peace, however, the presence of these and other Indonesian national organizations (DDII, HTI, and others) have grown in the province. Likewise, models of Islamic education developed in Java and elsewhere in Indonesia made inroads into Aceh, including the influential network of "modern *pesantren*" on the model of the famous school of Gontor that opened a campus in Aceh in 2008.[28] These developments have been facilitated by the work of the new and newly reconstituted state Shari'a institutions discussed in the preceding chapters.

[26] The Forum Silaturrahmi Ulama Perempuan se-Nanggroe Aceh Darussalam was held at the Hermes Palace Hotel and sponsored by Mitra Sejati Perempuan Indonesia. See Siti Zalikha Ibrahim, "Santri Menemukan Jati Diri," in Ahmadun Yosi Herfanda (ed.), *Menuju Syariat Islam Kaffah: Pikiran dan Pengalaman Santri Aceh dalam menuntut Ilmu dan Hubungannya dengan Perbuatan Nyata* (Banda Aceh: Lepena, 2008), 74.

[27] M.C. Ricklefs, *Islamisation and Its Opponents in Java: A Political, Social, Cultural and Religious History, c. 1930 to the Present* (Singapore: NUS Press, 2012), 240–2.

[28] These developments have been described in more detail in Chapters 3 and 4.

CONSTRUCTING A NEW "SHARI'A SYSTEM" FOR INDONESIAN ACEH

Beyond facilitating the further integration of Acehnese Islam into broader Indonesian national standards of religious belief and practice, the state project of Shari'a implementation in Aceh has also been deployed as a bulwark against the kind of NGO-style "globalization" that both Acehnese ulama and the Indonesian central government viewed with suspicion. Jakarta-based conspiracy theorists and Islamist activists have used various media to aggressively argue that post-disaster reconstruction programs have opened the floodgates for Christian missionaries and Zionist agents attempting to turn the Acehnese away from the true path of Islam.[29] Within Aceh itself, Muslim intellectuals from the IAIN worked on developing new strategies to counter what some there perceived to be an invasion of anti-Islamic forces from the West. Their efforts included the development of new *da'wa* media and education programs to imprint proper Islamic morality upon the populace.[30] Other governmental institutions also mobilized in the name of Shari'a as a response to perceived foreign corruptions in more physically assertive ways.[31] The state implementation of Shari'a was thus seen by both local Islamic leaders and officers of the central Indonesian state as having the potential to protect Aceh from the threat of moral degradation from "westernizing" globalization, while at the same managing diverse projects of economic, political, and social development framed by international donors.

Like the BRR, the World Bank, and other stakeholders in Aceh's post-tsunami reconstruction, the ideological supporters of the new Shari'a system saw tremendous opportunities to transform society according to their own ideals of progress in the wake of the tsunami. The vision of the architects of this Islamic legal system has been thoroughly forward looking, and the first head of the State Shari'a Agency, Alyasa Abubakar, made a point of repeatedly arguing that, "Acehnese society does not want and will not try to turn back the clock."[32] Rather, the ideology of many

[29] See, for example, Rizki Ridyasmara, *Gerilya Salib di Serambi Mekkah: Dari Zaman Portugis Hingga Paska Tsunami* (Jakarta: Pustaka Al-Kautsar, 2006).

[30] Muhammad A.R., *Portret Aceh Pasca Tsunami: Mengintip Peran Dayah dalam Menghadapi Akulturasi Akhlak* (Aceh: Ar-Raniry Press, 2007), 83–114.

[31] For example, in August 2006, the WH forced their way into the UN compound in Banda Aceh and attempted to inspect staff bedrooms there. Fadlullah Wilmot, "Sharīʿah in Aceh: Panacea or Blight?" *Accord: An International Review of Peace Initiatives* 20 (2008) 77–8.

[32] Alyasa Abubakar, *Syari'at Islam*, 81. Indeed, even while some at times rhetorically evoke the past glories of the Acehnese sultanate during its seventeenth-century "golden age," returning to a pre-modern model of Islamic law is not the primary motivation of the majority of people involved with the current experiment in establishing a Shari'a system in Aceh.

advocates of Shariʿa implementation in contemporary Aceh is one with a vision of future-oriented social transformation, insisting on the need to move beyond "traditional" understandings toward a vision of Islam that actively engages with modern developments in fields including education, economics, and medicine.[33]

The degree to which the transformation of visions of Islam in Aceh has been linked to broader Indonesian national trends is explicitly emphasized in the official text of the "Clarification" (I. *Penjelasan*) of *Qanun No. 11/2002*.[34] This commentary on a regional regulation of Islamic belief and practice interprets the de-centralization legal restructuring that followed the collapse of the New Order in 1998, as presenting an opportunity to develop mechanisms for the state application of Islamic law. These reforms served to facilitate the promulgation of "Shariʿa-based" regional by-laws (I. *perda syariat*) by dozens of local governments across the archipelago over the years that followed.[35] In Aceh, however, moves in this direction were allowed to proceed further than anywhere else after the province was granted the authority to formally implement Islamic law under the 1999 Law on Special Autonomy for Aceh.[36]

At that time, the provincial government's rhetoric heralded this new local authority over the administration of religion and education as allowing for the development of state Shariʿa institutions that would foster the further Islamization of society. The five-year development plan for Aceh issued in 2001 proclaimed the intention of creating a society based on Islam in which the Shariʿa would be applied in its totality (I. *secara kaffah*) across all aspects of social life.[37] As discussed in the preceding chapters however, during the first five years of Special Autonomy the institutions of the Islamic legal system had a rather limited impact. The situation began to change dramatically after the December 2004 earthquake and tsunami, when a heightened level of public religiosity, combined with hopeful visions of a peaceful future and pervasive discourses about "total

[33] Alyasa Abubakar, *Syariʿat Islam*, 25.

[34] "Penjelasan atas Qanun Provinsi Nanggroe Aceh Darussalam Nomor 11 Tahun 2002 tentang Pelaksanaan Syariʿat Islam Bidang Aqidah, Ibadah, dan Syiʿar Islam," *Himpunan Peraturan Perundang-Undangan tentang Mahkamah Syarʿiyah di Provinsi Nanggroe Aceh Darussalam* (Banda Aceh: Mahkamah Syarʿiyah Propinsi NAD, 2006), 201–9.

[35] For a brief summary of the impact of de-centralization policies on the administration of Islamic law in Indonesia, see Mark E. Cammack and R. Michael Feener, "The Indonesian Islamic Legal System," in Mark E. Cammack, R. Michael Feener, and Clark B. Lombardi (eds.), *Islamic Legal Professionals in Contemporary Southeast Asia,* a special issue of *Pacific Rim Law & Policy Journal*, 21(1) (January 2012) 37.

[36] *Undang-Undang Republik Indonesia Nomor 44/1999 tentang Penyelenggaraan Keistimewaan Propinsi Daerah Istimewa Aceh.*

[37] *Rencana Strategis Provinsi NAD Tahun 2001–2005*, republished in: Alyasa Abubakar, *Bunga Rampai Pelaksanaan Syariat Islam: Pendukung Qanun Pelaksanaan Syariat Islam* (Banda Aceh: Dinas Syariat Islam Aceh, 2009), 20.

reconstruction," came together in ways that served to energize projects for reforming society through the application of Islamic law.

THE "LIVING LAW"

As discussed in Chapter 3, the work of developing and promoting the Islamization of law in Aceh was to a great extent carried out by academics associated with the National Institute for Islamic Studies (IAIN) in Banda Aceh. Many of the most prominent figures involved in these developments—including Alyasa Abubakar as Director of the DSI and Muslim Ibrahim as Director of the MPU—had also studied in Cairo.[38] There they, and many other Indonesians of their generation, had been exposed to understandings of Islamic law and its potential role in programs of social transformation that were characteristic of broader shifts in the programmatic vision of the Muslim Brotherhood at that time.[39] In their later careers back in Aceh, they worked to integrate these ideas about Shariʿa and social change into broader Indonesian understandings of law as a tool of development that were increasingly dominant during the New Order period. In the twenty-first century these understandings of Islamic law and social engineering were further re configured in relation to international discourses on post-disaster/post-conflict relief, reconstruction, and development. The recent historical evolution of these conversations clearly demonstrates the remarkable degree to which non-Muslim discourses on law and society have influenced contemporary formulations and interpretations of Shariʿa. Future work in the field of Islamic legal studies will need to expand its horizons and develop new approaches in order to better understand the increasingly complex effects of such diverse influences on modern Muslim societies.

In the early years of Aceh's Islamic legal system, another prominent IAIN academic, Syahrizal, urged the Acehnese to seize the opportunity of special autonomy to "establish Islamic law as the 'living law' in Aceh."[40] This particular form for expressing the desired goal of the new Islamic legal system is striking in the way that it engages with one of the most prominent and highly-contested concepts of legal thought debated among

[38] Alyasa Abubakar, took a master's degree in *uṣūl al-fiqh* from al-Azhar in 1980, and Muslim Ibrahim spent over a decade in Egypt as well (1973–1984), taking graduate degrees in *tarbiya* and *fiqh*.

[39] For an overview of these developments, see Barbara H.E. Zollner, *The Muslim Brotherhood: Hasan al-Hudaybi and Ideology* (Abingdon: Routledge, 2009).

[40] Syahrizal (ed.), *Kontekstualisasi Syariʿat Islam di Nanggroe Aceh Darussalam* (Banda Aceh: Ar-Raniry Press, 2003), vxi.

Indonesian jurists since the founding of the independent nation in 1945. In particular, it reveals a major shift in emphasis from understandings of law as a reflection of established social practice to law as a system for the normative prescription of ideal values.

"Living law" has long been the main rubric under which the Indonesian state has effected significant changes to the legal culture of the nation. In the early years of independence, mapping "the living law" of the country came to define the primary battleground for those arguing diverse positions across an increasingly wide gap between proponents of *adat* and Islam as sources for national law.[41] The centrality of the concept of "living law" in Indonesian legal thought had its origins in the field of *adat* (customary law) studies in the Dutch colonial period. The early development of *adat* law and its rise to prominence in official discourses on law and administration in the Netherlands East Indies were driven by the work of Cornelius van Vollenhoven.[42] In elaborating his influential model of *adat* law, van Vollenhoven developed conceptions of "living law" and legal pluralism that in many ways paralleled those of his Austrian contemporary Eugen Ehrlich.

Ehrlich summed up his magnum opus on the sociology of law with the sentence, "At the present as well as at any other time, the center of gravity of legal development lies not in legislation, nor in juristic science, nor in judicial decision, but in society itself."[43] Today Ehrlich is regarded as a founding figure in the sociology of law for his attempts at recasting the scope of jurists' work to consider aspects of the wider society of which they are a part—thus calling for lawyers to be trained in sociology, economics, and even psychology in addition to their legal studies.[44] As will

[41] Ratno Lukito, "Law and Politics in Post-Independence Indonesia: A Case Study of Religious and Adat Courts," in Arskal Salim and Azyumardi Azra (eds.), *Shariʿa and Politics in Modern Indonesia* (Singapore: Institute of Southeast Asian Studies Press, 2003), 21.

[42] For more on these developments, see Roy Ellen, "The Development of Anthropology and Colonial Policy in the Netherlands: 1800–1960," *Journal of the History of the Behavioral Sciences* 12 (1976) 303–24; C. Fasseur, *De Indologen: Ambtenaren voor de Oost, 1825–1950* (Amsterdam: Bert Bakker, 1993); and Peter J. Burns, *The Leiden Legacy: Concepts of Law in Indonesia* (Jakarta: PT Pradnya Paramita, 1999), 246–54.

[43] Eugen Ehrlich, *Fundamental Principles of the Sociology of Law* (Cambridge, MA: Harvard University Press, 1936), xv.

[44] Baudouin Dupret has compared Ehrlich's approach to that of Malinowski, with a shared emphasis on the ways that cultural ideals govern human interaction to produce "law" reflecting norms of social control: Baudouin Dupret, "What is Plural in the Law? A Praxiological Answer," *Égypte/Monde arabe*, Troisième série, 1 (2005), <http://ema.revues.org/index1869.html>, accessed 4 November 2010. The followers of van Vollenhoven, however, proved increasingly more amenable to lending their work on aspects of Indonesian society to the service of the courts and various branches of governmental administration. See Raymond Kennedy, "Applied Anthropology in the Dutch East Indies," *Transactions of the New York Academy of Sciences* 6.5 (1944) 157–62. For more on Ehrlich in relation to Dutch and Indonesian formulations of "living law," see Franz and Keebet von

be discussed further in due course, such an expansive view of the social dimension of legal change is something that is frequently echoed in the writings and everyday language of many of those directly involved with the design and operation of Aceh's contemporary Islamic legal system.

LEGAL INSTRUMENTALISM AND THE TECHNOCRATS

Over the course of its long career and development out of Dutch *adat* law discussions, the Indonesian concept of "living law" (I. *hukum yang hidup*) mutated in terms of its relative emphasis: From ethnographic description to ideological prescription. *Adat* law came to play a powerful symbolic role in the Indonesian nationalist movement, and as such it was integrated into the modernizing reform projects of Dutch-trained scholars like R. Soepomo, who was an influential figure in the drafting of independent Indonesia's first national constitution.[45] In the process, the nostalgic idealism of "custom" faded under the glare of various shades of revolutionary romanticism.[46] As the von Benda-Beckmanns have recently summarized these developments, the rhetoric of "living law" thus came to serve as a legitimizing trope for a kind of "*freie Rechtslehre*" in a way that became clearly contrary to the visions of "living law" advanced by van Vollenhoven and Ehrlich.[47]

These changes were deeply lamented by latter-day Indonesian proponents of *adat* law.[48] Notable among them was Mohamad Koesnoe, who argued that the foundation of the 1945 constitution—as outlined in the preamble—was fundamentally a "metaphysical" conception of law manifest in "normative principles."[49] The movement away from an idealist toward a more instrumentalist vision of law over subsequent decades of Indonesian history was, in his view, a reflection of the influence of Marxist

Benda-Beckmann, "The Social Life of Living Law in Indonesia," in Marc Hertogh (ed.), *Living Law: Reconsidering Eugen Ehrlich* (Oxford: Hart Publishing, 2009).

[45] Ab Massier, *The Voice of the Law in Transition: Indonesian Jurists and their Languages, 1915–2000* (Leiden: KITLV Press, 2008), 151.

[46] See, for example, R. Supomo, "Hukum Adat Dikemudian Hari berhubung dengan Pembinaan Negara Indonesia," in *Bab-Bab tentang Hukum Adat* (n.p.: Penerbitan Universitas, 1959), 5–20.

[47] Franz and Keebet von Benda-Beckmann, "The Social Life of Living Law in Indonesia," 187.

[48] Moh. Koesnoe, "Mengamati Konsep Hukum di Dalam Masyarakat Kita," in M. Ali Boediarto (ed.), *Kapita Selekta Hukum Adat: Suatu Pemikiran Baru* (Jakarta: Varia Peradilan—Ikatan Hakim Indonesia, 2002), 53–82.

[49] In his discussion, Koesnoe also references the work of Roscoe Pound on law as a "tool of social engineering"—something which he sees as facilitating the further deterioration of law to the point that its priorities, "*pada hakekatnya berfungsi sebagai manifesto politik dari penyusunannya yaitu penguasa.*" Koesnoe, "Mengamati Konsep Hukum," 58–71.

legal theory upon Soekarno's left-leaning government.[50] Even after the collapse of the regime in 1965, however, basic understandings of law in instrumentalist terms persisted and found new forms of expression from the Indonesian state. In 1973, they re-emerged in the Main Outlines of National Direction (GBHN) under the new idiom of "law as a tool [for national development]," which Koesnoe glossed as "law as an instrument to facilitate the advance of political objectives."[51] By this point, the ideal of law was clearly no longer to be a descriptive reflection of the actual norms active in society, as had been professed by earlier academic proponents of *adat* law.[52] Rather, law had come to be viewed as a means by which to define the ideals that society should be aspiring toward. This fundamental shift from description to prescription in dominant Indonesian philosophies of law allowed the state to legitimize its various agendas of restructuring and reform in a wide number of areas including the articulation of official understandings of Islamic law as "living *fiqh*."[53]

Over the course of the New Order period (1965–1998), the Indonesian government instituted an entire range of policies in which particular forms of Islamic law were pressed into the service of state projects of modernization and economic development. In the field of legislation, this was perhaps most clearly evident in the 1974 Marriage Act, as discussed in Chapter 5. As will be discussed further later in the chapter, there was a growing convergence of interests between Indonesian technocrats and Islamic *daʿwa* activists over the last decades of the twentieth century. At the same time, significant efforts were also being made to engage with rural *pesantren* and Traditionalist religious leadership to help forge agendas for promoting key aspects of Indonesian state developmentalism that could be seen as in accordance with a particular social vision of Islam.[54] Prominent ulama were, for example, recruited to produce Islamic justifications for government initiatives in what proved to be a very successful promotion

[50] Koesnoe, "Mengamati Konsep Hukum," 70. In particular, there is a clear aversion to the "legal nihilism" of Marxist legal philosophers in the line of Evgeny Pashukanis which provided, "a rationale for extraordinary state action ... if the conscious plan for reshaping society so demanded," Peter C. Caldwell, *Dictatorship, State Planning, and Social Theory in the German Democratic Republic* (Cambridge: Cambridge University Press, 2003), 61.

[51] Koesnoe, "Mengamati Konsep Hukum," 62.

[52] For a contemporary statement protesting against developments in this direction see, for example, Soediman Kartohadiprodjo, *Hukum Nasional: Beberapa Tjatatan* (Bandung: Binatjipta, 1968).

[53] In relation to the 1991 Indonesian Compilation of Islamic Laws (KHI), see John Bowen, *Islam, Law and Equality in Indonesia: An Anthropology of Public Reasoning* (Cambridge: Cambridge University Press, 2003), 190–2; Moch. Nur Ichwan, "Official Reform of Islam: State Islam and the Ministry of Religious Affairs in Contemporary Indonesia, 1966–2004," Ph.D. dissertation (Tilburg University, 2006), 127–35.

[54] R. Michael Feener, *Muslim Legal Thought in Modern Indonesia* (Cambridge: Cambridge University Press, 2007), 157–62.

of Indonesia's family planning program in the 1970s.[55] In Aceh, analogous institutions were the focus of state interventions via the IAIN, and later by the State Shariʿa Agency as well.

Both there and across Indonesia more generally, such piecemeal reforms were accommodated to Traditionalist Muslim structures of authority based in the *pesantren* and *dayah*. Islamic Modernists and Revivalists were, in general, open to ideas of even more comprehensive social transformation. Modernist visions of Islamic law as a "totalizing system" had been known in Aceh since the mid-twentieth century, and promoted by PUSA and the leadership of the Darul Islam insurgency under Daud Beureueh. Beureueh used the term "*nizam*" as early as 1962 in the sense of "rules that can order human life on all levels—individual, communal, societal, and governmental, as well as in international relations."[56] This grand goal was, however, never realized under the Acehnese movement for the establishment of an Islamic state. Following the suppression of the Darul Islam in the 1960s, however, the Indonesian government appealed to Islamic norms to promote its own range of development programs in Aceh.

The Indonesian administration of Aceh under the New Order period was dominated by the developmentalist agendas of economists and other secular-trained experts who have come to be collectively referred to as "the technocrats." In the 1970s, John McDougall characterized their "ideology of modernity" as "mental enlightenment via material progress."[57] Stuart Schlegel described the situation as that of a technocratic civil government pushing for economic development in Banda Aceh, surrounded by "a sea of traditional peasant villagers" in which the ulama "remained the major rural political force."[58] These two worlds, moreover, were characterized by very different visions of modernizing social change:

> Development for the government officials and the academics means that technocratic advance is the proper course of historical change. What a Modernist modern Muslim ulama means by development is something quite different and he may want no part of economic and secular change. For the ulama and most village people of all streams, development indeed means such things as

[55] See, for example, Ali Yafie, "Doktrin Fiqh dalam Program Kependudukan," in *Teologi Sosial: Telaah Kritis Persoalan Agama dan Kemanusiaan* (Yogyakarta: LKPSM, 1997), 29–40.

[56] "Muqaddimah Pelaksanaan Unsur-unsur Sjariʿat Islam—9 April, 1962," in Analiansyah and Jamhuri, *Syariat Islam Di Nanggroe Aceh Darussalam: Inventarisasi Dokumen* (Banda Aceh: Dinas Syariat Islam Provinsi Nanggroe Aceh Darussalam, 2008), 95.

[57] John James McDougall, "The Technocrat's Ideology of Modernity," in Gloria Davis (ed.), *What is Modern Indonesian Culture?* (Athens: Ohio University Center for International Studies, 1979), 156.

[58] Stuart A. Schlegel, "Technocrats in a Muslim Society: Symbolic Community in Aceh," in Davis (ed.), *What is Modern Indonesian Culture?*, 237.

improved medical treatment, but primarily it means better mosques, a wider literacy in Arabic, and more people familiar with the Koran.[59]

In his presentation of the ways in which these diverse worlds interacted, Schlegel presented sketches of two prominent Acehnese technocrats of the late 1970s: one "typical of modernizing elite figures in most of the world" at that time—materialist, pragmatist, secularist, and aggressively flouting religious norms and traditional culture—and the other, a "pious" technocrat who displayed a commitment to normative Islamic belief and practice as popularly understood in Aceh. He concluded that the predominance of the latter type of technocrat in Aceh was responsible for their "tentative acceptance by Acehnese society at large because they share in the public symbols of its unity."[60] Schlegel presented these pious technocrats as representative of forms of Islam that were strikingly compatible with the New Order's developmentalist ideology in a way that marks them as a rather curious exception to dominant trends in the 1970s—or so it appeared at the time. From our present perspective of historical hindsight, however, his remarks read as extremely prescient perceptions of an early manifestation of a trend that developed significantly over the two decades that followed—that of increasing numbers of observant Muslims establishing themselves within the structures of the Indonesian state.[61]

By the 1990s, there was clearly an increasing convergence between the goals and orientations of "secular" and self-consciously "Islamic" technocrats in Indonesia. As noted earlier, however, already in the 1970s, McDougal had noted the penchant of secular technocrats not only to emphasize the importance of clearly structured organizations, but also their "puritanical" anxieties about the perceived weakening of moral norms in modern society.[62] Both of these characteristics were shared with the expanding class of upwardly mobile Muslims over the decades that followed. Indeed, even the kind of "mental and cultural enlightenment" espoused by secular economists and engineers overlapped with many of the same values that were later listed by the architects of Aceh's new Islamic legal system as desirable outcomes of Shari'a discipline.[63] Both

[59] Schlegel, "Technocrats in a Muslim Society," 244.

[60] Schlegel, "Technocrats in a Muslim Society," 245.

[61] These developments were signaled in a significant way with the establishment of the Association of Indonesian Muslim Intellectuals (ICMI) in 1990. See Robert W. Hefner, "Islam, State, and Civil Society: ICMI and the Struggle for the Indonesian Middle Class," *Indonesia* 56 (October 1993) 1–36.

[62] McDougall, "The Technocrat's Ideology of Modernity," 156–7.

[63] For example, Alyasa Abubakar's list of values that Shari'a implementation would serve to inculcate in society at large mentions: honesty, frugality, studiousness, diligence, loyalty, intelligence, and emotional maturity. *Syari'at Islam*, 85–6.

groups aimed not only for the technical implementation of particular developmentalist policies, but also the cultivation of specific kinds of subjectivities as the foundation for successful programs of modernization. Beyond the specific contexts of Indonesia and Islam, the intertwining of such material, political, and cultural dimensions in this project place the designers and functionaries of Aceh's state Shariʿa system solidly in company with Taylorian managerialists, technocratic engineers, and modernist architects in a shared devotion to "the trinity of 'unity, order, purity' as the guiding principles of any design."[64]

MODERN TRANSFORMATIONS OF MUSLIM JURISPRUDENCE

At work in all this are new configurations of law, moral authority, and state power reflecting the global order of modern nations. Such transformations of Islamic law are by no means novel to the Acehnese case. Wael Hallaq has noted that in the classical period, the Shariʿa presupposed and was dependent upon a "moral community" manifest in myriad informal structures.[65] In the absence of this in the modern period, the notion of a moral community was replaced with the more systematic and bureaucratic institutions of the state. Oussama Arabi has commented on the ways in which the formalization of Islamic law under Ottoman reforms presented a drastic shift from a fundamentally religious and theological conception of law to an instrumentalist, political conception, in which, "to an unprecedented degree, Shariʿa became a positive tool, a leverage at the service of state interests."[66] Through these modernizing transformations, there has been a marked shift in the relative emphasis on social maintenance vis-à-vis social engineering in dominant conceptions of Islamic law.

These developments were facilitated by the ascendance of previously constrained modes of "utilitarian" reasoning in Muslim jurisprudence.[67] Such approaches, framed in particular as they were by radically refashioned *fiqh* conceptions of "necessities" (Ar. *ḍarūriyyāt*) and "benefit"

[64] Mauro F. Guillén, *The Taylorized Beauty of the Mechanical: Scientific Management and the Rise of Modernist Architecture* (Princeton: Princeton University Press, 2006), 12.

[65] Wael B. Hallaq, *Sharīʿa: Theory, Practice, Transformations* (New York: Cambridge University Press, 2009), 544.

[66] Oussama Arabi, *Studies in Modern Islamic Law and Jurisprudence* (The Hague: Kluwer Law International, 2001), 192.

[67] For a discussion of the impact of the modern emergence of this strain of Muslim legal thought in Egypt, see Clark B. Lombardi, *State Law as Islamic Law in Modern Egypt: The Incorporation of the Sharīʿa into Egyptian Constitutional Law* (Leiden: E.J. Brill, 2006), 38–40.

(Ar. *maṣlaḥa*), have assumed a prominent place in modern Muslim legal thought.[68] The pervasive instrumentalism of this mode of Islamic reform makes it eminently amenable to prescriptive agendas of law as social engineering. Viewing the implementation of Islamic law in contemporary Aceh as a project for social transformation—rather than as simply a series of reactive measures to the perceived "crises of modernity" and/ or political machinations of national and local elites—can provide new perspectives on why the Shariʿa system has taken its present shape, and the extent of its accomplishments and failures. As will be discussed further in what follows, this general tone of instrumentalism in modern *fiqh* can be productively examined in relation to particular trends in non-Muslim jurisprudence and social theory that have contributed to contemporary understandings of law as a tool of social engineering.

ISSUES OF IMPLEMENTATION

In addressing the effectiveness of the implementation of Islamic law, Barry Hooker has proposed a list of basic tests, according to which a legal system must: (1) state criteria by which their validity can be tested, (2) be capable of effective implementation by public officials, and (3) extract a basic level of compliance from the population. In his assessment of the situation in 2008, the Aceh's state Shariʿa system had failed these tests.[69] It is hard to argue otherwise. Indeed, on nearly every indicator that one might use to evaluate the success of their attempts at creating a new legal order, the results are less than impressive. Well beyond Hooker's criteria, the implementation of Islamic law in Aceh appears to have fallen short on key indices such as its effectiveness in new institution building, public confidence in the legal system, and an actual impact on crime rates. The project of state Shariʿa is, moreover, frequently characterized as disappointing by many local proponents of the system itself.[70]

Cases involving gambling, alcohol consumption, and *khalwat* have never to date amounted to a significant portion of the caseload of Aceh's Shariʿa

[68] Wael B. Hallaq, *A History of Islamic Legal Theories* (Cambridge University Press, 1997), 164–74, 219.

[69] M.B. Hooker, *Indonesian Syariah: Defining a National School of Islamic Law* (Singapore: ISEAS, 2008), 292.

[70] Part of this is connected to a perceived "lack of political will" to enforce Shariʿa on the part of Irwandi Yusuf, a former member of the Free Aceh Movement who was elected as Aceh's governor in 2007. On the disappointment with the government's performance in implementing Islamic law, and on the need to further develop *siyāsa* see, for example, Hasanuddin Yusuf Adan, *Syariʿat Islam di Aceh: Antara Implementasi dan Diskriminasi* (Banda Aceh: Adnin Foundation, 2008), 30–4; "WH dan Satpol PP Dituding Jalan Ditempat," *Rakyat Aceh* (17 August 2008) 5.

Courts, and across the province there has been a marked decrease in the number of such cases brought to court since 2007.[71] In general, Aceh's Shari'a Courts continue to follow patterns well attested at the national level and in terms of their actual day-to-day operation, most of their work involves issues of family law, and divorce in particular. They are in this sense run much like the Islamic courts (I. *Pengadilan Agama*) in other Indonesian provinces.[72] The other state institutions of Aceh's Islamic legal system have similarly little distinguished themselves over recent years. Given such a performance record in the sphere of formal legal institutions, there are legitimate questions as to what, exactly, a decade of Shari'a implementation in Aceh has actually accomplished.

Despite the apparent failure to deliver tangible results in the formal legal sphere, Shari'a nevertheless remains a defining referent at the center of public discussions on law and society in Aceh. Indeed, the impact of state programs of *sosialisasi* building upon the foundations of state-directed *da'wa* established over the past half-century has produced a remarkable reconfiguration of public discourse—one in which the future of Aceh as both an "Islamic society" and as part of the Indonesian Republic are now largely accepted as a given. Here, the importance of the project for developments beyond the areas of legislation and formal legal institutions becomes clear.

In articulating a view of the aims and accomplishments of state Shari'a in effecting social change, one Acehnese IAIN academic has argued:

> The success of Shari'a implementation is not measured solely by the number of cases decided by the courts or the extent to which the sentences they pronounce are formally executed. Rather the indication of success should be found in the decrease of violations of the Shari'a, and in the heightened awareness of the need to uphold the law of God as a protector and as a bearer of benefits for individuals, families and society.[73]

The point here about a decrease in the actual number of violations is empirically unsupportable (and highly dubious). Nevertheless, the role of Shari'a emphasized here as a means of heightening "awareness" (I. *kesadaran*) and providing broadly conceived "benefit" (I. *kemaslahatan*)

[71] Statistics compiled by Muhammad Yusuf, Panitera/Sekretaris Mahkamah Syari'iyah Aceh, 5 June 2009.

[72] The vast majority of the cases before the court continue to be related to divorce, followed in number by inheritance—and these cases are generally decided according to rules and norms commonly found in the decisions of religious courts elsewhere in Indonesia. These and other aspects of the court's practice have been discussed at length in Chapter 6.

[73] Syahrizal, "Strategi Pelaksanaan Syari'at Islam di Nanggroe Aceh Darussalam," in Azman Ismail (ed.), *Suara Khatib Baiturrahman* (Banda Aceh: Pengurus Masjid Raya Baiturrahman, 2006), 20–5.

for society clearly points to the ways in which the development of Aceh's Islamic legal system has been directed toward areas of concern that are well beyond the limits of black-letter law and the policy enactments of formal state institutions. As Brinkley Messick has demonstrated, in Muslim societies, the Shariʿa holds the place not merely of "law" in a conventional Western sense, but rather as "the centerpiece of societal discourse."[74] From this perspective, the project of implementing Islamic law in contemporary Aceh can be seen not only as a project of formal legal change, but also as aiming at far broader social transformations.

SOCIAL ENGINEERING

Social engineering and related terms in various European languages (*sociale ingenieurs, social ingenjörskonst,* etc.) have carried diverse progressive and pejorative connotations in different circles over the past century. Carl Marklund has referred to social engineering as an important aspect of modernity that can and should be approached in diverse ways, depending on particular contexts, as "utopian ideology, as a set of paternalistic-cum-scientistic practices in operation, as a metaphor of state authority, and as a rhetorical strategy within American industrial betterment and scientific management."[75] In some cases, the term social engineering has been deployed with reference to an "antipolitics" intended to circumvent the perceived failings of popular democracy,[76] and as a "rhetorical tool" implying strategies by which subject populations could be manipulated "in such a way that they came to 'love their servitude.' "[77] Karl Popper has vehemently critiqued what he referred to as "Utopian social engineering" as "most dangerous" for its "uncompromising radicalism."[78] Today, the term social engineering is often associated with the pursuit of "lethal utopias" in Nazi Germany and Stalin's Soviet Union.[79]

[74] Brinkley Messick, *The Calligraphic State: Textual Domination and History in a Muslim Society* (Berkeley: University of California Press, 1993), 3.

[75] Carl Marklund, "Adjusting Facts and Values—Reconciling Politics with Science: Some Notes on the Rhetorics of Social Engineering in Depression-Era Sweden and the USA," *Ideas in History* II.2 (2007) 10.

[76] John M. Jordan, *Machine-Age Ideology: Social Engineering and American Liberalism, 1911–1939* (Chapel Hill, NC: University of North Carolina Press, 1994).

[77] David Östlund, "A Knower and Friend of Human Beings, Not Machines: The Business Career of the Terminology of Social Engineering, 1894–1910," *Ideas in History* II.2 (2007) 48.

[78] Popper does, however, accept a more limited model of what he termed "piecemeal engineering" to deal with specific points of social policy. See Karl Popper, *The Open Society and Its Enemies: Volume One—The Spell of Plato* (New York: Routledge, 2008—originally published, 1945), 166–7, 174.

[79] Christopher R. Browning and Lewis H. Siegelbaum, "Frameworks for Social Engineering: Stalinist Schema of Identification and the Nazi Volksgemeinschaft," in Michael

These negative glosses on social engineering, however, can obscure important aspects of its earlier usage that were combined with idealistic agendas for the betterment of both communities and individual human lives. The earliest noted reference to "social engineers" (in the writings of the Dutch industrialist J.C. van Marken) emphasized the development of technical expertise in the "management" of "specifically human problems."[80] The influential Swedish academic Gunnar Myrdal explicitly introduced the values of "modern social democratic political ambitions"[81] to determine the direction of social engineering, proclaiming (in 1944), that "[w]e have today in social science a greater trust in the improvability of man and society than we have ever had since the Enlightenment."[82]

It should be noted here, however, that the tone of social engineering agendas was not exclusively secular, particularly in the United States where in the early twentieth century, a number of would-be social engineers also figured as "socio-religious uplifters" with support from "Christian Sociologists" such as Edwin Earp[83] and links to the (largely Protestant) Social Gospel movement through figures such as Josiah Strong.[84] Over the first half of the twentieth century, Roman Catholics in the United States were also developing their own visions of how faith commitments and the moral ideals they were understood to imply could be effectively mobilized in the service of agendas for social change—expressed in terms of the Church's "social mission."[85] Drawing on Pope Leo XIII's 1891 encyclical *Rerum Novarum*, the American Fr. John Ryan spearheaded the development of a "Program for Social Reconstruction" that contributed to the subsequent development of both the Catholic Worker movement during the Great Depression, and the New Deal policies of the American welfare state.[86]

Geyer and Sheila Fitzpatrick (eds.), *Beyond Totalitarianism: Stalinism and Nazism Compared* (New York: Cambridge University Press, 2009), 231–65.

80 Östlund, "A Knower and Friend," 66–74.

81 Johan Strang, "Overcoming the Rift Between 'Is' and 'Ought': Gunnar Myrdal and the Philosophy of Social Engineering," *Ideas in History* II.2 (2007) 144.

82 Gunnar Myrdal, *An American Dilemma: The Negro Problem and Modern Democracy* (New York: Harper and Brothers, 1944), 1023–24; cit. Strang, "Overcoming the Rift," 186.

83 Edwin L. Earp, *The Social Engineer* (New York: Eaton and Mains, 1911).

84 See Marklund, "Adjusting Facts and Values," 27–8; and Östlund, "A Knower and Friend," 63–5, 79–80.

85 Charles E. Curran, *The Social Mission of the U.S. Catholic Church: A Theological Perspective* (Washington DC: Georgetown University Press, 2011), 15–40.

86 Mark Massa, with Catherine Osborne, *American Catholic History: A Reader* (New York: NYU Press, 2008), 139–46; Marta Cook and John Halpin, "The Role of Faith in the Progressive Movement," (Washington DC: Center for American Progress, 2010), 9. <http://www.americanprogress.org/wp-content/uploads/issues/2010/10/pdf/progressive_traditions6.pdf>, accessed 22 August 2012.

More specific conceptions of law as a tool of social engineering have a further complex history in modern Western thought, ranging across discussions of political ideology and policy planning, as well as of jurisprudence. The broad scope of these discussions parallel, in a provocative way, contemporary discourses on Shariʿa among reform-minded Muslims in Aceh and elsewhere. In both cases, discussions of rules, norms, and social change extend well beyond the limits of black-letter law and formal legal institutions. In his introduction to the English translation of Ehrlich's *Grundlegung der Soziologie des Rechts*, the American philosopher of law Roscoe Pound called attention to the importance of established relations of family and community in the production and maintenance of social order.[87] Pound's own writings take into consideration diverse and overlapping interests while also emphasizing the need for religion and conceptions of morality to support law's work in engineering the creation of a just society.[88] Pound maintained that well beyond dealing with breaches of particular legal rules, judicial and administrative processes "have a function of guidance as well,"[89] and in fact, saw legal history as the record of "a continually more efficacious social engineering."[90] His conception of law in relation to social change was, however, far from radical, and might be better characterized as adaptive and realist, rather than idealistic and transformative. As one of his intellectual biographers has phrased it, conceptions of "organicism" played a major role in limiting the degree to which Pound's vision of the sociology of law could be placed in service of legal instrumentalism.[91] Later studies of Pound's jurisprudence have also noted the considerable divergence between his own views on law as social engineering and the uses to which the idea was put by later jurists and philosophers.[92]

Pound's work and its later creative (mis)appropriations are directly relevant to developments in Indonesian legal discourse, both Muslim and non-. As noted earlier, the English-language term "social engineering" appears to have been first introduced into Indonesian discussions of legal change through Pound's *Introduction to the Philosophy of Law*, which

[87] Roscoe Pound, "Introduction," in Ehrlich, *Fundamental Principles*, xxxiii.

[88] Although this approach to law is mentioned in many of Pound's writings, the most sustained treatment can be found in Roscoe Pound, *Social Control through Law* (New Haven: Yale University Press, 1942).

[89] See, for example, Roscoe Pound, "Sociology of Law and Sociological Jurisprudence," *The University of Toronto Law Journal* 5(1) (1943) 15.

[90] Roscoe Pound, *An Introduction to the Philosophy of Law* (New Haven: Yale University Press, 1955), 47.

[91] David Wigdor, *Roscoe Pound: Philosopher of Law* (Westport, CT: Greenwood Press, 1974), 207–32.

[92] Edward B. McLean, *Law and Civilization: The Legal Thought of Roscoe Pound* (Lanham, MD: University Press of America, 1992), 302–11.

initially appeared in Indonesian translation in 1963. It has been reprinted at least once every decade ever since.[93] Over this period, Pound's sociological jurisprudence was reinterpreted by Indonesian jurists as the foundation of what came to be referred to as "Development Law Theory" (I. *Teori Hukum Pembangunan*).[94] The idea of law as a tool of social engineering thus came to be deployed in the service of more pro-active programs of state-directed development, often in the form of the kind of hard legal instrumentalism to which Pound himself was generally opposed. There were, however, also important continuities in the Indonesian adoption of aspects of Pound's sociological jurisprudence, particularly in the recognition of the importance of cultural norms in informing the broader contexts for law in society. In light of this, he called for more serious engagement with "the whole field of social control which may be achieved by adjustment of human relations and ordering of human conduct through the action of politically organized society."[95] The continuing legacy of this vision of law and society is clearly evident in the ways that the contemporary project of Shari'a social engineering in Aceh works through education and "socialization" to pursue its aims well beyond the sphere of formal legal institutions.

Close connections between law, education and social order have, of course, had a long and complex course of development in the histories of Muslim societies extending back to the classical period. During the nineteenth century, some modernizing Muslim rulers undertook new patterns of intervention into legal education that facilitated transformations that Wael Hallaq has characterized as "fundamental and everlasting changes in the legal system."[96] Since that time, new models of both law and education imported from the West have had a transformative impact on the ways in which Muslims in many parts of the world understand Islam, the Shari'a, and its function in society.[97]

[93] In the Indonesian translation, the term "social engineering" is given in its original English form and glossed as: "*suatu usaha jang terus-menurus makin berguna untuk pembangunan masjarakat, dengan menerapkan hukum-hukum dan sosiologis jang telah ditetapkan untuk mentjapai tudjuan-tudjuan sosial yang chusus dan diakui.*" Roscoe Pound, *Pengantar Filsafat Hukum* (Jakarta: Bhratara, 1963), 66.

[94] Sidharta, "Posisi Pemikiran Teori Hukum Pembangunan dalam Konfigurasi Aliran Pemikiran Hukum (sebuah diagnosis awal)," in Shidarta (ed.), *Mochtar Kusuma-Atmadja dan Teori Hukum Pembangunan: Eksistensi dan Implikasi* (Jakarta: Epistema Institute, 2012), 9–80.

[95] Roscoe Pound, *The Ideal Element in Law—Tagore Law Lectures, 1948* (Calcutta: Calcutta University Press, 1958), 179.

[96] Hallaq, *Sharīʿa*, 135.

[97] On the diverse transformative effects of modern styles of education in Muslim societies, see Dale F. Eickelman, *Knowledge and Power in Morocco: The Education of a Twentieth Century Notable* (Princeton: Princeton University Press, 1985); and the essays collected in Robert W. Hefner and Muhammad Qasim Zaman (eds.), *Schooling Islam: The Culture and Politics of Modern Muslim Education* (Princeton: Princeton University Press, 2007). I have

With a surge in social and political and social activism across the Muslim world since the late twentieth century, schools and other educational programs have played an important role in defining and disseminating popular understandings of Islamic law in contemporary society. These aspects of the "Islamic Trend" have been discussed by Gregory Starrett with particular reference to the function of state educational institutions employed in projects of social engineering: "Having a captive audience, the school represents an ideal laboratory for social engineering, particularly if the knowledge imparted to children is taken home to their families."[98] If this is true for the Egyptian day schools studied by Starrett, then all the more so for Acehnese *dayah*—the local Islamic "boarding schools," which have been described by local supporters of the Shariʿa system as "24-hour laboratories for socialization."[99]

STATE SHARIʿA AND SOCIAL CHANGE

The central focus of the state Shariʿa project as articulated by those directly involved with its design and operation is often expressed in terms of "social engineering" through law. The institutions developed for the administration of Islamic law in contemporary Aceh have, however, often been most active outside of the formal legal sphere. Instead the Ulama Council, the State Shariʿa Agency, and the Wilayatul Hisbah have dedicated much of their limited resources to programs for the "socialization" of Islamic religious values and norms of social behavior. While the development of new legislation has stalled and the number of cases involving existing *qanun* comprise only a small fraction of the caseload of the Shariʿa Courts, state Shariʿa as a project of public education has had effects at the levels of both individual behavior and social life that are potentially more enduring than the passing of any specific piece of legislation, the establishment of any particular governmental agency, or the ephemeral electoral victory of a political party. This in fact appears to have been the very intention of the architects of this project of social engineering, recalling a crucial point from the twentieth-century Western legal and philosophical discourses that informed the historical development of Indonesian understandings of sociological jurisprudence.

discussed the impact of modern educational reforms on Indonesian understandings of Islamic law at length in *Muslim Legal Thought*.

[98] Gregory Starrett, *Putting Islam to Work: Education, Politics and Religious Transformation in Egypt* (Berkeley: University of California Press, 1998), 116.

[99] See, for example, Hasbi Amiruddin, *Menatap Masa Depan Dayah di Aceh* (Banda Aceh: Yayasan Pena, 2008), 21.

As Roscoe Pound expressed it in his introduction to Ehrlich's major work on "living law," "the inner order maintained by the rules of conduct recognized and generally followed as binding . . . function notwithstanding the dissolution of a political order."[100]

This is not to deny that there are important factors involved with the formal state apparatus at work here, including manipulations of elite politics at various levels. As other observers of contemporary Aceh have already devoted extensive discussion to such issues, this study has aimed not to reproduce, but rather to complement that existing and expanding body of work. My intention here has been to open some new space for discussions of the implementation of Islamic law in contemporary Aceh that take into account some of the broader religious, intellectual, and cultural developments that inform it. For while the politics of the conflict between GAM and the Indonesian central government provided the opportunity for advocates of the Islamization of law to promote their agenda and gain access to new state resources, this political context did not itself determine the broader social aims and substantive content of Islamic law in contemporary Aceh. Underlying the form and function of the Islamic legal system is a complex history of evolving understandings of Shariʿa and society that has yet to receive the attention it deserves in international scholarship.

As an abstraction of ideals of social justice, communal harmony, public morality, and personal piety, the concept of "Shariʿa" allows for a considerable range of understandings and interpretations.[101] In different contexts, it has thus come to be deployed in support of myriad social and political agendas, ranging from conservative to radical, repressive to emancipatory. The particular case of Aceh discussed here presents a project of state Shariʿa implementation in which the elaboration of *daʿwa* agendas for religious and social reform that had taken shape in the twentieth century came to be amplified and reconfigured through complex engagements with elements of western sociological jurisprudence and with global discourses on reconstruction and development introduced to Aceh by different international organizations in the post-disaster/post-conflict period. Mapping the diverse and multi-vectored developments of modern Muslim thinking about law and society makes it

[100] Pound, "Introduction," xxxiii.

[101] As noted, for example, in the context of the state implementation of Islamic law in Pakistan even when local Muslims were critical of particular government Islamization programs, they were not adverse to the concept of Shariʿa as such—seeing Islam as "a symbol of the good, the correct, the moral, and the right." Richard Kurin, "Islamization: A View from the Countryside," in Anita M. Weiss (ed.), *Islamic Reassertion in Pakistan: The Application of Islamic Laws in a Modern State* (New York: Syracuse University Press, 1986), 115–28.

clear that conventional wisdom on calls for the implementation of Islamic law as expressions of identity politics and/or atavistic dreams of a return to the time of the Prophet is insufficient to understand the complexity and dynamism of evolving understandings of Shariʿa and society in the contemporary world. Instead we need to devote more careful and critical attention to the particular forms and contents of expressions of Islamic law, as well as to the specific contexts in which they are made in modern Muslim societies.

The case of state Shariʿa in post-disaster/post-conflict Aceh presents an extraordinary case in which to examine both the aspirational extent of and the practical limits to the application of Islamic law as a state-directed project of social engineering. This book has explored the ways in which various state Shariʿa institutions have developed and pursued this agenda, presenting in the process a fine-grained picture of both the structural design and the everyday work of one of the most complex experiments with the implementation of Islamic law in the contemporary world. As noted in the previous chapters, however, the state Shariʿa project in Aceh has not met with the success for which its supporters have hoped. At one level, this should, perhaps, come as no surprise given both the broad ambitions of the project and the reality of the time lag that characterizes any effort at using legal reform to foster new public attitudes and patterns of behavior.[102] The situation is, moreover, far more complicated than just that.

Aceh is today home to a particularly vibrant public sphere in which diverse sectors of Acehnese society advance a range of contesting visions for the future of state and society in Aceh.[103] Popular opprobrium for the enforcement measures of the WH and the political resistance of various parties to expanding the scope of state Shariʿa have marked significant limits to the ability of state Shariʿa institutions to control the direction of social change over recent years. While some critics argue that the Islamic legal system is simply in need of calibrated reform in order to make it more effective and beneficial to society, others see the entire project as fundamentally flawed. Such critics espouse rather different visions of

[102] Commenting on such attempts with the administration of Islamic law in modern Egypt, Ron Shaham has remarked: "The effects of legal reform are not immediately seen because a long period of time has to pass until the public internalizes new modes of behavior." See *Family and the Courts in Modern Egypt: A Study Based on Decisions by the Sharīʿa Courts, 1900–1955* (Leiden: Brill, 1997), 235.

[103] For studies of the persistence, resistance, and reconfigurations of various "unofficial" expressions and experiences of Islam in contemporary Aceh, see R. Michael Feener, David Kloos, and Annemarie Samuels (eds.), *Islam and the Limits of the State: Reconfigurations of Ritual, Doctrine, Community, and Authority in Contemporary Aceh* (Leiden: Brill, forthcoming).

Figure 9.2. Erecting the infrastructure of a modern Islam in East Aceh, symbolized by the concrete forms of construction projects to replace older mosques with new ones. Ambitious—but often stalled—mosque-building programs have made unfinished structures on recently cleared building sites a common sight across the province today. (Photo by R. Michael Feener)

Aceh's future through arguments expressed in non-confessional terms of rights, equality, and good governance rather than in terms of Shariʿa norms of public morality. The idea of implementing Islamic law as a project of social engineering is thus an important—but far from the only—vision of the future for Aceh's Muslim community, and the work of reconstituting society in the post-disaster/post-conflict period remains unfinished.

APPENDIX I

Abbreviations and Glossary

The terms below are from Indonesian/Malay (I.) except where specifically noted as Acehnese (Ac.); Arabic (Ar.); Dutch (D.); Japanese (Jp.); Javanese (Jv.); or Ottoman Turkish (OT).

ABRI	Angkatan Bersenjata Republik Indonesia/The Indonesian Armed Forces
adat	local custom
algojo	officer tasked with carrying out caning penalties for those convicted of offenses against state Shariʿa in Aceh
ARI	Asia Research Institute, National University of Singapore
BAPPENAS	Badan Perencanaan Pembangunan Nasional/ National Development Planning Agency
BKI	Bijdragen tot de Taal-, Land-, en Volkenkude
BRR	Badan Rehabilitasidan Rekonstruksi/Rehabilitation and Reconstruction Agency
BSOAS	Bulletin of the School of Oriental and African Studies
bupati	district head
CoHA	Cessation of Hostilities Agreement
Daerah Istimewa	Special Region
dakwah (Ar. *daʿwa*)	Islamic religious propagation
Darul Islam	armed insurrection against the Indonesian Republic to establish Aceh as an Islamic state
dayah (Ac.)	Acehnese religious boarding school
DDII	Dewan Dakwah Islamiyah Indonesia
desa percontohan	"model village"
dhikr (Ar.)	Sufi ritual "remembrance" of God
DI	Darul Islam
Dinas Syariat Islam	State Shariʿa Agency
DPRA	Dewan Perwakilan Rakyat Aceh/Aceh Provincial Legislative Assembly
DSI	Dinas Syariat Islam/State Shariʿa Agency

fiqh (Ar.)	Islamic jurisprudence
GAM	Gerakan Aceh Merdeka/Free Aceh Movement
gampong (Ac.)	village
GBHN	Garis-Garis Besar Haluan Negara/Main Outlines of National Direction
geucik (Ac.)	village head
GUPPI	Gabungan Usaha Perbaikan Pendidikan Islam
ḥajj	Muslim pilgrimage to Mecca
HDC	Henri Dunant Centre
HMI	Himpunan Mahasiswa Islam
HRW	Human Rights Watch
HTI	Hizbut Tahrir Indonesia
HUDA	Himpunan Ulama Dayah Aceh
ḥudūd (Ar. s. *ḥadd*)	stipulated Qurʾānic punishments for crimes against Islamic law
IAIN	Institut Agama Islam Indonesia/State Islamic Studies Institute
ICAIOS	International Center for Aceh and Indian Ocean Studies (Banda Aceh)
ICG	International Crisis Group
ijtihād (Ar.)	independent jurisprudential reasoning
imeum meunasah (Ac.)	village-level religious leader
ITB	Institut Teknologi Bandung/Bandung Institute of Technology
Jaksa	Public Prosecutor
Jawi	Malay written in a modified form of the Arabic script
jilbab	Muslim women's headscarf
JMBRAS	Journal of the Malaysian Branch, Royal Asiatic Society
JRAS	Journal of the Royal Asiatic Society
JSEAH	Journal of Southeast Asian History
kabupaten	district
kaluët (Ac.)	Sufi ritual withdrawal for meditiation and prayer
KAMMI	Kesatuan AksiMahasiswa Muslim Indonesia
kecamatan	sub-district
khalwat	inappropriate association between marriagable men and women

KHI	Kompilasi Hukum Islam/Compilation of Islamic Laws
LOGA	Law on Governing Aceh
LRRD	Linking Relief, Rehabilitation and Development
MA	Mahkamah Agung (Indonesian Supreme Court)
MAA	Majlis Adat Aceh/Aceh State Adat Council
madhhab (Ar.)	established "school" of Islamic jurisprudence
Mahkamah Syariah	Shariʿa Court
Majelis Ulama	Council of Ulama
meunasah (Ac.)	traditional village institution, used for basic Islamic education, prayer, and other communal functions
MPU	Majelis Permusyawaratan Ulama/Aceh's Ulama Council
MS	Mahkamah Syariah/Shariʿa Court
muhtasib desa	village-level officer for the enforcement of Islamic law
MUI	Majelis Ulama Indonesia/Indonesian National Ulama Council
MUNA	Majelis Ulama Nanggroe Aceh
NAD	Nanggroe Aceh Darussalam/State of Aceh, Abode of Peace
New Order	the authoritarian developmentalist state in Indonesia under Suharto (1965–1998)
NGO	Non-Governmental Organization
NU	Nadhlatul Ulama
NUS	National University of Singapore
PA	Partai Aceh
Partai Aceh	Provincial political party led by former GAM members
PBB	Partai Bulan Bintang/Crescent and Star Party
Pengadilan Agama	Religious Court
perang sabi (Ac.)	"holy war"
Perda	Peraturan Daerah/Regional Regulation
Perti	Pergerakan Tarbijah Islamijah
pesantren (Jv.)	traditional Islamic boarding school
PKI	Partai Komunis Indonesia/Indonesian Communist Party
PKS	Partai Keadilan Sejahtera/Prosperity and Justice Party
pl.	plural

PN	Pegawai Negeri/Civil Servant
PPNS	Penyidik Pegawai Negeri Sipil/Civil Service Investigator
PTAIN	Perguruan Tinggi Agama Islam Negeri/State Islamic Junior College
PUSA	Persantuan Ulama Seluruh Aceh/ All Aceh Union of Ulama
qāḍī (Ar.)	Shariʿa court judge
qanun (OT *qanūn*)	term used for regional regulations, including Islamic legislation in contemporary Aceh
rangkang (Ac.)	"pavillion" at a traditional Islamic religious school in Aceh
Reformasi	the post-New Order period of "Reform" in Indonesia
Replita	Rencana Pembangunan Lima Tahun/Five Year Development Plan
RTA	Rabithah Taliban Aceh
s.	singular
Sehülislam (OT)	highest ranking Islamic scholar in the Ottoman Empire
Shūkyō hōin (Jp.)	Shariʿa Court system established under the Japanese wartime occupation of Indonesia
SIRA	Sentral Informasi Referendum Aceh
sosialisasi	term commonly used in connection with projects for the public promotion of state Shariʿa
STAIN	Sekolah Tinggi Agama Islam Negeri/Indonesian State Islamic Studies Junior College
suluk	Sufi ritual practice
syiar (Ar. *shiʿār*)	"symbolism" of Islam
T.	Teuku
tarbiya (Ar.)	education
taʿzīr (Ar.)	discretionary punishments administered by state authorities for infractions against Islamic law
Teuku (Ac.)	Title traditionally used by the Acehnese landed aristocracy
Teungku (Ac.)	Title used by Acehnese ulama
Tgk.	Teungku
ulama (Ar. *ʿulamāʾ*)	an Islamic religious scholar; in Indonesia, this Arabic plural form is also used to refer to an individual scholar
ulèëbalang (Ac.)	the traditional Acehnese landed aristocracy

umat (Ar. *umma*)	Islamic community
VOC	Verenigde Oost-Indische Compagnie/Dutch East India Company
waḥdat al-wujūd (Ar.)	Sufi doctrine of the "Unity of Being"
WH	Wilayatul Hisbah
Wilayatul Hisbah	Aceh's "Shari'a Police"
yayasan	foundation
YICM	Yayasan Insan Cita Madani
zakāt (Ar.)	Islamic religious almsgiving
zinā (Ar.)	fornication

APPENDIX II

Chronology of Events[1]

1873	First Dutch invasion of Aceh
1903	Surrender of last sultan, Muhammad Daud Syah and the leadership of the Acehnese resistance to the Dutch
1919	The Dutch colonial administration establishes an Advisory Board of Ulama in Aceh
1939	Foundation of PUSA unites reform istulamaunder Daud Buereueh
1942	Members of the "Fujiwara Kikan" associated with PUSA help to prepare the groundwork for the Japanese invasion of Aceh
1944	Japanese wartime occupation administration establishes a system of Islamic religious courts in Aceh
1945	Japanese surrender to Allied Powers at the end of WWII Indonesian independence declared at Jakarta
1946	Violent "Social Revolution" ends *ulèëbalang* authority in Aceh
1947	Daud Beureueh, then serving as Indonesia's military governor of Aceh, extends state control over Acehnese *madrasas*
1948	Republican Sumatra formally divided into three Provinces, making Aceh nominally part of North Sumatra
1949	Indonesian Vice Premier Sjafruddin Prawiranegara authorizes the establishment of Aceh Province
1951	Aceh merged back into the province of North Sumatra
1953	Daud Beureueh proclaims Aceh part of the Negara Islam Indonesia (NII), launching the Darul Islam movement of armed conflict with the Indonesian Republic
1957	Aceh re-established as a province, with Ali Hasjmy appointed as governor
	New provincial regulation of Aceh's Shari'a Courts
1959	Negotiations lead to end of Darul Islam rebellion, in return for "Special Area" status. These provisions granted Aceh a greater degree of control over the administration of religion, custom and education. Daud Beureueh himself, however, refuses to submit until 1962
1960	Founding of the Faculty of Shari'a at the State Institute for Islamic Studies (IAIN) Ar-Raniry in Banda Aceh
1961	Passage of local by-laws limiting the sale and consumption of alcohol in Aceh
1963	Passage of provincial legislation on "Syiar Islam"

[1] This timeline of Aceh history builds upon a chronology of events prepared by Michelle Ann Miller and Anthony Reid for *Verandah of Violence: The Background to the Aceh Problem* (Singapore: NUS Press, 2006). I would like to thank them both for their generous permission to draw upon their work here.

1965	Coup attempt against Army leadership; General Suharto seizes control in Jakarta; massacres of communists across Indonesia, including in Aceh
1965	Founding of Aceh's Ulama Council
1966	Suharto replaces Sukarno as President; beginning of the New Order period
1968	Founding at Banda Aceh of the first Faculty of Dakwah in the Indonesian IAIN system
	Provincial bill on the implementation of "Elements of Shariʿa Law" struck down by the Indonesian Interior Minister
1971	Mobil discovers natural gas in North Aceh; Production begins 1977
1973	Indonesia's "Main Outlines of National Direction" (GBHN) calls for the use of law as a "tool" in the service of national development
1974	Passage of a new Indonesian code of Muslim marriage law; expanding the role of Islamic Religious Courts
1974–79	Indonesia's second Five Year Development Plan (Replita II) further stipulates the importance of law as part of national development projects
1976	Hassan Di Tiro declares "the independence of Aceh, Sumatra" thus launching the Free Aceh Movement (GAM)
1977	Beginning of counter-insurgency operations by the Indonesian armed forces
1979	Hassan di Tiro leaves Aceh; much of GAM's leadership is killed or fled to Malaysia
1982	Ali Hasjmy becomes head of Aceh's Ulama Council
1985	Indonesian national regulation recognizes the appointment of female Shariʿa Court judges
1987–89	GAM fighters obtain military training in Libya
1989	GAM begins serious strikes against the Indonesian military in Aceh, prompting strong retaliation and a further escalation of violence
1989	Major reforms of Indonesia's Islamic court system outlined in the Religious Judicature Act
1990–91	Indonesian military advances push much of GAM's leadership into exile abroad
1991	Presidential Instruction on the *Compilation of Islamic Law*
1998	Suharto forced to resign, thus ending the New Order and the beginning of a new period of "Reform" (I. *Reformasi*)
	B.J. Habibie becomes Indonesia's new president, after which he agreed to a referendum on independence for East Timor and called for a de-escalation of violence in Aceh
1999	Mounting campaign for a referendum on independence for Aceh; instead a Special Autonomy Law was passed with provisions for the implementation of Islamic law
	Abdurrahman Wahid becomes President
2000	Henri Dunant Centre begins work on the peace process between GAM and Jakarta
	Passage of first substantive Regional Regulation on the administration of Islamic law in Aceh

2001	Megawati becomes President and signs the Nanggroe Aceh Darussalam (NAD) Autonomy Law, which came into effect 2002.
2002	Peace talks resume in Geneva; Cessation of Hostilities Agreement (CoHA) signed
2002	Passing of new *qanun* on Islamic religious observance
2003	Governor Abdullah Puteh indicted for corruption
	Susilo Bambang Yudhoyono becomes president
	New *qanun* passed on gambling, alcohol, and *khalwat*
2004	Massive earthquake and tsunami strikes Aceh, killing thousands
	Foreign disaster relief and reconstruction agencies begin arriving in Aceh
2005	Peace agreement in Helsinki between GAM leadership and Indonesian Government
	First application of caning punishments for violations of Aceh's *qanun*
2006	Acehnese autonomy restructured with the Law on Governing Aceh (LOGA)
	Former GAM figure Irwandi Yusuf elected as governor
2007	Aceh's Ulama Council fatwa on "deviant teachings"
2009	Partai Aceh, headed by former GAM members and supporters, obtains a plurality of seats in the Provincial Legislative Assembly
	Passing of a Shariʿa Criminal Code (*Qanun Jinaya*) by the outgoing, Golkar-dominated Provincial Legislative Assembly
2010	District-level regulation on modest Muslim dress passed in West Aceh
2012	Former GAM affiliate Zaini Abdullah becomes governor after the electoral defeat of incumbent Irwandi Yusuf

APPENDIX III

Key Analytical Terms[1]

Basic Epistemological Distinctions

Traditionalism	Acceptance of the four Sunni Schools of Law (*madhhabs*) as valid guides to knowing Islam. Traditionalism usually recognizes that these legal traditions are subject to change and redefinition. It commonly involves tolerance towards locally derived cultural expressions, acceptance of Sufism, and a gradualist approach toward Islamization.
Traditionalist	One who, or that which, adheres to Traditionalism
Modernism	An approach to knowing Islam which denies that the four Sunni Schools of Law are authoritative guides and which relies fundamentally upon human reason in understanding revelation. This commonly involves a disregard for socio-historical contexts but openness to modern learning as a way of enhancing the power of reason. It is principally opposed to what it sees as the medieval obscurantism of Traditionalism, may reject local cultural expressions, and is at least suspicious of Sufism.
Modernist	One who, or that which, embraces Modernism
Revivalism	An approach to knowing Islam which denies that the four Sunni Schools of Law are authoritative guides and which aspires to revive a pristine universal Islam as in the time of the Prophet and his Companions. Its epistemology rests on cognition of Revelation as found in the Qur'ān and *ḥadīth* through divine guidance. Revivalism normally distrusts the application of human reason and denies that understandings of revelation may legitimately change over time or that Islam may evolve in changing socio-historical contexts. It commonly rejects local cultural expressions and regards Sufismas a source of heresy.
Revivalist	One who, or that which, adheres to Revivalism

[1] These analytical terms and their definitions grew from discussions over several months with colleagues in a research project at the National University of Singapore, in which Prof. M.C. Ricklefs was Principal Investigator, and I was co-PI. Chaider Bamualim was also involved. Several colleagues at NUS and overseas also gave valuable comments and suggestions for these terms. These terms and definitions are also outlined and employed in M.C. Ricklefs, *Islamisation and its Opponents in Java, c. 1930 to the Present* (Singapore: NUS Press, 2012), 514–16.

Socio-Religious Process

Islamism	A project whose principal locus of activity is the state. It seeks a more perfect political order by establishing state institutions and/or controlling existing ones so as to impose deeper Islamization, achieve greater justice, and safeguard the integrity of the Muslim community. Islamism is most commonly associated with Modernist and Revivalist thought and sometimes (but not necessarily) validates the use of force to achieve its objectives. It usually seeks social conformity and, where it is tolerant of other faiths, normally expects them to accept a position subordinate to Islamic dominance.
Islamist	One who, or that which, embraces Islamism
Da'wa	A project whose principal locus of activity is at the level of the society. It seeks a more perfect social order by actively propagating what it regards as a correct understanding of the faith, its moral standards, and its ritual obligations.
Liberalism	A project whose principal locus of activity is the individual. It seeks greater individual freedom in religious and other matters, so long as no harm is done to the rights of others. Liberalism is found amongst Traditionalists and Modernists, but is rare among Revivalists. It is generally suspicious of the role of government in religious affairs and opposed to the use of force in any context. It commonly prioritizes associated values such as social and gender equality, freedom of thought, interfaith harmony, social pluralism, and economic progress.
Liberal	One who, or that which, embraces Liberalism

Social and Political Projects

Islamization	A process of deepening commitment to standards of normative Islamic belief, practice, and religious identity. Those standards are subject to contestation among groups and individuals. Islamization as an objective is associated with all of the epistemological approaches described previously.

References

1. Archives

Arsip Propinsi Aceh (Aceh Provincial Archives, Banda Aceh).

Koninklijk Instituut voor Taal-, Land- en Volkenkunde (KITLV Library, Leiden).

2. Bibliography

10 Tahun Darussalam dan Hari Pendidikan (Banda Aceh: Yayasan Pembina Darussalam, 1969).

"10 Tips Meningkatkan Kemampuan Sosialisasi Anda ala Dale Carnegie," <http://www.scribd.com/doc/5593201/Dale-Carnegie-Tips>, accessed 29 March 2012,

Abdul Aziz, Imam Tholkhah, and Soetarman S. (eds.), *Gerakan Islam Kontemporer di Indonesia* (Jakarta: Pustaka Firdaus, 1989).

Abidin Nurdin, "Ulama dan Proses Legislasi: Mengkaji Legitimasi Lembaga Ulama Aceh," in Arskal Salim and Adlin Sila (eds.), *Serambi Mekkah yang Berubah: Views from Within* (Jakarta: Pustaka Alvabet, 2010), 93–120.

Abu-Manneh, Butrus, "Khalwa and Rabita in the Khalidi Order," in M. Gaborieau, A. Popovic, and T. Zarcone (eds.), *Naqshbandis: cheminements et situation actuelle d'un order mystique musulman* (Istanbul: Éd. Isis, 1990), 283–302.

Abubakar Atjeh, "Kebangkitan dunia baru Islam di Indonesia," in Lothrop Stoddard, *Dunia baru Islam* [Indonesian translation of *The New World of Islam*] (Jakarta: Panitia Penerbit, 1966), 295–332.

Aceh Tanah Rencong (Banda Aceh: Pemerintah Provinsi Nanggroe Aceh Darussalam, 2008).

Achmad Zaini, "Mawdudi's Conception of the Islamic State," in *Islam and Development: A Politico-Religious Response* (Yogyakarta: Permika Montreal, 1997), 163–99.

Achyar Zein, "Kriteria Tindak Pidana Dalam Al-Qur'an," Ph.D. dissertation (Banda Aceh: Institut Agama Islam Negeri Ar-Raniry Darussalam, 2010).

Affan Ramli, *Merajam Dalil Syariat* (Banda Aceh: Bandar Publishing, 2010).

Aguswandi, and Judith Large (eds.), Reconfiguring Politics: The Indonesia–Aceh Peace Process, special issue of *Accord: An International Review of Peace Initiatives* 20(2008). <http://www.c-r.org/accord-article/reconfiguring-politics-indonesia-aceh-peace-process>, accessed 30 July 2012.

Ahmad Fuad Effendi, Amir Hamzah Wiryosukarto, et al., *K.H. Imam Zarkasyi dari Gontor: Merintis Pesantren Modern* (Ponorogo: Gontor Press, 1996).

Alaiddin Koto, *Pemikiran Politik Perti* (Persatuan Tarbiyah Islamiyah), 1945–1970 (Jakarta: Nimas Multima, 1997).

Alam, Muzaffar, and Sanjay Subrahmanyam, *Writing the Mughal World: Studies on Culture and Politics* (New York: Columbia University Press, 2012).

Alfian, "The Ulama in Acehnese Society," in Ahmad Ibrahim, Sharon Siddique, and Yasmin Hussain (eds.), *Readings on Islam in Southeast Asia* (Singapore: Institute of Southeast Asian Studies, 1985), 82–6.

Ali Saifullah HA, "Darussalaam: Pondok Modern Gontor," in *Pesantren dan Pembaharuan* (Jakarta: LP3ES, 1985), 134–54.

Ali Yafie, "Doktrin Fiqh dalam Program Kependudukan," in *Teologi Sosial: Telaah Kritis Persoalan Agama dan Kemanusiaan* (Yogyakarta: LKPSM, 1997), 29–40.

Alibasjah Talsya, *Sedjarah dan Dokumen-dokumen Pemberontakan di Atjeh* (Jakarta: Penerbit Kesuma, 1955).

Alyasa Abubakar, *Sekilas Syariat Islam di Aceh* (Banda Aceh: Dinas Syariat Islam, 2005).

Alyasa Abubakar, "Pembinaan Generasi Muda dalam Islam," in Azman Ismail (ed.), *Suara Khatib Baiturrahman* (Banda Aceh: Pengurus Masjid Raya Baiturrahman, 2006).

Alyasa Abubakar, *Kajian Undang-Undang Pemerintahan Aceh dan Essay Tentang Perempuan, Perkahwinan dan Perwalian Anak* (Banda Aceh: Dinas Syariat Islam, 2007).

Alyasa Abubakar, *Penerapan Syariat Islam di Aceh: Upaya Penyusunan Fiqih dalam Negara Bangsa* (Banda Aceh: Dinas Syariat Islam, 2008).

Alyasa Abubakar, *Syariʿat Islam di Provinsi Nanggroe Aceh Darussalam: Paradigma, Kebijakan dan Kegiatan* (Banda Aceh: Dinas Syariat Islam, 2003—5th edition, 2008).

Alyasa Abubakar, *Bunga Rampai Pelaksanaan Syariat Islam: Pendukung Qanun Pelaksanaan Syariat Islam* (Banda Aceh: Dinas Syariat Islam Aceh, 2009).

Alyasa Abubakar, *Wilayatul Hisbah: Polisi Pamong Praja dengan Kewenangan Khusus di Aceh* (Banda Aceh: Dinas Syariʿat Islam Provinsi Aceh, 2009).

Alyasa Abubakar, and Marah Halim, *Hukum Pidana Islam di Provinsi Nanggroe Aceh Darussalam* (Banda Aceh: Dinas Syariat Islam, 2006).

Amiruddin Idris, and Wildan, "Pelaksanaan Pendidikan di Kabupaten Bireuen: Tinjauan Historis terhadap Al Muslim Peusangan," in T. H. Thalhas and Choirul Fuad Yusuf (eds.), *Pendidikan dan Syariat Islam di Nanggroe Aceh Darussalam dan 8 Undang-Undang Terkait* (Jakarta: Galura Pase, 2007).

Amirul Hadi, *Islam and State in Sumatra: A Study of Seventeenth-Century Aceh* (Leiden: Brill, 2004).

Amirul Hadi, "Exploring Acehnese Understandings of Jihad: A Study of Hikayat Prang Sabi," in R. Michael Feener, Patrick Daly, and Anthony Reid (eds.), *Mapping the Acehnese Past* (Leiden: KITLV Press, 2011), 183–98.

Amirullah M. Diyah, Mustafa Ahmad, and Azhari Ali, *Pokok Pikiran MPU Aceh Utara* (white paper issued by the North Aceh MPU, 3 February 2006).

Amirullah M. Diyah, "Makalah Peran Majelis Permusyawaratan Ulama dalam Penerapan Syariʿat Islam," unpublished PowerPoint slides presented at the MPU Kab. Aceh Utara, 2009.

Amnesty International, "Indonesian Government Must Repeal Caning Bylaws in Aceh," 22 May 2001, <http://www.amnesty.org/en/news-and-updates/indonesian-government-must-repeal-caning-bylaws-aceh-2011-05-20>, accessed 20 June 2012.

Amnesty International, "Indonesia: Repeal Cruel New Stoning and Caning Law," *Amnesty International Public Statement*, 17 September 2009, <http://www.amnesty.org/en/news-and-updates/news/indonesia-must-repeal-cruel-new-stoning-caning-law-20090917>, accessed 5 July 2012.

Ampuh Devayan, and Murizal Hamzah (eds.), *Polemik Penerapan Syariat Islam di Aceh* (Banda Aceh: YICM, 2007).

Analiansyah, and Jamhuri, *Syariat Islam Di Nanggroe Aceh Darussalam: Inventarisasi Dokumen* (Banda Aceh: Dinas Syariat Islam Provinsi Nanggroe Aceh Darussalam, 2008).

Anas M. Yunus, *Gerakan Kebangkitan Aceh Kumpulan Karya Sejarah M. Junus Djamil* (Bandung: Bina Biladi Press, 2009).

Andaya, Leonard, *Leaves of the Same Tree: Trade and Ethnicity in the Straits of Melaka* (Honolulu: University of Hawai'i Press, 2008).

Anderson, J.N.D., "Law as a Social Force in Islamic Culture and History," *Bulletin of the School of Oriental and African Studies* 20.1/3 (1957) 13–40.

Andi Mahdi (ed.), *Polemik Penerapan Syariat Islam di Aceh* (Banda Aceh: Yayasan Insan Cita Madani, 2007).

Arabi, Oussama, *Studies in Modern Islamic Law and Jurisprudence* (The Hague: Kluwer Law International, 2001).

Arfiansyah, "The Politicization of Shariʿah: Behind the Implementation of Shariʿah in Aceh, Indonesia," Ph.D. dissertation (Montreal: McGill University, 2010).

Arief Subhan, "Jamʿiyat Istijmāʿ al-juhūd li iṣlāḥ al-tarbiyya al-Islāmiyya (GUPPI): Tajdīd fī al-tarbiyya al-Islāmiyya ʿan ṭarīq al-siyāsa," *Studia Islamika* 5(3) (1998) 129–54.

Arief Subhan, "The Indonesian Madrasah: Islamic Reform and Modernization of Indonesian Islam in the Twentieth Century," in Azyumardi Azra, Kees van Dijk, and Nico J.G. Kaptein (eds.), *Varieties of Religious Authority: Changes and Challenges in 20th Century Indonesian Islam* (Singapore: Institute of Southeast Asian Studies, 2010), 127–38.

Arifin, M.T., *Gagasan Pembaharuan Muhammadiyah dalam Pendidikan* (Jakarta: Pustaka Jaya, 1987).

Armia Ibrahim, *Proses Hukum Terhadap Pelanggaran Qanun-Qanun Syariʿat Islam* (Aceh: Bahan Pembekalan Qanun-Qanun Syariʿat Islam Bagi Ulama/Tokoh Perempuan se Kota Banda Aceh, 2010).

Arskal Salim, "Epilogue: Shariʿa in Indonesia's Current Transition: An Update," in Arskal Salim and Azyumardi Azra (eds.), *Shariʿa and Politics in Modern Indonesia* (Singapore: ISEAS, 2003).

Arskal Salim, "Muslim Politics in Indonesia's Democratisation: The Religious Majority and the Rights of Minorities in the Post-New Order Era," in Ross

McLeod and Andrew MacIntyre (eds.), *Indonesia: Democracy and the Promise of Good Governance* (Singapore: ISEAS Press, 2007), 115–27.

Arskal Salim, *Challenging the Secular State: The Islamization of Law in Modern Indonesia* (Honolulu: University of Hawai'i Press, 2008).

Arskal Salim, *Politics, Criminal Justice and Islamisation in Aceh* (Melbourne: Melbourne Law School Asian Law Centre, 2009), <http://www.lindseyfederation.law.unimelb.edu.au>, accessed 2 February 2011.

al-Āshī, Ismāʿīl b. ʿAbd al-Muṭṭalib, *Jamʿ jawāmiʿ al-muṣannafāt* (Cairo: Muṣṭafā al-Bābī al-Halabī, 1925).

al-Āshī, Ismāʿīl b. ʿAbd al-Muṭṭalib, *Tāj al-muluk al-muraṣṣaʿ bi anwāʿ al-durār wa'l-jawāhir al-manẓūmāt* (Cairo: Muṣṭafā al-Bābī al-Halabī, 1938).

Aspinall, Edward, "Modernity, History and Ethnicity: Indonesian and Acehnese Nationalism in Conflict," in Damien Kingsbury and Harry Aveling (eds.), *Autonomy and Disintegration in Indonesia* (London: RoutledgeCurzon, 2003), 128–47.

Aspinall, Edward, *The Helsinki Agreement: A More Promising Basis for Peace in Aceh?* (Washington: East-West Center, 2005).

Aspinall, Edward, *Islam and Nation: Separatist Rebellion in Aceh, Indonesia* (Stanford, CA: Stanford University Press, 2009).

Aspinall, Edward, "Whither Aceh?" *Inside Indonesia* 62 (April–June 2000), <http://www.insideindonesia.org/edition-62-apr-jun-2000/whither-aceh-3007555>, accessed 30 July 2012.

Aspinall, Edward, and Harold A. Crouch, "The Aceh Peace Process: Why it Failed," *East-West Center Policy Studies* (Washington, DC: East-West Center, 2003).

Assyaukanie, Luthfi, *Islam and the Secular State in Indonesia* (Singapore: ISEAS Press, 2009).

Atho Mudzhar, Mohamad, *The Fatwas of the Council of Indonesian Ulama: A Study of Islamic Legal Thought in Indonesia, 1975–1988* (Jakarta: INIS, 1993).

Atho Mudzhar, Mohamad, "The Ulama, the Government, and Society in Modern Indonesia: The Indonesian Council of Ulama Revisited," in Johan Meuleman (ed.), *Islam in the Era of Globalization: Muslim Attitudes towards Modernity and Identity* (Jakarta: INIS, 2001), 315–26.

Atho Mudzhar, Mohamad, *Islam and Islamic Law in Indonesia: A Socio-Historical Approach* (Jakarta: Office of Religious Research, Development and Training – Ministry of Religious Affairs, 2003).

Ayang Utriza Nway, "Adakah Penerapan Syariat di Acheh: Tinjauan Sejarah Hukum di Kesultanan Acheh," *Jurnal Gelombang Baru* IV (2009): 17–62.

Azman Ismail, *Syariat Islam di Nanggroe Aceh Darussalam* (Banda Aceh: Dinas Syariat Islam, 2007).

Azra, Azyumardi, *Islam Substantif: Agar Umat Tidak Jadi Buih* (Bandung: Mizan, 2000).

Azra, Azyumardi, "The Indonesian Marriage Law of 1974: An Institutionalization of the Shariʿa for Social Change," in Arskal Salim and Azyumardi Azra (eds.), *Shariʿa and Politics in Modern Indonesia* (Singapore: ISEAS Press, 2003), 76–95.

Azra, Azyumardi, Dina Afrianty, and Robert W. Hefner, "Pesantren and Madrasa: Muslim Schools and National Ideas in Indonesia," in Robert W. Hefner and Muhammad Qasim Zaman (eds.), *Schooling Islam: The Culture and Politics of Modern Muslim Education* (Princeton University Press, 2006).

Badan Rehabilitasi dan Rekonstruksi (BRR), *Finance: The Seven Keys to Effective Aid Management* (Jakarta: Multi Donor Fund/UNDP, 2009).

Badan Rehabilitasi dan Rekonstruksi (BRR), *Religion, Social Culture: Revitalizing the Dignity of Society* (Jakarta: Multi Donor Fund/UNDP, 2009).

Badan Rehabilitasi dan Rekonstruksi (BRR), *Tsunami: From Disaster to the Emergence of Light* (Jakarta: Multi Donor Fund/UNDP, 2009).

Badan Rehabilitasi dan Rekonstruksi (BRR) and International Partners, *Aceh and Nias One Year after the Tsunami: The Recovery Effort and Way Forward* (Banda Aceh: BRR NAD-Nias, 2005).

Badan Rehabilitasi dan Rekonstruksi (BRR) and International Partners, *Aceh and Nias: Two Years after the Tsunami: 2006 Progress Report* (Banda Aceh: BRR NAD-Nias, 2006).

Badruzzaman Ismail (ed.), *Amal Bakti Empat Windu Majelis Ulama Aceh Tahun 1965–1997* (Aceh: Majelis Permusyawaratan Ulama Provinsi Nanggroe Aceh Darussalam, 2002).

Baihaqi A.K. "Ulama dan Madrasah Aceh," in Taufik Abdullah (ed.), *Agama dan Perubahan Sosial* (Jakarta: CV. Rajawali, 1983).

al-Banjārī, Muḥammad Arshad b. ʿAbd Allāh *Sabīl al-muhtadīn lil-tafaqquh fī amr al-dīn* (Singapore: al-Ḥaramayn, n.d.), 2 vols.

Barker, Joshua, "Vigilantes and the State," *Social Analysis* 50.1 (2006) 203–7.

Barnett, Michael, *Empire of Humanity: A History of Humanitarianism* (Ithaca: Cornell University Press, 2011).

Barter, Shane Joshua, "Ulama, the State, and War: Community Islamic Leaders in the Aceh Conflict," *Contemporary Islam* 5 (2011) 19–36.

Basiq Djalil, A., *Peradilan Agama di Indonesia: Gemuruhnya Politik Hukum (Hk. Islam, Hk. Barat, dan Hk. Adat) dalam Rentang Sejarah Bersama Pasang Surut Lembaga Peradilan Agama Hingga Lahirnya Peradilan Syariat Islam Aceh* (Jakarta: Kencana Prenada Media Group, 2006).

Beaulieu, Augustin de, *Mémoires d'un voyage aux Indes Orientales, 1619–1622*, ed. Denys Lombard (Paris: Maisonneuve et Larose, 1996).

Bedir, Murteza, "Fikih to Law: Secularization through Curriculum," *Islamic Law and Society* 11.3 (2004) 378–401.

Benda, Harry J., *The Crescent and the Rising Sun: Indonesian Islam under the Japanese Occupation, 1942–1945* (The Hague: W. van Hoeve Ltd., 1958).

Benda-Beckmann, Franz and Keebet von, "The Social Life of Living Law in Indonesia," in Marc Hertogh (ed.), *Living Law: Reconsidering Eugen Ehrlich* (Oxford: Hart Publishing, 2009).

Berg, L.W.C. van den, "Over de devotie der Naqsjibendijah in den Indischen Archipel," *Tijdschrift voor Indische Taal-, Land-, en Volkenkunde* 28.2 (1883): 158–75.

Berg, L.W.C. van den, "Het Mohammedaansche Godsdienstonderwijs op Java en Madoera en de daarbij gebruikte Arabische Boeken," *Tijdschrift voor Indische Taal-, Land- en Volkenkunde* 31 (1886) 518–55.

Birchok, Daniel, "Sojourning on Mecca's Verandah: Place, Temporality, and Islam in an Indonesian Province," Ph.D. dissertation (Ann Arbor: University of Michigan, 2013).

Birchok, Daniel, "Locating the Descendants of ʿAlī in Southwest Aceh: The Places of ʿAlid Piety in Late 20th-century Seunagan," in Chiara Formichi and R. Michael Feener (eds.), *Shiʿism in Southeast Asia: ʿAlid Piety and Sectarian Constructions* (London: Hurst, forthcoming).

Blueprint for the Reform of the Supreme Court of Indonesia (Jakarta: The Supreme Court of Indonesia, 2003).

Boland, B.J., *The Struggle of Islam in Modern Indonesia* (The Hague: Martinus Nijhoff, 1971).

Botiveau, Bernard, *Loi Islamique et droit dans le sociétés arabes* (Paris: Karthala, 1993).

Bowen, John R., *Muslims through Discourse: Religion and Ritual in Gayo Society* (Princeton: Princeton University Press, 1993).

Bowen, John R., *Islam, Law and Equality in Indonesia: An Anthropology of Public Reasoning* (Cambridge: Cambridge University Press, 2003).

Bowen, John R., "Fairness and Law in an Indonesian Court," in R. Michael Feener and Mark E. Cammack (eds.), *Islamic Law in Contemporary Indonesia: Ideas and Institutions* (Cambridge, MA: Harvard University Press, 2007), 170–92.

Bowrey, Thomas, *A Geographical Account of Countries Round the Bay of Bengal*, ed. Richard Temple (Cambridge: Hakluyt Society, 1905).

Braginsky, Vladimir, "Structure, Date and Sources of Hikayat Aceh Revisited: The Problem of Mughal-Malay Literary Ties," *Bijdragen tot de Taal-, Land- en Volkenkunde* 162.4 (2006) 441–67.

Brinkgreve, Francine, and Retno Sulistianingsih (eds.), *Sumatra: Crossroads of Cultures* (Leiden: KITLV Press, 2009).

Brown, Nathan J., "Shariʿa and State in the Modern Middle East," *International Journal of Middle East Studies* 29.3 (August 1997) 359–76.

Brown, Nathan J., "Egypt: Cacophony and Consensus in the Twenty-first Century," in Robert Hefner (ed.), *Sharia Politics: Islamic Law and Society in the Modern World* (Bloomington: Indiana University Press, 2011), 94–120.

Browning, Christopher R., and Siegelbaum, Lewis H., "Frameworks for Social Engineering: Stalinist Schema of Identification and the Nazi Volksgemeinschaft," in Michael Geyer and Sheila Fitzpatrick (eds.), *Beyond Totalitarianism: Stalinism and Nazism Compared* (New York: Cambridge University Press, 2009), 231–65.

Bruinessen, Martin van, "Kitab Kuning: Books in Arabic Script Used in the Pesantren Milieu," *BKI* 146 (1990) 226–69.

Bruinessen, Martin van, *Tarekat Naqsyabandiyah di Indonesia* (Bandung: Mizan, 1992).

Bruinessen, Martin van, "Divergent Paths from Gontor: Muslim Educational Reform and the Travails of Pluralism in Indonesia," in Freek L. Bakker and Jan Sihar Aritonang (eds.), *On the Edge of Many Worlds* (Zoetermeer: Uitgeverij Meinema, 2006), 152–62.

Bruinessen, Martin van, "After the Days of Abû Qubays: Indonesian Transformations of the Naqshbandiyya-Khâlidiyya," *Journal of the History of Sufism* 5 (2007) 225–51.

Bruinessen, Martin van, "Traditionalist and Islamist Pesantrens in Contemporary Indonesia," in Farish A. Noor, Yoginder Sikand, and Martin van Bruinessen (eds.), *The Madrasa in Asia: Political Activism and Transnational Linkages* (Amsterdam: Amsterdam University Press, 2008), 217–45.

Buchanan-Smith, Margaret, and Simon Maxwell, "Linking Relief and Development: An Introduction and Overview," *Institute of Development Studies Bulletin* 25.4 (1994) 2–16.

Buehler, Michael, "Decentralisation and Local Democracy in Indonesia: The Marginalisation of the Public Sphere," in Edward Aspinall and Marcus Mietzner (eds.), *Problems of Democratisation in Indonesia: Elections, Institutions and Society* (Singapore: Institute of Southeast Asian Studies, 2010).

Bünte, Marco, *Regionale Autonomie in Indonesien: Wege zur erfolgreichen Dezentralisierung* (Hamburg: IFA, 2003).

Burke, Edmund, *Reflections on the Revolution in France – and on the proceedings in certain societies in London relative to that event*, ed. Conor Cruise O'Brien (London: Penguin Books, 1986).

Burns, Peter J., *The Leiden Legacy: Concepts of Law in Indonesia* (Jakarta: PT Pradnya Paramita, 1999).

Bush, Robin, "Regional Shariʿa Regulations in Indonesia: Anomaly or Symptom" in Greg Fealy and Sally White (eds.), *Expressing Islam: Religious Life and Politics in Indonesia* (Singapore: ISEAS Press, 2008), 174–91.

Bustami Abubakar, "Respon Masyarakat Bireun terhadap Pelaksanaan," in Syahrizal (ed.), *Dimensi Pemikiran Hukum dalam Implementasi Syariat Islam di Aceh* (Banda Aceh: Dinas Syariat Islam Provinsi Nanggroe Aceh Darussalam, 2007).

Bustami Abubakar (ed.), *Ulama dan Politik: Menyongsong Aceh Baru* (Lhokseumawe: Lembaga Studi Islam dan Masyarakat Aceh/STAIN Malikussaleh, 2011).

Bustanul Arifin, "Kompilasi: Fiqih dalam Bahasa Undang-undang," *Pesantren* 2.2 (1985) 25–30.

Byron, G.G., *The Two Foscari: An Historical Tragedy* (Paris: A. and W. Galignani, 1822).

Calder, Norman, *Islamic Jurisprudence in the Classical Era* (Cambridge: Cambridge University Press, 2010).

Caldwell, Peter C., *Dictatorship, State Planning, and Social Theory in the German Democratic Republic* (Cambridge: Cambridge University Press, 2003).

Calinescu, Matei, *Five Faces of Modernity: Modernism, Avant-garde, Decadence, Kitsch, Postmodernism* (Durhan: Duke University Press, 1987).

Cammack, Mark E., "Islamic Law in Indonesia's New Order," *International and Comparative Law Quarterly* 38.1 (1989) 53–73.

Cammack, Mark E., "Indonesia's 1989 Religious Judicature Act: Islamization of Indonesia or Indonesianization of Islam," *Indonesia* 63 (April 1997) 143–68.

Cammack, Mark E., "The Indonesian Islamic Judiciary," in R. Michael Feener and Mark E. Cammack (eds.), *Islamic Law in Contemporary Indonesia: Ideas and Institutions* (Cambridge, MA: Harvard University Press, 2007), 146–69.

Cammack, Mark E., and R. Michael Feener, "Joint Marital Property in Indonesian Customary, Islamic, and National Law," in Peri Bearman, Wolfhart Heinrichs, and Bernard G. Weiss (eds.), *The Law Applied: Contextualizing the Islamic Shariʿa* (London: I.B. Tauris, 2008), 92–115.

Cammack, Mark E., and R. Michael, Feener, "The Indonesian Islamic Legal System," in Mark E. Cammack, R. Michael Feener, and Clark B. Lombardi (eds.), *Islamic Legal Professionals in Contemporary Southeast Asia*, a special issue of *Pacific Rim Law and Policy Journal* 21.1 (January 2012) 13–42.

Cammack, Mark E., R. Michael Feener, and Clark B. Lombardi (eds.), *Islamic Law and Islamic Legal Professionals in Southeast Asia*, a special issue of *Pacific Rim Law and Policy Journal* 21.1 (2012).

Cammack, Mark E., Lawrence A. Young, and Tim Heaton, "Legislating Social Change in an Islamic Society: Indonesia's Marriage Law," *The American Journal of Comparative Law* 44.1 (1996): 45–73, reprinted in Tim Lindsey (ed.), *Indonesia: Law and Society*, 2nd edition (Annandale: The Federation Press, 2008).

Casale, Giancarlo, *The Ottoman Age of Exploration* (Oxford: Oxford University Press, 2010).

Castles, Lance, "Notes on the Islamic School at Gontor," *Indonesia* 1 (June 1966) 30–45.

Chairuddin Shobari, "Pelaksanaan Syariat Islam di Aceh Sebagai Instrumen Menghadapi Milenium ke III," in Syamsul Rijal (ed.), *Syariat Islam dan Paradigma Kemanusiaan* (Banda Aceh: Dinas Syariat Islam, 2008).

Clark, John, et al., *Rebuilding a Better Aceh and Nias: Preliminary Stocktaking of the Reconstruction Effort Six Months After the Earthquake and Tsunami* (Jakarta: World Bank, 2005).

Consultative Group on Indonesia, *Notes on Reconstruction: The December 26, 2004 Natural Disaster* (Jakarta: BAPPENAS, 2005).

Cook, Marta, and John Halpin *"The Role of Faith in the Progressive Movement,"* (Washington DC: Center for American Progress, 2010), <http://www.americanprogress.org/wp-content/uploads/issues/2010/10/pdf/progressive_traditions6.pdf>, accessed 22 August 2012.

Cook, Michael, *Commanding Right and Forbidding Wrong in Islamic Thought* (Cambridge: Cambridge University Press, 2000).

Cribb, Robert, *Historical Atlas of Indonesia* (Honolulu: University of Hawaii Press, 2000).

Crouch, Harold, *Political Reform in Indonesia after Soeharto* (Singapore: ISEAS Press, 2010).

Crouch, Melissa, "Stretching the Scope of Special Autonomy in Aceh: The Controversial Qur'an Requirement for Election Candidates," *The Australian Journal of Asian Law* 11.1 (2009) 135–41.

Curran, Charles E., *The Social Mission of the U.S. Catholic Church: A Theological Perspective* (Washington DC: Georgetown University Press, 2011).

Dadi Darmadi, "IAIN dalam Wacana Intelektual Islam Indonesia," in Komaruddin Hidayat and Hendro Prasetyo (eds.), *Problem dan Prospek IAIN: Antologi Pendidikan Tinggi Islam* (Jakarta: Departemen Agama RI, 2000), 333–68.

Dahm, Bernhard, *Soekarno and the Struggle for Indonesian Independence*, revised and updated edition of *Sukarnos Kampf um Indonesiens Unabhängigkeit* (Ithaca: Cornell University Press, 1969).

Daly, Patrick, *Zero Hour: Post-disaster Recovery and Reconstruction* (forthcoming).

Damanhur bin Abbas, et al., *Tsunami dan Kisah Mereka* (Banda Aceh: Badan Arsip Provinisi NAD, 2006).
Damanhuri, "Aktualisasi Penerapan Syariat Islam," in Syamsul Rijal (ed.), *Syariat Islam dan Paradigma Kemanusiaan* (Banda Aceh: Dinas Syariat Islam, 2008), 25–50.
Damsté, H.T., "Hikajat Prang Sabi," *Bijdragen tot de Taal-, Land- en Volkenkunde* 84 (1928) 545–609.
"Darul Amin Gontor 10 Meunasah Baro, Seulimeum, Aceh," *Wardun: Warta Dunia Pondok Modern Darussalam Gontor* 61 (2008) 66–8.
Daud Beureueh, "Muqaddimah Pelaksanaan Unsur-unsur Sjariʿat Islam," in Analiansyah and Jamhuri (eds.), *Syariat Islam Di Nanggroe Aceh Darussalam: Inventarisasi Dokumen* (Banda Aceh: Dinas Syariat Islam Provinsi Nanggroe Aceh Darussalam, 2008).
Daud Zamzani, Nuruzzahri Yahya, Hasanoel Bashry HG, Muchtar A. Wahab, and Ismail Ya'kub (eds.), *Pemikiran Ulama Dayah Aceh* (Banda Aceh: BRR, 2007).
Davison, Roderic H., *Reform in the Ottoman Empire, 1856–1876* (Princeton: Princeton University Press, 1963).
Departemen Kaderisasi DPP Partain Keadilan Sejahtera, *Manajemen Tarbiyah: Anggota Pemula* (Jakarta: PT Syaamil Cipta Media, 2003).
Kamus Besar Bahasa Indonesia, Edisi Keempat (Jakarta: Pusat Bahasa/PT Gramedia Pustaka Utama, 2008).
Dewan Paripurna Ulama, *Kenduri Kematian* (Lhokseumawe: Majelis Permusyawaratan Ulama (MPU) Kota Lhokseumawe, 2004).
Dewan Perwakilan Rakyat Daerah, *Sidang Ke-IV Dewan Perwakilan Rakyat Daerah Gotong Rojong Propinsi Daerah Istimewa Atjeh* (Banda Aceh: Secretariat D. P. R. D. – GR Prop. Daerah Istimewa Aceh, 1968).
Dien, M.Y. Izzi, "Taʿzīr," *Encyclopædia of Islam*, Second Edition, Brill Online, 2012, <http://referenceworks.brillonline.com/entries/encyclopaedia-of-islam-2/tazir-SIM_7475>, accessed 27 June 2012.
Dijk, C. van, *Rebellion under the Banner of Islam: The Darul Islam in Indonesia* (The Hague: Martinus Nijhoff, 1981).
Dina Afrianty, "Local Women's NGOs and the Reform of Islamic Law in Aceh: Case Study of MISPI," Ph.D. dissertation (Melbourne: University of Melbourne, 2010).
Djajadiningrat, Hoesein, "Critisch Overzicht van de in Maleische Werken Vervatte Gegevens over de Geschiedenis van het Soeltanaat van Atjeh," *Bijdragen tot de Taal-, Land- en Volkenkunde* 65 (1911) 135–265.
Drewes, G.W.J. (ed.), *Hikajat Potjut Muhamat* (The Hague: Martinus Nijhoff, 1979).
Drewes, G.W.J. (ed.), *Two Acehnese Poems: Hikajat Ranto and Hikajat Teungku di Meuke* (The Hague: Martinus Nijhoff, 1980).
Drexler, Elizabeth F., *Aceh, Indonesia: Securing the Insecure State* (Philadelphia: University of Pennsylvania Press, 2008).
Dua Windu Kodam-I/Iskandar Muda (Jakarta: Sejarah Militer Kodam-I/Iskandar Muda, 1972).
Duke, Alastair, Gillian Lewis, and Andrew Pettegree (eds.), *Calvinism in Europe, 1540–1610: A Collection of Documents* (Manchester: Manchester University Press, 1992).

Dupret, Baudouin "What is Plural in the Law? A Praxiological Answer," Égypte/ Monde arabe, *Troisième série*, 1 (2005), <http://ema.revues.org/index1869.html>, accessed 4 November 2010.

Earp, Edwin L., *The Social Engineer* (New York: Eaton and Mains, 1911).

Ehrlich, Eugen, *Fundamental Principles of the Sociology of Law* (Cambridge, MA: Harvard University Press, 1936).

Eickelman, Dale F., *Knowledge and Power in Morocco: The Education of a Twentieth Century Notable* (Princeton: Princeton University Press, 1985).

Eka Srimulyani, *Mahmud Yunus' Islamic Educational Thought: Tracing and Contextualizing Islamic Educational Reform in Indonesia* (Banda Aceh: Ar-Raniry Press, 2008).

Eka Srimulyani, "Syariat Islam melalui Tiga Educational Networks (Keluarga, Sekolah dan Masyarakat)," in Eka Srimulyani (ed.), *Filosofi Pendidikan Berbasis Syariat dalam Educational Networks* (Banda Aceh: Dinas Syariat Islam Provinsi Nanggroe Aceh Darussalam, 2008).

Eka Srimulyani, "Teungku Inong Dayah: Female Religious Leaders' Authority and Agency in Contemporary Aceh," in R. Michael Feener, David Kloos and Annemarie Samuels (eds.), *Islam and the Limits of the State: Reconfigurations of Ritual, Doctrine, and Authority in Contemporary Aceh* (Leiden: Brill, forthcoming).

Ellen, Roy, "The Development of Anthropology and Colonial Policy in the Netherlands: 1800–1960," *Journal of the History of the Behavioral Sciences* 12 (1976) 303–24.

Emon, Anver M., "Ḥuqūq Allāh and Ḥuqūq al-ʿIbād: A Legal Heuristic for a Natural Rights Regime," *Islamic Law and Society* 13.3 (2006) 325–91.

Endang Saifuddin Anshari, "The Jakarta Charter of June 1945: A History of the Gentleman's Agreement between the Islamic and the Secular Nationalists in Modern Indonesia," M.A. thesis (Montreal: McGill University Institute of Islamic Studies, 1976).

Endang Saifuddin Anshari, *Piagam Jakarta, 22 Juni 1945: Sebuah Konsensus Nasional tentang Dasar Negara Republik Indonesia, 1945–1949* (Jakarta: Gema Insani Press, 1997).

Euis Nurlaelawati, *Modernization, Tradition and Identity: The Kompilasi Hukum Islam and Legal Practice in the Indonesian Religious Courts* (Amsterdam: Amsterdam University Press, 2010).

Fahd, T., *"Taʿzīr," Encyclopaedia of Islam*, 2nd edition (Brill Online, 2012), <http://referenceworks.brillonline.com/entries/encyclopaedia-of-islam-2/shiar-SIM_6921>, accessed 27 June 2012.

Fajran Zain, "WH Juga Manusia," in Fajran Zain (ed.), *Rangkeum 2009: Olah-pikir Aceh Institute di Media* (Banda Aceh: Aceh Institute Press, 2010), 187–91.

Fakhri, "Syarʿiat Islam Yang Kaffah: Suatu Pendekatan Komunikasi," in Zaki Fuad Chalil (ed.), *Melihat Syariat Islam Dari Berbagai Dimensi* (Banda Aceh: Dinas Syariat Islam, 2007).

Fakhri S., "Urgensi Syariat Islam Dalam Mengantisipasi Bencana Alam di NAD," in Syamsul Rijal (ed.), *Dinamika dan Problematika Penerapan Syariat Islam* (Banda Aceh: Dinas Syariat Islam, 2007), 50–72.

Fakhriati, *Menelusuri Tarekat Syattariyah di Aceh Lewat Naskah* (Jakarta: Departmen Agama RI Badan Litbang dan Diklat Puslitbang Lektur Keagamaan, 2008).

Fasseur, C., *De Indologen: Ambtenaren voor de Oost, 1825–1950* (Amsterdam: Bert Bakker, 1993).

Fauzi Saleh, "Eksistensi Akidah Dalam Penegakan Syariah: Kesiapan Mental Menerima Penerapakan Syariat Islam," in *Islam* (Banda Aceh: Dinas Syariat Islam Provinsi Nanggroe Aceh Darussalam, 2007).

Federspiel, Howard M., *Islam and Ideology in the Emerging Indonesian State: The Persatuan Islam (PERSIS), 1923–1957* (Leiden: Brill, 2001).

Feener, R. Michael, "Indonesian Movements for the Creation of a 'National Madhhab,'" *Islamic Law and Society* 9.1 (2001) 83–115.

Feener, R. Michael, *Muslim Legal Thought in Modern Indonesia* (Cambridge: Cambridge University Press, 2007).

Feener, R. Michael, "New Networks and New Knowledge: Migrations, Communications and the Refiguration of the Muslim Community in the Nineteenth and Early Twentieth Centuries," in Robert Hefner (ed.), *The New Cambridge History of Islam*, vol. 6 (Cambridge: Cambridge University Press, 2010), 39–68.

Feener, R. Michael, "Southeast Asian Localisations of Islam and Participation within a Global Umma, c. 1500–1800," in Anthony Reid and David Morgan (eds.), *The New Cambridge History of Islam*, vol. 3 (Cambridge: Cambridge University Press, 2010), 470–503.

Feener, R. Michael, "The Acehnese Past and its Present State of Study," in R. Michael Feener, Patrick Daly, and Anthony Reid (eds.), *Mapping the Acehnese Past* (Leiden: KITLV Press, 2011), 1–24.

Feener, R. Michael, "Hand, Heart and Handphone: State Shariʿa in the Age of the SMS," *Contemporary Islam* 7.1 (2013) 15–32.

Feener, R. Michael, David Kloos, and Annemarie Samuels (eds.), *Islam and the Limits of the State: Reconfigurations of Ritual, Doctrine, and Authority in Contemporary Aceh* (Leiden: Brill, forthcoming).

Feith, Herbert, *The Decline of Constitutional Democracy in Indonesia* (Ithaca: Cornell University Press, 1962).

Feldman, Noah, *The Fall and Rise of the Islamic State* (Princeton: Princeton University Press, 2008).

Fenwick, Stuart, "Yusman Roy and the Language of Devotion: 'Innovation' in Indonesian Islam on Trial," *Studia Islamika* 18.3 (2011) 497–529.

Formichi, Chiara, *Islam and the Making of the Nation: Kartosuwiryo and Political Islam in Twentieth-Century Indonesia* (Leiden: KITLV Press, 2012).

Foucault, Michel, *Discipline and Punish: The Birth of the Prison*, trans. Alan Sheridan (New York: Vintage Books, 1977).

Fuad Jabali, and Jamhari (eds.), *IAIN dan Modernisasi Islam di Indonesia* (Jakarta: UIN Jakarta Press, 2003).

Geertz, Clifford, *The Interpretation of Cultures* (New York: Basic Books, 1973), 87–125.

Gillett, Margaret, "The IAIN in Indonesian Higher Education," *Muslim Education Quarterly* 8.1 (1990) 21–32.

Gobée, E., and Adriaanse, C. (eds.), *Ambtelijke adviezen van C. Snouck Hurgronje, 1899–1936*, vol. I ('s-Gravenhage: Nijhoff, 1957).

Göksoy, İsmail Hakkı, "Ottoman-Aceh Relations as Documented in Turkish Sources," in R. Michael Feener, Patrick Daly, and Anthony Reid (eds.), *Mapping the Acehnese Past* (Leiden: KITLV Press, 2010), 65–96.

Good, Byron, and DelVecchio-Good, Mary-Jo (PIs), *Psychosocial Needs Assessment of Communities Affected by the Conflict in the Districts of Pidie, Bireuen and Aceh Utara* (Jakarta: International Organization for Migration, 2006).

Good, Erich, and Ben-Yehuda, Nachman, *Moral Panics: The Social Construction of Deviance* (Oxford: Blackwell Publishing, 1994).

Gorski, Philip S., *Disciplinary Revolution: Calvinism and the Rise of the State in Early Modern Europe* (Chicago: University of Chicago Press, 2003).

Gould, James W., "Sumatra: America's Pepperpot, 1784–1873," *Essex Institute Historical Collections* XCII (1956) 83–152; XCII (1956) 203–51; XCII (1956) 295–348.

Graf, Arndt, "Reading the Tsunami and the Helsinki Accord: 'Letters to the Editor' in Serambi Indonesia, Banda Aceh," in Arndt Graf, Susanne Schröter, and Edwin Wieringa (eds.), *Aceh: History, Politics and Culture* (Singapore: ISEAS Publishing, 2010), 287–99.

Großmann, Kristina, "Handlungsräume muslimischer Aktivistinnen: Nach der Einführung der Syariat Islam und dem Tsunami in Aceh, Indonesien," Ph.D. dissertation (Frankfurt am Main: Johann Wolfgang Goethe-Ūniversitāt, 2012).

Großmann, Kristina, "Women's Rights Activists and the Drafting Process of the Islamic Criminal Law," in R. Michael Feener, David Kloos, and Annemarie Samuels (eds.), *Islam and the Limits of the State: Reconfigurations of Ritual, Doctrine, and Authority in Contemporary Aceh* (Leiden: Brill, forthcoming).

Guillén, Mauro F., *The Taylorized Beauty of the Mechanical: Scientific Management and the Rise of Modernist Architecture* (Princeton: Princeton University Press, 2006).

Guillot, Claude, and Ludvik Kalus, *Les monuments funéraires et l'histoire du sultanat de Pasai à Sumatra, XIII*[e]*-XVI*[e] *siècles* (Paris: Association Archipel, 2008).

Habiburrahman, *Rekonstruksi Hukum Kewarisan Islam di Indonesia* (Jakarta: Kencana Prenada Media Group, 2011).

Haider Ala Hamoudi, and Cammack, Mark E., *Islamic Law in Modern Courts* (Alphen aan den Rijn: Wolters Kluwer, 2013).

Haim, S., *The Shorter Persian-English Dictionary* (Tehran: Farhang Moaser, 1985).

Hallaq, Wael B., *A History of Islamic Legal Theories* (Cambridge University Press, 1997).

Hallaq, Wael B., "Can the Shariʿah be Restored?" in Yvonne Y. Haddad and Barbara F. Stowasser (eds.), *Islamic Law and the Challenges of Modernity* (Walnut Creek: Altamira Press, 2004), 21–53.

Hallaq, Wael B., *Sharīʿa: Theory, Practice, Transformations* (New York: Cambridge University Press, 2009).

Hamdani Daud, and Tgk. Azhari, *Pembahasan Masaalah Qunut Dalam Shalat* (Lhokseumawe: Majelis Permusyawaratan Ulama Aceh Utara, 2006).

Hamdiah Latief, "Persatuan Ulama Seluruh Aceh (PUSA): Its Contributions to Education Reforms in Aceh," M.A. thesis (Montreal: McGill University, 1992).

Hanstein, Thoralf, *Islamisches Recht und Nationales Recht: Eine Unstersuchung zum Einfluß des Islamischen Rechts auf die Entwicklung des modernen Familienrechts am Beispiel Indonesiens*, 2 vols. (Frankfurt: Peter Lang, 2002).

Harist Muzani, "Syariat tanpa Simbol," (12 December 2010), <http://www.acehinstitute.org/index.php?option=com_content&view=article&id=385:syariat-tanpa-simbol&catid=74:paradigma-islam>, accessed 18 July 2011.

Hasanuddin Yusuf Adan, *Politik dan Tamaddun Aceh* (Banda Aceh: Adnin Foundation Aceh, 2006).

Hasanuddin Yusuf Adan, *Syariʿat Islam di Aceh: Antara Implementasi dan Diskriminasi* (Banda Aceh: Adnin Foundation, 2008).

Hasbi Amiruddin, *Perjuangan Ulama Aceh di Tengah Konflik* (Yogyakarta: Ceninnets Press, 2004).

Hasbi Amiruddin, "Dayah: Lembaga Pendidikan Tertua Masyarakat Aceh," in T.H. Thalhas and Choirul Fuad Yusuf (eds.), *Pendidikan dan Syariat Islam di Nanggroe Aceh Darussalam* (Jakarta: Galura Pase, 2007).

Hasbi Amiruddin (ed.), *Aceh: Serambi Mekka* (Banda Aceh: Pemerintah Provinsi Nanggroe Aceh Darussalam, 2008).

Hasbi Amiruddin, *Menatap Masa Depan Dayah di Aceh* (Banda Aceh: Yayasan Pena, 2008).

Hasbi Amiruddin, "Prof. H. A. Hasjmy (Rektor IAIN Ar-Raniry Periode 1977–1982)," in *Biografi Rektor IAIN Ar-Raniry: Kepemimpinan IAIN Ar-Raniry dari Masa ke Masa* (Banda Aceh: Ar-Raniry Press, 2008).

Hasjmy, A., *Kapita Selekta Islam: Kumpulan Pidato-Ceramah-Khuthbah* (Banda Aceh: Privately Printed, Yayasan Ali Hasjmy, no date).

Hasjmy, A., "Konsepsi Ideal Darussalam," in *10 Tahun Darussalam dan Hari Pendidikan* (Banda Aceh: Yayasan Pembina Darussalam, 1969), 25–78.

Hasjmy, A., *Hikajat Prang Sabi Mendjiwai Perang Atjeh Lawan Belanda* (Banda Aceh: Pustaka Faraby, 1971).

Hasjmy, A., *Dustur Daʿwah—Menurut Al-Quran* (Jakarta: Bulan Bintang, 1974).

Hasjmy, A., "Tugas Fakultas Dakwah: Membina Manusia Pembangun," in *Majalah Pengetahuna/Kebudayaan Sinar Darussalam* (Banda Aceh: Yayasan Pembina Darussalam/Studi Klub Islam Darussalam, 1975).

Hasjmy, A., *Dakwah Islamiyah dan Kaitannya dengan Pembangun Manusia: Pidato Pengukuhan sebagai Guru Besar Luar Biasa dalam Ilmu Dakwah* (Banda Aceh: IAIN, 1978).

Hasjmy, A., "Laporan Tahunan Rektor," *Buku Tahunan Hari Jadi ke-XVII IAIN Jamiʿah Ar-Raniry* (Banda Aceh: IAIN, 1980).

Hasjmy, A., *Pokok-pokok pikiran sekitar Dakwah Islamiyah: Sebuah Tinjauan tentang Sifat, Sasaran, dan Cara-cara Pelaksanaan Dakwah* (Banda Aceh: Majelis Ulama Propinsi Daerah Istimewa Aceh, 1981).

Hasjmy, A., "Kemungkinan-kemungkinan Islam di Abad XV," in *Bahan-bahan Penataran Imam dan Khatib* (Banda Aceh: Majelis Ulama se Daerah Istimewa Aceh, 1981).

Hasjmy, A., "Islam Menjiwai Alam Pikiran Melayu Lama: Sebuah Studi tentang Naskah Tua Safinatul Hukkam," in *Apa Tugas Sastrawan sebagai Khalifah Allah* (Surabaya: Bina Ilmu, 1984).

Hasjmy, A., *Di Mana Letaknya Negara Islam?* (Surabaya: Bina Ilmu, 1984).
Hasjmy, A., *Semangat Merdeka: 70 Tahun Menempuh Jalan Pergolakan and Perjuangan Kemerdekaan* (Jakarta: Bulan Bintang, 1985).
Hasjmy, A., *Ulama Aceh Mujahid Pejuang Kemerdakaan dan Pembangun Tamadun Bangsa* (Jakarta: Bulan Bintang, 1997).
Hatina, Meir, "Restoring a Lost Identity: Models of Education in Modern Islamic Thought," *British Journal of Middle Eastern Studies* 33.2 (2006) 179–97.
Hattori, Mina, *"The Tradition of Kitab Learning at Pondok Pesantren in Indonesia,"* (Tokyo: Sophia University Institute of Asian Cultures Working Paper Series, 2012), 47–70.
Hefner, Robert W., "Islam, State, and Civil Society: ICMI and the Struggle for the Indonesian Middle Class," *Indonesia* 56 (October 1993) 1–36.
Hefner, Robert W., "Islamic Schools, Social Movements, and Democracy in Indonesia," in Robert W. Hefner (ed.), *Making Modern Muslims: The Politics of Islamic Education in Southeast Asia* (Honolulu: University of Hawai'i Press, 2009), 55–105.
Hefner, Robert W., and Muhammad Qasim Zaman (eds.), *Schooling Islam: The Culture and Politics of Modern Muslim Education* (Princeton: Princeton University Press, 2007).
Heru Cahyono, *Peranan Ulama dalam Golkar, 1971–1980: Dari Pemilu sampai Malari* (Jakarta: Pustaka Sinar Harapan, 1992).
Heru Cahyono, "Portret Kelembagaan Gampong yang Lumpuh di Meuria, Kecamatan Matangkuli, Kabupaten Aceh Utara," in Irine Hiraswati Gayatri (ed.), *Runtuhnya Gampong di Aceh: Studi Masyarakat Desa yang Bergejolak* (Yogyakarta: Pustaka Pelajar, 2008).
Himpunan Peraturan Perundang-Undangan Produk Departemen Agama RI, Tahun 1981 (Jakarta: Proyek Perencanaan Peraturan Perundangan Keagamaan Tahun Anggaran, 1982).
Himpunan Peraturan Perundang Undangan tentang Mahkamah Syar'iyah di Provinsi Nanggroe Aceh Darussalam (Banda Aceh: Mahkamah Syar'iyah Propinsi NAD, 2006).
Himpunan Undang-Undang, Keputusan Presiden, Peraturan Daerah/Qanun, Instruksi Gubernor berkaitan Pelaksanaan Syari'at Islam, edisi ketujuh (Banda Aceh: Dinas Syariat Islam, 2009).
Hindley, Donald, *The Communist Party of Indonesia, 1951–1963* (Berkeley: University of California Press, 1964).
Hocking, William Ernest, *Present Status of the Philosophy of Law and of Rights* (New Haven: Yale University Press, 1926).
Hocking, William Ernest, *The Coming World Civilization* (New York: Harper, 1956).
Holle, K.F., "Mededeelingen over de devotie der Naqsjibendijah in den Ned. Indischen Archipel," *Tijdschrift voor Indische Taal-, Land-, en Volkenkunde* 31 (1886) 67–81.
Holtzappel, Coen J.G., "The Regional Governance Reform in Indonesia, 1999–2004," in Coen J.G. Holtzappel and Martin Ramstedt (eds.), *Decentralization and Regional Autonomy in Indonesia: Implementation and Challenges* (Singapore: ISEAS, 2009), 1–48.

Honna, Jun, "Military Ideology in Response to Democratic Pressure during the Late Suharto Era: Political and Institutional Contexts," *Indonesia* 67 (April 1999) 77–126.

Hooker, M.B., *Indonesian Islam: Social Change through Contemporary Fatawa* (Crows Nest, NSW: Allen and Unwin, 2003).

Hooker, M.B., *Indonesian Syariah: Defining a National School of Islamic Law* (Singapore: ISEAS, 2008).

Human Rights Watch, *Policing Morality: Abuses in the Application of Shariʿa in Aceh, Indonesia* (New York: HRW, 2010). Available online at: <http://www.hrw.org/sites/default/files/reports/indonesia1210WebVersionToPost.pdf>, accessed 22 May 2012.

Husein Segaf, Suminto, Chatibul Umam, and Ali Ibrahim (eds.), *Ulama dan Pembangunan* (Jakarta: Panitia Musyawarah Nasional I Majelis Ulama Seluruh Indonesia, 1976).

Ibn Baṭṭūṭa, *Riḥla: Tuḥfat al-nuẓẓar fī gharāʾib al-amṣār wa ajāʾib al-asfār* (Beirut: Dār al-sharq al-ʿarabī, n.d.).

Ibrahim (ed.), *Pengantar Hukum Islam di Indonesia* (Jakarta: Departemen Agama, 1965).

Institut Agama Islam Negeri (IAIN), *Buku Tahunan IAIN 'Al-Djamiʿah Al-Islamijah Al-Hukumijah' 1960–1962* (Jogjakarta: IAIN 'Al-Djamiʿah Al-Islamijah Al-Hukumijah', 1962).

Institut Agama Islam Negeri (IAIN), *Die Natalis Ke-I Djamiʿah Ar-Raniry* (Banda Aceh: Panitia Perajaan Dies Natalis Ke-I I.A.I.N., Djamiʿah Ar-Raniry Darussalam, 1963).

Institut Agama Islam Negeri (IAIN), *Kenang2-an Die Natalis Ke-I Djamiʿah Ar-Raniry* (Banda Aceh: Panitia Perajaan Dies Natalis Djamiʿah Ar-Raniry Darussalam, 1963).

Institut Agama Islam Negeri (IAIN), *Risalah: Fakultas Dakwah dan Publisistik I.A.I.N. Djamiʿah Ar-Raniry Darussalam* (Aceh: Bahagian Publikasi Fakultas Dakwah, Publisistik Darussalam Banda Atjeh, 1969).

Institut Agama Islam Negeri (IAIN), *Seminar Adat yang Bertentangan dengan Syariʿat* (Banda Aceh: Lembaga Research dan Survey IAIN Jamiʿah Ar-Raniry Darussalam, Banda Aceh, 1975).

Institut Agama Islam Negeri (IAIN), *Sewindu Fakultas Dakwah* (Banda Aceh: IAIN Jamiʿah Ar-Raniry, 1975).

Institut Agama Islam Negeri (IAIN), *15 Tahun Institut Agama Islam Negeri Jamiʿah Ar-Raniry Darussalam Banda Aceh, 5 Okt 1963 – 5 Okt 1978* (Banda Aceh: Panita Harijadi Ke-XV IAIN Jamiʿah Ar-Raniry, 1978).

Institut Agama Islam Negeri (IAIN), *DwiWindu: Fakultas Tarbiyah I.A.I.N. Jamiʿah Ar-Raniry, 15 Des. 1962 – 15 Des. 1978* (Banda Aceh: Fakultas Tarbiyah I.A.I.N. Jamiʿah Ar-Raniry, 1978).

International Crisis Group, "Aceh: Can Autonomy Stem the Conflict?" *ICG Asia Report* No. 18 (27 June 2001), <http://www.crisisgroup.org/~/media/Files/asia/south-east-asia/indonesia/Aceh%20Can%20Autonomy%20Stem%20the%20Conflict.pdf>, accessed 28 August 2012.

International Crisis Group, "Aceh: Why the Military Option Still Won't Work," *Indonesia Briefing* (9 May 2003), <http://www.crisisgroup.org/~/media/

Files/asia/south-east-asia/indonesia/B026%20Aceh%20Why%20The%20Military%20Option%20Still%20Wont%20Work.pdf>, accessed 28 August 2012.

International Crisis Group, "Aceh: How Not to Win Hearts and Minds," *Indonesia Briefing* (23 July 2003), <http://www.crisisgroup.org/~/media/Files/asia/south-east-asia/indonesia/B027%20Aceh%20How%20Not%20to%20Win%20Hearts%20and%20Minds.pdf>, accessed 28 August 2012.

Irfan Awwas, *Trilogi kepemimpinan Negara Islam Indonesia* (Yogyakarta: Uswah, 2008).

Isa Sulaiman, "Islam et propaganda anti-néerlandaise: Abdullah Arief et le Seumangat Atjeh, 1945–1946," *Archipel* 30 (1985) 207–17.

Isa Sulaiman, "Les Ulèebalang, les Ulémas, et les enseignants de madrasah: La lutte pour le pouvoir local en Aceh de 1942 à 1951," Ph.D. dissertation (Paris: Écoles des Hautes Études en Sciences Sociales, 1985).

Isa Sulaiman, and Klinken, Gerry van, "The Rise and Fall of Governor Puteh," in Henk Schulte Nordholt and Gerry van Klinken (eds.), *Renegotiating Boundaries: Local Politics in Post-Suharto Indonesia* (Leiden: KITLV Press, 2007), 235–48.

Iskandar Ibrahim, "Syariat Islam Yang Solutif," in Syamsul Rijal (ed.), *Syariat Islam dan Paradigma Kemanusiaan* (Banda Aceh: Dinas Syariat Islam, 2008).

"Islam dan Perdamaian: Dari Hudaibiyah ke Helsinki," *Aceh Forum*, 29 June 2006, <http://www.acehforum.or.id/archive/index.php/t-2447.html>, accessed 17 July 2012.

Ismuha, *Sejarah Singkat Majelis Ulama Propinsi Daerah Istimewa Aceh* (Banda Aceh: Majelis Ulama Propinsi Daerah Istimewa Aceh, 1983).

Ismuha, "Ulama Aceh dalam Perspektif Sejarah," in Taufik Abdullah (ed.), *Agama dan Perubahan Sosial* (Jakarta: CV. Rajawali, 1983).

Ismuha, Baihaqi A.K., and Dalminis Noor, "Pengaruh PUSA terhadap Reformasi di Aceh," in Usman Said (ed.), *Agama, Perkembangan dan Pembangunan* (Jakarta: Proyek Pembinaan Perguruan Tinggi Agama/IAIN di Pusat – Direktort Pembinaan Perguruan Tinggi Agama Islam, 1980), 39–67.

Ito, Takeshi, "The World of the Adat Aceh: A Historical Study of the Sultanate of Aceh," Ph.D. dissertation (Canberra: Australian National University, 1984).

Jailani, "Implementasi Syari'at Islam di Aceh (Peluang dan Tantangan Membangun Sistem Pemerintahan yang Bersih dan Berwibawa)," in Azman Ismail (ed.), *Syariat Islam di Nanggroe Aceh Darussalam* (Banda Aceh: Dinas Syariat Islam, 2007), 104–23.

Jamaluddin, A. (team leader/Ketua), *Konsep Pendidikan Agama Islam di Semua Jenjang Pendidikan dan Kerjasama Lembaga Pendidikan Formal dengan Lembaga Pendidikan Informal* (Bireuen: Official document issued by the Majelis Permusyawaratan Ulama Kabupaten Bireuen, 2008).

Joll, Christopher M., *Muslim Merit Making in Thailand's Far-South* (Dordrecht: Springer, 2012).

Jordan, John M., *Machine-Age Ideology: Social Engineering and American Liberalism, 1911–1939* (Chapel Hill, NC: University of North Carolina Press, 1994).

Julianto Saleh, *Pemaknaan Kejadian Tsunami dan Perilaku Keberagamaan Masyarakat Pasca Tsunami* (Banda Aceh: Pusat Latihan Penelitian Ilmu-Ilmu Sosial, 2005).

Kadı, Ismail Hakkı, Peacock, Andrew, and Gallop, Annabel Teh, "Writing History: The Acehnese Embassy to Istanbul, 1849–1852," in R. Michael Feener, Patrick Daly, and Anthony Reid (eds.), *Mapping the Acehnese Past* (Leiden: KITLV Press, 2010), 163–82.

Kahin, Audrey R., *Islam, Nationalism and Democracy* (Singapore: NUS Press, 2012).

Kalus, Ludvik, and Claude Guillot, "Note sur le sultanat de Peudada, fin XVe- début XVIe [Épigraphie islamique d'Aceh. 5]," *Archipel* 83 (2012) 7–15.

Kamali, Mohammad Hashim, *Principles of Islamic Jurisprudence* (Cambridge: Islamic Texts Society, 1991).

Kamus Besar Bahasa Indonesia (Jakarta: Pusat Bahasa, 2008).

Kaoy Syah, H.M., and L. Hakiem, *Keistimewaan Aceh Dalam Lintasan Sejarah. Proses Pembentukan UU No. 44/1999* (Jakarta: Pengurus Besar Al Jamʿiyatul Washliyah, 2000).

Kaptein, Nico J.G. (ed.), *The Muhimmāt al-Nafāʾis: A Bilingual Meccan Fatwa Collection for Indonesian Muslims from the End of the Nineteenth Century* (Jakarta: INIS: 1997).

Katz, Marion Holmes, "The Ḥadd Penalty for Zinā: Symbol or Deterrent? Texts from the Early Sixteenth Century," in Paul M. Cobb (ed.), *The Lineaments of Islam: Studies in Honor of Fred McGraw Donner* (Leiden: Brill, 2012), 351–78.

Kell, Tim, *The Roots of the Acehnese Rebellion, 1989–1992* (Ithaca: Cornell Modern Indonesia Project, 1995).

Kennedy, James, Joseph Ashmore, Elizabeth Babister, and Ian Kelman, "The Meaning of 'Build Back Better': Evidence From Post-Tsunami Aceh and Sri Lanka," *Journal of Contingencies and Crisis Management* 16.1 (2008) 24–36.

Kennedy, Raymond, "Applied Anthropology in the Dutch East Indies," *Transactions of the New York Academy of Sciences* 6.5 (1944) 157–62.

Kholid Santosa, *Jejak-jejak Sang Pejuang Pemberontak: Pemikiran, Gerakan and Ekspresi Politik S.M. Kartosuwirjo dan Daud Beureueh* (Bandung: Sega Arsy, 2006).

Khomeini, Ayatollah, *Islam and Revolution: Writings and Declarations of Imam Khomeini*, trans. by Hamid Algar (Berkeley: Mizan Press, 1981).

Kingsbury, Damien, *The Politics of Indonesia* (New York: Oxford University Press, 2005).

Kingsbury, Damien, *Peace in Aceh: A Personal Account of the Helsinki Peace Process* (Jakarta: PT Equinox Publishing, 2006).

Kingsbury, Damien, "Political Reconstruction in Aceh," in Matthew Clarke, Ismet Fanany, and Sue Kenny (eds.), *Post-Disaster Reconstruction: Lessons from Aceh* (London: Earthscan, 2010), 61–78.

Kloos, David, "Becoming Better Muslims: Religious Authority and Ethical Improvement in Aceh, Indonesia," Ph.D. dissertation (Amsterdam: Vrije Universiteit, 2013).

Knysh, Alexander, *Ibn ʿArabi in the Later Islamic Tradition: The Making of a Polemical Image in Medieval Islam* (Albany: State University of New York Press, 1999).

Kobayashi, Yasuko, *Indonesia tenkaisuru isuramu* (Nagoya: Daigaku Shuppankai, 2008).

Koesnoe, Moh., "Mengamati Konsep Hukum di Dalam Masyarakat Kita," in M. Ali Boediarto (ed.), *Kapita Selekta Hukum Adat: Suatu Pemikiran Baru* (Jakarta: Varia Peradilan – Ikatan Hakim Indonesia, 2002).

Kraus, Werner, *Zwischen Reform und Rebellion: Über die Entwicklung des Islams in Minangkabau (Westsumatra) zwischen den beiden Reformbewegungen der Padri (1837) und der Modernisten (1908): Ein Beitrag zur Geschichte der Islamisierung Indonesiens* (Wiesbaden: Franz Steiner Verlag, 1984).

Kraus, Werner, "Some Notes on the Introduction of the Naqshbandiyya-Khalidiyya into Indonesia," in M. Gaborieau, A. Popovic and T. Zarcone (eds.), *Naqshbandis: cheminements et situation actuelle d'un order mystique musulman* (Istanbul and Paris: Éd. Isis, 1990), 691–706.

Kraus, Werner, "The Shattariyya Sufi Brotherhood in Aceh," in Arndt Graf, Susanne Schröter, and Edwin Wieringa (eds.), *Aceh: History, Politics and Culture* (Singapore: ISEAS Publishing, 2010), 212–24.

Kurin, Richard, "Islamization: A View from the Countryside," in Anita M. Weiss (ed.), *Islamic Reassertion in Pakistan: The Application of Islamic Laws in a Modern State* (New York: Syracuse University Press, 1986), 115–28.

Kushimoto, Hiroko, "Ajaran Sesat (deviant teachings): The Official Views on Sufism in Malaysia," *Proceedings of the KIAS/SIAS Joint International Workshop "Struggling Muslims in the Modern and Present-day Eras: Political, Social, and Religious Aspects of their Endeavours* (Tokyo: Sophia University, 22 February 2012).

Labrousse, Pierre, and Farida Soemargono, "De l'Islam comme morale du développmement: L'action des bureaux de propagation de la foi (Lembaga Dakwah) vue de Surabaya," *Archipel* 30 (1985) 219–28.

Laffan, Michael, "Lightning Angels and Prayers for the Nation: Reading the Fatwas of the Jamiʿah Ahlith Thoriqoh al-Muʿtabaroh," in R. Michael Feener and Mark E. Cammack (eds.), *Islamic Law in Contemporary Indonesia: Ideas and Institutions* (Cambridge, MA: Harvard University Press, 2007), 66–80.

Laffan, Michael, "Understanding al-Imam's Critique of Tariqa Sufism," in Azyumardi Azra, Kees van Dijk, and Nico J.G. Kaptein (eds.), *Varieties of Religious Authority: Changes and Challenges in 20th Century Indonesian Islam* (Singapore: ISEAS Press, 2010), 27–35.

Laffan, Michael, *The Makings of Indonesian Islam: Muslims, Orientalists and Entwined Visions of a Sufi Tradition* (Princeton: Princeton University Press, 2011).

Lange, Christian, *Justice, Punishment, and the Medieval Muslim Imagination* (Cambridge: Cambridge University Press, 2008).

Langen, K.F.H. van, "De Inrichting van het Atjehsche Staatsbestuur onder het Sultanaat," *Bijdragen tot de Taal- Land- en Volkenkunde van Nederlandsch-Indië* 37.1 (1888) 382–471.

Lee, Kam Hing, *Education and Politics in Indonesia, 1945–1965* (Kuala Lumpur: University of Malaya Press, 1995).

Lev, Daniel S., *Islamic Courts in Indonesia: A Study in the Political Bases of Legal Institutions* (Berkeley: University of California Press, 1972).

Lev, Daniel S., "Judicial Institutions and Legal Culture in Indonesia," in Claire Holt, with Benedict R. O'G. Anderson and James Siegel (eds.), *Culture and Politics in Indonesia* (Ithaca: Cornell University Press, 1972), 255–97.

Liaw, Yock Fang, *Undang-Undang Melaka* (The Hague: Martinus Nijhoff, 1976).

Lindsey, Tim, "The Criminal State: Premanisme and the New Indonesia," in Grayson J. Lloyd and Shannon L. Smith (eds.), *Indonesia Today: Challenges of History* (Lanham, Md.: Rowman & Littlefield, 2001), 283–307.

Lindsey, Tim, and M.B. Hooker, with Ross Clarke and Jeremy Kingsley, "Shariʿa Revival in Aceh," in R. Michael Feener and Mark E. Cammack (eds.), *Islamic Law in Contemporary Indonesia: Ideas and Institutions* (Cambridge, MA: Harvard University Press, 2007).

Lindsey, Tim, and Mas Achmad Santosa, "The Trajectory of Law Reform in Indonesia," in Tim Lindsey (ed.), *Indonesia: Law and Society*, 2nd edition (Annandale: The Federation Press, 2008), 2–22.

Lombard, Denys, *Le sultanat d'Atjéh au temps d'Iskandar Muda* (Paris: École Française d'Extrême-Orient, 1967).

Lombardi, Clark B., *State Law as Islamic Law in Modern Egypt: The Incorporation of the Sharīʿa into Egyptian Constitutional Law* (Leiden: E.J. Brill, 2006).

Longhurst, Richard, "Conceptual Frameworks for Linking Relief and Development," *Institute of Development Studies Bulletin* 25.4 (1994) 17–23.

Maccoby, Eleanor E., "Historical Overview of Socialization Research and Theory," in Joan E. Grusec and Paul D. Hastings (eds.), *Handbook of Socialization Theory and Research* (New York: The Guilford Press, 2007), 13–41.

Machmudi, Yon, *Islamising Indonesia: The Rise of the Jemaah Tarbiyah and the Prosperous Justice Party (PKS)*. (Canberra: Australian National University E Press, 2008).

Madinier, Rémy, *L'Indonésie, entre démocratie musulmane et Islam intégral: Histoire du parti Masjumi, 1945–1960* (Paris: Karthala, 2012).

Mahdi Syihab, "Penegakan Syariat: Etnografi Aksi Razia Santri Dayah di Aceh Utara," in Arskal Salim and Adnin Sila (eds.), *Serambi Mekkah yang Berubah* (Banda Aceh: Aceh Research Training Institute, 2010), 57–91.

Mahkamah Syariʿah, *Yurisprudensi Mahkamah Syariʿah Provinsi Nanggroe Aceh Darussalam Perkara Jinayat* (Banda Aceh: Mahkamah Syariʿah Provinsi NAD, 2007).

Mahmud Yunus, *Sejarah Pendidikan Islam* (Jakarta: Hidakarya Agung, 1985).

Majelis Permusyawaratan Ulama (MPU), *Berjabat Tangan (Mushafahah) antara Laki-laki dan Perempuan Ajnabiyah menurut Hukum Islam* (Lhokseumawe: Majelis Permusyawaratan Ulama Kota Lhokseumawe, 2005).

Majelis Permusyawaratan Ulama (MPU), *Kajian Komisi 'A' Majelis Permusyawaratan Ulama (MPU) Kota Lhokseumawe No. 247/ 2006 tentang Korupsi, Kolusi dan Nepotisme (KKN) serta Money Politik* (Commission report – MPU Kota Lhokseumawe, 2006).

Majelis Permusyawaratan Ulama (MPU), *Kesimpulan Musyawarah Ulama Kabupaten Aceh Utara dan Kota Lhokseumawe tentang Keramaian Malam* (Circular letter issued on 20 July, 2006).

Majelis Permusyawaratan Ulama (MPU), *Kumpulan Fatwa-fatwa Majelis Ulama Propinsi Daerah Istimewa Aceh tahun 1965 s/d 31 Maret 1979* (Banda Aceh: Sekretariat Majelis Permusyawaratan Ulama, 2006).

Majelis Permusyawaratan Ulama (MPU), *Materi Pembakalan Pembinaan Calon Linto dan Dara Baro (CALINDA)*, (Lhoksuemawe: Majelis Permusyawaratan Ulama Kota Lhokseumawe, 2007).

Majelis Permusyawaratan Rakyat, *Ketetapan-ketetapan Majelis Permusyawaratan Rakyat Indonesia Tahun 1993* (Jakarta: B7 Pusat, 1993).
Majelis Ulama Propinsi Daerah Istimewa Aceh dalam rangka Serah Terima Jabatan Gubernur Kepala Daerah Istimewa Aceh 1968 s/d 1977 (Banda Aceh: Sekretariat Majelis Ulama Daerah Istimewa Aceh, 1977).
Mannan Nur, *Studi Tentang Dayah di Samalanga* (Banda Aceh: Pusat Penelitian Ilmu-Ilmu Sosial, 1975).
Marah Halim, "Sistem Penegakan Hukum dalam Pelaksanaan Syariat Islam di NAD," in Syahrizal (ed.), *Dimensi Pemikiran Hukum dalam Implementasi Syariat Islam di Aceh* (Banda Aceh: Dinas Syariat Islam Provinsi Nanggroe Aceh Darussalam, 2007), 36–74.
Mardani, *Hukum Acara Perdata Peradilan Agama dan Mahkamah Syari'ah* (Jakarta: Sinar Grafika, 2009).
Marklund, Carl, "Adjusting Facts and Values—Reconciling Politics with Science: Some Notes on the Rhetorics of Social Engineering in Depression-Era Sweden and the USA," *Ideas in History* II(2) (2007) 9–42.
Marzuki Wahid, and Rumadi, *Fiqih Madzhab Negara: Kritik Atas Politik Hukum Islam di Indonesia* (Yogyakarta: LKiS, 2001).
Massa, Mark, with Catherine Osborne, *American Catholic History: A Reader* (New York: NYU Press, 2008).
Massier, Ab, *The Voice of the Law in Transition: Indonesian Jurists and their Languages, 1915–2000* (Leiden: KITLV Press, 2008).
Al-Māwardī, Abī al-Ḥasan 'Alī b. Muhammad b. Ḥabīb al-Baṣrī al-Baghdādī al-Māwardī, *Kitāb al-aḥkām al-sulṭāniyya wa al-will-aḥkām al-sulṭ* (Beirut: al-Maktabat al-'Aṣriyya, n.d.).
Mawdudi, Abu'l-A'la, *The Islamic Law and Constitution* (Lahore: Islamic Publications, n.d.).
McDougall, John James, "The Technocrat's Ideology of Modernity," in Gloria Davis (ed.), *What is Modern Indonesian Culture?* (Athens: Ohio University Center for International Studies, 1979).
McKinnnon, E. Edwards, "Beyond Serandib: A Note on Lambri at the Northern Tip of Aceh," *Indonesia* 46 (1988) 103–21.
McLean, Edward B., *Law and Civilization: The Legal Thought of Roscoe Pound* (Lanham, MD: University Press of America, 1992).
Messick, Brinkley, *The Calligraphic State: Textual Domination and History in a Muslim Society* (Berkeley: University of California Press, 1993).
Meuleman, Johan, "The Institut Agama Islam Negeri at the Crossroads: Some Notes on the Indonesian State Institutes for Islamic Studies," in Johan Meuleman (ed.), *Islam in the Era of Globalization: Muslim Attitudes towards Modernity and Identity* (Jakarta: INIS, 2001).
Meuleman, Johan Hendrik and Henri Chambert-Loir, "Les Instituts islamiques publics indonésiens," in Nicole Grandin and Marc Gaborieau (eds.), *Madrasa: La transmission du savoir dans le monde musulman* (Paris: Éditions Arguments, 1997), 199–216.
Miller, Michelle Ann, *Rebellion and Reform in Indonesia: Jakarta's Security and Autonomy Policies in Aceh* (Abingdon: Routledge, 2009).

Miller, Michelle Ann, "The Role of Islamic Law (Sharia) in Post-Tsunami Reconstruction," in Matthew Clarke, Ismet Fanany, and Sue Kenny (eds.), *Post-Disaster Reconstruction: Lessons from Aceh* (London: Earthscan, 2010), 29–60.

Miller, Michelle Ann, and R. Michael Feener, "Emergency and Islamic Law in Aceh," in Victor Ramraj and Arun Thiruvengadam (eds.), *Law and Emergency Powers in Asia: Exploring the Limits of Legality* (Cambridge, UK; New York: Cambridge University Press, 2010), 213–36.

Misri A. Muchsin, Hasnuddin Yusuf Adan, Muhammad AR, and Khairuddin, Bukhari, *Buku Panduan Pelaksanaan Syariʿat Islam Bagi Birokrat* (Banda Aceh: Dinas Syariʿat Islam, 2008).

Missbach, Antje, *Separatist Conflict in Indonesia: The Long-Distance Politics of the Acehnese Diaspora* (Abingdon: Routledge, 2011).

Mizan Sya'roni, "Muslim-Government Relation in the Indonesian New Order: Making Sense of the Nahdlatul Ulama's Withdrawal from Practical Politics," in Sri Mulyati (ed.), *Islam and Development: A Politico-Religious Response* (Yogyakarta: Permika Montreal, 1997), 255–92.

Morris, Eric E., "Islam and Politics in Aceh: A Study of Center-Periphery Relations in Indonesia," Ph.D. dissertation (Ithaca: Cornell University, 1983).

Muhamad Hisyam, "The Preparatory Committee for Implementation of Sharia (KPPSI): An Islamic Resurgence in South Sulawesi," in Ikuya Tokor (ed.), *Islam in Southeast Asia: Transnational Networks and Local Contexts* (Tokyo: Tokyo University of Foreign Studies, 2009).

Muhammad, "Partisipasi Masyarakat dalam Penegakan Hukum Pada Qanun-Qanun Aceh," in Syamsul Rijal (ed.), *Syariat Islam di Aceh: Problematika Implementasi Syariah* (Banda Aceh: Dinas Syariat Islam, 2009).

Muhammad A.R., *Portret Aceh Pasca Tsunami: Mengintip Peran Dayah dalam Menghadapi Akulturasi Akhlak* (Aceh: Ar-Raniry Press, 2007).

Muhammad Imaduddin Abdul Rahim, *Kuliah Tauhid* (Bandung: Pustaka-Perpustakaan Salman ITB, 1980).

M. Kamal Hassan, "The Influence of Mawdūdī's Thought on Muslims in Southeast Asia: A Brief Survey," *The Muslim World* 93 (July/October 2003) 429–64

Muhammad Suhaili Sufyan, *Busana Islami di Nanggroe Syariat* (Banda Aceh: Dinas Syariat Islam, 2008).

Muhibbuddin Waly, *Ayah Kami: Maulana Syeikh Haji Muhammad Waly al-Khalidy/ Teungku Syeikh Haji Muda Waly* (Singapore: JBW Printers and Binders Pte. Ltd., 1993).

Mujiburrahman, "The Politics of Shariah: The Struggle of the KPPSI in South Sulawesi," in Martin van Bruinessen (ed.), *Contemporary Developments in Indonesian Islam: Explaining the 'Conservative Turn'* (Singapore: ISEAS, 2013).

Mukhtar Aziz, "Tinjauan Historis Pelaksanaan Syariat Islam di NAD," in T.H. Thalhas (ed.), *Pendidikan dan Syariat Islam di Nanggroe Aceh Darussalam dan 8 Undang-Undang Terkait* (Jakarta: Galura Pase, 2007).

Multi Donor Fund, *Implementing Projects, Achieving Results: 18 Months of the Multi Donor Fund for Aceh and Nias—Progress Report III* (Jakarta: 2006).

Muslim Ibrahim, "Sejarah Syari'at Islam di Bumi Aceh," in Rusjdi Ali Muhammad (ed.), *Kontekstualisasi Syari'at Islam di Nanggroe Aceh Darussalam* (Banda Aceh: Ar-Raniry Press, 2003).

Muslim Ibrahim, *Penahapan dalam Legislasi dan Penerapan Syari'at Islam* (Jakarta: Cahaya Ilahi, 2006).

Muslim Thahiry, Khairizzaman, and Abidin Nurdin (eds.), *Wacana Pemikiran Santri Dayah Aceh* (Banda Aceh: BRR, PKPM Aceh & Wacana Press, 2006).

Mustofa Syarif, *Administrasi Pesantren* (Jakarta: PT Paryu Barkah, 1981).

Myrdal, Gunnar, *An American Dilemma: The Negro Problem and Modern Democracy* (New York: Harper and Brothers, 1944).

Nakamura, Hisako, *Conditional Divorce in Indonesia*, Cambridge, MA: Harvard Law School Islamic Legal Studies Program Occasional Publications No. 7 (July 2006).

Nasr, Seyyed Vali Reza, *Vanguard of the Islamic Revolution: The Jama'at-i Islami of Pakistan* (London: I.B. Tauris, 1994).

Natsir, M., *Demokrasi di bawah Hukum* (Jakarta: Penerbit Media Da'wah, 2002—based upon lectures given in 1966).

Nazamuddin, Agussabti, and Syamsudin Mahmud, "Economic Modernization and its Influence on the Social System in Aceh," in Arndt Graf, Susanne Schröter, and Edwin Wieringa (eds.), *Aceh: History, Politics and Culture* (Singapore: ISEAS Publishing, 2010), 81–98.

Nishi, Yoshimi, "Among Bangsa, Keturunan and Daerah: Peace-building and Group Identity in the Law on Governing Aceh, 2006," in Yamamoto Hiroyuki, Anthony Milner, Kawashima Midori, and Arai Kazuhiro (eds.), *Bangsa and Umma: Developments of People-grouping Concepts in Islamized Southeast Asia* (Kyoto: Kyoto University Press, 2011).

Nonaka, Yo, "Isuraamuni motoduku jikohenkakuni yoru shakaikaikakuno kokoromi—Indonesia no daigakudaawaundouno rekishito shisou," Ph.D. dissertation (Tokyo: Keio University, 2011).

Nonaka, Yo, "Indonesiano daigakudaawaundou saikou: Saruman mosukuniokeru isuraamuundou no shisou to gendaitekiigi," *SOIAS Research Paper Series 7* (Tokyo: Sophia University Institute of Asian Cultures, 2012).

Noorhaidi Hasan, "Islamizing Formal Education: Integrated Islamic Schools and a New Trend in Formal Education in Indonesia," *S. Rajaratnam School of International Studies, Working Paper* No. 172 (Singapore: RSIS, 2009).

Nourouzzaman Shiddiqi, *Jeram-Jeram Peradaban Muslim* (Yogyakarta: Pustaka Pelajar, 1996).

Nur Ahmad Fadhil Lubis, "The State's Legal Policy and the Development of Islamic Law in Indonesia's New Order," in Arskal Salim and Azyumardi Azra (eds.), *Shari'a and Politics in Modern Indonesia* (Singapore: ISEAS, 2003), 48–75.

Nur El Ibrahimy, M., *Tgk. M. Daud Beureueh: Perannya dalam Pergolakan di Aceh*, (Jakarta: Gunung Agung, 1982).

Nur Ichwan, Moch., "Official Reform of Islam: State Islam and the Ministry of Religious Affairs in Contemporary Indonesia, 1966–2004," Ph.D. dissertation (Tilburg University, 2006).

Nur Ichwan, Moch.,"The Politics of Sharīʿatization: Central Governmental and Regional Discourses of Sharīʿa implementation in Aceh," in R. Michael Feener and Mark E. Cammack (eds.), *Islamic Law in Contemporary Indonesia: Ideas and Institutions* (Cambridge, MA: Harvard University Press, 2007), 193–215.

Nur Ichwan, Moch., "Ulama and Politics: Majelis Ulama Indonesia in the Early Reformation Era," in Moch. Nur Ichwan and Noorhaidi Hasan (eds.), *Moving with the Times: The Dynamics of Contemporary Islam in a Changing Indonesia* (Yogyakarta: UIN Sunan Kalijaga, 2007).

Nur Ichwan, Moch., "Official Ulema and the Politics of Re-Islamization: The Majelis Permusyawaratan Ulama, Sharīʿatization and Contested Authority in Post-New Order Aceh," *Journal of Islamic Studies* 22.2 (2011) 183–214.

Oepen, Manfred, and Karcher, Wolfgang with Kingham, Robert (eds.), *The Impact of Pesantren in Education and Community Development in Indonesia* (Berlin: Fredrich-Naumann Stiftung, 1988).

Olle, John, "The Majelis Ulama Indonesia versus 'Heresy': The Resurgence of Authoritarian Islam," in Gerry van Klinken and Joshua Barker (eds.), *State of Authority: The State in Society in Indonesia* (Ithaca: Cornell University Southeast Asia Program, 2009).

Oman Fathurahman, *Tarekat Syattariyah di Minangkabau; Teks dan Konteks* (Jakarta: KITLV, 2008).

Östlund, David, "A Knower and Friend of Human Beings, Not Machines: The Business Career of the Terminology of Social Engineering, 1894–1910," *Ideas in History* II.2 (2007) 43–82.

Otto, Benjamin, and Otto, Jan Michiel, "Aceh's Wilayatul Hisbah (Sharīʿa Police): Practices and Perceptions," in R. Michael Feener, David Kloos, and Annemarie Samuels (eds.), *Islam and the Limits of the State: Reconfigurations of Ritual, Doctrine, Community and Authority in Contemporary Aceh* (Leiden: Brill, forthcoming).

Otto, Jan Michiel (ed.), *Sharia Incorporated: A Comparative Overview of the Legal Systems of Twelve Muslim Countries in Past and Present* (Leiden: Leiden University Press, 2010).

Otto Syamsuddin Ishak, *Dari Maaf ke Panik Aceh: Sebuah Sketsa Sosiologi-Politik* (Jakarta: Tifa, Lembaga Studi Pers dan Pembangunan, 2008).

Palmer, Blair, "Services Rendered: Peace, Patronage and Post-Conflict Elections in Aceh," in Edward Aspinall and Marcus Mietzner (eds.), *Problems of Democratisation in Indonesia: Elections, Institutions and Society* (Singapore: ISEAS, 2010), 286–306.

Panduan Program Strata Satu (S-1) Sekolah Tinggi Agama Islam (STAI) Al-Aziziyah Samalanga Tahun Akademik 2005–2006 (Samalanga: Sekolah Tinggi Agama Islam Al-Aziziyah, 2005).

Peters, Rudolph, "From Jurists' Law to Statute Law or What Happens When the Shariʿa is Codified," in B.A. Roberson (ed.), *Shaping the Current Islamic Reformation* (London: Frank Cass, 2003), 82–95.

Peters, Rudolph, *Crime and Punishment in Islamic Law: Theory and Practice from the Sixteenth to the Twenty-first Century* (New York: Cambridge University Press, 2005).

Phillips, Wendell, *Speeches, Lectures and Letters* (Boston: Lee and Shepard Publishers, 1884).

Piekaar, A.J., *Atjèh en de Oorlog met Japan* ('s-Gravenhage-Bandung: N. V. Uitgeverij W. van Hoeve, 1949).
Pijper, G.F., "Nieuwe godsdienstige denkbeelden in Benkoelen," *Fragmenta Islamica: Studiën over het Islamisme in Nederlandsch-Indië* (Leiden: E. J. Brill, 1934), 159–82.
Platzdasch, Bernhard, *Islamism in Indonesia: Politics in the Emerging Democracy* (Singapore: ISEAS Press, 2009).
Pohl, Florian, "Religious Education and Secularization: Indonesia's Pesantren Tradition and Civil Society," Ph.D. dissertation (Philadelphia: Temple University, 2007).
Pompe, Sebastiaan, *The Indonesian Supreme Court: A Study of Institutional Collapse* (Ithaca: Cornell Southeast Asia Program, 2005).
Popper, Karl, *The Open Society and Its Enemies: Volume One—The Spell of Plato* (New York: Routledge, 2008—originally published, 1945).
Porter, Donald J., *Managing Politics and Islam in Indonesia* (London: Routledge, 2002).
Pound, Roscoe, *Social Control through Law* (New Haven: Yale University Press, 1942).
Pound, Roscoe, "Sociology of Law and Sociological Jurisprudence," *The University of Toronto Law Journal* 5.1 (1943) 1–20.
Pound, Roscoe, *An Introduction to the Philosophy of Law* (New Haven: Yale University Press, 1955).
Pound, Roscoe, *The Ideal Element in Law—Tagore Law Lectures*, 1948 (Calcutta: Calcutta University Press, 1958).
Pound, Roscoe, *Pengantar Filsafat Hukum, diterjmahkan dari edisi yang diperluas oleh Moh. Radjab* (Jakarta: Bhratara, 1963).
Prasetyo, Stanley Adi, and Birks,Teresa, "Background and Political Situation in Aceh," in Olle Törnquist, Stanley Adi Prasetyo, and Teresa Birks (eds.), *Aceh: The Role of Democracy for Peace and Reconstruction*, 2nd edition (Jogjakarta: PCD Press, 2010), 47–72.
Priyono, A.E., "Post-DOM Aceh: The Escalation of State Terror and Resistance of Civil Society Movements," in Stanley Adi Prasetyo, A.E. Priyono, and Olle Törnquist (eds.), *Indonesia's Post-Soeharto Democracy Movement* (Jakarta: DEMOS, 2003), 513–41.
Pusat Daʿwah Islam Indonesia (Jakarta: Sekreteriat Pusat Daʿwah Islam Indonesia, Masjid Istiqlal, 1970).
Putnam, George Granville, *Salem Vessels and Their Voyages—Series I: A History of the Pepper Trade with the Island of Sumatra* (Salem, Massachusetts: The Essex Institute, 1924).
Ratno Lukito, "Law and Politics in Post-Independence Indonesia: A Case Study of Religious and Adat Courts," in Arskal Salim and Azyumardi Azra (eds.), *Sharīʿa and Politics in Modern Indonesia* (Singapore: Institute of Southeast Asian Studies Press, 2003).
Redhouse, James W., *A Turkish and English Lexicon: Shewing in English the Significations of the Turkish Terms* (Constantinople: Printed for the American Mission by A.H. Boyajian, 1890/reprinted İstanbul: Çağrı Yayınları, 1992).

Regulation of the President of Republic of Indonesia Number 30 Year 2005 on Master Plan for Rehabilitation and Reconstruction for the Regions and People of the Province of Nanggroe Aceh Darussalam and Nias Islands of the Province of North Sumatra (Jakarta: Republic of Indonesia, 2005).

Reid, Anthony (ed.), *The Contest for North Sumatra: Atjeh, the Netherlands, and Britain, 1858–1898* (Kuala Lumpur: University of Malaya Press, 1969).

Reid, Anthony, *Blood of the People: Revolution and the End of Traditional Rule in Northern Sumatra* (Kuala Lumpur: Oxford University Press, 1979).

Reid, Anthony, *Witnesses to Sumatra: A Travellers' Anthology* (Kuala Lumpur: Oxford University Press, 1995).

Reid, Anthony (ed.), *Verandah of Violence: The Background to the Aceh Problem* (Singapore: Singapore University Press, 2006).

Reid, Anthony, "Islam in South-East Asia and the Indian Ocean littoral, 1500–1800: Expansion, Polarisation, Synthesis," in Anthony Reid and David Morgan (eds.), *The New Cambridge History of Islam*, vol. 3 (Cambridge: Cambridge University Press, 2010), 427–69.

Renoe, Curtis E. "Legal Texts and Truths: The Interactive Production of Fact in Indonesian Criminal Trials," Ph.D. dissertation (New Haven: Yale University, 2002).

Reza Idria, "Mesin Syariat," *Jurnal Gelombang Baru* IV (2009) 12.

Reza Idria, "Muslim Theological Perspectives on Natural Disasters: The Case of Indonesian Earthquakes and Tsunami of 2004," M.A. thesis (Leiden: Leiden University, 2010).

Ricklefs, M.C., "Religion, Politics and Social Dynamics in Java: Historical and Contemporary Rhymes," *Indonesia Update Keynote Speech*, Australian National University, Canberra, 7 September 2007.

Ricklefs, M.C., *Islamisation and Its Opponents in Java: A Political, Social, Cultural and Religious History, c. 1930 to the Present* (Singapore: NUS Press, 2012).

Riddell, Peter G., *Islam and the Malay-Indonesian World: Transmission and Responses* (London: Hurst and Company, 2001).

Ridwan Hasan (ed.), *Islam and Globalization: Challenges and Opportunities to the Future Renaissance* (Aceh: Unimal Press, 2010).

Riesebrodt, Martin, *The Promise of Salvation: A Theory of Religion* (Chicago: University of Chicago Press, 2010).

Rifki Rosyad, "A Quest for True Islam: A Study of the Islamic Resurgence Movement among the Youth in Bandung, Indonesia," M.A. thesis (Canberra: Australian National University, 1995).

Rist, Manfred, "Economic Development of Aceh since 1945," in Arndt Graf, Susanne Schröter, and Edwin Wieringa (eds.), *Aceh: History, Politics and Culture* (Singapore: ISEAS Publishing, 2010), 99–119.

Rizki Ridyasmara, *Gerilya Salib di Serambi Mekkah: Dari Zaman Portugis Hingga Paska Tsunami* (Jakarta: Pustaka Al-Kautsar, 2006).

al-Rānīrī, Nūr al-Dīn Muḥammad Jīlānī b. ʿAlī b. Ḥasanjī b. Muḥammad b. Ḥumayd, *Ṣirāt al-Mustaqīm fī fiqh madhhab al-Shāfiʿī* (Cairo: al-Bābī al-Ḥalabī 1937).

Roeslan Abdulgani, "Prof. Ali Hasjmy sebagai Pembangun Jembatan Kepercayaan antara Pusat dan Daerah Berdasarkan Islamisme-Nasionalisme sesuai

Pancasila," in Badruzzaman Ismail (ed.), A. Hasjmy, *Aset Sejarah Masa Kini Dan Masa Depan: Delapan Puluh Tahun Melalui Jalan Raya Dunia* (Jakarta: Bulan Bintang, 1994), 17–22.

Roff, William R., "Patterns of Islamization in Malaysia, 1890s–1990s: Exemplars, Institutions and Vectors," *Studies of Islam and Society in Southeast Asia* (Singapore: NUS Press, 2009), 97–115.

Rosimanidar, "Wacana Madrasah Modern Dalam Persaingan Global," in Ridwan Hasan (ed.), *Islam and Globalization: Challenges and Opportunities to the Future Renaissance* (Aceh: Unimal Press, 2010), 499–506.

Rusjdi Ali Muhammad, *Revitalisasi Syarʿiat Islam di Aceh: Problem, Solusi dan Implementasi* (Jakarta: Logos Wacana Ilmu, 2003).

Rusjdi Ali Muhammad, *Revitalisasi Syariat Islam di Aceh: Problem, Solusi, dan implementasi menuju Pelaksanaan Hukum Islam din Nanggroe Aceh Darussalam* (Banda Aceh: Ar-Raniry Press, 2003).

Ryter, Loren, "Youth, Gangs and the State in Indonesia," Ph.D. dissertation (Seattle: University of Washington, 2002).

Ryter, Loren, "Reformasi Gangsters," *Inside Indonesia*, (April 2005), <http://www.insideindonesia.org/weekly-articles-82-apr-jun-2005/reformasi-gangsters-2407177>, accessed 30 July 2012.

Safrina, "Luka Aceh Syariat Atau Aceh Lukai Syariat," 5 November 2010, <http://lidahtinta.wordpress.com/2010/11/05/luka-aceh-syariat-atau-aceh-lukai-syariat>, accessed 27 August 2012.

Safwan Idris, *Mengemban Amanah Allah: Reaktualisasi Syariat Islam dan Masa Depan Pendidikan di Aceh* (Pidato Pengukuhan Jabatan Guru Besar Tetap dalam Ilmu Pendidikan pada Fakultas Tarbiyah IAIN Ar-Raniry, Banda Aceh, 1999).

Saleh Suhaidy, *Buku Pegangan Teungku Imeum Meunasah* (Aceh: Dinas Syariat Islam Provinsi Nanggroe Aceh Darussalam, 2007, reprinted 2009).

Samuels, Annemarie, "After the Tsunami: The Remaking of Everyday Life in Banda Aceh, Indonesia," Ph.D. dissertation (Leiden: Leiden University, 2012).

Santos, Gabriel A., *Reforming the Broken Body: Church and State after Disaster* (Eugene, OR: Cascade Books, 2009).

Sarity Pawiloy, *Madrasah Islam Modern* (Banda Aceh: Pusat Latihan Penelitian Ilmu-Ilmu Sosial, 1974).

Schacht, Joseph, "Problems of Modern Islamic Legislation," *Studia Islamica* 12 (1960) 99–129.

Schlegel, Stuart A., "Technocrats in a Muslim Society: Symbolic Community in Aceh," in Gloria Davis (ed.), *What is Modern Indonesian Culture?* (Athens: Ohio University Center for International Studies, 1979), 232–48.

Semerdjian, Elyse, *Off the Straight Path: Illicit Sex, Law, and Community in Ottoman Aleppo* (Syracuse University Press, 2008).

Sevea, Terenjit, "Making Medinas in the East: Islamic Connections and Progressive Islam," in R. Michael Feener and Terenjit Sevea (eds.), *Islamic Connections: Muslim Societies in South and Southeast Asia* (Singapore: ISEAS, 2009), 149–74.

Shaham, Ron, *Family and the Courts in Modern Egypt: A Study Based on Decisions by the Sharīʿa Courts, 1900–1955* (Leiden: Brill, 1997).

Shaham, Ron, "Western Scholars on the Role of the 'Ulamā' in Adapting the Sharī'a to Modernity: A Critical Review," in Meir Hatina (ed.), *Guardians of Faith in Modern Times: 'Ulamā' in the Middle East* (Leiden: E.J. Brill, 2009), 171–92.
Shaham, Ron, *The Expert Witness in Islamic Courts: Medicine and Crafts in the Service of Law* (Chicago: University of Chicago Press, 2010).
Shidarta, "Posisi Pemikiran Teori Hukum Pembangunan dalam Konfigurasi Aliran Pemikiran Hukum (sebuah diagnosis awal)," in Shidarta (ed.), *Mochtar Kusuma-Atmadja dan Teori Hukum Pembangunan: Eksistensi dan Implikasi* (Jakarta: Epistema Institute, 2012), 9–80.
Shiraishi, Saya, "Aceh under the Japanese Occupation: Rival Leaders in Aceh Besar and Pidie," M.A. thesis (Tokyo: International Christian University, 1975).
Sidel, John T., *Riots, Pogroms, Jihad: Religious Violence in Indonesia* (Singapore: NUS Press, 2007).
Siegel, James T., *The Rope of God* (Berkeley: University of California Press, 1969).
Siegel, James T., *Shadow and Sound: The Historical Thought of a Sumatran People* (Chicago: University of Chicago Press, 1979).
Siegel, Jim T., "Syariat Islam di Acheh," *Jurnal Gelombang Baru* IV (2009) 105–6.
Sieh, Kerry, "The Sunda Megathrust: Past, Present and Future," in Patrick Daly, R. Michael Feener, and Anthony Reid (eds.), *From the Ground Up: Perspectives on Post-Tsunami and Post-Conflict Aceh* (Singapore: ISEAS Press, 2012), 1–22.
[Al-Singkel] Teungku Sjeich Abdurrauf alias Teungku Tjhik Sjiah Kuala, *Mir'at at-Tullab Fi Tashil Ma'rifat Ahkam Ash-Syar'iyyah li'l Malik Al-Wahhab/Tjermin bagi mereka jang menuntut Ilmu Fiqih pada memudahkan mengenai segala Hukum Sjara' Allah* (Banda Aceh: Universitas Syiah Kuala, 1971).
Siti Musdah Mulia, with Mark E. Cammack, "Toward a Just Marriage Law: Empowering Indonesian Women through a Counter Legal Draft to the Indonesian Compilation of Islamic Law," in R. Michael Feener and Mark E. Cammack (eds.), *Islamic Law in Contemporary Indonesia: Ideas and Institutions* (Cambridge, MA: Harvard University Press, 2007), 128–45.
Siti Zalikha H. Ibrahim, *Menuju Syariat Islam Kaffah* (Banda Aceh: Lapena Institute for Culture and Society, 2008).
Siti Zalikha Ibrahim, "Santri Menemukan Jati Diri," in Ahmadun Yosi Herfanda (ed.), *Menuju Syariat Islam Kaffah: Pikiran dan Pengalaman Santri Aceh dalam menuntut Ilmu dan Hubungannya dengan Perbuatan Nyata* (Banda Aceh: Lepena, 2008), 27–80.
Smillie, Ian, "Relief and Development: The Struggle for Synergy," Thomas J. Watson Jr. *Institute for International Studies Occasional Papers #33* (Providence: Brown University, 1998).
Smith, Catherine, "War, Medicine and Morality in Aceh: An Ethnography of 'Trauma' as an Idiom of Distress," Ph.D. dissertation (Canberra: Australian National University, 2012).
Snouck Hurgronje, C., *The Achehnese*, 2 vols., trans. A.W.S. O'Sullivan (Leiden: E. J. Brill, 1906).
Soediman Kartohadiprodjo, *Hukum Nasional: Beberapa Tjatatan* (Bandung: Binatjipta, 1968).

Soedirman, "Dasar Pikiran Majelis Ulama Indonesia tentang Proyek-proyek Pembangunannya," *Majelis Ulama: Untuk Informasi dan Komunikasi Intern* 8 (August 1982) 7–16.

Spiegel, Paul, "The Relief-Reconstruction-Development Dynamic: A New approach to the Concept of Linking Relief, Reconstruction, and Development," *Refuge* 17.4 (October 1998) 33–7.

Sri Suyanta, *Pola Hubungan Ulama dan Umara: Kajian Tentang Pasang Surut Peran Ulama Aceh* (Jakarta: Universitas Islam Negeri (UIN) Syarif Hidayatullah, 2005).

Sri Suyanta, Nurjannah Ismail, Muhammad Maulana, Emk Elidar, and Muhammad Yasir (eds.), *Buku Panduan—Pelaksanaan Syarʿiat Islam Untuk Remaja, Pelajar dan Mahasiswa* (Banda Aceh: Dinas Syariʿat Islam, 2008).

Sri Widodo, and Ikhwan Nursyujoko (eds.), *99 Tangan Tuhan di Aceh: Misteri dan Keajaiban di Balik Tsunami* (Jakarta: Yayasan Air Mata, 2005).

Standardisasi Pengadilan Agama (Jakarta: Direktorat Pembinaan Badan Peradilan Agama Islam, 1980).

Stange, Gunnar, and Patock, Roman, "From Rebels to Rulers and Legislators: The Political Transformation of the Free Aceh Movement (GAM) in Indonesia," *Journal of Current Southeast Asian Affairs* 29.1 (2010) 95–120.

Starrett, Gregory, *Putting Islam to Work: Education, Politics and Religious Transformation in Egypt* (Berkeley: University of California Press, 1998).

Steenbrink, Karel A., *Pesantren, Madrasah, Sekolah: Pendidikan Islam dalam Kurun Moderen* (Jakarta: LP3ES, 1986).

Stockmann, Petra, *Indonesian Reformasi as Reflected in Law: Change and Continuity in Post-Suharto Era Legislation on the Political System and Human Rights* (Münster: LIT Verlag, 2004).

Strang, Johan, "Overcoming the Rift Between 'Is' and 'Ought': Gunnar Myrdal and the Philosophy of Social Engineering," *Ideas in History* II.2 (2007) 143–78.

Sukarno, *Under the Banner of Revolution* (Jakarta: Publication Committee, 1966).

Sukarno, and Adams, Cindy, *Soekarno: An Autobiography, as told to Cindy Adams* (Indianapolis: The Bobbs-Merrill Company, Inc., 1965).

Sulaiman Tripa, *Perang Melawan Khalwat di Aceh: Pelaksanaan Qanun Khalwat dan Profil Kasus Khalwat dalam Harian Serambi Indonesia, 15 January 2007–15 Januari 2008* (Banda Aceh: Pustaka Novum, 2008).

Suparlan Suryopratondo, Abd. Rachman Saleh, Marwan Saridjo,*and* Mustofa Syarif *(eds.), Kapita Selekta Pondok Pesantren* (Jakarta: PT Paryu Barkah, 1976).

Supomo, R., *Bab-Bab tentang Hukum Adat* (n.p.: Penerbitan Universitas, 1959).

Surjadi, A., *Daʿwah Islam dengan Pembangunan Masjarakat Desa* (Bandung: Rivanty, 1971), 94–9.

Suryadi, "Shaikh Daud of Sunur: Conflict between Reformists and the Shattariyyah Sufi Order in Rantau Pariaman in the First Half of the Nineteenth Century," *Studia Islamika* 8.3 (2001) 57–124.

Syahrizal (ed.), *Kontekstualisasi Syariʿat Islam di Nanggroe Aceh Darussalam* (Banda Aceh: Ar-Raniry Press, 2003).

Syahrizal, "Strategi Pelaksanaan Syariʿat Islam di Nanggroe Aceh Darussalam," in Azman Ismail (ed.), *Suara Khatib Baiturrahman* (Banda Aceh: Pengurus Masjid Raya Baiturrahman, 2006), 20–5.

Syahrizal Abbas, "Pelaksanaan Syariʿat Islam di Aceh Dalam Kerangka Sistem Hukum Nasional," in Syahrizal (ed.), *Dimensi Pemikiran Hukum dalam Implementasi Syariat Islam di Aceh* (Banda Aceh: Dinas Syariat Islam Provinsi Nanggroe Aceh Darussalam, 2007), 2–13.

Syahrizal Abbas, *Syariʿat Islam di Aceh: Ancangan Metodologis dan Penerapannya* (Aceh: Dinas Syaria'at Islam Provinsi Aceh, 2009).

Syariat Islam Akan Membawa Aceh Makin Tertinggal, <http://www.topix.com/forum/world/malaysia/T0VS2NMLQI3J75M0S>, accessed 22 August 2012.

Syed Muhammad Naguib al-Attas, *Rānīrī and the Wujūdiyah of 17th Century Acheh* (Kuala Lumpur: Monographs of the Malaysian Branch Royal Asiatic Society, 1966).

Syukrinur A. Gani, "Syariat Islam dan Dakwah," in Zaki Fuad Chalil (ed.), *Melihat Syariat Islam Dari Berbagai Dimensi* (Banda Aceh: Dinas Syariat Islam, 2007).

Tanter, Richard, and Young, Kenneth (eds.), *The Politics of Middle Class Indonesia* (Clayton: Monash University Centre of Southeast Asian Studies, 1990).

At-Tarusani, Jalaluddin, *Safinat Al-Hukkam fi Takhlish Al-Khashsham* (Banda Aceh: Dinas Syariʿat Islam Provinsi Nanggroe Aceh Darussalam/Fakultas Syariʿah IAIN Ar-Raniry, 2004).

Taufik Abdullah, *Schools and Politics: The Kaum Muda Movement in West Sumatra, 1927–1933* (Ithaca: Cornell University SEAP, 1971).

Taufik Al Mubarak, *Aceh Pungo* (Banda Aceh: Bandar Publishing, 2009).

Taylor, Jean Gelman, "Aceh Histories in the KITLV Images Archive," in R. Michael Feener, Patrick Daly, and Anthony Reid (eds.), *Mapping the Acehnese Past* (Leiden: KITLV Press, 2011), 199–239.

Telford, John, "Disaster Recovery: An International Humanitarian Challenge?" in Patrick Daly, R. Michael Feener, and Anthony Reid (eds.), *From the Ground Up: Perspectives on Post-Tsunami and Post-Conflict Aceh* (Singapore: ISEAS Press, 2012), 25–39.

Telford, John, J. Cosgrove, and R. Houghton, *Joint Evaluation of the International Response to the Indian Ocean Tsunami: Synthesis Report* (London: Tsunami Evaluation Coalition (TEC), 2006).

Teuku Abdullah Sanny, *Tsunami Aceh* (Banda Aceh: Pemerintah Provinsi Nanggroe Aceh Darussalam, 2008).

Teuku Ibrahim Alfian, "Aceh and the Holy War (Prang Sabil)," in Anthony Reid (ed.), *Verandah of Violence: The Background to the Aceh Problem* (Singapore: Singapore University Press, 2006), 109–20.

Thalhas, T.H., and Choirul Fuad Yusuf (eds.), *Pendidikan dan Syariat Islam di Nanggroe Aceh Darussalam dan 8 Undang-Undang Terkait* (Jakarta: Galura Pase, 2007).

Tyan, Emile, *Histoire de l'organisation judicaire en pays d'Islam* (Leiden: E.J. Brill, 1960).

Udjang Tholib, "The Relation between the Qanun and the Shariʿa in the Ottoman Empire (15th–17th Centuries)," in *Islam and Development: A Politico-Religious Response* (Yogyakarta: Permika Montreal, 1997), 45–59.

Ujong Rimba, *Risalah Majlis Ulama Daerah Istimewa Aceh: Sumbangan Pikiran untuk Musyawarah Majlis Ulama se Indonesia yang berlangsung di Jakarta sejak tanggal 21 s/d 27 Juli, 1975* (n.p. – typescript KITLV Library, Leiden # M q 1176N I).

Vandewalle, Dirk, *Libya since Independence: Oil and State-building* (Ithaca: Cornell University Press, 1998).

Velde, J.J. van de, *De Godsdienstige rechtspraak in Nederlandsch-Indië, Staatsrechtlijk beschouwd* (Leiden: Drukkerij A Vros, 1928).

Veltman, T.J., "Nota over de Geschiedenis van het Landschap Pidië," *Tijdschrift van het Bataviaasch Genootschap van Kunsten en Wetenschappen* 58 (1919) 71–88.

White, Philip, and Lionel Cliffe, "Matching Response to Context in Complex Political Emergencies: 'Relief,' 'Development,' 'Peace-building' or Something In-Between?" *Disasters* 24.4 (2000) 314–42.

Wickham, Carrie Rosefsky, *Mobilizing Islam: Religion, Activism, and Political Change in Egypt* (New York: Columbia University Press, 2002).

Wieringa, Edwin, "The Dream of the King and the Holy War against the Dutch: The 'Kôteubah' of the Acehnese Epic, 'Hikayat Prang Gômpeuni,'" *Bulletin of the School of Oriental and African Studies* 61.2 (1998) 298–308.

Wieringa, Edwin, "A Tale of Two Cities and Two Modes of Reading: A Transformation of the Intended Function of the Syair Mekah dan Madinah," *Die Welt des Islams* 42.2 (2002) 174–206.

Wieringa, Edwin, "God Speaks through Natural Disasters, but What Does He Say? Islamic Interpretations in Indonesian Tsunami Poetry," in Arndt Graf, Susanne Schröter, and Edwin Wieringa (eds.), *Aceh: History, Politics and Culture* (Singapore: ISEAS Publishing, 2010), 313–33.

Wigdor, David, *Roscoe Pound: Philosopher of Law* (Westport, CT: Greenwood Press, 1974).

Wilmot, Fadlullah, "Sharīʿah in Aceh: Panacea or Blight?" *Accord: An International Review of Peace Initiatives* 20 (2008) 76–9.

World Bank, "Literacy rate, youth total (% of people ages 15–24)," <http://data.worldbank.org/indicator/SE.ADT.1524.LT.ZS/countries>, accessed 1 August 2012.

Wormser, Paul, *Le Bustan al-Salatin de Nuruddin ar-Raniri: Réflexions sur le role culturel d'un étranger dans le monde Malais au XVII*[e] *siècle* (Paris: Cahiers d'Archipel, 2012).

Yahya Harahap, "Informasi Materi Kompilasi Hukum Islam: Mempositifkan Abstraksi Hukum Islam," in Cik Hassan Bisri (ed.), *Kompilasi Hukum Islam dan Peradilan Agama dalam Sistem Hukum Nasional* (Jakarta: Logos Wacana Ilmu, 1999), 21–80.

Yayasan Insan Cita Madani, *Hasily Survey YICM tentang Penerapan Qanun-Qanun Syariat Islam* (Banda Aceh: YICM, 2007).

Zainal Abidin Ahmad, *Memperkembang dan Mempertahankan Pendidikan Islam di Indonesia* (Jakarta: Bulan Bintang, 1976), 108–13.

Zaman, Muhammad Qasim, *The Ulama in Contemporary Islam: Custodians of Change* (Princeton: Princeton University Press, 2002).

Zaman, Muhammad Qasim, "Epilogue: Competing Conceptions of Religious Education," in Robert W. Hefner and Muhammad Qasim Zaman (eds.), *Schooling Islam: The Culture and Politics of Modern Muslim Education* (Princeton: Princeton University Press, 2006), 242–68.

Zarkasyi, "Penerapan Syariat Islam di Aceh," in Siti Zalikha H. Ibrahim (ed.), *Menuju Syariat Islam Kaffah* (Banda Aceh: Lapena Institute for Culture and Society, 2008).

Ziemek, Manfred, *Pesantren dalam Perubahan Sosial* (Jakarta: P3M, 1986).
Zollner, Barbara H.E., *The Muslim Brotherhood: Hasan al-Hudaybi and Ideology* (Abingdon: Routledge, 2009).

3. Legislation and Executive Decisions (in Chronological Order)

Staatsblad No. 152/1882 - Ordonnantie van den Gouverneur Generaal bevattende bepalingen omtrent de samenstelling enz. der priesterraden op Java en Madura. Reprinted in Thoralf Hanstein, *Islamisches Recht und Nationales Recht: Eine Unstersuchung zum Einfluß des Islamischen Rechts auf die Entwicklung des modernen Familienrechts am Beispiel Indonesiens* (Frankfurt: Peter Lang, 2002), 140–1.
Aceh Syu Rei (Undang-Undang) no. 12/ Tahun Syowa 19, 2 Gatsu, 13 Nichi (13 February, 1944).
Keputusan No. 35 Sidang Pekerdja Dewan Perwakilan Aceh Pada Hari Rabu Tanggal 3 December 1947.
Peraturan Pemerintah Nomor 29/Tahun 1957 tentang Pembentukan Pengadilan Agama/Mahkamah Sjar'ijah di Propinsi Aceh, Pasal 2.
Peraturan Pemerintah Nomor 45/Tahun 1957 tentang Pembentukan Pengadilan Agama/Mahkamah Sjar'ijah di luar Djawa dan Madura.
Peraturan Daerah Aceh Nomor 17/1958 tentang Larangan Membuat, Memasukkan, Memperdagangkan, Menyimpan dan Meminum Minuman Keras di Daerah Propinsi Daerah Istimewa Aceh.
Surat Keputusan Perdana Menteri Republic Indonesia Nomor 1/missi/59/Tgl. 26 Mei, 1958.
Penetapan Menteri Agama Nomor 35/Tahun 1960.
Penetapan Menteri Agama Nomor 43/Tahun 1960.
Peraturan Peresiden Republik Indonesia Nomor 11/Tahun, 1960.
Peraturan Daerah/Tingkat Ke II Atjeh Timur Nomor 4/Tahun 1961 tentang Mengatur Pedjualan Minuman Keras.
Peraturan Daerah/Tingkat Ke II Atjeh Tengah Nomor 36/Tahun 1961 tentang Mengatur Pendjualan Makanan dan Minuman Keras.
Keputusan Penguasa Perang Nomor KPTS/PEPERDA -061/3/62 tentang Kebidjaksanan Pelaksanaan Unsur-unsur Sjari'at Islam bagi Pemeluk-pemelluknja di Daerah Istimewa Atjeh.
Pernyataan Nomor B-71/1/DPRD-RG/1962.
Peraturan Daerah Istimewa Atjeh Nomor 1/Tahun 1963 tentang Pelaksanaan Sjiar Agama Islam.
Peraturan Daerah Propinsi Daerah Istimewa Atjeh Nomor 1/1966 tentang Pedoman Dasar Majlis Mermusjawaratan Propinsi Daerah Istimewa Atjeh.
Peraturan Daerah Propinsi Daerah Istimewa Atjeh Nomor 6/1966 tentang Larangan Membuat, Memasukkan, Memperdagangkan, Menjimpan dan Menimbun Minuman Keras.
Peraturan Daerah Propinsi Daerah Istimewa Aceh Nomor 6/1968 tentang Ketentuan-ketentuan Pokok Pelaksanaan Unsur-unsur Sjari'at Islam.
Undang-Undang Republik Indonesia Nomor 1/Tahun 1974 tentang Perkawinan.
Rencana Pembangunan Lima Tahun Kedua/Tahun 1974/75 s.d. 1978/79.

Keputusan Menteri Agama Republik Indonesia Nomor 13/Tahun 1981 tentang Klasifikasi Pengadilan Tinggi Agama dan Pengadilan Agama se Indonesia.

Undang-Undang Nomor 7/Tahun 1989 tentang Peradilan Agama.

Peraturan Daerah Istimewa Aceh Nomor 4/Tahun 1999 tentang Larangan Minuman Beralkohol di Propinsi Daerah Istimewa Aceh.

Undang-Undang Republik Indonesia Nomor 22/Tahun 1999 tentang Pemerintahan Daerah.

Undang-Undang Republik Indonesia Nomor 44/1999 tentang Penyelenggaraan Keistimewaan Propinsi Daerah Istimewa Aceh.

Peraturan Daerah Propinsi Daerah Istimewa Aceh Nomor 4/Tahun 2000 tentang Perubahan Pertama atas Peraturan Daerah Nomor 4/Tahun 1999.

Peraturan Daerah Nomor 5/Tahun 2000 tentang Pelaksanaan Syariat Islam di Provinsi Daerah Istimewa Aceh.

Peraturan Daerah Propinsi Daerah Istimewa Aceh Nomor 7/Tahun 2000 tentang Penyelenggaraan Kehidupan Adat.

Instruksi Gubernur Daerah Istimewa Aceh Nomor 05/INSTR/2000/Tahun 2000 tentang Pembudayaan Kemakmuran Masjid dan Meunasah dalam Provinsi Daerah Istimewa Aceh.

Peraturan Dearah Aceh Nomor 7/Tahun 2000 tentang Penylelenggaraan Adat.

Undang-Undang Republik Indonesia Nomor 18/Tahun 2001 tentang Otonomi Khusus bagi Provinsi Daerah Istimewa Aceh sebagai Provinsi Nanggroe Aceh Darussalam.

Peraturan Daerah Nomor 33/2001 tentang Pembentukan Susunan Organisasi dan/ Tata Kerja Dinas Syariat Islam Propinsi Daerah Istimewa Aceh.

Instruksi Gubernur Propinsi Nanggroe Aceh Darussalam Nomor 04/INSTR/2002/ Tahun 2002 tentang Larangan Judi (Maisir), Buntut, Taruhan dan Sejenisnya yang Mengandung Unsur-Unsur Perjudian dalam Propinsi Nanggroe Aceh Darussalam.

Instruksi Gubernur Provinsi Nanggroe Aceh Darussalam Nomor 05/INSTR/2002/ Tahun 2002 tentang Tata Pergaulan/Khalwat antara Pria dan Wanita dalam Provinsi Nanggroe Aceh Darussalam.

Qanun Provinsi Aceh Nomor 10/Tahun 2002 tentang Peradilan Syariat Islam.

Qanun Provinsi Nanggroe Aceh Darussalam Nomor 10/Tahun 2002 tentang Peradilan Syariat Islam.

Qanun Provinsi Nanggroe Aceh Darussalam Nomor 11/Tahun 2002 tentang Pelaksanaan Syariat Islam bidang Aqidah, Ibadah dan Syiʿar Islam.

Surat Edaran Gubernur Provinsi Nanggroe Aceh Darussalam 536/20976/Tahun 2002 tentang Larangan Minuman Beralkohol (Khamar).

Qanun Nomor 5/Tahun 2003 tentang Pemerintahan Gampong dalam Provinsi Nanggroe Aceh Darussalam.

Qanun Provinsi Nanggroe Aceh Darussalam Nomor 9/2003 tentang Hubungan/ Tata Kerja Majelis Permusyawaratan Ulama dengan Eksekutif, Legislatif dan Instansi lainnya.

Qanun Provinsi Nanggroe Aceh Darussalam Nomor 12/Tahun 2003 tentang Minuman Khamar dan Sejenisnya.

Qanun Provinsi Nanggroe Aceh Darussalam Nomor 13/Tahun 2003 tentang Maisir (Perjudian).

Qanun Provinsi Nanggroe Aceh Darussalam Nomor 14/Tahun 2003 tentang Khalwat (Mesum).

Keputusan Presiden Republik Indonesia Nomor 11/Tahun 2003 tentang Mahkamah Syar'iyah Provinsi di Provinsi Nanggroe Aceh Darussalam.

Keputusan Bersama Gubernur, Kepala Kepolisian Daerah, Kepala Kejaksaan Tinggi, Ketua Mahkamah Syar'iyah Provinsi, Ketua Pengadilan Tinggi dan Kepala Kantor Wilayah Departemen Kehakiman dan HAM Provinsi Nanggroe Aceh Darussalam Nomor: 26/PKS/2004, Nomor: SKEP/62/VIII/2004, Nomor: B-1229/N.1/08/2004, Nomor: MSY. P/K/HK.009/614/2004, Nomor: W1.D1.UM.01.10-1116, Nomor: W1. UM.01.08-1604 tentang Operasionalisasi Kewenangan Mahkamah Syar'iyah.

Qanun Provinsi Aceh Nomor 7/Tahun 2004 tentang Pengelolaan Zakat.

Keputusan Gubernur Nomor 01/Tahun 2004 tentang Organisasi dan Tata Kerja Wilayatul Hisbah.

Keputusan Presiden Republik Indonesia Nomor 21/Tahun 2004 tentang Pengalihan Organisasi, Administrasi dan Finansial di Lingkungan Peradilan Umum dan Peradilan Usaha Negara dan Peradilan Agama ke Mahkamah Agung.

Undang-Undang Nomor 10/Tahun 2004 tentang Tatacara Undang-undang.

Peraturan Gubernor Provinsi Nanggroe Aceh Darussalam Nomor 10/Tahun 2005 tentang Petunjuk/Teknis Pelaksanaan Uqubat Cambuk.

Undang-Undang Republik Indonesia Nomor 3/20006 tentang Perubahan atas Undang-Undang Nomor 7/1989 tentang Peradilan Agama.

Undang-Undang Republik Indonesia Nomor 11/Tahun 2006 tentang Pemerintahan Aceh (Law on Governing Aceh/LoGA).

Peraturan Gubernur Provinsi Nanggroe Aceh Darussalam Nomor 41/Tahun 2009 tentang Susunan Organisasi dan/Tata Kerja Unit Pelaksana/Teknis Dinas Pada Dinas Syariat Islam Provinsi Nanggroe Aceh Darussalam.

Qanun Propinsi Aceh Nomor 2/Tahun 2009 tentang Majelis Permusyawaratan Ulama.

Qanun Propinsi Aceh Nomor --- /2009 tentang Hukum Acara Jinayat.

Qanun Propinsi Aceh Nomor --- /2009 tentang Hukum Jinayat.

Peraturan Bupata Aceh Barat Nomor 5/2010 tentang Penegakan Syariat Islam dalam Pemakaian Busana Islami di Kabupaten Aceh Barat.

Keputusan Bersama Gubernor Aceh, Panglima Komando Daerah Militer Iskandar Muda, Kepala Polisi Daerah Aceh, Kepala Kejaksaan Tinggi Aceh, dan Kepala Kantor Wilayah Kementerian Agama Aceh Nomor 450.1/165/2011, KEP/216/IV/2011, KEP/65/IV/2011, KEP-073/N.1/Dsp.5/04/2011, KW.01.1/4/ HM.00.1/766/2011 tentang Larangan Kegiatan Aliran Millata Abraham di Aceh.

Peraturan Gubernor Aceh Nomor 9/2011 tentang Larangan Kegiatan Aliran Millata Abraham di Aceh.

4. Fatwas and Ulama Council Decisions (in Chronological Order)

Keputusan Musyawarah Alim Ulama Se-Daerah Provinsi Daerah Istimewa Aceh (26 November 1967).

Keputusan Komisi A Majelis Ulama Provinsi Daerah Istimewa Aceh mengenai Masalah Thariqat (22 March 1972).

Keputusan Komisi A Majelis Ulama Provinsi Daerah Istimewa Aceh mengenai Bangunan diatas Kuburan (23 March 1972).

Keputusan Komisi A Majelis Ulama Provinsi Daerah Istimewa Aceh (7 November 1974).

Hasil Keputusan Raker Majelis Ulama Keb.Aceh Timor yang Berlangsusng dari tanggal 31 January s/d 2 Bebruari 1975 di Langsa.

Fatwa Majelis Ulama Provinsi Daerah Istimewa Aceh tentang Khutba Hari Raya (8 December 1975).

"Pernyataan Majelis Ulama Indonesia tentang Pemilu/Tahun 1977," Bulletin Majelis Ulama Indonesia—Untuk Informasi dan Komunikasi Intern 12 (Banda Aceh: Sekretariat MUI, March 1977), Arsip Propinsi Aceh - 338/53.

Keputusan Rapat Kerja Komisi A Majelis Ulama Provinsi Daerah Istimewa Aceh tentang Ajaran Makrifatullah dan Ajaran Ahmad Arifin (16 July 1978).

Keputusan Rapat Kerja Komisi A Majelis Ulama Provinsi Daerah Istimewa Aceh tentang Talfiq (16 July 1978).

Majlis Ulama Daerah Istimewa Aceh, Surat perihal Pembaharuan Sistim Pendidikan Nasional (Nomor 420/MU/101), 9 February 1979.

Tauhsiyah Majlis Permusyawaratan ʿulamāʾ Kota Lhokseumawe Nomor 94/2004 tentang Surat Selebaran.

Kumpulan Fatwa-fatwa Majelis Ulama Daerah Istimewa Aceh (Banda Aceh: MPU, 2005).

Taushiyah Majelis Permusyawaratan Ulama (MPU) Kota Lhokseumawe Nomor 247/2006 tentang Pemilihan Kepala Daerah dan Walikota/ wakil Walikota Lhokseumawe.

Fatwa Majelis Permusyawaratan Ulama Nanggroe Aceh Darussalam Nomor 04/2007 tentang Pedoman Identifikasi Aliran Sesat.

Fatwa Majelis Permusyawaratan Ulama Nanggroe Aceh Darussalam Nomor 07/2008 tentang Thariqat Naqsyabandiyah di Kebun Ubi, Aceh Tamiang.

Fatwa Majelis Permusyawaratan Ulama Provinsi Nanggroe Aceh Darussalam Nomor 451/1167/2008 tentang Beberapa Masalah Aqidah, Syariʿah (Fiqh) dan Akhlak.

Taushiyah Majelis Permusyawaratan Ulama (MPU) Nomor 6/2008 tentang Peringatan/Tsunami dan Menyambut/Tahun Baru (Tahun Baru Hijriyah dan Miladiyah).

Muzakarah Ulama Se Kabupaten Aceh Utara Dilaksanakan pada Tanggal 15 s/d 16 Juli 2009 oleh Majelis Mermusyawaratan Ulama (MPU) Kabupaten Aceh Utara di Gedung Hasbi Ash Shiddiqi, Moun Gedung Kota Lhokseumawe, Thema: 'Melalui Muzakarah Ulama-Umara kita Tingkatkan Pemahaman Hukum Syariʿah' (unpublished official report compiled by the North Aceh MPU, 2009).

Majelis Permusyawaratan Aceh, Kesimpulan Mubahasah Ulama Aceh/Terhadap Pemahaman yang Menimbulkan Bid'ah dan Syubhat (3 August 2009).

5. Court Decisions and Documents (in Chronological Order)

Keputusan Mahkamah Agung Nomor 1/Tahun 1977 tentang Jalan Pengadilan dalam Pemeriksaan Kasasi dalam Perkara Perdata dan Perkara Pidana oleh Pengadilan Agama dan Pengadilan Militer.

Surat Edaran Mahkamah Agung Nomor 04/1977 perihal Pelaksanaan Jalan Pengadilan Pemeriksaan Kasasi dalam Perkara Perdata dan Pidana oleh Peradilan Agama dan Peradilan Militer.

Peraturan Mahkamah Agung Republik Indonesia Nomor 2/Tahun 2003 tentang Prosedur Mediasi di Pengadilan.

Keputusan Ketua Mahkamah Agung Republik Indonesia tentang Pelimpahan Sebagian Kewenangan dari Peradilan Umum kepada Mahkamah Syarʿiyah Provinsi di Provinsi Nanggroe Aceh Darussalam Nomor: KMA/070/SK/X2004.

Putusan Mahkamah Syariah Provinsi Aceh Nomor 03/JN/2006/1/4Sy-Prov.

Putusan Mahkamah Syariah Lhokseumawe 04/JN/2006/MSy.Lsm.

Putusan Nomor 151/Pdt.G/2006/MSy-Lsm (Lhokseumawe, 25 January 2007).

Putusan Mahkmah Agung Republik Indonesia No. 02K/AG/JN/2007.

Peraturan Mahkamah Agung Republik Indonesia Nomor 1/Tahun 2008 tentang Prosedur Mediasi di Pengadilan.

Putusan Mahkamah Syariah Banda Aceh, A. Muslim/Mary bte. Tjong Tjun (28 May 2008).

"Estate of H. Zainal Bachri," *Putusan Mahkamah Provinsi Nomor 13/2008* (26 March 2008).

6. Newspaper and Magazine Articles (Organized by Publication, and Listed in Chronological Order)

Aceh Independen "WH dan Satpol PP Jalan diTempat," *Aceh Independen* (1 December 2008), 6.

"Unjuk Rasa Syariat Islami Ricuh: Polisi dan Mahasiswa Kejar-kejaran," *Aceh Independen* (31 December 2008), 1–2.

Muhibuddin Hanafiah, "Ketika Ulama Merespon Zaman," *Aceh Independen* (20 February 2009), 10.

"Dayah Mabdaul Ulum Al Aziziyyah," *Aceh Independen* (6 March 2009), 14.

"Aktifkan Pengajian Antisipasi Ajaran Sesat," *Aceh Independen* (25 March 2009), 4

"Dayah Warisan Ulama Aceh," *Aceh Independen* (24 April 2009), 14.

Antara News

"Dunia Islam," *Antara News* (22 November 1949).

BBC Online

"Aceh Gamblers Caned in Public," *BBC News* online (24 June 2005), <http://news.bbc.co.uk/2/hi/asia-pacific/4618595.stm>, accessed 25 June 2012.

"On Patrol with Aceh's Sharīʿa Law Police,"*BBC News* online (2 February 2010), <http://news.bbc.co.uk/2/hi/8481289.stm>, accessed 20 June 2012.

Berita Indonesia

"Memperloeas Sjiar Islam," *Berita Indonesia* (10 October 1946), 2.

Gema Baiturrahman

Ali Mochtar Ngabalin, "Refleksi Musibah Orang Aceh," *Gema Baiturrahman* (3 January 2011), 2.

Harian Aceh

"Togel Marak di Bireuen: Dinas Syariat Islam Dituding 'Tutup Mata'," *Harian Aceh* (12 April 2007), 5.

"Warga Tuding Dinas Syariat Islam Pilih Kasih," *Harian Aceh* (21 April 2007), 1, 11.

"Ketua PN Sabang Tidak Dihukum: Masyarakat Minta Dinas Syariat Islam Dibubarkan," *Harian Aceh* (24 April 2007), 1.

"Pelaksana Syariah Tak Adil Rakyat Kecil Dihukum, Orang Berada Lolos," *Harian Aceh* (6 November 2007), 2.

"Kinerja Polhut dan WH Dipertanyakan," *Harian Aceh* (10 November 2008), 13.

"Dinas Syariat Islam Aceh Barat Rekrut Tenaga Kontrak WH," *Harian Aceh* (12 December 2008), 15.

"Minta Syariat Islam, Rumah Walikota Langsa Didemo," *Harian Aceh* (27 January 2009), 14.

"Dinas Syariat Islam Dituding Menambah Ayat Al Quran," *Harian Aceh* (12 February 2009), 15.

"Karang Taruna Diharapkan Ikut Tegakkan Syariat Islam," *Harian Aceh* (18 February 2009), 3.

"Ekses Ceramah Menyesatkan: MPU Akan Panggil Tgk Kasim," *Harian Aceh* (6 June 2009), 5.

"Peran WH Belum Maksimal," *Harian Aceh* (8 June 2009), 5.

"Ulama Diminta Tingkatkan Pelaksanaan SI," *Harian Aceh* (11 August 2009), 1.

"Syariat Islam di Agara Belum Maksimal," *Harian Aceh* (11 August 2009), 11.

"Warga Bireuen Pro Aktif Mengawal Syariat Islam," *Harian Aceh* (18 August 2009), 3.

Thayeb Loh Angen, "Membangun Peradaban Aceh Baru," *Harian Aceh* (13 November 2009), 10.

"Ideologi di Balik Pakaian Ketat," *Harian Aceh* (16 November 2009), 2.

"Penerapan Syariat Islam Masih 'Dangkal'," *Harian Aceh* (22 December 2009), 5.

"HMI Desak WH Dikembalikan ke Dinas Syariat Islam," *Harian Aceh* (27 December 2009), 5.

"Rekrutmen Wilayatul Hisbah Akan Diperketat," *Harian Aceh* (19 January 2010), 3.

"Pemerintah dan WH Jangan Impoten," *Harian Aceh* (12 April 2010), 3.

"Gempar Buka Rental Rok di Perbatasan Aceh Barat," *Harian Aceh* (17 June 2010), 14.

"Asoh Buka Posko Pengumpulan Rok," *Harian Aceh* (28 June 2010), 14.

"WH Aceh Besar Kekurangan Personil," *Harian Aceh* (1 July 2010), 3.

"Pengelola Café Keluhkan Sikap WH," *Harian Aceh* (26 October 2010), 14.

"Dinas Syariat Islam dan MPU Dinilai Gagal," *Harian Aceh* (10 November 2010), 14.

Harian Duta

"Pentingnya Seminar Mengali Ajaran2 Agama untuk Mendorong Pembangunan," *Harian Duta* I.23 (5 November 1974), 1, 4.
"Majlis Alam UlamaTinjau Proyek L.N.G.," *Harian Duta* II.78 (23 May 1975), 1, 4.

International Herald Tribute

Jane Perlez, "In Aceh, Islamic Law is Taking Hold, *International Herald Tribune* (2 August 2006), 1, 4.

Jakarta Post

"A Stone To Throw," *The Jakarta Post* (16 September 2009), 6.
Erwinda Maulia and Hotli Simanjuntak, "Government To Review Aceh's Stoning By-law," *The Jakarta Post* (17 September 2009), 1.

Kontras

"Syariat Islam yang Kaffah," *Kontras* (25 February 2007), 2.

Metro Aceh

"Peserta Suluk Mengamuk, Tiga Santri Tewas Ditikam; Dayah Sa'adatun Banjir Darah," *Metro Aceh* (13 September 2008), 1.
"Nikah Siri Bawa Petaka—Dituduh Mesum, Janda-Duda Mandi Air Parit," *Metro Aceh* (30 October 2008), 1–2.
"Bolos Sekolah, Lima Pelajar SMA Ketangkap WH," *Metro Aceh* (20 November 2008), 1–2.
"Mulut Pezina Dibroti Warga," *Metro Aceh* (7 May 2009), 1–2.
"Aspirasi," *Metro Aceh* (12 October 2009), 6.
"Aspirasi," *Metro Aceh* (13 October 2009), 6.
"Aspirasi," *Metro Aceh* (14 October 2009), 6.
"Aspirasi," *Metro Aceh*(19 October 2009), 6.
"Saling Raba Tubuh di Tempat Gelap—Pasangan Mesum Kena Gimbal," *Metro Aceh* (1 December 2009), 2.
"Digerebek Lalu Diarak Massa—Janda dan Penarik Ojek Bertindih di Semak Belukar," *Metro Aceh* (13 February 2010), 1–2.
"Hukuman Cambuk Tak Adil," *Metro Aceh* (15 November 2010), 6.

New York Times

Feldman, Noah, "Why Sharia?" *New York Times* (16 March 2008): <http://www.nytimes.com/2008/03/16/magazine/16Shariah-t.html?pagewanted=all>, accessed 23 August 2012.
Norimitsu Onishi, "Extremism Spreads across Indonesian Penal Code," *New York Times* (27 October 2009): <http://www.nytimes.com/2009/10/28/world/asia/28stoning.html>, accessed 25 June 2012.

Prohaba

"Kinerja WH Bireuen Dipertanyakan," *Prohaba* (19 January 2009), 2.

Dedi Iskandar, "Razia Busana Ketat, WH Bagi Rok Gratis," *Prohaba* (21 August 2010), 1.

Radio Nederland Online

"Perempuan Aceh Barat Dilarang Pakai Celana," *Radio Nederland Online* (16 November 2009), archived at: <http://id.shvoong.com/law-and-politics/law/1946717-perempuan-aceh-barat-dilarang-pakai>, accessed 22 May 2012.

Rakyat Aceh

"Legislatif Setujui Gaji WH," *Rakyat Aceh* (26 January 2007), 2.

"Penegakan Syariat Islam Belum Sempurna," *Rakyat Aceh* (7 February 2007), 5.

"Tegakkan Syariat Islam, WH Langsa Harus Tegas," *Rakyat Aceh* (29 March 2007), 7.

"Kinerja Dinas Syariat Islam Lamban," *Rakyat Aceh* (11 April 2007), 4.

"Dinas Syariat Islam Bantah Lamban dalam Bekerja," *Rakyat Aceh* (16 April 2007), 3.

"Oknum WH Mesum Harus Dihukum," *Rakyat Aceh* (21 April 2007), 11.

"Imeum Meunasah Dibekali," *Rakyat Aceh* (7 August 2007), 2.

"WH Rekrut Anggota Baru," *Rakyat Aceh* (11 August 2007), 2.

"Dana WH Perlu Ditingkatkan," *Rakyat Aceh* (3 September 2007), 2.

"Dinas SI Diminta Perketat Pengawasan," *Rakyat Aceh* (3 September 2007), 3.

"Hukum Cambuk Tidak Melanggar HAM," *Rakyat Aceh* (7 September 2007), 4.

"Ulama Jadi Benteng Masuknya Aliran Sesat," *Rakyat Aceh* (10 November 2007), 3.

"5,000 Terompet Disita," *Rakyat Aceh* (2 January 2008), 2.

"Pemko Bersedia Menggaji WH," *Rakyat Aceh* (27 January 2008), 2.

"Dayah Terima Kitab Seumeubeut," *Rakyat Aceh* (27 January 2008), 7.

"Enam Pelaku Maisir Dicambuk," *Rakyat Aceh* (19 April 2008), 1, 11.

"Desak WH Jadi Penyidik Sipil," *Rakyat Aceh* (15 May 2008), 2.

"68 Tengku Imum Gampong Terima Honor," *Rakyat Aceh* (30 May 2008), 3.

"Ratusan Tengku Seumebeut Terima Honor," *Rakyat Aceh* (2 July 2008), 4.

"WH dan Satpol PP Dituding Jalan Ditempat," *Rakyat Aceh* (17 August 2008), 5.

"Polisi Syariah Digugat: Bertindak Melebihi Polisi," *Rakyat Aceh* (30 August 2008), 2.

"Ahmadiyah 'Haram' di Aceh," *Rakyat Aceh* (26 November 2008), 1–2.

"Satpol PP WH Lhokseumawe Kurang Personil," *Rakyat Aceh* (18 December 2008), 4.

"Penerapan SI Harus Dimulai dari Keluarga Sendiri," *Rakyat Aceh* (11 January 2009), 3.

"Syariat Islam Lemah: KAMMI Demo Rumah Walikota," *Rakyat Aceh* (27 January 2009), 1–2.

"Abaikan Agama, Aceh Semakin Hancur," *Rakyat Aceh* (2 February 2009), 1–2.

"Pelanggaran Syariat Islam Cenderung Meningkat," *Rakyat Aceh* (10 February 2009), 3.

"Bolos Sekolah, Lima Pelajar Ditertibkan," *Rakyat Aceh* (26 February 2009), 4.
"Personil WH di Aceh Timur Belum Maksimal," *Rakyat Aceh* (12 March 2009), 7.
"Kembalikan WH ke Dinas Syariat Islam," *Rakyat Aceh* (30 May 2009), 4.
"Kembalikan WH ke Dinas Syariat Islam," *Rakyat Aceh* (7 June 2009), 6.
"Pelaksanaan Syariat Islam Belum Maksimal," *Rakyat Aceh* (3 July 2009), 4.
"Dayah Harus Direvilitasi," *Rakyat Aceh* (20 July 2009), 4.
"Warning! PNS Nongkrong Jam Kerja—Satpol PP Aktifkan Razia," *Rakyat Aceh* (14 October 2009), 5.
"Bangun Dayah Sambil Bentengi Perbatasan," *Rakyat Aceh* (27 October 2009), 3.
"Peringatan Bagi Kaum Perempuan—Pakai Celana Jeans Ketat Digunting," *Rakyat Aceh* (29 October 2009), 1–2.
"Gubernur BelumTerapkan Qanun Jinayat: Ribuan Massa Demo Akbar," *Rakyat Aceh* (9 November 2009), 1–2.
"180 Pengurus Masjid Diberi Pelatihan," *Rakyat Aceh* (21 November 2009), 3.
"WH Diminta Serius Awasi Pelanggaran Syariat Islam," *Rakyat Aceh* (23 November 2009), 3.
"Penganut Sekta Salek Buta Sesat dan Murtad," *Rakyat Aceh* (6 January 2010), 1–2.
"Program 100 Hari Kasatpol PP dan WH—Siswa Bolos Ditangkap," *Rakyat Aceh* (28 January 2010), 1–2.
"Anggarah Habis, Syariat Islam Kandas," *Rakyat Aceh* (15 February 2010), 1–2.
"WH Seperti Macan Ompong," *Rakyat Aceh* (21 April 2010), 4.
"Dakwah Ramadhan Digelar di 40 Gampong," *Rakyat Aceh* (12 August 2010), 3.
"WH Minta Dikembalikan ke Dinas SI," *Rakyat Aceh* (5 October 2010), 3.
"Tiga Tahun Baju Dinas Tak Berganti," *Rakyat Aceh* (10 October 2010), 5.
"MPU Acut dan Dinas SI Sepakat: Kutuk Aliran Sesat," *Rakyat Aceh* (19 October 2010), 4.
"Aliran Millata Abraham Hancurkan Islam," *Rakyat Aceh* (21 October 2010), 13.
"Dewan Minta Dinas Syariat Islam Pro Aktif," *Rakyat Aceh* (4 November 2010), 5
"Moral Pemimpin Patut Dipertanyakan," *Rakyat Aceh* (19 December 2010), 4.
"Tgk Dayah Akan Dapat Gaji," *Rakyat Aceh* (22 December 2010), 3.

Serambi

"PII dan Forsima Sosialisasikan Syariat Islam," *Serambi* (9 March 2007), 13.
"Dilarang Lakukan Pengajian: Tengku Syahrul Mengadu ke Dewan," *Serambi* (9 March 2007), 19.
"Tak Semua Pelaku Khalwat Harus Dicambuk," *Serambi* (3 April 2007), 5.
"Kadis Syariat Islam Aceh Utara: Tak Semua Pelaku Khalwat Harus Dicambuk," *Serambi* (3 April 2007), 9.
"Penerapan Syariat Islam Belum Maksimal," *Serambi* (19 April 2007), 3.
"Diaktifkan, Tim Terpadu Syariat Islam," *Serambi* (19 April 2007), 13.
"DSI Kota Serius Tegakkan Syariat," *Serambi* (21 April 2007), 2.
"Pelaksanaan Syariat Islam Kurang Bergema," *Serambi* (23 April 2007), 13.
"Pembayaran Diyat Perlu Payung Hukum," *Serambi* (2 July 2007), 10.
"MPU Larang Ajaran Hendri Dikembangkan di Abdya," *Serambi* (20 July 2007), 1.
"Ada Apa Dengan Syariat Islam di Aceh," *Serambi* (3 August 2007), 4.
"BRR Latih Daʿi Perempuan," *Serambi* (13 August 2007), 2.

"Pendaftaran Anggota WH Diperpanjang," *Serambi* (22 August 2007), 10.
"Penegakan Syariat Islam Diperketat di Aceh Jaya," *Serambi* (27 August 2007), 4.
"Syariat Islam Mati Suri di Tamiang," *Serambi* (29 August 2007), 3.
"Polisi Akan Dampingi WH," *Serambi* (30 August 2007), 13.
"Pembekalan Wawasan Imeum Selesai," *Serambi* (31 August 2007), 4.
"Lagi, Santri Gelar Razia," *Serambi* (22 October 2007), 10.
"Siswa Dibimbing Syariat Islam," *Serambi* (6 November 2007), 7.
"Wagub Muhammad Nazar: Masyarakat Tak Berwenang Lakukan Razia Syariat," *Serambi* (23 November 2007), 1.
"Calon WH Pidie Dites Baca Khutbah," *Serambi* (8 February 2008), 15.
"WH Aceh Barat Empat Bulan Tak Terima Gaji," *Serambi* (8 April 2008), 17.
"WH Aceh Barat Lima Bulan belum Bergaji," *Serambi* (13 May 2008), 21.
"Manajemen Dayah Harus Diubah," *Serambi* (7 August 2008), 10.
Irwan Adaby, "HarapanTerhadap Syariat," *Serambi* (13 August 2008), 30.
"Dakwah Jadi 'Senjata' Pemantapan Syariat," *Serambi* (16 August 2008), 28.
"Dinas Syariat Islam Gelar Safari Pekan," *Serambi* (17 September 2008), 21.
"Dinas Syariat Rekrut 26 WH," *Serambi* (12 December 2008), 21.
"Ketua MPU Aceh Barat: Penerapan Syariat Islam di Aceh Masih Ragu-Ragu," *Serambi* (24 December 2008), 22.
"264 Peserta Ikut Tes WH," *Serambi* (30 December 2008), 17.
"Pemerintah Diminta Serius Terapkan Syariat Islam," *Serambi* (31 December 2008), 1–2.
"Razia Pelanggaran Syariat Harus Ditingkatkan," *Serambi* (27 March 2009), 9.
"WH Dikembalikan ke Dinas Syariat Islam," *Serambi* (15 April 2009), 17.
Mahbub Fauzie, "Dakwah dan Sosial Umat Islam," *Serambi* (17 April 2009), 30.
"26 Petugas WH Aceh Barat Lulus Seleksi," *Serambi* (20 April 2009), 29.
"WH Empat Bulan Tak Bergaji," *Serambi* (25 April 2009), 13.
"WH Banda Aceh Kenakan Seragam Satpol PP," *Serambi* (26 April 2009), 3.
"MPU Aceh Evaluasi Pelaksanaan Syariat," *Serambi* (5 May 2009), 7.
"Tgk Ahmad Silet Bantah Bawa Aliran Sesat," *Serambi* (10 May 2009), 19.
"Kembalikan WH ke Dinas Syariat Islam," *Serambi* (15 May 2009), 22.
"Dinas Syariat Islam Bantu Muallaf," *Serambi* (2 July 2009), 33.
"Tahun 2010, Dinas Syariat Islam Pijay Kerja Ekstra," *Serambi* (16 July 2009), 25.
"Dinas SI Sosialisasi Qanun," *Serambi* (4 August 2009), 17.
"Banyak Eksekusi Cambuk belum Dilaksanakan: Kadis Syariat Islam Dituding Suap," *Serambi* (7 August 2009), 9.
"Grand Mufti Suriah: Syariat IslamTidak Mengedepankan Hukuman," *Serambi* (15 October 2009), 1.
"Dana WH Tahun 2009 belum Disalurkan," *Serambi* (7 January 2010), 3.
"Kualitas WH Harus Ditingkatkan," *Serambi* (22 January 2010), 2.
"Satpol PP/WH Akan Razia Pegawai Bolos," *Serambi* (28 January 2010), 20.
"WH Kembali Digabung ke Dinas Syariat," *Serambi* (25 March 2010), 13.
"WH Harus Dikembalikan ke DSI," *Serambi* (2 May 2010), 14.
"Revisi Raqan Jinayat Tak Masuk Prioritas," *Serambi* (4 May 2010), 1.
"MPU Abdya Dukung Pengembalian WH ke DSI," *Serambi* (5 May 2010), 24.
"Patroli WH di Pantai Meureudu Diprotes," *Serambi* (12 May 2010), 19.
"Gubernur Minta Ulama Tidak Lepas Tangan," *Serambi* (18 May 2010), 1.

"Tim WH Intensifkan Razia di Kota—Wanita Bercelana Jeans Dibagi Rok," *Serambi* (24 June 2010), 17.
"WH Harus Dikembalikan ke Dinas Syariat Islam," *Serambi* (28 June 2010), 3.
"Diduga Ajaran Aliran Sesat: Ratusan Orang Gerebek Rumah Warga," *Serambi* (2 August 2010), 19.
"KAMMI Unjuk Rasa di Dinas Syariat Islam," *Serambi* (7 August 2010), 17.
"Pelaksanaan Syariat Islam Masih Kabur," *Serambi* (7 August 2010), 21.
"MPU Keluarkan Fatwa Thariqat Muktabarah," *Serambi* (9 August 2010), 3.
"Plafon Anggaran Syariat Islam Dinilai Minim," *Serambi* (19 October 2010), 20.
"Soal CD Pendangkalan Akidah: MPU Bireuen Didesak Keluarkan Fatwa," *Serambi* (20 November 2010), 9.
"Ulama Kutuk Insiden Perampokan Ranto Peureulak," *Serambi* (21 November 2010), 13.
"Mahasiswa Minta Syariat Islam Ditegakkan," *Serambi* (7 December 2010), 17.
"WH Pidie Diminta Aktif," *Serambi* (9 December 2010), 16.
"WH Pidie Diminta Perbaiki Kinerja," *Serambi* (10 December 2010), 19.
"Wagub Aceh: Pengikut Aliran Sesat Digaji Rp 15 Juta," *Serambi* (4 April 2011), 1.
"4 Pengikut Tgk. Aiyub Disidangkan MPU Bireuen," *Serambi* (4 April 2011), 13.
"Polisi Masih Amankan Anggota Millah Abraham," *Serambi* (7 April 2011), 1.
"Puluhan Ribu Massa Demo Aliran Sesat," *Serambi* (8 April 2011), 1, 11.
"MPU Tidak Infokan Nama Aliran Sesat," *Serambi* (13 April 2011), 1–2.
"Amnesty International Diminta Pahami Aceh," *Serambi* (24 May 2011), 1.

The Straits Times

Lynn Lee, "Aceh's Human Rights Record under Scrutiny," *The Straits Times* (2 December 2010), A16.

Tabloid/Tabangun Aceh

"Dayah Samalanga Menuju Era Baru," *Tabloid Tabangun Aceh* (7 August 2007), 5.

Waspada

"Penerapan SI di Subulussalam Lemah," *Waspada* (13 July 2007), 24.
"Razia Jilbab Diprotes Warga Aceh Tamiang," *Waspada* (24 October 2007), 3.
"Maksiat Merajalela, SI Tamiang Hanya Razia Jilbab," *Waspada* (27 October 2007), 3.
"Warga Nikahkan Pasangan Khalwat," *Waspada* (31 October 2007), 7.
"Penerapan SI Butuh Peran Negara," *Waspada* (6 November 2007), 17.
"Puluhan Calon WH Ujian Seleksi," *Waspada* (13 March 2008), 19.
"Kepala Dinas Syariat Islam Diminta Berani Tindak Bawahan," *Waspada* (14 March 2008), 16.
"Pelaksanaan Syariat Islam Jalan Ditempat," *Waspada* (29 March 2008), 12.
"KAMMI: Kinerja Dinas SI Menurun," *Waspada* (31 October 2008), 16.
"Ulama Aceh Bahas Fiqih Anti Korupsi," *Waspada* (28 November 2008), 7.
"Rekrutmen Satpol PP dan WH Diam-diam," *Waspada* (29 November 2008), 7.

"HMI Kecewa Syariat Islam di Aceh 'Jalan Ditempat'," *Waspada* (21 February 2009), 11.
"Hukum Cambuk Mulai Pudar," *Waspada* (27 April 2009), 23.
"Nasib WH Bireuen, 4 Bulan Belum Terima Gaji," *Waspada* (27 April 2009), 23.
"Bangkitkan Pendidikan Dayah," *Waspada* (27 April 2009), 24.
"Minim Dana, Kantor WH Ditutup," *Waspada* (23 June 2010), 7.
"Wilayatul Hisbah Terkendala Dana," *Waspada* (24 August 2010), 7.
"Ulama Hukum Berat Penyiksa Sumiati," *Waspada* (19 November 2010), 3.
"Penerapan Syariat Islam Menurun," *Waspada* (3 December 2010).
"Amnesty Internasional Minta Indonesia: Stop Hukum Cambuk di Aceh," *Waspada* (23 May 2011), 1.
"Ulama Aceh Tanggapi Amnesty Internasional," *Waspada* (23 May 2011), 1.

Waspada Online

"WH Bireuen ke DSI," *Waspada Online* (25 March 2010), <http://www.waspada.co.id/index.php?option=com_content&view=article&id=99946>, accessed 4 November 2011.
"Bupati Aceh Barat Minta Pendatang Pakai Rok," *Waspada Online* (29 May 2010), <http://www.waspada.co.id/index.php?option=com_content&view=article&id=118393>, accessed 22 December 2011.
"MPU Aceh: TerorTermasuk Dosa Besar," *Waspada Online* (1 July 2010), <http://www.waspada.co.id/index.php?option=com_content&view=article&id=127022:mpu-aceh-teror-termasuk-dosa-besar&catid=13&Itemid=26>, accessed 12 October 2011.
"Maksiat Marak di Lokasi Waduk," *Waspada Online* (15 July 2010), <http://www.waspada.co.id/index.php?option=com_content&view=article&id=130054:maksiat-marak-di-lokasi-waduk&catid=13:aceh&Itemid=26>, accessed 21 August 2012.
"Pemilik Kafe Bentrok dengan Aparat," *Waspada Online* (30 November 2010), <http://www.waspada.co.id/index.php?option=com_content&view=article&id=159605:pemilik-kafe-bentrok-dengan-aparat&catid=13&Itemid=26>, accessed 21 August 2012.

Index